שִׁירֵי יְדִידוֹת

PARSHAH & TEHILLIM

HAND IN HAND

SEFER BEREISHIS

YERACHMIEL GOLDMAN

Shirei Yedidos:
Parshah & Tehillim Hand In Hand – Bereishis

First Edition – First Impression – September 2024

© Copyright 2024 by Yerachmiel (Jeremy) Goldman

ALL RIGHTS RESERVED

No part of this book, in whole or in part, may be used, stored, reproduced, transmitted, or translated in any form or by any means whatsoever, manually or electronically, including without limitation, photocopying, recording, or by any information storage and retrieval system, without prior written permission from the author/copyright holder, except by a reviewer who wishes to quote brief passages in connection with a review written for inclusion in newspapers or magazines. The rights of the author/copyright holder will be strictly enforced.

Cover design and layout by

MK Design

designbymkdesign@gmail.com

Attribution of original icon of G-clef and moon
(first appearing on 6th page): Vecteezy.com

For dedication opportunities, comments, questions, etc.,
the author can be contacted at ParshahandTehillim@gmail.com

To purchase this *sefer* see Amazon.com or contact the author.

In memory of

Rudolph and Gertrude Goldman *z"l*

and

Murray and Gloria Fox *z"l*

We are delighted to

support our friend and mentor

Yerachmiel Goldman

on the first of many *sifrei kodesh* he will, G-d willing, produce.

In memory of

Martin Paul Solomon

מנשה בן אברהם יעקב ז"ל

His loving wife, children, and

grandchildren

לזכרון עולם

האי גברא חסיד וענייו

מרדכי הלל בן הרב יחזקאל יהודה

למשפחת אייז ז"ל

שעסק באמת ובאמונה

בצרכי ציבור ובעול כל אדם

והשפיע לאנשים אין מספר,

דיבורו בחכמה ובנחת

וכל מעשיו בשלום ושמחה.

משפחת טנדלר

לעילוי נשמת

אבי מורי

שלמה ישעיהו בן טודרוס ז"ל

איש שעשה משפט ואהב חסד והצנע לכת עם ה'

Dedicated in loving memory
of our dear father

Shlomo Groll *z"l*

He inspired us through his devotion to family,
love of learning, acts of kindness,
and his zeal to perform justice
and walk modestly with Hashem.

He is deeply missed.

Avraham and Dina Groll

TABLE OF CONTENTS

Haskamos (in alphabetical order) 20

- Rabbi Shmuel Brazil,
  Rosh HaYeshiva, Yeshivas Zeev HaTorah, Jerusalem, Israel

- Rabbi Reuven Feinstein,
  Rosh HaYeshiva, Yeshiva of Staten Island, NY

- Rabbi Naftali Jaeger,
  Rosh HaYeshiva, Sh'or Yoshuv Institute, Lawerence, NY

- Rabbi Shmuel Kamenetsky,
  Rosh HaYeshiva, Talmudical Yeshiva of Philadelphia, PA

- Rabbi Mordechai Tendler,
  Rav, New Hempstead Kehillah, New Hempstead, NY

- Rabbi Yechezkel Zweig,
  Menahel, Bais Yaakov High School of Baltimore, MD

Acknowledgments 27

Introduction 32

Chapter 1: Parshas Bereishis & Tehillim 139 43

Introduction: The Tehillim/Bereishis Connection / The Many Connections Between Parshas Bereishis & Tehillim 139 / Downfall Through Daas / Repair Through Daas / Atah Chonein Le'Adam Daas / Adam's Personal Connection to Dovid HaMelech / The Human Condition / Hashem's Foreknowledge Versus Man's Free Will / Creation of Man / Knowledge and Regret / Attempted Escape from Hashem / Moshiach Ties It All Together / From Fleeing to

Friendship / The Fright of the First Sunset / The Terror of the Changing Times / The Darkness of Galus and Light of Geulah / Tehillim 139, Bereishis, and Pesach / Darkness Has No Intrinsic Effect on Hashem / The Human Mind and Childbirth / Thanking Hashem for Body and Soul / Adam: The First to Thank Hashem / The Moment When the Daas Finally "Clicks" / The Greatness of the Jewish Soul / The Wonders of Creation / The Creation and Actual Formation of Man / In Hashem's Book All Are Recorded / Hashem Is Above and Beyond Time / The Yamim Noraim: Days of Awe / Our Infinite God and His Torah and Friendship / Our Infinite God and His Master Plan / Hashem Chose the Jewish People as His Own / Coping with and Combating Rishus (Evil) / The Hiding of the Hidden Light / Rebuke of the Non-Believers / The Serpent, Its Sins, and Its Punishments / Why Evil Exists at All / A Final Flourish of Daas / May Hashem's Daas Reveal Our Purity / The Double Daas That Hints to Shabbos / Daas in the Haftarah Elevates Us Beyond the Rules of Nature / Our Role in the Tikkun of the Cheit / Overcoming the Sadness of Sin / Hashem's Sadness / From This World to the World to Come / Closing Remarks on the Bereishis-Tehillim Connection

Chapter 2: Parshas Noach & Tehillim 29 89

Introduction: Diving In / The Many Connections Between Parshas Noach & Tehillim 29 / Sons of the Mighty Ones / Honor Restored / The "Oz" of Destruction and of Torah / Havu La'Hashem: "Havu" Unto God / The Voice of Hashem Heard Through Mighty Waters / The Voice of Hashem as Power and Wrath / The Mystical Power of Hashem's Voice in Our Homes Even Today / The Voice of Hashem as Deadly Heat / Hidden References to the Rainbow / References to Cham and His Offspring / The Animals in the Ark / Hashem Bestows Oz (Torah) and Shalom (Peace) / Additional Themes in Parshas Noach & Tehillim 29 / Tehillim 29 and Its Connection to Shemoneh Esrei / Noach's Connection to Shemoneh Esrei: Mei Noach / Searching for Hidden References to Noach in Shemoneh Esrei / Shemoneh Esrei Is a Wave / The Brachah of Gevuros Is the Perfect Storm / The First Generations and Their Lack of Daas in Atah Chonein / Noach the Tzaddik's Rise and Fall in Al Ha'tzaddikim / V'La'Malshinim's Connection to Tehillim 29 and the Flood / Marcheshvan, Mabul, and Moving Mouths / Noach and Family

TABLE OF CONTENTS

Inspire Shomeia Tefillah / The Sweet Smell of Sacred Sacrifices / Their Chammas Was an Insult to Shemoneh Esrei / Hashem La'Mabul Yashav: Hashem at the Flood Sat Enthroned / The Hidden Name of Hashem and Its Power of Healing / "Hashem Oz" in Tehillim 29 Corresponds to the Blessing of Refaeinu / Every Shemoneh Esrei Concludes with Healing and Peace / Healing and Peace Intertwined with Yedidus / Finding the Hidden Name of Hashem in Refaeinu

Chapter 3: Parshas Lech Lecha & Tehillim 110 122

Preface: Avraham, Are We the Children That You Dreamed Of? / Introduction: Where Is the Avraham of Chessed? / The Many Connections Between Parshas Lech Lecha & Tehillim 110 / Avraham Is the Focal Point of Tehillim 110 / Eliezer: Eved and Author / Avraham Coronated as King and Prince of God / Malki-Tzedek and His Allegiance to Avraham / Avraham Becomes Kohen Forever / The Right Hand of Hashem / Volunteers to Fight At His Side / Holy from Birth / Avraham's Pleasant and Rebellious Youth / Fear After the Fight / Avraham: Kohen and King / Hashem Crushed Kings and Made Miracles Against Monarchs / Avraham: First to Call Hashem "Adon" / Allusions to the Slavery in Egypt / The War Song of Avram / Pausing to Ponder Past Improprieties / Lech Lecha from and into the Valley of the Shadow of Death / To March into Gehinnom for a Heavenly Cause / And Avraham Laughed / Conclusion: Yes, We're the Children That You Dreamed Of

Chapter 4: Parshas Vayeira & Tehillim 11 153

Introduction: The Common Denominator is the Destruction of Sedom / The Many Connections Between Parshas Vayeira & Tehillim 11 / Taking Refuge in Hashem / Wandering, but Finding Home / Lot's Escape from Sedom / A Hint to Moav and to Balak / Flying Like a Bird / Yishmael's Attempts to Murder Yitzchak / The Upright of Heart / Avraham's Introspection After Inability to Save Sedom / The Unsuccessful Upbringing of Yishmael / Hashem's Personal Attention to All / Stricter Scrutiny of the Tzaddik / A Hint to Avraham's Ten Tests / Hashem's Hatred of Eisav, Yishmael, and

Their Descendants / Destruction of Sedom Described / The Inspiration of Tzidkus / Pinpoint Perfection of Hashgachah Pratis / Yearning to See Hashem's Face / Avraham, Hashem, and the Three Travelers / How Can Akeidas Yitzchak Be Missing?

Chapter 5: Parshas Chayei Sarah & Tehillim 45 181

Preface: Lecha Dodi Likras Kallah / Introduction: A Tribute to the Beauty of Avraham Avinu and Sarah Imeinu / The Many Connections Between Parshas Chayei Sarah & Tehillim 45 / Roses for the Beloved / The First Jewish King and Queen / The Precision of Avraham's Words and Intentions / Avraham's Grace and Beauty on Earth and in Heaven / Avraham's Abundance of Blessings / Here, the Sword Remained Sheathed / A Quick Reference to Bris Milah / Rivkah and Yitzchak's "First Sight" / Military Might, from the "Almighty" Hashem / To Crush Your Enemies / Military Might and Monarchy, from the "Almighty" Hashem / Just a Reflection of the Kingship of Hashem / Avraham's Love: For Others and for Hashem / The Milah and Fine Middos are More Fragrant than Myrrh / From King's Daughter to Maidservant / Willingness to Leave One's World and Wants Behind / Rivkah: Inclined Toward Chessed / Avraham: The Grade "A" of Adam and Adon / Only Gifts from God / The Tzenius of the Jewish Woman / Rivkah as Kallah: Her Bridal Canopy, Train, and Veil / Simcha In Hashem's Palace and In Our Homes / To Laugh at the Day of Death / Proper Succession from Father to Son, and the Mother's Role Therein / Remember the Name / Tehillim 45 and the Story of Yitzchak and Rivkah / A Closing Blessing of Eishes Chayil "Me" Yimtza

Chapter 6: Parshas Toldos & Tehillim 36 216

Preface: I Loved Yaakov. And Eisav I Hate / Introduction: To Be or Not To Be An Eved Hashem / Yitzchak Avinu as an Eved Hashem / Eisav's Refusal to Be an Eved Hashem / Yaakov Avinu as an Eved Hashem / Hashem, Grant Us a Yetzer Tov to Be Your Eved / The Many Connections Between Parshas Toldos & Tehillim 36 / The Eved Hashem Is the True Victor / Criticism of the Wickedness of Eisav / Eisav the Wicked, Despite His Father and His Mother / Eisav's Ability to Deceive / The Battle of Emes and Sheker / Eisav's

TABLE OF CONTENTS

Premeditated Wickedness / The Rasha and Tzaddik: Affecting Heaven and Earth / Of Mountains and Monsters / A Quick Reconnect with the Avos and Each Precious Jew / The World to Come and the Beis HaMikdash: Home / Water Wells of Torah, Brachah, and the Beis HaMikdash / The True Light Is Hashem's and Should Not Be Taken Lightly / The Mystical Formula of the Tallis Prayer / Toldos, Tehillim, and the Tallis / The Hand Grasping the Heel / The Downfall of Our Enemies / Eisav: Exiles, the Holocaust, and World War III / A Closing Song of Battle and Blessing

Chapter 7: Parshas Vayeitzei & Tehillim 3 251

Introduction: The Experiences of Yaakov and Dovid Intertwined / The Many Connections Between Parshas Vayeitzei & Tehillim 3 / Consolation and Calamity from Closeness / Yaakov's Many Tzaros: Problems / Yaakov's Many Tzaros: Rival Wives / The Spiritual Dangers Posed by Lavan / The Dangers Posed by All of the Exiles / Striking Back at Evil Through Trust and Prayer / Yaakov's Head Is Heavenly / Gateway to Heaven: The Voice of Prayer and the Beis HaMikdash / Even While We Sleep, Hashem Protects Us / The Bedtime Prayer and Tehillim 3 / Ha'malach Ha'goel / Torah Twenty-Four Hours a Day/Seven Days a Week / Waking Up with Hashem / Break His Teeth / Kisses of the Enemy / Hashem, Please "Arise" and Redeem Us / The Brachos of Yitzchak to Yaakov to Us All / The Theme of Yeshuah / The Avos and Hashem as Ozer, U'Moshia, U'Magen / Why "Moshia" When Yaakov (and Dovid) Are "Ozer"?

Chapter 8: Parshas Vayishlach & Tehillim 140 285

Introduction: A Plea for Victory While on the Brink of Battle / The Many Connections Between Parshas Vayishlach & Tehillim 140 / Yaakovs' Victories Are for All Time / Eisav Is Pure Death / Eisav's Heart Beats Only Evil and War / The Destruction of Shechem in Eisav-Like Fashion / Eisav Followed by a Long Line of Jewish Foes / Wickedness Like the Original Serpent / Fear of Spiders / Dovid HaMelech's Connection to Spiders / The Hands of Eisav / Eisav and Yishmael: Each Is the Anti-Yedid / To Trap and Trip Up the Tzaddik

/ Yaakov's Connection to Tefillas Haderech / Taryag Mitzvos Shamarti / Arrogant Antoninus and Proud Rabbi Yehudah HaNasi / The Power and Style of Prayer / A Chanukah Connection / Yaakov's Connection to Sukkos / The Day of the Kiss / A Plea That Hashem Not Listen to the Wicked / Would Hashem Ever Side with Evil? / Eisav's Death by Decapitation / May the Reshaim Suffer in Gehinnom Forever / Let the Hunter Become the Hunted / Katonti Mikol Ha'chassadim: Yaakov's Immense Humbleness / A Befitting Conclusion to Yaakov in Parshas Vayishlach / The Wounded Tzaddik Is Still a Tzaddik / The Warriors Who Fight For and Praise Hashem / The Dwellings of the Upright in Both Worlds / From Facing Evil to Face-to-Face with Hashem / Eradicating the Eisav and Evil That Lurks Within

Chapter 9: Parshas Vayeishev & Tehillim 112 328

Introduction: Yaakov and His Sons Around the Shabbos Table / The Many Connections Between Parshas Vayeishev & Tehillim 112 / The Jewish Father / A Desire for Mitzvos / A True Man Fears Only Hashem / These Are the Offspring of Yaakov: Yosef / The Mighty Yaakov and Sons / The Sons of Yaakov: The First Mighty and Upright "Generation" / Yaakov: From Rags to Riches, He Remained Reserved / Homeless, Yosef Created a Home for Others / Yosef HaTzaddik: Tzaddik Yesod Ha'olam / Zarach and Yosef: Seeing Light Amidst the Darkness / Flashes of Chanukah / Chanukah and the Mystical Number Thirteen / Yosef's Successes in Egypt: Due to Chein / Yosef as Provider to All / A Tribute to the Jewish Wife / Other Famous References to the Tzaddik / Tales of Terrible and Tearful Tidings / Yaakov's Reaction to Yosef's "Death" / Yosef's Reaction to Dire Warnings / Yosef's Apparent Death: Fearless Toward Man, but Fearful of God / Is It Fitting to Feel Fear? / Yosef's Rise to Power in Egypt / The Aleph-Beis Connection / The Coat of Many Colors / The Seductiveness of Potiphar's Wife and its Impact / Yosef and Moshiach Ben Yosef's Power to Defeat Edom / Care for Kavod and Avoiding Embarrassment / Our Modern-Day Revenge

TABLE OF CONTENTS

Chapter 10: Parshas Mikeitz & Tehillim 40 371

Introduction: Place Your Hope in Hashem, and Only Hashem / Yosef's Prolonged Imprisonment / What Did Yosef Do Wrong? / Hashem's, and Only Hashem's, Salvation / Other Example of Yosef's "Moshia" Missteps / Recap and Digging Deeper / Establishing the Yitzchak-Yosef Connection to "Elokim" / Additional Yitzchak-Yosef & Moshia-Elokim Connections in Parshas Mikeitz & Tehillim 40 / Yosef's Release from Prison / The "New Song" of Yosef / Yosef's Mistaken Reliance on the Sar HaMashkim / Our Own Personal Elokim / Of Wonders and Wisdom / Hashem Wants to Hear Our Tefillos / Bitul to Hashem with Heartfelt Love / Mutual Faith That Hashem Will Save / The Simchah of Salvation / Though Destitute, Din Will Deliver Without Delay / Culmination of the Yitzchak-Yosef & Elokim-Moshia Connections / Additional Connections Between Parshas Mikeitz & Tehillim 40 / Torah's Study and Wisdom Saves from Gehinnom / A Spark of Chanukah / Footsteps Ascending the Steps to Pharaoh's Throne / Songs Amidst the Sorrow / Az Yashir in the Merit of Yosef / The Attribute of Sincere Tribute / Yosef's Skill of Listening / The Mysterious "Megillos" of Mitzrayim / Torah from One's Essence / Recognizing Miracles of All Types / The "World of Prayer" / Haunting References to the Sons of Yaakov / Zechus Avos / The Ultimate Coverup / We Always Need Hashem, and Must Always Ask For More / Yosef and His Hair / The Reaction of the Brothers / The Attempted Murder of Yosef / Yosef's Final Rebuke of His Brothers / No Delays

Chapter 11: Parshas Vayigash & Tehillim 48 416

Introduction: The Unity of Yerushalayim and Yaakov & Sons: Yachdav / The Many Connnections Between Parshas Vayigash & Tehillim 48 / Sons of Korach and Sons of Yaakov / Korach's Redemption / Experience Yerushalayim and the Beis HaMikdash / Our Monday Morning Tour of Yerushalayim / The Yosef-Binyamin Yearning for Yerushalayim / Berlin Is Not Yerushalayim / The Monday Shir Shel Yom and Yosef / Fairest of Sites: References to Yosef / Beis HaMikdash: Teshuvah and Joy to All / The Immeasurable Joy of Yaakov and of Our Kings / Hashem Is Our

Stronghold / When the Kings Clash and Then Reconcile / The Reaction of the Brothers to Yosef's Revealing Himself / Yosef's Visceral Reaction That Could Not Be Held Back / The Loss of Rochel Looms Over All / Yissachar and Zevulun / Wishing to be Shipwrecked in Eretz Yisrael / Yaakov's Soul and Spiritual Status, Restored / To See It with Your Own Eyes / Goshen and the Ever-Available Mikdash Me'at / Reexamining the Emphasis on "Elokim" / Time for the Brothers to Celebrate / Israel: Traveling To and Fro, To and Fro / The Continuity of the Jewish People Guaranteed / A Farewell Message of Parental Love and Care

Chapter 12: Parshas Vayechi & Tehillim 41.............. 456

Introduction: Sickness, Death, and Olam HaBa / The Many Connections Between Parshas Vayechi & Tehillim 41 / Joy In and With Hashem, Even in Illness / Rising to Ruach Hakodesh Amidst Illness / Focus on the Future Time, for a Great Future Awaits / The Mitzvah of Visiting the Sick / Intelligent Interactions with the Ill / Lessons for Life and Death / Yaakov Was the First to Ever Become Sick / Delving Into the Description of "Dal" / Appreciate Life / Yosef at Yaakov's Deathbed / A Time to Die / Healing Through Chein / Healing Through Teshuvah / Ha'malach Ha'goel: Protection from All Evil / Death Should Not Be Confused with Evil / The Brothers Doubt Yosef's Sincerity and Fear Him / The Greatness of Yaakov and Yosef Amidst the Evil / Hints to the Original Dispute between the Brothers and Yosef / The Life and Death of Eisav HaRasha / The Origins of Yaakov and Eisav / The Serpent Is the Heel, At the Heel, Who Does Not Heal / Metaso Sheleimah: His Bed Was Whole / Torah Is the Ultimate Protection / Yaakov Remained the Ish Tam Forever / Supporting the Wholehearted / Concluding Connections to Yaakov and the World to Come / Chazzak Chazzak Ve'nischazeik

Conclusion to Sefer Bereishis: *V'Zakeinu L'Gadel*............. 495

About the Author 502

Rav Shmuel Brazil
Rosh HaYeshiva

Yeshivas Zeev HaTorah
14 Shimon Chacham
Jerusalem, Israel

יז חודש אדר תשפ"א

ירושלים עיר הקודש

My Dear Talmid Yerachmiel שליט"א,

Even since the day you entered my *shiur* in Yeshiva Shor Yoshuv, I realized the burning passion you possessed for learning and for transmitting Torah to others. Although you eventually got married and left the *Beis Medrash* to join the work force, in my heart I know that you never really joined but still, even until today, you remain in the *Beis Medrash*.

Your public *shiurim* that you have given over the many years are inspiring, insightful, enjoyable and personal growth oriented.

Now you are bringing to the *Olam Hatorah* an incredible unique *sefer* that connects a specific *perek* of *Tehillim* to a specific *Parshas HaShavua*. In this new work of yours you weave together a tapestry of connections and *peirushim* between the two, enriching the reader with both a deeper understanding in the *Parsha* and an appreciation of the insightful hinted messages that lie in the few words of the *pessukim* of Dovid Hamelech.

The thoughts and lessons that you express in your *sefer* "*Parsha & Tehillim* Hand in Hand" lends a new perception and understanding to everyday challenges and advises the reader how to tackle and overcome them.

I bench you that Hashem should continue to give you the ability to be *marbitz* Torah as you are now, and to enlighten those who seek to bond closer with *Hashem Yisbarach*.

Rabbi Reuven Feinstein
1880 Drumgoole Road East
Staten Island, New York 10309

שלי' ראובן פיינשטיין
ראש הישיבה
ישיבה דסטעטן אייילענד

י"א אדר תשפ"א

To my dear great-nephew, HaRav Yerachmiel SHLIT"A,

The understanding and appreciation of both Parsha and Tehillim today is unfortunately lacking. The appreciation and power of Tehillim as well as wisdom and insight gained from learning each Parsha is perhaps one of the greatest losses of this generation.

Your Sefer "Shirei Yedidos – Parsha and Tehillim Hand-In-Hand" is written with clarity and knowledge that represents a clear understanding of the unique topic at hand. I have reviewed several portions of this Sefer and found them to be engaging and thought provoking.

The gates to heaven never shut to sincere prayers and Tehillim. Understanding Parsha gives us both an insight and appreciation of the depth of wisdom of Hashem. The study of Tehillim and Parsha, as well as your unique approach which combines the two, cannot be overstated! The very foundation of Yiddishkeit is the study of Hashem's Torah.

HaRav Yerachmiel, his most Chashoova wife Naomi and their family should be benched with Hatzlacha and Siyata Dishmaya to be marbitz Torah and mikadash Sheim Shamayim, and together with Klal Yisroel see the redemption and greet Melech HaMoshiach speedily in our days.

B'Birkas HaTorah, your great-uncle,

Reuven Feinstein

RABBI NAFTALI JAEGER
ROSH HaYeshiva

בס"ד

שמואל קמנצקי
Rabbi S. Kamenetsky

2018 Upland Way
Philadelphia, PA 19131

Home: 215-473-2798
Study: 215-473-1212

בע"ה ד' ניסן ושנת

לאחר היד היוחדלא קצפחוד שטעא
ספו אורי ישועת הרב אהרתה שליט"א
אבל תק ס' דין ורצל לפרסר מסו רבים
שוראי לא דעי אלהרת וקבלה תא קאיט
עם דעת, אין דעווח לאבע דיני אלרה ישאלו
הקפה דין הדעת.

דעי הוראתי לאד אוצרתק כאוב יאש
עמ תולד חלא קצ אא באסצה אלע חדר ישו
קלפ קלות קשה דעי יאלרה, ולבסוף יאלו
כאב דאלא שא

דורי חיים ואלו ל"ז
הוארק ולא

Rabbi Mordecai Tendler
Rav, New Hempstead Kehillah
665 Union Road, New Hempstead, NY 10977
Phone / Voicemail: (845) 354-4948
Fax: (845) 362-3130
E-Mail: rtofnh@aol.com

בס"ד

מרדכי טנדלר
תלמיד מובהק לטבא וגאון
רב משה פיינשטיין זצוק"ל
רב ואב"ד דקנ"א ניו העמפסטעד ש"י ק"ק

מחבר ספרים "מסורת משה"י ו"מעשה משה"

כ' אדר תשפ"א

ידידי וחביבי מהר"ר ירחמיאל גולדמן שליט"א חתן אחי הגאון רב אהרון ברוך שליט"א, כתב ספר מאוד מחודש בשם "פרשת ותהלים יד בידי". קראתי כמה מפרקיו על ספר בראשית. הספר בסיס על ההשקפה שיש יחס וקשר בן פרשיות החומש ופרקי תהלים.

הספר נכתב בלשון מבואר ומעניין, ומלא חכמה ועמקות בבקיאות, וראוי להתפיסה ולפרסמה. והלואי זכה המחבר לגמור כל הפרשיות ולהמשיך לכתוב עוד ספרים להגדיל תורה ולהאדירה.

ונזכה כולנו בקרוב להרמת קרן התורה ולגאולה השלימה.

הכותב לכבוד התורה,

מרדכי טנדלר

BAIS YAAKOV SCHOOL FOR GIRLS

RABBI YECHEZKEL ZWEIG, PRINCIPAL • EVA WINER HIGH SCHOOL
443.548.7700 X 110 • RABBIZWEIG@BAISYAAKOV.NET

Lower Elementary School
Preschool
Rabbi Yitzchok Sanders
Principal

Upper Elementary School
Rabbi Yochanon Stein
Principal

11111 Park Heights Avenue
Owings Mills, MD 21117
443.548.7700
Lower Elementary x 4
Upper Elementary x 3

Rabbi Benjamin Steinberg
Middle School
Rabbi Moshe Frohlich
Principal

6400 Smith Avenue
Baltimore, MD 21209
443.548.7700 x 2

Eva Winer High School
Rabbi Yechezkel Zweig
Principal

Rabbi Yehoshua Shapiro
Associate Principal

Mrs. Elise Wolf
General Studies Principal

6302 Smith Avenue
Baltimore, MD 21209
443.548.7700 x 1

Executive Office
Rabbi Zalman Nissel
Chief Executive Officer

Rabbi Aaron Gross
Director of Development

Rabbi Yaacov Siwica
Vice President, Development

6300 Smith Avenue
Baltimore, MD 21209
443.548.7700 x 5

Officers
Moshe Dov Shurin, *President*
David E. Feinberg, *Vice President*
Ari Krupp, *Treasurer*
Tzvi Schwartz, V.P. & *Secretary*
Jacob I. Shane, V.P., *Finance*
Dr. Yoel Jakobovits,
Chair, Va'ad Hachinuch

www.baisyaakov.net
Bais Yaakov is a beneficiary
of the Associated Jewish Community
Federation of Baltimore

ערב יום הקדוש, תשפ"ב   9/15/21

My yedid, R' Yerachmiel Goldman, נ"י, asked for words of support for his most original and scholarly endeavor, his beautiful sefer connecting the weekly Parshiyos with counterpart Perakim of Sefer Tehilim. Any sefer explicating Dovid Hamelech's שירות to the רבש"ע will automatically contain matters of interest to the women of כלל ישראל, who have so fervently adopted these תהילות into their daily routine and service of ה'. While it is not for me to assess the high quality of the writer's gifted analysis and commentary, I can proudly comment on the person of R' Yerachmiel. Having davened with him and earned his friendship over the years, I can think of no one more suited to this worthwhile endeavor than he. Although an attorney by trade, R' Yerachmiel's תפילות, demeanor, and עבודה could easily lead any outsider to mistakenly assume that he serves in a כלי קדש capacity within our community. His sefer reflects the טהרה of his devotion to תפילה and עבודת ה' and mirrors the cadence of his beautiful, soft, sing-song davening and learning that have so entranced and inspired me and others over the years. May R' Yerachmiel's sefer merit the reception it surely deserves, and may it ennoble its readers through his deep insights and heartfelt devotion.

Respectfully,

Rabbi Yechezkel Zweig
Menahel, Bais Yaakov Eva Winer High School of Baltimore

ACKNOWLEDGMENTS

In *Tehillim* 32, Dovid HaMelech proclaims: "וְהַבּוֹטֵחַ בַּה׳, חֶסֶד יְסוֹבְבֶנּוּ – One who trusts in Hashem, *chessed* – kindness, surrounds him."[1]

These words have intrigued, inspired, and even haunted me since hearing them as a child, sung by Yerachmiel Begun's Miami Boys Choir. Consequently, as a young yeshiva student learning in the Old City of Yerushalayim, each Friday I made sure to complete my Shabbos preparations early so that I could return to the *beis medrash*. There, in a quiet and dimmed study hall, while looking out at the Kosel and the Har HaBayis, I would recite *Tehillim* 32 slowly, deliberately, and lovingly as I davened to Hashem and thought of family and loved ones of the past, of the present, and even of the future. In particular, I would concentrate on this phrase, "וְהַבּוֹטֵחַ בַּה׳, חֶסֶד יְסוֹבְבֶנּוּ," singing it over and over again to try to absorb it into my heart, continuing even as the lights would be switched back on and as my fellow *talmidim* would repopulate the *beis medrash* in the moments before the *kedushah* of Shabbos arrived.

As is every *pasuk*, phrase, and word in *Tehillim*, the above phrase is multi-layered. It means that one who trusts in Hashem will merit to be surrounded by the *chessed* of Hashem, and as a result, will himself be the direct **recipient** of that *chessed*. It also means that one who trusts in Hashem will merit to be surrounded by the *chessed* of Hashem, but, as a result, will seek to emulate Hashem and strive to **bestow** *chessed* upon others. Both are powerful understandings.

Yet, the *p'shat* I am most conscious and appreciative of is the following: one who trusts in Hashem, *chessed* will surround him **in the form of other people**. Good people, caring people, giving people – people

---

[1] *Tehillim* 32:10.

who bestow *chessed*, and not just their *"own" chessed* but the *chessed* of **Hashem** upon him, upon his loved ones, and upon all those in his life, such that a flurry of *chessed*, even a whirlwind of *chessed*, is an ever-present reality.

Baruch Hashem, that is how I feel, and that is how I have always felt. I am the **beneficiary** of "חֶסֶד יְסוֹבְבֶנּוּ," in the form of Hashem's *chessed* lovingly conveyed by *people* in my life serving as Hashem's emissaries. It started with my wonderful parents, grandparents, siblings, aunts, uncles, cousins, and my many *rebbeim*, teachers, and friends, to which were added over the years, *baruch Hashem*, my precious wife, Naomi, my in-laws, and my dear children, along with more family, more *rebbeim*, more teachers, and more friends (*kein yirbu*). They, **you**, are all a vital part of the "חֶסֶד יְסוֹבְבֶנּוּ" of my life.

With this *sefer* as well, *baruch Hashem*, there are so many people, so many bestowers of "חֶסֶד יְסוֹבְבֶנּוּ" to acknowledge and thank.

Cherished advisors include Rabbi Mordechai Tendler; Rabbi Shmuel and Rebbitzen Brazil; Rabbi Yaakov Berger; Rabbi Elchanan Shoff; Rabbi Gedalia Oppen; Rabbi Shlomo Horwitz; Rabbi Yehoshua Kurland; Rabbi Shlomo Shulman; Rabbi Aryeh Lebowitz; Rabbi Binyamin Marwick; Rabbi Ariel Shoshan; Rabbi Lazer and Mindy Shapiro; Rabbi Raffi Bilek; Rabbi Tzvi Finkelstein; Rabbi Moshe Hubner; my in-laws, Rabbi Aron and Esther Tendler; my parents, Hon. Ronald and Janet Goldman; Rabbi Dr. Michael Shmidman; Dr. Avi Shmidman; Dr. Janet Sunness; Dr. Sheldon Tajerstein; Chaim Wealcatch; David Kramer; Yoni Sebbag; Eli Drabkin; Mrs. Karyn Toso; Ari Zoldan; Avraham Groll; Yitzchak Tendler; Avi Goldenberg; Howard Berger; Shoshana Warn; Deena Goldman; Asher Blum; Rabbi Nachman Schachter; Binyomin Wolf; Nissan Selah; Avi Dear; Shalom Goldman; and Shifra Goldman.

Lay editors include my wife, Naomi Goldman; Hon. Ronald Goldman; Rabbi Yechezkel Zweig; Larry Solomon; Dr. Dovid Lewis; Rabbi Avi Shapiro; Rabbi Yehuda Finkelstein; Hillel Goldman; and Sima Goldman.

ACKNOWLEDGMENTS

A very special thank you to Mrs. Rochel Naiman, whose role as primary editor of this *sefer* is invaluable. Despite joining late in the process, Mrs. Naiman's editing skills, attention to detail, Torah knowledge, and deep sensitivity toward the subject matter, have *b'ezras Hashem* elevated this *sefer* on every level.

Tremendous *hakaras hatov* to Mrs. Minky Kohn of MK Design for her collaboration, creativity, and commitment to this project. It was a real *zechus* to work with you.

Thank you as well to those whose dedications are contained in this *sefer*. May Hashem fulfill all the desires of your heart *l'tov*.

In addition, *hakaras hatov* to the *rebbeim* and *talmidei chachamim* of my youth who made an indelible impression on me: Rabbi Moshe Teitelbaum, Rabbi Zvi Bajnon, Rabbi Yehuda Shmulewitz, Rabbi Yechezkel Lehrer, Dr. Mark Sicklick, Dr. Andrew Sicklick, Dr. Yaakov Shalev, and Rabbi David Lapa *zt"l*, as well as my favorite high school English teacher, Mrs. Susan Ackerman, who took notice of and encouraged my writing.

Perhaps most of all, the blessing of "חֶסֶד יְסוֹבְבֶנּוּ" manifested itself around my *mishpachah's* Shabbos table, when on a weekly basis we would discuss the connections between the *Parshas HaShavua* and its corresponding *kapitel*[2] *Tehillim*. What tremendous *nachas* it was when my children would each open a *Sefer Tehillim* and parse through each word and phrase in search of a connection or *chiddush*. Thank you, Sima Ariella and Moshe Dovid, Chaim Zev, Shifra Gittel, Shalom Eliyahu, and Yisroel Yosef. May that *nachas* only continue, as we, as a family, continue to craft and study future volumes of this *sefer* together, *b'ezras Hashem*.

Finally, thank you to my *eishes chayil*, Naomi Miriam. Born into a family of true *gadlus baTorah*, I am humbled by the unwavering love, advice, and support that you provide to me always, and I look forward to

---

[2] *Kapitel* is synonymous with *"perek"* and "chapter" of *Tehillim*.

the years to come, as together we strive to embody "חֶסֶד יְסוֹבְבֶנּוּ" and serve Hashem, inspire others, and help bring *Moshiach Tzidkeinu*.

Be'yedidus,

Yerachmiel Goldman
Elul 5784/September 2024
Baltimore, Maryland

INTRODUCTION

"עַל כֵּן אֲדַבֵּר בָּךְ נִכְבָּדוֹת, וְשִׁמְךָ אֲכַבֵּד בְּשִׁירֵי יְדִידוֹת – Therefore I will speak of You [Hashem] in glorious terms, and Your Name I shall honor with songs of belovedness."[1]

The Torah, read and studied weekly in the *Parshas HaShavua*, has always been the foundation of Jewish learning and spiritual growth, while *Tehillim* has sustained the faith and belief of generations of Jewish solace seekers.

While Torah and *Tehillim* are often considered to be separate and distinct entities within the framework of Tanach,[2] in actuality they are very much intertwined. The Gemara in *Taanis*[3] states that upon discovering a lesson found in *Mishlei* that Rabbi Yochanan did not immediately recognize as having a source in the Torah itself, he exclaimed in bewilderment: "מִי אִיכָּא מִידֵּי דִּכְתִיבִי בִּכְתוּבֵי דְּלָא רְמִיזִי בְּאוֹרְיָיתָא – Is there anything that is written in the *Kesuvim* that is not alluded to in the Torah?" Such a possibility was unthinkable to Rabbi Yochanan, for Hashem's Torah is infinite and all-encompassing. As *Rashi* explains, the Torah is the foundation of the writings of the *Neviim* and *Kesuvim*, and all such writings have an earlier basis in the Torah itself.[4]

Of course, *Kesuvim* includes all of Dovid HaMelech's writings in *Sefer Tehillim*, and thus all of *Tehillim* has a basis in the Torah. In fact, the Gemara in *Yevamos*[5] describes the exhilarating moment when Dovid

---

[1] From the *tefillah Anim Zemiros*.
[2] Tanach, or תַּנַ״ךְ, is the abbreviation for Torah, *Neviim*, and *Kesuvim*, which comprise the totality of the twenty-four books of the Jewish Scripture.
[3] *Taanis* 9a.
[4] *Rashi, Taanis* 9a.
[5] *Yevamos* 77a.

INTRODUCTION

HaMelech discovered an allusion to *himself* in the Torah. He discerned an association between the Torah's word "הַנִּמְצָאֹת – that were found"[6] used in connection with the rescue of Lot's daughters from Sedom (both of whom would be progenitors of the Davidic Dynasty), and the similar such opening word used in the Divinely inspired phrase in *Tehillim*: "מָצָאתִי דָּוִד עַבְדִּי; בְּשֶׁמֶן קָדְשִׁי מְשַׁחְתִּיו – I found Dovid, My servant; with My holy oil I have anointed him."[7] Moreover, the Gemara[8] reveals that Dovid memorialized this thrilling and personal discovery in another statement in *Tehillim*: "אָז אָמַרְתִּי, הִנֵּה בָאתִי בִּמְגִלַּת סֵפֶר כָּתוּב עָלָי – Then I said: Behold have I come with the Scroll of the Book that is written for *me*!"[9]

Perhaps just as astounding is the following revelation from the *sefer Degel Machaneh Ephraim*.[10] Expounding on the *pasuk* in *Tehillim*: "לִי קִוּוּ רְשָׁעִים לְאַבְּדֵנִי; עֵדֹתֶיךָ אֶתְבּוֹנָן – Against me did the wicked hope to destroy me; but Your testimonies I contemplate,"[11] he writes:

> כִּי יָדוּעַ שֶׁדָּוִד הַמֶּלֶךְ עָלָיו הַשָּׁלוֹם חִבֵּר הַסֵּפֶר תְּהִלִּים חֲמִשָּׁה סְפָרִים כְּנֶגֶד חֲמִשָּׁה חֻמְשֵׁי תּוֹרָה, **נִמְצָא כָּלוּל וְגָנוּז בּוֹ כָּל הַתּוֹרָה כֻּלָּהּ**, וְהָיִינוּ כְּשֶׁבָּאוּ עָלָיו צָרוֹת – דֶּרֶךְ מָשָׁל הַזֵּיפִים וַיֹּאמְרוּ וְכוּ' – אָז חִבֵּר קַפִּיטֶל תְּהִלִּים (תְּהִלִּים נד), **שֶׁהִסְתַּכֵּל בְּאוֹתִיּוֹת וְתֵבוֹת שֶׁל אוֹתוֹ הַצָּרָה, וְנִתְגַּלָּה לוֹ עַל יְדֵי זֶה אֵיזֶה אוֹר מִן הַתּוֹרָה וְחִבֵּר כְּנֶגְדּוֹ קַפִּיטֶל תְּהִלִּים, שֶׁבְּוַדַּאי יֵשׁ כְּנֶגְדּוֹ אֵיזֶה פָּרָשָׁה מִן הַתּוֹרָה**, וְהוּא שֶׁאָמַר "לִי קִוּוּ רְשָׁעִים לְאַבְּדֵנִי" – קִוּוּ לְשׁוֹן אֲסִיפָה וְהָיִינוּ שֶׁנֶּאֶסְפוּ עָלַי רְשָׁעִים לְאַבְּדֵנִי, וְעַל יְדֵי זֶה "עֵדוֹתֶיךָ אֶתְבּוֹנָן" – וְהָיִינוּ שֶׁעַל יְדֵי זֶה נִתְגַּלֶּה לִי אוֹר הַתּוֹרָה וְהָעֵדוּת.

It is known that Dovid HaMelech, *alav ha'shalom*, composed *Sefer Tehillim* in five books corresponding to the five books of the Torah. **As such, incorporated into *Tehillim* and hidden within it is the entirety of the Torah.** Therefore, when *tzaros* (challenges and

---

[6] *Bereishis* 19:15.
[7] *Tehillim* 89:21.
[8] *Yevamos* 77a.
[9] *Tehillim* 40:8.
[10] *Degel Machaneh Ephraim, Parshas Chayei Sarah.*
[11] *Tehillim* 119:95.

PARSHAH & TEHILLIM HAND IN HAND

problems) came upon Dovid, for example when the Ziffim [who were members of Dovid's own tribe] said [and betrayed his whereabouts to Shaul HaMelech, as described in *I Shmuel* 23:19–29], it was then that Dovid composed *Tehillim* 54, **for Dovid looked deeply into the letters and words of that particular *tzarah*, and by virtue of doing so, a certain light from the Torah was revealed to him, by which he composed that chapter of *Tehillim*, for certainly there is a particular *parshah* (portion) of the Torah corresponding to it.** And that is what is written: "Against me did the wicked קוו, hope, to destroy me," but קוו is also an expression of gathering, meaning that while the wicked actually gathered against me to destroy me, because of that/during that time: "Your testimonies I contemplate," and through doing so it was revealed to me the light of the Torah and its testimonies.

The nineteenth-century Torah scholar, Rabbi Yitzchak Baer *zt"l*, also known as Rabbi Isaac Seligman Baer, highlighted the relationship between each *Parshas HaShavua* in the Torah and a specific *kapitel* of *Tehillim*, thereby reinforcing the combination of these two mainstays of Jewish thought and experience. His *Siddur Avodas Yisrael* (originally published by Rödelheim Press in 1868) contains an enigmatic list revealing that each *Parshas HaShavua* has a corresponding *kapitel Tehillim*. An authoritative version of the *Siddur Avodas Yisrael* republished in 1901 contains the list[12] and is accompanied by the following note: "מִזְמוֹרִים שֶׁנּוֹהֲגִים לוֹמַר בְּכָל שַׁבָּת וְשַׁבָּת מֵעִין הַפָּרְשִׁיּוֹת" – translated as "Psalms that are customarily recited each

---

[12] Note that the list is printed on page 962 of the 1901 printing of the *Siddur Avodas Yisrael*. Note further that some more recent reprints of the *Siddur Avodas Yisrael* are limited to only 740 total pages, with pages omitted presumably to cut costs and/or to reduce the bulkiness of the siddur rather than due to inaccuracies and the like. Unfortunately, in some reprinted editions, the *Parshah/Tehillim* list is omitted. Finally, please note that at the time of the printing of this *sefer*, the author does not have a copy of the original 1868 printing.

and every Shabbos as appropriate for each *Parshas HaShavua*." Indeed, it appears that it was an established *minhag* for individuals to recite the applicable *kapitel* each Shabbos, thus creating an additional layer of connection to the weekly *Parshah*.

ArtScroll as well, in its more recent versions of *Tehillim*, reprinted the list under the heading of "Sabbath Psalms," and states the following: "*Siddur Avodas Yisrael* lists Psalms to recite each Sabbath of the year, corresponding to the respective Torah readings."

In both such instances, the *Parshah* & *Tehillim* list consists of the following:

See Table on the following page.

Parshah & Tehillim – to be recited each Shabbos, per *Siddur Avodas Yisrael*

Sefer Bereishis סֵפֶר בְּרֵאשִׁית		Sefer Shemos סֵפֶר שְׁמוֹת		Sefer Vayikra סֵפֶר וַיִּקְרָא		Sefer Bamidbar סֵפֶר בַּמִּדְבָּר		Sefer Devarim סֵפֶר דְּבָרִים	
Bereishis בְּרֵאשִׁית	139 קלט	Shemos שְׁמוֹת	99 צט	Vayikra וַיִּקְרָא	50 נ	Bamidbar בַּמִּדְבָּר	122 קכב	Devarim דְּבָרִים	137 קלז
Noach נֹחַ	29 כט	Va'eira וָאֵרָא	46 מו	Tzav צַו	107 קז	Naso נָשֹׂא	67 סז	Va'eschanan וָאֶתְחַנַּן	90 צ
Lech Lecha לֶךְ לְךָ	110 קי	Bo בֹּא	77 עז	Shemini שְׁמִינִי	128 קכח	Behaalosecha בְּהַעֲלֹתְךָ	68 סח	Eikev עֵקֶב	75 עה
Vayeira וַיֵּרָא	11 יא	Beshalach בְּשַׁלַּח	66 סו	Tazria תַזְרִיעַ	106 קו	Shelach שְׁלַח	64 סד	Re'eh רְאֵה	97 צז
Chayei Sarah חַיֵּי שָׂרָה	45 מה	Yisro יִתְרוֹ	19 יט	Metzora מְצֹרָע	120 קכ	Korach קֹרַח	5 ה	Shoftim שֹׁפְטִים	17 יז
Toldos תּוֹלְדוֹת	36 לו	Mishpatim מִשְׁפָּטִים	72 עב	Acharei Mos אַחֲרֵי מוֹת	26 כו	Chukas חֻקַּת	95 צה	Ki Seitzei כִּי תֵצֵא	32 לב
Vayeitzei וַיֵּצֵא	3 ג	Terumah תְּרוּמָה	26 כו	Kedoshim קְדֹשִׁים	15 טו	Balak בָּלָק	79 עט	Ki Savo כִּי תָבוֹא	51 נא
Vayishlach וַיִּשְׁלַח	140 קמ	Tetzaveh תְּצַוֶּה	65 סה	Emor אֱמֹר	42 מב	Pinchas פִּינְחָס	50 נ	Nitzavim נִצָּבִים	81 פא
Vayeishev וַיֵּשֶׁב	112 קיב	Ki Sisa כִּי תִשָּׂא	75 עה	Behar בְּהַר	112 קיב	Mattos מַטּוֹת	111 קיא	Vayeilech וַיֵּלֶךְ	65 סה
Mikeitz מִקֵּץ	40 מ	Vayakhel וַיַּקְהֵל	61 סא	Bechukosai בְּחֻקֹּתַי	105 קה	Mas'ei מַסְעֵי	49 מט	Haazinu הַאֲזִינוּ	71 עא
Vayigash וַיִּגַּשׁ	48 מח	Pekudei פְקוּדֵי	45 מה					V'zos Habrachah וְזֹאת הַבְּרָכָה	12 יב
Vayechi וַיְחִי	41 מא								

© Copyright 2024 – Yerachmiel Goldman, from the *sefer* שִׁירֵי יְדִידוּת: *Parshah & Tehillim Hand In Hand*

INTRODUCTION

Reciting the designated *kapitel* each Shabbos enables us to complete a mini-synthesis of Tanach, as we intertwine the *Parshas HaShavua* (Torah), the *Haftarah* (*Neviim*), and *Tehillim* (*Kesuvim*).

Furthermore, this recitation provides a new perspective from which to approach, analyze, and *live* the *Parshas HaShavua*.

The above custom and list were not claimed by Rabbi Baer as his own original insight or *chiddush*. Rabbi Baer describes this practice as a pre-existing *minhag* among Klal Yisrael, and sources have been found dating this *minhag* at least as far back as the Geonic Period, and specifically to Rabbeinu Hai Gaon who lived in the eleventh century.[13]

While the designated *kapitel* could certainly have been recited individually, the general practice was for the entire congregation to recite the *kapitel* in unison each Shabbos morning during the powerful *eis ratzon* of the removal of the *Sefer Torah* from the *aron kodesh*.[14] While still practiced during Rabbi Baer's time in the mid-1800s, sadly, it is apparent that this practice has become a lost *mesorah*. Perhaps it is a lost *mesorah* that we, *b'ezras Hashem*, can help to restore.

The *Parshah & Tehillim* list provided by the *Siddur Avodas Yisrael* is enigmatic because it does not include an explanation of the connections between the *Parshas HaShavua* and its corresponding *kapitel Tehillim* but rather only codifies them. Often, the connections are not self-evident or seem to be tenuous or limited when left only to a cursory review.

---

[13] *Sefer Shimush Tehillim of Rabbeinu Hai Gaon*, p. 16; see also *Otzar Dinim U'Minhagim*, pp. 433-434.
[14] *Sefer Shimush Tehillim*, p. 16.

As someone who cherishes the opportunity to perform the mitzvah of *shenayim mikra v'echad targum* each week,[15] as well as someone who longs to be a student and soldier of Dovid HaMelech, this mysterious interplay between *Parshah* and *Tehillim* certainly captured my imagination. It also captured the imagination of my precious daughter, Shifra, who, as part of our bonding in preparation for her upcoming bas mitzvah, recited each applicable *kapitel Tehillim* with me every Shabbos of year 5780, and together we brainstormed each week and all year long, into years 5781 and 5782 in an effort to try to uncover the many hidden connections.

While we would quickly be struck by a common theme or recall or discover a famous Gemara, Midrash, or *divrei Chazal* clearly linking the *Parshah* and the *kapitel*, that connection, strong as it was, only accounted for a small portion of the *kapitel* and a fraction of the much longer *Parshah*. Unsatisfied by what seemed like an incomplete connection, our process required further study, investigation, creativity, and of course above all, *siyata d'Shmaya*, in order to discover many additional common links throughout. Our approach was framed by the words of *Rashi*[16] who so encouragingly states: "Let the text of Scripture be explained in its simplest meaning, with each word spoken in its appropriate context; then let the homiletical interpretation be expounded, as it says: 'Are My words not like fire, says Hashem, and as a hammer shatters a rock'[17] and divides the rock into many sparks and shards." So too, the Torah contains many varied and distinct meanings and interpretations, each reflecting a different aspect of Hashem's singular truth.

Baruch Hashem, as a result of our bas mitzvah preparations, this *sefer* developed and covers *Sefer Bereishis*, revealing and explaining the many connections between each *Parshah* from *Bereishis* through *Vayechi* and

---

[15] The mitzvah of reading the text of the weekly *Parshah* twice, and then once more with the commentary of *Onkelos* (or *Rashi*). See *Brachos* 8a–b.

[16] *Rashi, Shemos* 6:9.

[17] *Yirmiyahu* 23:29.

INTRODUCTION

its corresponding *kapitel Tehillim*. To orient the reader, each chapter of this *sefer* is tied to a particular *Parshah* and begins with the Hebrew/English translation of the applicable *kapitel Tehillim*.[18] The *Parshas HaShavua* usually serves as the backdrop for the analysis, which springs to life from a deep focus on the Divinely inspired words and phrases composed by Dovid HaMelech in each *kapitel*. Put another way, while it is important to bear the particular *Parshah* in mind, it is the *kapitel Tehillim* itself that is the initial focus. Flowing in whatever direction and redirection Dovid HaMelech may have taken the *kapitel*, we then attempt to understand how it relates back to the *Parshah*. Essentially, this *sefer* attempts to analyze the *Parshas HaShavua* from a new vantage point: we "see" through the eyes of Dovid HaMelech, based on the focus and content of the applicable *kapitel Tehillim*. As such, the approach and style of each chapter may vary from chapter to chapter, as well as within a chapter itself. For example, it may include a combination of broad thematic associations, more detailed and nuanced *pasuk*-by-*pasuk* interconnections, and word associations between the Torah and *Tehillim*.

This work on *Sefer Bereishis* reflects the first of five volumes which will, *b'ezras Hashem*, cover the full spectrum of *Parshiyos HaShavua* in an effort to further reveal another small layer of what we all believe and know to be the Divine unity of all of Hashem's Torah.

At a minimum, my hope is that, along with the mainstay of the *leining* of the *Parshas HaShavua* in shul each Shabbos, the learner of this *sefer* will be inspired to recite the *Parshah's* corresponding *kapitel Tehillim* each Shabbos. The thought that we can thereby collectively revive the lost *mesorah* described by the *Siddur Avodas Yisrael* and which has ancient roots dating back more than a thousand years to the Geonic Period is

---

[18] The English translation of each *kapitel Tehillim* is modeled after the ArtScroll Interlinear Tehillim, with some changes by the author of this *sefer*. The Hebrew text of each *kapitel Tehillim* is gleaned from Mechon Mamre with some punctuation changes by the author of this *sefer*.

electrifying! *B'ezras Hashem*, this forgotten tradition will be revitalized and reimplemented among Klal Yisrael. At least, let's start with me and you.

Additionally, my hope is that the contents of this *sefer* will be incorporated into the reader's weekday and Shabbos Torah-learning experience, and that Jews will begin to appreciate anew the *Parshah*, the *kapitel Tehillim*, and their inter-connectivity from innovative and deeper perspectives. This will include not only those provided in this *sefer*, but also other connections made by Chazal that may have been intentionally or unintentionally omitted here, and even the reader's own *chiddushim*.

Of course, as with anything, *hachanah*, preparation, is key. The more deeply and thoroughly one immerses himself in the *kapitel* and the *Parshah*, the more benefit one will glean from this *sefer*.[19] For example, just as some begin to study the *Parshas HaShavua* days in advance of Shabbos, a recitation of the applicable *kapitel Tehillim* in advance – throughout the upcoming week in preparation for Shabbos – will enable one to absorb the *kapitel*'s words, content, meaning, flow, rhythm, rhyme, *kedushah*, and the *deveikus ba'Hashem* that it brings. Doing so will help create a deeper appreciation of the contents of this *sefer*, as well as an even deeper appreciation for both *Tehillim* and the *Parshas HaShavua*.

A special by-product of the above is that doing so will undoubtedly make Dovid HaMelech a stronger presence in our homes and hearts each Shabbos. Moreover, combining Dovid's experiences and messages in *Tehillim* with those of Hashem's servant, Moshe Rabbeinu, can propel us and our families to levels of learning, understanding, and *kedushah* we never dared dream of.

Most importantly, the hope is that this *sefer*, respectfully and lovingly titled שִׁירֵי יְדִידוֹת: *Parshah & Tehillim Hand In Hand*, will reveal how both the clear as well as the hidden messages of Moshe Rabbeinu in the שִׁירָה,

---

[19] That said, every chapter of this *sefer* has been divided into numerous sub-chapters, each of which can be learned and appreciated on its own.

song, that is the Torah, and the messages of Dovid HaMelech in the שִׁירָה that is *Tehillim*, join יָד בְּיָד, hand-in-hand, to reveal the messages of, and bring us ever closer to, the Divine Author behind both works.

Our beloved Hashem is our Ultimate יְדִיד נֶפֶשׁ, with Whom we strive to live our lives יָד בְּיָד: proverbially clutching His hand as a child securely holds on to his father; shaking hands with Him in a manner symbolic of two יְדִידִים who share a genuine friendship; and lovingly holding His hand like two inseparable and forever loyal דּוֹדִים, beloveds.

Yehi ratzon, it is my fervent wish that the readers of this *sefer*, Klal Yisrael as a whole, and most importantly, *Hashem Yisbarach*, accept this *sefer* in fulfillment of the following statement of the Gemara[20] that I have carried in my soul for so many years:

יָבוֹא יָדִיד בֶּן יָדִיד, וְיִבְנֶה יָדִיד לְיָדִיד, בְּחֶלְקוֹ שֶׁל יָדִיד, וְיִתְכַּפְּרוּ בּוֹ יְדִידִים

"May a beloved, the son of a beloved, build a beloved for the Beloved, in the portion of a beloved, and through that, may atonement be achieved by the beloveds,"

kein yehi ratzon.

---

[20] *Menachos* 53a.

CHAPTER 1

PARSHAS BEREISHIS & TEHILLIM 139
פָּרָשַׁת בְּרֵאשִׁית / תְּהִלִּים קלט

תְּהִלִּים קלט — TEHILLIM 139

1 For the conductor, by Dovid, a psalm. Hashem, You have scrutinized me, and You Know.	א לַמְנַצֵּחַ לְדָוִד מִזְמוֹר; ה' חֲקַרְתַּנִי וַתֵּדָע.
2 You know my sitting down and my rising up; You understand my thought from afar.	ב אַתָּה יָדַעְתָּ שִׁבְתִּי וְקוּמִי; בַּנְתָּה לְרֵעִי מֵרָחוֹק.
3 The path [that I travel] and [the place] where I lie down You encompass; [with] all my ways You are familiar.	ג אָרְחִי וְרִבְעִי זֵרִיתָ; וְכָל דְּרָכַי הִסְכַּנְתָּה.
4 For the word is not yet on my tongue, behold, Hashem, You knew it all.	ד כִּי אֵין מִלָּה בִּלְשׁוֹנִי, הֵן ה' יָדַעְתָּ כֻלָּהּ.
5 Back and front you have restricted me, and You have laid upon me the palm of Your hand.	ה אָחוֹר וָקֶדֶם צַרְתָּנִי, וַתָּשֶׁת עָלַי כַּפֶּכָה.
6 Concealed is knowledge from me; exalted, I am incapable of it.	ו פְּלִיאָה דַעַת מִמֶּנִּי; נִשְׂגְּבָה, לֹא אוּכַל לָהּ.

7	Where can I go from Your spirit, and where from Your Presence can I flee?	ז אָנָה אֵלֵךְ מֵרוּחֶךָ, וְאָנָה מִפָּנֶיךָ אֶבְרָח.
8	If I ascend up to heaven, there You are; and if I make my bed in the lowest depths, behold, You are there.	ח אִם אֶסַּק שָׁמַיִם, שָׁם אָתָּה; וְאַצִּיעָה שְּׁאוֹל, הִנֶּךָּ.
9	Were I to take up wings of dawn, were I to dwell in the distant west.	ט אֶשָּׂא כַנְפֵי שָׁחַר, אֶשְׁכְּנָה בְּאַחֲרִית יָם.
10	Even there Your hand leads me, and grasps me does Your right hand.	י גַּם שָׁם יָדְךָ תַנְחֵנִי, וְתֹאחֲזֵנִי יְמִינֶךָ.
11	Were I to say: "Surely darkness will shadow me," then the light would be illuminated around me.	יא וָאֹמַר: אַךְ חֹשֶׁךְ יְשׁוּפֵנִי; וְלַיְלָה אוֹר בַּעֲדֵנִי.
12	Even the darkness is not too dark for You; and night like the day shines, the darkness is the same as the light.	יב גַּם חֹשֶׁךְ לֹא יַחְשִׁיךְ מִמֶּךָּ; וְלַיְלָה כַּיּוֹם יָאִיר, כַּחֲשֵׁיכָה כָּאוֹרָה.
13	For You have created my mind; You have covered me in the womb of my mother.	יג כִּי אַתָּה קָנִיתָ כִלְיֹתָי; תְּסֻכֵּנִי בְּבֶטֶן אִמִּי.
14	I thank You because awesomely, wondrously am I [fashioned]; wondrous are Your works, and my soul knows it well.	יד אוֹדְךָ עַל כִּי נוֹרָאוֹת נִפְלֵיתִי; נִפְלָאִים מַעֲשֶׂיךָ, וְנַפְשִׁי יֹדַעַת מְאֹד.
15	Not hidden was my frame from You; when I was fashioned in concealment, when I was knit together in the lowest parts of the earth.	טו לֹא נִכְחַד עָצְמִי מִמֶּךָּ; אֲשֶׁר עֻשֵּׂיתִי בַסֵּתֶר, רֻקַּמְתִּי בְּתַחְתִּיּוֹת אָרֶץ.

CHAPTER 1: BEREISHIS & TEHILLIM 139

16 My unshaped form was seen by Your eyes, and in Your book, all were recorded; [though] in many days they will be fashioned, to Him they are as one.

טז גׇּלְמִי רָאוּ עֵינֶיךָ וְעַל סִפְרְךָ כֻּלָּם יִכָּתֵבוּ; יָמִים יֻצָּרוּ (וְלֹא) וְלוֹ אֶחָד בָּהֶם.

17 To me, how glorious are Your thoughts, God! How very great are their core ideas!

יז וְלִי מַה יָּקְרוּ רֵעֶיךָ אֵ-ל; מֶה עָצְמוּ רָאשֵׁיהֶם.

18 Were I to count them, more than the grains of sand would be their number; even if I were to be constantly awake and always with You.

יח אֶסְפְּרֵם, מֵחוֹל יִרְבּוּן; הֱקִיצֹתִי וְעוֹדִי עִמָּךְ.

19 Would that You would slay, God, the wicked, and men of blood [to whom I would say] "Depart from me!"

יט אִם תִּקְטֹל, אֱ-לוֹהַּ, רָשָׁע, וְאַנְשֵׁי דָמִים סוּרוּ מֶנִּי.

20 Those who pronounce Your Name for wicked schemes, it is taken in vain by Your enemies.

כ אֲשֶׁר יֹמְרוּךָ לִמְזִמָּה; נָשֻׂא לַשָּׁוְא עָרֶיךָ.

21 For indeed, those who hate You, Hashem, I hate them, and with those who rise up against You, I quarrel.

כא הֲלוֹא מְשַׂנְאֶיךָ, ה', אֶשְׂנָא; וּבִתְקוֹמְמֶיךָ אֶתְקוֹטָט.

22 With the utmost hatred I hate them; enemies they have become to me.

כב תַּכְלִית שִׂנְאָה שְׂנֵאתִים; לְאוֹיְבִים הָיוּ לִי.

23 Examine me, God, and know my heart; test me and know my thoughts.

כג חׇקְרֵנִי אֵ-ל וְדַע לְבָבִי; בְּחָנֵנִי וְדַע שַׂרְעַפָּי.

24 And see if a way of sadness/rebellion is within me; and lead me in the way of the world/eternity.

כד וּרְאֵה אִם דֶּרֶךְ עֹצֶב בִּי; וּנְחֵנִי בְּדֶרֶךְ עוֹלָם.

45

INTRODUCTION: THE TEHILLIM / BEREISHIS CONNECTION

The connection between *Tehillim* 139 and *Parshas Bereishis* is not immediately evident from a simple reading of the texts. Moreover, *Tehillim* 139 is not a psalm that describes Creation with beautifully vivid imagery, nor does it overtly describe Adam HaRishon's story and struggles, as *Parshas Bereishis* does. Nonetheless, as we journey together through *Tehillim* 139 using the prism of *Parshas Bereishis*, we will see the remarkable and numerous connections between the two, so much so, that we will almost feel that Dovid HaMelech's psalm is not only speaking *about Parshas Bereishis*, but is speaking *on behalf* of Adam HaRishon! Furthermore, at times it will feel as if it is actually Adam *himself* who is speaking – speaking to Hashem, and to us. Amazingly, there is an opinion in the *Midrash Tehillim* that the original composer of *Tehillim* 139 was, in fact, Adam HaRishon![1]

As we approach *Parshas Bereishis* (and all the *Parshiyos HaShavua* that follow) with the additional benefit of its accompanying *kapitel Tehillim*, may we be *zocheh* to channel the forthcoming insights, emotions, prayers, and *pesukim* toward deeper closeness to Hashem and His Torah.

---

[1] *Midrash Tehillim, Shocher Tov* 139. See also *Bava Basra* 14b and *Rashi* there.

THE MANY CONNECTIONS BETWEEN PARSHAS BEREISHIS & TEHILLIM 139

Pasuk 1:

לַמְנַצֵּחַ לְדָוִד מִזְמוֹר;

ה' חֲקַרְתַּנִי וַתֵּדָע

For the conductor, by Dovid, a psalm.
Hashem, You have scrutinized me, and You know.

Pasuk 2:

אַתָּה יָדַעְתָּ שִׁבְתִּי וְקוּמִי;

בַּנְתָּה לְרֵעִי מֵרָחוֹק

You know my sitting down and my rising up;
You understand my thought from afar.

Pasuk 4:

כִּי אֵין מִלָּה בִּלְשׁוֹנִי,

הֵן ה' יָדַעְתָּ כֻלָּהּ

For the word is not yet on my tongue,
behold, Hashem, You knew it all.

Downfall Through *Daas*

Before a Jew passes away, there is a custom that he or she should try to take a drink of water in order to make one last *brachah* and say: "בָּרוּךְ אַתָּה ה' אֱ-לֹהֵינוּ מֶלֶךְ הָעוֹלָם שֶׁהַכֹּל נִהְיֶה בִּדְבָרוֹ – Blessed are You Hashem, our God, King of the world, who brings everything into being by His word." Doing so is a final declaration that all of Creation, including the person himself, exists only by virtue of the kindness of Hashem. It is a final statement of *hakaras hatov* for all the goodness that Hashem has bestowed upon the person in his lifetime and a recognition of Hashem as Creator of the vast world in which he himself was blessed to be a part.

Then, if time and circumstance (or, more accurately, if *Hashem*) allows, the Jew will rush to recite *Borei Nefashos*, the *brachah* said *after* drinking, in which he declares: "בָּרוּךְ אַתָּה ה' אֱ-לֹהֵינוּ מֶלֶךְ הָעוֹלָם בּוֹרֵא נְפָשׁוֹת רַבּוֹת וְחֶסְרוֹנָן עַל כָּל מַה שֶׁבָּרָאתָ לְהַחֲיוֹת בָּהֶם נֶפֶשׁ כָּל חָי, בָּרוּךְ חֵי הָעוֹלָמִים – Blessed are You Hashem, our God, King of the world, Who creates the many souls and their deficiencies; for all that You create to give life to the living soul, blessed is the Life-Giver of the worlds."[2] And with that final statement the Jew is then ready to relinquish, or rather return, that soul to Hashem.[3]

In *Borei Nefashos*, one acknowledges not only his own God-given and intrinsically holy soul, but also his own חֶסְרוֹנָן, deficiencies; he recognizes that all human beings are created imperfect by Divine design. However, there is one exception to this rule of universal imperfection: the first man himself. Indeed, Adam HaRishon was created perfect; physically, mentally, and spiritually – perfect in every way, so much so that Chazal teach us that when the angels saw Adam HaRishon they wanted to sing to him the famous praise "קָדוֹשׁ קָדוֹשׁ קָדוֹשׁ"[4] – to declare him infinitely holy, thinking that he was the embodiment of Hashem Himself.[5] Even after they realized that he was not God, they still excitedly served him, delivering

---

[2] Interestingly, located outside of the burial shrine of the *Chida* on *Har Hamenuchos*, is an elegant water station with the *brachos* of *Shehakol* and *Borei Nefashos* prominently displayed, designed to encourage visitors of the cemetery to say these *brachos* and thereby perform a *living Kiddush HaShem*.

[3] Note that the foregoing is not to the exclusion of the *vidui* prayer to be said at death and/or such prominent and succinct *pesukim* such as the famed "שְׁמַע יִשְׂרָאֵל ה' אֱ-לֹהֵינוּ ה' אֶחָד".

[4] *Yeshayahu* 6:3.

[5] *Yalkut Shimoni, Bereishis* 23.

CHAPTER 1: BEREISHIS & TEHILLIM 139

him delicacies of roasted meat and wine in an effort to minister to this perfect being.[6]

In fact, the Midrash states that at the time Hashem created Adam HaRishon, He took him to pass before all the trees of Gan Eden and said to him: "See My creations, how pleasant and praiseworthy each is, and all that I created, I created for you; תֵּן דַּעְתְּךָ – use your knowledge, and take heed not to damage and destroy My world."[7] Hashem's words "תֵּן דַּעְתְּךָ – use your knowledge," were supposed to resonate powerfully with Adam, who was being taught that it was *specifically* his Divinely bestowed דַּעַת (*daas*), that would *prevent* him from sinning and damaging Hashem's world, and that from the outset his *daas* was sufficient for him to appreciate and utilize Hashem's world to the fullest.

We can now sense the irony here even more acutely. Adam's desire for דַּעַת, which Hashem directly told him was not lacking or needed, transformed his one and only mitzvah[8] into history's first and gravest sin: eating from the עֵץ הַדַּעַת טוֹב וָרָע – the Tree of Knowledge of Good and Evil. It was a sin that led to the struggles and mortality of his progeny for all generations to follow[9] until the time of Moshiach, the Messianic Era, when the world will once again overflow with Hashem's original and pure דַּעַת, as Yeshayahu HaNavi states: "כִּי מָלְאָה הָאָרֶץ דֵּעָה אֶת ה', כַּמַּיִם לַיָּם מְכַסִּים – For the earth will be full of the דֵּעָה – knowledge of Hashem, as the waters cover the sea."[10]

Repair Through *Daas*

Therefore, it is fitting that Dovid HaMelech commences *Tehillim* 139, which corresponds to *Parshas Bereishis*, with an emphasis on the

---

[6] *Sanhedrin* 59b.
[7] *Koheles Rabbah* 7:13.
[8] E.g., *Rashi* to *Bereishis* 3:7, from *Bereishis Rabbah* 19:6.
[9] *Bereishis* 3:19.
[10] *Yeshayahu* 11:9.

word and concept of דַּעַת by placing the *shoresh*, root-word, of דַּעַת immediately in *pesukim* 1, 2, and 4:

- *Pasuk* 1: "ה' חֲקַרְתַּנִי וַתֵּדָע" – Hashem, You have scrutinized me, and You know."
- *Pasuk* 2: "אַתָּה יָדַעְתָּ שִׁבְתִּי וְקוּמִי" – You know my sitting down and my rising up."
- *Pasuk* 4: "הֵן ה' יָדַעְתָּ כֻלָּהּ" – Behold, Hashem, You knew it all."

The *Midrash Tehillim*[11] expounds upon the reference to *daas* in *pasuk* 1 as a multifaceted statement by Adam HaRishon himself: Adam HaRishon recognized Hashem's omniscience, and specifically: (1) Hashem's *knowledge* of Adam's need for a mate, since the word "יָדַע" in Biblical terminology often connotes knowledge of an intimate nature;[12] (2) Hashem's *knowledge* involved in the precise placement of Adam in Gan Eden, hinted in the word "שִׁבְתִּי," which can also mean "my dwelling"; and (3) Hashem's *knowledge* of Adam's sin and banishment from the Garden of Eden, alluded to in the word "קוּמִי," which connotes "getting up" and "going" after Adam was expelled. Moreover, through the plain meaning of the initial four *pesukim*, we see a "*chazakah*," a three-fold reference to *daas* and the knowledge possessed by God, as well as *Adam's* understanding that Hashem possesses complete knowledge about every aspect of man.

But there is more. When we approach the text with the mindset that this *kapitel* is intricately tied to *Parshas Bereishis*, we perceive Dovid HaMelech's yearning – and through him, yearn ourselves as well to bring a *tikkun*, rectification, to Adam HaRishon's sin of eating from the *Eitz HaDaas*. When we recite this *kapitel* with *kavanah* – concentration and focus – by accentuating the words, phrases, and concepts that emphasize

---

[11] *Midrash Tehillim, Shocher Tov* 139.
[12] E.g., *Bereishis* 4:1.

daas, we can accomplish something monumental: with each word of prayer, we too can contribute to the *tikkun* of the sin of the *Eitz HaDaas*.

Atah Chonein Le'Adam Daas

In addition, we can now acquire a deeper understanding of the fourth blessing of *Shemoneh Esrei*, which begins with "אַתָּה חוֹנֵן לְאָדָם דַּעַת – You [Hashem] graciously bestow knowledge upon man." This is not simply a general introduction about Hashem granting knowledge to human beings, but rather "לְאָדָם" is a reference to Adam HaRishon himself, to whom Hashem first granted *daas* and who serves as a warning and reminder to us that when requesting "דֵּעָה בִּינָה וְהַשְׂכֵּל" – wisdom, insight, and discernment," this needs to be requested properly. The desired knowledge must be recognized as emanating from Hashem and Hashem alone: "אַתָּה – You" Hashem, "מֵאִתְּךָ – from You," does the knowledge flow. Furthermore, the desired knowledge should be viewed as flowing from Hashem's willingness to be "חוֹנֵן" – to show us חֵן, Divine grace, and to bestow upon us a מַתְּנַת חִנָּם, a gift, and not something that we self-generate as Adam tried to do. And perhaps most importantly, we must consider the purpose for which we request such knowledge. The next *brachah* in *Shemoneh Esrei*, the *brachah* of *Hashiveinu*, provides an answer. We ask for knowledge for the holy purposes of knowing and observing Torah, performing *avodas Hashem*, and achieving a complete *teshuvah* – repentance that returns us closer to Hashem and even elevates us to stand before Him. Sadly, these purposes were rejected by Adam when he disobeyed Hashem and ate from the *Eitz HaDaas*.

Remarkably, but perhaps not surprisingly, *Tehillim* 139 will continue to emphasize דַּעַת in *pesukim* 6, 14, and twice in the penultimate *pasuk* 23, as we will discuss below.

Pasuk 1:
לַמְנַצֵּחַ לְדָוִד מִזְמוֹר
For the conductor, by Dovid, a psalm.

Adam's Personal Connection to Dovid HaMelech

"By Dovid" or "To Dovid" alludes to the *tikkun* of Adam HaRishon through Dovid HaMelech himself. The *Zohar Hakadosh*[13] teaches that Hashem revealed to Adam HaRishon all the future generations that would ever exist. When Adam saw that Dovid was not destined to live but was supposed to die through a miscarriage, Adam became terrified and donated seventy years of his own life to Dovid. Through Adam's benevolence, Dovid would survive, excel, and grow to become Dovid Melech Yisrael, to whom we refer as "חַי וְקַיָּם – living and enduring."[14]

In the future, Dovid will be able to repay Adam HaRishon's generosity through his descendant, the *Melech HaMoshiach*. With the arrival of Moshiach, each Jew will obtain the same status that Adam had before he sinned – the ultimate *tikkun* of the *cheit* (sin) of the *Eitz HaDaas*. In a circle of kindness, Adam's gift of seventy years will ultimately result in his own *tikkun*. As a beautiful hint to this powerful triumvirate of Adam, Dovid, and Moshiach, my *rebbi*, Rabbi Shmuel Brazil, is fond of saying that the word אָדָם (Adam) is comprised of the letters א, ד, מ – which are the *roshei teivos* (first letters of the words) of אָדָם, דָּוִד, מָשִׁיחַ!

Pasuk 2:
אַתָּה יָדַעְתָּ שִׁבְתִּי וְקוּמִי;
בַּנְתָּה לְרֵעִי מֵרָחוֹק
You know my sitting down and my rising up;
You understand my thought from afar.

---

[13] *Zohar Hakadosh, Chelek aleph* 91b.
[14] *Rosh Hashanah* 25a.

Pasuk 3:

אָרְחִי וְרִבְעִי זֵרִיתָ;
וְכָל דְּרָכַי הִסְכַּנְתָּה

**The path [that I travel] and [the place] where I lie down
You encompass; [with] all my ways You are familiar.**

Pasuk 4:

כִּי אֵין מִלָּה בִּלְשׁוֹנִי,
הֵן ה' יָדַעְתָּ כֻלָּהּ

**For the word is not yet on my tongue,
behold, Hashem, You knew it all.**

The Human Condition

The connections to Adam HaRishon abound. Interestingly, *pesukim* 2 through 4 describe all aspects of Adam's (and mankind's) ordinary human life and functions: שִׁבְתִּי (sitting), קוּמִי (standing), רֵעִי (thought), רֵעִי (also excretion), אָרְחִי (walking and travel), וְרִבְעִי (lying down and sleeping), וְכָל דְּרָכַי (all of man's ways), and מִלָּה בִּלְשׁוֹנִי (speech). In addition, the phrase "וְרִבְעִי זֵרִיתָ" can be interpreted as a double reference to the facets of marital relations, conception, and family life.[15] How apropos for a *kapitel* connected to the story of the creation of mankind!

In addition, the description of these many bodily and physical functions serves as an acknowledgment that Adam HaRishon (contrary to what the angels initially thought) was not God nor was he even remotely similar to Hashem, and is consistent with the third *Ani Maamin*[16] which states: "I believe with a faith that is complete that the Creator blessed be His Name is not physical and is not subject to phenomena that are physical, and that

---

[15] *Midrash Tehillim, Shocher Tov* 139.
[16] The *"Ani Maamins"* are the Thirteen Principles of Faith, based upon the formulation of the *Rambam* in *Peirush HaMishnayos, Sanhedrin, perek* 10.

there is no comparison to Him whatsoever."[17] These *pesukim* are an admission, and an admonition, that Adam HaRishon was unlike Hashem and was indeed just a man.

Pasuk 4:

כִּי אֵין מִלָּה בִּלְשׁוֹנִי,
הֵן ה' יָדַעְתָּ כֻלָּהּ

**For the word is not yet on my tongue,
behold, Hashem, You knew it all.**

Hashem's Foreknowledge Versus Man's Free Will

This statement that Hashem is aware of a person's words before those words are even uttered (or for that matter, even thought),[18] incisively addresses the complex and controversial topic of Hashem's foreknowledge versus mankind's God-given ability to exercise free will. While this seeming paradox is beyond the scope of this *sefer*,[19] it is certainly appropriate for this topic to be referenced in *Tehillim* 139 because *Parshas Bereishis* recounts the first – and most infamous – decisions ever made by mankind, including Adam and Chavah's choice to eat from the *Eitz Hadaas* and Kayin's cold-blooded murder of Hevel.

Pasuk 5:

אָחוֹר וָקֶדֶם צַרְתָּנִי,
וַתָּשֶׁת עָלַי כַּפֶּכָה

**Back and front You have restricted me,
and You have laid upon me the palm of Your hand.**

---

[17] Translation from the ArtScroll Interlinear Siddur.
[18] See also *Rambam*'s Thirteen Principles of Faith, *Ani Maamin* #10.
[19] For additional information on this topic, see e.g., the *Rambam's Shemoneh Perakim*, *perek* 8.

Creation of Man

Although this *pasuk* contains Dovid HaMelech's humbling description of man's inability to physically move forward or backward without Hashem, and certainly not in a spiritually upward and uplifted trajectory, this *pasuk* is also quite famous in the context of the story of Adam HaRishon himself.

"אָחוֹר וָקֶדֶם צַרְתָּנִי" – Back and front You have restricted me." Here, the word "צַרְתָּנִי" can also mean "You formed me," and is a reference to the astounding phrase in *Bereishis*: "זָכָר וּנְקֵבָה בָּרָא אֹתָם" – male and female He created them."[20] The Midrash[21] explains that Hashem initially created Adam with "two faces" in a single body, in which one side was male and one side was female, connected back-to-back with two "fronts." Later, the Torah informs us that Hashem took Adam's "צַלְעֹתָיו" – commonly translated as "one of his ribs" – and fashioned a separate female, Chavah.[22] In fact, the accurate definition of the word צַלְעֹתָיו is not his rib, but rather "his side." Therefore, according to Chazal, the phrase "Back and front You have formed me" refers to the initial creation of Adam with a male form on one side and a female form on the other side.

"וַתָּשֶׁת עָלַי כַּפֶּכָה" – And You have laid upon me the palm of Your hand." By no coincidence, we are treated to a cross-reference to *Tehillim* 139 directly in *Rashi's* commentary on the *pasuk* in *Parshas Bereishis*: "וַיִּבְרָא אֱ-לֹהִים אֶת הָאָדָם בְּצַלְמוֹ – And God created man in his image."[23] *Rashi*[24] clarifies that the "image" referred to there is not "God's image,"[25] but rather refers to the fact that Hashem actually crafted Adam using a unique

---

[20] *Bereishis* 1:27.
[21] *Bereishis Rabbah* 8:1.
[22] *Bereishis* 2:21.
[23] *Bereishis* 1:27.
[24] *Rashi, Bereishis* 1:27, from *Kesubos* 8a.
[25] That Adam was created in "God's image" is indeed true, but according to *Rashi*, that concept is instead expressed in the very next phrase "בְּצֶלֶם אֱ-לֹהִים בָּרָא אֹתוֹ – in the image of God He created him."

stamp or mold that was specifically created for *him*. While everything else was created through God's *word*, Adam was the creation of God's "*hands*," which is an expression of Hashem's personal involvement, interest, and love for Adam. There, *Rashi* cites the phrase from our *pasuk* 5: "וַתָּשֶׁת עָלַי כַּפֶּכָה" – And You have laid upon me the palm of Your hand" as a testimony to the above description of how Adam was fashioned personally and lovingly by Hashem.

Additionally, "וַתָּשֶׁת עָלַי כַּפֶּכָה" is interpreted in the Gemara as referring to Hashem's tragic shrinking of Adam from his original size following the sin of the *Eitz HaDaas*.[26] Originally, Adam's physical and spiritual stature were so immense that he spanned the distance of earth to heaven when standing, and encircled the earth from head to toe when lying down.[27] However, after the *cheit*, Hashem used the same "hands" that had so lovingly formed Adam to punish and diminish him, as expressed by Hashem's "laying His palm upon" Adam to constrict and shrink him.[28]

Pasuk 6:
פְּלִיאָה דַעַת מִמֶּנִּי;
נִשְׂגְּבָה, לֹא אוּכַל לָהּ
Concealed is knowledge from me;
too exalted, I am incapable of it.

Knowledge and Regret

Only six *pesukim* into the *kapitel*, we already find a fourth reference to *daas*: "פְּלִיאָה דַעַת מִמֶּנִּי."

---

[26] *Sanhedrin* 39a.

[27] *Sanhedrin* 38b.

[28] Note that the Torah in *Shemos* 33:22 uses a similar expression in a *positive* manner to describe Hashem's shielding of Moshe Rabbeinu from His Presence using the palm of His hand: "וְשַׂכֹּתִי כַפִּי עָלֶיךָ" – And I shall cover you with the palm of My hand." This similarity is clearly intentional, as Moshe performed many *tikkunim* for Adam HaRishon.

In the context of *Parshas Bereishis*, this *pasuk* is an admission and lament by Adam that eating from the *Eitz HaDaas* did not provide him with more wisdom. Rather, since he had not simply eaten from the Tree of Knowledge but from the "עֵץ הַדַּעַת טוֹב וָרָע – the Tree of Knowledge of Good and Evil,"[29] his mind became murky. Moreover, Chazal tell us that before Adam sinned, the *yetzer hara*, the evil inclination, existed *outside* of Adam. However, once he sinned, the evil became a part of him.[30] As a result, he became driven by an intermingling of good and evil, and his outlook became confused, making his choices more difficult. Unwittingly, Adam trapped himself – and all future generations – in the struggle between good and evil.

In addition, as my daughter Shifra cleverly pointed out, the phrase "לֹא אוּכַל לָהּ" has a dual meaning in this context: not only does it mean "I am incapable of it [such knowledge]," but the word אוּכַל is a play on the word "אוֹכֵל – to eat," as if Adam himself is declaring and lamenting in this *pasuk*: "I should *not* have *eaten* from the Tree of Knowledge" – לֹא אוֹכֵל לָהּ!

Pasuk 7:
אָנָה אֵלֵךְ מֵרוּחֶךָ,
וְאָנָה מִפָּנֶיךָ אֶבְרָח
**Where can I go from Your spirit,
and where from Your Presence can I flee?**

Pasuk 8:
אִם אֶסַּק שָׁמַיִם, שָׁם אָתָּה;
וְאַצִּיעָה שְּׁאוֹל, הִנֶּךָּ
**If I ascend to heaven, there You are;
and if I make my bed in the lowest depths,
behold, You are there.**

---

[29] *Bereishis* 2:17.
[30] *Rashi, Bereishis* 2:25, from *Bereishis Rabbah* 19:9.

Attempted Escape from Hashem

Pesukim 7 and 8 are particularly powerful and made famous by many *baalei mussar*, as they express a desire to run away from Hashem.

Rav Shimshon Pincus explains that whether we want to admit it or not, sometimes a Jew has the desire to escape and abandon all expectations, rules, regulations, responsibilities, and restrictions. He may wish to forsake it all and just run away from Hashem. Yet that is impossible; one cannot run away from Hashem. Hashem is omnipresent. Hashem is omniscient. So, what is such a desperate Jew to do?

He should run away from Hashem *to* Hashem! "אֶבְרַח מִמְּךָ, אֵלֶיךָ – I will run away from You, *to* You!"[31] Rav Pincus provides us with a beautiful parable: one Purim he decided to dress up as a bear in full costume including claws and ferocious teeth. When he came home, his young child saw a bear enter their home, was frightened, and tried to run away and hide. The *rebbetzin*, Chaya Mindel Pincus, explained and reassured her child saying, "It's not a bear; it's Tatty. It's Tatty."

It's Tatty? The child only saw a frightening bear and wanted to run away! However, instinctively trusting that, somehow, this terrifying bear was also Tatty, the child frantically ran *from* Tatty *to* Tatty, and grabbed hold of and hugged the bear, his father in disguise. Rav Pincus quickly removed the mask and lifted his child, embracing him and reassuring him that he was safe in his loving father's arms.

Rav Pincus derived from this experience the explanation of the *pasuk* "דֹּב אֹרֵב הוּא לִי – A bear waiting in ambush He is to me."[32] Sometimes Hashem appears to us as if He is a petrifying bear waiting to attack or punish, but in reality, it is just an illusion, just an elaborate costume. The bear is really "Tatty," our *Avinu She'ba'Shamayim*, and, although we

---

[31] *Piyyut Kesser Malchus*, by Rabbi Shlomo Ibn Gabirol.
[32] *Eichah* 3:10.

sometimes want to run *away* from Him – since we cannot – we must run away from Him *to* Him!

Amazingly, we find not one but two similar situations in *Parshas Bereishis*. First, Adam HaRishon and Chavah, having eaten from the *Eitz HaDaas*, literally tried to run away and hide from Hashem. "They heard the sound of Hashem Elokim walking in the garden toward the direction of the sun, and the man and his wife hid from Hashem Elokim among the trees of the garden."[33] Of course, while Hashem immediately confronted Adam in his futile game of hide-and-seek, He did so in a manner designed not to startle Adam but to enable Adam to engage Hashem in conversation in the hope that he would confess and repent.[34]

Similarly, after Kayin murdered his brother Hevel, Hashem confronted Kayin, asking "Where is Hevel your brother?"[35] thereby initiating conversation with him through calm words in the hope that he too would repent.[36] Nevertheless, as *Rashi* explains, Kayin tried to lie to Hashem, thinking he could deceive God and escape God's knowledge and retribution.[37] Furthermore, in response to Hashem's punishment, Kayin later proclaimed: "וּמִפָּנֶיךָ אֶסָּתֵר – And from Your Presence can I be hidden?"[38] thereby admitting to Hashem (and to himself) that there is no hiding or escaping from Him.

Both Adam and Kayin tried to run away from Hashem – the former literally, and the latter figuratively – but it is all the same. Although both were punished by Hashem, Hashem's goal was to teach them, and to teach us, that there is no running away from Hashem, nor is there any possibility of deceiving Him. While we are not perfect, part of the beauty of Hashem's infiniteness is that there is no sin too terrible for Hashem to address and

---

[33] *Bereishis* 3:8.
[34] *Rashi, Bereishis* 3:9.
[35] *Bereishis* 4:9.
[36] *Rashi, Bereishis* 4:9.
[37] *Rashi, Bereishis* 4:9, from *Bamidbar Rabbah* 19:11.
[38] *Bereishis* 4:14.

forgive. Even if we experience a moment or a period in which we want to run away from Hashem, we must instead run and return *to* Hashem, into the embrace of our loving Tatty, our *Avinu She'ba'Shamayim*.

Pasuk 9:

אֶשָּׂא כַנְפֵי שַׁחַר,
אֶשְׁכְּנָה בְּאַחֲרִית יָם

**Were I to take up wings of dawn,
were I to dwell in the distant west.**

Moshiach Ties It All Together

This statement is not just one of dramatic imagery further describing an attempt to flee from Hashem. Chazal tell us that King Shemever, later mentioned in the Torah as one of the Five Kings who battled the Four Kings in the time of Avraham Avinu,[39] actually "took up wings" and placed an artificial limb on himself to be able to fly and leap heavenward in rebellion against Hashem.[40] Similarly, in *Parshas Noach* the *Dor Haflagah*, the Generation of Disunion, attempted to build a tower to the skies in order to rebel and fight against Hashem in His domain.[41]

Yet, as terrible as that was, the expression "בְּאַחֲרִית יָם" – in the distant west" can be seen as an allusion to the term "אַחֲרִית הַיָּמִים" – the End of Days," a synonym for the Era of Moshiach.[42] As mentioned earlier, the time of Moshiach will be marked by the revelation of God on earth ushered in by Moshiach ben Dovid, a *tzaddik* from the Davidic Dynasty, who will bring about the culmination of אָדָם (Adam) as alluded to in the acronym of אָדָם, דָּוִד, מָשִׁיחַ. At that glorious time, every Jew and non-Jew alike will recognize that all of mankind – many of whom have tried to escape from

---

[39] *Bereishis* 14:2.
[40] *Rashi, Bereishis* 14:2, from *Midrash Tanchuma, Lech Lecha* 8.
[41] *Bereishis* 11:4. See also *Rashi, Bereishis* 11:1.
[42] Based on *Rashi, Devarim* 34:2, from *Sifrei, Devarim* 357.

CHAPTER 1: BEREISHIS & TEHILLIM 139

God since the dawn of time, or worse, to attack and rebel against God – will be blessed to escape *into* Hashem's warm embrace forever and ever.

Pasuk 10:
גַּם שָׁם יָדְךָ תַנְחֵנִי,
וְתֹאחֲזֵנִי יְמִינֶךָ
Even there Your hand leads me,
and grasps me does Your right hand.

From Fleeing to Friendship

"גַּם שָׁם – Even there" refers to the "אַחֲרִית יָם – distant west" described in *pasuk* 9 as a faraway land to which one might try to "escape" from Hashem. Even there, Hashem still accompanies us lovingly.

Furthermore, the double-expression "יָדְךָ" and "יְמִינֶךָ" used to describe Hashem's "hand" are a personification and an expression of יְדִידוּת, friendship and belovedness. For the word "יְדִיד – beloved" is a combination of יָד-יָד, hand-hand, or "hand-in-hand" in friendship and love.

This *pasuk* expresses that even the audacious and failed escape from Hashem mentioned in *pesukim* 7–9 became an opportunity for the greatest closeness with Hashem and culminated in belovedness – even friendship – with Hashem. In this way, the Jew lives his life walking hand-in-hand with Hashem in a world of יְדִידוּת.

This poignant imagery of יְדִידוּת is also present in the *Haftarah* to *Parshas Bereishis*. After the opening *pasuk* in which Hashem reintroduced Himself as the creator of heaven and earth and as the provider of souls and all life, the *pasuk* states: "I am Hashem; in righteousness I have called you וָאַחְזֵק בְּיָדֶךָ – and I have taken hold of your hand; I have protected you... to be a light for the nations."[43]

---

[43] *Yeshayahu* 42:5–6.

Pasuk 11:
וָאֹמַר: אַךְ חֹשֶׁךְ יְשׁוּפֵנִי;
וְלַיְלָה אוֹר בַּעֲדֵנִי

**Were I to say: "Surely darkness will shadow me,"
then the light would be illuminated around me.**

The Fright of the First Sunset

The Gemara tells us that soon after the *cheit* of Adam, nighttime set in naturally. However, since Adam had never experienced a sundown, he was frightened that the darkness was a result of his sin and that he and the world would be relegated to live in darkness forever – or worse, that because of him the world was ending. He and Chavah cried all night long and fasted, expecting the world to be returned to emptiness and nothingness. Of course, at the proper time, Hashem had the sun rise again, and Adam acknowledged what he then understood to be a natural phenomenon by sacrificing a *korban* in gratitude to Hashem.[44] The foregoing episode is clearly alluded to here in *pasuk* 11: "Were I to say, 'Surely darkness will shadow me,' then the light would be illuminated around me."

The Terror of the Changing Times

In addition, the *Talmud Yerushalmi* directly associates *pasuk* 11 and the word "יְשׁוּפֵנִי" with Hashem's famous curse of the Serpent.[45] When the *Nachash* is cursed, the Torah twice uses similar verbiage: "הוּא יְשׁוּפְךָ רֹאשׁ וְאַתָּה תְּשׁוּפֶנּוּ עָקֵב – He [mankind] will crush you [the Serpent] on the head, and you will hiss at his heel,"[46] which expresses the mutual danger that man and snake pose to one another. The *Yerushalmi*, as explained by the

---

[44] *Avodah Zarah* 8a.
[45] *Yerushalmi, Avodah Zarah* 1:2.
[46] *Bereishis* 3:15.

P'nei Moshe, describes the worry and panic that Adam HaRishon experienced throughout the initial time period in which the nights were longer than the days. Specifically, Adam proclaimed in terror the words "אַךְ חֹשֶׁךְ יְשׁוּפֵנִי." Tormented by the increasing darkness and quivering among the shadows, Adam feared that the darkness would provide an opportunity for the Serpent to kill him in fulfillment of "וְאַתָּה תְּשׁוּפֶנּוּ עָקֵב." So great was Adam's terror that as soon as the days started to become longer than the nights, he established the first man-made holiday in celebration of the increased light and his having survived unscathed.

The Darkness of *Galus* and Light of *Geulah*

In addition, darkness symbolizes *galus*, exile, while light is the symbol of *geulah*, redemption. As with Adam's experience, the Jewish experience of exile, the night, will not last forever. In fact, the exiles themselves were predestined and were even hinted to in the second *pasuk* of the Torah: "וְהָאָרֶץ הָיְתָה תֹהוּ וָבֹהוּ, וְחֹשֶׁךְ עַל פְּנֵי תְהוֹם" – The land was emptiness and nothingness, with darkness upon the face of the deep."[47] Chazal explain this four-fold frightening expression as a reference to the four main Jewish exiles of *Bavel* (Babylonia), *Paras U'Maddai* (Persia and Media), *Yavan* (Greece), and *Edom* (the Roman Empire).[48] Yet, the *pasuk* continues with the phrase: "וְרוּחַ אֱ-לֹהִים מְרַחֶפֶת עַל פְּנֵי הַמָּיִם" – And the spirit of God was hovering over the face of the waters,"[49] in which Chazal see immediate consolation in the promise that despite all the darkness and difficulties, the spirit and light of Moshiach is also predestined to eventually arrive.[50]

A similar concept is also found in the basic explanation of *pasuk* 12 below.

---

[47] *Bereishis* 1:2.
[48] *Bereishis Rabbah* 2:5.
[49] *Bereishis* 1:2.
[50] *Bereishis Rabbah* 2:5.

Pasuk 12:
גַּם חֹשֶׁךְ לֹא יַחְשִׁיךְ מִמֶּךָ;
וְלַיְלָה כַּיּוֹם יָאִיר,
כַּחֲשֵׁיכָה כָּאוֹרָה

**Even darkness is not too dark for You;
and night like the day shines,
the darkness is the same as the light.**

Tehillim 139, *Bereishis*, and Pesach

The well-known middle phrase of *pasuk* 12, "וְלַיְלָה כַּיּוֹם יָאִיר," is a reference to Pesach and *Yetzias Mitzrayim*. This phrase is a source for the fact that the night of the Exodus, commemorated on the night(s) of our Pesach Seder, has a halachic status of "nights that are like day," filled with the light of redemption. For example, though *Hallel* is typically only said during the daytime, we recite it on the evening of the Seder because the Seder night has the status of day.[51]

This sudden hint to Pesach is not out of place in *Tehillim* 139 and *Parshas Bereishis*, as there are numerous teachings of Chazal that associate and find parallels between *Yetzias Mitzrayim* and Hashem's creation of the world. A famous, but sometimes overlooked, example of this can be found in the Friday night *Kiddush* when we say: "וְשַׁבָּת קָדְשׁוֹ בְּאַהֲבָה וּבְרָצוֹן הִנְחִילָנוּ זִכָּרוֹן לְמַעֲשֵׂה בְרֵאשִׁית. כִּי הוּא יוֹם תְּחִלָּה לְמִקְרָאֵי קֹדֶשׁ זֵכֶר לִיצִיאַת מִצְרָיִם – And His holy Shabbos with love and favor He gave us a heritage, a remembrance of the work of Creation. For Shabbos is the first day to be called 'holy,' a remembrance to the Exodus from Egypt." Indeed, *Bereishis* and the Exodus are very much intertwined: just as *Bereishis* was the birth of mankind, *Yetzias Mitzrayim* was the birth of the Jewish People.

---

[51] E.g., *Ohr Hachaim, Shemos* 13:8.

Darkness Has No Intrinsic Effect on Hashem

Finally, we must point out the very important phrase: "כַּחֲשֵׁיכָה כָּאוֹרָה – the darkness is the same as the light," which means that literally everything that happens to mankind, and even everything that occurs throughout the vast universe, has no intrinsic effect on Hashem "בְּעֶצֶם," at His Essence. He is omnipotent and omniscient, and nothing transpires or is done "outside" of Him or impacts Him against His will. Thus, to Hashem at His core (so to speak), even the proverbial "darkness" that the world may experience is the same as the "light."[52]

Pasuk 13:
כִּי אַתָּה קָנִיתָ כִלְיֹתָי;
תְּסֻכֵּנִי בְּבֶטֶן אִמִּי
For You have created my mind;
You have covered me in the womb of my mother.

The Human Mind and Childbirth

In *pasuk* 13 (and continuing through pasuk 16), although the composer Dovid HaMelech is speaking, the words could just as easily have been those of Adam HaRishon!

The phrase "כִּי אַתָּה קָנִיתָ כִלְיֹתָי" and its reference to the "mind" refers to Hashem having created mankind with the capabilities of the שֵׂכֶל, intelligence. Starting of course with Adam, the Torah states: "נַעֲשֶׂה אָדָם בְּצַלְמֵנוּ כִּדְמוּתֵנוּ – Let us make man in our image and like our form."[53] *Rashi* explains, "כִּדְמוּתֵנוּ: לְהָבִין וּלְהַשְׂכִּיל – In our form: [with the ability] to understand and to comprehend."[54]

---

[52] E.g., *Aish Kodesh*, *Noach* 1941.
[53] *Bereishis* 1:26.
[54] *Rashi*, *Bereishis* 1:26, from *Bereishis Rabbah* 8:11, and *Chagigah* 16a.

In addition, Hashem gave Adam the mitzvah of *peru u'revu*, to be fruitful and multiply.[55] When the first child was born, he was named Kayin because "קָנִיתִי אִישׁ אֶת ה'" – I have acquired a man with Hashem,"[56] in recognition of the unique "partnership" that Adam, Chavah, and Hashem formed in the conception, development, and birth of the child.[57] The symmetrical use of the *shoresh* of the word "קוֹנֶה" in the expressions of "כִּי אַתָּה קָנִיתָ כִלְיֹתָי" and "קָנִיתִי אִישׁ אֶת ה'" surely alludes to the above.

Finally, the phrase "תְּסֻכֵּנִי בְּבֶטֶן אִמִּי" is a praise to God and reinforces the fact that as intelligent as humans may be, and as profoundly and prolifically as science and technology may develop, it is really Hashem alone Who invented and controls the process of conception, pregnancy, and birth,[58] and Who enables mankind to reproduce and endure.[59]

Pasuk 14:
אוֹדְךָ עַל כִּי נוֹרָאוֹת נִפְלֵיתִי;
נִפְלָאִים מַעֲשֶׂיךָ, וְנַפְשִׁי יֹדַעַת מְאֹד
I thank You, because awesomely, wondrously am I [fashioned]; wondrous are Your works, and my soul knows it well.

Thanking Hashem for Body and Soul

In this *pasuk*, Adam thanks Hashem for creating his physical body and his spiritual soul, declaring "...wondrously am I [fashioned]... my soul knows it well." In addition, the *shoresh* of the word נִפְלָא, wondrous, is

---

[55] *Bereishis* 1:28.
[56] *Bereishis* 4:1.
[57] *Rashi, Bereishis* 4:1, from *Bereishis Rabbah* 22:2.
[58] E.g., *Taanis* 2b. See also *Midrash Tanchuma, Pekudei* 3.
[59] Nonetheless, we must acknowledge that Adam would not be able to declare about himself that he "was fashioned in his mother's womb," since Adam did not have a "natural" birth but was rather fashioned from the *adamah*, from the earth, by the hand of Hashem Himself.

used twice in the above phrase: "נִפְלֵיתִי" and "נִפְלָאִים." The precision of this terminology is striking because Chazal describe the uniting of the two greatest opposites – the physical and mortal body intertwined with the spiritual and eternal soul – as the biggest "פֶּלֶא," the greatest of wonders. As such, the *brachah* of *Asher Yatzar* concludes with the statement: "רוֹפֵא כָל בָּשָׂר וּמַפְלִיא לַעֲשׂוֹת – Hashem, the Healer of all flesh and the performer of wonders," in reference to the ultimate wonder that is a healthy body and a healthy soul functioning in tandem.[60]

In fact, it seems clear that the opening words of the *Asher Yatzar* prayer: "אֲשֶׁר יָצַר אֶת הָאָדָם – [Hashem] Who formed the man," are derived from the Torah's reference to Adam HaRishon himself in *Parshas Bereishis*: "Hashem Elokim planted a garden in Eden, to the east, and placed there אֶת הָאָדָם אֲשֶׁר יָצָר – the man whom He had fashioned"![61]

Adam: The First to Thank Hashem

*P*asuk 14 also contains the word "אוֹדְךָ – I thank You." The *Midrash Tehillim*[62] tells us that Adam, for all his self-inflicted flaws, was also the very first to thank Hashem.

Adam was created on the first Friday, sinned in the tenth hour, was judged in the eleventh hour, and was banished from Gan Eden in the twelfth hour. As his guilty sentence was about to be rendered and his punishment swiftly administered, Shabbos suddenly entered and removed him. Shabbos then interceded as a defender on Adam's behalf and respectfully argued before Hashem: "Master of the worlds, in all six days of Creation no man was ever punished in the world, and yet You would start punishment and render Your first negative decree toward man on my

---

[60] This is also why Chazal have us say *Asher Yatzar* each morning and then immediately follow it with the *brachah* of *Elokai Neshamah*; first a *brachah* focused on the body but which concludes with a reference to both body and soul, and then a second *brachah* focusing entirely on the soul.

[61] *Bereishis* 2:8.

[62] *Midrash Tehillim, Shocher Tov* 92.

day, on Shabbos? Is that my holiness? Is that my rest and tranquility?" Thus, because of Shabbos, Hashem relented and Adam was spared from death and Gehinnom.

Once Adam saw the power of Shabbos, he wanted to shower praise upon Shabbos and proclaimed: "מִזְמוֹר שִׁיר לְיוֹם הַשַּׁבָּת – A psalm, a song for the day of Shabbos."[63] However, the ever-modest Shabbos said: "Do you want to praise me? Instead, both you and I will give praise to Hashem," as the next *pasuk* continues: "טוֹב לְהֹדוֹת לַה' – It is good to thank Hashem!"

So too, here in *pasuk* 14 the word "אוֹדְךָ – I thank You," alludes to Adam HaRishon's life-saving experience with Shabbos that enabled and inspired him to become the trailblazer in giving thanks to Hashem.

The Moment When the *Daas* Finally "Clicks"

This *pasuk* also captures the moment in which things finally "clicked" in Adam's mind. We once again find the *shoresh* of the word "דַעַת" in the phrase "וְנַפְשִׁי יֹדַעַת מְאֹד – And my soul knows it well." These words are part of a statement by Adam that combines his "אוֹדְךָ" of "thanksgiving" with his "אוֹדְךָ" of "acknowledgment" as he expresses a penetrating cognizance of his blunder in having eaten from the *Eitz HaDaas*. He realized that his actions were completely unnecessary, for Hashem had initially formed his body and soul with all the *daas* he could ever need – and perhaps even more than he needed. Adam now realized that he was originally created with a "נֶפֶשׁ יֹדַעַת – knowing soul," a soul of *daas* – and even more so, a soul of "דַעַת מְאֹד – much *daas*!"

This is also the phrase that captures the moment in which Adam finally understood the gravity of his sin. Here, Adam proclaims that partaking from the *Eitz HaDaas* was an action performed in direct disregard of Hashem's only commandment to him, and that he now understands the far-reaching implications of his transgression: "וְנַפְשִׁי יֹדַעַת מְאֹד – my soul knows full well" what a terrible *aveira* I committed.

---

[63] *Tehillim* 92:1.

The Greatness of the Jewish Soul

In addition, with the words "וְנַפְשִׁי יֹדַעַת," the reference to *daas* is used specifically in conjunction with the נֶפֶשׁ, the human soul, which contains the key element of humanity. Man is called a "נֶפֶשׁ חַיָּה."[64] *Rashi* describes this as not only a "living soul" (which animals too possess), but also as "*de'ah v'dibbur*," the faculties of knowledge/reasoning and speech, which are capabilities unique to humans and thus define and distinguish mankind from beast.[65]

Yet, Hashem's *greatest* creation is not the human soul. Hashem's greatest creation is the *Jewish* soul, which Hashem breathed into us directly from Himself, and which is a "*chelek Elokah me'maal*," literally "a part of God from above."[66]

The Wonders of Creation

Finally, in the phrase "נִפְלָאִים מַעֲשֶׂיךָ," Adam is not only acknowledging the wonders of his *own* creation but also the wonders of the entire Universe, as seen in the use of the *shoresh* of the word "מַעֲשֶׂה" in the phrase "נִפְלָאִים מַעֲשֶׂיךָ," which alludes to "מַעֲשֵׂה בְרֵאשִׁית" – Creation in all its towering totality.

Pasuk 15:
לֹא נִכְחַד עָצְמִי מִמֶּךָּ;
אֲשֶׁר עֻשֵּׂיתִי בַסֵּתֶר,
רֻקַּמְתִּי בְּתַחְתִּיּוֹת אָרֶץ

**Not hidden was my frame from You;
when I was fashioned in concealment,
when I was knit together in the lowest parts of the earth.**

---

[64] *Bereishis* 2:7.
[65] *Rashi, Bereishis* 2:7. See also *Targum Onkelos, Bereishis* 2:7.
[66] *Iyov* 31:2. See also e.g., *Tanya, perek* 2.

Pasuk 16:

גָּלְמִי רָאוּ עֵינֶיךָ...

My unshaped form was seen by Your eyes...

The Creation and Actual Formation of Man

In *pesukim* 15 and 16, it is as if Adam HaRishon continues to speak about his own creation.

While the traditional meaning of *pasuk* 15 refers to the forming of a child in the concealment of his mother's womb, here Adam is also describing his *own* creation by the hand of Hashem, Who formed him "בַּסֵּתֶר," in the utmost of concealment possible, since no other human being yet *existed* to whom Adam's creation could be revealed!

In addition, "בְּתַחְתִּיּוֹת אָרֶץ" is a clear reference to Adam having been created from the very soil of the *earth* itself; from the very אֲדָמָה from which he derived his name, אָדָם.

The description of the actual formation of Adam HaRishon's physical body is described in *pasuk* 16. Specifically, the phrase "גָּלְמִי רָאוּ עֵינֶיךָ – My unshaped form was seen by Your eyes" is a reference to Adam having been formed and kneaded like dough from a shapeless mass of water-saturated soil[67] to a clod of earth like a "*golem*" (the same *shoresh* as the word גָּלְמִי) until he was deemed ready for the Spirit of Hashem to be breathed into him, thereby incorporating the living soul into his otherwise lifeless body.

Pasuk 16:

גָּלְמִי רָאוּ עֵינֶיךָ

וְעַל סִפְרְךָ כֻּלָּם יִכָּתֵבוּ;

יָמִים יֻצָּרוּ (וְלֹא) וְלוֹ אֶחָד בָּהֶם

---

[67] *Rashi, Bereishis* 2:6.

> **My unshaped form was seen by Your eyes,**
> **and in Your book, all were recorded;**
> **[though] in many days they will be fashioned,**
> **to Him they are as one.**

In Hashem's Book All Are Recorded

Pasuk 16 continues to reveal additional nuances about Adam HaRishon. The phrase "וְעַל סִפְרְךָ כֻּלָּם יִכָּתֵבוּ" – And in Your book all were recorded," can be interpreted on multiple levels.

First, it is a reference to the *pasuk* in *Parshas Bereishis*: "זֶה סֵפֶר תּוֹלְדֹת אָדָם – This is the account [literally, "book"] of the descendants of Adam,"[68] which introduces the sub-portion of *Parshas Bereishis* that lists the ten generations from Adam to Noach.

It is also a reference to the highly detailed account of Adam's creation in the Torah's opening *Parshah* of *Bereishis*, with "סִפְרְךָ" referring to the "*Sefer Torah*" in general.

Finally, "Your book" is a reference to a completely different type of book. *Targum Onkelos* defines "Your book" as "סֵפֶר דָּכְרָנָךְ" – the *Sefer Ha'zichronos*, Book of Remembrances."[69] This is the same book referred to in the famed and stirring prayer of *Unesaneh Tokef* said tearfully each Rosh Hashanah and Yom Kippur by Ashkenazi Jewry. It is a book that Hashem maintains and in which He inscribes the names, spiritual status, and even the signature of each human being, young and old. It is the book that Hashem opens on Rosh Hashanah and Yom Kippur and in which our good deeds and our misdeeds are recorded, along with our decree and Godly-intended trajectory for the year to come. It seems logical that Adam, the very first person in all of Creation, would be the very first name recorded in the *Sefer Ha'zichronos*, and it is fitting that Dovid HaMelech refers to this book here in *Tehillim 139*.

---

[68] *Bereishis* 5:1.
[69] *Targum Onkelos, Tehillim* 139:16.

Hashem Is Above and Beyond Time

Then, in perfect stride, comes the phrase "יָמִים יֻצָּרוּ, (וְלֹא) וְלֹו אֶחָד בָּהֶם – [Though] in many days they will be fashioned, to Him they are as one."

These words remind us that Hashem initially created everything in the world on day one of Creation even though the creations were not revealed or permanently fixed into place until later during the six-day process.[70]

In addition, this phrase is an allusion to Hashem as the Creator of time and space, while still maintaining His lofty status above and beyond time and space as reflected in His very Name of י-ה-ו-ה, the Name that signifies הָיָה הֹוֶה וְיִהְיֶה – past, present, and future converged into one.

The *Yamim Noraim*: Days of Awe

Yet Chazal learn from the phrase "יָמִים יֻצָּרוּ, (וְלֹא) וְלֹו אֶחָד בָּהֶם" something more: Hashem Himself has a singular day that is unique beyond all the days that He created, and that special day is Yom Kippur.[71] Thus, "יָמִים" here need not refer to just ordinary days, but rather to the "יָמִים נוֹרָאִים," the Days of Awe that begin with the thirty days of Elul. In fact, Elul is also alluded to here by the *kri u'kesiv* in which "לֹא" was originally written but the main intent and translation is "לֹו." When those two words are combined, they contain the letters that spell אֱלוּל. These days lead into Rosh Hashanah, the days when we celebrate not only Hashem's Creation and daily re-creation of the world, but also the coronation of Hashem as King of the world and as our own personal *Melech*. On these days we "crown" the *Melech*. In addition, Rosh Hashanah is not actually the anniversary of the first day of Creation, but rather the anniversary of the sixth day of Creation, the day that Adam was created, because "אֵין מֶלֶךְ

---

[70] *Rashi, Bereishis* 1:14, from *Bereishis Rabbah* 12:4.
[71] *Tanna D'bei Eliyahu, perek aleph.*

בְּלֹא עָם – A king is not a king without subjects."[72] Thus, Adam's creation marks the first moments when Hashem's true *malchus* on earth began.

Nevertheless, as noted above, the *Tanna D'bei Eliyahu* understands the phrase "יָמִים יֻצָּרוּ, (וְלֹא) וְלוֹ אֶחָד בָּהֶם" as referring to Yom Kippur, Hashem's most special day of all, since Hashem only created the world in order to bestow *chessed*, lovingkindness, upon mankind. This is confirmed by the famous dictum of "עוֹלָם חֶסֶד יִבָּנֶה" – The world was built on Hashem's kindness"[73] and continues to be rebuilt every moment for the purpose of Hashem granting kindness to it. It should therefore come as no surprise that Hashem's most cherished day is Yom Kippur, the day singled out for מְחִילָה סְלִיחָה וְכַפָּרָה, forgiveness, pardon, and atonement,[74] when we can be forgiven for our transgressions and thereby "re-permit" Hashem to shower His *chessed* upon us.[75]

Yet, *seforim* such as the works of Slonim, the *Yesod Ha'Avodah* and the *Darchei Noam*, tell us that Yom Kippur is uniquely special because it is the day most opportune for the *pintele Yid* – that tiny, pure point in the Jewish soul – to cling to Hashem in purity. It is the day when we can rise like (and beyond) even the angels, and connect to the true *adam*, the true man, and be elevated to the level of Adam HaRishon before the *cheit*. This, too, is alluded to in the expression of Yom Kippur as "וְלוֹ אֶחָד בָּהֶם:" to Him (וְלוֹ), among us (בָּהֶם), is only אֶחָד, referring to "שְׁמַע יִשְׂרָאֵל ה' אֱ-לֹהֵינוּ ה' אֶחָד"[76] which we passionately proclaim at the apex of the most exalted moment on the most exalted day, at the end of the *Neilah* prayer in the last seconds of Yom Kippur. In that moment, each Jew – every man, woman, and child – becomes the embodiment of what it means to be a true *adam*.

---

[72] Rabbeinu Bachya, *Bereishis* 38:30; *Likutei Moharan* 49.
[73] *Tehillim* 89:3.
[74] From the Yom Kippur *Shemoneh Esrei*.
[75] In addition, the aforementioned concepts of *teshuvah* and forgiveness are *themselves* examples of Hashem's vast *chessed*.
[76] *Devarim* 6:4.

Pasuk 17:
וְלִי מַה יָּקְרוּ רֵעֶיךָ אֵ-ל;
מֶה עָצְמוּ רָאשֵׁיהֶם

**To me, how glorious are Your thoughts, God!
How very great are their core ideas.**

Our Infinite God and His Torah and Friendship

Here is the acknowledgment and declaration that we cannot even *hope* to fully understand the magnitude of the infinite depth of Hashem's thoughts and intentions. Interestingly, the ArtScroll Tehillim employs none other than *Maaseh Bereishis* itself as the prime illustration of the meaning behind this *pasuk*: "Contemplating merely the general categories of the unfathomable Divine power and wisdom evident in Creation would completely overwhelm the most brilliant mind, even ignoring the countless, exacting details of each and every one of those categories."

Nonetheless, Hashem gifted us with "רֵעֶיךָ," His "thoughts," in the form of the *Torah She'bichsav*, the Written Torah, as well as the *Torah She'baal Peh*, the Oral Torah. Each is infinite and perfect,[77] providing us with the full spectrum of understanding and guidance that we, as Jews, require both to navigate this world and to earn a place in *Olam Haba*, the World to Come.

Even more astoundingly, "רֵעֶיךָ" also means "friendship," and refers to the most precious and everlasting friendship of all: friendship with Hashem. As the *pasuk* in *Mishlei* beckons to us: "רֵעֲךָ וְרֵעַ אָבִיךָ אַל תַּעֲזֹב – Your friend and the friend of your father, do not forsake."[78] *Rashi* in the Gemara Shabbos says of the friend referred to here: "זֶה הקב"ה – this is Hashem!"[79]

---

[77] E.g., *Tehillim* 19:8.
[78] *Mishlei* 27:10.
[79] *Rashi, Shabbos* 31a. See also *Targum Onkelos, Tehillim* 139:17.

While the above approaches to the meaning of "רֵעֶיךָ" can each stand alone, in the context of *Tehillim* 139:17 we can also combine the two as follows: awareness, focus, devotion, and loyalty to Hashem's "רֵעֶיךָ – thoughts" as conveyed in the Torah will enable us to merit having Hashem as "רֵעֶיךָ – our friend" throughout our lives in both *Olam Hazeh* and *Olam Haba*.[80]

Our Infinite God and His Master Plan

It should be noted that the phrase "וְלִי מַה יָּקְרוּ רֵעֶיךָ אֵ-ל" is cited in the Gemara[81] in the following context: "זֶה סֵפֶר תּוֹלְדֹת אָדָם – This is the account of the descendants of Adam."[82] This teaches that Hashem showed Adam HaRishon a prophetic vision of every generation and *dorshav*, its expounders, and every generation and *chochamav*, its wise men. When Hashem showed Adam a vision of Rabbi Akiva, the famed Torah scholar and martyr who died with the word "אֶחָד" of *Shema* on his holy lips, Adam rejoiced in Rabbi Akiva's Torah yet was saddened by his death. Adam then proclaimed none other than the words: "וְלִי מַה יָּקְרוּ רֵעֶיךָ אֵ-ל" – How glorious are Your thoughts, God," in recognition that even though Adam was unable to fully comprehend all of Hashem's ways, he maintained absolute faith that Hashem's ways were just and glorious. As an interesting support to this Gemara, Rabbi Yisrael Ephraim Cutler[83] writes that the phrase "יָּקְרוּ רֵעֶיךָ" has a *gematria* (numerical value) of 616, which is the same combined *gematria* as אֲקִיבָא בֶּן יוֹסֵף and רַבִּי עֲקִיבָא בֶּן יוֹסֵף (616).

We can also add that Adam specifically used the Name "אֵ-ל," which connotes both power and kindness, *chozek* and *chessed*,[84] in recognition of Hashem's incomprehensibly complex master plan for the world, which

---

[80] E.g., *Bilvavi Mishkan Evneh, chelek aleph, perek* 29 and 36.
[81] *Sanhedrin* 38b.
[82] *Bereishis* 5:1.
[83] *Kuntrus Abitah Niflaos*, p. 67.
[84] E.g., *Shabbos Malkesa*, by Rabbi Shimshon Pincus, p. 21.

as the aforementioned Gemara reveals, was already fully in place from the very start of Creation.

All the above is yet another illustration of how Dovid HaMelech's holy words in *Tehillim* 139 not only echo, but mirror, the words spoken by Adam HaRishon thousands of years prior.

Pasuk 18:
אֶסְפְּרֵם, מֵחוֹל יִרְבּוּן;
הֱקִיצֹתִי וְעוֹדִי עִמָּךְ

Were I to count them, more than the grains of sand would be their number; even if I were to be constantly awake and always with You.

Hashem Chose the Jewish People as His Own

The description of "חוֹל – grains of sand" conveys an overwhelming sense of the infinite wisdom involved in Creation, since each and every grain of sand was itself a complete "creation" of Hashem יֵשׁ מֵאַיִן, *ex nihilo*. Its imagery engenders a sense of the earth's formation: its soil, the sand beneath one's toes, and the ground upon which we walk.

In addition, Chazal[85] found a reference to the Jewish People in the very first word of the Torah, "בְּרֵאשִׁית," and explain that Hashem created the world "בִּשְׁבִיל יִשְׂרָאֵל שֶׁנִּקְרְאוּ רֵאשִׁית תְּבוּאָתֹה" – for [the Nation of] Yisrael who are called 'the first of His crop.'"[86] Similarly, we find a reference to the Jewish People in *Tehillim* 139, even though its *Bereishis*-related subject matter predates the formation of Am Yisrael. Here in the phrase "מֵחוֹל יִרְבּוּן – More than the grains of sands would be their number" we find a reference to the Jewish People, who are throughout the entirety of the Torah likened by Hashem to the sand of the earth, as in the blessing Hashem gave to

---

[85] *Rashi, Bereishis* 1:1, from *Bereishis Rabbah* 4:36.
[86] *Yirmiyahu* 2:3.

Avraham following *Akeidas Yitzchak*: "I shall surely bless you and surely increase your offspring like the stars of the heavens, וְכַחוֹל אֲשֶׁר עַל שְׂפַת הַיָּם – and like the חוֹל – sand on the seashore."[87]

Pasuk 18 continues: "הֱקִיצֹתִי, וְעוֹדִי עִמָּךְ – Even if I were to be constantly awake and always with You," which at first engenders a sense of the frailty of the human condition. Man is dismayed that he is not always with Hashem. Man is troubled that he cannot remain awake nor conscious and cognizant of the busy and complex world around him. Unlike Hashem, we must sleep; we are vulnerable and limited; and our lives are like the tiny grains of sand falling quietly in an hourglass. Yet, the truth is that despite our limitations and faults, we *are* "עוֹדִי עִמָּךְ – always with You." Hashem chose our people – a historically scant, meek, and vulnerable people – the Jewish People, to be His *Am Segulah*, treasured nation. He breathed within us a Jewish soul and gave us His gift of the Torah – אַשְׁרֵינוּ מַה טוֹב חֶלְקֵנוּ – How fortunate we are to be Hashem's chosen people, the *Am Ha'nivchar*! "קֻדְשָׁא בְּרִיךְ הוּא וְאוֹרַיְתָא וְיִשְׂרָאֵל חַד הוּא" – The Holy One blessed be He, the Torah, and Yisrael, are all one.[88]

To be "עוֹדִי עִמָּךְ – always with You," is both our dream and our reality.

Pasuk 19:
אִם תִּקְטֹל, אֱ-לוֹהַּ, רָשָׁע;
וְאַנְשֵׁי דָמִים סוּרוּ מֶנִּי
**Would that You would slay, God, the wicked,
and men of blood, [to whom I say] "Depart from me!"**

Coping With and Combating *Rishus* (Evil)

Pasuk 19 (and continuing through *Pasuk* 22) shifts gears to the topic of combating *rishus*, evil, in the world. Evil, a terrible reality, only

---

[87] *Bereishis* 22:17. See also *Bava Basra* 8a.
[88] E.g., *Aruch HaShulchan, Yoreh De'ah* 246:1; *Likutei Moharan* 251.

became a reality once Adam HaRishon sinned by eating from the Tree of Knowledge of Good and Evil and unleashed the *yetzer hara* upon himself and upon the world.

Two terms here are essential to our understanding. First, the term "תִּקְטֹל" means "to kill," which is an expression of death. Because of Adam HaRishon's sin, God brought death and mortality into the world as a punishment (as well as a *tikkun*). Second, the word "רָשָׁע" in *Tehillim* 139 reminds us that wicked men abound in *Parshas Bereishis*. In addition to Adam and Kayin who sinned gravely, we are also told of Yaval who built houses for idolatry,[89] Yuval who played the harp and flute to play music for idolatry,[90] Tuval Kayin who improved upon the craft of Kayin by making weapons for murderers,[91] the *tzaddik* Chanoch whom Hashem removed from the world before his time because of concern that he might regress to doing evil,[92] the *Bnei Elokim* who would force themselves on brides before they entered their marriage canopy,[93] the Nefillim who fell from heaven and made the world fall,[94] the Giborim who were mighty in their rebellion against Hashem,[95] and the Anshei HaSheim who were given wicked nicknames symbolic of the destruction that they caused.[96]

In addition, the expression "אַנְשֵׁי דָמִים – men of blood," recalls Kayin's murder of Hevel and Hashem's lament: "קוֹל דְּמֵי אָחִיךָ צֹעֲקִים אֵלַי מִן הָאֲדָמָה – The sound of your brother's *blood* cries out to Me from the ground."[97]

Indeed, because of all this *rishus*, even before the conclusion of *Parshas Bereishis* Hashem already reconsidered and even regretted

---

[89] *Rashi, Bereishis* 4:20.
[90] *Rashi, Bereishis* 4:20.
[91] *Rashi, Bereishis* 4:22.
[92] *Rashi, Bereishis* 5:24.
[93] *Rashi, Bereishis* 6:2.
[94] *Rashi, Bereishis* 6:4.
[95] *Rashi, Bereishis* 6:4.
[96] *Rashi, Bereishis* 6:4.
[97] *Bereishis* 4:10.

(*kiv'yachol*) having made man and was therefore intent on bringing the *Mabul* to flood and destroy the world.[98]

Pasuk 20:
אֲשֶׁר יֹמְרוּךָ לִמְזִמָּה;
נָשׂוּא לַשָּׁוְא עָרֶיךָ
Those who pronounce Your name for wicked schemes, it is taken in vain by Your enemies.

The Hiding of the Hidden Light

This *pasuk* is essentially a description of the wicked who misappropriated powers granted to them by Hashem in the form of the misuse of Hashem's Holy Name.

We see the first such example of a misappropriation early in the Torah: "וַיַּרְא אֱ-לֹהִים אֶת הָאוֹר כִּי טוֹב וַיַּבְדֵּל אֱ-לֹהִים בֵּין הָאוֹר וּבֵין הַחֹשֶׁךְ" – God saw that the light was good, and God separated between the light and the darkness."[99] This is actually a reference to a unique light, the *ohr ha'ganuz* – hidden light, which Hashem saw would be misused by the wicked and therefore hid before it could be utilized for evil purposes. Yet, Hashem preserved this light for the *tzaddikim* in the future time of Moshiach.[100]

Rebuke of the Non-Believers

In the *sefer Chochmah U'Mussar*, the Alter of Kelm cites the phrase "אֲשֶׁר יֹמְרוּךָ לִמְזִמָּה" to succinctly admonish the ancient philosophers and people even today who do not believe in God; who believe that the world always existed and was not the "creation" of God; and/or who believe that while God exists, He is unconcerned, uninvolved, and detached from all

---

[98] *Bereishis* 6:5–8.
[99] *Bereishis* 1:4.
[100] *Rashi, Bereishis* 1:4, from *Chagigah* 12a and *Bereishis Rabbah* 3:6.

that transpires in the world. Instead, says the Alter, if one but looks at the spectacle of nature, and beyond even that, if one but looks at the Jewish soul, one cannot help but know with certainty that Hashem exists, that Hashem controls the world, and that Torah was gifted to the Jewish People directly from Hashem Himself![101]

Pasuk 21:
הֲלוֹא מְשַׂנְאֶיךָ, ה', אֶשְׂנָא;
וּבִתְקוֹמְמֶיךָ אֶתְקוֹטָט
For indeed those who hate You, Hashem, I hate them, and with those who rise up against You, I quarrel.

The Serpent, Its Sins, and Its Punishments

In this *pasuk* we find references to the first and most nefarious villain in all *Parshas Bereishis* and the first creation to display hatred toward Hashem: the *Nachash*, the Serpent. Whether it was his lust for Chavah, his thirst for power, or just innate wickedness, his persuasion of Chavah to eat from the *Eitz HaDaas* led to the undoing of Hashem's world (*kiv'yachol*) and in so doing, revealed his hatred for Hashem and for Hashem's creations.

Consistent with the statement in *pasuk* 21 of: "Those who hate You, I hate them," in *Parshas Bereishis* Hashem punished the Serpent with animosity and fear between itself and mankind, as Hashem told the Serpent: "I will put enmity between you and the woman, and between your offspring and her offspring."[102] Furthermore, in the word "וּבִתְקוֹמְמֶיךָ" – and those who rise up against You," we find an additional and interesting reference to the Serpent. Chazal tell us that the *Nachash* was not originally created as having to slither on its belly; it was created with legs and the

---

[101] *Chochmah U'Mussar*, pp. 61-62.
[102] *Bereishis* 3:15.

ability to stand vertically and with קוֹמְמִיּוּת, *komemiyus*, an expression of standing upright, with stature and pride.[103] It was only as a punishment for inciting Chavah – and through her, Adam – to eat from the *Eitz HaDaas*, that the Serpent was punished and lost the gift of *komemiyus* by having his legs cut off.[104] The *Nachash* was thereby relegated to lowliness, to slither upon its belly and eat the dust of the earth as a punishment that was designed *middah k'neged middah*, measure for measure: because the Serpent personified the wickedness of "וּבְתִקוֹמְמֶיךָ" and rose up against Hashem with *komemiyus*, it lost the blessing of *komemiyus*.

In contrast to the *Nachash*, the Jewish People are blessed with *komemiyus* in a positive way. With the coming of Moshiach, which will be the time when the *cheit* of the *Eitz HaDaas* and all other sins that followed it will be eradicated, we will return to Eretz Yisrael and *Yerushalayim Habenuyah* with *komemiyus*, as we daven each day: "וַהֲבִיאֵנוּ לְשָׁלוֹם מֵאַרְבַּע כַּנְפוֹת הָאָרֶץ וְתוֹלִיכֵנוּ קוֹמְמִיּוּת לְאַרְצֵנוּ – Hashem will bring us in peace from the four corners of the earth and lead us to our land with upright stature and the pride of *komemiyus*."[105]

Pasuk 22:
תַּכְלִית שִׂנְאָה שְׂנֵאתִים;
לְאוֹיְבִים הָיוּ לִי

**With the utmost hatred I hate them;
enemies they have become to me.**

Why Evil Exists at All

At this point, Dovid HaMelech bravely steps into the breach created by Adam's sin and is willing, and even eager, to wage war against the enemies of Hashem. In so doing, he embodies the powerful battle cry

---

[103] *Rashi, Bereishis 3:14, from Bereishis Rabbah 20:5.*
[104] *Rashi, Bereishis 3:14; Avos D'Rav Nosson 1:7.*
[105] From the *tefillah Ahavah Rabbah*. See also *Bircas Hamazon*.

of "אֹהֲבֵי ה' שִׂנְאוּ רָע" [106] – Those who love Hashem hate evil" and begins to put into effect the much-needed *tikkun* for Adam HaRishon through the embodiment of the Adam-Dovid-Moshiach connection previously discussed.

Of course, if we stop for a moment and contemplate, these *pesukim* beg the question: if Hashem created the world to revolve around *chessed* – "עוֹלָם חֶסֶד יִבָּנֶה"[107] – then how and why is there evil in the world at all?

While these are complex topics, a basic approach is that evil exists in the world due to Adam HaRishon's sin and continues to exist as a result of *bechirah chofshis*, free will, with which Hashem empowers mankind. In addition, per the primary theme of the *Daas Tevunos* of the *Ramchal*, while evil was certainly not the original intent of God (*kiv'yachol*), the existence and even proliferation of evil in the world will ultimately lead to the highest possible magnification of *Kiddush HaShem*, sanctification of the Name in the future time of Moshiach when Hashem will transform an impure and evil world into a world of pure goodness in the blink of an eye. Moreover, says the *Ramchal*, the more depraved and debased the evil is now, the greater and more exalted will be the revelation of *Kiddush HaShem* and *Yichud Hashem* (the Oneness of Hashem) in the future, when Hashem will forever eradicate evil and transform the world into a place of morality and righteousness through the culmination of the ultimate Adam-Dovid-Moshiach *tikkun*.

Pasuk 23:
חָקְרֵנִי אֵ-ל וְדַע לְבָבִי;
בְּחָנֵנִי וְדַע שַׂרְעַפָּי

**Examine me, God, and know my heart;
test me and know my thoughts.**

---

[106] *Tehillim* 97:10.
[107] *Tehillim* 89:3.

A Final Flourish of *Daas*

In this penultimate *pasuk* of *Tehillim* 139, Dovid HaMelech ends with a two-fold flourish of the *shoresh* of "דַּעַת – knowledge" and states: "חָקְרֵנִי אֵ-ל וְדַע לְבָבִי; בְּחָנֵנִי וְדַע שַׂרְעַפָּי" – Examine me, God, and know my heart; test me and know my thoughts."

May Hashem's *Daas* Reveal Our Purity

This dual expression of *daas* provides the *kapitel* with its final allusions to Adam's sin of the *Eitz HaDaas*. Yet here, Dovid HaMelech is asking, even challenging, Hashem to use His Godly knowledge to reveal Dovid's purity of heart and mind. By extension, this will reveal the purity of heart and mind possessed by the entire Jewish People, whom Dovid as our quintessential human king and the great-great-grandfather-to-be of the *Melech HaMoshiach*, represents.

The Double *Daas* That Hints to Shabbos

In addition, this double mention of *daas* brings the number of mentions of *daas* in *Tehillim* 139 to a total of seven, which symbolizes that the sin of the *Eitz HaDaas* adulterated and damaged Hashem's world which He created and then rested from during a seven-day period. In addition, the two-fold mention of *daas* here as the respective sixth and seventh mentions of *daas* would thus correspond to days six and seven of Creation. It is therefore apropos that these last two mentions of *daas* are tied together, combined in a single *pasuk*, for that is consistent with the famous teaching of Chazal that the moment of transition from the end of the first Friday (day six) into the start of the first Shabbos (day seven) was something that only Hashem Himself was capable of discerning, but to man the days appeared to be intermingled.[108]

---

[108] *Rashi, Bereishis* 2:1, from *Bereishis Rabbah* 10:9.

Daas in the Haftarah Elevates Us Beyond the Rules of Nature

It must also be noted that the very last *pasuk* in the *Haftarah* to *Parshas Bereishis* contains an emphasis on the concept of *daas* as well: "אַתֶּם עֵדַי נְאֻם ה', עַבְדִּי אֲשֶׁר בָּחָרְתִּי; לְמַעַן תֵּדְעוּ וְתַאֲמִינוּ לִי וְתָבִינוּ כִּי אֲנִי הוּא, לְפָנַי לֹא נוֹצַר אֵל וְאַחֲרַי לֹא יִהְיֶה – You are My witness, swears Hashem, and My servant, whom I have chosen; לְמַעַן תֵּדְעוּ – so that you will *know* Me and believe in Me, and understand that I am He; before Me nothing was created by a god and after Me it shall not be!"[109]

The above reference to *daas*, combined with the references to *daas* in *Tehillim* 139, brings the grand total to eight, which is a special number in the context of *Maaseh Bereishis*.

Creation included Hashem's laws of nature, *teva*, which ironically sometimes *disguise* Hashem's presence in the world such that man becomes less cognizant of Hashem as the Creator rather than more acutely aware of Him, as the above-quoted *pasuk* from the *Haftarah* laments. While the number seven represents nature bound by a weekly cycle of seven days, the number eight is the first number that adds upon – even transcends – the number seven. Therefore, the number eight symbolizes *le'maalah min ha'teva*, above and beyond nature – almost supernatural. As such, the number eight is designed to reconnect us to Hashem, Who is simultaneously within nature and above and beyond it.

Furthermore, the supernatural number eight also represents the time of Moshiach, which is the goal of *Maaseh Bereishis*. In that time, Hashem will allow both mankind and the so-called "natural world" – plagued by famine, sickness, and death – to be restored to the level of Adam HaRishon and *Maaseh Bereishis* as Hashem *originally* created.

---

[109] *Yeshayahu* 43:10.

Our Role in the *Tikkun* of the *Cheit*

Just as importantly, whenever we learn, recite, daven, or better yet, pour out our hearts to Hashem with a focus on each mention of *daas* in this *kapitel Tehillim* 139, we too become vital participants in repairing the *cheit* of Adam HaRishon.

How much more so must this be true when we learn, recite, and immerse ourselves in this *kapitel* specifically on Shabbos *Parshas Bereishis* itself!

Pasuk 24:
וּרְאֵה אִם דֶּרֶךְ עֹצֶב בִּי;
וּנְחֵנִי בְּדֶרֶךְ עוֹלָם
And see if a path of sadness/rebellion is within me;
and lead me in the way of the world/eternity.

Overcoming the Sadness of Sin

The reference here to "עֹצֶב – sadness," is very much on point, for Hashem's curse of both Adam and Chavah includes references to "עִצָּבוֹן," sadness/suffering.

Regarding Chavah, Hashem used a double expression of sadness: "הַרְבָּה אַרְבֶּה עִצְּבוֹנֵךְ וְהֵרֹנֵךְ, בְּעֶצֶב תֵּלְדִי בָנִים" – I will greatly increase your sadness/suffering and your pregnancy; in sadness/pain you shall bear children."[110]

To Adam, Hashem said: "אֲרוּרָה הָאֲדָמָה בַּעֲבוּרֶךָ, בְּעִצָּבוֹן תֹּאכֲלֶנָּה" – Accursed is the ground because of you; through sadness/suffering shall you eat of it."[111]

Yet here in *pasuk* 24, when Dovid HaMelech passionately proclaims "וּרְאֵה אִם דֶּרֶךְ עֹצֶב בִּי" – rhetorically declaring to Hashem that there is *no*

---

[110] *Bereishis* 3:16.
[111] *Bereishis* 3:17.

sadness to be found within him – it is as if Dovid HaMelech, on his own behalf and on behalf of Adam and Chavah, is respectfully declaring to Hashem that despite all the difficulties and punishments and suffering endured by mankind, the God-fearing among man will *not* succumb to despair because they know that it is all a part of the will of Hashem. Dovid HaMelech refused to be despondent, and so must we.

Hashem's Sadness

In addition, at the very end of *Parshas Bereishis*, the Torah states: "וַיִּנָּחֶם ה' כִּי עָשָׂה אֶת הָאָדָם בָּאָרֶץ; וַיִּתְעַצֵּב אֶל לִבּוֹ – And Hashem reconsidered having made Man on earth, and He was pained/saddened in His heart."[112] According to one interpretation in *Rashi*, Hashem was mourning the impending destruction of His handiwork which would take place in *Parshas Noach*.[113] Furthermore, although Hashem knew in advance that mankind was destined to sin, He did not refrain from creating them because of the *tzaddikim* who were destined to arise from among them.[114] Nevertheless, the merciful Hashem was "וַיִּתְעַצֵּב" and felt sadness over what was to transpire.

In response to this, the pronouncement by Dovid HaMelech here in *pasuk* 24 of "וּרְאֵה אִם דֶּרֶךְ עֹצֶב בִּי" is a promise to remain hopeful. And, perhaps, this pasuk is also a request that Hashem Himself remain hopeful because *tzaddikim* yet endure and thrive in this world, thereby serving as a testament to the *success* of Hashem's Creation.

From This World to the World to Come

In addition, how appropriate it is that the final word in the *kapitel* corresponding to *Parshas Bereishis* – in which Hashem reveals a

---

[112] *Bereishis* 6:6.
[113] *Rashi, Bereishis* 6:6, from *Bereishis Rabbah* 27:4.
[114] *Rashi, Bereishis* 6:6, from *Bereishis Rabbah* 27:4 and *Bereishis Rabbah* 8:4.

behind-the-scenes, detailed view of His creation of the world – is the word "עוֹלָם – world."

Moreover, it is appropriate that Dovid HaMelech, though having just proclaimed himself as pure of thought, eager to serve Hashem (*pasuk* 23), and devoid of any rebelliousness (*pasuk* 24) still requests: "וּנְחֵנִי – and lead me." Here, Dovid beseeches Hashem for His guidance in navigating the pitfalls of our complicated world marred by the sin of Adam HaRishon. Though bolstered and brave, Dovid only yearns to navigate this world together with Hashem.

Of course, Dovid HaMelech is not singularly focused on this transient, physical world. Rather, "עוֹלָם" can also mean "eternally," which indicates that Dovid is simultaneously focused on the *additional* world that Hashem created: "עוֹלָם הַבָּא – the World to Come." That more spiritual world is the goal and destination of every Jew and the ultimate reason why this physical world was created by Hashem during *Maaseh Bereishis* in the first place. As the *Ramchal* so famously articulates at the very start of *Mesillas Yesharim*, the purpose of this world is to provide us with the opportunity to *earn* our eternal reward of "לְהִתְעַנֵּג עַל ה' וְלֵהָנוֹת מִזִּיו שְׁכִינָתוֹ – to rejoice in Hashem and derive [spiritual] pleasure from the radiance of His Divine Presence" in the World to Come.[115]

Closing Remarks on the *Bereishis-Tehillim* Connection

In light of the above, we can now see and feel more deeply the many connections between *Parshas Bereishis* and *Tehillim* 139, a *kapitel* that does indeed contain the story of *Parshas Bereishis* interwoven throughout its very core. Like *Parshas Bereishis*, *Tehillim* 139 tells the story of Creation, the struggles of Adam HaRishon, Kayin, and other figures and events of the *Parshah*, and of the failings and challenges that mankind faces each precious day.

---

[115] *Mesillas Yesharim, perek alef.*

But perhaps even more importantly, *Tehillim* 139 provides each of *us* with the opportunity to daven to Hashem using the voice of Dovid HaMelech, intertwined with the voice of Adam HaRishon, and joined by a voice that is uniquely ours.

CHAPTER 2

PARSHAS NOACH & TEHILLIM 29

פָּרָשַׁת נֹחַ / תְּהִלִּים כט

TEHILLIM 29 — תְּהִלִּים כט

1 A psalm by Dovid: ascribe to Hashem, you sons of the powerful; ascribe to Hashem honor and might.

א מִזְמוֹר לְדָוִד: הָבוּ לַה' בְּנֵי אֵלִים; הָבוּ לַה' כָּבוֹד וָעֹז.

2 Ascribe to Hashem the honor due His Name; bow down to Hashem in the splendor of holiness.

ב הָבוּ לַה' כְּבוֹד שְׁמוֹ; הִשְׁתַּחֲווּ לַה' בְּהַדְרַת קֹדֶשׁ.

3 The voice of Hashem is upon the waters, the God of Glory thunders; Hashem is upon vast waters.

ג קוֹל ה' עַל הַמָּיִם, אֵ-ל הַכָּבוֹד הִרְעִים; ה' עַל מַיִם רַבִּים.

4 The voice of Hashem [comes] in power; the voice of Hashem [comes] in majesty.

ד קוֹל ה' בַּכֹּחַ; קוֹל ה' בֶּהָדָר.

5 The voice of Hashem breaks the cedar trees; Hashem breaks the cedars of Lebanon.

ה קוֹל ה' שֹׁבֵר אֲרָזִים; וַיְשַׁבֵּר ה' אֶת אַרְזֵי הַלְּבָנוֹן.

6	He makes them prance about like a calf; Lebanon and Siryon like young *re'eimim*.	וַיַּרְקִידֵם כְּמוֹ עֵגֶל; לְבָנוֹן וְשִׂרְיֹן כְּמוֹ בֶן רְאֵמִים.	ו
7	The voice of Hashem cleaves with flames of fire.	קוֹל ה' חֹצֵב לַהֲבוֹת אֵשׁ.	ז
8	The voice of Hashem shakes the wilderness; Hashem shakes the wilderness of Kadesh.	קוֹל ה' יָחִיל מִדְבָּר; יָחִיל ה' מִדְבַּר קָדֵשׁ.	ח
9	The voice of Hashem frightens the deer and strips bare the forests; and in His Temple, all will proclaim "Glory."	קוֹל ה' יְחוֹלֵל אַיָּלוֹת, וַיֶּחֱשֹׂף יְעָרוֹת; וּבְהֵיכָלוֹ-כֻּלּוֹ אֹמֵר כָּבוֹד.	ט
10	Hashem at the Flood sat enthroned; Hashem sits enthroned as King forever.	ה' לַמַּבּוּל יָשָׁב; וַיֵּשֶׁב ה' מֶלֶךְ לְעוֹלָם.	י
11	Hashem will give strength to His nation; Hashem will bless His nation with peace.	ה' עֹז לְעַמּוֹ יִתֵּן; ה' יְבָרֵךְ אֶת עַמּוֹ בַשָּׁלוֹם.	יא

INTRODUCTION: DIVING IN

Take a look at the words of *Tehillim* 29 and dip your toes into its waters; get your feet wet. Then daven its words, letting yourself sway back and forth, transforming yourself into a wave. Feel the intensity of its ebb and flow, your ebb and flow.

As you say "הָבוּ לַה' בְּנֵי אֵלִים," start to see the clouds forming from above.

CHAPTER 2: NOACH & TEHILLIM 29

With "הָבוּ לַה' כָּבוֹד וָעֹז," be shocked by the thunder's power and awed by the splendor of the lightning's flash.

As you say "הָבוּ לַה' כְּבוֹד שְׁמוֹ," feel the raindrops pattering on your shoulders, lightly, even innocently. Are these rains of blessing?

And with "קוֹל ה' עַל הַמָּיִם" the downpour begins, along with an uneasy feeling that something is out of the ordinary; something is different.

With "קוֹל ה' בַּכֹּחַ," there are sheets of rain like the Plague of Darkness; no one can move, and the terror sets in. But there is still time to do *teshuvah*; the evil world can still repent.

"קוֹל ה' בֶּהָדָר," and the earth rumbles; it explodes as the lower waters rise to combine with the waters from above. It is almost too late. Almost.

With "קוֹל ה' שֹׁבֵר אֲרָזִים," roads, homes, and marketplaces are flooded and battered, and the fatalities begin. Why won't anyone repent?

"קוֹל ה' חֹצֵב לַהֲבוֹת אֵשׁ," and the waters become fiery, unsurvivable. But will at least those still safe on the mountaintops be moved to make amends?

With "קוֹל ה' יָחִיל מִדְבָּר," the earth is entirely caught in chaos; the world has become a single, giant, and infuriated ocean. It is too late; no one outside the Ark remains.

"קוֹל ה' יְחוֹלֵל אַיָּלוֹת" expresses the incredible power, the unimaginable destruction of human and beast, young and old. Yet, try to understand and appreciate the Godly retribution.

"וּבְהֵיכָלוֹ- כֻּלּוֹ אֹמֵר כָּבוֹד," and through it all the angels echo from above already declaring "*Kavod*!" Give honor to Hashem.

While the above utilizes some poetic license, *Tehillim* 29 does indeed correspond to *Parshas Noach* and the story of the Flood, brought by Hashem to destroy His world to rebuild it anew from the righteous Noach and his small family of seven.

> PARSHAH & TEHILLIM HAND IN HAND

THE MANY CONNECTIONS BETWEEN PARSHAS NOACH & TEHILLIM 29

Pasuk 10:

ה' לַמַּבּוּל יָשָׁב;

וַיֵּשֶׁב ה' מֶלֶךְ לְעוֹלָם

Hashem at the Flood sat enthroned;
Hashem sits enthroned as King forever.

Hashem at the Flood Sat Enthroned

Tehillim 29 is part of our Friday night *Kabbalas Shabbos* davening and is also said every Shabbos day as we return the *Sefer Torah* to the *aron kodesh*. That *Tehillim* 29 is connected to *Parshas Noach* is abundantly clear from its second-to-last *pasuk*, *pasuk* 10: "ה' לַמַּבּוּל יָשָׁב; וַיֵּשֶׁב ה' מֶלֶךְ לְעוֹלָם – Hashem at the Flood sat enthroned; Hashem sits enthroned as King forever."

Indeed, the *Midrash Tehillim* states that "ה' לַמַּבּוּל יָשָׁב" teaches that Hashem יָשָׁב, sat in *din*, strict judgment, against the wicked at the time of the Flood. Furthermore, "וַיֵּשֶׁב ה' מֶלֶךְ לְעוֹלָם" reveals that in response to Noach's *korbanos* (animal sacrifices) soon after the Flood, "נִתְיַישְּׁבָה דַעְתּוֹ – [Hashem's] mind 'sat' at ease" and caused Him to thereafter show *rachamim*, mercy, to the world.[1]

As we shall see, *Tehillim* 29 contains many additional fascinating and insightful hidden connections to *Parshas Noach* that will *b'ezras Hashem* inspire us in our *avodas Hashem*.

---

[1] *Midrash Tehillim, Shocher Tov* 29.

Pasuk 1:
בְּנֵי אֵלִים
Sons of the mighty ones.

Sons of the Mighty Ones

"בְּנֵי אֵלִים" is a reference to the children of Avraham, Yitzchak, and Yaakov. The Gemara[2] teaches that the Avos HaKedoshim are referred to as "אֵילֵי הָאָרֶץ – mighty ones of the land"[3] due to their *tzidkus* and inner strength. The Avos immediately follow Noach as the Torah's protagonists and stars throughout *Sefer Bereishis* and were instrumental in publicizing *Hashem's* presence and might ("אֵילֵי") throughout a world ("הָאָרֶץ") that Hashem had erased in the time of Noach.

In fact, the *Zohar Hakadosh* further intertwines *Tehillim* 29 with the Avos when it references other phrases contained in this chapter and states: "קוֹל ה' עַל הַמָּיִם – דָּא אַבְרָהָם. קוֹל ה' בַּכֹּחַ – דָּא יִצְחָק. קוֹל ה' בֶּהָדָר – דָּא יַעֲקֹב" – 'The voice of Hashem is upon the waters' – this refers to Avraham. 'The voice of Hashem [comes] in power' – this refers to Yitzchak. 'The voice of Hashem [comes] in majesty' – this refers to Yaakov."[4]

Pesukim 1, 2, 3, and 9:
כָּבוֹד
Honor.

Honor Restored

Pesukim 1, 2, 3, and 9 each reference the word "כָּבוֹד – honor." These *pesukim* initially hint to the *lack* of *kavod* by mankind toward their fellow man and toward God prior to the *Mabul*. They also refer to the

---

[2] *Rosh Hashanah* 32a.
[3] *Yechezkel* 17:13.
[4] *Zohar Hakadosh* 3:31b, quoting portions of *Tehillim* 29:3–4.

subsequent *kavod Shamayim*, honor toward God in heaven, that resulted from the *Mabul*. First, Hashem's honor was restored among the generation of the Flood when they were punished and eradicated by Hashem. Additionally, the angels witnessed the destruction and recognized the power of Hashem and the honor due to Him. Subsequently, Noach and his family appreciated Hashem's honor through their experience of survival. The restoration of *kavod Shamayim* ultimately culminated with the Avos HaKedoshim and Bnei Yisrael, who would remember the lessons of the *Mabul* and serve Hashem while striving to properly emulate His might and His mercy and thereby bring honor to His Name.

Pesukim 1 and 12:
עֹז
Power.

The "*Oz*" of Destruction and of Torah

Pesukim 1 and 12 each reference the word "עֹז – power" but within two different contexts. *Pasuk* 1 refers to Hashem's power and might in bringing the destructive Flood. Yet *pasuk* 12, in the famous phrase: "ה' עֹז לְעַמּוֹ יִתֵּן," refers to Hashem "granting power to His nation Israel" in the form of:

- Torah, e.g., "אַתָּה וַאֲרוֹן עֻזֶּךָ – You and the Ark of Your עֹז, strength,"[5] referring to the Torah into which Hashem looked and created the world;[6]
- Mitzvos, such as the mitzvah of tefillin that is referred to as the עֹז of, and for, the Jewish People;[7] and

---

[5] *Tehillim* 132:8.
[6] *Midrash Tanchuma, Bereishis* 1.
[7] *Brachos* 6a.

- Closeness to Hashem Himself, e.g., "ה' עֹז לָמוֹ – Hashem [Himself] is עֹז, strength, for them [the Jewish People]."[8]

Pesukim 1 and 2:
הָבוּ לַה'
Ascribe to Hashem.

Havu La'Hashem: "*Havu*" Unto God

Pesukim 1 and 2 contain an initial emphasis on the phrase "הָבוּ לַה'," which is used three times. הָבוּ is a difficult word to translate: *Rashi* and the *Malbim* say that it means "prepare" for Hashem; *Metzudas Dovid* says "praise" Hashem; the *Radak* says "give" to Hashem; the ArtScroll Tehillim translates it as "render" to Hashem; and we have translated it as "ascribe" to Hashem.

Irrespective of its specific translation, on a deeper level the common denominator of "הָבוּ" is that it implies a lack that needs to be fulfilled or completed. More urgently, הָבוּ is a *directive* to do so; the listener must be *told* to prepare/praise/give/render/ascribe because he is not doing so naturally on his own. These are appropriate sentiments for the debased and vile generation of the Flood.

In addition, the same *shoresh* of הָבוּ appears three times in *Parshas Noach* in the context of *Migdal Bavel*, the Tower of Babel, in the form of the word "הָבָה," which *Rashi* says means "come" and "prepare." First the people stated: "הָבָה נִלְבְּנָה לְבֵנִים – Come, let us make bricks"[9] for nefarious purposes, and then they said: "הָבָה נִבְנֶה לָּנוּ עִיר וּמִגְדָּל וְרֹאשׁוֹ בַשָּׁמַיִם וְנַעֲשֶׂה לָּנוּ שֵׁם – Come, let us build us a city, with a tower with its top in the heavens, and let us make a name for ourselves"[10] in rebellion against Hashem. The third and final use of the word הָבָה was said by Hashem: "הָבָה, נֵרְדָה וְנָבְלָה

---

[8] *Tehillim* 28:8.
[9] *Bereishis* 11:3.
[10] *Bereishis* 11:4.

שָׁם שְׂפָתָם" – Come, let us descend and confuse their language there."[11] *Rashi* explains this final use in a two-fold approach. These words are an expression of Hashem's judgment performed with extreme humility by calling upon His Heavenly court.[12] Additionally, this is an expression of Hashem judging *middah k'neged middah*: the people sinned with expressions of הָבָה and were thus punished with an expression of הָבָה.[13] That the same root-expression of "הָבוּ" is similarly such an important word in the tapestry of *Tehillim* 29 is truly remarkable.

Pasuk 3:
קוֹל ה' עַל הַמָּיִם,
אֵ-ל הַכָּבוֹד הִרְעִים;
ה' עַל מַיִם רַבִּים

**The voice of Hashem is upon the waters,
the God of Glory thunders;
Hashem is upon vast waters.**

The Voice of Hashem Heard Through Mighty Waters

Rashi on *Tehillim* 29 explains this *pasuk* (and the entire *kapitel*) in a different historical context, seeing in it a reference to the waters of *Krias Yam Suf* (the Splitting of the Reed Sea). Nevertheless, this *pasuk* certainly contains imagery reminiscent of the Flood of Noach as well. In fact, second only to the explicit statement of "ה' לַמַּבּוּל יָשָׁב" in *pasuk* 10, this *pasuk* with its double reference to water and reference to thunder screams out: *Mabul*!

---

[11] *Bereishis* 11:7.
[12] *Rashi, Bereishis* 11:7, from *Sanhedrin* 38b.
[13] *Tanchuma Yashan, Noach* 25.

Pasuk 3 also brings with it a change in emphasis, as we are introduced to a new recurring theme: "קוֹל ה׳ – the voice of Hashem," as will be discussed below.

Pesukim 3, 4, 5, 7, 8, and 9:
קוֹל ה׳
The voice of Hashem.

The Voice of Hashem as Power and Wrath

Pesukim 3–5 and 7–9 each utilize the theme of "קוֹל ה׳ – the voice of Hashem," which resonates throughout the *kapitel*.

- *Pasuk* 3: "The voice of Hashem is upon the waters."
- *Pasuk* 4: "The voice of Hashem [comes] in power; the voice of Hashem [comes] in majesty."
- *Pasuk* 5: "The voice of Hashem breaks cedar trees."
- *Pasuk* 7: "The voice of Hashem cleaves with flames of fire."
- *Pasuk* 8: "The voice of Hashem shakes the wilderness."
- *Pasuk* 9: "The voice of Hashem frightens the deer and strips bare the forests."

These are all striking expressions of the קוֹל ה׳ reverberating in power and wrath during the *Mabul* and then echoing throughout a virtually empty world following the Flood.

The Mystical Power of Hashem's Voice in Our Homes Even Today

The Gemara in *Pesachim*[14] contains esoteric and mystical discussions about the concept of evil spirits in various contexts and provides warnings on how to prevent attracting them and/or how to ward them off. The Gemara teaches that one should not drink water on Tuesday nights or

---

[14] *Pesachim* 112a.

PARSHAH & TEHILLIM HAND IN HAND

Friday nights in the dark,[15] lest he bring danger upon himself due to the threat of *ruach ra'ah*, evil spirits that are able to lurk in the darkness on these specific evenings. However, if a person is thirsty on one of these nights and the room is dark, which can often occur on a Friday night when we are forbidden to turn on the lights due to Shabbos, how can one drink water without endangering himself from evil spirits? The first of many remedies that the Gemara provides is that "one should recite the seven 'קוֹלוֹת – voices' that Dovid said over the water and then drink."

What are these "seven voices"? The answer is *pesukim* 3 through 5 and 7 through 9 of *Tehillim* 29, which contain the words קוֹל ה' seven times! Additionally, it is interesting to note that the Gemara uncharacteristically writes out all seven phrases explicitly rather than just referencing them or bringing them in abbreviated form, further highlighting their significance.

Furthermore, the *Maharsha* comments that while most of these *pesukim* do not actually mention *water* at all, we can still understand each use of the "voice of Hashem" as a reference to water. The *Maharsha* points us to the *first* mention of קוֹל ה' in the phrase "קוֹל ה' עַל הַמָּיִם" – The voice of Hashem is upon the waters." On the strength of this first reference to water, *all* the remaining קוֹלוֹת are referred to by the Gemara as "over the water," thus further highlighting the power of the phrase "קוֹל ה' עַל הַמָּיִם."[16]

The above Gemara teaches that *Tehillim* 29 takes on an association with water throughout, and that the words of this *kapitel* have the power to ward off harmful spirits attracted by the drinking of water. Such notions are certainly apropos for this *kapitel*, which corresponds to *Parshas Noach* and revolves so heavily around the waters of the *Mabul*. Even more powerful is this Gemara's teaching that *Tehillim* 29 contains the mystical power to *protect* us from the hidden harmful effects of water in our own homes even today.

---

[15] *Rashbam, Pesachim* 112a.
[16] *Maharsha, Pesachim* 112a.

Pasuk 7:
קוֹל ה' חֹצֵב לַהֲבוֹת אֵשׁ
The voice of Hashem cleaves with flames of fire.

The Voice of Hashem as Deadly Heat

"קוֹל ה' חֹצֵב לַהֲבוֹת אֵשׁ" and its reference to flames and burning fire reminds us that the *Mabul* was much more than just water: it was liquid that contained a deadly combination of sulfur and fiery heat as well.[17] The Gemara explains that this too was *middah k'neged middah* because "בְּרוֹתְחִין קִלְקְלוּ וּבְרוֹתְחִין נִדּוֹנוּ. בְּרוֹתְחִין קִלְקְלוּ – בַּעֲבֵירָה, וּבְרוֹתְחִין נִדּוֹנוּ" – With boiling they acted corruptly, and with boiling they were punished. With a boiling substance they acted corruptly – by engaging in immorality – and with boiling water [of the flood] they were punished."[18]

Hidden References to the Rainbow

On its surface, *Tehillim* 29 lacks any reference to the קֶשֶׁת, rainbow, the famous symbol in *Parshas Noach* representing Hashem's promise never to bring another flood to destroy mankind, no matter how terrible their sins.[19] The rainbow not only is a sign of Hashem's abundant Divine mercy, but also is a sign to those who see it to correct their ways. The rainbow reflects Hashem's dissatisfaction with the spiritual state of the generation in which a rainbow appears. As a result, despite its colors and attraction, the appearance of a rainbow is actually a קְלָלָה, a curse, and a sign of אָרוּר, accursedness.[20] For that reason, we are instructed not to stare at a rainbow for the purpose of indulging in its physical beauty,[21] nor

---

[17] *Rashi, Bereishis* 6:14, from *Sanhedrin* 108b.
[18] *Rosh Hashanah* 12a.
[19] *Bereishis* 9:8–17.
[20] *Kesubos* 77b.
[21] *Chagigah* 16a.

are we to point out and show the rainbow to others, as one should neither enjoy nor encourage others to enjoy an accursed thing.[22]

Indeed, *Tehillim* 29 does not explicitly contain the word קֶשֶׁת, nor does it contain any of the other key words used by the Torah in connection with the rainbow, such as בְּרִית, covenant,[23] or אוֹת, sign.[24] Nonetheless, upon closer examination of *pesukim* 7 and 8, and specifically the ת and the שׁ of the phrase "לַהֲבוֹת אֵשׁ" that concludes *pasuk* 7, and the very next letter which is the ק of "קוֹל" that begins *pasuk* 8, we see that together these letters can be combined to spell the word "קֶשֶׁת" – rainbow!

It must be noted that these three letters of the word קֶשֶׁת are interrupted by a seemingly stray א from the word "אֵשׁ" in *pasuk* 7. As a result of this seemingly extraneous א, the hidden reference to the rainbow might seem to be sullied. However, there is a famous *yesod* that ties in the א perfectly. The question is asked: why does the Torah begin with a ב, the second letter of the Hebrew language, and not with an א, which is the first letter? The answer is because א stands for אָרוּר while ב stands for בָּרוּךְ.[25] We can now understand that the presence of the letter א amidst the letters that spell קֶשֶׁת is extremely apropos, for both the א and the קֶשֶׁת are unique symbols of אָרוּר and קְלָלָה, accursedness.

It should also be noted that the hints to קֶשֶׁת and אָרוּר span two *pesukim*, carrying over from one *pasuk* to the next. This alludes to the phenomenon and structure of the rainbow itself, whose appearance in the sky spans from one side of the horizon to the other.

Finally, the fact that the word קֶשֶׁת is hidden within *Tehillim* 29 and not overtly revealed is consistent with the *halachah* noted above that one should not show the rainbow to others due to its accursed status.

---

[22] *Mishnah Berurah* 229:1.
[23] *Bereishis* 9:9, 11–13, 15–17.
[24] *Bereishis* 9:12–13, and 17.
[25] *Yerushalmi, Chagigah* 2:1; *Bereishis Rabbah* 1:10; *Midrash Tanchuma, Bereishis* 5.

References to Cham and His Offspring

It is also interesting to note that the events in the Torah following that of the rainbow is the episode in which Noach planted a vineyard, became drunk, and was victimized by his son Cham.[26] As a result, Noach declared in punishment to Cham: "אָרוּר כְּנָעַן; עֶבֶד עֲבָדִים יִהְיֶה לְאֶחָיו – Cursed is Canaan; a slave of slaves shall he be to his brothers."[27] There, the concept of "אָרוּר" appears yet again, in close proximity to the episode of the accursed rainbow!

In addition, the Torah tells us that the rejected Cham had a grandson named "לְהָבִים,"[28] which literally means "flames," because he and his family had faces that resembled a flame.[29] That the aforementioned hints to קֶשֶׁת and אָרוּר are primarily found in *pasuk* 7 of *Tehillim* 29 is remarkable because in that same *pasuk* the word "לַהֲבוֹת – flames" is also mentioned: "קוֹל ה' חֹצֵב לַהֲבוֹת אֵשׁ."

Pesukim 6 and 9:
עֵגֶל... רְאֵמִים... אַיָּלוֹת...
calf... re'eimim... deer...

The Animals in the Ark

Pasuk 6 refers to a calf and to the *re'eimim*, which is a type of horned animal often translated as aurochs (extinct wild oxen), buffalo, reindeer, or even unicorn.[30] *Pasuk* 9 refers to a deer. These references allude to a fundamental aspect of the account of Noah's Ark, for every child knows that the Ark housed not only Noach's wife and small family,

---

[26] *Bereishis* 9:20–27.
[27] *Bereishis* 9:25.
[28] *Bereishis* 10:13.
[29] *Rashi, Bereishis* 10:13.
[30] ArtScroll Interlinear Chumash, *Sefer Bamidbar*, p. 297, fn. 6.

but a select and holy[31] few of every single animal, creature, and bug that existed upon the face of the earth in order to ensure these creatures' survival during the Flood and their repopulation on the earth in the *Mabul's* aftermath. It is therefore no coincidence that *Tehillim* 29 contains rare references to three distinct types of animals: the עֵגֶל and רְאֵמִים in *pasuk* 6 and the אַיָּלוֹת in *pasuk* 9. While just a small sampling of animals, the three-fold "*chazakah*" mention of animals is certainly appropriate to find in the *kapitel* that corresponds to *Parshas Noach*.

Pasuk 11:
ה' עֹז לְעַמּוֹ יִתֵּן;
ה' יְבָרֵךְ אֶת עַמּוֹ בַשָּׁלוֹם
Hashem will give strength to His nation;
Hashem will bless His nation with peace.

Hashem Bestows *Oz* (Torah) and *Shalom* (Peace)

This concluding *pasuk* of *Tehillim* 29 is particularly well known. On the heels of the prior *pasuk* that explicitly describes Hashem enthroned on high during the *Mabul*, here we are reminded of the *purpose* of the *Mabul*: to reset the world through the progeny of Noach and specifically through his son Shem, from whom would emerge Avraham Avinu and Klal Yisrael, Hashem's "עַם הַנִּבְחָר – Chosen Nation."

Furthermore, with the word "עַמּוֹ – *His* nation" used not once but twice in this lone *pasuk*, we see the emphasis on Hashem's personal selection of, and connection to, the Jewish People to whom (as previously discussed) Hashem grants Torah, mitzvos, and even a personalized connection with Hashem Himself.

Finally, all of the above takes place under the framework of "שָׁלוֹם – peace," which is the ultimate preserver of all blessings. As the Mishnah

---

[31] *Rashi, Bereishis* 6:20, from *Sanhedrin* 108b.

teaches at the end of *Uktzin*: "לֹא מָצָא הַקָּדוֹשׁ בָּרוּךְ הוּא כְּלִי מַחֲזִיק בְּרָכָה לְיִשְׂרָאֵל אֶלָּא הַשָּׁלוֹם – The Holy One, blessed be He, found no vessel that could contain blessing for Israel except for that of peace, as it is written: "ה' עֹז לְעַמּוֹ יִתֵּן; ה' יְבָרֵךְ אֶת עַמּוֹ בַשָּׁלוֹם."[32]

ADDITIONAL THEMES IN PARSHAS NOACH & TEHILLIM 29

B'*ezras Hashem*, the remainder of this chapter will focus on two main themes that further unify *Tehillim* 29 and *Parshas Noach*:

(1) Noach's connection to *Shemoneh Esrei* and the power of *tefillah*.

(2) Hashem's ability to heal, even through destruction, and the "*yedidus*," friendship and belovedness, with Hashem that such paradoxical healing engenders.

TEHILLIM 29 AND ITS CONNECTION TO SHEMONEH ESREI

The Gemara in *Brachos*[33] inquires as to the source of the eighteen blessings of *Shemoneh Esrei*. Interestingly, Rav Hillel the son of Rav Shmuel bar Nachmani states that they correspond to the eighteen mentions

---

[32] *Uktzin* 3:12.
[33] *Brachos* 28b.

of Hashem's Divine Name of י-ה-ו-ה said by Dovid HaMelech in *Tehillim* 29.

The Gemara in *Rosh Hashanah*[34] elaborates further: the first blessing in *Shemoneh Esrei*, known as *Avos*, is based upon the phrase in pasuk 1 of *Tehillim* 29, "הָבוּ לַה' בְּנֵי אֵלִים," in reference to our "mighty" forefathers Avraham, Yitzchak, and Yaakov, also known as the "אֵילֵי הָאָרֶץ – mighty ones of the land."[35] The second blessing of *Shemoneh Esrei*, known as *Gevuros*, is based upon the continuation of *pasuk* 1, "הָבוּ לַה' כָּבוֹד וָעֹז," which references "power" and is very similar in meaning to *gevurah*. The third blessing of *Shemoneh Esrei*, known as *Kedushos*, is based upon *Tehillim* 29's phrase in *pasuk* 2: "הָבוּ לַה'... בְּהַדְרַת קֹדֶשׁ." Thus, the first three *brachos* of *Shemoneh Esrei* parallel the first three expressions of *Tehillim* 29 – in order.

We find yet another example of this parallel in the shared concluding word of both *Shemoneh Esrei* and *Tehillim* 29: שָׁלוֹם. And although the Gemara does not further elaborate or trace the connections in *Tehillim* 29 to the content of the remaining blessings of *Shemoneh Esrei*, the Gemara does explicitly state that the total of eighteen blessings is derived from *Tehillim* 29's eighteen mentions of י-ה-ו-ה.[36]

Noach's Connection to *Shemoneh Esrei*: *Mei Noach*

In light of the above, we must consider the following question: since *Tehillim* 29 is the source for the eighteen *brachos* of *Shemoneh Esrei*, and since *Tehillim* 29 corresponds to *Parshas Noach*, what then, if any, is the connection between *Parshas Noach* and *Shemoneh Esrei*?

The *Haftarah* to *Parshas Noach* twice uses the expression "מֵי נֹחַ – the waters of Noach," to describe the *Mabul*.[37] The same expression is also

---

[34] *Rosh Hashanah* 32a.
[35] *Yechezkel* 17:13.
[36] *Brachos* 28b.
[37] *Yeshayahu* 54:9.

CHAPTER 2: NOACH & TEHILLIM 29

used in the Shabbos day *zemer*, *Yonah Matzah*. On the surface, מֵי נֹחַ is a title given to the Flood as a *reward* to Noach for having been the patriarch of the world's sole-surviving family; "waters of Noach" is a badge of honor.

However, others, including the *Zohar Hakadosh*,[38] understand מֵי נֹחַ to be a criticism, even an indictment, of Noach. While Noach did spend 120 years building the Ark in patient fulfillment of Hashem's hope that others would heed the warnings and repent, ultimately Noach influenced no one at all. However, the real criticism lies in the fact that Noach failed to take it a step further: Noach failed to daven for the sake and safety of his generation. Unlike Avraham Avinu who would later daven repeatedly for the sinister cities of Sedom and Amorah,[39] Noach never attempted to pray that Hashem should have mercy on the world. As such, מֵי נֹחַ is a stigma and a condemnation of Noach for what seems like a combination of self-centeredness, a lack of faith in man's ability to improve, or worse yet, a lack of faith in the extent of Hashem's Divine mercy. Whatever the case, Noach failed to daven on behalf of the Generation of the Flood. Therefore, the waters of the Flood are forever called מֵי נֹחַ in his name, for he bears a personal responsibility for neglecting to stave off the deluge through heartfelt prayer to Hashem.

Nonetheless, after Noach and his family spent the better part of a year aboard the Ark,[40] sailing through an otherwise empty world and toiling day and night to feed and pamper the myriad of wildlife on board with them, the Torah tells us "...וַיִּזְכֹּר אֱ-לֹהִים אֶת נֹחַ – God remembered Noach and all the beasts and animals that were with him in the Ark, and God caused a spirit to pass over the earth, and the waters subsided."[41] On the opening words וַיִּזְכֹּר אֱ-לֹהִים, *Rashi* explains that the Name אֱ-לֹהִים represents *middas ha'din*, the Divine attribute of strict judgment. However, that

---

[38] *Zohar Hakadosh, Vayikra*, 3:15a.

[39] *Bereishis, Perek* 18.

[40] *Rashi, Bereishis* 8:14.

[41] *Bereishis* 8:1.

attribute was transformed into *middas ha'rachamim*, the Divine attribute of mercy, because it was the specific description of God as אֱ-לֹהִים that functioned mercifully here to cause the deadly waters to subside. Indeed, the Gemara elaborates that this transformation was triggered by the prayers of the righteous, for the prayers of *tzaddikim* are compared to a pitchfork: just as the pitchfork lifts and flips the grain from place to place on the threshing floor, so too the *tefillos* of *tzaddikim* overturn the mindset of Hashem from what appears to be אַכְזָרִיּוּת, cruelty, to His attribute of mercy.[42]

Therefore, the above reveals that Noach did, in fact, daven to Hashem and thereby caused the Flood to conclude.[43] The Flood is still derogatorily called מֵי נֹחַ, for Noach only davened *after* the Flood and for his *own* sake and that of his family; nonetheless, we do find that Noach *did* ultimately daven to Hashem.

In fact, it seems that Noach's prayer is one of the earliest references to prayer alluded to in the Torah. While Adam HaRishon was the very first to daven to Hashem (ironically also a prayer focused on water, in which Adam prayed to bring the first rainfall to saturate the earth and trigger the growth of vegetation),[44] it must be noted that this episode took place *prior* to Adam's sin, when he was still in mankind's original and perfect state. However, it was Noach, the more "ordinary" man, albeit a *tzaddik*, who was the very first "ordinary" person to daven!

Therefore, considering the above, we now have a deeper understanding of why *Tehillim* 29, the source for the eighteen blessings of *Shemoneh Esrei*, is also tied to the *Parshas HaShavua* in which Noach is the focal point.

---

[42] *Sukkah* 14a.

[43] A similar teaching is found in the *Midrash Tehillim* as well, which indicates that not only Noach but also his family members davened for the Flood to end (see *Midrash Tehillim,* Shocher Tov 29).

[44] *Rashi* to *Bereishis* 2:5, from *Chullin* 60b.

CHAPTER 2: NOACH & TEHILLIM 29

Searching for Hidden References to Noach in *Shemoneh Esrei*

We can now take the above a step further, perhaps even into uncharted territory. Since *Parshas Noach* is connected to *Tehillim* 29, and since *Tehillim* 29 is the basis for the eighteen *brachos* of *Shemoneh Esrei*, is it possible to find connections to Noach and/or the *Mabul* within *Shemoneh Esrei* itself?

After all, Avraham, Yitzchak, and Yaakov are mentioned by name in *Shemoneh Esrei* in the first blessing of *Avos*, and are each, in chronological order, alluded to in the first three blessings.[45] Dovid HaMelech is mentioned by name in the blessings of *V'LiYerushalayim* and *Es Tzemach Dovid*. Moshe Rabbeinu and Aharon HaKohen and his sons are mentioned in *Bircas Kohanim* each morning before *Sim Shalom*, and Moshe Rabbeinu is mentioned by name each Shabbos during the *Shacharis Shemoneh Esrei*. So why not Noach?

Were one to argue that Noach was not part of Klal Yisrael and/or was undeserving of being mentioned in *Shemoneh Esrei*, we need only look to the famed Rosh Hashanah *Mussaf Shemoneh Esrei*, which contains the vital formula of *Malchius*, *Zichronos*, and *Shofros*. There, in the middle of the *Zichronos* portion of *Shemoneh Esrei*, we find Noach prominently mentioned by name, and in fact, the *pasuk* mentioned is "וַיִּזְכֹּר אֱ-לֹהִים אֶת נֹחַ," the same *pasuk* cited above from *Bereishis*[46] which as previously noted is one of the earliest instances of prayer. In addition, the Rosh Hashanah *Mussaf Shemoneh Esrei* includes a beautiful introduction praising both Hashem and Noach:

> Also Noach lovingly did You remember, and You recollected him with the themes of salvation and mercy, when You brought the

---

[45] See e.g., *Derech Hashem*, chelek 4, perek 6, os 11; *Nefesh Shimshon: Siddur HaTefillah*, p. 387.
[46] *Bereishis* 8:1.

waters of the Flood to destroy all flesh because of the evil of their deeds. Consequently, remembrance of him came before You, Hashem our God, to multiply his descendants like the dust of the world, and his offspring like the sand by the sea. As it is written in Your Torah: "וַיִּזְכֹּר אֱ-לֹהִים אֶת נֹחַ – And God remembered Noach… and the waters subsided."[47]

Thus, the Rosh Hashanah *Mussaf Shemoneh Esrei* serves as a clear precedent that Noach *is* worthy of mention in *Shemoneh Esrei*. Still, considering Noach's connection to *Tehillim* 29 and the eighteen blessings of *Shemoneh Esrei* said each *weekday*, the question remains: can we find references to Noach in the *daily Shemoneh Esrei* prayer?

While Noach is clearly not mentioned by name in the daily *Shemoneh Esrei*, we can indeed suggest several instances in which Noach and/or the *Mabul* are either directly connected to or alluded to in this central *tefillah*.

Shemoneh Esrei Is a Wave

Every *Shemoneh Esrei* begins with our taking three steps backward and then three steps forward. *Shemoneh Esrei* concludes that way as well. Backward and forward, backward and forward – an ebb and flow, much like a wave. In addition, while *Shemoneh Esrei* requires us to stand in place with feet locked together, much of our time saying this prayer includes movement: the backward and forward start and finish, our *shuckling* and swaying back and forth and/or side to side, and our multiple bowings to Hashem during *Shemoneh Esrei*. Considered this way, *Shemoneh Esrei* can be thought of as us flowing very much like a wave. How much more so when we are together with ten, fifty, a hundred, a thousand, eighty thousand strong at a Siyum HaShas! We literally look like a massive ocean comprised of individual waves merging into one, and we sense this, too. *Shemoneh Esrei* itself can be a Noach moment.

---

[47] Translated from the ArtScroll Rosh Hashanah Machzor.

CHAPTER 2: NOACH & TEHILLIM 29

The *Brachah* of *Gevuros* Is the Perfect Storm

Half the year, starting on *Shemini Atzeres* – which is never more than two weeks away from *Parshas Noach* and the month of Marcheshvan in which the *Mabul* began – we add to the second blessing of *Shemoneh Esrei*, known as the *brachah* of *Gevuros*, the praise "מַשִּׁיב הָרוּחַ וּמוֹרִיד הַגֶּשֶׁם – [Hashem] Who makes the wind blow, and brings down the rain." These daily references to wind and rain, starting around the time of *Parshas Noach* and the month of the *Mabul* – and specifically in the context of the blessing of *Gevuros* which emphasizes Hashem's power and strength, including the phrase "מֶלֶךְ מֵמִית וּמְחַיֶּה – King who causes death and restores life," – all combine to make the "perfect storm," as the expression goes. This, too, can be a Noach moment.

The First Generations and Their Lack of *Daas* in *Atah Chonein*

In the fourth blessing called *Atah Chonein*, we daven to Hashem for wisdom, insight, and discernment, beginning the *brachah* with the introductory words: "אַתָּה חוֹנֵן לְאָדָם דַּעַת וּמְלַמֵּד לֶאֱנוֹשׁ בִּינָה." As noted earlier, this phraseology need not be simply understood as a general introduction to man being granted wisdom from God, rather on a deeper level the "אָדָם" mentioned here is a reference to the *original* אָדָם – Adam HaRishon.[48] Furthermore, the word "אֱנוֹשׁ" mentioned here can mean more than "mankind:" this term can be a reference to the "דוֹר אֱנוֹשׁ," the generation of evil-doers who preceded the Generation of the Flood, one-third of whom were killed by Hashem in a lesser-known flood of relatively minor magnitude as a punishment and warning to all who remained.[49] Unfortunately, it was a warning that went unheeded by the survivors, to

---

[48] See Chapter 1, *Parshas Bereishis* & *Tehillim* 139.
[49] *Bereishis Rabbah* 23:11.

the point that *Parshas Noach's* worldwide destructive *Mabul* was the world's only hope for long-term success.

Thus, the blessing of *Atah Chonein,* in which we ask Hashem to grant us *daas,* contains references to Adam HaRishon who sinned through the *Eitz HaDaas* – and contains references to the *Dor Enosh* who did not use their *daas* to take *mussar* from that initial flood – and therefore certainly alludes to the Torah's next key generation of Noach as well. This generation used its *daas* for evil and ignored the warning signs even from Noach himself, whom they saw toiling for more than a century to construct the Ark in the hope that they would be influenced toward good and avoid the devastating Flood. This, too, can be a Noach moment.

Noach the *Tzaddik*'s Rise and Fall in *Al Ha'tzaddikim*

In the blessing known as *Al Ha'tzaddikim,* we pray for the righteous *tzaddikim*, devout *chassidim*, elders of Hashem's nation, the remnant of the Jewish scholars and scribes, and even for ourselves, ultimately asking "וְלֹא נֵבוֹשׁ כִּי בְךָ בָּטָחְנוּ" – may we not be embarrassed because in You [Hashem] we trust." Famously, the first *pasuk* of *Parshas Noach* refers to Noach as an "אִישׁ צַדִּיק – a righteous man."[50] Thus, the expression in *Shemoneh Esrei* of "עַל הַצַּדִּיקִים" may very well include Noach together with all *tzaddikim* of every generation. In addition, the inclusion of the request, "May we not be embarrassed," is unfortunately a sentiment relevant to Noach, who later in life became intoxicated and was violated by his own son Cham in a most shameful way.[51] Thus, the words of *Al Ha'tzaddikim* – which express that *tzaddikim* must be cherished, and that even a *tzaddik* can plummet so terribly *chas v'shalom* – are important lessons to us all. In this we find another Noach moment.

---

[50] *Bereishis* 6:9.
[51] *Bereishis* 9:21–22, and *Rashi* there.

V'LaMalshinim's Connection to *Tehillim* 29 and the Flood

Although *Shemoneh Esrei* literally means "eighteen," it is widely known that *Shemoneh Esrei* has evolved to comprise nineteen blessings from *Avos* through *Sim Shalom*. In response to the rampant threat of heretical Jews slandering religious Jews to the anti-Semitic Roman government following the destruction of the Second Beis HaMikdash, a nineteenth blessing called *V'LaMalshinim* was inserted into *Shemoneh Esrei*.[52] At first, this might seem to be contradictory to the Gemara mentioned earlier which explained that the eighteen blessings of *Shemoneh Esrei* were numbered as such to specifically correspond to the eighteen times that י-ה-ו-ה is stated in *Tehillim* 29. However, there appears to be a textual basis for a nineteenth blessing in *Tehillim* 29 as well. Indeed, the Gemara[53] teaches that the additional blessing of *V'LaMalshinim* is drawn from the fact that *Tehillim* 29 contains a nineteenth mention of the Name of God, albeit the different Name of "א-ל," found in the phrase "א-ל הַכָּבוֹד הִרְעִים."[54] א-ל is a Name of judgment rather than the merciful Name of י-ה-ו-ה. It is thus an appropriate Name for the blessing of *V'LaMalshinim*, a blessing borne of harsh circumstances and betrayal and one in which we ask Hashem to reveal His power by taking revenge on the enemies of the Jewish People, both enemies from without and from within. Furthermore, this nineteenth mention is specifically found in a *pasuk* that cries out "*Mabul*:" "קוֹל ה' עַל הַמָּיִם, אֵ-ל הַכָּבוֹד הִרְעִים; ה' עַל מַיִם רַבִּים" – The voice of Hashem is upon the waters, א-ל, the God of Glory thunders, Hashem is upon vast waters." Incredibly, we find yet another a Noach moment.

---

[52] *Brachos* 28b.
[53] *Brachos* 28b.
[54] *Tehillim* 29:3.

Marcheshvan, *Mabul*, and Moving Mouths

Chazal tell us that the *Mabul* began in the month of Cheshvan, which is also more accurately known as מַרְחֶשְׁוָן – Marcheshvan,[55] or "bitter Cheshvan." In addition to the month's association with the Flood, a well-known reason that this month received the moniker of "bitter" is because Marcheshvan is devoid of Jewish holidays.

However, Rav Shimshon Pincus[56] so beautifully explains that Marcheshvan comes from the expression found in the Gemara: "מְרַחֲשִׁין שִׂפְוָותַיְיהוּ – [their] lips were moving" to connote whispering words of Torah.[57] As such, Marcheshvan is not a name of bitterness but rather a name that expresses the intrinsic status of every Jew during this month, for it is a month that follows the month of Tishrei. At that time, our lips and hearts were filled daily with extraordinary amounts of Torah and especially *tefillah*: prayers of *Selichos*, Rosh Hashanah, Yom Kippur, Sukkos, Hoshana Rabbah, Shemini Atzeres, and Simchas Torah. The name Marcheshvan conveys that the inspiration of Tishrei continues throughout the following month, during which our lips remain constantly whispering, singing, and proclaiming words of Torah and *tefillah*. Of course, paramount among all *tefillos* is our precious *Shemoneh Esrei*, which is so deeply connected to *Tehillim* 29 and to Noach. This is a Noach moment.

Noach and Family Inspire *Shomeia Tefillah*

The powerful *brachah* of *Shema Koleinu* concludes: "בָּרוּךְ אַתָּה ה' שׁוֹמֵעַ תְּפִלָּה – Blessed are You Hashem, Who hears prayer." Remarkably, there is a Midrash[58] that cites the *pasuk*: "וַיִּזְכֹּר אֱ-לֹהִים אֶת נֹחַ – And Hashem

---

[55] *Rashi, Bereishis* 7:11, from *Rosh Hashanah* 11b; see also e.g., *Taanis* 10a.
[56] *Sichos Rav Shimshon Pincus – Sukkos*, p. 195.
[57] *Chagigah* 3a.
[58] See *Otzar Midrashim – Aggadas Tefillas Shemoneh Esrei*.

remembered Noach,"[59] explaining that Hashem listened to the prayers of Noach and the rest of his family living in the Ark. Their prayers, explains the Midrash, were literally the inspiration and foundation for the prayer and reality of "שׁוֹמֵעַ תְּפִלָּה!" This, too, is a Noach moment.

The Sweet Smell of Sacred Sacrifices

On holidays during which the Kohanim ascend to *duchan* and publicly recite *Bircas Kohanim*, the *brachah* of *Retzei* is augmented to include the *tefillah* called *V'seiareiv*, in which we beseech Hashem that our *tefillos* be as pleasing to Him as *korbanos*. Among other things, this change alters the traditional concluding blessing of "בָּרוּךְ אַתָּה ה' הַמַּחֲזִיר שְׁכִינָתוֹ לְצִיּוֹן – Blessed are You Hashem, Who returns His Divine Presence to Zion" to "בָּרוּךְ אַתָּה ה' שֶׁאוֹתְךָ לְבַדְּךָ בְּיִרְאָה נַעֲבוֹד – Blessed are you Hashem, for You alone with awe do we serve." In this context, "serve" refers to both *tefillah* and *korbanos*. In expounding the phrase: "וַיֵּשֶׁב ה' מֶלֶךְ לְעוֹלָם – Hashem sits as King forever,"[60] the Midrash[61] teaches that in response to Noach's post-*Mabul korbanos*, Hashem's "mind sat at ease" by the *reiach ha'nichoach*, sweet smell, of Noach's sacrifices.[62] As a result, Hashem had mercy on the world, and, says the Midrash, in that moment the phrase "שֶׁאוֹתְךָ לְבַדְּךָ בְּיִרְאָה נַעֲבוֹד" was born. Yet another Noach moment.

Their *Chammas* Was an Insult to *Shemoneh Esrei*

This last explanation was devised by my beloved daughter Shifra as we sat together learning and discussing *Tehillim* 29 on Shabbos *Parshas Noach* in the year 2019.

---

[59] *Bereishis* 8:1.
[60] *Tehillim* 29:10.
[61] *Otzar Midrashim – Aggadas Tefillas Shemoneh Esrei*.
[62] *Bereishis* 8:21.

The Torah in *Parshas Noach* tells us this terrible fact: "מָלְאָה הָאָרֶץ חָמָס – the earth was filled with *chammas*."[63] *Rashi* explains that the death sentence of the Generation of the Flood was sealed only on account of *chammas*, the sin of robbery.[64] How interesting that the evil characteristic of robbery is a characteristic in utter contradiction to everything that *Shemoneh Esrei* represents!

The majority of *Shemoneh Esrei* contains *bakashos*, requests, made to our God Who is the one and only true Being capable of fulfilling our needs and desires. Our *bakashos* indicate our faith and recognition that Hashem, and only Hashem, is our true source of success.

In contrast, *chammas*, robbery, is in direct conflict with such faith and recognition. Since Hashem is our sole source of blessing, there certainly should be no need to take advantage of others by stealing, and, in fact, doing so is not only an isolated *aveirah*, but also is a blatant contradiction to our turning to Hashem in prayer as the source of fulfillment of our *bakashos*.

In addition, building on the inspiration of Shifra's insight, we can add that *chammas* is not only a violation of mitzvos *bein adam l'Makom*, between man and God, but is, of course, also a violation of mitzvos *bein adam l'chaveiro*, between man and his fellow man. Indeed, the Generation of the Flood was completely wiped out while other evil generations were permitted to live because the *Dor Hamabul* was uniquely wicked in that they lacked any semblance of unity among mankind.[65] This lack of unity is also in direct contrast to the words of *Shemoneh Esrei* which, while a private prayer, we say from the start through *Sim Shalom* entirely in plural and on behalf of *all* Jews, not just the individual.

Thus, the *chammas* of the generation of the Flood was the antithesis of everything that *Shemoneh Esrei* stands for. That generation's very

---

[63] *Bereishis* 6:13.
[64] *Rashi, Bereishis* 6:13, from *Sanhedrin* 108a.
[65] *Rashi, Bereishis* 11:9.

existence was an affront to the beauty of *Shemoneh Esrei*, and they needed to be eradicated.

Moreover, when *we* daven *Shemoneh Esrei* and thereby show our faith in Hashem and our care for our fellow Jew, we further distance ourselves from the depraved sins of the *Dor Hamabul*.

Considering the above, we can now be *melamed zechus* – find meritorious justification – for Noach's decision to refrain from davening to save his generation. For how could he daven to save mankind when its very nature had devolved into the opposition of everything that davening and *Shemoneh Esrei* embody?

This is the final Noach moment.

HASHEM LA'MABUL YASHAV: HASHEM AT THE FLOOD SAT ENTHRONED

A cornerstone of the connection between *Parshas Noach* and *Tehillim* 29 is *pasuk* 10 of *kapitel* 29: "י-ה-ו-ה לַמַּבּוּל יָשָׁב; וַיֵּשֶׁב י-ה-ו-ה מֶלֶךְ לְעוֹלָם – Hashem at the Flood sat enthroned; Hashem sits enthroned as King forever."

The following approach will focus on a single aspect of this *pasuk* that is not widely known, and that will *b'ezras Hashem* open for us, our loved ones, and all Klal Yisrael the gates of *refuah* – healing, and the gates of *yedidus* – friendship and belovedness.

The Hidden Name of Hashem and Its Power of Healing

There is a beautiful *sefer* on *Tehillim* titled *Tefillas Mordechai – Derushim Lechol Cheftzeihem*, written by Rabbi Mordechai Wulliger of Yeshivas Torah Vodaath approximately fifty years ago.

PARSHAH & TEHILLIM HAND IN HAND

On *pesukim* 10 and 11 of *Tehillim* 29: יְ-ה-ו-ה לַמַּבּוּל יָשָׁב; וַיֵּשֶׁב יְ-ה-ו-ה מֶלֶךְ לְעוֹלָם. יְ-ה-ו-ה עֹז לְעַמּוֹ יִתֵּן; יְ-ה-ו-ה יְבָרֵךְ אֶת עַמּוֹ בַשָּׁלוֹם, Rabbi Wulliger writes as follows (paraphrased from Hebrew):

> *The seforim ha'kedoshim* explain that a Name of Hashem, the Name יל״י, is one of the seventy-two Holy Names of Hashem and emanates from the *roshei teivos* of the phrase "לְמַעַן יֵחָלְצוּן יְדִידֶיךָ" – So that Your beloved ones may be released."[66] This Name is *mesugal*[67] for *refuah* because the word יֵחָלְצוּן refers to healing as seen in the expression of the Gemara: "חֲלָצַתּוּ חַמָּה" – the fever released him."[68]

Rabbi Wulliger then retells an impactful story from his father, who once traveled in his youth (in the mid-1800s) with his *rebbe* the Baal Yitav Lev of Sighet to be *mevaker cholim* the Maharam Schick, who was ill and close to the time of his passing. When it was time to take leave, as a parting blessing the Yitav Lev extended his hand and grasped the hand of the Maharam Schick and said to him: "In the Gemara in *Brachos* there is an account that Rabbi Yochanan, as part of his visit to the sick, told the ill person to give him his hand, יְהַב לֵיהּ יְדֵיהּ, and on contact, the sick person was healed."[69] The Yitav Lev, still holding the hand of the ailing Maharam Schick, explained that this specific expression and the actions of Rabbi Yochanan aroused the Holy Name of יל״י and its healing power, thus restoring the health of the sick person. This, too, was the parting blessing of the Yitav Lev to the Maharam Schick. In this manner, Rabbi Mordechai Wulliger concludes the story in the name of his father.

Rabbi Wulliger continues, יְ-ה-ו-ה לַמַּבּוּל יָשָׁב also contains the *roshei teivos* of the Holy Name יל״י. And the remainder of the *pasuk*, וַיֵּשֶׁב יְ-ה-ו-ה מֶלֶךְ לְעוֹלָם, reveals to us that the world after the *Mabul* was indeed healed

---

[66] *Tehillim* 60:7. See also *tefillas Elokai Netzor* in *Shemoneh Esrei*.
[67] *Mesugal* here connotes "capable" and "opportune."
[68] *Brachos* 34b.
[69] *Brachos* 5b.

in a spiritual sense as Hashem once again sat on His throne as the world's undisputed King.

Let us pause to ponder and elaborate on Rav Wulliger's explanation. *Tehillim* 29:10 secretly contains the Divine Name of י"לי, which effectuates *healing*, not wrath or vengeance, and which was on full display during the *Mabul*. While Hashem showed His supremacy during the *Mabul*, a curative, not destructive, power was released into the world through the Holy Name י"לי. At first this seems counterintuitive because the *Mabul* eradicated virtually all of mankind, not healed it. However, the *Mabul* was a form of "constructive destruction." It was an annihilation of the evildoers of the world for the sake of curing and rebuilding the world through the *tzaddik* Noach and his family. Through the devastation of the *Mabul*, Hashem healed and rehabilitated the spiritual status of the world for Noach and for all subsequent generations.

"*Hashem Oz*" in *Tehillim* 29 Corresponds to the Blessing of *Refaeinu*

Rabbi Wulliger continues and quotes the Gemara (discussed earlier in this chapter) that says that the eighteen mentions of י-ה-ו-ה in *Tehillim* 29 are the basis for the eighteen blessings of *Shemoneh Esrei*,[70] among which is the blessing of *Refaeinu* in which we request that Hashem heal us both physically and spiritually. He then connects the power of healing to the final *pasuk* of *Tehillim* 29, that of: "י-ה-ו-ה עֹז לְעַמּוֹ יִתֵּן; י-ה-ו-ה יְבָרֵךְ אֶת עַמּוֹ בַשָּׁלוֹם – Hashem will give strength to His nation; Hashem will bless His nation with peace."

Specifically, Rabbi Wulliger reveals that the *brachah* of *Refaeinu* corresponds to "י-ה-ו-ה עֹז לְעַמּוֹ יִתֵּן – Hashem will give strength to His nation." In this instance, the term עֹז refers to the Torah,[71] which heals and

---

[70] *Brachos* 28b.
[71] E.g., *Tehillim* 132:8: "אַתָּה וַאֲרוֹן עֻזֶּךָ – You and the Ark of Your strength."

revitalizes us. We see support for this in the Mishnah in *Pirkei Avos*:[72] "So great is Torah which confers life to its practitioners in both this world and in the World to Come, as it says,[73] 'כִּי חַיִּים הֵם לְמֹצְאֵיהֶם וּלְכָל בְּשָׂרוֹ מַרְפֵּא – For they [the teachings of the Torah] are life to those who find them, and to his entire flesh מַרְפֵּא, a healing.'" By means of the עֹז of Torah, Hashem grants עֹז: strength, health, healing, and life, to the learner and keeper of the Torah.

Every *Shemoneh Esrei* Concludes with Healing and Peace

Similarly, says Rabbi Wulliger, the closing statement of "י-ה-ו-ה יְבָרֵךְ אֶת עַמּוֹ בַשָּׁלוֹם – Hashem will bless His nation with peace" refers to the understanding of Chazal that "אִם אֵין שָׁלוֹם אֵין כְּלוּם – if there is no peace, then there is nothing," and "הַשָּׁלוֹם שָׁקוּל כְּנֶגֶד הַכֹּל – Peace is equal to everything."[74]

Rabbi Wulliger explains – and unfortunately, we know all too well – that so many sicknesses can develop simply from the *fear* of possible war or danger, as opposed to the actual war or danger itself. Even the *emotion* of fear alone physically impacts the person's health. This all begins with the *heart,* upon which the person relies first and foremost as Shlomo HaMelech teaches: "מִכָּל מִשְׁמָר נְצֹר לִבֶּךָ, כִּי מִמֶּנּוּ תּוֹצְאוֹת חַיִּים – More than you guard anything, safeguard your heart, for from it are the sources of life."[75] Therefore, *Tehillim* 29 concludes with a blessing for *shalom* because not only is *shalom* itself a *brachah*, *shalom* impacts all other facets of our lives, and in particular our health and wellbeing.

---

[72] *Pirkei Avos* 6:7.
[73] *Mishlei* 4:22.
[74] *Rashi, Vayikra* 26:6, from *Sifra, Bechukosai* 1.
[75] *Mishlei* 4:23.

CHAPTER 2: NOACH & TEHILLIM 29

For the same reason, *Shemoneh Esrei's* final *brachah*, *Sim Shalom*, ends with the blessing of *shalom* and has its own origins in the final words of *Tehillim* 29: "יְ-הֹ-וָ-ה יְבָרֵךְ אֶת עַמּוֹ בַשָּׁלוֹם."[76]

Healing and Peace Intertwined with *Yedidus*

To build further upon Rav Wulliger's *yesodos*, like Rabbi Yochanan and the Yitav Lev before us, we too correlate the *tefillah* of *Elokai Netzor* and its powerful expression of "לְמַעַן יֵחָלְצוּן יְדִידֶיךָ" – So that Your beloved ones may be released,"[77] as a call to unleash Hashem's Holy Name of Healing. Here, "ילי" clearly serves within the *Shemoneh Esrei* as a message of *yedidius*, friendship and belovedness, between us and Hashem. Furthermore, we then immediately daven for *shalom* and say: "עֹשֶׂה שָׁלוֹם בִּמְרוֹמָיו הוּא יַעֲשֶׂה שָׁלוֹם עָלֵינוּ וְעַל כָּל יִשְׂרָאֵל" – [Hashem] Who bestows peace in His heavens, may He make peace on us and on all the Jewish People," which reinforces that feeling of harmony, belovedness, and *yedidus* among all Jews.

It is surely no coincidence that just like the last two *pesukim* of *Tehillim* 29 – the *kapitel* that is the source for the structure and content of *Shemoneh Esrei* – conclude with words of *yedidus*, healing, and *shalom*, the same is true of *Shemoneh Esrei* itself: when we step backward and officially end every *Shemoneh Esrei*, we do so with prayers that revolve around the "ילי" hidden Holy Name of healing, intertwined with *yedidus* and the *shalom* that it brings.

---

[76] *Tehillim* 29:11. Indeed, most major *tefillos* conclude with the word שָׁלוֹם. For example, in addition to being the final word of *Shemoneh Esrei*, שָׁלוֹם is the final word of *Bircas Hamazon*, *Kaddish*, and *Bircas Kohanim*.

[77] Note that the word יֵחָלְצוּן has many different meanings including released, healed, strengthened, and armed, all of which are powerful *kavanos* for us to have at the end of *Elokai Netzor*.

PARSHAH & TEHILLIM HAND IN HAND

Finding the Hidden Name of Hashem in *Refaeinu*

Based on the above, one would expect to find the formula for healing, the Divine Name of י"ל, mentioned in the *brachah* of *Refaeinu* itself.[78] But is that Name found there at all?

The *Yehi Ratzon* prayer that can be added to the *brachah* of *Refaeinu* gives us the opportunity to personalize the *brachah* by inserting the names of specific individuals in need of physical or spiritual healing. Amazingly, the last few words of the *Yehi Ratzon* are "בְּתוֹךְ שְׁאָר חוֹלֵי יִשְׂרָאֵל," which does indeed contain the letters of י"ל without interruption.

Incredible as that may be, one might still wonder about the main body of the *Refaeinu brachah*: why is there no mention of י"ל there? Upon closer examination of the *brachah* we find that *Refaeinu* concludes with "Blessed are You Hashem, רוֹפֵא חוֹלֵי עַמּוֹ יִשְׂרָאֵל, Who heals the sick of His people Israel." There too, the *tefillah* contains the same hidden healing formula in the words: "חוֹלֵי יִשְׂרָאֵל" – "י"ל".

This would be spectacular, except that the formula is interrupted by another word: "עַמּוֹ." At first blush, this is disappointing and difficult to understand. Why would the authors of *Shemoneh Esrei*, the famed and holy *Anshei Knesses Hagedolah* (the Men of the Great Assembly) among whom were actual Prophets, interrupt the Name of healing, and especially do so with a seemingly superfluous word like עַמּוֹ?

In light of Rabbi Wulliger's insights above, we can understand how this all fits together beautifully. *Pasuk* 10 of *Tehillim* 29 contains the phrase י-ה-ו-ה לַמַּבּוּל יָשָׁב, with the formula of the hidden Name of Hashem י"ל that triggers the power of healing. The very next *pasuk* concludes the *kapitel* with another healing-like *pasuk* as Rabbi Wulliger explained, the *pasuk* of: "י-ה-ו-ה עֹז לְעַמּוֹ יִתֵּן; י-ה-ו-ה יְבָרֵךְ אֶת עַמּוֹ בַשָּׁלוֹם." There, remarkably, the word "עַמּוֹ" appears not once but twice!

---

[78] For a possible reference to the Divine Name of י"ל mentioned in *Parashas Noach*, see *Bereishis* 7:4.

CHAPTER 2: NOACH & TEHILLIM 29

This emphasis on עַמּוֹ specifically in the context of healing reveals to us that the word עַמּוֹ in *Refaeinu* is of course not an unnecessary or unfortunate interruption, but rather is part and parcel of, and provides an added dimension to, the healing formula of י"לי itself.

After all, we and the ill among us are all "עַמּוֹ;" we are all "הָעָם שֶׁלּוֹ," Hashem's nation. Based on this holy designation alone, we are deserving of עֹז and health, and שָׁלוֹם and peace, from our wonderful and merciful Hashem Who "healed" the *Dor Hamabul* with the Divine Name of י"לי, and Who can and will cure those of our nation, *His* nation, who are in need.

CHAPTER 3

PARSHAS LECH LECHA & TEHILLIM 110

פָּרָשַׁת לֶךְ לְךָ / תְּהִלִּים קי

TEHILLIM 110 — תְּהִלִּים קי

1	To Dovid, a psalm. The word of Hashem to my master: Wait at My right, until I make your enemies a footstool for your feet.
2	The rod of your strength will be sent by Hashem from *Tzion*; rule in the midst of your enemies!
3	Your people volunteer on the day of your military campaign; because of your splendorous holiness from conception, from the dawn, you retain the dew-like freshness of your youth.
4	Sworn has Hashem and He will not reconsider: You shall be a Kohen forever, because you are *malki-tzedek* (a king of righteousness).

א לְדָוִד מִזְמוֹר;
נְאֻם ה' לַאדֹנִי:
שֵׁב לִימִינִי, עַד אָשִׁית
אֹיְבֶיךָ הֲדֹם לְרַגְלֶיךָ.

ב מַטֵּה עֻזְּךָ יִשְׁלַח ה' מִצִּיּוֹן;
רְדֵה בְּקֶרֶב אֹיְבֶיךָ.

ג עַמְּךָ נְדָבֹת בְּיוֹם חֵילֶךָ;
בְּהַדְרֵי קֹדֶשׁ
מֵרֶחֶם מִשְׁחָר,
לְךָ טַל יַלְדֻתֶיךָ.

ד נִשְׁבַּע ה' וְלֹא יִנָּחֵם,
אַתָּה כֹהֵן לְעוֹלָם;
עַל דִּבְרָתִי מַלְכִּי-צֶדֶק.

CHAPTER 3: LECH LECHA & TEHILLIM 110

5 The Lord is at your right; He crushes on the day of His anger, kings.	ה אֲדֹנָ-י עַל יְמִינְךָ; מָחַץ בְּיוֹם אַפּוֹ מְלָכִים.
6 He will judge the nations that are filled with corpses; He will crush the leader of the mighty land.	ו יָדִין בַּגּוֹיִם, מָלֵא גְוִיּוֹת; מָחַץ רֹאשׁ עַל אֶרֶץ רַבָּה.
7 From a river [of enemy blood] along the way he shall drink; therefore, may he [proudly] lift his head.	ז מִנַּחַל בַּדֶּרֶךְ יִשְׁתֶּה; עַל כֵּן יָרִים רֹאשׁ.

PREFACE: AVRAHAM, ARE WE THE CHILDREN THAT YOU DREAMED OF?

Avraham, are we the children that you dreamed of?
Are we that shining star you saw at night?
You know it's true, we still call you avinu.
Our father, our pride, we've got your soul inside; take us home.

From the song "Avraham," by Eighth Day.

Ever since I first heard this song, I've been haunted by its lyrics and melody, especially the opening words[1] of the chorus: "Avraham, are

---

[1] Truthfully, I am even more intrigued about the phrase "Are we that shining star you saw at night?" which also applies to *Parshas Lech Lecha* (see *Bereishis* 15:5 and *Rashi* there). That Avraham gazed down (not up) at the same stars that we see even today, and that one of those stars corresponds to me, and one to you, and another one to her… and that Avraham saw "our" star and cherished

we the children that you dreamed of?" It has forced me to ask myself some serious questions:

Am I a good child, a loyal child to Avraham? Would he recognize me? Would he claim me as his own? Would he be proud of me? Would he love me? Would he even *like* me?

What does he expect of me? What would give him "*Yiddishe nachas?*" For me to be perfect, of course. Or at least to be as perfect as possible, right? Or maybe just as perfect a "me" as I can be.

But that's such a high standard, perhaps too high. Yet don't I usually expect that high a bar to be consistently reached by my own children? Aren't I sometimes disappointed?

What about that child who, on occasion, displays a certain... guile, or laziness, or even insensitivity? Why do I get so upset at him for not being the perfect "him," and yet subconsciously and on occasion overtly, favor him or penalize him? Perhaps because I know that his guile, laziness, and insensitivity... came from me.

INTRODUCTION: WHERE IS THE AVRAHAM OF *CHESSED*?

The above is probably not what the reader expects (or wants) from a preface to *Parshas Lech Lecha*, the first of three *parshiyos* that revolve around Avraham Avinu. Avraham is widely known as the very embodiment of *chessed*, as Michah HaNavi states: "תִּתֵּן אֱמֶת לְיַעֲקֹב, חֶסֶד

---

it, and through it cherished *us*, has captivated me. But this analysis is beyond our scope here. So, for the moment, please contemplate this on your own, just as I hope to continue to do as I gaze at the stars so far away and at the Torah's words so near.

לְאַבְרָהָם – Grant truth to Yaakov, kindness to Avraham."[2] Indeed, Avraham is called the *Amud HaChessed*, Pillar of Kindness.[3]

Yet, Avraham may not have been born with a propensity toward kindness.[4] After all, Avraham was born into a barbaric world where murder, idolatry, and adultery were rampant, and in which the absence of fear of God did nothing to engender care and compassion among mankind.

As Rav Shimshon Pincus teaches, Avraham's drive for *chessed* was an *acquired* trait.[5] Avraham recognized at either the age of three, forty, forty-eight, or fifty (there are varying opinions)[6] that Hashem was the Creator and the active and kind caretaker of the world, stirring him to see his own actions and responsibilities, as well as those of the entire world around him, through the prism of *Hashem's chessed*. Henceforth, everywhere he looked he saw the *middas ha'chessed* of Hashem, God's Divine attribute of kindness. From sky to ground, mountain to sea, angel to man, in Avraham's heart it was all declaring: "*Chasdei Hashem!*" As such, Avraham discovered the mitzvah referred to as "וְהָלַכְתָּ בִּדְרָכָיו – And you shall walk in His ways"[7] expounded upon by *Rashi* to mean: "הוא רחום וְאַתָּה תְּהֵא רחום, הוא גּוֹמֵל חֲסָדִים וְאַתָּה גּוֹמֵל חֲסָדִים – He is merciful, and you shall be merciful; He bestows lovingkindness, and you should bestow lovingkindness."[8] This principle both inspired and *required* Avraham to become Hashem's emissary of His *chessed* to the world. As a result of this realization, says Rav Pincus, Avraham *developed* into the paradigm of human *chessed* in this world; he was *not* *created* that way.

---

[2] *Michah* 7:20.
[3] Based on *Pirkei Avos* 1:2.
[4] E.g., *Ohr HaTzafun* by Rav Nosson Tzvi Finkel, the Alter of Slabodka, *chelek beis*, p. 199.
[5] See *Nefesh Shimshon: Siddur HaTefillah*, pp. 395–396.
[6] E.g., *Rambam, Hilchos Avodah Zarah* 1:3.
[7] *Devarim* 28:9.
[8] *Rashi, Devarim* 11:22, from *Sifrei, Devarim* 49.

The *meforshim* on *Tehillim* 110, including *Rashi* and the *Metzudas Dovid*, explain that *Tehillim* 110 *explicitly* refers to Avraham Avinu and his experiences throughout *Parshas Lech Lecha*. However, as we will explore in this chapter, *Parshas Lech Lecha* and *Tehillim* 110 actually seem to be focused on the "pre-*chessed*" version of Avraham Avinu. Indeed, when we focus on *Tehillim* 110 and use it to reframe our learning of *Parshas Lech Lecha*, we see Avraham Avinu in an atypical light. Avraham will navigate a dark and dangerous world filled with cruelty and lawlessness, a world that even pushes him into combat and bloodshed, all as forcefully reflected in the words and theme of *Tehillim* 110.

Tehillim 110 is not a *kapitel* of *chessed*. It is a battle cry. *Tehillim* 110 is a *kapitel* of war.

THE MANY CONNECTIONS BETWEEN PARSHAS LECH LECHA & TEHILLIM 110

While *Tehillim* 110 is certainly applicable to Dovid HaMelech as the focal point, *Rashi's* first approach is different. *Rashi* explains that the opening phrase "נְאֻם ה׳ לַאדֹנִי" in *pasuk* 1 and the entire *kapitel* refer to Avraham Avinu. Therefore, *Rashi* begins his explanation of *Tehillim* 110 as follows: "רַבּוֹתֵינוּ דְּרָשׁוּהוּ בְּאַבְרָהָם אָבִינוּ, וַאֲנִי אֲפָרְשֶׁנּוּ כְּדִבְרֵיהֶם" – Our Rabbis interpreted it as referring to Avraham Avinu, and I shall explain according to their words."[9]

---

[9] *Rashi, Tehillim* 110:1. Thereafter, *Rashi* brings a second, completely different avenue of interpretation, which revolves around Dovid HaMelech.

Pasuk 1:
לְדָוִד מִזְמוֹר; נְאֻם ה' לַאדֹנִי:
שֵׁב לִימִינִי, עַד אָשִׁית אֹיְבֶיךָ הֲדֹם לְרַגְלֶיךָ

To Dovid, a psalm. The word of Hashem to my master: Wait at My right, until I make your enemies a footstool for your feet.

Avraham Is the Focal Point of *Tehillim* 110

Rashi says that "לַאדֹנִי" refers to Avraham, upon whom the world conferred such a title as seen later in *Parshas Chayei Sarah* when the community of Bnei Cheis addressed Avraham with the respectful expression: "שְׁמָעֵנוּ אֲדֹנִי – hear us, our master."[10]

The continuation of the *pasuk*, according to *Rashi*, directly connects to *Parshas Lech Lecha* as the phrase "עַד אָשִׁית אֹיְבֶיךָ – until I make your enemies" refers to Amraphel and his allies. Specifically, it is a reference to the infamous coalition of the Four Kings led by Kedarlaomer and Amraphel, who defeated the more numerous Five Kings and captured Avraham's relative Lot. It was against them that Avraham would wage war, and it was they whom Avraham defeated as part of his rescue effort to save Lot, to subdue the greater evil, and bring renown to Hashem.[11]

In addition, continues *Rashi*, Amraphel was Avraham's former nemesis, Nimrod, whose nickname אַמְרָפֶל was derived from "אָמַר פֹּל – said fall." This was in reference to Nimrod's decree years earlier that Avraham should fall into a flaming furnace, which was followed by an actual attempt to kill Avraham by throwing him into the fiery furnace known as the *kivshan ha'aish* at Ur Kasdim.[12]

---

[10] *Bereishis* 23:6.
[11] *Bereishis* 14:1–16.
[12] *Rashi, Bereishis* 14:1, from *Eruvin* 53a; *Rashi, Bereishis* 11:28, from *Bereishis Rabbah* 38:13.

Eliezer: *Eved* and Author

The *Metzudas Dovid*[13] attributes the original authorship of *Tehillim* 110 to Eliezer, the servant of Avraham. Eliezer had been approached by idol worshippers who had witnessed Avraham's remarkable victory against the Four Kings and were astonished. They asked Eliezer how Avraham, with such small numbers (either 318 newly religious initiates[14] or with just Eliezer himself[15]) was able to achieve victory. Eliezer responded by composing and declaring *Tehillim* 110, ascribing Avraham's triumph not to his bravery, skilled military maneuvers, nor even to luck, but rather to Avraham's relationship with Hashem.

Avraham Coronated as King and Prince of God

On the phrase, "שֵׁב לִימִינִי, עַד אָשִׁית אֹיְבֶיךָ הֲדֹם לְרַגְלֶיךָ – Wait at My right, until I make your enemies a footstool for your feet," the Midrash says that this refers specifically to the post-war episode at Emek Shaveh, the Valley of Equals, also known as Emek HaMelech, Valley of the King. There, all the surviving kings and nations of the world became "equal" and like-minded by declaring Avraham their sovereign, thereby humbling themselves and falling before Avraham as a proverbial "footstool for his feet."[16] In addition, according to *Rashi*, it was there that Avraham also received the title of *Nesei Elokim*, Prince of God, from the leaders of the other nations.[17] By referring to *Elokim*, these leaders demonstrated that they attributed Avraham's successes to his closeness with God. This recognition was a tremendous *Kiddush HaShem*.

---

[13] *Metzudas Dovid, Tehillim* 110:1.
[14] *Bereishis* 14:14.
[15] *Rashi, Bereishis* 14:14.
[16] *Midrash Tanchuma, Lech Lecha* 13.
[17] *Rashi, Bereishis* 14:17.

Pasuk 2:
מַטֵּה עֻזְּךָ יִשְׁלַח ה' מִצִּיּוֹן;
רְדֵה בְּקֶרֶב אֹיְבֶיךָ
The rod of your strength will be sent by Hashem from Tzion; rule in the midst of your enemies!

Malki-Tzedek and His Allegiance to Avraham

The phrase "מַטֵּה עֻזְּךָ יִשְׁלַח ה' מִצִּיּוֹן" is explained by *Rashi*[18] as referring to the post-war episode in *Parshas Lech Lecha*[19] in which Hashem sent Malki-Tzedek, otherwise known as Noach's son Shem,[20] to feed Avraham's exhausted troops bread and wine.

While *Rashi* on *Tehillim* 110 does not elaborate on the source of this connection, it seems that the word "מַטֵּה" is the reference to "bread" as in the expression: "מַטֵּה לֶחֶם – staff of bread."[21] The word "צִיּוֹן," meaning the holy city of Yerushalayim then known as Shalem, refers to Malki-Tzedek, who was also known as "*Melech Shalem* – King of Shalem."[22]

It must be noted that it was Malki-Tzedek who went to Avraham because it was Malki-Tzedek whose grandchildren were killed by Avraham in battle. Malki-Tzedek personally came and fed Avraham to make it clear that he felt no animosity toward Avraham, but rather felt only admiration, loyalty, and a sincere desire to make peace.[23]

Avraham Becomes Kohen Forever

Interestingly, the Gemara[24] *directly* connects the *pesukim* in *Parshas Lech Lecha* describing Malki-Tzedek's actions of peace and blessing

---

[18] *Rashi, Tehillim* 110:2.
[19] *Bereishis* 14:18.
[20] *Rashi, Bereishis* 14:18, from *Nedarim* 32b.
[21] *Vayikra* 26:26.
[22] *Targum Onkelos, Bereishis* 14:18.
[23] *Rashi, Bereishis* 15:1.
[24] *Nedarim* 32b.

toward Avraham[25] with the *pesukim* in *Tehillim* 110:1 and 4. In so doing, the Gemara reveals that Hashem originally intended the *Kehunah*, Jewish Priesthood, to come from Shem/Malki-Tzedek. However, in the above-referenced *pesukim* in *Lech Lecha*, Malki-Tzedek erroneously praised Avraham prior to praising Hashem, and as a result of that indiscretion Hashem stripped him of the *Kehunah* and instead bestowed it upon the future family of *Avraham* of whom it is written: "אַתָּה כֹהֵן לְעוֹלָם – you shall be a Kohen forever."[26]

Pasuk 1:
שֵׁב לִימִינִי
Wait at My right.

Pasuk 5:
אֲדֹנָ-י עַל יְמִינְךָ
The Lord is at your right.

The Right Hand of Hashem

The dual references to the protective "right" of Hashem in *pasuk* 1: "שֵׁב לִימִינִי – Wait at My right," and in *pasuk* 5: "אֲדֹנָ-י עַל יְמִינְךָ – The Lord is at your right," emphasize the right hand and right side. These references symbolize the loving Divine attributes of *rachamim* and *chessed*, of which Avraham was to become the embodiment.

In addition, these references parallel two *pesukim* from the *Haftarah* of *Parshas Lech Lecha*, a prophecy given through Yeshayahu HaNavi and which contains Hashem's stirring declaration: "אַבְרָהָם אֹהֲבִי – Avraham, who loved Me."[27] There too, Yeshayahu emphasized the "right" in reference to Hashem and His relationship with Avraham: "אַל תִּירָא כִּי עִמְּךָ

---

[25] *Bereishis* 14:18–19.
[26] *Tehillim* 110:4.
[27] *Yeshayahu* 41:8.

אָנִי, אַל תִּשְׁתָּע כִּי אֲנִי אֱלֹהֶיךָ; אִמַּצְתִּיךָ אַף עֲזַרְתִּיךָ, אַף תְּמַכְתִּיךָ בִּימִין צִדְקִי – "Fear not, for I am with you, do not stray for I am your God; I have strengthened you, even helped you, even supported you with My righteous right hand,"[28] and "כִּי אֲנִי ה' אֱ-לֹהֶיךָ מַחֲזִיק יְמִינֶךָ; הָאֹמֵר לְךָ אַל תִּירָא, אֲנִי עֲזַרְתִּיךָ" – For I am Hashem your God, Who grasps your right hand, Who says to you: Fear not, for I help you."[29]

Furthermore, each of the above statements by Yeshayahu contains a reference to protection from fear in the form of "אַל תִּירָא – fear not," which further connects to Hashem's encouragement of Avraham in *Parshas Lech Lecha*: "אַל תִּירָא אַבְרָם, אָנֹכִי מָגֵן לָךְ; שְׂכָרְךָ הַרְבֵּה מְאֹד" – Fear not, Avram, I am a shield for you; your reward is very great."[30]

Pasuk 3:
עַמְּךָ נְדָבֹת בְּיוֹם חֵילֶךָ
Your people volunteer on the day of your military campaign.

Volunteers to Fight At His Side

According to *Rashi*, this phrase refers to the fact that when Avraham was trying to amass an army to fight the Four Kings, it was specifically Avraham's "עַמְּךָ – his people," who were אֹהֲבֶיךָ, those who loved him, who volunteered to fight at his side.[31]

These people were also known as Avraham's חֲנִיכָיו, his initiates, whom he introduced to Hashem's mitzvos.[32] The Torah also refers to these people as יְלִידֵי בֵיתוֹ, children born into his home, for they converted to the service of Hashem and were thus considered to be like newborns.[33] Finally, by

---

[28] *Yeshayahu* 41:10.
[29] *Yeshayahu* 41:13.
[30] *Bereishis* 15:1.
[31] *Rashi, Tehillim* 110:3.
[32] *Bereishis* 14:14, and *Rashi* there.
[33] *Bereishis* 14:14, and *Rashi* there.

virtue of the Torah that Avraham taught them, he was not only their teacher but was even tantamount to their father: Avraham bestowed both worldly life and helped to ensure their afterlife as a loving father should.[34] In this light, these people truly epitomized the concept of "עַמְּךָ," Avraham's people, in both body and soul.

Also volunteering in Avraham's army were Aner, Eshkol, and Mamre, Avraham's friends, confidants, and advisers.[35] Essentially, all those who knew Avraham loved him, and they proved that love with "נְדָבֹת," by volunteering and dedicating[36] themselves to Avraham's cause – and even rushing to fight at his side despite the imminent dangers.

Pasuk 3:
בְּהַדְרֵי קֹדֶשׁ מֵרֶחֶם
Because of your splendorous holiness from conception.

Holy from Birth

Rashi explains that all the loyalty Avraham received from others and all his successes were attributable to the grandeur of the holiness of his birth from his mother's womb.[37] However, such an explanation is difficult to understand because Avraham was born into a family of idolaters who were not God-fearing at all. Therefore, the exalted birth referred to here seems not to be a literal description; rather, it refers to Avraham's independent recognition of his Creator at the early age of three, an age so young that it is essentially comparable to achieving holiness immediately from birth.

It also bears mention that in *Parshas Lech Lecha*, Hashem promised Avraham that he would eventually have a son from Sarah Imeinu,

---

[34] Based upon *Kiddushin* 30b.
[35] *Bereishis* 14:24, and *Rashi* to *Bereishis* 14:13.
[36] E.g., *Shemos* 25:2, and *Rashi* there.
[37] *Rashi*, *Tehillim* 110:3.

Yitzchak, whom Chazal explain *was* literally "sanctified from the womb." Indeed, Hashem states in the Torah: "וְאֶת בְּרִיתִי אָקִים אֶת יִצְחָק – And I will establish My covenant with Yitzchak,"[38] upon which the *Avudraham*[39] explains that the word אָקִים contains the *roshei teivos* of the phrase "אֲשֶׁר קִדַּשׁ יְדִיד מִבֶּטֶן – Who sanctified the beloved from the womb." We cite this reference to Yitzchak Avinu even today as part of every *bris milah* service,[40] for Yitzchak was literally already sanctified and holy unto Hashem from the time he was in his mother's womb, and we yearn for all newborns to reflect such *kedushah* as well.

Pasuk 3:
מִשְׁחָר, לְךָ טַל יַלְדֻתֶיךָ
From the dawn, you retain the dewlike freshness of your youth.

Avraham's Pleasant and Rebellious Youth

Rashi explains that Avraham's youth was as pleasant and delicate as the morning dew.[41] However, this demands explanation because Avraham's youth was marked by a family environment steeped in idol worship. Furthermore, it is widely known that Avraham's efforts to overcome his environment entailed the destruction of his father's precious idols as part of a rebellion against his family, his neighborhood, their gods, and their entire misguided world. We will examine this more closely later in this chapter, but for now we can simply understand the meaning behind *Rashi's* statement as follows: rebelliousness, when that rebellion is directed against *evil*, is a rebellion for the sake of goodness and

---

[38] *Bereishis* 17:21.
[39] *Avudraham, Hilchos Brachos, shaar* 9.
[40] *Tosefta, Brachos* 6.
[41] *Rashi, Tehillim* 110:3.

righteousness and is therefore as pleasant and delicate to Hashem as the pure and revitalizing dew of the dawn.

Pasuk 4:
נִשְׁבַּע ה' וְלֹא יִנָּחֵם
Sworn has Hashem and He will not reconsider.

Fear After the Fight

Rashi reveals that Avraham was worried that Hashem would punish him for the many soldiers he had killed in the battles against the Four Kings.[42] In this light, our phrase conveys Hashem's reassurance to Avraham that he had done no wrong, and that Hashem would not withdraw the goodness He promised him, for "sworn has Hashem and He will not reconsider" any of the rewards and blessings promised to Avraham.

As noted above, even Malki-Tzedek, whose own grandchildren were among the kings and soldiers killed by Avraham's hand in battle, bore him no ill will and initiated peace with him after the war, showing genuine respect for Avraham. Indeed, the righteous Avraham had reached the cherished and esteemed level of meriting "וּמְצָא חֵן וְשֵׂכֶל טוֹב בְּעֵינֵי אֱ-לֹהִים וְאָדָם" – finding favor and good understanding in the eyes of God and man,"[43] and as a result, he had nothing to fear.

Pasuk 4:
אַתָּה כֹהֵן לְעוֹלָם;
עַל דִּבְרָתִי מַלְכִּי־צֶדֶק
You shall be a Kohen forever,
because you are *malki-tzedek* [a king of righteousness].

---

[42] *Rashi, Tehillim* 110:4; *Rashi, Bereishis* 15:1.
[43] *Mishlei* 3:4.

Avraham: Kohen and King

As noted above, this phrase is essentially a summary of the Gemara which describes how the *Kehunah* was withdrawn from Shem ben Noach and reassigned to Avraham's future progeny.[44]

On a more basic level, this phrase alludes to the very *title* "*malki-tzedek*" itself, which literally means "king of righteousness." While Shem ben Noach bore that moniker, it was an even more appropriate title for Avraham. Since Avraham was the true reflection of the Ultimate King of Righteousness, it is to Avraham that *Tehillim* 110:4 correctly refers with the words "You are *malki-tzedek*!"

Pasuk 5:
אֲדֹנָ-י עַל יְמִינְךָ;

מָחַץ בְּיוֹם אַפּוֹ מְלָכִים

The Lord is at your right;
He crushes on the day of His anger, kings.

Hashem Crushed Kings and Made Miracles Against Monarchs

Rashi explains that Hashem was at Avraham's right side accompanying him at every step in the war against the Four Kings, teaching us that Avraham was only an emissary of Hashem; it was *Hashem* Who crushed the nefarious kings in battle.[45]

Indeed, Chazal tell of the many miracles that Hashem performed for and through Avraham during this war. For example, the Midrash teaches that the expression "מָגֵן – shield" of Avraham[46] also refers in this context

---

[44] *Nedarim* 32b.
[45] *Rashi, Tehillim* 110:5.
[46] Note that the famous expression "מָגֵן אַבְרָהָם," which is the concluding phrase of the first blessing of *Shemoneh Esrei*, is itself an expression derived from

to a מָגִנָּא, an amulet or charm that Hashem bestowed upon Avraham to provide him with protection, and which miraculously created confusion and contention among his adversaries.[47]

In addition, Hashem enabled Avraham to simply throw dust and chaffs of wheat at his enemies, miraculously transforming them into arrows and spears as they left Avraham's holy hand.[48] This extraordinary episode is also referenced in the *Haftarah* to *Parshas Lech Lecha*:

מִי הֵעִיר מִמִּזְרָח, צֶדֶק יִקְרָאֵהוּ לְרַגְלוֹ; יִתֵּן לְפָנָיו גּוֹיִם וּמְלָכִים יַרְדְּ, יִתֵּן כֶּעָפָר חַרְבּוֹ כְּקַשׁ נִדָּף קַשְׁתּוֹ. יִרְדְּפֵם, יַעֲבוֹר שָׁלוֹם; אֹרַח בְּרַגְלָיו לֹא יָבוֹא – Who aroused [Avraham] from the east, who would proclaim His [Hashem's] righteousness at every footstep? Let Him place nations before him [Avraham], and may he dominate kings, may he give like dust, his sword, and like shredded straw, his bow. Let him pursue them and pass over peacefully on a path where his feet had never come before.[49]

The same must be true of us: when our enemies are vanquished, when the race is won, when the lucrative deal is closed, or when the *masechta* is completed, the credit and praise must be given to Hashem, Who has been there with us, lovingly and protectively, at our right side.

Avraham: First to Call Hashem "*Adon*"

The use of the Divine Name "אֲדֹנָי" here (and even the use of the non-sacred term "אֲדֹנִי" in *pasuk* 1 referring to Avraham) is most apropos, as the Gemara tells us that no one had ever referred to Hashem as אָדוֹן until Avraham Avinu called Hashem אָדוֹן.[50] Indeed, the source for this is

---

Parshas Lech Lecha (*Bereishis* 15:1); see also *Rashi*, *Bereishis* 12:2, from *Pesachim* 117b.
[47] *Midrash Tanchuma, Lech Lecha* 15.
[48] *Midrash Tanchuma, Lech Lecha* 15.
[49] *Yeshayahu* 41:2–3.
[50] *Brachos* 7b.

Avraham's statement in *Parshas Lech Lecha*: "וַיֹּאמַר: אֲדֹנָ-י יֱ-הֹ-וִ-ה, בַּמָּה אֵדַע כִּי אִירָשֶׁנָּה – And he said: *Adona-i Elokim*, whereby shall I know that I am to inherit it?"[51]

We can also suggest that Avraham's unprecedented use of the Name אֲדֹנָ-י would explain why *Shemoneh Esrei* includes the introductory *pasuk* of "אֲדֹנָ-י שְׂפָתַי תִּפְתָּח וּפִי יַגִּיד תְּהִלָּתֶךָ – *Adona-i* open my lips, so that my mouth may declare Your praise."[52] While *Shemoneh Esrei* begins with the *brachah* of *Avos* which mentions all three of the Patriarchs, *Avos* is nevertheless considered to be Avraham's *brachah* as supported by the concluding words of "מָגֵן אַבְרָהָם." Similarly, the addition of אֲדֹנָ-י שְׂפָתַי תִּפְתָּח to begin *Shemoneh Esrei* is designed to draw our attention to the Divine Name of "אֲדֹנָ-י," the Name innovated by none other than Avraham.

Pasuk 6:
יָדִין בַּגּוֹיִם,
מָלֵא גְוִיּוֹת;
מָחַץ רֹאשׁ עַל אֶרֶץ רַבָּה

**He will judge the nations
that are filled with corpses;
He will crush the leader of the mighty land.**

Pasuk 7:
מִנַּחַל בַּדֶּרֶךְ יִשְׁתֶּה;
עַל כֵּן יָרִים רֹאשׁ

**From a river [of enemy blood]
along the way he shall drink;
therefore, may he [proudly] lift his head."**

---

[51] *Bereishis* 15:8.
[52] *Tehillim* 51:17.

Allusions to the Slavery in Egypt

Here *Rashi*[53] veers away from the theme of direct connections to Avraham to explain these final *pesukim* in reference to the infamous Pharaoh of *Sefer Shemos* who enslaved Bnei Yisrael in Egypt. In fact, Pharaoh's punishment is described here in these last two *pesukim* of *Tehillim* 110 even more gruesomely than in the Torah!

Nonetheless, prior to sharing the foregoing explanation, *Rashi*[54] also sees in these *pesukim* an allusion to the famous episode known as the *Bris Bein Habesarim*, when Hashem entered a timeless covenant with Avraham and his future offspring. Included with the promise of Eretz Yisrael, Hashem foretold to Avraham the exile and slavery that would befall his descendants in Egypt. Of course, the *Bris Bein Habesarim* occurred in none other than *Parshas Lech Lecha*.[55]

---

[53] Rashi, Tehillim 110:6.
[54] Rashi, Tehillim 110:6.
[55] Bereishis 15:13–14.

THE WAR SONG OF AVRAM

As shown throughout this chapter, Chazal and in particular *Rashi* on *Tehillim* 110 are abundantly clear that *kapitel* 110 is a companion piece to *Parshas Lech Lecha*.

Yet, perhaps lost in the beauty of Chazal's interpretations and in the rise of Avraham as a heroic superpower in an evil and lawless world, is the fact that *Tehillim* 110 is a war song, a battle cry disguised as a *kapitel Tehillim*. It contains numerous militant expressions, such as:

> I make your enemies a footstool for your feet. The rod of your strength will be sent by Hashem… rule in the midst of your enemies! Your people volunteer on the day of your military campaign… The Lord is at your right; He crushes on the day of His anger, kings. He will judge the nations that are filled with corpses, He will crush the leader of the mighty land. From a river [of enemy blood] along the way he shall drink; therefore, may he [proudly] lift his head.

The last two sentences (*pesukim* 6 and 7) are also used to form the conclusion of the Shabbos *tefillah*, *Av HaRachamim*, the prayer dedicated to Jewish martyrs who were killed *Al Kiddush HaShem* and whose spilled blood we pray that Hashem avenge. This only adds to the intensity here.

Of course, war is not intrinsically bad; fighting on the side of good against evil is certainly a noble cause. Nonetheless, in light of its combative content, *Tehillim* 110 is also not the *kapitel* of *chessed* that one might have expected to correspond to the introductory *Parshah* of Avraham Avinu, the *Amud HaChessed* and the epitome of kindness.

PARSHAH & TEHILLIM HAND IN HAND

Therefore, considering the firmly established and intimate connection of *Tehillim* 110 to *Parshas Lech Lecha*, we can suggest that the protagonist of *Parshas Lech Lecha* is not quite yet the "Avraham" we claim as our forefather. Instead, for a total of the first 110 *pesukim* through which we meet him,[56] he is referred to in the Torah as "Avram," the father of the nation of Aram, a land that would forever remain alien and irrelevant to the Jewish People.[57] He was not yet our beloved "Avraham" Avinu until the *end* of *Parshas Lech Lecha* when his name was changed by Hashem from Avram to Avraham,[58] thereby transforming his entire essence and granting him the opportunity for wholeness and perfection in his entire 248 limbs.[59] This renaming includes the performance of his *bris milah*,[60] enabling him to father the Jewish People in purity.

Yes, the person of whom *Tehillim* 110 speaks is only Avram, who was still in the process of being cleansed by Hashem through his experiences in navigating a world teeming with cruelty, lawlessness, bloodshed, and war. During these experiences Avram had the blessing of Hashem's accompaniment at his right side. In this manner, Avram transcended his upbringing, his environment, and even his very essence, earning the honor of becoming the forefather of the Jewish People known as our beloved Avraham Avinu.

Pausing to Ponder Past Improprieties

Yet, let us pause for a moment to consider whether this approach is even appropriate. For example, there is an opinion in the Gemara

---

[56] *Bereishis* 11:26–17:5. It is certainly no coincidence that said 110 *pesukim* correspond to *Tehillim* 110.
[57] *Rashi, Bereishis* 17:5.
[58] *Bereishis* 17:5.
[59] *Rashi, Bereishis* 17:1, from *Nedarim* 32b: the *gematria* of the name "אַבְרָהָם" is 248.
[60] *Bereishis* 17:24; *Rashi* to *Bereishis* 17:1.

CHAPTER 3: LECH LECHA & TEHILLIM 110

that states we are forbidden to refer to Avraham Avinu as "Avram,"[61] as it is no longer his name and no longer captures his essence, just as we are told not to remind a *baal teshuvah* about his past.[62]

However, every single day of the year in *tefillas Shacharis* we refer to Avraham Avinu as Avram, although it is often overlooked, or rather eclipsed, by the *Hallelukahs* and *Az Yashir* that surround it. Nevertheless, in the *tefillah* that begins with the phrase *"Atah Hu Hashem Levadecha,"* we daven to Hashem and say: "אַתָּה הוּא ה' הָאֱ-לֹהִים אֲשֶׁר בָּחַרְתָּ בְּאַבְרָם וְהוֹצֵאתוֹ מֵאוּר כַּשְׂדִּים וְשַׂמְתָּ שְׁמוֹ אַבְרָהָם, וּמָצָאתָ אֶת־לְבָבוֹ נֶאֱמָן לְפָנֶיךָ – It is You Who are Hashem the God, אֲשֶׁר בָּחַרְתָּ בְּאַבְרָם – Who chose *Avram* and brought him out of Ur Kasdim and changed his name to Avraham, and You found his heart faithful before You."[63] There we *do* in fact refer to Avraham as Avram as we recount what occurred to Avram in the past and even praise Hashem for it.[64]

As for not shying away from the past, we need look no further than our precious Pesach Haggadah where Chazal tell the story of *Yetzias Mitzrayim* specifically from the vantage point of "מַתְחִיל בִּגְנוּת וּמְסַיֵּים בְּשֶׁבַח – we begin with denigration, and end with praise" by starting with the telling of the shame of our Nation's idolatrous past and concluding with the triumphant song of *Dayeinu*.[65] There we recite this paragraph:

> מִתְּחִלָּה עוֹבְדֵי עֲבוֹדָה זָרָה הָיוּ אֲבוֹתֵינוּ... – In the beginning our forefathers were worshippers of idols, but now *HaMakom* [Hashem] has brought us to His service, as it is said: 'And Yehoshua spoke to the whole nation: Thus has Hashem, God of Israel, spoken: Your father dwelt in olden times beyond the river [Euphrates], Terach, the father of Avraham and the father of Nachor, and they served other gods.

---

[61] *Brachos* 13a.
[62] *Bava Metzia* 58b.
[63] *Nechemiah* 9:7.
[64] *Brachos* 13a.
[65] *Pesachim* 116a.

And I took your father Avraham from beyond the river and led him throughout all the land of Canaan, and I multiplied his offspring and gave him Yitzchak, and to Yitzchak I gave Yaakov... and Yaakov and his sons went down to Egypt.[66]

That the above is said out loud, toward the very start of the Seder, by each and every Jewish family, men, women, and specifically even children, is proof that we, as a nation, do not hide from our past but rather view it as part of our national success story in rising from the deepest depths of idolatry to the highest of heights: that of Am Yisrael's closeness to Hashem.

Lech Lecha From and Into the Valley of the Shadow of Death

Therefore, we will now re-explore *Parshas Lech Lecha* through the grisly lens of *Tehillim* 110, whose tone and intensity parallels that of the "pre-*chessed*" *Avram* who had to steer his life through a wicked and perilous world bursting with unkindness, brutality, and mayhem, and which even forced him to engage in conflict, violence, and necessary killing. However, we will also clearly see that in each such interaction, even "Avram" remained moral and *yashar*, protected and guided by Hashem Himself.

Nevertheless, the description of the life of Avram in the Torah and from Chazal, spanning from the end of *Parshas Noach* through *Parshas Lech Lecha* until Hashem changed his name to Avraham,[67] could without exaggeration be described as the fulfillment of Dovid HaMelech's famous statement: "גַּם כִּי אֵלֵךְ בְּגֵיא צַלְמָוֶת, לֹא אִירָא רָע, כִּי אַתָּה עִמָּדִי" – Even though I walk in the valley of the shadow of death, I will not fear evil, for You are

---

[66] *Yehoshua* 24:2–4.
[67] *Bereishis* 11:26–17:5.

CHAPTER 3: LECH LECHA & TEHILLIM 110

with me,"[68] as evidenced by the following list of terrifying experiences endured by Avram:

- **Buried Alive.** *Pirkei D'Rabi Eliezer*[69] reveals that from the moment that Avram was born, the heads of the kingdoms, led by Nimrod, wanted to kill him. No rationale or motive is provided. For his own protection, Avram was hidden under the ground for thirteen years and did not see the light of the sun or the glow of the moon. After thirteen years in darkness and isolation, Avram emerged speaking *lashon hakodesh*, despising the worship of *asheira trees* and idols, trusting in the protective shade of his Creator, and proclaiming to Hashem: "אַשְׁרֵי אָדָם בֹּטֵחַ בָּךְ – Fortunate is the man who places his trust in You."[70]

- **Imprisoned.** Avram was then imprisoned for ten years in two different prisons, either by Nimrod or by his very own father Terach as punishment for destroying his family's collection of idols.[71]

- *Kivshan Ha'aish*. At the end of these ten years, Avram was summoned and, instead of being freed, was cast by Nimrod into the infamous *kivshan ha'aish*, the fiery furnace of Ur Kasdim. Yes, they threw him, alive, into a burning furnace. Yet, Hashem extended His right hand to Avram and saved him from death: "I am Hashem who took you out of Ur Kasdim."[72] It should be noted that the Midrash teaches that from Avram's perspective, he had completely surrendered his soul to die *Al Kiddush HaShem*.[73] Avram did not expect to survive, nor did he rely on a miracle; he was fully prepared to perish.

---

[68] *Tehillim* 23:4.
[69] *Pirkei D'Rabi Eliezer, perek* 26.
[70] *Tehillim* 84:13.
[71] *Pirkei D'Rabi Eliezer, perek* 26.
[72] *Bereishis* 15:7.
[73] *Midrash Tanchuma, Lech Lecha* 2.

- **Haran's Death**. Although Avram was miraculously saved from the *kivshan ha'aish*, his brother Haran was not. Chazal tell us that Haran did not pledge any allegiance, but rather waited to pick the winning side, only later siding with Avram once Avram emerged unscathed from the fire. However, Haran was thereafter cast into the flames by Nimrod and was burned alive.[74]
- **Shalom Bayis**. Haran was not only the father of Lot; he was also the father of Avram's wife, Sarai. As Sarai's father, Haran's death under such circumstances must have been exceptionally tragic for Avram and Sarai. That Avram's dwindling family unit was able to stay intact and maintained *shalom bayis* and harmony in the home may be considered yet another hidden miracle.
- **Childless**. The Torah then testifies that Sarai, Avram's *eishes chayil*, "was barren and had no child."[75] Avram too, according to his astrological sign, was not originally destined to have a son worthy of being his heir.[76] No words can properly describe the heartache of childlessness.
- **Terach Dead**. The Torah itself engages in a rare "cover-up" of sorts, as it informs the reader, not in chronological order, that Avram's father Terach died many decades before the actual date of his death. *Rashi* explains why: so that Avram's leaving in response to the commandment of "*Lech Lecha*" should not trigger criticism from his community that would claim he had abandoned his father in his old age and failed to properly honor him.[77] This of a father who was a *rasha* and was considered like the living dead,[78] and who (as noted above) worshipped idols, imprisoned Avram, and handed him over to Nimrod to be killed! Such was the

---

[74] *Rashi, Bereishis* 11:28.
[75] *Bereishis* 11:30.
[76] *Rashi, Bereishis* 15:5, from *Shabbos* 156a.
[77] *Rashi, Bereishis* 11:32.
[78] *Rashi, Bereishis* 11:32.

level of two-facedness and hypocrisy of the generation of Avram.[79]

- **Unrequited Love**. In the Mirrer Yeshiva Haggadah,[80] a sombering insight is brought in the name of the Mirrer Mashgiach Rav Yechezkel Levenstein. Rav Levenstein explains that while Avram recognized Hashem at the young age of three, Hashem only first spoke to him with the commandment of "*Lech Lecha*" at the age of seventy-five. Thus, Avram had lived for seventy-two years as an iconoclast, dedicated only to Hashem, and yet he did so without any overt communication or reassurance *from* Hashem. Moreover, instead of becoming depressed or weakening in his resolve, throughout those seven decades Avram continued to use this lack of reciprocity to perfect his *emunah* in Hashem, in Whom he believed and trusted. We often take for granted that Hashem spoke with Avram. Therefore, the thought that Avram actually endured Hashem's unrequited love for so long only adds to our appreciation of Avram's faith.

- **Blessings to Balance**. While *Parshas Lech Lecha* begins with an uplifting prophecy and promise of blessings, *Rashi* notes that many of these blessings were bestowed upon Avram only to counteract the negative effects of being forced away from home to journey into the unknown.[81] Put another way, these blessings were in large part only designed to balance out the hardships and afflictions suffered by Avram.

---

[79] It should be noted that all the above bullet points took place *prior* to *Parshas Lech Lecha,* in *Parshas Noach*! Moreover, many commentators learn that Avraham's famous "ten tests" from Hashem did not begin until the prophecy of "*Lech Lecha,*" such that the above are not considered among his most important challenges from Hashem. What Avram endured is truly unfathomable.

[80] *Mirrer Yeshiva Haggadah*, p. 121.

[81] *Rashi, Bereishis* 12:2.

- **Shechem**. The Torah tells us that Avram traveled to Shechem,[82] and *Rashi*[83] explains that Avram davened to Hashem there. This seems to be the earliest allusion in the Torah to Avram davening and as such is undoubtedly a special moment for Avram and for us. However, the *simchah* of this moment is dashed when we learn that Avram only stopped to daven in Shechem because he foresaw that the sons of Yaakov would wage war there[84] in a controversial attempt to rescue and avenge the honor of their sister Dinah, who was violated there. It was an episode that disturbed Yaakov Avinu from that moment onward, so much so that he took issue with his sons even as he lay on his deathbed.[85] That Avram's very first revealed prayers were uttered in response to the burden of such a prophetic vision is heartrending.
- **Murder and Kidnapping**. Forced to leave Eretz Canaan due to a famine designed by Hashem to specifically test his resolve, Avram found himself in the horrific position of having to worry that he would be murdered in cold blood and his wife stolen from him.[86] Nonetheless, despite the best efforts of Avram and Sarai to hide[87] and to disguise their relationship,[88] Sarai was ultimately kidnapped by Pharaoh and required Divine intervention in order to remain unharmed and untouched.
- **Loyalty to Lot**. The shepherds of Avram and Lot had a dispute that culminated in the two parting ways and Lot heading to the depraved land of Sedom.[89] This must certainly have been a difficult and disappointing outcome for Avram. Hashem then

---

[82] *Bereishis* 12:6.
[83] *Rashi, Bereishis* 12:6, from *Bereishis Rabbah* 39:15.
[84] *Rashi, Bereishis* 12:6, from *Bereishis Rabbah* 39:15.
[85] *Bereishis* 49:5–7.
[86] *Bereishis* 12:12.
[87] *Rashi, Bereishis* 12:14.
[88] *Bereishis* 12:12.
[89] *Bereishis* 13:1–13.

immediately spoke to Avram, enabling Chazal to present a crucial insght: the entire time the wicked Lot was with Avram, Hashem separated from and did not communicate (at least at length) with Avram.[90] This shows that Avram's familial loyalty to Lot (and/or perhaps more so to Lot's sister, Avram's wife Sarai) came at the expense of his closeness to Hashem.

- **War Against Kings**. *Bereishis perek* 14 recounts Avram's war against the notorious Four Kings led by Kedarlaomer and Avram's archenemy Nimrod to rescue Lot and to defeat the wicked. Though terribly outnumbered, Avram did not refrain from rushing headlong into battle and risking his life. He swiftly defeated the tyrannical monarchs, even giving chase to fleeing enemies to eradicate evil by the sword. Although not our typical image of him, Avram was the first brave soldier in the *tzvaos Hashem*, the army of God. While certainly admirable and the model for our current day *Tzahal* (may Hashem protect them), in hindsight we all know the successful outcome. Yet consider how frightening it must have been for Avram to go out to battle, or if not for Avram then for his wife Sarai and their household, unaware if Avram would survive.

- **King of the Wicked**. After the war, Avram came face to face and even conversed with the depraved King of Sedom, ruler of arguably the most immoral city in the history of the world. There, Avram was coronated as king of the surviving rulers and nations. At first, this seems like a great personal honor, and yet we must consider that it was a responsibility thrust upon Avram. Avram "*Halvri*," who had always situated himself *away* from the immorality of the world by placing himself "*mei'eiver hanahar*," on the other side of the river,[91] was suddenly chosen to be

---

[90] *Rashi, Bereishis* 13:14.
[91] *Bereishis* 14:13, and *Rashi* there.

monarch, or perhaps only a figurehead, of territory that included the nefarious Sedom and Amorah, cities with no hope for rehabilitation (as we know from the next *Parshah*, *Vayeira*). Avram certainly did not want to be the king of misfits and murderers!

- **Fear of Lost Reward.** *Bereishis perek* 15 begins with Hashem appearing to Avram after the war and telling him: "Fear not, Avram, I am a shield for you; your reward is very great." *Rashi* explains from the Midrash[92] that Avram was afraid: he feared that due to the miracles performed for him and because he had taken the lives of so many (albeit *reshaim*), he might have received his full reward for all his prior acts of righteousness, or worse, opened himself up to Hashem's retribution. Avram's fear was so strong that Hashem Himself came to reassure Avram that He would shield him from punishment and that his reward would continue to be great.

- **Fear From Killing.** *Pirkei D'Rabi Eliezer*[93] explains Avram's fear differently: he was afraid and concerned that among all the soldiers he killed, was it possible that there was not a single *tzaddik* among them? If so, Avram felt terror and guilt that he had done an irreparable wrong. Such a virtuous, yet sad, thought. Fortunately, Hashem answered that there was no stain or wrongdoing in anything that Avram had done during the war, as all those who were killed were deserving of death.

- ***Bris Bein Habesarim.*** *Bereishis perek* 15 is then highlighted by the *Bris Bein Habesarim*, the Covenant Between the Parts,[94] in which Hashem promised the Land of Israel to Avram and his

---

[92] *Rashi, Bereishis* 15:1, from *Bereishis Rabbah* 44:4.
[93] *Pirkei D'Rabi Eliezer, perek* 27.
[94] *Bereishis* 15:7–21.

offspring, but which involved numerous dark elements and frightening symbolism:

- o The cutting of various animals in half was a bloody undertaking and symbolized that the other nations of the world would gradually be cut off and destroyed.[95]
- o A bird of prey descended upon the carcasses, and Avram drove it away, symbolizing that Dovid HaMelech would come and attempt to annihilate the pagan nations. However, Hashem would not allow the defeat of our enemies to be completed until much later in history through Dovid's descendant, the *Melech HaMoshiach*.[96]
- o A deep sleep fell upon Avram, and he suddenly felt a terrible dread and darkness overcome him. This is an allusion to the struggles and darkness of the Jewish People in the numerous exiles that would follow.[97]
- o Hashem then informed Avram that his offspring would be enslaved in Egypt for 400 years,[98] which was tragic news for the founding father of the Jewish People to hear. Even more terrible was that the slavery was a punishment caused by Avram's own questioning of Hashem[99] when he stated: "How shall I know that I am to inherit it?"[100] in reference to the Land of Israel.[101]
- o Hashem promised to avenge the Jewish Nation not only from Egypt through the Ten Plagues, but also to punish

---

[95] *Rashi, Bereishis* 15:10.
[96] *Rashi, Bereishis* 15:11.
[97] *Rashi, Bereishis* 15:12.
[98] *Bereishis* 15:13.
[99] *Nedarim* 32a; *Targum Yonasan, Bereishis* 15:13; see also *Mesillas Yesharim* 4:22.
[100] *Bereishis* 15:8.
[101] *Rashi, Bereishis* 15:6.

the four primary nations who would exile us[102] by hurling them down to Gehinnom.[103] Even these positive promises foretold a dark future for the Jewish People and for the nations who were destined to torment them.

- **Hagar**. *Bereishis perek* 16 focuses on the conflict between Avram's wife Sarai and his concubine, Hagar, who was banished by Divine decree until she was willing to subjugate herself to Sarai. Hagar would go on to give birth to Yishmael, the forefather of the Arab nations, who terrorize and brutalize the Jewish People to this day.

- **Yishmael**. Hashem informed Avram that Yishmael would be a wild man, a hunter, whose hand would be in everything for banditry, and that the hand of others would oppose him to hate and attack him.[104] For anyone, much less a *tzaddik* like Avram, this prediction had to be terribly disappointing and embarrassing – not exactly "the child that one dreams of."

To March into Gehinnom for a Heavenly Cause

Each of the approximately twenty situations discussed above could be considered a tragedy, each almost too much to bear, each a miniature Gehinnom on earth. When considered together, it is *impossible* to bear, if not for Hashem's Divine guidance and Avram's willing subservience to the *ratzon Hashem*, the Divine's desire.

Here, in a harrowing *Parshas Lech Lecha* that is now more understandably paralleled by a graphic and haunting *Tehillim* 110, we see Avram literally rise from the ashes, bounced from Godly test to Godly trial to Godly tribulation, all as part of a cleansing process to merit the honor

---

[102] *Bereishis* 15:13–14, and *Rashi* there.
[103] *Rashi, Bereishis* 15:17, from *Pirkei D'Rabi Eliezer, perek* 28.
[104] *Bereishis* 16:12, and *Rashi* there.

of becoming the forefather of the Jewish People, known as "Avraham" – as he is so aptly renamed by God Himself later in *Parshas Lech Lecha*.[105]

And Avraham Laughed

For those who truly take the lessons of this chapter to heart and (perhaps for the first time) empathize with and feel sadness for Avram, I would like to try and leave you with one final thought of *nechamah*, consolation. Just a few *pesukim* after Avram's name is changed to Avraham, the Torah reveals that he did a very unexpected thing: "וַיִּצְחָק – he laughed."[106] It was not a sarcastic laugh nor a doubting laugh nor an ironic laugh nor an angry laugh, but rather a laugh of joy, of rejoicing.[107] The start of Avraham's metamorphosis from Avram to Avraham was marked by *simchah*, joy and laughter, in Hashem's promise that he and Sarah would soon have a son aptly named יִצְחָק meaning "will laugh," who would be the very first of Avraham's countless "shining stars."

Conclusion: Yes, We're the Children That You Dreamed Of

As we learn through *Parshas Lech Lecha*, and *live* through *Parshas Lech Lecha*, let us intertwine these experiences with the recitation of *Tehillim* 110. By so doing, may we grow ever closer to Avraham Avinu, and, of course, to Hashem; and may the power of *Tehillim* 110 be a *zechus* for Divine Protection for us and for all of Klal Yisrael, just as Hashem protected our shared father, Avraham.

And now we can conclude with the poignant finale of the song with which this chapter was started, and which refers to each and every one of *us*:

---

[105] *Bereishis* 17:5.
[106] *Bereishis* 17:17.
[107] *Rashi* and *Targum Onkelos*, *Bereishis* 17:17.

Avraham, yes, we're the children that you dreamed of.
And we're that shining star you saw at night.
You know it's true, that's why we call you avinu.
Our father our pride, we've got your soul inside; take us home.
Our father our pride, we've got your soul inside; take us home.
Our father our pride, we've got your soul inside; take us home.
Take us home.

CHAPTER 4

PARSHAS VAYEIRA & TEHILLIM 11

פָּרָשַׁת וַיֵּרָא / תְּהִלִּים יא

TEHILLIM 11 — תְּהִלִּים יא

1 For the conductor, by Dovid. In Hashem I have taken refuge. How [dare] you say about my soul [to me]: "Flee from your mountain like a bird!"	א לַמְנַצֵּחַ לְדָוִד; בַּה' חָסִיתִי, אֵיךְ תֹּאמְרוּ לְנַפְשִׁי: נוּדִי הַרְכֶם צִפּוֹר.
2 For, behold, the wicked bend the bow, ready their arrow on the bowstring, to shoot in the dark at the upright of heart.	ב כִּי הִנֵּה הָרְשָׁעִים יִדְרְכוּן קֶשֶׁת, כּוֹנְנוּ חִצָּם עַל יֶתֶר, לִירוֹת בְּמוֹ אֹפֶל לְיִשְׁרֵי לֵב.
3 When the foundations are destroyed, the righteous man, what has he accomplished?	ג כִּי הַשָּׁתוֹת יֵהָרֵסוּן; צַדִּיק, מַה פָּעָל.
4 Hashem is in the abode of His holiness, Hashem, in heaven is His throne; His eyes behold, His eyelids scrutinize mankind.	ד ה' בְּהֵיכַל קָדְשׁוֹ, ה' בַּשָּׁמַיִם כִּסְאוֹ; עֵינָיו יֶחֱזוּ, עַפְעַפָּיו יִבְחֲנוּ בְּנֵי אָדָם.

5 Hashem, the righteous one He examines, but the wicked and the lover of violence His soul despises.	ה ה', צַדִּיק יִבְחָן, וְרָשָׁע וְאֹהֵב חָמָס שָׂנְאָה נַפְשׁוֹ.
6 He will rain down upon the wicked, coals; fire and brimstone, and a burning blast is their allotted portion.	ו יַמְטֵר עַל רְשָׁעִים פַּחִים; אֵשׁ וְגָפְרִית, וְרוּחַ זִלְעָפוֹת מְנָת כּוֹסָם.
7 For righteous is Hashem, those of righteous deeds He loves; the upright will behold His face.	ז כִּי צַדִּיק ה', צְדָקוֹת אָהֵב; יָשָׁר יֶחֱזוּ פָנֵימוֹ.

INTRODUCTION: THE COMMON DENOMINATOR IS THE DESTRUCTION OF SEDOM

The most straightforward connection between *Tehillim* 11 and *Parshas Vayeira* is *pasuk* 6 of the *kapitel*: "יַמְטֵר עַל רְשָׁעִים פַּחִים; אֵשׁ וְגָפְרִית, וְרוּחַ זִלְעָפוֹת מְנָת כּוֹסָם," which describes Hashem's raining down coals, fire, brimstone, and burning winds upon the wicked, which is eerily similar to the description of Hashem's destruction of Sedom and Amorah in *Parshas Vayeira*: "וַה' הִמְטִיר עַל סְדֹם וְעַל עֲמֹרָה גָּפְרִית וָאֵשׁ, מֵאֵת ה' מִן הַשָּׁמָיִם – And Hashem rained down upon Sedom and Amorah brimstone and fire, from Hashem from the heavens."[1]

Indeed, *Tehillim* 11 focuses on Hashem's punishment of the wicked and rewarding of the righteous, the quintessence of which is encapsulated

---

[1] *Bereishis* 19:24.

CHAPTER 4: VAYEIRA & TEHILLIM 11

in *Parshas Vayeira*. This is the *Parshah* that emphasizes Hashem's love for Avraham Avinu and contrasts that love with Hashem's destruction of Sedom and Amorah, the symbols of wickedness for all time.

In *Parshas Vayeira* the distinction between good and evil is clear, and each receive the repayment they deserve. Throughout history, however, that outcome was not always so apparent, as the wicked *rasha* often rose to a position of superiority that enabled him to lord over the righteous *tzaddik*.

According to the *Malbim*,[2] in *Tehillim* 11 Dovid HaMelech is rebuking those of his generation who doubted and complained due to their shaken faith in the *hashgachah* of Hashem. God's omniscient and attentive eye on the world was hidden from these skeptics and thus gave the appearance of Hashem abandoning the world to chance and not rendering *mishpat*, proper judgment.

In *pasuk* 4, Dovid does not deny this perception but explains that while Hashem is indeed enthroned on high, distinct from man and seemingly indifferent to his actions, in reality: "עֵינָיו יֶחֱזוּ, עַפְעַפָּיו יִבְחֲנוּ בְּנֵי אָדָם," Hashem is simultaneously watching and scrutinizing all. Furthermore, as *pasuk* 5 makes clear: "ה', צַדִּיק יִבְחָן, וְרָשָׁע וְאֹהֵב חָמָס שָׂנְאָה נַפְשׁוֹ," Hashem often tests the *tzaddik* while simultaneously longing for his success, yet He despises the evil actions of the *rasha*.

Indeed, says the *Malbim*, Dovid is explaining to the scoffers and cynics that the feelings they are experiencing are all part of the method in which Hashem challenges mankind. For if Hashem would punish the *rasha* immediately, there would be no place for *bechirah* – free will, or for reward and punishment, and though such a prompt and strong response would result in all of mankind exactaly serving Hashem, it would be a servitude borne from fear of retribution rather than free choice. In contrast, when Hashem *hides* His *hashgachah*, only then can mankind truly be tested. Then the righteous distinguish themselves as serving Hashem out

---

[2] *Malbim, Tehillim* 11.

of truth and sincerity – exponentially increasing their reward, possibly in this world and certainly in the World to Come. The same is true of the *reshaim*: their apparent success attained through evil is only transient, and it will be followed by a Godly reckoning. Whether this reckoning will be meted out in this world, as was the case with the destruction of Sedom and Amorah, in the afterlife, or both, is for Hashem to decide – but their punishment is guaranteed.

THE MANY CONNECTIONS BETWEEN PARSHAS VAYEIRA & TEHILLIM 11

Pasuk 1:

לַמְנַצֵּחַ לְדָוִד; בַּה' חָסִיתִי,

אֵיךְ תֹּאמְרוּ לְנַפְשִׁי:

נוּדִי הַרְכֶם צִפּוֹר

For the conductor, by Dovid. In Hashem I have taken refuge. How [dare] you say about my soul [to me]: "Flee from your mountain like a bird."

Taking Refuge in Hashem

Here the scoffers urge Dovid HaMelech to abandon his faith in Hashem, yet Dovid proclaims that it is with Hashem, and only Hashem, that he finds refuge, safety, and protection. "בַּה' חָסִיתִי," *in* Hashem, *with* Hashem; closeness to Hashem is the safest place to be.

Avraham Avinu was also granted safety and security from Hashem and blessed to just "be" with Hashem, as we find in the opening story of *Parshas Vayeira* when Hashem appeared to Avraham specifically on his third and most painful day following his *bris milah* to be *mevaker cholim*

CHAPTER 4: VAYEIRA & TEHILLIM 11

and visit the sick and recovering Avraham. Yes, God himself appeared to Avraham to inquire about his well-being.[3] And although this visit seems to have been initiated by *Hashem*, it was really *Avraham* who initiated the connection by fulfilling Hashem's commandment and passing His test, circumcising himself in his old age.

This is the meaning of "בַּה' חָסִיתִי:" to *be* with Hashem, safe and sound.

Wandering, but Finding Home

In the phrase "נוּדִי הַרְכֶם" – flee to the mountain," נוּדִי can also means to "wander," like the similar expression of "נָע וָנָד" in the curse of Kayin.[4] It is no coincidence that the Jewish People are referred to as "the wandering Jew," for Avraham Avinu was the first to personify the title when Hashem appeared to him and told him on two separate occasions, once in *Parshas Lech Lecha* and once in *Parshas Vayeira*, to just "go," "לֶךְ לְךָ,"[5] without even informing him of the destination.[6] Additionally, in *Parshas Vayeira* Avraham explained to Avimelech why he was justified in protecting himself by introducing Sarah as his sister rather than his wife: because "הִתְעוּ אֹתִי אֱ-לֹהִים" – God caused me to wander,"[7] on which *Rashi* says "מְשׁוֹטֵט וָנָד," to roam and move from place to place,[8] constantly encountering wicked people who would desire Sarah and seek to eliminate her husband.

Despite Avraham's challenges of "נוּדִי," he *did* find a temporary destination at the end of *Parshas Vayeira* in the form of a הַר, a mountain. This was not just any mountain, but Har HaMoriah, the location of *Akeidas Yitzchak*, and the future location of the Beis HaMikdash – Hashem's *bayis* – His home. If there ever was a true "הַרְכֶם," which is an expression of

---

[3] Rashi, Bereishis 18:1, from Bava Metzia 86b.
[4] Bereishis 4:12.
[5] Bereishis 12:1 and 22:2.
[6] Rashi, Bereishis 12:1, from Bereishis Rabbah 39:9.
[7] Bereishis 20:13.
[8] Rashi, Bereishis 20:13.

"הַר שֶׁלָּכֶם – *your* mountain," it was *this* mountain that Avraham found, destined forever to be the holiest place on earth because it is the place where the Divine Presence resides.

Lot's Escape from Sedom

*P*asuk 1 states: "לְנַפְשִׁי: נוּדִי הַרְכֶם צִפּוֹר – About my soul: flee from your mountain like a bird!" Having to flee like a bird to save one's very soul is an expression reminiscent of the flight of Lot and his family from the obliteration of Sedom in *Parshas Vayeira*. The angels begged him: "הִמָּלֵט עַל נַפְשֶׁךָ – Flee for your life/for your soul,"[9] which parallels the phrase "לְנַפְשִׁי: נוּדִי – About my soul: flee." Moreover, Lot was specifically told: "הִמָּלֵט הָהָרָה – flee to the mountain,"[10] which parallels the word "הַרְכֶם – your mountain."

A Hint to Moav and to Balak

*I*n addition, it is eerie to see the use of the word "צִפּוֹר" here in the context of Hashem saving the lives of Lot and his two daughters, thereby ensuring the continuation of his progeny. For *Parshas Vayeira* also contains the story of the incestuous union of Lot and his daughters, which led to the birth and naming of the original Moav, the progenitor of the Moabite nation.[11] A noteworthy and nefarious descendant of Lot and Moav would be the Moabite King Balak, who would infamously enlist the wicked Prophet Bilaam to curse the Jewish People in the desert.[12] The evil King Balak's father, himself a direct descendant of Moav and Lot, was named צִפּוֹר.[13]

---

[9] *Bereishis* 19:17.
[10] *Bereishis* 19:17.
[11] *Bereishis* 19:37.
[12] *Parshas Balak: Bamidbar, Perakim* 22–24.
[13] *Bamidbar* 22:2.

Flying Like a Bird

The reference to a bird in the phrase "נוּדִי... צִפּוֹר – Flee... like a bird," also refers to the Jewish People as a nation, who are often compared to birds.[14] Moreover, Am Yisrael is often specifically compared to a *yonah*, a dove, which is a symbol of peace. Chazal teach that just as a dove is only saved by its wings, so too the Jewish People are protected by the mitzvos we perform.[15]

Additionally, in *Parshas Lech Lecha* at the *Bris Bein Habesarim*, the various larger cattle were sliced in half symbolizing the destruction of the other nations, yet "וְאֶת הַצִּפֹּר לֹא בָתָר" – the two smaller birds were left untouched. They remained whole to teach that the צִפּוֹר, which represents Klal Yisrael, are "קַיָּמִים לְעוֹלָם – will last forever."[16]

Upon reflection, we see that while Lot had to *flee* like a bird, the Jewish People soars heavenward like one.

Pasuk 2:
כִּי הִנֵּה הָרְשָׁעִים יִדְרְכוּן קֶשֶׁת,
כּוֹנְנוּ חִצָּם עַל יֶתֶר,
לִירוֹת בְּמוֹ אֹפֶל לְיִשְׁרֵי לֵב

**For, behold, the wicked bend the bow,
ready their arrow on the bowstring,
to shoot in the dark at the upright of heart.**

Yishmael's Attempts to Murder Yitzchak

This description of the *reshaim* aiming their bow and arrow to shoot at the righteous directly corresponds to how Yishmael manifested his hatred toward Yitzchak in *Parshas Vayeira*. Under the guise of playfulness

---

[14] E.g., Rashi, Bereishis 15:10; Shir Hashirim 2:14. See also e.g., Gitten 45a.
[15] *Brachos* 53b.
[16] Rashi, Bereishis 15:10, from *Pirkei D'Rabi Eliezer, perek* 28.

or sport, Yishmael attempted to kill young Yitzchak by luring him outside to the field and using his bow to shoot arrows at him – all to become Avraham's sole heir. "כְּמִתְלַהְלֵהַּ הַיֹּרֶה זִקִּים חִצִּים וָמָוֶת – As a madman shoots fireball, arrows, and death,"[17] so did Yishmael act toward Yitzchak. He would claim that he was merely jesting, but his true intent was to kill.[18]

Furthermore, the bow and arrow are mentioned two additional times in *Parshas Vayeira*, each instance in the context of Yishmael and in association with acts of *rishus*.

First, when Yishmael was deathly ill in the desert, the Torah reveals that his mother, Hagar, cast him off under a tree and distanced herself from him "הַרְחֵק כִּמְטַחֲוֵי קֶשֶׁת – a number of bowshots away."[19] This is interpreted by Chazal as an act of selfishness or even cruelty by Hagar, who did not force herself to remain by Yishmael's side and comfort him in what seemed like the last moments before his impending death.[20]

A few *pesukim* later, the Torah tells us that Yishmael survived and "וַיְהִי רֹבֶה קַשָּׁת – he became an archer"[21] who used his skills not as a hunter nor as a sportsman, but rather for banditry through robbing desert travelers.[22]

Unfortunately, Yishmael's bow and arrow has evolved into the even more deadly and destructive form of missiles and rockets, which his terrorist progeny often fire into Eretz Yisrael from Gaza up to Lebanon, aimlessly and indiscriminately, ruthlessly trying to harm the children of Yitzchak Avinu even to this day. May Hashem protect Am Yisrael from the *rishus* and violence of Yishmael always, and bring an end to his terror forever.

---

[17] *Mishlei* 26:18.
[18] *Rashi, Bereishis* 21:9, from *Bereishis Rabbah* 53:11.
[19] *Bereishis* 21:16.
[20] *Rashi, Bereishis* 21:16, and *Be'er Yitzchak*.
[21] *Bereishis* 21:20.
[22] *Rashi, Bereishis* 21:20, from *Midrash Tanchuma, Shemos* 1.

The Upright of Heart

❝לְיִשְׁרֵי לֵב – to the upright of heart," is a reference to the Avos – Avraham, Yitzchak and Yaakov – who are known as יְשָׁרִים, straight and upright in their righteousness. In fact, all of *Sefer Bereishis* is referred to as "סֵפֶר הַיָּשָׁר" due in large part to its prominent portrayal of the Avos.[23]

As we will see, this theme of the Avos as each being a יָשָׁר and collectively being יְשָׁרִים will be a recurring topic in this *sefer*. As such, the *kapitelach Tehillim* corresponding to *Sefer Bereishis* contain numerous references to this exalted word and concept.

Pasuk 3:
כִּי הַשָּׁתוֹת יֵהָרֵסוּן;

צַדִּיק, מַה פָּעָל

When the foundations are destroyed,
the righteous man, what has he accomplished?

Avraham's Introspection After Inability to Save Sedom

❝When the foundations are destroyed" certainly refers to the destruction of Sedom and Amorah. Moreover, "the righteous man, what has he accomplished," can be understood as a statement by Avraham about *himself* in the context of the destruction of Sedom and Amorah. This is apparent in two ways. First, we read of Avraham's strong sense of responsibility to daven to Hashem for the salvation of these evil cities' inhabitants;[24] and second, we learn of Avraham's sense of helplessness when he is unable to save them.[25]

---

[23] *Avodah Zarah* 25a. See also *Haamek Davar*, Introduction to *Sefer Bereishis*.
[24] *Bereishis* 18:23–32.
[25] *Bereishis* 18:33, and *Rashi* there.

While there can be no doubt that Avraham fully accepted Hashem's final decree of annihilation of these wicked cities and their inhabitants, the Torah contains two mysterious *pesukim* as the cities are being razed and inundated by smoke and flames:

> Avraham rose early in the morning to the place where he had stood before Hashem. And he gazed down upon Sedom and Amorah and upon the entire surface of the land of the plain and saw; and behold, the smoke of the earth rose like the smoke of a lime pit.[26]

The Torah does not reveal Avraham's specific thoughts at this moment. But the Torah does tell us that Avraham returned to the same place – the place where he had previously davened and had even "battled" with Hashem through prayer – to save these cities.[27]

Even with Avraham's perfect faith in Hashem, we must recall that Avraham was blessed (or burdened) with many roles and responsibilities toward the other nations. The Gemara[28] teaches that the name Avraham itself stood for his status as the "אַב הֲמוֹן גּוֹיִם – father of a multitude of nations."[29] He embodied the *Amud HaChessed*, Pillar of Kindness, toward all.[30] Moreover, *Rashi* informs us that Avraham was even the beloved king of the nations and *Nesi Elokim*, Prince of God, having been anointed as such at Emek Shaveh by all the world's kingdoms, including the kings of Sedom and Amorah themselves.[31] In fact, the Torah goes so far as to explain that even *Hashem* felt compelled to reveal to Avraham His plan to destroy Sedom[32] because how could He "destroy the children and not inform the father; the father who is someone who loves Me?"[33]

---

[26] *Bereishis* 19:27–28.

[27] *Rashi, Bereishis* 18:23.

[28] *Shabbos* 105a.

[29] *Bereishis* 17:5.

[30] Based on *Pirkei Avos* 1:2.

[31] *Rashi, Bereishis* 14:17.

[32] *Bereishis* 18:17.

[33] *Rashi, Bereishis* 18:17, from *Bereishis Rabbah* 49:2.

Therefore, it is logical to consider that at least part of what Avraham might have been feeling upon gazing down at the smoldering cities is a lament akin to *pasuk* 3 of *Tehillim* 11:

- "כִּי הַשָּׁתוֹת יֵהָרֵסוּן," when the foundations of Sedom and Amorah are destroyed,
- "צַדִּיק," the righteous man, me, Avraham, the father of many nations, even the wicked ones,
- "מַה פָּעָל," what have I accomplished, when in the end I was unable to save them?

The Unsuccessful Upbringing of Yishmael

"כִּי הַשָּׁתוֹת יֵהָרֵסוּן; צַדִּיק, מַה פָּעָל" as cited above includes these two references: "destroyed foundations" and "צַדִּיק, מַה פָּעָל" – the *tzaddik's* sense of failure, powerlessness, and guilt. In addition to our initial understanding, these phrases can also be interpreted in the context of Avraham's feelings about the unsuccessful upbringing of Yishmael.

In *Parshas Lech Lecha* we learn that Avraham beseeched Hashem: "לוּ יִשְׁמָעֵאל יִחְיֶה לְפָנֶיךָ,"[34] which *Rashi* interprets as "Would that Yishmael should grow up to be God-fearing."[35] Later in *Parshas Vayeira* we learn (as noted above) that Yishmael attempted to murder Yitzchak in cold blood and was ultimately banished to the desert by Sarah, Avraham, and Hashem.[36] Indeed, the Torah states: "וַיֵּרַע הַדָּבָר מְאֹד בְּעֵינֵי אַבְרָהָם עַל אוֹדֹת בְּנוֹ – The matter greatly distressed Avraham regarding his son."[37] *Rashi* explains that the distress included Avraham's anguish upon having heard that Yishmael had adopted evil behavior. Even more, *Rashi* states that Avraham uncharacteristically went so far as to *hate* Yishmael because he had fallen so terribly into sin.[38]

---

[34] *Bereishis* 17:18.
[35] *Rashi, Bereishis* 17:18.
[36] *Bereishis* 21:12–14.
[37] *Bereishis* 21:11.
[38] *Rashi, Bereishis* 21:11, from *Midrash Tanchuma, Shemos* 1.

How sad and disturbing: Avraham's own son was such a wicked outcast that he was ultimately despised by even his own righteous father! Indeed, one can genuinely feel Avraham's anguish and empathize with him as we recite these words that are now even more haunting: "כִּי הַשָּׁתוֹת יֵהָרֵסוּן; צַדִּיק, מַה פָּעָל."

Pasuk 4:

ה' בְּהֵיכַל קָדְשׁוֹ,

ה' בַּשָּׁמַיִם כִּסְאוֹ;

עֵינָיו יֶחֱזוּ, עַפְעַפָּיו יִבְחֲנוּ בְּנֵי אָדָם

Hashem is in the abode of His holiness,
Hashem, in heaven is His throne;
His eyes behold, His eyelids scrutinize mankind.

Hashem's Personal Attention to All

Although Hashem is high above in His holy realm and enthroned upon the heavens, as the *Malbim* emphasized in the Introduction to this chapter, Hashem is all-seeing and concerned with both the actions of mankind as a whole and with each person individually.

That such personal attention is bestowed by Hashem upon Avraham at the start of *Parshas Vayeira*[39] in the form of a personal *bikkur cholim* visit is spellbinding enough. That Hashem also showed such personal attention to the likes of the debased Lot as he was rescued from Sedom,[40] and to the outcasts Yishmael and Hagar as their lives were jeopardized in the desert,[41] is further proof of the reality of Hashem's *hashgachah pratis*.

Surpassing even that, we find that Hashem even gave personal attention to the depraved inhabitants of Sedom and Amorah. In *Parshas Vayeira*,

---

[39] *Bereishis* 18:1.
[40] *Bereishis*, *Perek* 19.
[41] *Bereishis* 21:17–19.

Hashem states: "אֵרְדָה נָּא וְאֶרְאֶה, הַכְּצַעֲקָתָהּ הַבָּאָה אֵלַי עָשׂוּ כָּלָה; וְאִם לֹא, אֵדָעָה — I will descend and see: if they acted in accordance with its outcry which came to Me, then destruction! And if not, I will know."[42] There, Hashem came down from on high, so to speak, to perform a personal investigation of Sedom and Amorah even though because of Hashem's omniscience doing so was completely unnecessary. *Rashi* explains that Hashem was teaching future Jewish judges to refrain from issuing a verdict in capital cases except through "seeing," i.e., examining the issues carefully and personally, despite the judge's elevated status, wisdom, and experience.[43]

Hashem was leading by example and showing us that nothing and no one is too small or trivial even for Him. The hope is that we, too, recognize Hashem's ability to synthesize greatness and humility, and that we emulate this *middah* ourselves in our interactions with others.

Pasuk 5:
ה', צַדִּיק יִבְחָן,
וְרָשָׁע וְאֹהֵב חָמָס שָׂנְאָה נַפְשׁוֹ
Hashem, the righteous one He examines,
but the wicked and the lover of violence
His soul despises.

Stricter Scrutiny of the *Tzaddik*

The expression "ה', צַדִּיק יִבְחָן" teaches that Hashem examines and scrutinizes the *tzaddik* much more closely than He does the *rasha*, which is a cornerstone of the *Malbim's* explanation described above. This Godly approach is illustrated throughout *Parshas Vayeira* where we learn of the many challenges that confronted the righteous Avraham, including the destruction of Sedom and Amorah,[44] Avimelech's abduction of

---
[42] *Bereishis* 18:21.
[43] *Rashi, Bereishis* 18:21, from *Midrash Tanchuma, Bereishis* 18.
[44] *Bereishis, Perek* 19.

Sarah,[45] the banishment of Yishmael and Hagar,[46] and of course, *Akeidas Yitzchak*.[47]

Additionally, in the context of *Parshas Vayeira*, "צַדִּיק" is also a reference to Avimelech, who in his own defense to Hashem after having stolen Sarah away from Avraham, nonetheless refers to himself as a *tzaddik* and pleads: "אֲדֹנָ-י, הֲגוֹי גַּם צַדִּיק תַּהֲרֹג – My Master, a nation, even a righteous one, would You kill?"[48] Of course, that Avimelech was focused on *tzidkus* at all was no doubt inspired and reinforced by *Avraham's* very presence.

A Hint to Avraham's Ten Tests

The phrase "ה', צַדִּיק יִבְחָן" is particularly fundamental in the context of the story of Avraham Avinu. As the *Midrash Tehillim* on this *pasuk* reminds us, the word "יִבְחָן" is synonymous with נִסָּיוֹן, test,[49] and thus alludes to the famous ten tests that Hashem put Avraham through. *Pirkei Avos* teaches: "עֲשָׂרָה נִסְיוֹנוֹת נִתְנַסָּה אַבְרָהָם אָבִינוּ וְעָמַד בְּכֻלָּם, לְהוֹדִיעַ כַּמָּה חִבָּתוֹ שֶׁל אַבְרָהָם אָבִינוּ – With ten trials was Avraham Avinu tested, and he withstood them all, to make known how great was the love of Avraham Avinu for Hashem."[50] While *Rashi*[51] and the *Rambam*[52] differ in opinion as to what the ten tests were, both agree that the incidents in *Parshas Vayeira* of the driving away of Yishmael and Hagar and *Akeidas Yitzchak* were among the ten, and that *Akeidas Yitzchak* was the final and most difficult test of all.

---

[45] *Bereishis, Perek 20.*
[46] *Bereishis, Perek 21.*
[47] *Bereishis, Perek 22.*
[48] *Bereishis 20:4.*
[49] *Midrash Tehillim, Shocher Tov 11.*
[50] *Pirkei Avos 5:3.*
[51] *Rashi, Pirkei Avos 5:3.*
[52] *Rambam, Peirush HaMishnayos, Pirkei Avos 5:3.*

The *Zohar Hakadosh*[53] quotes *Tehillim* 11:5 and draws a direct parallel between "ה׳, צַדִּיק יִבְחָן" and the concept of נִסָּיוֹן, explaining as follows: Hashem is well aware that the *tzaddik's emunah* is unswerving. If so, why does He test him at all? Hashem does so not for His own sake, but for the sake of the *tzaddik* – to raise the status of the *tzaddik* in the eyes of the world. So did Hashem do to Avraham at *Akeidas Yitzchak*: "וְהָאֱ-לֹהִים נִסָּה אֶת אַבְרָהָם – And God tested Avraham."[54] However, "נִסָּה" does not only mean "tested." It is also an expression of "הָרִימוּ נֵס – lift up a sign/raise a banner,"[55] so that all the world can see the success and faith of Avraham Avinu. This, concludes the *Zohar*, is an approach that Hashem initiated with Avraham and has continued to use with many *tzaddikim* to this very day.

Hashem's Hatred of Eisav, Yishmael, and Their Descendants

"וְרָשָׁע וְאֹהֵב חָמָס, שָׂנְאָה נַפְשׁוֹ – But the wicked and the lover of violence, His soul despises." This statement that Hashem hates the wicked surely includes the inhabitants of Sedom and Amorah. However, in this context, these words have an even more specific meaning behind them.

The use of the word "רָשָׁע" is not simply generic but can refer specifically to the nations spawned from Eisav, whom Chazal refer to as "עֵשָׂו הָרָשָׁע – Eisav the wicked."[56] This includes the Roman Empire, known as the "אֻמָּה הָרְשָׁעָה – wicked nation,"[57] which destroyed the Second Beis HaMikdash and in whose exile we have been trapped for more than two thousand years.

Furthermore, the use of the word "חָמָס" is a clear reference to Hagar's son Yishmael and their progeny, the Arab nations. In *Parshas Lech Lecha*

---

[53] *Zohar Hakadosh* 1:139b.
[54] *Bereishis* 22:1.
[55] *Yeshayahu* 62:10.
[56] E.g., *Rashi, Bereishis* 32:7.
[57] E.g., the Chanukah *tefillah Maoz Tzur*.

when Sarah Imeinu was struggling with the complexities of the tripartite relationship between herself, Hagar, and Avraham, Sarah argued with and even cursed Avraham by stating: "חֲמָסִי עָלֶיךָ – may the חָמָס, injustice, done to me, be placed upon you!"[58] It is no coincidence that one of the most notorious terrorist organizations in modern times is the Arab terrorist group that the terrorists themselves proudly named חָמָס (Hamas)!

Regarding these wicked individuals and nations, "שָׂנְאָה נַפְשׁוֹ," Hashem's very soul, *kiv'yachol*, despises them all. Furthermore, any modicum of success that they may have is but part of Hashem's broader process of testing the righteous – "ה', צַדִּיק יִבְחָן," while sometimes punishing the wicked more slowly and methodically, as explained by the *Malbim* cited in the Introduction to this chapter.

Pasuk 6:
יַמְטֵר עַל רְשָׁעִים פַּחִים;
אֵשׁ וְגָפְרִית, וְרוּחַ זִלְעָפוֹת מְנָת כּוֹסָם

He [Hashem] will rain down upon the wicked, coals; fire and brimstone, and a burning blast is their allotted portion.

Destruction of Sedom Described

As explained in more detail in the Introduction to this chapter, this *pasuk* summarizes the annihilation of Sedom and Amorah, which was miraculous, swift, and powerful.

It also serves as a warning to other nations who may try to cross Am Yisrael that their efforts will ultimately be in vain and self-destructive, as we saw, for example, during the miracles of the ten plagues in Egypt and at many other times in Jewish history. Although such *nissim geluyim*, revealed miracles, are less common today, the overt miracles of the past

---

[58] *Bereishis* 16:5, and *Rashi* there.

serve as a reminder that even Hashem's so-called "natural world" is *itself* a miracle, filled with constant *nissim nistarim*, hidden miracles, that we should not take for granted.[59]

Pasuk 7:
כִּי צַדִּיק ה', צְדָקוֹת אָהֵב;
יָשָׁר יֶחֱזוּ פָנֵימוֹ

For righteous is Hashem, those of righteous deeds He loves; the upright will behold His face.

The Inspiration of *Tzidkus*

On a basic level, this *pasuk* is applicable to Avraham, who was himself a *tzaddik* and who was inspired by *Hashem's tzidkus*.

In addition to tracking the sojourns of Avraham, *Parshas Vayeira* includes several additional connections to concepts revolving around *tzidkus*.

For example, as noted above, Avimelech proudly considered himself a *tzaddik*,[60] also seeking, no doubt, to follow in Avraham's footsteps.

Interestingly, in Avraham's prayers to save Sedom, Avraham focuses on the possibility that its inhabitants may include *tzaddikim*. Therefore, he begins his prayer with the question: "הַאַף תִּסְפֶּה צַדִּיק עִם רָשָׁע – Will You even obliterate the righteous with the wicked?"[61] Surprisingly, Avraham's dialogue with Hashem in defense of Sedom uses the *shoresh* of the word צַדִּיק a total of seven times!

In addition, when one contemplates the phrase "כִּי צַדִּיק ה', צְדָקוֹת אָהֵב," one will appreciate its depths, for it is a declaration that Hashem is a *tzaddik* and righteous, and that He loves people who perform righteous deeds.

---

[59] E.g., *Ramban, Shemos* 13:16.
[60] *Bereishis* 20:4.
[61] *Bereishis* 18:23.

Furthermore, it must be noted that the above does not say that Hashem loves the *tzaddik*, but rather that Hashem loves "צְדָקוֹת – righteous *deeds*." For us on a personal level, this means that we don't have to feel pressured to suddenly transform ourselves into *tzaddikim* (although that should be our long-term goal). Instead, with each singular good deed, with each proper decision, with even a *moment* of *tzidkus*, we become even more beloved to Hashem.

My *rebbi*, Rabbi Shmuel Brazil, told us of the Chassidim who finally gathered the courage to ask their Rebbe how he became such a *tzaddik*. His answer: "One *bechirah* at a time." All it takes is one good choice, followed by one more, followed by one more...

Pinpoint Perfection of *Hashgachah Pratis*

On a more philosophical level, the phrase "כִּי צַדִּיק ה', צְדָקוֹת אָהֵב – For righteous is Hashem; those of righteous deeds He loves," goes right to the heart of the *Malbim's* approach to *Tehillim* 11: *Tehillim* 11 is Dovid HaMelech's response to those who observe the world around them with eyes that lack *emunah* in Hashem and therefore have their trust in God shaken by their mistaken belief that Hashem is not properly meting out *mishpat* and may even have disconnected Himself from the world.

Interestingly, it is Avraham Avinu himself who asks similar questions of Hashem in *Parshas Vayeira* when initiating his plea on behalf of Sedom: "הַאַף תִּסְפֶּה צַדִּיק עִם רָשָׁע – Will You even obliterate the righteous with the wicked?"[62] Avraham bravely continues: "חָלִלָה לְּךָ מֵעֲשֹׂת כַּדָּבָר הַזֶּה, לְהָמִית צַדִּיק עִם רָשָׁע, וְהָיָה כַצַּדִּיק כָּרָשָׁע; חָלִלָה לָּךְ, הֲשֹׁפֵט כָּל הָאָרֶץ לֹא יַעֲשֶׂה מִשְׁפָּט – It would be profane for You to do such a thing, to bring death upon the righteous with the wicked; that the righteous will be like the wicked. It would be profane for You. Shall the Judge of all the earth not do justice?"[63]

---

[62] *Bereishis* 18:23.
[63] *Bereishis* 18:25.

However, after challenging Hashem's *mishpat* in a reverent manner, and after advocating on behalf of Sedom to the best of his ability within the parameters of justice and righteousness, Avraham understood that Hashem's answer of "No" to sparing Sedom was *itself* the epitome of "כִּי צַדִּיק ה', צְדָקוֹת אָהֵב." God's righteousness manifested itself in the punishment of the wicked, together with pinpoint perfection of *hashgachah pratis* by simultaneously rescuing Lot and his daughters in the merit of the *tzaddik*, Avraham Avinu.

Yearning to See Hashem's Face

The final phrase of "יָשָׁר יֶחֱזוּ פָנֵימוֹ – The upright will behold His face," concludes *Tehillim* 11 with words of inspiration. It is a reference to the intense and intimate closeness of Hashem toward those who are "יָשָׁר," led by the Avos – Avraham, Yitzchak and Yaakov, also known as יְשָׁרִים (as discussed above).

As for the connection to seeing Hashem's face, this is of course allegorical as we know that Hashem has no physical form.[64] Thus "seeing Hashem's face" means to better understand His ways and feel His closeness. The Avos were certainly on this level, having communicated with Hashem prophetically, which is the epitome of *deveikus ba'Hashem*.

Furthermore, there is a clear connection between the imagery of Hashem's "פָּנִים – face/closeness," and Avraham Avinu specifically, in the daily *Shemoneh Esrei brachah* of *Sim Shalom*. There we daven the words: "בָּרְכֵנוּ אָבִינוּ כֻּלָּנוּ כְּאֶחָד בְּאוֹר פָּנֶיךָ" – Bless us, our Father [Hashem], all of us as one, with the light of Your face." The *Eitz Yosef*[65] explains that in this context the word "כְּאֶחָד" does not only mean "as one," but also is a special request that we be blessed just as *Avraham Avinu* was and is blessed, for Avraham Avinu is referred to as "אֶחָד," as it says in the *Navi Yechezkel*:

---

[64] E.g., *Rambam's Thirteen Principles of Faith, Ani Maamin* #3.
[65] *Eitz Yosef, Siddur Otzar HaTefillah.*

"אֶחָד הָיָה אַבְרָהָם – Avraham was one."[66] As such, we come full circle: *Shemoneh Esrei begins* with references to Avraham in the *brachah* of *Avos* and also *ends* with reference to Avraham in *Sim Shalom*.

Thus, the intent in *Sim Shalom* is two-fold: that Hashem bless "all of us as one" and that Hashem bless us even to the exalted extent that He blessed the one and only Avraham Avinu.

And for what blessings do we ask? The first of our list of requests is actually "בְּאוֹר פָּנֶיךָ:" we are asking to be blessed "with the light of Your face," a statement similar to "יָשָׁר יֶחֱזוּ פָנֵימוֹ – the upright will behold His face." We ask to be blessed with the closeness to Hashem that Avraham experienced.

Moreover, *Sim Shalom* continues with the statement: "כִּי בְאוֹר פָּנֶיךָ נָתַתָּ לָּנוּ ה' אֱ-לֹהֵינוּ תּוֹרַת חַיִּים וְאַהֲבַת חֶסֶד וּצְדָקָה וּבְרָכָה וְרַחֲמִים וְחַיִּים וְשָׁלוֹם – for from the light of Your face You have given us, Hashem, our God, the Torah of life and a love of kindness, righteousness, blessing, compassion, life, and peace." While many tend to emphasize one or more of the words "Torah of life and a love of kindness, righteousness, blessing, compassion, life, and peace," the greatest of all the requests mentioned above is actually "כִּי בְאוֹר פָּנֶיךָ נָתַתָּ לָּנוּ: ה' אֱ-לֹהֵינוּ – for from the light of Your face You have given us: Hashem, our God!" Hashem has given us the gift of having *Him* as our God, including the gift of His "face" in the form of the ability to be spiritually close to Him. The greatest gift is closeness to Hashem.

To whom do we have to be thankful for enabling such a blessing, the ultimate blessing of closeness to God Himself? We have to thank the first person to recognize Hashem, and the one who earned and granted us that blessing as our rightful heritage – Avraham Avinu.

---

[66] *Yechezkel* 33:24.

AVRAHAM, HASHEM, AND THE THREE TRAVELERS

Parshas Vayeira's story of the destruction of Sedom, involving Hashem's punishment of the wicked and closeness to the righteous, is clearly the main theme of *Tehillim* 11. Nonetheless, we should pause to ponder why the famous opening story of Avraham excusing himself from Hashem's presence to do *chessed* with the three *Malachim* seems to be missing from *Tehillim* 11.

Upon close analysis, the opening episode with the three *Malachim* is indeed found in *Tehillim* 11 when we consider its enigmatic first *pasuk*: "בַּה' חָסִיתִי. אֵיךְ תֹּאמְרוּ לְנַפְשִׁי: נוּדִי" – In Hashem I have taken refuge. How [dare] you say about my soul [to me]: Flee."

The opening word of the *Parshah* is "וַיֵּרָא,"[67] which means Hashem "appeared," for indeed Hashem appeared to Avraham specifically then, on the third and most painful day following his circumcision, to be *mevaker cholim*, to visit the sick and recovering Avraham.[68] However, more than the pain of the *bris milah* was Avraham's distress at being unable to show hospitality to passing travelers, as there weren't any due to the oppressive heat brought by Hashem so as not to inconvenience Avraham while he was recuperating. Nonetheless, once Avraham showed Hashem that he was truly aggrieved by the lack of *chessed* opportunities, Hashem brought three angels to Avraham disguised as men.[69]

---

[67] *Bereishis* 18:1.
[68] *Rashi, Bereishis* 18:1, from *Bava Metzia* 86b.
[69] *Rashi, Bereishis* 18:1, from *Bava Metzia* 86b.

Upon seeing the men, Avraham said: "וַיֹּאמַר: אֲדֹנָ-י, אִם נָא מָצָאתִי חֵן בְּעֵינֶיךָ, אַל נָא תַעֲבֹר מֵעַל עַבְדֶּךָ."[70] *Rashi* provides two explanations based on the word "אֲדֹנָ-י." The first is that it is a non-sacred term of "lord" or "master," and that Avraham was speaking to the leader of the three travelers and asking him: "My lord, if I find favor in your eyes, please do not pass from before your servant," but rather stay, you weary travelers, and permit me to bestow kindness upon you.[71] *Rashi's* other explanation is that "אֲדֹנָ-י" here is sacred and refers to Hashem. Avraham was requesting of Hashem: "My Lord, if I find favor in Your eyes, please do not pass from before Your servant," but rather, Hashem, please wait for me while I welcome the visitors and take care of their needs.[72]

Rashi's second explanation is illustrative of the Gemara's statement: "גְּדוֹלָה הַכְנָסַת אוֹרְחִין מֵהַקְבָּלַת פְּנֵי שְׁכִינָה" – Greater is the mitzvah of hospitality toward guests than even *kabbalas p'nei haShechinah* – receiving the face of the Divine Presence of Hashem."[73] As a proof, the Gemara cites the above *pasuk*[74] in which Avraham seemingly asked of Hashem that he be temporarily excused from Hashem's Presence to perform the *chessed* of *hachnasas orchim*.

The above is quite complex and raises many questions, chief among them why Avraham could not perform **both** *hachnasas orchim* and *kabbalas p'nei haShechinah*. After all, was it not Avraham's main purpose in bestowing *chessed* to combine emulating Hashem and spreading the glory of Hashem to the world? If so, is it not at the very least ironic that Avraham would have to *disconnect* from Hashem to emulate and publicize Him?

To make the question even stronger, many *seforim*, especially those of a Chassidic nature, abound with lessons and instructions for achieving and

---

[70] *Bereishis* 18:3.
[71] *Rashi, Bereishis* 18:3.
[72] *Rashi, Bereishis* 18:3, from *Shabbos* 127a.
[73] *Shabbos* 127a.
[74] *Bereishis* 18:3.

CHAPTER 4: VAYEIRA & TEHILLIM 11

maintaining *deveikus ba'Hashem*, cleaving and closeness to Hashem – not just in the privacy of one's home or under the privacy of one's tallis, but rather in any and every situation: when learning, when sharing *divrei Torah*, when relaxing, when working, and even when interacting with ordinary people.[75] If such levels of *deveikus* were attainable 300 years ago and even today, then certainly Avraham Avinu was on a high enough level to maintain that connection as well.

While this is a complicated subject, we can offer a number of answers:

1. *Deveikus ba'Hashem* has many different levels, few of which are as high as the level of *kabbalas p'nei haShechinah* that Avraham Avinu experienced at the start of *Parshas Vayeira,* which was a level akin to the Divine Presence in the Beis HaMikdash. It is an extremely elevated manifestation of Divine closeness that seems to have been initiated by Hashem for a select few. While *deveikus ba'Hashem* can be maintained while simultaneously focusing on other things (albeit with great difficulty, much practice, and with *siyata d'Shmaya*), *kabbalas p'nei haShechinah* cannot, as it requires a person's complete and undivided attention, and anything less would be an insult to Hashem.

2. It is possible that Avraham *was* able to interact with others and still maintain his focus on *kabbalas p'nei haShechinah*, but he asked to take leave of Hashem out of modesty and/or out of proper *middos* and courtesy because he would be adding a second, albeit simultaneous, focus to the equation.

3. It is possible that Avraham *was* able to interact with others and still maintain his focus on *kabbalas p'nei haShechinah*, but he asked to take leave of Hashem through an abundance of caution in case his

---

[75] E.g., *Likuttim Yekarim* of the Maggid of Mezeritch, *simanim* 50–52, 54, 59. See also *Bilvavi Mishkan Evneh*, chelek aleph, for a masterful guide on how to achieve and maintain *deveikus ba'Hashem*.

focus slipped at some point as a result of adding a second, albeit simultaneous, focus to the equation.

4. In the *sefer Nachlas Tzvi* by Rabbi Meshulam Fayish Tzvi Gross, he asks a different question based on the above premise that Avraham was prepared to take leave of the *Shechinah*.[76] From where did Avraham *himself* learn the rule of "גְּדוֹלָה הַכְנָסַת אוֹרְחִין מֵהַקְבָּלַת פְּנֵי שְׁכִינָה"? How did he know that he was doing the right thing? Rabbi Gross suggests that Avraham came to this conclusion through his own *sevarah*, reasoning. There is a *pasuk* in *Tehillim* that states: "כִּי יַעֲמֹד לִימִין אֶבְיוֹן" – For He [Hashem] stands at the right of the destitute."[77] One who requires *hachnasas orchim* is considered an אֶבְיוֹן and is therefore accompanied by Hashem's Divine Presence. Therefore, says Rabbi Gross, when one bestows hospitality on someone in need and welcomes him as a guest, at that moment the bestower of kindness is also simultaneously fulfilling *kabbalas p'nei haShechinah* and welcoming *Hashem*, Who is standing beside the recipient. Avraham Avinu was able to determine that *hachnasas orchim* is greater than *kabbalas p'nei haShechinah* alone, because *hachnasas orchim* includes **both** *hachnasas orchim* and *kabbalas p'nei haShechinah* together. Therefore, when Avraham asked permission to take leave of Hashem's *Shechinah*, he was not doing so at the *expense* of *kabbalas p'nei haShechinah*. Rather, Avraham was trying to take his experiencing of *kabbalas p'nei haShechinah* and to *add* to it the precious mitzvah of *hachnasas orchim*, which would allow him to simultaneously bestow *chessed* and *remain* blessed with *kabbalas p'nei haShechinah*.

We can now return to our original question of why Avraham's experience with the three *Malachim* does not seem to be included in

---

[76] *Nachlas Tzvi, Parshas Vayeira*, p. 35.
[77] *Tehillim* 109:31.

CHAPTER 4: VAYEIRA & TEHILLIM 11

Tehillim 11. Armed with the above understandings, and especially with the *yesod* of Rabbi Gross, we can now suggest that it *is* alluded to in the opening phrase of *Tehillim* 11: "בַּה' חָסִיתִי. אֵיךְ תֹּאמְרוּ לְנַפְשִׁי: נוּדִי" – In Hashem I have taken refuge. How [dare] you say about my soul [to me]: Flee."

To the scoffers and evildoers, it may have appeared that Avraham Avinu was fleeing and departing from the Divine Presence of Hashem to focus on simple stranger who, to make matters worse, actually looked like idol worshippers or even Arabs, all in what would seem to be a terrible affront to Hashem. Yet, the opposite is true: "בַּה' חָסִיתִי" – In Hashem I have taken refuge." Throughout Avraham Avinu's recovery he was surrounded by Hashem's Presence; he was as close to Hashem as humanly possible. In addition, Avraham's level of *kabbalas p'nei haShechinah* was maintained both when he was alone with Hashem and even when he was interacting with the strangers to fulfill the great mitzvah of *hachnasas orchim*, a mitzvah that *itself* caused *kabbalas p'nei haShechinah*.

Furthermore, upon close reading of *Tehillim* 11:1, here it is as if Dovid HaMelech, on Avraham's behalf, took umbrage at the scoffers' accusation.

Alternatively, in light of the *Parshah-Tehillim* connection that is the subject of this *sefer*, it can even be said that Avraham *himself* was taking umbrage at the accusation that he would sacrifice his closeness to Hashem.

As such, we can now read the *pasuk* as follows: "בַּה' חָסִיתִי – I *have* taken refuge in Hashem," and "אֵיךְ תֹּאמְרוּ לְנַפְשִׁי נוּדִי" – How [dare] you say of my soul [to me] that I tried to flee" from closeness to Hashem! How dare you!

Indeed, after the travelers departed, the Torah itself provides the following affirmation: "וְאַבְרָהָם עוֹדֶנּוּ עֹמֵד לִפְנֵי ה'" – Avraham was still standing before Hashem,"[78] indicating that the original closeness between Avraham and Hashem was maintained and that nothing was forfeited or lost.

---

[78] *Bereishis* 18:23.

HOW CAN *AKEIDAS YITZCHAK* BE MISSING?

As was mentioned above, *Parshas Vayeira's* story of the destruction of Sedom is quite evident in *Tehillim* 11, and we have now shown that even Avraham's interaction with Hashem and the three *Malachim* can be found in its words. Taking this one step further, we must consider an additional quandary concerning the content of *Tehillim* 11: How can it be that arguably the most important part of *Parshas Vayeira* – *Akeidas Yitzchak* – is not explicitly referenced in *Tehillim* 11?

Akeidas Yitzchak[79] is the story of the sacrificial binding of Yitzchak by his father at the behest of Hashem, Who was only testing Avraham and at the very last moment ordered him to withdraw his knife from Yitzchak's throat. Yitzchak was promptly replaced on the altar with the famous *ayil*, the ram that Hashem had prepared during the creation of the world[80] and which Avraham found nearby caught in the thicket by its horns. *Akeidas Yitzchak* is the account we recite in the davening and relive each morning in the *Korbanos* section of the *Shacharis* prayer. It is the experience we call upon in the Torah reading of Rosh Hashanah as a merit for Klal Yisrael. It is the event we, and even Hashem, are reminded of when we hear the shofar's blast.

For *Akeidas Yitzchak* not to be emphasized or even mentioned in the *kapitel* that corresponds to *Parshas Vayeira* is truly a dilemma. Perhaps it *is* mentioned, and I missed it; in truth, the nuances of Hashem's Torah are "עָמֹק עָמֹק, מִי יִמְצָאֶנּוּ" – deep, so deep, who can find it?"[81]

---

[79] *Beresishis* 22:1–19.
[80] *Pirkei Avos* 5:8.
[81] *Koheles* 7:24.

But then it suddenly struck me: perhaps the original author of *Tehillim* 11, Dovid HaMelech through Divine inspiration *intentionally omitted* references to *Akeidas Yitzchak* from *Tehillim* 11.

You see, like Avraham, Dovid also endured a God-given test involving a child sacrifice: the rebellion of his own son Avshalom, who sought to kill his father Dovid and usurp the throne of Israel. In the end, however, although Dovid wanted Avshalom's life to be spared, Avshalom was killed. In reaction, Dovid was heartbroken and dejectedly proclaimed: "בְּנִי אַבְשָׁלוֹם בְּנִי בְנִי אַבְשָׁלוֹם, מִי יִתֵּן מוּתִי אֲנִי תַחְתֶּיךָ, אַבְשָׁלוֹם בְּנִי בְנִי" – Oh my son Avshalom, my son, my son Avshalom! Would I had died in your stead, Oh Avshalom, my son, my son!"[82] Rather than celebrating the quelled rebellion, Dovid's victory was transformed into a time of personal, and even national, mourning as he grieved for his son and triggered a confusing time of introspection among the entire Jewish People.

In addition, it must be noted that Avshalom's fatal flaw was his pride, highlighted by pride in his hair. Indeed, the *Navi* discusses Avshalom's pride in his hair in detail, even stating the monetary value of his hair which he cut only once a year and with much fanfare.[83] It was this pride in his hair that led to his being punished, *middah k'neged middah*, via his hair. During the rebellion as he was riding on his mule, his hair became ensnared on a giant overhanging tree, leaving him trapped and hanging from the tree between heaven and earth, unable to free himself, as Gehinnom opened below him. He was trapped because of his hair and was ultimately surrounded and executed by the men of Dovid's general, Yoav, who promptly blew a shofar as a sign of victory.[84]

On one hand, we have *Akeidas Yitzchak*, and on the other hand we have Avshalom's rebellion. The parallels between these two "child sacrifices" and the very different outcomes, with each ultimate *korban* – the *ayil* and

---

[82] *II Shmuel* 19:1.
[83] *II Shmuel* 14:25–26.
[84] *II Shmuel* 18:9–16.

Avshalom – entangled in the thicket by its proud horns and its proud hair respectively, and the connection of each to the shofar, are startling.

While Avraham's story forever solidified his place as *avinu*, our father, the tragic story of Dovid and Avshalom might have been too much for Dovid HaMelech, in his role as a father, to bear, especially when and if compared with the eternal success and merit of *Akeidas Yitzchak*.

That is not to say, *chas v'shalom*, that Dovid HaMelech did not relinquish himself to the *ratzon Hashem* as it related to Avshalom, or that Dovid HaMelech did not value and cherish the merit of *Akeidas Yitzchak*, for of course he did. However, to include the *Akeidah* in *Tehillim* 11 was perhaps too much, too personal, too raw, even for the highest caliber *tzaddik*, even for Dovid HaMelech, to bear. We can now understand why *Tehillim* 11 might be silent on the topic of the *Akeidah*, especially since *Tehillim* was composed with Divine inspiration, thus requiring Dovid to be *b'simchah* to receive that Divine inspiration.

CHAPTER 5

PARSHAS CHAYEI SARAH & TEHILLIM 45

פָּרָשַׁת חַיֵּי שָׂרָה / תְּהִלִּים מה

תְּהִלִּים מה – TEHILLIM 45

1	For the conductor, upon *shoshanim*, by the sons of Korach; a *maskil*, a song of belovedness.	א לַמְנַצֵּחַ עַל שֹׁשַׁנִּים לִבְנֵי קֹרַח; מַשְׂכִּיל שִׁיר יְדִידֹת.
2	My heart is excited with a good matter, I say that my actions are for the king; my tongue is like the quill of a skillful scribe.	ב רָחַשׁ לִבִּי דָּבָר טוֹב, אֹמֵר אָנִי, מַעֲשַׂי לְמֶלֶךְ; לְשׁוֹנִי עֵט סוֹפֵר מָהִיר.
3	You are more beautiful than other men, grace is poured upon your lips; therefore, God has blessed you forever.	ג יָפְיָפִיתָ מִבְּנֵי אָדָם, הוּצַק חֵן בְּשִׂפְתוֹתֶיךָ; עַל כֵּן בֵּרַכְךָ אֱ-לֹהִים לְעוֹלָם.
4	Gird your sword upon your thigh, mighty one, your glory and your majesty.	ד חֲגוֹר חַרְבְּךָ עַל יָרֵךְ, גִּבּוֹר, הוֹדְךָ וַהֲדָרֶךָ.
5	And in your majesty, overcome and ride for the sake of truth and righteous humility; and may you be guided to awesome deeds by your right hand.	ה וַהֲדָרְךָ, צְלַח רְכַב עַל דְּבַר אֱמֶת וְעַנְוָה צֶדֶק; וְתוֹרְךָ נוֹרָאוֹת יְמִינֶךָ.

6	Your arrows are sharp, nations beneath you fall, [the arrows sink] into the heart of the enemies of the king.	ו חִצֶּיךָ שְׁנוּנִים, עַמִּים תַּחְתֶּיךָ יִפְּלוּ בְּלֵב אוֹיְבֵי הַמֶּלֶךְ.
7	Your throne is from God, it is forever and ever; for the scepter of integrity is the scepter of your kingdom.	ז כִּסְאֲךָ אֱ-לֹהִים עוֹלָם וָעֶד; שֵׁבֶט מִישֹׁר, שֵׁבֶט מַלְכוּתֶךָ.
8	You have loved righteousness and hated wickedness; therefore, God has anointed you, your God, with the oil of gladness from among your peers.	ח אָהַבְתָּ צֶּדֶק וַתִּשְׂנָא רֶשַׁע, עַל כֵּן מְשָׁחֲךָ אֱ-לֹהִים אֱ-לֹהֶיךָ, שֶׁמֶן שָׂשׂוֹן מֵחֲבֵרֶךָ.
9	Myrrh, aloes, and cassia are the fragrance of all your garments; from palaces of ivory, from those which have gladdened you.	ט מֹר וַאֲהָלוֹת קְצִיעוֹת כָּל בִּגְדֹתֶיךָ; מִן הֵיכְלֵי שֵׁן, מִנִּי שִׂמְּחוּךָ.
10	Daughters of kings are your visitors; erect stands the queen at your right in the golden jewelry of Ophir.	י בְּנוֹת מְלָכִים בִּיקְּרוֹתֶיךָ; נִצְּבָה שֵׁגַל לִימִינְךָ בְּכֶתֶם אוֹפִיר.
11	Hear, daughter, and see, and incline your ear; forget your people, and the house of your father.	יא שִׁמְעִי בַת וּרְאִי, וְהַטִּי אָזְנֵךְ; וְשִׁכְחִי עַמֵּךְ וּבֵית אָבִיךְ.
12	Then the king will desire your beauty; for he is your master, therefore, bow down to him.	יב וְיִתְאָו הַמֶּלֶךְ יָפְיֵךְ; כִּי הוּא אֲדֹנַיִךְ, וְהִשְׁתַּחֲוִי לוֹ.
13	And daughter of Tyre, with gifts your favor has been sought by the wealthiest of the nation.	יג וּבַת צֹר, בְּמִנְחָה פָּנַיִךְ יְחַלּוּ עֲשִׁירֵי עָם.

14 Every honorable princess dwells within; made of settings of gold is her raiment.	יד כָּל־כְּבוּדָּה בַת־מֶלֶךְ פְּנִימָה; מִמִּשְׁבְּצוֹת זָהָב לְבוּשָׁהּ.
15 In embroidered apparel she will be brought to the king; the maidens in her train, her companions, are also led to you.	טו לִרְקָמוֹת תּוּבַל לַמֶּלֶךְ; בְּתוּלוֹת אַחֲרֶיהָ, רֵעוֹתֶיהָ, מוּבָאוֹת לָךְ.
16 They are brought with gladness and joy; they enter the palace of the king.	טז תּוּבַלְנָה בִּשְׂמָחֹת וָגִיל; תְּבֹאֶינָה בְּהֵיכַל מֶלֶךְ.
17 Succeeding your fathers will be your sons; you will appoint them leaders throughout the land.	יז תַּחַת אֲבֹתֶיךָ יִהְיוּ בָנֶיךָ; תְּשִׁיתֵמוֹ לְשָׂרִים בְּכָל־הָאָרֶץ.
18 I will make your name remembered in all generations; therefore, the nations will acknowledge you forever and ever.	יח אַזְכִּירָה שִׁמְךָ בְּכָל־דֹּר וָדֹר; עַל־כֵּן עַמִּים יְהוֹדֻךָ לְעֹלָם וָעֶד.

PREFACE: LECHA DODI LIKRAS KALLAH

As we usher in the Shabbos of *Parshas Chayei Sarah*, we will say: "לְכָה דוֹדִי לִקְרַאת כַּלָּה, פְּנֵי שַׁבָּת נְקַבְּלָה – Come, my Beloved [Hashem], to greet the bride, the presence of Shabbos, let us welcome/greet." Homiletically, as a special *kavanah* for *Parshas Chayei Sarah*, we can refocus these words as follows:

לְכָה – Come, Avraham Avinu, who obeyed Hashem's commandment of לֶךְ לְךָ and left his old life behind, together with his God-fearing wife, Sarah

Imeinu, who accompanied and aided him; and come, Avraham Avinu, who obeyed Hashem's commandment of לֶךְ לְךָ yet a second time, ready to perform the *Akeidah*, and whose God-fearing son, Yitzchak Avinu, accompanied and aided him.

דּוֹדִי – Hashem's beloved Avraham, who is called a דּוֹד, a יָדִיד, a beloved of Hashem, along with Hashem's beloved Yitzchak, who was the original יְדִיד מִבֶּטֶן, beloved from birth. Whom, together with their beloved Sarah, were *themselves* connected, and connected *others*, to the Ultimate דּוֹד: Our beloved Hashem.

לִקְרַאת כַּלָּה – To greet the bride, Rivkah Imeinu, the כַּלָּה of *Parshas Chayei Sarah*, the first Jewish bride in the Torah, and the first Jewish wedding of Am Yisrael. Rivkah Imeinu, whose marriage to Yitzchak we all joyfully re-experience on Shabbos *Parshas Chayei Sarah*.

פְּנֵי שַׁבָּת – Rivkah, who restored a Shabbos-like presence to the world when her own presence returned the holiness of Sarah Imeinu to the world, for when Rivkah entered her bridal tent Hashem restored the famous light that stayed lit from Shabbos eve to Shabbos eve. Rivkah, whose presence filled Yitzchak's void caused by his mother Sarah's passing, and who provided her new husband with the Shabbos-like *menuchah* – comfort and solace – that he yearned for.

נְקַבְּלָה – Let us greet, together with *Hashem Yisbarach*, Avraham and Sarah, the *chosson* Yitzchak, and *Shabbos Kodesh*, let us greet our Shabbos Bride Rivkah Imeinu, and let us all welcome her into the family once again, on Shabbos *Parshas Chayei Sarah* and always.

INTRODUCTION:
A TRIBUTE TO THE BEAUTY OF AVRAHAM AVINU AND SARAH IMEINU

Tehillim 45 corresponds to *Parshas Chayei Sarah* – the *Parshah* that contains Sarah Imeinu's passing, Avraham's purchase of Me'aras Hamachpeilah as a burial place for Sarah, Avraham's sending of his servant Eliezer to search for a wife for Yitzchak, the discovery of Rivkah Imeinu as the destined bride, and Avraham's remarriage to Hagar – all before Avraham's own passing as memorialized at the *Parshah's* end.

Tehillim 45 can be studied on many levels and from many perspectives, including:

(1) through the eyes of Dovid HaMelech observing his own life;

(2) as a lesson of prerequisites for prospective Jewish kings;

(3) as a prophetic vision and song of praise by the surviving sons of Korach;

(4) as a homage to Torah scholars in general;[1]

(5) as a tribute to the uniqueness of the Jewish soul; and

(6) as a futuristic vision and celebration of the *Melech HaMoshiach*.[2]

Nevertheless, we will analyze *Tehillim* 45 from the perspective of its connection to *Parshas Chayei Sarah*, and in so doing we will discover that just as *Parshas Chayei Sarah* begins with Avraham's eulogy of Sarah Imeinu,[3] *Tehillim* 45 is itself a tribute to, and even a eulogy for, none other than Avraham Avinu as well. Of course, a tribute and eulogy of Avraham Avinu would not be complete without also emphasizing the splendor and

---

[1] *Rashi, Tehillim* 45.
[2] *Radak, Tehillim* 45.
[3] *Bereishis* 23:2.

kedushah of his relationship with Sarah Imeinu and their individual and collective impact on the world, on their children, and on Klal Yisrael forever and ever. As we shall uncover, all the foregoing is intertwined within the poetry and power of *Tehillim* 45.

To set the tone with a clear example from Chazal, the Midrash explains that the expression in *pasuk* 3 of *Tehillim* 45: "יָפְיָפִיתָ מִבְּנֵי אָדָם, הוּצַק חֵן בְּשְׂפְתוֹתֶיךָ – You are more beautiful than other men, grace is poured upon your lips," refers to the physical and spiritual grace and charm of Avraham Avinu.[4]

Moreover, the very first person in the entire Torah to be identified as "beautiful" was Sarah Imeinu, as the *pasuk* reveals: "וַיֹּאמֶר אֶל שָׂרַי אִשְׁתּוֹ הִנֵּה נָא יָדַעְתִּי כִּי אִשָּׁה יְפַת מַרְאֶה אָתְּ – He [Avraham] said to Sarai his wife: Behold, now I have known that you are women of beautiful appearance,"[5] which *Rashi* explains is referring to her physical beauty.[6] It is especially poignant to note that when the Torah conveys Sarah's beauty to us, it does not do so through an objective narrative as is the Torah's usual approach, but rather describes her beauty as seen through the eyes of her own husband, Avraham Avinu, and yet still does so in a matter that underscores the *tzenius* of their relationship.[7]

In addition, when we are first introduced to Rivkah in *Parshas Chayei Sarah*, the *pasuk* describes her as being "טֹבַת מַרְאֶה מְאֹד – exceedingly fair to look upon."[8]

Of course, Judaism does not venerate the physical, and thus the emphasis on the physical beauty of Avraham, Sarah, and Rivkah is just an illustration of the outward manifestation of their spiritual, inner beauty; their charm was a reflection of their *kedushah*.

---

[4] *Bereishis Rabbah* 59:5.
[5] *Bereishis* 12:11.
[6] *Rashi, Bereishis* 12:11.
[7] E.g., *Rashi, Bereishis* 12:11, from *Midrash Tanchuma, Lech Lecha* 5.
[8] *Bereishis* 24:16.

CHAPTER 5: CHAYEI SARAH & TEHILLIM 45

A famous example of this is found at the very beginning of *Parshas Chayei Sarah*. The Torah describes Sarah Imeinu's lifespan as "100 years, and 20 years, and 7 years,"[9] with the numbers divided into separate units to teach us a valuable lesson. *Rashi* explains that at the old age of 100, Sarah was like a 20 year-old with respect to purity from sin; and at the age of 20, she was like a 7 year-old in regard to her natural, unadulterated beauty.[10] *Rashi* concludes with the statement that "all of Sarah's life was equal in goodness."[11] A similar explanation is provided regarding the Torah's description of Avraham's lifespan of "100 years, and 70 years, and 5 years,"[12] which teaches that Avraham left this world without sin despite living to an advanced age and having had many diverse interactions and life experiences.[13]

Indeed, the theme of physical and spiritual יֹפִי, beauty, is interwoven throughout *Tehillim* 45. The *shoresh* of the word יֹפִי appears not only in *pasuk* 3 but is explicitly used again in *pasuk* 12 with the statement "וְיִתְאָו הַמֶּלֶךְ יָפְיֵךְ; כִּי הוּא אֲדֹנַיִךְ" – Then the [K]ing will desire your beauty; for [H]e is your master" in reference to Hashem's love and desire for Avraham and Sarah who were beautiful in every way, including seeing the beauty in others and in everything in Hashem's world around them.

Thus, to summarize by borrowing from a famous and powerful line from *Eishes Chayil*, which by no coincidence Chazal[14] reveal was actually Avraham's eulogy for Sarah Imeinu: "שֶׁקֶר הַחֵן וְהֶבֶל הַיֹּפִי, אִשָּׁה יִרְאַת ה' הִיא תִתְהַלָּל – Grace is deceitful, and יֹפִי – [physical] beauty is vain; but a woman who fears Hashem, she shall be praised."[15] Avraham spoke these

---

[9] *Bereishis* 23:1.
[10] *Rashi, Bereishis* 23:1, from *Bereishis Rabbah* 58:1.
[11] *Rashi, Bereishis* 23:1.
[12] *Bereishis* 25:8.
[13] *Rashi, Bereishis* 25:8.
[14] *Midrash Tanchuma, Chayei Sarah* 4.
[15] *Mishlei* 31:30.

words in accurate admiration and praise of his beloved wife Sarah, and the moral lessons contained therein are also true of Avraham himself.

THE MANY CONNECTIONS BETWEEN PARSHAS CHAYEI SARAH & TEHILLIM 45

Pasuk 1:

לַמְנַצֵּחַ עַל שֹׁשַׁנִּים לִבְנֵי קֹרַח;
מַשְׂכִּיל שִׁיר יְדִידֹת

For the conductor, upon *shoshanim*, by the sons of Korach; a *maskil*, a song of belovedness.

Roses for the Beloved

The phrases "עַל שֹׁשַׁנִּים... שִׁיר יְדִידֹת" – Upon roses... a song of belovedness," opens the *kapitel* with a feeling of love and harmony.

The words "עַל שֹׁשַׁנִּים" are tantamount to a husband lovingly handing his wife a fresh bouquet of roses. Like the *pasuk* in *Shir HaShirim*: "כְּשׁוֹשַׁנָּה בֵּין הַחוֹחִים, כֵּן רַעְיָתִי בֵּין הַבָּנוֹת" – As a rose standing among the thorns, so is My beloved among the daughters,"[16] so does Klal Yisrael stand out among the nations, and so was Sarah Imeinu the most prominent among the women of her time and for all time.

The expression "שִׁיר יְדִידֹת – song of belovedness," further signifies the *shalom bayis* of Avraham and Sarah, who lived יָד בְּיָד, hand-in-hand and in harmony, and who taught others to live a life of יְדִידוּת with Hashem. As the Gemara famously says, when there is *shalom* and harmony between

---

[16] *Shir HaShirim* 2:2.

husband and wife, they merit to have the Presence of the *Shechinah* dwelling in their home.[17]

Pasuk 2:

רָחַשׁ לִבִּי דָּבָר טוֹב,

אֹמֵר אָנִי, מַעֲשַׂי לְמֶלֶךְ;

לְשׁוֹנִי עֵט סוֹפֵר מָהִיר

**My heart is excited with a good matter,
I say that my actions are for the king;
my tongue is like the quill of a skillful scribe.**

The First Jewish King and Queen

The word "לְמֶלֶךְ – for the king," in *pasuk* 2 marks the first of many mentions of the *shoresh* of מַלְכוּת – kingship, in *Tehillim* 45, a *shoresh* that also appears in *pesukim* 6, 7, 10, 12, 14, 15, and 16. Indeed, *Tehillim* 45 is filled with descriptions of royalty, including, for example, the *shoresh* of the word "הָדָר – majesty," which appears in *pesukim* 4 and 5.

In connection with Avraham's purchase of Me'aras Hamachpeilah, *Rashi* teaches that the property was blessed with an ascension in greatness when its ownership was transferred from Efron, a commoner, to Avraham, a king.[18]

Furthermore, as we discussed in Chapter 3 (on *Parshas Lech Lecha* & *Tehillim* 110), during the post-war assembly of the Five Kings at Emek Shaveh that became known as Emek HaMelech, Valley of the King, all the surviving monarchs and representatives of the nations of the world united in appointing Avraham as their sovereign and king. A tremendous *Kiddush HaShem* ensued as Avraham also earned the title *Nesi Elokim*,

---

[17] *Sotah* 17b.
[18] *Rashi, Bereishis* 23:17.

Prince of God, for the nations of the world attributed Avraham's victory to Divine intervention.[19]

Similarly, Sarah was elevated to queenly status by Hashem Himself when her name was changed from Sarai, meaning "my ruler," to Sarah, "ruler over all."[20]

Yet, beyond the prestige of Avraham and Sarah themselves, *pasuk* 2 of *Tehillim* 45 encapsulates their true focus in the phrase: "אֹמֵר אָנִי, מַעֲשַׂי לְמֶלֶךְ – I say that my actions are for the King," all for Hashem and His Kingship. Avraham and Sarah were not preoccupied with their own royal status, as they always saw themselves and their actions as being dedicated to Hashem, the true King, our מֶלֶךְ מַלְכֵי הַמְּלָכִים הַקָּדוֹשׁ בָּרוּךְ הוּא.

The Precision of Avraham's Words and Intentions

"לְשׁוֹנִי עֵט סוֹפֵר מָהִיר – My tongue is like the quill of a skillful scribe" is both a beautiful and insightful expression. For a *Sefer Torah* to be halachically acceptable, it must be written by a *sofer* trained in all the many required *kavanos*, including that the Torah be written *lishmah* and with the proper intentions behind each of Hashem's Divine Names.

Likewise, Avraham Avinu's interactions with mankind were performed *lishmah*, for their "own" sake: for the sake of the mitzvah and for the sake of Hashem, without any ulterior motives such as the desire for reward that cheapen the actions and thought behind them. Like the writings of a skilled and holy *sofer*, Avraham infused precision and perfection in his every word, every act, and every intention.

Pasuk 3:

יְפֵיפִיתָ מִבְּנֵי אָדָם,

הוּצַק חֵן בְּשִׂפְתוֹתֶיךָ;

עַל כֵּן בֵּרַכְךָ אֱ-לֹהִים לְעוֹלָם

---

[19] *Rashi, Bereishis* 14:17.
[20] *Rashi, Bereishis* 17:15, from *Brachos* 13a.

CHAPTER 5: CHAYEI SARAH & TEHILLIM 45

**You are more beautiful than other men,
grace is poured upon your lips;
therefore, God has blessed you forever.**

Avraham's Grace and Beauty on Earth and in Heaven

As noted in the Introduction to this chapter, *pasuk* 3 focuses intently on praise of Avraham; his *middos*, grace, and influence, as well as the spiritual beauty he and his wife Sarah possessed.

The Midrash explains that Avraham was even greater "מִבְּנֵי אָדָם" – greater than the sons of the very *first* man, Adam HaRishon, and greater than the sons of Noach who reestablished mankind after the Flood.[21] As a result, Hashem desired to continuously beautify Avraham with renown on the earth below as well as in the realms of the angels above.[22]

In addition, the imagery in the phrase "הוּצַק חֵן בְּשְׂפְתוֹתֶיךָ" is stunning: Avraham had grace and charm poured upon his lips, and he had grace and charm pouring *from* his lips. Every word that flowed from Avraham's holy mouth made its listeners feel good about themselves, redirected them to see the many gifts in their own lives, and inspired them to praise and thank *Hashem* as the source of this goodness. Clearly, Avraham dedicated himself to "the other" and connecting that "other" to Hashem.

Furthermore, the Midrash[23] describes *pasuk* 3 as praising Avraham as follows: "יָפְיָפִיתָ מִבְּנֵי אָדָם – You are more beautiful than other men: נִתְיַפִּית בָּעֶלְיוֹנִים – You are beautiful in the upper realms,[24] and נִתְיַפִּית בַּתַּחְתּוֹנִים – You are beautiful in the lower realms, as the Bnei Cheis proclaimed in *Parshas Chayei Sarah*: 'נְשִׂיא אֱ-לֹהִים אַתָּה בְּתוֹכֵנוּ – You are a Prince of God in our midst.'"[25] Avraham's beauty was neither merely physical nor merely spiritual; his beauty was transcendent, as it influenced everyone

---

[21] *Midrash Tanchuma, Lech Lecha* 18.
[22] *Bereishis Rabbah* 59:5.
[23] *Bereishis Rabbah* 59:5.
[24] Based on *Yeshayahu* 33:16–17.
[25] *Bereishis* 23:6.

and everything around him and even ascended and impacted heaven above.

Avraham's Abundance of Blessings

The phrase referring to Godly *brachah* in *pasuk* 3: "עַל כֵּן בֵּרַכְךָ אֱ-לֹהִים לְעוֹלָם," certainly alludes to the Torah's statement in *Parshas Chayei Sarah*: "וַה' בֵּרַךְ אֶת אַבְרָהָם בַּכֹּל" – Hashem blessed Avraham with everything,"[26] which *Rashi* explains is the blessing of a son, Yitzchak, born from the union of Avraham and Sarah.[27]

Although it is true that "עַל כֵּן בֵּרַכְךָ אֱ-לֹהִים לְעוֹלָם" refers to Yitzchak Avinu, who was Avraham's righteous heir without whom all of Avraham's blessing would have been for naught,[28] the promise and power of Hashem's *brachah* to Avraham did not begin and end there; rather, *brachah* is a major theme throughout *Parshiyos Lech Lecha*, *Vayeira* and *Chayei Sarah*.

In *Parshas Lech Lecha*, Hashem promised Avraham from the start: "וְאֶעֶשְׂךָ לְגוֹי גָּדוֹל, וַאֲבָרֶכְךָ וַאֲגַדְּלָה שְׁמֶךָ, וֶהְיֵה בְּרָכָה. וַאֲבָרֲכָה מְבָרְכֶיךָ וּמְקַלֶּלְךָ אָאֹר; וְנִבְרְכוּ בְךָ כֹּל מִשְׁפְּחֹת הָאֲדָמָה – And I will make from you a great nation, and I will bless you, and make your name great; and you will be a blessing. And I will bless those who bless you, and the one who curses you I will curse; and all the families of the earth will be blessed through you."[29] There, Hashem's blessings flowed with five separate expressions of "בְּרָכָה" combined into a single statement. Indeed, *Rashi* and other commentators provide unique details about each expression, revealing a large scope of Godly blessings showered upon Avraham.

---

[26] *Bereishis* 24:1.
[27] *Rashi*, *Bereishis* 24:1, from *Tanchuma Yashan, Chayei Sarah* 6.
[28] E.g., *Bereishis* 15:2–3.
[29] *Bereishis* 12:2–3.

CHAPTER 5: CHAYEI SARAH & TEHILLIM 45

In *Parshas Vayeira* toward the conclusion of *Akeidas Yitzchak*, Hashem once again promises Avraham an influx of blessing that includes a three-fold mention of "בְּרָכָה:"

כִּי בָרֵךְ אֲבָרֶכְךָ, וְהַרְבָּה אַרְבֶּה אֶת זַרְעֲךָ כְּכוֹכְבֵי הַשָּׁמַיִם, וְכַחוֹל אֲשֶׁר עַל שְׂפַת הַיָּם; וְיִרַשׁ זַרְעֲךָ אֵת שַׁעַר אֹיְבָיו. וְהִתְבָּרְכוּ בְזַרְעֲךָ כֹּל גּוֹיֵי הָאָרֶץ, עֵקֶב אֲשֶׁר שָׁמַעְתָּ בְּקֹלִי – That I shall surely bless you and surely increase your offspring like the stars of the heavens and like the sand of the seashore; and your offspring shall inherit the gate of its enemy. And all of the nations of the earth shall bless themselves by your offspring, because you have listened to My voice.[30]

Rav Shimshon Pincus explains that this expression is so unique because it is the first blessing in the Torah received by both Avraham and his living successor, Yitzchak, and is a blessing not only received by them personally but also imparted by Hashem to their future descendants. As such, like a flask or bottle that preserves a precious wine, these *pesukim* hold within them the power to preserve and protect all blessings. Therefore, these are vital *pesukim* for us to say each morning in *Shacharis* as part of the *Korbanos tefillah*, as they serve as an impenetrable safeguard of the many blessings and requests that we daven for daily. Rav Pincus adds to the urgency of davening these *pesukim* (and all of *Akeidas Yitzchak*) by stating that just as one will not pour out an abundance of precious wine unless the recipient has a vessel within which to contain it, so too Hashem is more likely to bestow blessing in instances in which the blessing will be properly preserved rather than wasted or lost.[31] It is the recitation of *Akeidas Yitzchak* that preserves our *brachos*, requests, and *tefillos*.

Finally, toward the end of *Parshas Chayei Sarah*, the Torah states: "וַיִּתֵּן אַבְרָהָם אֶת כָּל אֲשֶׁר לוֹ לְיִצְחָק" – Avraham gave all that he had to Yitzchak."[32] *Rashi* explains that Avraham conveyed his own God-given

---

[30] *Bereishis* 22:16–17.
[31] See *Nefesh Shimshon: Siddur HaTefillah*, p. 129 and 132.
[32] *Bereishis* 25:5.

power to dispense *brachah* to Yitzchak.[33] Hashem had previously told Avraham that the power of blessing was placed into Avraham's hand to bless whomever he desired,[34] and Avraham transferred that power of *brachah* to Yitzchak. In addition, there is a contrasting Midrash[35] on the *pasuk*: "וַיְהִי אַחֲרֵי מוֹת אַבְרָהָם, וַיְבָרֶךְ אֱ-לֹהִים אֶת יִצְחָק בְּנוֹ – And it was after the death of Avraham that Hashem blessed Yitzchak his son,"[36] which teaches that although the power to bless was given to Avraham, he was afraid to transmit that power to Yitzchak because he foresaw that the wicked Eisav would come from him. Instead, Avraham said: "יָבֹא בַּעַל הַבְּרָכוֹת וִיבָרֵךְ אֶת אֲשֶׁר יִיטַב בְּעֵינָיו – Let the Master of blessings come and bless whoever will be good in His eyes." As a result, Hashem personally blessed Yitzchak. In the end, both Midrashim make clear that the all-important blessings of Hashem to Avraham were transferred to Yitzchak.

Considering the above examples, the statement in *Tehillim* 45 of "עַל כֵּן בֵּרַכְךָ אֱ-לֹהִים לְעוֹלָם" is clearly applicable to Avraham Avinu, perhaps more so than anyone else in history.

We must also add that Hashem bestowed these blessings *middah k'neged middah*. One of Avraham's primary values was the desire to influence *others* to bless Hashem, as we find regarding the famous אֵשֶׁל of Avraham.[37] There, Avraham would welcome strangers, providing them with food, drink, and lodging, and asking in return only that they fulfill his selfless request: "בָּרְכוּ לְמִי שֶׁאֲכַלְתֶּם מִשֶּׁלּוֹ – Bless Him of Whom you have eaten."[38] As a result, Avraham merited to be the recipient of Hashem's ultimate and unlimited *brachos*.

---

[33] *Rashi, Bereishis* 25:5, from *Bereishis Rabbah* 61:6.
[34] *Rashi, Bereishis* 12:2.
[35] *Bereishis Rabbah* 61:6.
[36] *Bereishis* 25:11.
[37] *Bereishis* 21:33.
[38] *Rashi, Bereishis* 21:33, from *Sotah* 10a.

Pasuk 4:

חֲגוֹר חַרְבְּךָ עַל יָרֵךְ,

גִּבּוֹר, הוֹדְךָ וַהֲדָרֶךָ

**Girst your sword upon your thigh,
mighty one, your glory and your majesty.**

Here, the Sword Remained Sheathed

Although Avraham showed himself to be a mighty warrior in *Parshas Lech Lecha* by defeating the wicked Four Kings, in his dealings with the Bnei Cheis at the start of *Parshas Chayei Sarah* "his sword remained girded at his thigh," sheathed and unbrandished. Avraham approached not by using the tools of war but through his classic attribute of *yashrus* despite his God-given claim to the land and that each passing second meant that his deceased wife lay unburied. There, Avraham's "הוֹדְךָ וַהֲדָרֶךָ – majesty and splendor," was revealed through his peaceful and honest dealings rather than through impatience or violence.

This is further supported by *pasuk* 5 which directly follows: "וַהֲדָרְךָ, צְלַח רְכַב עַל דְּבַר אֱמֶת וְעַנְוָה צֶדֶק – And in your majesty, overcome, and ride for the sake of truth and righteous humility," reemphasizing Avraham's majestic *yashrus* in the form of honesty, humility, and truth rather than the powers of eminent domain or brute force that were also at his disposal.

A Quick Reference to *Bris Milah*

It should also be noted that the use in *pasuk* 4 of the somewhat uncommon word "יָרֵךְ – thigh," is a term mentioned not once but twice in *Parshas Chayei Sarah* in connection with Avraham. Indeed, Avraham uses the same *shoresh* when he states: "שִׂים נָא יָדְךָ תַּחַת יְרֵכִי – Place now your hand under my thigh"[39] in reference to Avraham's high regard for the

---

[39] *Bereishis* 24:2.

precious mitzvah of *bris milah* located near the thigh. This mitzvah was so dear to Avraham because it was his very first commandment and was fulfilled through pain.[40] Shortly thereafter, the Torah describes the oath that Avraham had Eliezer swear, thereby obligating him to find a wife for Yitzchak: "וַיָּשֶׂם הָעֶבֶד אֶת יָדוֹ תַּחַת יֶרֶךְ אַבְרָהָם אֲדֹנָיו, וַיִּשָּׁבַע לוֹ – And the servant placed his hand under the thigh of Avraham his master and swore to him."[41] This was an oath taken all the more seriously since it was specifically sworn over the precious *bris milah*. Indeed, the Midrash explicitly expounds *Tehillim* 45:4 in reference to Avraham and states as follows: "חֲגוֹר חַרְבְּךָ עַל יָרֵךְ, גִּבּוֹר, תֵּן אֶת הַמִּילָה בֵּין יְרֵכֶיךָ, וְהוּא הוֹדְךָ וַהֲדָרֶךָ – Gird your sword upon your thigh, you who desire to be mighty, and perform the *bris milah* between your thighs, and it will be your glory and majesty."[42]

Pasuk 5:
וַהֲדָרְךָ, צְלַח רְכַב
עַל דְּבַר אֱמֶת וְעַנְוָה צֶדֶק;
וְתוֹרְךָ נוֹרָאוֹת יְמִינֶךָ

And in your majesty, overcome and ride for the sake of truth and righteous humility; and may you be guided to awesome deeds by your right hand.

Rivkah and Yitzchak's "First Sight"

Incredibly, the words "רְכַב – ride" and "וַהֲדָרְךָ – your majesty" also tie in beautifully to *Parshas Chayei Sarah* as the *shorashim* of both words are used in the *Parshah*. When Rivkah saw Yitzchak for the very first time from afar, she was riding (רְכַב) towards him, as the *pasuk* says: "וַתִּרְכַּבְנָה

---

[40] *Rashi, Bereishis* 24:2, from *Bereishis Rabbah* 59:8.
[41] *Bereishis* 24:9.
[42] *Midrash Tanchuma, Lech Lecha* 18.

עַל הַגְּמַלִּים – they rode upon the camels."[43] And what did Rivkah see? She saw Yitzchak and beheld that he was "הָדוּר – majestic."[44] Indeed, Rivkah's first sight of Yitzchak left her astonished by the majesty of his holiness because Yitzchak was davening *Minchah* and looked like an awesome and awe-inspiring angel of Hashem.[45]

Pasuk 6:

חִצֶּיךָ שְׁנוּנִים,
עַמִּים תַּחְתֶּיךָ יִפְּלוּ,
בְּלֵב אוֹיְבֵי הַמֶּלֶךְ

**Your arrows are sharp,
nations beneath you fall,
[the arrows sink] into the heart
of the enemies of the king.**

To Crush Your Enemies

The sudden shift to these more violent expressions used in *pasuk* 6, with an emphasis on crushing one's "אוֹיְבִים – enemies," alludes to God's blessing to Avraham in *Parshas Vayeira* at the conclusion of *Akeidas Yitzchak*: "וְיִרַשׁ זַרְעֲךָ אֵת שַׁעַר אֹיְבָיו – And your offspring shall inherit the gate of its enemy."[46]

Furthermore, *Rashi*[47] directly connects that *pasuk* to the similar *brachah* bestowed upon Rivkah by her mother and brother in *Parshas Chayei Sarah*. Just before Rivkah departed to marry Yitzchak they stated:

---

[43] *Bereishis* 24:61.
[44] *Rashi, Bereishis* 24:64, from *Bereishis Rabbah* 60:15.
[45] *Haamek Davar, Bereishis* 24:64, from *Bereishis Rabbah* 60:15.
[46] *Bereishis* 22:17.
[47] *Rashi, Bereishis* 24:60.

"וְיִירַשׁ זַרְעֲךָ אֵת שַׁעַר שֹׂנְאָיו" – And may your offspring inherit the gate of those who hate them."[48]

Yes, the wording in *pasuk* 6 takes a violent turn, but just as we find in the *Al HaNissim tefillah* when we even thank Hashem "וְעַל הַמִּלְחָמוֹת" – for the wars," being on the side of good sometimes requires facing, fighting, and unapologetically crushing the enemies of the good.

Pasuk 7:
כִּסְאֲךָ אֱ-לֹהִים עוֹלָם וָעֶד;
שֵׁבֶט מִישֹׁר, שֵׁבֶט מַלְכוּתֶךָ

**Your throne is from God, it is forever and ever;
for the scepter of integrity
is the scepter of your kingdom.**

Military Might and Monarchy, from the "Almighty" Hashem

Pasuk 6 emphasizes Avraham's might and military prowess, which reached great heights in *Parshas Lech Lecha* and resulted in his coronation over the nations. However, it is *pasuk* 7 that reveals the *reality*: it was Avraham's *"yashrus,"* his uprightness and integrity expressed in the word "מִישֹׁר," and not his militarily conquests, that caused him to be crowned king. Furthermore, it was a kingship not *taken* but *bestowed* upon him by the Almighty Hashem: "כִּסְאֲךָ אֱ-לֹהִים" – Your throne is from God."

Just a Reflection of the Kingship of Hashem

It must be noted that Avraham's kingship was uniquely special precisely because it reflected the Kingship of Hashem. Avraham himself said in *Parshas Chayei Sarah*: "בַּה' אֱ-לֹהֵי הַשָּׁמַיִם וֵא-לֹהֵי הָאָרֶץ" – By Hashem, God of

---

[48] *Bereishis* 24:60.

the heavens and God of the earth."[49] *Rashi* explains that Avraham was declaring that in addition to Hashem having *always* been known as the God of the heavens, it was actually *Avraham* who helped make Hashem known as the God of the *earth*.[50] Indeed, Avraham proudly stated that Hashem became more regularly recognized and discussed by man due to the living *Kiddush HaShem* that Avraham and his wife Sarah exemplified and through their joint efforts to inspire and convert men and women, respectively, to the service of Hashem.[51] The greatness of Avraham was that the greatness was not his; it was Hashem's. All Avraham did was reflect that greatness and shine its light back onto Hashem for all to see.

Pasuk 8:

אָהַבְתָּ צֶּדֶק וַתִּשְׂנָא רֶשַׁע,

עַל כֵּן מְשָׁחֲךָ אֱ-לֹהִים אֱ-לֹהֶיךָ,

שֶׁמֶן שָׂשׂוֹן מֵחֲבֵרֶךָ

You have loved righteousness and hated wickedness; therefore, God has anointed you, your God, with the oil of gladness from among your peers.

Avraham's Love: For Others and for Hashem

This *pasuk* seems to be a tailor-made description of Avraham Avinu, and the Midrash confirms it.

The Midrash specifically states that "אָהַבְתָּ צֶּדֶק וַתִּשְׂנָא רֶשַׁע" refers to Avraham: Avraham, who tried to find some modicum of merit even in the nefarious people of Sedom; Avraham, in whom Hashem recognized the special characteristic of loving to justify the actions of others; Avraham, whose only hatred was the hatred of finding guilt in Hashem's creations.

---

[49] *Bereishis* 24:3.
[50] *Rashi, Bereishis* 24:3, from *Bereishis Rabbah* 59:8.
[51] *Rashi, Bereishis* 12:5, from *Sanhedrin* 99b.

As a reward, "עַל כֵּן מְשָׁחֲךָ אֱ-לֹהִים אֱ-לֹהֶיךָ, שֶׁמֶן שָׂשׂוֹן מֵחֲבֵרֶיךָ," Hashem anointed Avraham with the oil of gladness and optimism in a measure more abundant than He bequeathed to anyone else. Avraham, as the quintessential advocate of all people, even including the wicked, was worthy of being anointed as their king.[52]

In addition, on the word "מֵחֲבֵרֶיךָ – from among your peers," the Midrash[53] compares Avraham to others before him and explains that Hashem said to Avraham: "From the time of Noach until you, over the course of a full ten generations, I did not speak to even a single one of them, except to you, as it says: "וַיֹּאמֶר ה' אֶל אַבְרָם, לֶךְ לְךָ מֵאַרְצְךָ וּמִמּוֹלַדְתְּךָ וּמִבֵּית אָבִיךָ אֶל הָאָרֶץ אֲשֶׁר אַרְאֶךָּ – Hashem said to Avram, 'Go for yourself from your land, from your birthplace, and from your father's house to the land that I will show you.'"[54] Avraham eclipsed all others; he had no equal among mankind.

Finally, the inclusion of the word "אָהַבְתָּ – you loved," is particularly striking here, for Avraham is widely known as the exemplar of the characteristic of אַהֲבַת ה', love of God. Hashem Himself attests to this through Yeshayahu HaNavi: "אַבְרָהָם אֹהֲבִי – Avraham, who loved Me,"[55] which we read in the *Haftarah* for *Parshas Lech Lecha*. Even more poignantly, Hashem *reciprocated* Avraham's love, as seen for example in the daily *Korbanos* section of davening when we refer to ourselves as "בְּנֵי אַבְרָהָם אֹהַבְךָ – the children of Avraham whom You love," and in the Friday night *zemer Kol Mekadesh*, when we proudly self-identify as "דּוֹרְשֵׁי ה' זֶרַע אַבְרָהָם אוֹהֲבוֹ – Seekers of Hashem, offspring of Avraham His beloved."

---

[52] *Bereishis Rabbah* 49:9.
[53] *Bereishis Rabbah* 49:9.
[54] *Bereishis* 12:1.
[55] *Yeshayahu* 41:8.

Pasuk 9:

מֹר וַאֲהָלוֹת קְצִיעוֹת כָּל בִּגְדֹתֶיךָ;
מִן הֵיכְלֵי שֵׁן, מִנִּי שִׂמְּחוּךָ

**Myrrh, aloes, and cassia are the fragrance
of all your garments; from palaces of ivory,
from those which have gladdened you.**

The *Milah* and Fine *Middos* are More Fragrant than Myrrh

The *Midrash Tanchuma* explains that this *pasuk* refers to Avraham who is called "מר," one of the aromatic ingredients of the *ketores*, the spice-incense offering burned twice each day in the Beis HaMikdash on the *Mizbeiach HaZahav*, the Golden Altar. Specifically, says the Midrash, this comparison teaches that Avraham's cut foreskin and blood was more pleasant to Hashem than even the sweet fragrances of myrrh and *levonah*.[56]

Rav Shimshon Rafael Hirsch explains that the sweet-smelling and far-reaching fragrance of the *ketores* symbolizes the Jewish People's responsibility to make *all* their actions pleasing to Hashem. Even our mundane perfumes, garments, and homes must be used to bring joy to others and to inspire and elevate them. This is an extremely high bar to reach, but is a level that we, as the children of Avraham, can attain.

Pasuk 10:

בְּנוֹת מְלָכִים בְּיִקְּרוֹתֶיךָ;
נִצְּבָה שֵׁגַל לִימִינְךָ בְּכֶתֶם אוֹפִיר

**Daughters of kings are your visitors;
erect stands the queen at your right in the golden
jewelry of Ophir.**

---

[56] *Midrash Tanchuma, Vayeira* 2.

From King's Daughter to Maidservant

The phrase "בְּנוֹת מְלָכִים" is a praise of both Avraham and Sarah, to whom a "daughter of kings" was delivered in the form of Hagar, daughter of Pharaoh, ruler of Egypt. *Rashi* explains in *Parshas Lech Lecha* that when Pharaoh saw the miracles performed for Sarah at his expense, he said: "Better that my daughter should be a maidservant in the house of Sarah and not the main wife in another household," and presented his daughter to Sarah as a servant.[57] In addition, the word "שֵׁגַל" refers to a Queen as well as to a concubine,[58] the latter of which Hagar eventually became to Avraham at Sarah's behest.[59]

Pasuk 11:

שִׁמְעִי בַת וּרְאִי, וְהַטִּי אָזְנֵךְ;
וְשִׁכְחִי עַמֵּךְ וּבֵית אָבִיךְ

**Hear, daughter, and see, and incline your ear;
forget your people, and the house of your father.**

Willingness to Leave One's World and Wants Behind

The *Midrash*[60] states that this *pasuk* is a direct parallel to Hashem's first recorded commandment to Avraham: "לֶךְ לְךָ מֵאַרְצְךָ וּמִמּוֹלַדְתְּךָ וּמִבֵּית אָבִיךָ, אֶל הָאָרֶץ אֲשֶׁר אַרְאֶךָּ – Go for yourself from your land, from your birthplace, and from your father's house to the land that I will show you."[61] In addition, the *Midrash* explains that "וְשִׁכְחִי עַמֵּךְ וּבֵית אָבִיךְ" refers specifically to Avraham's rejection of idol worship.

Of course, Sarah was always by Avraham's side and shared his religious devotion and commitment to serving Hashem as the one true

---

[57] *Rashi, Bereishis* 16:1.
[58] *Rashi, Devarim* 28:30; *Rosh Hashanah* 4a.
[59] *Bereishis* 16:2.
[60] *Midrash Tanchuma, Lech Lecha* 3.
[61] *Bereishis* 12:1.

CHAPTER 5: CHAYEI SARAH & TEHILLIM 45

God, and it was she who encouraged and personally presided over the conversion of women into the service of Hashem.[62] Sarah was a true "בַּת" of Hashem and influenced many other women to become the same.

Furthermore, "שִׁמְעִי בַת וּרְאִי, וְהַטִּי אָזְנֵךְ; וְשִׁכְחִי עַמֵּךְ וּבֵית אָבִיךְ" – Hear, daughter, and see, and incline your ear; forget your people, and the house of your father," can just as easily be said about Rivkah, who in *Parshas Chayei Sarah* left her entire family, land, and life to follow a stranger (Eliezer) in order to marry Yitzchak who was also a stranger to her.

Rivkah: Inclined Toward *Chessed*

This *pasuk's* use of the expression "וְהַטִּי אָזְנֵךְ" – incline your ear" deserves analysis regarding its connection to Rivkah. Rivkah was chosen as a match for Yitzchak because of her *chessed* in providing water to Eliezer at his request and then also volunteering to provide water to his many camels. When Eliezer davened to Hashem and established a sign to determine the worthy wife for Yitzchak, Eliezer used a similar expression that included the word "הַטִּי" and stated: "הַטִּי נָא כַדֵּךְ וְאֶשְׁתֶּה" – Incline please your jug so that I may drink."[63]

This symmetry of words further supports the expectation of Eliezer that one's willingness to bend and share one's *water* is a sign of willingness to also bend and share one's "אָזְנֵךְ," *ear*, i.e., one's time, energy, and focus with someone else who is in need, reflecting both a desire to perform *chessed* of a physical nature as well as *chessed* of an emotional and spiritual nature.

These are all characteristics Rivkah possessed even at a young age and were further proven when she willingly left her old world behind to join the family of Avraham and Sarah, renowned for their unparalleled altruism and *chessed*.

---

[62] *Rashi, Bereishis* 12:5, from *Sanhedrin* 99b.
[63] *Bereishis* 24:14.

Pasuk 12:
וְיִתְאָו הַמֶּלֶךְ יָפְיֵךְ;
כִּי הוּא אֲדֹנַיִךְ, וְהִשְׁתַּחֲוִי לוֹ
**Then the king will desire your beauty;
for he is your master, therefore, bow down to him.**

Avraham: The Grade "A" of Adam and *Adon*

This *pasuk* as translated above can be understood as referring to Avraham because it contains the word "יָפְיֵךְ" and thus refers to the יוֹפִי and beauty of Avraham discussed in the Introduction to this chapter and in *pasuk* 3 above. Furthermore, as discussed in Chapter 3 in the context of *Parshas Lech Lecha* and *Tehillim* 110, Avraham was crowned by the leaders of his generation as "מֶלֶךְ" over the world. Furthermore, the *shoresh* of "אֲדֹנַיִךְ" bespeaks a connection unique to Avraham, for the Gemara teaches that it was Avraham who was the very first person to refer to Hashem as "אָדוֹן – Master."[64]

That *pasuk* 12 contains the words "אֲדֹנַיִךְ – your master" and "וְהִשְׁתַּחֲוִי – bow" is even more remarkable because during Avraham's interaction with the Bnei Cheis in *Parshas Chayei Sarah*, they refer to Avraham specifically as "master" using the *shoresh* of the word אָדוֹן a total of three times,[65] and Avraham twice bows down to them as a sign of modesty, mutual appreciation, and respect.[66]

On an even deeper level, this *pasuk* can be understood through *Hashem's* perspective as a declaration of His love for Avraham. With this approach, we can translate as follows: "וְיִתְאָו הַמֶּלֶךְ יָפְיֵךְ; כִּי הוּא אֲדֹנַיִךְ – Then the King [Hashem] will desire your [Avraham's] beauty; for He [Hashem] is your [Avraham's] Master." Clearly, Avraham possessed pristine *middos* on a supreme level. It is Avraham of whom it was said in *pasuk* 3:

---

[64] *Brachos* 7b.
[65] *Bereishis* 23:6, 11, and 15.
[66] *Bereishis* 23:7 and 12.

"יְפָיְפִיתָ מִבְּנֵי אָדָם – You are more beautiful than other men" – your *middos tovos* are beautiful in the upper realms, and you are beautiful in the lower realms as exemplified by Avraham's conduct with the Bnei Cheis at the start of *Parshas Chayei Sarah*.[67] Furthermore, such exemplary conduct serves as a catalyst for Hashem to *continuously* beautify Avraham and bless him with fame in both the earthly and heavenly worlds.[68] Amazingly, doing so was for Avraham's benefit as well as for *Hashem's* benefit (*kiv'yachol*), for Avraham was perceived by the world as Hashem's representative. As such, honor given to Avraham was tantamount to honor of Hashem, a fact recognized by the Bnei Cheis who referred to Avraham as "נְשִׂיא אֱ-לֹהִים – Prince of God."[69]

Finally, considering the above, the concluding words in *pasuk* 12 of *Tehillim* 45 can be understood in two ways:

(1) "וְהִשְׁתַּחֲוִי לוֹ" means "therefore bow to Him [Hashem]," declaring that even Avraham should/will lovingly bow to Hashem; and

(2) "וְהִשְׁתַּחֲוִי לוֹ" means "therefore [other nations should] bow to him [to Avraham]," because as a result of Hashem's intimate relationship with Avraham, the subservience of the nations to Avraham is actually a manifestation of their true desire to serve Hashem.

Pasuk 13:
וּבַת צֹר, בְּמִנְחָה
פָּנַיִךְ יְחַלּוּ עֲשִׁירֵי עָם
**And daughter of Tyre, with gifts
your favor has been sought
by the wealthiest of the nation.**

---

[67] *Bereishis Rabbah* 59:5.
[68] *Bereishis Rabbah* 59:5.
[69] *Bereishis* 23:6.

PARSHAH & TEHILLIM HAND IN HAND

Only Gifts from God

The phrase "בְּמִנְחָה פָנֶיךָ יְחַלּוּ עֲשִׁירֵי עָם" – With gifts your favor has been sought by the wealthiest of the nation" alludes to the many times that Avraham was showered with wealth and gifts from world leaders: by Pharaoh in *Bereishis* 12:15; by Melech Sedom in *Bereishis* 14:21 (but which Avraham declined); by Avimelech to Avraham in *Bereishis* 20:14; and by Avimelech to Sarah in *Bereishis* 20:16.

Ultimately, however, Avraham divested himself of these gifts and riches that had come from less holy or even unholy sources by relinquishing them to the Bnei Keturah (Avraham's other sons from Hagar). Instead, Avraham chose to retain only those blessings that were overtly provided to him directly from Hashem.[70]

Pasuk 14:
כָּל כְּבוּדָּה בַת מֶלֶךְ פְּנִימָה;
מִמִּשְׁבְּצוֹת זָהָב לְבוּשָׁהּ

**Every honorable princess dwells within;
made of settings of gold is her raiment.**

The *Tzenius* of the Jewish Woman

The expression "כָּל כְּבוּדָּה בַת מֶלֶךְ פְּנִימָה" – Every honorable princess dwells within," is a classic reference to the *tzenius* and modesty of the Jewish woman, as exemplified by Sarah Imeinu and Rivkah Imeinu.

In *Parshas Vayeira*'s discussion between Avraham and the three guests, the Torah recounts: "וַיֹּאמְרוּ אֵלָיו, אַיֵּה שָׂרָה אִשְׁתֶּךָ; וַיֹּאמֶר, הִנֵּה בָאֹהֶל – They said to him: 'Where is Sarah your wife?' And he said 'Behold, in the tent.'"[71] *Rashi* explains that the angels knew full well where Sarah Imeinu was, but that they nonetheless asked Avraham of her whereabouts in order

---

[70] *Rashi, Bereishis* 25:6.
[71] *Bereishis* 18:9.

to highlight Sarah's modesty, further endearing her to her husband.[72] *Rashi* also comments that Avraham's response of "Behold, in the tent," is comparable to saying "She is modest,"[73] and other commentators say it is equivalent to saying "In the tent, *of course!*" indicating that Avraham was well aware of Sarah's modesty and was extremely proud of it.[74]

Interestingly, when we are first introduced to Rivkah, she was *not* "in the tent" but rather was being utilized, and perhaps exploited, by her wicked family as a water-drawer and carrier. This forced her out of the home and to the water wells, which were frequented by men of the field and as such were not safe places for a young girl to be going alone. Nevertheless, the Torah tells us that Rivkah was not only beautiful but also "בְּתוּלָה וְאִישׁ לֹא יְדָעָהּ,"[75] chaste and virtuous despite the environment in which she lived and worked.

Indeed, the expression "בַּת מֶלֶךְ" very much endures even today as an expression of the Jewish woman's quality of modesty and as an inspirational reminder to each Jewish female to safeguard and preserve that modesty. For after all, like Sarah Imeinu and Rivkah Imeinu before her, she is the daughter of the מֶלֶךְ מַלְכֵי הַמְּלָכִים, our King, King of Kings: Hashem.

Pasuk 15:
לִרְקָמוֹת תּוּבַל לַמֶּלֶךְ;

בְּתוּלוֹת אַחֲרֶיהָ, רֵעוֹתֶיהָ, מוּבָאוֹת לָךְ

In embroidered apparel she will be brought to the king;
the maidens in her train, her companions,
are also led to you.

---

[72] *Rashi, Bereishis* 18:9, from *Bava Metzia* 87a.
[73] *Rashi, Bereishis* 18:9.
[74] See *Divrei Dovid* and *Emes L'Yaakov*.
[75] *Bereishis* 24:16.

PARSHAH & TEHILLIM HAND IN HAND

Rivkah as *Kallah*: Her Bridal Canopy, Train, and Veil

The *Malbim* on *Tehillim* 45 interprets this *pasuk* as referring to an embroidered bridal canopy, a *chuppah*, to which the bride is escorted by her friends. What a fitting image for *Parshas Chayei Sarah*, the *Parshah* of tribute to the Jewish home of Avraham and Sarah as well as the story of the marriage of Yitzchak and Rivkah.

In addition, in describing Rivkah's journey to meet her future husband, the Torah tells us: "וַתָּקָם רִבְקָה וְנַעֲרֹתֶיהָ, וַתִּרְכַּבְנָה עַל הַגְּמַלִּים, וַתֵּלַכְנָה אַחֲרֵי הָאִישׁ; וַיִּקַּח הָעֶבֶד אֶת רִבְקָה וַיֵּלַךְ – And Rivkah arose with her maidens, and they rode upon the camels and went after the man; the slave took Rivkah and went,"[76] which describes Rivkah and her wedding procession's journey with Eliezer to meet Yitzchak. This *pasuk* parallels *Tehillim* 45:15, which describes a beautifully clothed woman escorted, along with her companions, to the king – in this case Yitzchak – whose royal status as *tzaddik* and son of Avraham was further elevated with the added status of "חָתָן דּוֹמֶה לְמֶלֶךְ – a groom has a status of a king."[77]

Finally, the reference to "לִרְקָמוֹת," which is a type of feminine clothing, alludes to Rivkah's use of her own clothing – a veil – to cover herself immediately upon being told that she was in Yitzchak's line of sight, as the Torah states: "וַתִּקַּח הַצָּעִיף, וַתִּתְכָּס – She then took the veil and she covered herself"[78] in an act of modesty.

Pasuk 16:
תּוּבַלְנָה בִּשְׂמָחֹת וָגִיל;
תְּבֹאֶינָה בְּהֵיכַל מֶלֶךְ
**They are brought with gladness and joy;
they enter the palace of the king.**

---

[76] *Bereishis* 24:61.
[77] *Pirkei D'Rabi Eliezer, perek* 16.
[78] *Bereishis* 24:65.

CHAPTER 5: CHAYEI SARAH & TEHILLIM 45

Simcha In Hashem's Palace and In Our Homes

The references to "שִׂמְחָה" and joy are allusions to the dictum: "עִבְדוּ אֶת ה' בְּשִׂמְחָה; בֹּאוּ לְפָנָיו בִּרְנָנָה – Serve Hashem with gladness; come before Him with joyous song,"[79] which undoubtably permeated Avraham and Sarah's home. Their home was built on the foundations of *chessed*, connection to Hashem, and performance of His mitzvos, and as such, although it may have looked like a simple tent, it was a "הֵיכַל מֶלֶךְ" – palace of the King [Hashem]" here on earth.

This *pasuk* also alludes to the "שִׂמְחָה" of the "שִׂמְחַת חָתָן וְכַלָּה – the gladness/celebration of the groom and bride" experienced by Yitzchak and Rivkah in *Parshas Chayei Sarah*. Fittingly, the expression of "שִׂמְחַת וְגִיל" utilizes two of the same words said to newlyweds in blessing and praise throughout their days of *Sheva Brachos*: אֲשֶׁר בָּרָא שָׂשׂוֹן וְשִׂמְחָה, חָתָן וְכַלָּה, גִּילָה רִנָּה דִּיצָה וְחֶדְוָה, אַהֲבָה וְאַחְוָה, וְשָׁלוֹם וְרֵעוּת – Blessed are You, Hashem... Who created joy and gladness (שִׂמְחָה), groom and bride, rejoicing (גִּילָה), glad song, pleasure and delight, love and brotherhood, and peace and companionship."[80] Furthermore, the phrase "הֵיכַל מֶלֶךְ – palace of the King [Hashem]," is reminiscent of the expression: "שֶׁהַשִּׂמְחָה בִּמְעוֹנוֹ – In Whose [Hashem's] palace is gladness," said at the start of *Bircas Hamazon* during *Sheva Brachos*.[81]

To Laugh at the Day of Death

On an even deeper level, in the context of *Parshas Chayei Sarah* the emphasis in *pasuk* 16 to the experience of happiness and joy in the words "שִׂמְחַת וְגִיל" as one enters the royal inner chambers known as the "הֵיכַל מֶלֶךְ," is an allusion to the famous expression in *Eishes Chayil*: "וַתִּשְׂחַק לְיוֹם אַחֲרוֹן – And she laughs at her last day,"[82] the day of death.

---

[79] *Tehillim* 100:2.
[80] *Kesubos* 8a.
[81] *Kesubos* 8a.
[82] *Mishlei* 31:25.

Originally said by Avraham as part of his eulogy for Sarah,[83] it is a declaration that Sarah was so righteous that she had nothing to fear even in death, for surely a most elevated place is reserved for her in the World to Come.

Thus, the words "תְּבֹאֶינָה בְּהֵיכַל מֶלֶךְ," can be interpreted as an expression of welcoming Sarah Imeinu into the heavenly palace of the King of Kings in Gan Eden, in which her passing from this world to the next was accompanied not by sadness or regret, but by "שְׂמָחֹת וָגִיל," great gladness and joy, paralleling the laughter and joy of "וַתִּשְׂחַק לְיוֹם אַחֲרוֹן."

Pasuk 17:
תַּחַת אֲבֹתֶיךָ יִהְיוּ בָנֶיךָ;
תְּשִׁיתֵמוֹ לְשָׂרִים בְּכָל הָאָרֶץ

**Succeeding your fathers will be your sons;
you will appoint them leaders throughout the land.**

Proper Succession from Father to Son, and the Mother's Role Therein

This *pasuk* corresponds to the conclusion of *Parshas Chayei Sarah* where the Torah tells us that Avraham sent away the Bnei Keturah who were his other sons from Hagar[84] and gave all that he had to the righteous Yitzchak,[85] including both material wealth and the God-given power to bestow blessings upon others.[86] This was the culmination of Sarah's insistence: "כִּי לֹא יִירַשׁ בֶּן הָאָמָה הַזֹּאת עִם בְּנִי עִם יִצְחָק" – For the son of that slave woman shall not inherit with my son, with Yitzchak,"[87] and was

---

[83] *Midrash Tanchuma, Chayei Sarah* 4.
[84] *Bereishis* 25:6.
[85] *Bereishis* 25:5.
[86] *Rashi, Bereishis* 25:5; *Bereishis Rabbah* 61:6.
[87] *Bereishis* 21:10.

CHAPTER 5: CHAYEI SARAH & TEHILLIM 45

the fulfillment of Hashem's promise: "כִּי בְיִצְחָק יִקָּרֵא לְךָ זָרַע,"[88] that through Yitzchak, and only through Yitzchak, will offspring be considered from Avraham. These offspring were to become "שָׂרִים בְּכָל הָאָרֶץ – leaders throughout the land" in the form of the Jewish People, and who would emulate not only their forefather Avraham, but their matriarch Sarah, whose very name "שָׂרָה" bears the same *shoresh* as "שָׂרִים" and stands for righteous authority and leadership on a global scale.[89]

Similarly, the *Haftarah* to *Parshas Chayei Sarah*[90] focuses on Batsheva's frankness with her husband Dovid HaMelech when advocating for their son Shlomo to be the one to fill Dovid's place on the throne of Am Yisrael. While the holy Nasan HaNavi echoed Batsheva's words, and while Dovid certainly was aware that it was the *ratzon Hashem* that Shlomo succeed him as king, we must also consider the content and tone of the concluding *pesukim* of the *Haftarah*. Those words poignantly convey the vast love and respect shared between Dovid and Batsheva. It is therefore apparent that Dovid's loyalty and devotion toward Batsheva also played a strong role in his decision to select their son Shlomo as his successor.[91]

Furthermore, in *Parshas Toldos*, it was Rivkah who was the driving force in ensuring that the righteous Yaakov, rather than the wicked Eisav, would receive Yitzchak's Godly blessings. In so doing, Rivkah helped guaranty that the three-fold link in the chain of Am Yisrael beginning with

---

[88] *Bereishis* 21:12.
[89] *Rashi, Bereishis* 17:15; *Brachos* 13a.
[90] *I Melachim* 1:1–31.
[91] It is worth noting that according to the *Zohar Hakadosh* (*Zohar Chadash, Chukas* 61), the opening phrase of *Tehillim* 45: "שִׁיר יְדִידֹת" – Song of belovedness" conveys a *double* connotation of belovedness by using the plural word יְדִידֹת. There, Dovid HaMelech received prophesy of another song that utilized the double expression of שִׁיר – that of שִׁיר הַשִּׁירִים – which would ultimately be written by Shlomo HaMelech, Dovid's son with Batsheva, in recognition and praise of Hashem and Bnei Yisrael.

Avraham and continuing to Yitzchak would intertwine with Yaakov and be eternally augmented through Yaakov's holy sons.

Finally, this theme of ensuring continuity from father to son is also found in connection with Rivkah in *Parshas Chayei Sarah*, as seen in her family's parting blessing to her: "אֲחֹתֵנוּ, אַתְּ הֲיִי לְאַלְפֵי רְבָבָה – Our sister, may you come to be thousands of myriads."[92] According to *Rashi*, this was a blessing that Hashem's post-*Akeida brachah* for Avraham (and Yitzchak) to become a numerous and great nation should be fulfilled *only* through Rivkah.[93] And indeed it was, in the form of Rivkah's son Yaakov who is the focal point of the *parshiyos* that follow.

In all such instances, it was the Jewish *mothers*, Sarah, Rivkah, and Batsheva, who ensured the proper succession from father to son, and in doing so, safeguarded the continuity and *kedushah* of Am Yisrael.

Pasuk 18:
אַזְכִּירָה שִׁמְךָ בְּכָל דֹּר וָדֹר;
עַל כֵּן עַמִּים יְהוֹדוּךָ לְעֹלָם וָעֶד

I will make your name remembered in all generations; therefore, the nations will acknowledge you forever and ever.

Remember the Name

On one level, the phrase "אַזְכִּירָה שִׁמְךָ בְּכָל דֹּר וָדֹר – I will make your name remembered in all generations" refers to the remembrance of *Avraham's* name in every generation.

Even more importantly, however, this refers to the remembrance of *Hashem's* Name in every generation.

---

[92] *Bereishis* 24:60.
[93] *Rashi, Bereishis* 24:60.

In truth, such remembrances are essentially one and the same, as the Torah reveals to us in a powerful *pasuk* in *Parshas Vayeira*: "כִּי יְדַעְתִּיו לְמַעַן אֲשֶׁר יְצַוֶּה אֶת בָּנָיו וְאֶת בֵּיתוֹ אַחֲרָיו, וְשָׁמְרוּ דֶּרֶךְ ה', לַעֲשׂוֹת צְדָקָה וּמִשְׁפָּט".[94] According to *Rashi*, this *pasuk* means that Hashem declared that He knows and cherishes Avraham because Avraham will command his sons about Hashem and will teach them to keep Hashem's ways by performing acts of charity and justice.[95] In other words, Hashem ultimately chose Avraham because Avraham's priority was to ensure the continuity of the דֶּרֶךְ ה', the ways of Hashem.

Thus, Avraham epitomized both aspects of "אַזְכִּירָה שִׁמְךָ בְּכָל דֹּר וָדֹר," for it was Avraham's goal to ensure that his own actions and reputation be forever associated with, and give glory to, Hashem, and that Hashem's Name be remembered and cherished by all generations to come.

TEHILLIM 45 AND THE STORY OF YITZCHAK AND RIVKAH

It must be noted that in focusing primarily upon Avraham and Sarah, *Tehillim* 45 does not emphasize the more major focus of *Parshas Chayei Sarah*: the story of Eliezer's mission in finding Rivkah as a wife for Yitzchak. Remarkably, this mission spans a grand total of 67 *pesukim*, approximately two-thirds of the *Parshah*.

We can suggest that since the purpose of Yitzchak's shidduch was to ensure the continuity of Avraham's family and the continuation of the

---

[94] *Bereishis* 18:19.
[95] *Rashi, Bereishis* 18:19.

nascent Jewish People, Yitzchak and Rivkah's union was an extension of Avraham and Sarah's story. In other words, in *Tehillim* 45 Yitzchak and Rivkah's story is not eclipsed by Avraham and Sarah's, but rather is part and parcel of it.

As a support to this, the Torah's very detailed account of Eliezer's mission culminates with the *pasuk*: "וַיְבִאֶהָ יִצְחָק הָאֹהֱלָה שָׂרָה אִמּוֹ, וַיִּקַּח אֶת רִבְקָה וַתְּהִי לוֹ לְאִשָּׁה, וַיֶּאֱהָבֶהָ; וַיִּנָּחֵם יִצְחָק אַחֲרֵי אִמּוֹ – And Yitzchak brought her into the tent, Sarah his mother; he married Rivkah, and she became his wife, and he loved her. And Yitzchak was consoled after his mother."[96] Noting the unusual phraseology of "into the tent, Sarah his mother," *Rashi* explains that Yitzchak brought Rivkah into the tent and behold, she was like Sarah his mother. This meant that Rivkah became the mirror image of his mother Sarah, for when Sarah was alive, a candle would remain burning from Shabbos eve to Shabbos eve; Divine blessing would be bestowed upon the family's dough; and a cloud, representing the *Shechinah*, Hashem's Divine Presence, would be constantly stationed over Avraham and Sarah's tent. When Sarah died, all three of these holy miracles ceased. However, with the arrival of Rivkah, each of these three blessings returned.[97]

Furthermore, in connection with the above-quoted *pasuk*,[98] the *Zohar Hakadosh*[99] reveals that just as Yitzchak's facial appearance was like Avraham's such that whoever saw Yitzchak knew without a doubt that Avraham sired Yitzchak, so too Rivkah's appearance was identical to that of Sarah. More imporantly, the *Zohar* says that the specific expression of "שָׂרָה אִמּוֹ" teaches that Rivkah was like Sarah in all her holy actions and refined conduct. The Brisker Rav adds that although immediately upon his return Eliezer informed Yitzchak of the many miracles performed for him in finding Rivkah and bringing her back, Yitzchak did not take Rivkah for

---

[96] *Bereishis* 24:67.
[97] *Rashi, Bereishis* 24:67, from *Bereishis Rabbah* 60:16.
[98] *Bereishis* 24:67.
[99] See *Sefer B'Shem Omro, Bereishis* 24:67.

CHAPTER 5: CHAYEI SARAH & TEHILLIM 45

a wife until he first saw her holy actions and *middos tovos*.[100] Finally, as the *Ramban* explains, Yitzchak was deeply pained by the loss of his mother and could find no comfort until Rivkah entered his life. For Rivkah was like Sarah his mother in that she possessed the same righteousness and talents, and as such, Yitzchak was able to find comfort from the loss of Sarah through Rivkah.[101]

Indeed, the prototypical Jewish home, relationship, and life that was exemplified by the marriage of Avraham Avinu and Sarah Imeinu was reestablished by their son and daughter-in-law, Yitzchak Avinu and Rivkah Imeinu.

Thus, the story of Avraham and Sarah is also the story of Yitzchak and Rivkah. It is a story they share in *Parshas Chayei Sarah*, and it is a story they share in *Tehillim* 45.

A Closing Blessing of *Eishes Chayil* "*Me*" *Yimtza*

Yehi ratzon, that like Avraham and Sarah, and like Yitzchak and Rivkah, may we each be blessed to have fulfilled in us "אֵשֶׁת חַיִל, מִי יִמְצָא – A woman of valor, who can find."[102]

For the women among us, may *you* be the fulfillment of "A woman of valor: 'me' יִמְצָא!" May that woman of valor be found **in me**! Me, I, I **am** her. "Me" יִמְצָא, *baruch Hashem*!

And for the men among us, may *you* be the fulfillment of "A woman of valor: 'me' יִמְצָא!" May that woman of valor be found **by me**! Me, I, I **found** her. "Me" יִמְצָא, *baruch Hashem*!

---

[100] See *Sefer B'Shem Omro, Bereishis* 24:67.
[101] *Ramban, Bereishis* 24:67.
[102] *Mishlei* 31:10.

CHAPTER 6

PARSHAS TOLDOS & TEHILLIM 36

פָּרָשַׁת תּוֹלְדוֹת / תְּהִלִּים לו

TEHILLIM 36 — תְּהִלִּים לו

1	For the conductor, by the servant of Hashem, by Dovid.	א לַמְנַצֵּחַ לְעֶבֶד ה' לְדָוִד.
2	The speech of transgression to the wicked is in my heart, and there shall be no fear of God before his eyes.	ב נְאֻם פֶּשַׁע לָרָשָׁע בְּקֶרֶב לִבִּי; אֵין פַּחַד אֱ-לֹהִים לְנֶגֶד עֵינָיו.
3	For it smoothed the way before him in his eyes, that He should find his iniquity to hate him.	ג כִּי הֶחֱלִיק אֵלָיו בְּעֵינָיו; לִמְצֹא עֲוֹנוֹ לִשְׂנֹא.
4	The words of his mouth are evil and deceit; he has ceased contemplating to do good.	ד דִּבְרֵי פִיו, אָוֶן וּמִרְמָה; חָדַל לְהַשְׂכִּיל לְהֵיטִיב.
5	Evil he devises on his bed; he stands on a path of no good, evil he does not disdain.	ה אָוֶן יַחְשֹׁב עַל מִשְׁכָּבוֹ; יִתְיַצֵּב עַל דֶּרֶךְ לֹא טוֹב, רָע לֹא יִמְאָס.
6	Hashem, unto the heavens is Your kindness; Your faithfulness reaches to the upper heights.	ו ה' בְּהַשָּׁמַיִם חַסְדֶּךָ; אֱמוּנָתְךָ עַד שְׁחָקִים.

7 Your righteousness is like the mighty mountains, Your judgments are like the great deep waters; both man and beast You save, Hashem.	ז צִדְקָתְךָ כְּהַרְרֵי אֵ-ל, מִשְׁפָּטֶיךָ תְּהוֹם רַבָּה; אָדָם וּבְהֵמָה תוֹשִׁיעַ, ה'.
8 How precious is Your kindness, God! Mankind in the shadow of Your wings takes refuge.	ח מַה יָּקָר חַסְדְּךָ אֱ-לֹהִים; וּבְנֵי אָדָם בְּצֵל כְּנָפֶיךָ יֶחֱסָיוּן.
9 They will be sated from the abundance of Your house; and from the stream of Your delights, You give them to drink.	ט יִרְוְיֻן מִדֶּשֶׁן בֵּיתֶךָ; וְנַחַל עֲדָנֶיךָ תַשְׁקֵם.
10 For with You is the source of life; by Your light may we see light.	י כִּי עִמְּךָ מְקוֹר חַיִּים; בְּאוֹרְךָ נִרְאֶה אוֹר.
11 Extend Your kindness to those who know You, and Your righteousness/charity to the upright of heart.	יא מְשֹׁךְ חַסְדְּךָ לְיֹדְעֶיךָ; וְצִדְקָתְךָ לְיִשְׁרֵי לֵב.
12 Let not come to me the foot of arrogance, and let the hand of the wicked not move me.	יב אַל תְּבוֹאֵנִי רֶגֶל גַּאֲוָה; וְיַד רְשָׁעִים אַל תְּנִדֵנִי.
13 There fell the practitioners of evil; they were thrust down and were not able to rise.	יג שָׁם נָפְלוּ פֹּעֲלֵי אָוֶן; דֹּחוּ וְלֹא יָכְלוּ קוּם.

PREFACE:
I LOVED YAAKOV. AND EISAV I HATE

נְאֻם ה' – וָאֹהַב אֶת יַעֲקֹב. וְאֶת עֵשָׂו שָׂנֵאתִי.

The words of Hashem – yet I loved Yaakov.
And Eisav I hated.

Malachi 1:2–3, Haftarah of Parshas Toldos

INTRODUCTION:
TO BE OR NOT TO BE AN *EVED HASHEM*

Tehillim 36 begins with the *pasuk*: "לַמְנַצֵּחַ לְעֶבֶד ה' לְדָוִד – For the conductor, by the *eved* of Hashem, by Dovid." This opening formula is extremely unique, appearing only one other time in all of *Tehillim*.[1] It contains a reference to an *eved*, slave, or as we often prefer to translate it using the less offensive term, servant. However, this is no ordinary, lowly *eved* but rather an *Eved Hashem*, a proud servant, even a willing slave, to God Himself![2]

---

[1] In *Tehillim* 18. Even in other formulations, the word עֶבֶד appears in only two other opening *pesukim* in all of *Sefer Tehillim*, in *Tehillim* 113 and 135.

[2] Note that when reciting *Tehillim* 36, one should be careful not to miss the opportunity to focus on the fact that one is saying the famous expression "*Eved Hashem*." For when reciting this *kapitel*, one pronounces the phrase "עֶבֶד ה'" as "*eved Adona*-i." While that is indeed the proper pronunciation, one

CHAPTER 6: TOLDOS & TEHILLIM 36

For a Jew, to become a true *Eved Hashem* is among the loftiest of goals and highest of accomplishments.[3] Even Moshe Rabbeinu, whose greatness encompassed every facet of life, is described in the Torah (and in our *Shacharis* davening each day) as "וּבְמֹשֶׁה עַבְדּוֹ – And in Moshe, His [Hashem's] *eved*."[4] Similarly, in our Shabbos *Shacharis Shemoneh Esrei* we state: "יִשְׂמַח מֹשֶׁה בְּמַתְּנַת חֶלְקוֹ, כִּי עֶבֶד נֶאֱמָן קָרָאתָ לּוֹ – Moshe rejoiced in the gift of his portion: that a faithful *eved* did You [Hashem] call him." Dovid HaMelech as well, although a king, proudly proclaimed of himself and his upbringing: "אָנָּה ה' כִּי אֲנִי עַבְדֶּךָ, אֲנִי עַבְדְּךָ בֶּן אֲמָתֶךָ – Please, Hashem, for I am Your *eved*; I am Your *eved*, the son of Your maidservant."[5]

Nevertheless, it should not be misconstrued that to be a true *Eved Hashem* is a goal reserved for Gedolim. Rather, if true subservience is a goal of the Gedolim, then surely such subservience should be a goal that each one of us should also strive to achieve.

Thus the desire, even longing, to be an *Eved Hashem*, is the perfect introduction for the *Kapitel Tehillim* connected to *Parshas Toldos*. For *Parshas Toldos* explores the lives of Yitzchak Avinu and Yaakov Avinu, each of whom was a true עֶבֶד ה' of the highest magnitude.

Yitzchak Avinu as an *Eved Hashem*

Yitzchak was the first person in history to be "*frum* from birth," as the expression goes. Yitzchak was born into the holy home of Avraham and Sarah, yet he still chose for *himself* whether to proceed on the path of Hashem and what direction and form that path would take. In the opening phrase of every *Shemoneh Esrei* we say: "אֱ-לֹהֵי אַבְרָהָם אֱ-לֹהֵי יִצְחָק וֵא-לֹהֵי יַעֲקֹב – The God of Avraham, the God of Yitzchak, and the God of Yaakov," and the commentators on the siddur teach us that the repetition

---

must be careful not to accidentally overlook this commonly used yet most meaningful of expressions: "Eved Hashem."

[3] E.g., *Shabbos Malkesa*, p. 36.
[4] *Shemos* 14:31.
[5] *Tehillim* 116:16.

of the word אֱ-לֹהֵי for each of the Avos reveals that each one of the Avos independently sought out, investigated, and chose Hashem as his own God, of his own accord and own free will.[6]

However, in this endeavor Yitzchak was unique, since he was the first of the Avos to be born into a religious home, and from within that holy environment Yitzchak was the first to choose to *remain* an *Eved Hashem* – to stay on that path.

Yet even the *type* of path that Yitzchak chose was unique to him. Yitzchak's father, Avraham, is famously known as the *Amud HaChessed*, Pillar of Kindness, and is the epitome of the characteristics of *ahavah*, love; *rachamim*, mercy; *gadol*, greatness; and *tuv*, unlimited goodness of Hashem. These are but a few of the different but interrelated characteristics that were embodied in Avraham, and which shaped Avraham's worship of Hashem.

However, Yitzchak's path was different – some might even say the respectful *opposite* of his father. For Yitzchak is the epitome of the attribute of *gevurah*, might and power (as well as self-control), and *yirah*, fear, even to the extent of being associated with Hashem as "פַּחַד יִצְחָק – [the] fear of Yitzchak."[7] His path as an *Eved Hashem* was based upon *din* and *mishpat,* strict judgment, and limiting the *tuv* and goodness of Hashem to a more measured amount. Yitzchak is also identified as the *Amud HaAvodah*, Pillar of Service, of Hashem. Whether through prayer, through his daily life and conduct, through *korbanos* in the form of animal sacrifices, or even through *korbanos* when he offered his very *self* as a sacrifice to Hashem at the *Akeidah*, Yitzchak as the symbol of עֲבוֹדָה (which bears the same *shoresh* as עֶבֶד), in addition to all of the other attributes cited above, is, in a style all his own, the embodiment of an עֶבֶד ה'.

---

[6] E.g., *Eitz Yosef, Siddur Otzar HaTefillah*.
[7] *Bereishis* 31:42 and 31:53.

Eisav's Refusal to Be an *Eved Hashem*

Parshas *Toldos* also tells the story of the divergent paths of Yitzchak's twin sons, Yaakov and Eisav. Their competition for the *bechorah* (birthright) and for the blessings of their father, boiled down to the question of which brother would become a true *Eved Hashem*. To be fair, there are even opinions that both brothers could have risen to the occasion, each becoming an *Eved Hashem*. For example, one school of thought is that Yaakov was to serve Hashem through *ruchniyus*, spirituality, while Eisav would serve Hashem through *gashmiyus*, earthiness and materialism.[8] Another school of thought is that Yaakov was to have been the exemplar of service of Hashem amidst perfect piety, while Eisav would have been the exemplar of service of Hashem amidst constant battle with the *yetzer hara*.[9] In either case, the two brothers could have formed a perfect unit, a perfect team, whose progeny would have together led all mankind on a path dedicated to Hashem regardless of one's predispositions, desires, and drives.

Yet as seen throughout *Parshas Toldos* and its commentaries, from the pivotal age of thirteen, Eisav was already dedicated to the path of evil, submerging himself in trickery, robbery, even murder and adultery, and eventually marrying numerous wives all of whom were unabashed idol worshippers. Eisav not only sold his birthright to Yaakov, but he belittled that very birthright, proving that Eisav only viewed the *bechorah* as a hindering weight upon him that would ultimately crush him when he refused to change his ways.[10]

Evidently, Eisav interpreted *Eved Hashem* as "slavery," an unwanted burden with rules and restrictions that would enslave and kill him, and of which he wanted no part. Eisav was unwilling and therefore unworthy even to be a proud "servant" of Hashem. Eisav quickly lost everything

---

[8] Based upon *Michtav Me'Eliyahu*.
[9] Based upon the *Tanya*.
[10] E.g., *Rashi, Bereishis* 25:32.

even remotely connected to what an *Eved Hashem* represents. Sadly, in the end and for all eternity, Eisav is known as Eisav HaRasha, Eisav the Wicked.

Appropriately and even ironically as only Hashem in His majesty can do, Eisav, who so despised the responsibility of being an *Eved Hashem* and loathed the imagined burden of slavery (or even servitude) when casting off the yoke of Heaven from upon himself, in so doing actually *became a slave* on multiple levels. In addition to becoming a slave to the *yetzer hara* – which evidently did not disturb him – he also became an unwilling slave to his brother Yaakov. At the end of *Parshas Toldos* when Yitzchak seems not to possess any remaining blessings to bestow upon Eisav, Yitzchak states: "הֵן גְּבִיר שַׂמְתִּיו לָךְ וְאֶת כָּל אֶחָיו נָתַתִּי לוֹ לַעֲבָדִים" – Behold, a lord have I made him [Yaakov] over you, and all his brethren I have given to him as slaves."[11] *Rashi* elaborates that Yitzchak told Eisav: "Of what benefit and use is a blessing to you? If you will acquire possessions, they are Yaakov's, for I have made him a master over you, וּמַה שֶּׁקָּנָה עֶבֶד קָנָה רַבּוֹ – and whatever a *slave* acquires, his master acquires it from him."[12]

Yaakov Avinu as an *Eved Hashem*

In contrast, *Parshas Toldos* introduces us to Yaakov Avinu, who would be forever known for his unparalleled attributes of *emes*, truth; *tiferes*, splendor; *kedushah*, holiness; *nora*, awesomeness; and, of course, as the *Amud HaTorah*, Pillar of Torah. Yaakov would prove to be the perfect synthesis of the *chessed* of Avraham and the *gevurah* of Yitzchak, resulting in the exact amount of *tuv*/goodness needed, and which amount Hashem will precisely provide in the perfect measure that the soul requires.[13]

---

[11] *Bereishis* 27:37.
[12] *Rashi, Bereishis* 27:37, from *Bereishis Rabbah* 67:5.
[13] E.g., *Nefesh Shimshon: Siddur HaTefillah*, p. 390.

CHAPTER 6: TOLDOS & TEHILLIM 36

In *Parshas Toldos* we are clearly introduced to the Yaakov of "Torah," whose *yetzer tov* directed him from the pivotal age of thirteen and who is described as: "וְיַעֲקֹב אִישׁ תָּם, יֹשֵׁב אֹהָלִים,"[14] meaning that he possessed the characteristic of purity developed through sitting in the tents of Torah and plumbing its depths.[15] Yaakov was not only a willing "servant of Hashem," but rather through his toil in Torah day and night would even consider the title "*slave* of Hashem" to be the highest of honors. As we say every morning in the *tefillah* of *Hodu* in a double reference to Yaakov (who would later also be named Yisrael): זֶרַע יִשְׂרָאֵל עַבְדּוֹ בְּנֵי יַעֲקֹב בְּחִירָיו – Offspring of Yisrael His *eved*, children of Yaakov, His chosen one."[16]

Thus, Yaakov was much more than a holy son born into the home of Yitzchak and the esteemed grandson of Avraham. Yaakov developed a religious approach unique to himself; yet in doing so, like his father and grandfather before him, he was also the epitome of an *Eved Hashem*.

Moreover, Yaakov was not only the one true *Eved Hashem* among Yitzchak's sons. Yaakov also recognized that Eisav was *not*.[17] Thus, says the Torah commentator known as the *Mesiach Ilmim*, Yaakov did not lure the birthright away from Eisav for Yaakov's own sake, but rather he did so out of respect for Hashem. For Yaakov knew that the responsibility of *avodah*, including the performance of sacrificial services that their father Yitzchak and Hashem held so very dear should not be performed by a *rasha* such as Eisav.[18] עֲבוֹדָה, as the very term itself suggests, must be performed by an עֶבֶד ה'.

Considering all of the above, it is extraordinary that *Tehillim* 36 – which parallels *Parshas Toldos* – begins with the unique phrase: "לַמְנַצֵּחַ לְעֶבֶד ה' לְדָוִד" – For the conductor, by the *eved* of Hashem, by Dovid."

---

[14] *Bereishis* 25:27.
[15] E.g., *Rashi, Bereishis* 25:27.
[16] *I Divrei Hayamim* 16:13.
[17] E.g., *Rashi, Bereishis* 25:31.
[18] *Rashi, Bereishis* 25:3.

Hashem, Grant Us a *Yetzer Tov* to Be Your *Eved*

It must also be stated that a true *Eved Hashem* is the "freest" person of all. For the moral responsibilities of Hashem's Torah and Hashem's mitzvos provide us with the opportunity to truly exercise our own free will, to find direction and meaning in life, and to unlock within the mitzvos the vital roadmap to the afterlife, *Olam Haba*. As Chazal tell us: "אֵין לְךָ בֶן חוֹרִין אֶלָּא מִי שֶׁעוֹסֵק בְּתַלְמוּד תּוֹרָה – There is no free man like one who is immersed in the study of Torah."[19]

In light of the above, let us begin our in-depth study of *Tehillim* 36 and its connection to *Parshas Toldos* with the following *tefillah* to Hashem, which we can each say as part of a "special *tefillah*" (as my dear father lovingly refers to it) every Friday night in the *Ribbon Kol Ha'Olamim* prayer printed right after *Shalom Aleichem*, and which concisely contains elements of all we have discussed in the Introduction above:

> וְתֵן בָּנוּ יֵצֶר טוֹב לְעָבְדְּךָ בֶּאֱמֶת וּבְיִרְאָה וּבְאַהֲבָה – Hashem, may You instill within us the *yetzer tov* [the desire to do good] to serve You [*to be an Eved Hashem*] with truth/honesty [in the manner of Yaakov], with fear [in the manner of Yitzchak], and with love [in the manner of Avraham]

just as the Avos HaKedoshim did, each in his own unique way.

---

[19] *Pirkei Avos* 6:2.

THE MANY CONNECTIONS BETWEEN PARSHAS TOLDOS & TEHILLIM 36

Pasuk 1:
לַמְנַצֵּחַ לְעֶבֶד ה' לְדָוִד

For the conductor, by the servant of Hashem, by Dovid.

The *Eved Hashem* Is the True Victor

As noted in the Introduction to this chapter, the term "*Eved Hashem*" is particularly apropos to *Parshas Toldos*, which focuses on the lives of two of the original *Ovdei Hashem*: Yitzchak Avinu and Yaakov Avinu.

In addition, *Parshas Toldos* contains Yitzchak's second prophetic encounter. There, Hashem introduces Himself as the God of Yitzchak's father Avraham and then promises Yitzchak general blessings as well as a specific *brachah* of abundant offspring. Why such great reward? Hashem explains: "בַּעֲבוּר אַבְרָהָם עַבְדִּי" – because of Avraham, My *eved*,"[20] thus establishing a link between Avraham, Yitzchak, Yaakov, and beyond, all intertwined in an honored and holy chain of *avdus*: being an *Eved Hashem*.

Finally, while the word "לַמְנַצֵּחַ" means "for the conductor" in reference to the person who was to lead the singing of this *kapitel* in the Beis HaMikdash, לַמְנַצֵּחַ also means "for the *victor*," as the word נִצָּחוֹן means victory. In this context, the Midrash says that the "victor" refers to Yaakov, who despite his struggles with the aggressive and deadly Eisav in *Parshas Toldos* (and later in *Parshas Vayishlach*), always emerged victorious,

---

[20] *Bereishis* 26:24.

thanks to his righteousness and to the accompanying *siyata d'Shmaya* bestowed upon him.[21]

In our own lives as well, we must always remember that no matter what the outcome appears to be, even if it does not turn out exactly as we had planned or hoped, one who conducts himself as an *Eved Hashem* is the true מְנַצֵּחַ, the true victor.

Pasuk 2:
נְאֻם פֶּשַׁע לָרָשָׁע בְּקֶרֶב לִבִּי; אֵין פַּחַד אֱ-לֹהִים לְנֶגֶד עֵינָיו

The speech of transgression to the wicked is in my heart, and there shall be no fear of God before his eyes.

Criticism of the Wickedness of Eisav

On a basic level, this entire *pasuk* can be interpreted as a strong criticism of the wickedness of Eisav.

According to *Rashi*, the word "פֶּשַׁע" as used in this *pasuk* does not simply mean "transgression" but rather "Transgression" with a capital "T," i.e., the *Yetzer Hara* itself,[22] which clearly gained control over and fed fuel to the fire of the ultimate *rasha* – Eisav HaRasha. Thus, the phrase "פֶּשַׁע לָרָשָׁע" refers to the *Yetzer Hara's* domination of Eisav's thoughts and actions.

Moreover, evil was very much "בְּקֶרֶב לִבִּי," entrenched in Eisav's לֵב, heart, already from the start. *Rashi* tells us that even as a fetus, Eisav would attempt to escape from the womb when his mother passed places of idol worship.[23]

The expression "אֵין פַּחַד אֱ-לֹהִים" teaches that Eisav possessed neither fear nor awe of God. In addition, on a more personal level in the life of

---

[21] *Midrash Tehillim, Shocher Tov* 36.
[22] *Rashi, Tehillim* 36:2.
[23] *Rashi, Bereishis* 25:22, from *Bereishis Rabbah* 63:6.

Eisav, "אֵין פַּחַד אֱ-לֹהִים" alludes to the fact that Eisav did not even possess a respectful fear and awe of his own *father*, Yitzchak, who is associated with פַּחַד as seen in the Torah's phraseology "פַּחַד יִצְחָק,"[24] and whose holy *middos* represented the Divine Name of strict judgment, the Name "אֱ-לֹהִים."

Moreover, Eisav's sins were performed "לְנֶגֶד עֵינָיו," just out of the line of sight of his righteous father, and sometimes even right before his eyes, thus exploiting his father's physical disability of blindness. Worse, Chazal teach us that Eisav bore responsibility for that disability, as Yitzchak's עֵינָיו, eyes, were blinded by the smoke and incense of the idol worship of Eisav's wives.[25]

As tragic as all this is, even more egregious are Eisav's sins unabashedly performed "לְנֶגֶד עֵינָיו," before the eyes of *Hashem*, Who sees all.

Eisav the Wicked, Despite His Father and His Mother

It must be noted that *Rashi's* commentary throughout *Parshas Toldos* includes a multitude of Midrashim and other proofs from *Torah She'baal Peh* that focus on Eisav's wickedness, and (as noted above) some of these sources even indicate that Eisav was predestined to be a *rasha* from the womb.[26]

If so, can Eisav be blamed for his wickedness? The answer is, yes, he can; and he is.

True, Eisav certainly appears to have had a God-given predisposition to *rishus* as symbolized by his physical appearance: ruddy and hairy and representative of tendencies toward animalistic behavior and bloodshed.[27] Nevertheless, like everyone else, Eisav was capable of *bechirah* – to

---

[24] *Bereishis* 31:42 and 31:53.
[25] *Rashi, Bereishis* 27:1, from *Midrash Tanchuma, Toldos* 8.
[26] E.g., *Rashi, Bereishis* 25:23, and *Rashi, Bereishis* 25:24, from *Bereishis Rabbah* 63:8.
[27] *Rashi, Bereishis* 25:25, from *Bereishis Rabbah* 63:8.

choose whether to listen to his *yetzer hara* or his *yetzer tov*, whether to be evil or to be good.

A prime example of the proper use of *bechirah* is Eisav's own mother, Rivkah Imeinu. In just the second *pasuk* of *Parshas Toldos*, Rivkah is reintroduced once again as the daughter of Besuel and sister of Lavan[28] (also commonly referred to as "Lavan HaRasha"). *Rashi* explains that this repetition is actually an expression of praise: Rivkah was the daughter of a *rasha*, the sister of a *rasha*, and was raised in a land of *reshaim*; yet she did *not* learn from their wicked deeds nor did she emulate their wicked behavior.[29] Lest we think that Rivkah was somehow naturally impervious to evil, the very next *pasuk* states that when Yitzchak and Rivkah davened for children, "Hashem allowed Himself to be entreated by him [Yitzchak]."[30] *Rashi* points out, by *him*, but not by *her*, for as the Gemara teaches, the prayer of a *tzaddik* who is the child of a *rasha* (as was the case with Rivkah) is not comparable to the prayer of a *tzaddik* who is the child of a *tzaddik* (as was the case with Yitzchak).[31]

Thus, Chazal's consecutive teachings about Eisav's righteous mother Rivkah and her upbringing surrounded by *rishus* proves to us – and could have, and *should* have proven to *Eisav* as well – that one can elevate oneself above wickedness. Despite still being somewhat saddled by that wickedness, one can nonetheless burst forth into a life of Torah and *tzidkus*, if only he or she truly desires to do so.

For *not* having done so, and for instead succumbing to his base desires, Eisav is very much to blame for becoming Eisav HaRasha.

---

[28] *Bereishis* 25:20.

[29] *Rashi, Bereishis* 25:20, from *Bereishis Rabbah* 63:4.

[30] *Bereishis* 25:21.

[31] *Rashi, Bereishis* 25:21, from *Yevamos* 64a.

Pasuk 3:
כִּי הֶחֱלִיק אֵלָיו בְּעֵינָיו;
לִמְצֹא עֲוֹנוֹ לִשְׂנֹא
**For it smoothed the way before him in his eyes,
that He should find his iniquity to hate him.**

Eisav's Ability to Deceive

The aforementioned force known as "Transgression" or the *Yetzer Hara*, continued to aid and abet and "הֶחֱלִיק – smooth the way" for Eisav, who used his smooth-talking words to ensnare unsuspecting men to their deaths[32] and women to illicit behavior.[33] Even someone as wise as Yitzchak was tricked into thinking that Eisav was a *tzaddik*. The Torah tells us: "כִּי צַיִד בְּפִיו – For ensnaring was in his mouth"[34] referring to the mouth of Eisav who would entrap Yitzchak and deceive him with words,[35] insincerely asking intricate halachic questions of his father such as how does one tithe salt and straw.[36] Eisav was already aware that these items were exempt from such requirements but nevertheless asked in order to make himself seem like an inquisitive and sincere *shomer mitzvos* in the eyes of his father. In doing so, Eisav not only tried to deceive Yitzchak; Eisav tried to deceive himself.

In this context, the word "בְּעֵינָיו – in his eyes," conveys a double meaning. This word refers to Eisav and his self-perception, and also refers to the eyes of Yitzchak, who was deceived into thinking that Eisav was meticulous in mitzvos.[37]

---

[32] E.g., *Rashi, Bereishis* 25:29, from *Bereishis Rabbah* 63:12.
[33] E.g., *Rashi, Bereishis* 26:34, from *Bereishis Rabbah* 65:1.
[34] *Bereishis* 25:28.
[35] *Rashi, Bereishis* 25:28.
[36] *Rashi, Bereishis*, 25:27.
[37] *Rashi, Bereishis*, 25:27.

However, the *Darchei Noam* of Slonim provides a startling insight regarding the ability of Eisav to deceive a *tzaddik* like Yitzchak, who although physically blind was certainly not spiritually blind. He explains that sometimes when a person, even a *rasha*, stands in front of a *tzaddik* and they look at one another's face and into each other's eyes, in that moment the *rasha* becomes a reflection of the *tzaddik* and transforms, albeit temporarily, into a *tzaddik* himself.

According to this beautiful understanding, we can explain the phrase "כִּי הֶחֱלִיק אֵלָיו בְּעֵינָיו" in a new light: when Eisav found himself standing in front of and "בְּעֵינָיו – in the eyes" of his holy father Yitzchak, the gruff and hairy Eisav "הֶחֱלִיק," became like one who is smooth, soft, and pure. Eisav became a reflection of his holy father who was not fooled but rather caused Eisav's deeply hidden and nearly non-existent goodness to surface whenever he was in Yitzchak's presence!

Nonetheless, Eisav's ability to excel in deceit and wickedness was all engineered by none other than Hashem. For what purpose? "לִמְצֹא עֲוֹנוֹ לִשְׂנֹא" – so that He should find his iniquity to hate him." Amazingly, this harsh sentiment is reiterated forcefully and clearly in the *Haftarah* of *Parshas Toldos* in which Hashem unequivocally states: "וָאֹהַב אֶת יַעֲקֹב. וְאֶת עֵשָׂו שָׂנֵאתִי – Yet I loved Yaakov. And Eisav I hated."[38]

Pasuk 4:

דִּבְרֵי פִיו אָוֶן וּמִרְמָה;
חָדַל לְהַשְׂכִּיל לְהֵיטִיב

**The words of his mouth are evil and deceit;
he has ceased contemplating to do good.**

---

[38] *Malachi* 1:2–3.

The Battle of *Emes* and *Sheker*

While similar to *pasuk* 3, this *pasuk* conveys even more meaning as it encapsulates the difference between Eisav and Yaakov.

For Eisav epitomized *sheker*, lies and falsehood, as conveyed in the expression: "דִּבְרֵי פִיו אָוֶן וּמִרְמָה" – The words of his mouth are evil and deceit." In addition, the specific use of the word "פִיו" relates back to the Torah's criticism of Eisav discussed above: "כִּי צַיִד בְּפִיו" – For ensnaring was in his mouth."[39]

In contrast, the "פִיו" of Yaakov was entirely *emes*, truth. As *Rashi* explains on the words "וְיַעֲקֹב אִישׁ תָּם,"[40] Yaakov "was not proficient in all the evil and deceit in which Eisav had expertise" but rather was wholesome and honest. *Rashi* adds, "Whatever was in Yaakov's heart, כֵּן פִיו, so too were the words of his mouth."[41] In this description we learn of Yaakov's signature characteristic: the *middah* of *emes*, the attribute of truth, as the *pasuk* says: "תִּתֵּן אֱמֶת לְיַעֲקֹב" – [Hashem] Grant truth to Yaakov."[42]

Amazingly, the commentators on *Tehillim* 36:4 explain that the remainder of the *pasuk* describes the fatal flaw of the *rasha*: that of "חָדַל לְהַשְׂכִּיל לְהֵיטִיב" – he has ceased contemplating to do good," by further tying such depraved phrase to the concept of *emes*. The *Metzudas Dovid* explains that the *rasha* specifically prevents himself from contemplating and investigating the *emes*, which would have helped him improve his ways.[43] Similarly, the *Malbim* laments that if the *rasha* would only stop for a moment to contemplate, he would find the *emes* in the form of Hashem's mitzvos, which are *tovim v'yesharim*, good and straight, and

---

[39] *Bereishis* 25:28.
[40] *Bereishis* 25:27.
[41] *Rashi, Bereishis* 25:27.
[42] *Michah* 7:20.
[43] *Metzudas Dovid, Tehillim* 36:4.

contain rehabilitative qualities that the *rasha* so desperately needs but refuses to acquire through facing or seeking the truth.[44]

Indeed, *pasuk* 4 of *Tehillim* 36 succinctly describes the true battle between Yaakov and Eisav: the battle between *emes* and *sheker*, between Torah truth and faithless falsehood.

Pasuk 5:
אָוֶן יַחְשֹׁב עַל מִשְׁכָּבוֹ;
יִתְיַצֵּב עַל דֶּרֶךְ לֹא טוֹב,
רָע לֹא יִמְאָס

**Evil he devises on his bed;
he stands on a path of no good,
evil he does not disdain.**

Eisav's Premeditated Wickedness

This entire *pasuk*, from start to finish, is a concise and accurate portrayal of Eisav's wickedness.

"אָוֶן יַחְשֹׁב עַל מִשְׁכָּבוֹ" describes the despicable *rishus* of one who actually lulls himself to sleep while planning acts of wickedness, and is surely a description befitting of Eisav HaRasha. The reference to "מִשְׁכָּבוֹ – his bed" also alludes to Eisav's adulterous acts[45] as well as to his idol worshipping wives.[46]

In the phrase "יִתְיַצֵּב עַל דֶּרֶךְ לֹא טוֹב – he stands on a path of no good," the word "יִתְיַצֵּב," standing, implies standing by and waiting with a certain consistency and eagerness, a certain tolerance, and a certain *patience* in devising his evil plans and waiting for them to come to fruition. Eisav displayed such "patience" after he lost Yitzchak's blessings to Yaakov.

---

[44] *Malbim, Tehillim* 36:4.
[45] *Rashi, Bereishis* 26:34.
[46] *Rashi, Bereishis* 26:35 and 27:1.

Despite his anger and thirst for revenge, Eisav vowed to wait to kill Yaakov after their father's death, however long that might take, and was even willing to wait an additional seven days through the *shiva* period.[47] Such was Eisav's stamina for the sake of sin.

Finally, the words "רַע לֹא יִמְאָס – evil he does not disdain" sharpen our outlook even more. Eisav disdained goodness, as the Torah tells us: "וַיִּבֶז עֵשָׂו אֶת הַבְּכֹרָה – and Eisav belittled the birthright."[48] On this, *Rashi* comments: "הֵעִיד הַכָּתוּב עַל רִשְׁעוֹ שֶׁבִּזָּה עֲבוֹדָתוֹ שֶׁל מָקוֹם – This *pasuk* testifies to his wickedness, that he belittled the service of the Omnipresent."[49] While Eisav claimed that he relinquished the *bechorah* because he feared that his unbridled sins would lead to his death (as mentioned above), his true motive was a lack of respect for the significance of the birthright and the significance of Hashem.

Unlike *pasuk* 3 of *Tehillim* 36 that refers to Eisav's skill of smooth-talking and can be construed as wickedness "in the moment," here *pasuk* 5 makes it abundantly clear that Eisav's wickedness was premeditated. It was a wickedness that dominated his very essence.

Pasuk 6:
ה' בְּהַשָּׁמַיִם חַסְדֶּךָ;

אֱמוּנָתְךָ עַד שְׁחָקִים

Hashem, unto the heavens is Your kindness;
Your faithfulness reaches to the upper heights.

The *Rasha* and *Tzaddik*: Affecting Heaven and Earth

Frighteningly, *Rashi* interprets this *pasuk* as a warning that the actions of evildoers can cause Hashem to remove His kindness and faithfulness from this world and to retreat to the upper realms away from

---

[47] Bereishis 27:41.
[48] Bereishis 25:34.
[49] Rashi, Bereishis 25:34.

mankind.[50] This lesson is certainly apropos in the context of Eisav HaRasha.

Nevertheless, the imagery here of Hashem high atop the heavens and in His lofty skies is also reminiscent of Yaakov, who at the start of next week's *Parshah, Vayeitzei,* fled from Eisav's wrath and then dreamt his famous prophetic dream in which we are told that Yaakov saw "סֻלָּם מֻצָּב אַרְצָה, וְרֹאשׁוֹ מַגִּיעַ הַשָּׁמָיְמָה – A ladder set earthward, and its top reached heavenward."[51] This was a prophecy conveying the message that Hashem's kindness and faithfulness from heaven would manifest itself on earth in the form of the many blessings and promises of safety and security that Yaakov received at that time.

Just as the wicked such as Eisav may cause Hashem to *remove* His active presence from this world and to withdraw to heaven away from mankind, so too the righteous such as Yaakov have the opposite effect: they cause Hashem's kindness and presence to span from heaven above to the earth below, bringing His Godly presence ever closer.

Pasuk 7:

צִדְקָתְךָ כְּהַרְרֵי אֵ-ל,

מִשְׁפָּטֶיךָ תְּהוֹם רַבָּה;

אָדָם וּבְהֵמָה תוֹשִׁיעַ, ה'

Your righteousness is like the mighty mountains;
Your judgments are like the great deep waters;
both man and beast You save, Hashem.

Of Mountains and Monsters

The phrase "כְּהַרְרֵי אֵ-ל – like the mighty mountains," refers to the Avos – Avraham, Yitzchak, and Yaakov – who are respectfully referred to

---

[50] *Rashi, Tehillim* 36:6.
[51] *Bereishis* 28:12.

CHAPTER 6: TOLDOS & TEHILLIM 36

as "הָרִים – mountains"[52] and who are our "הוֹרִים – parents." By no coincidence, we find that the Torah mentions all three of the Avos living together at the same time *only* in *Parshas* Toldos, as *Rashi* tells us that Avraham lived until Yaakov's thirteenth birthday.[53]

"מִשְׁפָּטֶיךָ" refers to Yitzchak Avinu, whose *middah* was that of מִשְׁפָּט, strict judgment. In *Parshas Toldos*, Yitzchak witnessed the *ultimate* "תְּהוֹם רַבָּה" when the vast and terrible depths of Gehinnom opened under Eisav's feet in Yitzchak's presence as they both realized that the blessings were given to someone else – Yaakov.[54]

"אָדָם וּבְהֵמָה תּוֹשִׁיעַ, ה'" refers to Hashem's unlimited mercy because He is willing to save not only a high caliber and great אָדָם such as Yaakov, but even a בְּהֵמָה, an animal, and by extension may even save a "beast" and monster such as Eisav. That Eisav is likened to a beast is clear from his hairy and furry exterior, and more so from his animalistic, hedonistic, and monstrous interior.

Indeed, this bestial description is more than figurative, for in *Parshas Toldos Rashi* describes Eisav's dishonest facade as characteristic of a swine, who when lying down stretches out its split hooves to hypocritically and incorrectly portray itself as pure and kosher.[55] In addition, in *Parshas Vayishlach* Eisav attempted to kill Yaakov by turning a kiss into a sudden bite aimed at the neck,[56] which is animal-like behavior, primitive and violent. Finally, the Gemara[57] teaches that in the time of Moshiach, Eisav's descendants, the wicked Roman Empire, will follow the lead of other nations and attempt to offer tribute to the *Melech HaMoshiach*, gifts that Hashem will overtly reject. Why? Not only because the gifts will be

---

[52] E.g., *Shir HaShirim* 2:8, and *Rosh Hashanah* 11a.
[53] *Rashi, Bereishis* 25:30.
[54] *Rashi, Bereishis* 27:33, from *Midrash Tanchuma, Toldos* 11, and *Bereishis Rabbah* 67:2.
[55] *Rashi, Bereishis* 26:34, from *Bereishis Rabbah* 65:1.
[56] *Bereishis Rabbah, Vayishlach* 78:9.
[57] *Pesachim* 118b.

offered with insincerity and from a source of impurity, but because Hashem will say: "גְּעַר חַיַּת, קְנֵה עֲדַת אַבִּירִים,"[58] which the Gemara explains to mean "Rebuke the *beast* [Edom] and embrace the Assembly of mighty ones [Yisrael]," confirming yet again that Hashem will forever accept the Jewish People but will reject and exclude the monstrosity that is Eisav and his wicked progeny.

It is truly frightening that two brothers, twins no less, could differ and diverge to such an extent, one rising to great heights symbolized by the giant mountains of "הַרְרֵי אֵ-ל," and the other falling to such low depths that he is likened to a "בְּהֵמָה."

Pasuk 8:
מַה יָּקָר חַסְדְּךָ אֱ-לֹהִים;
וּבְנֵי אָדָם בְּצֵל כְּנָפֶיךָ יֶחֱסָיוּן
How precious is Your kindness, God!
Mankind in the shadow of Your wings takes refuge.

A Quick Reconnect with the Avos and Each Precious Jew

Similar to the first three *brachos* of *Shemoneh Esrei*, this *pasuk* focuses primarily on praise of Hashem, and yet it also contains an underlying reconnection to the Avos:

- "חַסְדְּךָ" is an allusion to Avraham Avinu and the attribute of *chessed*, kindness.
- "אֱ-לֹהִים" is an allusion to Yitzchak Avinu and the attribute of *din*, the strict judgment intrinsic to this Name.
- "וּבְנֵי אָדָם בְּצֵל כְּנָפֶיךָ יֶחֱסָיוּן" is an allusion to Yaakov Avinu and the attribute of *emes*. As the *Radak*[59] explains, this phrase refers to

---

[58] *Tehillim* 68:31.
[59] *Radak, Tehillim* 36:8.

CHAPTER 6: TOLDOS & TEHILLIM 36

those who merit to find "refuge in the shadow of the wings" of Hashem in the World to Come. Who are those people worthy of such a blessing? The *Radak* answers: the "בְּנֵי אָדָם בֶּאֱמֶת" those who are sincere representations of the creation called man, and people who are connected to the *truth*, to the אֱמֶת that is the characteristic of Yaakov Avinu.

- Indeed, "מַה יָּקָר."

    "מַה יָּקָר" – how precious is each *middah tovah*!

    "מַה יָּקָר" – how precious are the Avos!

    "מַה יָּקָר" – how precious is each righteous Jew!

    "מַה יָּקָר" – how precious is Hashem!

Pasuk 9:
יִרְוְיֻן מִדֶּשֶׁן בֵּיתֶךָ;
וְנַחַל עֲדָנֶיךָ תַשְׁקֵם

They will be sated from the abundance of Your house; and from the stream of Your delights, You give them to drink.

The World to Come and the Beis HaMikdash: Home

The Gemara quotes this entire *pasuk* as the basis for the statement: "כָּל הַמַּרְעִיב עַצְמוֹ עַל דִּבְרֵי תוֹרָה בָּעוֹלָם הַזֶּה, הַקָּדוֹשׁ בָּרוּךְ הוּא מַשְׂבִּיעוֹ לְעוֹלָם הַבָּא – Whoever makes himself starving for words of Torah in this world, Hashem will satiate him in the Word to Come."[60] Torah is the path to *Olam HaBa*, our ultimate spiritual בַּיִת, home. This is certainly a description befitting of Yaakov Avinu, the Pillar of Torah.

"בֵּיתֶךָ" is a home. It was Eisav's wickedness and anger that forced Yaakov to flee from his land, his parents, and his home. Yet, when Yaakov

---

[60] *Sanhedrin* 100a.

awoke from his dream with the ladder in *Parshas Vayeitzei*, he realized that he had discovered another type of בַּיִת and proclaimed: "אֵין זֶה כִּי אִם בֵּית אֱלֹהִים, וְזֶה שַׁעַר הַשָּׁמָיִם – This is none other than the House of God, and this is the Gate of heaven."[61] He had discovered the future site of the Beis HaMikdash, Hashem's truest "home" on earth.

There, in the eminent and imminent Third Beis HaMikdash, the Jewish People will experience a "נַחַל" of sorts. As discussed in Chapter 3 on *Parshas Lech Lecha* & *Tehillim* 110, we are presented with a contrast. First, we read the frightening phrase in *Tehillim* 110:7: "מִנַּחַל בַּדֶּרֶךְ יִשְׁתֶּה – From a river [of enemy blood] along the way he shall drink," which refers to the tortured past, present, and (*lo aleinu*) future of Am Yisrael. However, *Tehillim* 36:9 contrasts this horror with the maginificent time of Moshiach and the rebuilt Third Beis HaMikdash, when Klal Yisrael will live within the safety and security of Hashem's holy בַּיִת. There, the Jewish People will merit to drink only from "וְנַחַל עֲדָנֶיךָ תַשְׁקֵם" – Hashem's river of delights."

Finally, *Olam Haba* as well is associated with the blessings of the "נַחַל," as, for example, the Gemara recounts that Rabbi Elazar ben Pedas was promised: "לְעָלְמָא דְּאָתֵי תְּלֵיסְרֵי נַהֲרְוָותָא דְמִשְׁחָא אֲפַרְסְמוֹן דָּכְיָין כְּפְרָת וְדִיגְלַת דְּמְעַנְּגַתְּ בְּהוּ – In the World to Come, thirteen rivers of pure balsam oil as large as the Euphrates and the Tigris Rivers for you to enjoy."[62] In addition, from the personalized expression of "עֲדָנֶיךָ," which can also mean "*your* Eden,*" the Midrash learns that "כָּל צַדִּיק וְצַדִּיק יֵשׁ לוֹ עֵדֶן בִּפְנֵי עַצְמוֹ – each and every righteous person will merit to have his own personal Gan Eden,"[63] his individualized בַּיִת within which to dwell and delight together with Hashem.

---

[61] *Bereishis* 28:17.
[62] *Taanis* 25a.
[63] *Vayikra Rabbah* 27:1.

Pasuk 10:
כִּי עִמְּךָ מְקוֹר חַיִּים;

בְּאוֹרְךָ נִרְאֶה אוֹר

For with You is the source of life;
by Your light may we see light.

Water Wells of Torah, *Brachah* and Beis HaMikdash

In *Parshas Toldos*, Hashem Who is the "מְקוֹר חַיִּים – Source of all life," provided Yitzchak with multitudes of wells filled with refreshing and life-giving water, wells referred to as "בְּאֵר מַיִם חַיִּים."[64]

In addition, Chazal famously compare water to the very Torah itself, as the Gemara states: "אֵין מַיִם אֶלָּא תּוֹרָה – There is no water except Torah."[65] Both water and Torah are a "מְקוֹר חַיִּים – source of life" for mankind.

In addition, the Midrash[66] explains that Yaakov Avinu also focused on the connection between Torah and water, for he attributed his worthiness of Yitzchak's *brachah* of "וְיִתֶּן לְךָ הָאֱלֹהִים מִטַּל הַשָּׁמַיִם – And may God give you of the dew of the heavens,"[67] to the very fact that he occupied himself with Torah. In other words, specifically because he surrounded himself with Torah, which is likened to water, he was blessed with the water-like substance of dew.

Furthermore, the *Ramban* teaches that the wells of *Parshas Toldos* are symbolic of the Beis HaMikdash: just as Yitzchak's wells were wickedly filled by enemies not once but twice, so too the Beis HaMikdash would twice be destroyed by our enemies. However, Yitzchak's third set of wells, which were dug in the location called Rechovot, were claimed without

---

[64] *Bereishis* 26:19.
[65] *Bava Kama* 82a.
[66] *Bereishis Rabbah* 66:1.
[67] *Bereishis* 27:28.

confrontation and struggle, just as the Third Beis HaMikdash will usher in a time of peace that will be firmly established forever.[68]

The True Light Is Hashem's and Should Not Be Taken Lightly

"בְּאוֹרְךָ נִרְאֶה אוֹר – by Your light may we see light." In the context of *Parshas Toldos*, this double expression of light parallels the double expression of "day" used by Yaakov when purchasing the birthright from Eisav. Yaakov said: "מִכְרָה כַיּוֹם אֶת בְּכֹרָתְךָ לִי – Sell, as this day, your birthright to me"[69] followed by "וַיֹּאמֶר יַעֲקֹב, הִשָּׁבְעָה לִי כַּיּוֹם, וַיִּשָּׁבַע לוֹ; וַיִּמְכֹּר אֶת בְּכֹרָתוֹ לְיַעֲקֹב – And Yaakov said: Swear to me as this day; he [Eisav] swore to him and sold his birthright to Yaakov."[70] *Rashi* explains that Yaakov's intent was for the sale of the birthright to be considered as an indisputable sale, with a validity as clear as the light of day.[71]

So too, says the Torah commentator Rav Chayun: Dovid HaMelech's words "בְּאוֹרְךָ נִרְאֶה אוֹר," express that Hashem's *chessed*, *tzidkus*, and *mishpat* are revealed and clear to us all, as clear as the light of day, and yet must never be taken for granted.[72]

Additionally, it must be noted that the double expression of "light" in "בְּאוֹרְךָ נִרְאֶה אוֹר – by Your light may we see light," reminds us of the holiday of Chanukah, the Festival of Lights, marked by its mitzvah of the lighting of the menorah in every Jewish home, and which begins on the twenty-fifth day of the month of Kislev, the month whose start often coincides with *Parshas Toldos*. Indeed, the holiday of Chanukah serves as a powerful reminder that we too must recognize the reality of בְּאוֹרְךָ נִרְאֶה אוֹר: true light does not emanate from Greek culture, from the modern day outside world, or from any other source, but rather only from Hashem.

---

[68] *Ramban, Bereishis 26:20.*
[69] *Bereishis 25:31.*
[70] *Bereishis 25:33.*
[71] *Rashi, Bereishis 25:31.*
[72] Rav Chayun, as cited in *Me'am Lo'ez, Tehillim 36:10.*

With its varied references to the water wells, the Beis HaMikdash, the clarity of Hashem's light, and Chanukah, what a sparkling and lluminating *pasuk* this is!

Pasuk 11:
מְשֹׁךְ חַסְדְּךָ לְיֹדְעֶיךָ;
וְצִדְקָתְךָ לְיִשְׁרֵי לֵב
**Extend Your kindness to those who know You,
and Your righteousness/charity to the upright of heart.**

The Mystical Formula of the Tallis Prayer

It must be noted that *pesukim* 8 through 11 are part of a mystical formula men say every day of the year as they recite a blessing on their tallis and are still wrapped within it. The tallis, with its tzitzis on all four corners, reminds us to perform all 613 mitzvos and even has the power to elevate our consciousness to the heights of Hashem's *Kisei HaKavod*.[73]

Indeed, the *Siddur Otzar HaTefillah* cryptically states: "וְסוֹדָם שֶׁל פְּסוּקִים אֵלּוּ רָם וְרַב לַמְקֻבָּלִים" – The secret behind these *pesukim* is exalted and vast to the Kabbalists." The details of that statement may be a mystery to many, but how poignant it is that when our heads and faces are literally enveloped in a shade and darkness of sorts caused by the tallis, the Jew can instead experience under that tallis the greatest of lights: "בְּאוֹרְךָ נִרְאֶה אוֹר," *Hashem's* light, together with all the other *brachos* and beauty contained in *pesukim* 8 through 11.

Toldos, Tehillim, and the Tallis

Chazal teach us that it was Avraham Avinu who merited the mitzvah of the blue-green techeiles strings of the tzitzis through his dealings

---

[73] *Menachos* 43b.

PARSHAH & TEHILLIM HAND IN HAND

with the King of Sedom in *Parshas Lech Lecha*.[74] However, since *pesukim* 8 through 11 of *Tehillim* 36 are part of the mystical formula recited while donning the tallis, the connection between Yaakov Avinu, *Parshas Toldos*, *Tehillim* 36, and the tallis must also be explored.

Ironically, when the Torah describes the first impression that Eisav gave as he exited the womb, the Torah states: "אַדְמוֹנִי, כֻּלּוֹ כְּאַדֶּרֶת שֵׂעָר – He was red, all of him was like a hairy mantle."[75] *Rashi* provides us with a visual image of Eisav's hairiness by saying that Eisav was full of hair like a cloak made of wool, stating that Eisav was "כְּטַלִּית שֶׁל צֶמֶר הַמְלֵאָה שֵׂעָר – like a tallis made of wool, full of hair."[76]

On a deeper level, however, the tallis links back to *Parshas Noach*, where the Torah tells of Noach's three sons after the Flood.[77] Cham, who desecrated or emasculated his father, was cursed. Shem led Yafes to their father's rescue and they were blessed. Shem and Yafes were two brothers working together to help remedy the wickedness of their remaining brother. What was the God-given reward to Shem for initiating the respectful covering of his father's nakedness? *Rashi* tells us he was rewarded with his *own* children from whom Avraham Avinu and the Jewish People would emerge. It was these descendants who were blessed with the privilege of the tallis and its accompanying tzitzis.[78] Needless to say, this episode of one brother's heroism in the face of another brother's wickedness and its connection to the tallis proves to be a striking parallel to Yaakov and Eisav, to *Parshas Toldos*, and to *Tehillim* 36 with its mystical connection to the tallis.

We should also add that the three Avos correspond to the three *parshiyos* that comprise the famed *Shema Yisrael* prayer. The first

---

[74] *Sotah* 17a.
[75] *Bereishis* 25:25.
[76] *Rashi, Bereishis* 25:25.
[77] *Bereishis, Perek* 9.
[78] *Rashi, Bereishis* 9:23.

paragraph of *Shema*, which revolves around the *mitzvas aseh d'Oraisa*[79] of *ahavas Hashem*, corresponds to Avraham Avinu. The second paragraph known as *VeHayah*, which revolves around acceptance of mitzvos and the *mitzvas aseh d'Oraisa* to believe in *se'char* and *onesh* (reward and punishment), involves *din* and *mishpat* and thus corresponds to Yitzchak Avinu. The third paragraph known as *VaYomer* corresponds to Yaakov Avinu, as it not only contains the *mitzvas aseh d'Oraisa* of remembering the Exodus from Egypt – which is the culmination of a process that began with Yaakov's initial descent to Mitzrayim in *Parshas Vayigash* – but also contains the *mitzvas aseh d'Oraisa* of tzitzis, which we hold lovingly in our hands and kiss repeatedly as we daven this section each morning.

Finally, the Gemara[80] teaches that the punishment for not wearing the inexpensive white strings of tzitzis is more severe than the punishment for not wearing the *techeiles* strings of tzitzis. The Gemara provides a *mashal* of a human king who commanded one servant to bring him a cement stamp with which to brand animals and then commanded a second servant to bring him a golden stamp. When neither servant delivered, the king was much angrier at the first servant for not bringing the cement stamp because it was made of materials that were far less expensive and thus much easier to obtain than the golden stamp. As such, the first servant had no good excuse for being unable to deliver. The same is true of the white versus the blue-green dyed tzitzis strings. Furthermore, *Tosafos* asks why tzitzis are compared to a cement stamp at all, and answers that a cement stamp was used to brand slaves to signify to which master they belonged. Similarly, says *Tosafos*, the tzitzis are "מֵעִיד עַל יִשְׂרָאֵל שֶׁהֵם עַבְדֵי הקב"ה" – a testimony on the Jewish People that they are the עַבְדֵי – servants, and even the willing 'slaves' of Hashem." With that discussion of tzitzis, we return full circle to the theme discussed in the Introduction to this chapter: the theme of dedication to Hashem as a true *Eved Hashem*.

---

[79] An affirmative active ("positive") Torah-commandment.
[80] *Menachos* 43b.

Pasuk 12:
אַל תְּבוֹאֵנִי רֶגֶל גַּאֲוָה;
וְיַד רְשָׁעִים אַל תְּנִדֵנִי
**Let not come to me the foot of arrogance,
and let the hand of the wicked not move me.**

The Hand Grasping the Heel

Amazingly, this penultimate *pasuk* of *Tehillim* 36 refers to a "יָד – hand" and a "רֶגֶל – foot." Of course, this parallels the famous words of the Torah at the start of *Parshas Toldos* detailing the birth of Yaakov and Eisav. Eisav was born first, "וְאַחֲרֵי כֵן יָצָא אָחִיו, וְיָדוֹ אֹחֶזֶת בַּעֲקֵב עֵשָׂו – And after that his brother [Yaakov] emerged with his hand grasping the heel of Eisav."[81]

The above contains important symbolism. As *Rashi* explains, the grasping of the heel is a sign that Eisav's descendants will not even have the chance to formally conclude their rule before Yaakov's descendants arise and usurp their power.[82] The implication is that the descendants of Yaakov will cause the downfall and destruction of the wicked kingdom of Eisav known as Edom[83] and the Roman Empire,[84] all as a stepping-stone to the swift reestablishment of their *own* kingdom in the Era of Moshiach; a kingdom that will restore the Davidic Dynasty and a kingdom of purity and holiness that will glorify the Name of Hashem.

Pasuk 13:
שָׁם נָפְלוּ פֹּעֲלֵי אָוֶן;
דֹּחוּ וְלֹא יָכְלוּ קוּם

---

[81] *Bereishis* 25:26.
[82] *Rashi, Bereishis* 25:26, from *Pirkei D'Rabi Eliezer, perek* 32.
[83] *Bereishis* 25:30.
[84] E.g., *Rashi, Bereishis* 25:23.

CHAPTER 6: TOLDOS & TEHILLIM 36

There fell the practitioners of evil;
they were thrust down and were not able to rise.

The Downfall of Our Enemies

This concluding *pasuk* continues to emphasize Hashem's promise that the Jewish People will ultimately overcome our enemies, who are also *Hashem's* enemies, in the time of Moshiach.

Specifically, "נָפְלוּ – falling," is a reference to the descendants of Yishmael, the Arabs. The very end of the previous *Parshah*, *Chayei Sarah*, concludes with a reference to the children of Yishmael: "עַל פְּנֵי כָל אֶחָיו נָפָל."[85] According to *Rashi*, this can be explained as "in the face of all his brothers he fell," alluding to the constant "נְפִילָה – downfall" of the descendants of Yishmael that started upon the death of Avraham and set them on a perpetual freefall ever since – as we see even to this day.[86]

Nonetheless, as cruel and maniacal as Yishmael's progeny are, the truest enemy, the real "פֹּעֲלֵי אָוֶן – practitioners of evil," are the descendants of Eisav–Edom–the Roman Empire, who are our primary national nemesis in this fourth and final exile, and who embody wickedness and the *yetzer hara* just as Eisav did. In the time of Moshiach with Hashem's help, they too will experience the accursed fate of "דֹּחוּ וְלֹא יָכְלוּ קוּם." They will be pushed away, thrust continuously downward even to Gehinnom, never to rise again.[87]

Frighteningly, the very last *pasuk* of *Parshas Toldos* teaches that Eisav specifically married the daughter of Yishmael and spawned children from her.[88] This unholy union of our two cruelest enemies only added to the vehement hatred and bloddshed that Klal Yisrael has endured throughout

---

[85] *Bereishis* 25:18.

[86] *Rashi, Bereishis* 25:18, from *Bereishis Rabbah* 62:5.

[87] E.g., *Midrash Tanchuma, Tzav* 2.

[88] *Bereishis* 28:9.

the centuries. Nevertheless, the time will come when these enemies will all collapse before Hashem and His Chosen Nation. Indeed, we so anxiously await and yearn to witness the time of "שָׁם נָפְלוּ פֹּעֲלֵי אָוֶן; דֹּחוּ וְלֹא יָכְלוּ קוּם."

EISAV: EXILES, THE HOLOCAUST, AND WORLD WAR III

On its surface, there is no doubt that *Tehillim* 36 is in large part a condemnation and admonition of *reshaim* and *rishus* in general. Yet, within its connection to *Parshas Toldos* we clearly see *Tehillim* 36 as a specific condemnation and admonition of Eisav HaRasha.

A study of *Parshas Toldos* when learned in tandem with *Rashi's* commentary attacks Eisav at every opportunity.[89] As we have seen in this chapter, words and phrases in the Torah that at first glance seem innocuous and/or simply descriptive are expounded upon by *Rashi* and Chazal to criticize, and even demonize, Eisav.

If you feel sympathy for Eisav at any point in his story, it is because you have a good Jewish heart. However, Chazal were not demonizing Eisav; they were exposing Eisav as the demon he was! As Rabbi Shimon Bar Yochai says: "הֲלָכָה הִיא בְּיָדוּעַ שֶׁעֵשָׂו שׂוֹנֵא לְיַעֲקֹב – It is an established fact and it is known that Eisav hates Yaakov."[90] As we know all too well, this statement is true not only of these original brothers, but also of their descendants throughout the ages.

---

[89] E.g., *Rashi*, *Bereishis* 25:23 and 25:24.
[90] *Rashi*, *Bereishis* 33:4, from *Sifrei*, *Bamidbar* 69.

CHAPTER 6: TOLDOS & TEHILLIM 36

Parshas Toldos begins with Shem, the son of Noach, telling Rivkah Imeinu through *ruach hakodesh* that the confused baby inside her was actually twins – one destined to be a *tzaddik* and the other a *rasha*. "וַיֹּאמֶר ה' לָהּ, שְׁנֵי גוֹיִם בְּבִטְנֵךְ וּשְׁנֵי לְאֻמִּים מִמֵּעַיִךְ יִפָּרֵדוּ; וּלְאֹם מִלְאֹם יֶאֱמָץ, וְרַב יַעֲבֹד צָעִיר – And Hashem said to her: Two nations are in your womb, and two regimes from your insides will be separated; and one regime will become strong through the other regime, and the elder shall serve the younger."[91] An ominous message indeed. Yet this message is not limited to Yaakov and Eisav as individuals but rather focuses on the nations that will emanate from them: Am Yisrael, of course, who will emerge from Yaakov and his twelve sons, and the nation of Edom, who will emerge from Eisav. In this light, the Torah teaches us here that there will be constant animosity and struggle between these two regimes.

Lest you think that the nation of Edom is unknown and unmarked on a modern-day map, that it is unrepresented in the United Nations, and that it is a nation which has assimilated and vanished from the earth, think again. To our horror, Edom is Amalek, *yemach shemam*; Edom is Ancient Greece; Edom is the Roman Empire; Edom is Nazi Germany, *yemach shemam*. Camouflaged at times, Edom is nevertheless everpresent. Edom is Eisav HaRasha.

Amalek is the Biblical archenemy of the Jewish People whose intrinsic evil is a discussion for another time, but whose *rishus* Hashem commanded us to remember every day.[92]

Ancient Greece's persecution of the Jewish People marked the third of the four Jewish exiles known as *Galus Yavan*. They desecrated the Second Beis HaMikdash during the period in which Hashem produced the miracles of Chanukah, and continued to persecute Am Yisrael even in Chanukah's aftermath.

---

[91] *Bereishis* 25:23.
[92] *Devarim* 25:17–19. See also the *Sheish Zechiros* – the Six Remembrances.

The Roman Empire destroyed the Second Beis HaMikdash. Their descendants and disciples were responsible for the Crusades that took millions of Jewish lives and in whose fourth and final exile known as *Galus Edom* we have been confined for over 2,000 years to this very day.

And of course, there was Nazi Germany, *yemach shemam*, whose wounds are too horrific and too fresh to even describe in this *sefer*.

This is Eisav. This is what we must hate. As Dovid HaMelech demands of us and then fortifies us: "אֹהֲבֵי ה' שִׂנְאוּ רָע, שֹׁמֵר נַפְשׁוֹת חֲסִידָיו, מִיַּד רְשָׁעִים יַצִּילֵם – Those who love Hashem must hate evil! He [Hashem] protects the lives of His devout ones, from the hand of the wicked He rescues them."[93]

True, over the millennia, millions of Jewish lives were lost, but the Godly guarantee is that the Jewish Nation will survive and thrive. Through it all, our people known as *rachmanim*, merciful, and *gomlei chassadim*, bestowers of lovingkindness,[94] must nonetheless hate evil.

Hate is such a strong and terrible word, but evil is such a strong and terrible presence. We must not succumb to evil, we must not tolerate it, we must not ignore it, and we certainly must not perpetuate it. We cannot allow ourselves to be deceived by Eisav and his descendants. They are not our friends. They are our enemies.

Tanach and Chazal tell us of the War of *Gog U'Magog*, Armageddon.[95] Then, in the moments before the culmination of purity and righteousness in the Era of Moshiach we and our children will have the great *zechus* of heading into battle as representatives of Yaakov Avinu in the most meaningful and final war ever to be known to mankind.

By doing so, we will serve as Hashem's agents to fulfill that most dangerous, heroic, and holy of visions described in the *pasuk* we say daily

---

[93] *Tehillim* 97:10.

[94] *Midrash Tehillim*, *Shocher Tov* 1.

[95] It is important to note that the War of *Gog U'Magog*, Armageddon, is *not* inevitable. It can be avoided if the Jewish People bring the Era of Moshiach due to our *merits*, in which case Moshiach will arrive through miracles and in a peaceful fashion (e.g., *Sanhedrin* 98a; *Ohr Hachaim*, *Devarim* 24:17).

and need to start saying with more intensity than ever before: "וְעָלוּ מוֹשִׁעִים בְּהַר צִיּוֹן לִשְׁפֹּט אֶת הַר עֵשָׂו; וְהָיְתָה לַה' הַמְּלוּכָה" – And the redeemers will ascend the mountain of Tzion to judge the mountain of Eisav, and to Hashem will be the Kingship,"[96] forever and ever and ever.

Yes, we will wage war while Hashem Himself will fight at our side in this final confrontation with Eisav and his descendants, as the prayer of *Anim Zemiros* so dramatically and graphically states: "צַח וְאָדוֹם לִלְבוּשׁוֹ אָדוֹם, פּוּרָה בְּדָרְכוֹ בְּבוֹאוֹ מֵאֱדוֹם" – He [Hashem] is white and crimson; His garments will be stained red [with enemy blood], as He tramples like in a winepress when He comes from Edom."

A Closing Song of Battle and Blessing

As a closing *tefillah* and *brachah* for *Tehillim* 36, for *Parshas Toldos*, and for the month of Kislev in which *Parshas Toldos* and Chanukah coincide, let us conclude with the final passage of the famed Chanukah prayer, *Ma'oz Tzur*, and beseech Hashem:

"חֲשׂוֹף זְרוֹעַ קָדְשֶׁךָ וְקָרֵב קֵץ הַיְשׁוּעָה" – Bare Your holy arm [Hashem] and hasten the final salvation."

"נְקֹם נִקְמַת דַּם עֲבָדֶיךָ מֵאֻמָּה הָרְשָׁעָה" – Avenge the vengeance of the blood of עֲבָדֶיךָ – Your servants from the nation that is wicked," in reference to Eisav and Edom.

"כִּי אָרְכָה לָּנוּ הַיְשׁוּעָה וְאֵין קֵץ לִימֵי הָרָעָה" – For long-delayed has been the salvation of Moshiach, and there appears to be no end to the days of evil."

"דְּחֵה אַדְמוֹן בְּצֵל צַלְמוֹן" – Repel the Red One [Eisav and Edom] to the nethermost shadow of Gehinnom;" and

"הָקֵם לָנוּ רוֹעִים שִׁבְעָה" – Reestablish for us the seven shepherds" – Avraham Avinu, Yitzchak Avinu, Yaakov Avinu, Yosef

---

[96] *Ovadyah* 1:21.

HaTzaddik, Moshe Rabbeinu, Aharon HaKohen, and Dovid HaMelech, with the coming of *Moshiach Tzidkeinu, b'miheirah b'yameinu.*

CHAPTER 7

PARSHAS VAYEITZEI & TEHILLIM 3

פָּרָשַׁת וַיֵּצֵא / תְּהִלִּים ג

TEHILLIM 3 — תְּהִלִּים ג

1	A psalm by Dovid, as he fled from Avshalom his son.	א מִזְמוֹר לְדָוִד, בְּבָרְחוֹ מִפְּנֵי אַבְשָׁלוֹם בְּנוֹ.
2	Hashem, how numerous are my tormentors! Many rise up against me!	ב ה', מָה רַבּוּ צָרָי; רַבִּים קָמִים עָלָי.
3	Many say of my soul: "There is no salvation for him from God, Selah."	ג רַבִּים אֹמְרִים לְנַפְשִׁי: אֵין יְשׁוּעָתָה לּוֹ בֵא-לֹהִים סֶלָה.
4	But You, Hashem, are a shield for me; for my honor/soul, and the One Who raises my head.	ד וְאַתָּה, ה', מָגֵן בַּעֲדִי; כְּבוֹדִי, וּמֵרִים רֹאשִׁי.
5	With my voice to Hashem I call out, and He answers me from His holy mountain, Selah.	ה קוֹלִי אֶל ה' אֶקְרָא; וַיַּעֲנֵנִי מֵהַר קָדְשׁוֹ סֶלָה.
6	I lay down and slept, yet I awoke, for Hashem supports me.	ו אֲנִי שָׁכַבְתִּי וָאִישָׁנָה; הֱקִיצוֹתִי כִּי ה' יִסְמְכֵנִי.

7	I fear not the tens of thousands of people that all around are deployed against me.
8	Rise up Hashem, save me, my God, for You struck all my enemies on the cheek; the teeth of the wicked You broke.
9	To Hashem is Salvation; upon Your people is Your blessing, Selah.

ז לֹא אִירָא מֵרִבְבוֹת עָם, אֲשֶׁר סָבִיב שָׁתוּ עָלָי.

ח קוּמָה ה', הוֹשִׁיעֵנִי אֱ-לֹהַי, כִּי הִכִּיתָ אֶת כָּל אֹיְבַי לֶחִי; שִׁנֵּי רְשָׁעִים שִׁבַּרְתָּ.

ט לַה' הַיְשׁוּעָה; עַל עַמְּךָ בִרְכָתֶךָ סֶּלָה.

INTRODUCTION: THE EXPERIENCES OF YAAKOV AND DOVID INTERTWINED

The connection between *Tehillim* 3 and *Parshas Vayeitzei* is evident from the start, as their respective heroes are on the run from those looking to kill them and are beset by potential dangers at every turn.

Tehillim 3 begins with the introductory *pasuk* of "מִזְמוֹר לְדָוִד, בְּבָרְחוֹ מִפְּנֵי אַבְשָׁלוֹם בְּנוֹ – A psalm by Dovid, as he fled from Avshalom his son," in reference to the distressing story of the nearly successful attempt by Avshalom to overthrow Dovid and usurp the throne.[1] Dovid was rendered a king forced to flee from his palace and city without his army to protect him and without a definite and safe destination. He composed this *kapitel* as a *tefillah* to Hashem, both to seek Hashem's salvation and to praise Him preemptively for having received that salvation, which Dovid felt assured would come. Although Dovid would eventually be victorious, in the

---

[1] *II Shmuel, Perakim* 15–19.

CHAPTER 7: VAYEITZEI & TEHILLIM 3

process his still beloved son Avshalom was killed, leaving Dovid bereaved and heartbroken (as we discussed at the end of Chapter 4 on *Parshas Vayeira* & *Tehillim* 11).[2]

Similarly, *Parshas Vayeitzei* begins with the phrase: "וַיֵּצֵא יַעֲקֹב מִבְּאֵר שָׁבַע, וַיֵּלֶךְ חָרָנָה – And Yaakov went out from Be'er Sheva and went to Charan."[3] This event is later described in *Parshas Vayishlach* using the words "בְּבָרְחוֹ מִפְּנֵי אָחִיו" – when he fled from his brother,"[4] an expression so similar to Dovid's "בְּבָרְחוֹ מִפְּנֵי אַבְשָׁלוֹם בְּנוֹ" here in *Tehillim* 3. Like Dovid, Yaakov was also on the run, having fled from his home due to the life-threatening danger posed to him by his very own brother, Eisav HaRasha.

Toward the end of the previous *Parshah*, Yaakov's mother Rivkah Imeinu, who was acutely aware of the peril that endangered Yaakov, encouraged Yitzchak to send Yaakov to her brother Lavan in Padan-Aram, partially for the purpose of seeking a wife from the house of Lavan[5] but primarily to secretly remove Yaakov from the danger posed by Eisav. However, Yaakov left only after having received additional parting blessings from Yitzchak, which explicitly included the blessings passed on to Yitzchak by Avraham,[6] thus enabling Yaakov to depart encouraged by the knowledge that the continuity of his holy father and grandfather

---

[2] It must be noted that here in *Parshas Vayeitzei* (*Bereishis* 3:31), *Rashi* quotes parts of two *pesukim* from *II Shmuel*, *Perek* 15 (*pesukim* 12 and 31), and both of these *pesukim* have to do with co-conspirators to Avshalom's rebellion! The *Rashi* is in the context of Yaakov's dealings with Lavan and the spotted and speckled cattle and seems to be simply explaining the meaning of "early bearing flocks." However, in quoting from those *pesukim* in *II Shmuel*, *Rashi* in *Parshas Vayeitzei* is, to some degree, drawing us into the world of Avshalom's rebellion and Dovid's escape in *Tehillim* 3. Perhaps this is a hint from *Rashi* to encourage us to connect the escapes of Yaakov and Dovid. At the very least, as Rabbi Shimshon Pincus might say, this seems to be yet another "wink from Hashem" regarding the *Parsha* & *Tehillim* connection.

[3] *Bereishis* 28:10.
[4] *Bereishis* 35:7.
[5] *Bereishis* 28:1–2.
[6] *Bereishis* 28:3–4.

would be perpetuated through him and his future offspring. In addition, Chazal tell us that Yaakov further fortified himself by stopping for fourteen years to study Torah with Eiver, the great-grandson of Shem ben Noach, at the famed Yeshivas Shem V'Eiver.[7]

Nevertheless, Yaakov ultimately ran from the danger of Eisav into the danger of Lavan HaArami, who is also disparagingly referred to as Lavan HaRama'i, Lavan the cheater/trickster.[8] Lavan was not only a swindler who tried to deceive Yaakov innumerable times but also an idol worshipper. Lavan is infamously described in the Pesach Haggadah as the one who "בִּקֵּשׁ לַעֲקֹר אֶת הַכֹּל – sought to uproot everything"[9] that was Torah-true from Yaakov and his progeny. Yaakov had fled from one threat into another, more dangerous threat: he fled from the physical threat of Eisav into the spiritual threat of Lavan.

Thus, the basic parallel between *Tehillim* 3 and *Parshas Vayeitzei* is two-fold. Both focus on the greatest of *tzaddikim*, Dovid HaMelech and Yaakov Avinu, who must run away from home to escape imminent danger but who then encounter equally precarious and dangerous situations. Additionally, both involved a danger coming from within their own families: from Dovid's own son Avshalom, and from Yaakov's own twin brother Eisav as well as his uncle (and eventual father-in-law) Lavan.

These connections can be taken a step further. There is a well-known question on the opening words of *Tehillim* 3: "מִזְמוֹר לְדָוִד – A psalm by Dovid," which also can be interpreted as "A song by Dovid."[10] It seems that Dovid had sung to Hashem in joy when fleeing from his rebellious and power-hungry son. How can that be? While the Gemara[11] asks this same question and provides a famous answer (see below on *pasuk* 1 of this

---

[7] *Rashi, Bereishis* 28:9.
[8] E.g., *Daas Zekainim, Bereishis* 29:22.
[9] Pesach Haggadah; see also *Rashi, Devarim* 26:5.
[10] E.g., *Metzudas Dovid* 3:1.
[11] *Brachos* 7b.

chapter), a lesser-known answer is brought by the *Midrash Tehillim*.[12] According to this source, Dovid looked at his own unnatural and seemingly hopeless situation "בְּבָרְחוֹ – as he fled," and found direct inspiration from the experiences of Yaakov Avinu and Moshe Rabbeinu. Dovid strengthened himself by focusing on the fact that the righteous Yaakov also had to undergo a "וַיִּבְרַח" and flee, as it says in *Hoshea* in reference to the events of *Parshas Vayeitzei* (and which, by no coincidence, is also part of the *Haftarah* to *Parshas Vayeitzei*): "וַיִּבְרַח יַעֲקֹב שְׂדֵה אֲרָם; וַיַּעֲבֹד יִשְׂרָאֵל בְּאִשָּׁה, וּבְאִשָּׁה שָׁמָר" – And Yaakov fled to the field of Aram; and Yisrael served for a wife, and for a wife he waited."[13] In addition, said Dovid, the righteous Moshe also had to "וַיִּבְרַח" and flee, as we see in *Shemos*: "וַיִּבְרַח מֹשֶׁה מִפְּנֵי פַרְעֹה" – And Moshe fled because of Pharaoh" after it became known that Moshe had killed a wicked Egyptian.[14] Inspired and reinvigorated by that realization, Dovid declared: "I, too, am fleeing just like them!"

Dovid then bravely and excitedly proclaimed: "זָכַרְתִּי מִשְׁפָּטֶיךָ מֵעוֹלָם ה', וָאֶתְנֶחָם – I remembered Your judgments of old, Hashem, and was comforted,"[15] and further declared: "I recall Your *middas ha'din*, attribute of strict judgment, with which You dealt with the original great ones, Yaakov and Moshe, and found comfort in this for myself."

Thus, not only does Dovid's experience in *Tehillim* 3 parallel that of Yaakov's in *Parshas Vayeitzei*, it is much more. As the above *Midrash Tehillim* reveals, Dovid not only composed *Tehillim* 3 while endangered and fleeing from Avshalom, but also had the emotional and spiritual strength to compose it as a "מִזְמוֹר – a joyous song." Dovid saw that his own plight and flight mirrored that of the very first *tzaddik* to be in such a predicament: the righteous Yaakov Avinu in *Parshas Vayeitzei*. It was this

---

[12] *Midrash Tehillim, Shocher Tov* 3.
[13] *Hoshea* 12:13.
[14] *Shemos* 2:15.
[15] *Tehillim* 119:52.

very reflection that provided Dovid with the *chizuk* and inspiration he so desperately needed!

With this background, we can now analyze the words of Dovid HaMelech in *Tehillim* 3 and find in them numerous additional connections to Yaakov Avinu in *Parshas Vayeitzei*.

THE MANY CONNECTIONS BETWEEN PARSHAS VAYEITZEI & TEHILLIM 3

Pasuk 1:

מִזְמוֹר לְדָוִד, בְּבָרְחוֹ מִפְּנֵי אַבְשָׁלוֹם בְּנוֹ

A psalm [a song] by Dovid, as he fled from Avshalom his son.

See the above Introduction which focuses on this *pasuk* in detail, including the connections between Yaakov Avinu and Dovid HaMelech and their similar challenge of "בְּבָרְחוֹ," having had to flee from Eisav and Avshalom, respectively.

Consolation and Calamity from Closeness

In the Introduction to this chapter, we discussed the answer of the *Midrash Tehillim* as to why and how Dovid was able to compose *Tehillim* 3 as a joyous song to Hashem, as a "מִזְמוֹר לְדָוִד – psalm/song by Dovid," rather than as a *lamentation* recounting the harrowing circumstances of his own son Avshalom rising against him in open rebellion to usurp his throne. Yet, the more traditional answer is found in the following Gemara.[16] Initially Dovid was informed through Divine prophecy that Hashem would be bringing upon him a rebellion from within his own home.[17] At first, Dovid was concerned that perhaps the uprising would be initiated by a slave or a *mamzer* who would act mercilessly toward Dovid and not show him any pity or compassion. However, once Dovid learned that the rebellion would be led by his very own son, the sensation that Dovid felt was one of joy: he was happy, consoled by the expectation that ultimately mercy would be shown to him by Avshalom, as it is the nature of a son to have mercy on his father.

In stark contrast, Eisav's bloodlust toward his brother Yaakov was received with no such joy. When Rivkah was informed through *ruach hakodesh*[18] that Eisav intended to kill Yaakov, Rivkah immediately warned Yaakov that he must run.[19] Rivkah also began to put into motion *Yitzchak's* approval of Yaakov leaving home, although based on reasons that focused on his finding a suitable wife[20] rather than Eisav's thirst for revenge. Even more striking is Rivkah's statement to Yaakov: "לָמָה אֶשְׁכַּל גַּם שְׁנֵיכֶם יוֹם אֶחָד" – Why should I be bereaved of both of you on the same day,"[21] which *Rashi* explains was an expression of Rivkah's genuine fear that Eisav would kill Yaakov. Rivkah also feared that even if Yaakov succeeded in defending himself and killing Eisav, Eisav's sons would then retaliate and kill Yaakov, bringing further calamity upon the family in a vicious cycle of murder.[22]

Therefore, unlike Dovid who saw a silver lining in the rebellion from within his family, Yaakov's predicament with Eisav involved no such expectation of mercy or hope for reconciliation – not by Yaakov, who even

---

[16] *Brachos* 7b.
[17] *II Shmuel* 12:11.
[18] *Rashi, Bereishis* 27:42.
[19] *Bereishis* 27:43.
[20] *Bereishis* 27:46.
[21] *Bereishis* 27:45.
[22] *Rashi, Bereishis* 27:45.

more than 20 years later in *Parshas Vayishlach* still feared a violent confrontation with Eisav,[23] nor even by Rivkah, Eisav's own mother.

Pasuk 2:
ה', מָה רַבּוּ צָרָי;
רַבִּים קָמִים עָלָי

Hashem, how numerous are my tormentors!
Many rise up against me!

Yaakov's Many *Tzaros*: Problems

Here the word "צָרָי" refers not only to tormentors, but also to צָרוֹת: problems and troubles in general, which is the traditional meaning of the word.

As the *Maharal* explains, each of the Avos were tested: Avraham was tested through abundance of blessing, Yitzchak was tested with physical suffering in the form of lost eyesight which rendered him as if dead, and "יַעֲקֹב נִתְנַסָּה מָה שֶׁהָיָה בַּעַל צָרָה" – Yaakov was tested in that he was a person to whom Hashem had given so many צָרוֹת – *tzaros*/problems."[24]

A powerful support to this can be found in *Parshas Mikeitz* when Yaakov finally conceded that he had no choice but to send his beloved Binyamin on a perilous journey down to Mitzrayim along with his other sons. Yaakov then prayed and blessed his sons using the Name of God: "אֵ-ל שַׁדָּ-י."[25] *Rashi* explains from the Midrash that the Name שַׁדָּ-י was specifically used by Yaakov to call upon Hashem Who had commanded: "דַּי – Enough!" when He stopped creating the world and/or created the world with boundaries and limits. So too, Yaakov davened: "Hashem should say דַּי, enough to my *tzaros* and troubles, for I have not had calm since my youth. I have had the *tzaros* of Lavan, *tzaros* of Eisav, *tzaros* of

---

[23] *Bereishis* 32:8 and 32:12.
[24] *Chiddushei Aggados, Sanhedrin* 107a.
[25] *Bereishis* 43:14.

CHAPTER 7: VAYEITZEI & TEHILLIM 3

Rochel, *tzaros* of Dinah, *tzaros* of Yosef, *tzaros* of Shimon, and now *tzaros* of Binyamin."[26]

Even earlier, in *Parshas Vayeitzei*, Yaakov implored his household to rid themselves of all hints of idolatrous objects so that he could properly construct an alter to "לָאֵ-ל הָעֹנֶה אֹתִי בְּיוֹם צָרָתִי – To the God Who answers me on the day of my *tzaros* – problems, troubles, and distress."[27]

In addition, in each weekday davening after the second *Ashrei*, we say *Tehillim* 20 which contains the *pasuk*: "יַעַנְךָ ה' בְּיוֹם צָרָה; יְשַׂגֶּבְךָ שֵׁם אֱ-לֹהֵי יַעֲקֹב – May Hashem answer you on the day of *tzarah*, distress; may you be made impregnable by the Name of the God of Yaakov."[28] There too, the *Midrash Tehillim* addresses the connection between *tzarah* and *Yaakov* specifically (as opposed to Avraham and Yitzchak) and states that Yaakov was the *Av* most beset by problems and *tzaros*. Therefore, we daven each day that Hashem, Who answered Yaakov in his many times of *tzarah*, should please answer us as well, and specifically answer us in Yaakov's merit for having confronted and withstood so many *tzaros*.[29]

Rav Yeruchum Olshin explains that Hashem intended for Yaakov to live a life of *tzaros* so that he would have the opportunity to display – and in so doing, teach *us* – that a Jew must have *emunah* that everything that happens is entirely the desire of Hashem and is for our benefit. We must love, thank, and bless Hashem for what appears to be good and for what appears to be bad – for since it all emanates from Hashem, it is all ultimately good. The conduit for this lesson is Yaakov Avinu and his steadfast *emunah* amidst a constant barrage of *tzarah*.[30]

Surely this can also be said of Dovid HaMelech, the author of the phrases "ה' מָה רַבּוּ צָרָי" and "יַעַנְךָ ה' בְּיוֹם צָרָה," and the king whose life was replete with *tzaros*, and yet whose lifelong conduct and crafting of *Sefer*

---

[26] *Rashi, Bereishis* 43:14, from *Midrash Tanchuma, Mikeitz* 10.
[27] *Bereishis* 35:3.
[28] *Tehillim* 20:2.
[29] *Midrash Tehillim, Shocher Tov* 20.
[30] *Yareiach LaMoadim, Chanukah.*

Tehillim itself, often from within the deepest throes of those *tzaros*, attests to his tremendous *emunah* in Hashem and ability to see the goodness of Hashem always.

A further testament to this *yesod* is Dovid's famous declaration: "לוּלֵא הֶאֱמַנְתִּי לִרְאוֹת בְּטוּב ה'" – Had I not believed/trusted that I would see the goodness of Hashem,"[31] I would have been lost.[32] This statement combines *emunah* and seeing the טוּב, goodness, of Hashem. Moreover, the placement of such a statement directly following the previous *pasuk* conveys the depth of Dovid's faith, for there Dovid exclaims: "אַל תִּתְּנֵנִי בְּנֶפֶשׁ צָרָי – Do not deliver me into the desire of my tormentors/my *tzaros*!"[33]

Thus, the phrase "ה' מָה רַבּוּ צָרָי" is befitting of both Dovid and Yaakov. In addition, these words remind us that although the *tzaros* may seem innumerable and insurmountable, they emanate not from evil nor from chance, but from *Hashem* – and specifically from His Name "י-ה-ו-ה," His attribute of mercy and kindness.

Yaakov's Many *Tzaros*: Rival Wives

"צָרָי" can also have an entirely different meaning. While it may be surprising to some, Torah law permits polygamy (although it was completely banned for Ashkenazi Jews in the tenth century by Rabbi Gershom ben Yehudah in his decree known as *Takanas Rebbeinu Gershom*). Interestingly, in Hebrew the word "צָרָה" is also the term used to describe the relationship between "co-wives," and is literally translated as "rival," while "צָרוֹת" describes multiple wives and is the plural word for "rivals." Of course, these co-wives are not required to be actual rivals, but

---

[31] *Tehillim* 27:13.
[32] See *Rashi, Brachos* 4a.
[33] *Tehillim* 27:12.

CHAPTER 7: VAYEITZEI & TEHILLIM 3

Chazal clearly chose this terminology carefully, hinting that such rivalry must be anticipated and is perhaps inevitable.[34]

Not coincidentally, an example of this terminology is found in *Parshas Vayeitzei*, as *Rashi* discusses Rochel Imeinu giving her maidservant Bilhah to Yaakov as "צָרָתָהּ – her rival wife," so that Rochel's family may be built through her, just as Sarah Imeinu had initially done with Hagar and Avraham.[35]

Therefore, "ה' מָה רַבּוּ צָרָי" can be interpreted as a statement applicable to Yaakov Avinu in proclaiming: "Hashem, how numerous are my wives!" in reference to his multiple marriages, all of which took place in *Parshas Vayeitzei*: first to Leah Imeinu due to the deception of Lavan, and then to Rochel Imeinu his originally intended bride, as well as his relationships with Bilhah and Zilpah who are sometimes referred to as the *Shefachos*, the Maidservants, but who also became wives.[36]

It should also be noted that the original reference by Dovid HaMelech to "צָרָי" in *Tehillim* 3:2 could also extend beyond "my problems" and on a deeper level also refer to *his* wives and familial relationships. For Dovid HaMelech ultimately married six wives[37] and had many other permissible concubines. Some of those unions were difficult, such as his marriage to Michal, the daughter of the prior King, Shaul. In addition, *Rashi* on the very next *pasuk* of *Tehillim* 3 teaches that Dovid's detractors accused him of impropriety in his relationship with Batsheva, whose union with Dovid would ultimately lead to the birth of Shlomo. Shlomo would go on to

---

[34] E.g., *Gitten* 23b.
[35] *Rashi, Bereishis* 30:3. See also *Rashi, Bereishis* 16:2 where *Rashi* uses the word צָרָתִי in the context of Sarah bringing Hagar into her home, although it must be noted that Hagar was not a true wife but rather only a concubine to Avraham and remained a maidservant to Sarah.
[36] See *Rashi, Bereishis* 29:34, where *Rashi* states in reference to Yaakov: "וְאַרְבַּע נָשִׁים יִשָּׂא – And that he would marry four wives," specifically calling all four women "wives" and stating that they were "married," thus ruling out the possibility that the Maidservants were only concubines.
[37] *II Shmuel* 3:2-5.

become Dovid's rightful and effective successor to the Jewish throne, as well as the builder of the First Beis HaMikdash, which were two of the loftiest and holiest successes of Am Yisrael and which Hashem purposefully engineered through Shlomo in order to evidence Dovid's lack of sin with regard to Batsheva.[38] However, the fact that Dovid required such vindication in the first place is a prime example of the complexities of his marriages. Finally, Avshalom, as part of his revolt against Dovid, had relations with Dovid's concubines specifically to solidify the authenticity of his rebellion and publicize his intention to usurp the throne.[39] As such, the *kavanah* expressed by Dovid in the statement "ה' מָה רַבּוּ צָרָי" contains the dual meaning of צָרַי as "my problems" and צָרַי as "my many wives."

Pasuk 3:
רַבִּים אֹמְרִים לְנַפְשִׁי:
אֵין יְשׁוּעָתָה לּוֹ בֵא-לֹהִים סֶלָה
Many say of my soul:
"There is no salvation for him from God, Selah."

The Spiritual Dangers Posed by Lavan

Pasuk 3 is a reference to Lavan HaRama'i. For while in *pasuk* 2 the expression of "רַבִּים קָמִים עָלָי – many rise up against me," refers to dangers in a *physical* sense such as the dangers posed by Eisav HaRasha, here the emphasis is an attack on the נֶפֶשׁ, "רַבִּים אֹמְרִים לְנַפְשִׁי," which is an attack on the Jewish soul.

As noted in the Introduction to this chapter, Lavan was not looking to harm Yaakov's family physically;[40] rather, his primary goal was בִּקֵּשׁ לַעֲקֹר אֶת הַכֹּל – to uproot the souls of a budding Jewish Nation by extinguishing

---

[38] E.g., *Nefesh Shimshon: Siddur HaTefillah*, pp. 188-198.
[39] *II Shmuel* 16:22.
[40] *Bereishis* 31:43, and *Rashi* there.

their connection to Torah and their connection to Hashem. It is for this reason that even the Pesach Haggadah, designed to focus on the evils of the physical slavery in Egypt, conveys that Lavan was even worse than Pharaoh, for Pharaoh tried to eradicate Jewish bodies and lives while Lavan tried to eradicate the Jewish soul.

While spiritual destruction was Lavan's long-term goal, on a day-to-day basis he also sought to deceive and cheat Yaakov at every opportunity, a tactic that could only have been so consistently and enthusiastically employed by one who either rejects Hashem or expects that his victim will not be protected by Hashem – that his victim is relegated to abandonment in the form of "אֵין יְשׁוּעָתָה לּוֹ בֵא-לֹהִים סֶלָה" – There is no salvation for him from God."

This approach is supported in our *Parshah*, when we read that Lavan, a devout idol worshipper typical of his times, frantically searched for his missing *terafim*, a type of idol.[41] As such, Lavan's many attempts to trick and defraud Yaakov were not just schemes driven by a desire for financial gain but were rather part of the spiritual war Lavan constantly waged against Yaakov. This was a war to prove "אֵין יְשׁוּעָתָה לּוֹ בֵא-לֹהִים סֶלָה" – that Yaakov was unprotected by Hashem. This fueled Lavan's hopes each time he tried to swindle Yaakov, and this must have continued to be his hope no matter how many times Hashem enabled Yaakov to prevail. Indeed, the word "סֶלָה" connotes something constant and consistent, thus reinforcing that Lavan never wavered from attempts to challenge and cheat Yaakov in order to discourage and demoralize Yaakov's faith in Hashem, or to at least negatively influence the faith of Yaakov's family.

Lavan was relentless in his attempts to undermine the spirituality and נֶפֶשׁ of the Jewish People. We too must be relentless in protecting and preserving the precious נֶפֶשׁ that is ours.

---

[41] *Bereishis* 31:32–35.

PARSHAH & TEHILLIM HAND IN HAND

The Dangers Posed by All of the Exiles

Pesukim 2 and 3 both contain the word "רַבִּים," while a third such similar expression in the word "רַבּוּ" is also found in *pasuk* 2. My *rebbi*, Rabbi Shmuel Brazil, taught that within the word רַבִּים, which means many or vast, there is a hidden reference to the far-reaching and long-lasting four exiles that Hashem has required the Jewish People to endure:

- The ר in רַבִּים stands for רוֹמִי – ancient Rome and the Roman Empire, the descendants of Eisav and Edom who destroyed the Second Beis HaMikdash and in whose exile we remain today even after more than 2,000 years. This is the fourth and final exile that we pray each day for Hashem to end with the coming of Moshiach (see Chapter 6).
- The ב in רַבִּים stands for בָּבֶל – Bavel and the Babylonian Empire, which destroyed the First Beis HaMikdash and began the first exile.
- The י in רַבִּים stands for יָוָן – the Greek Empire, descendants of Eisav who were the villains of Chanukah and the nation responsible for the third exile.
- The ם in רַבִּים stands for מָדַי – the nefarious פָּרָס וּמָדַי exile known as the Persian/Median Exile, the second exile, during which period the story of Purim took place.

In fact, the Midrash[42] says that the ladder upon which Yaakov saw angels traversing up and down was actually Hashem showing Yaakov a vision of the future exiles: first the Sar (ministering angel) of Bavel rising up the ladder seventy rungs and then descending; then the Sar of Madai rising up the ladder fifty-two rungs and descending; then the Sar of Yavan rising one hundred rungs and descending; and finally the Sar of Edom rising and rising with seemingly no end and no descent. Yaakov became

---

[42] *Midrash Tanchuma, Vayeitzei* 2.

fearful and asked Hashem whether perhaps Edom would never fall, to which Hashem responded: "וְאַתָּה אַל תִּירָא עַבְדִּי יַעֲקֹב נְאֻם ה', וְאַל תֵּחַת יִשְׂרָאֵל – Do not fear, my servant Yaakov, and do not be frightened Yisrael,"[43] for even if you had seen Edom rise all the way up to Me, from there I would cast him down!

Thus, the emphasis on "רַבִּים" in *Tehillim* 3 refers to much more than just the "many" personal enemies of Dovid HaMelech and Yaakov Avinu. It is an allusion to the archenemies of the Jewish People throughout the centuries, including Yaakov's brother and nemesis Eisav HaRasha, the founder and representative of Edom that signifies our present-day and final exile. Even more importantly, the emphasis on "רַבִּים" in *Tehillim* 3 reinforces our *emunah* by reminding us that each of the exiles is a key part of Hashem's broader plan for the Jewish People, which we were predestined to undergo and emerge from each time as an even greater nation.

Pasuk 4:
וְאַתָּה, ה', מָגֵן בַּעֲדִי; כְּבוֹדִי, וּמֵרִים רֹאשִׁי

**But You, Hashem, are a shield for me;
for my honor/soul, and the One Who raises my head.**

Striking Back at Evil Through Trust and Prayer

Here Dovid and Yaakov strike back at their enemies not with weapons but through the prayer of this very *pasuk*, which bespeaks an unflinching *bitachon* in Hashem:

- "וְאַתָּה"– You, directly addressing Hashem in an informal, personal manner, which conveys the closeness felt by the speaker.

---

[43] *Yirmiyahu* 30:10.

- "ה'" – Calling upon the Name of י-ה-ו-ה, which represents Divine *rachamim* and *chessed* without limit.
- "מָגֵן בַּעֲדִי" – Hashem is a shield for me, providing protection from danger. In addition, this expression calls upon the merit of Avraham Avinu, who received the blessings of מָגֵן אַבְרָהָם and whom Hashem promised to protect even *before* harm could approach him like a defensive shield in battle.
- "כְּבוֹדִי" – Literally means "my honor," but here it is also interpreted by the commentators as referring to "my soul" – the Jewish soul. Indeed, these two meanings are intertwined because the grandeur of the Jewish soul is the underlying reason for the importance of Jewish honor. In addition, this expression alludes to Lavan's vendetta against the Jewish soul, as discussed above.

Yaakov's Head Is Heavenly

The above *pasuk* concludes with the words: "וּמֵרִים רֹאשִׁי – and the One Who raises my head" in respectful pride.

The presence of the *shoresh* of the word רֹאשׁ here is a clear allusion to Yaakov Avinu, who in *Parshas Vayeitzei* is associated with numerous references to the word רֹאשׁ.

At the very start of *Parshas Vayeitzei*, the Torah states: "וַיֵּלֶן שָׁם כִּי בָא הַשֶּׁמֶשׁ, וַיִּקַּח מֵאַבְנֵי הַמָּקוֹם וַיָּשֶׂם מְרַאֲשֹׁתָיו; וַיִּשְׁכַּב בַּמָּקוֹם הַהוּא" – He spent the night there because the sun had set; he took from the stones of the place and he put them מְרַאֲשֹׁתָיו – around his head, and he lay down in that place."[44] There the Torah emphasizes Yaakov's רֹאשׁ, and *Rashi*[45] tells us that he put his head down to sleep for the first time in fourteen years specifically using stones to protect his head from dangerous animals. In addition, Chazal tell us that the stones all competed for Yaakov's attention and wanted to serve him, as each stone said: "עָלַי יָנִיחַ צַדִּיק אֶת רֹאשׁוֹ" – Upon

---

[44] *Bereishis* 28:11.

[45] *Rashi, Bereishis* 28:11, from *Bereishis Rabbah* 68:11.

me shall the *tzaddik* lay his head." So desperate was each stone to assist the righteous Yaakov that Hashem performed a miracle and combined them into a single stone to cushion his head.[46]

Furthermore, there Yaakov dreamed of the ladder, saw a vision of the angels ascending and descending it, and was blessed by Hashem with promises of protection and success. Yaakov awoke not only awed by those events, but also strengthened and invigorated. Chazal tell us that Yaakov's image is carved into the *Kisei HaKavod*, Hashem's Throne of Glory.[47] My *rebbi*, Rabbi Shmuel Brazil explained that the angels who went up and down the ladder were actually the exact same angels ascending and descending, back and forth in amazement, for they could not believe the sight they were seeing: the same person, Yaakov, whose ראש, head and face, were engraved on the Throne of Hashem at the top of the ladder above in heaven, was sleeping at the foot of the ladder below.

In addition, after awakening from that dream, the Torah tells us: "וַיִּקַּח אֶת הָאֶבֶן אֲשֶׁר שָׂם מְרַאֲשֹׁתָיו, וַיָּשֶׂם אֹתָהּ מַצֵּבָה; וַיִּצֹק שֶׁמֶן עַל רֹאשָׁהּ – And he [Yaakov] took the stone he had placed around his head and set it as a monument, and he poured oil over its head."[48] There, twice more, the *shoresh* of the word "ראש" is emphasized.

The many Torah and rabbinic references here to "ראש" in regard to Yaakov surely highlight the praise of Hashem as "וּמֵרִים ראשִׁי – the One Who raises my head." We are reminded that when striking back at evil through prayer, battle, or by whatever means the circumstances may require, a Jew must be directed by his ראש – his intellect – and not his fears or feelings, so that Hashem may raise that head proudly and victoriously.

Finally, it is important to note that these lessons are gleaned specifically from Yaakov, whose name is derived from the *eikev*, the lowly heel, but

---

[46] *Rashi, Bereishis* 28:11, from *Chullin* 91b.
[47] *Bereishis Rabbah* 68:12; *Chullin* 91b.
[48] *Bereishis* 28:18.

who instead represents the רֹאשׁ, the head, which is high atop the body. For it is the head that houses one's intelligence, and with the intellect leading, a Jew can perform acts that are heavenly.

Pasuk 5:
קוֹלִי אֶל ה' אֶקְרָא;
וַיַּעֲנֵנִי מֵהַר קָדְשׁוֹ סֶלָה
With my voice to Hashem I call out,
and He answers me from His holy mountain, Selah.

Gateway to Heaven: The Voice of Prayer and the Beis HaMikdash

The statement "קוֹלִי אֶל ה' אֶקְרָא" brings to mind the *original* power of the קוֹל, the "voice," and specifically the Jewish קוֹל engaged in prayer. This is famously derived from Yaakov Avinu, of whom it is said in *Parshas Toldos*: "הַקֹּל קוֹל יַעֲקֹב – The voice is the voice of Yaakov,"[49] which is the source for the Jewish power of *tefillah* and from which Dovid HaMelech and all Jews throughout the generations derive their inspiration to daven.

The phrase "וַיַּעֲנֵנִי מֵהַר קָדְשׁוֹ סֶלָה" alludes to Yaakov's dream with the ladder in *Parshas Vayeitzei*. This dream took place at none other than the future site of the Beis HaMikdash, often referred to as a "הַר," such as הַר הַמּוֹרִיָּה, הַר הַבַּיִת, and הַר צִיּוֹן, to which the expression "הַר קָדְשׁוֹ" here clearly refers.[50]

The linking of the concept of the power of prayer with the location of the Beis HaMikdash makes this *pasuk* particularly compelling. In *Parshas Vayeitzei*, Yaakov calls the site of the Beis HaMikdash "שַׁעַר הַשָּׁמַיִם – Gate of the Heavens,"[51] which means that it is a place of *tefillah*, a gateway to

---

[49] *Bereishis* 27:22.
[50] E.g., *Radak* and *Ibn Ezra* to *Tehillim* 3:5.
[51] *Bereishis* 28:17.

Hashem, the place where prayers can most easily ascend heavenward,[52] and the place aligned with the heavenly Beis HaMikdash above.[53] It is no wonder that when Yaakov awoke from his dream and realized he had slept in such a holy place, he immediately davened. He prayed to Hashem to safeguard him on his journey, to sustain him, and to allow him to eventually return to his father's home unscathed.[54] Yes, these were things he desperately desired and needed, but the main goal was the *tefillah* itself: to daven to Hashem, and to do so at the future site of the Beis HaMikdash.

To this day, Jews from all four corners of the earth longingly and lovingly face toward Hashem's "הַר קָדְשׁוֹ" when davening, and among our greatest joys is to daven at the *Kosel HaMaaravi*, which contains Hashem's *Shechinah*[55] and is the closest place to the actual הַר הַבַּיִת, Hashem's שַׁעַר הַשָּׁמָיִם.

Pasuk 6:
אֲנִי שָׁכַבְתִּי וָאִישָׁנָה;
הֱקִיצוֹתִי כִּי ה' יִסְמְכֵנִי
I lay down and slept,
yet I awoke, for Hashem supports me.

Even While We Sleep, Hashem Protects Us

The *Malbim* on this *pasuk* explains it in historical context, teaching that it refers to the traitorous advice that Dovid's former adviser Achitophel had given to Avshalom – to attack an exhausted Dovid specifically while he slept.[56] It was advice not ultimately followed but advice the *Malbim* says would have been successful – for indeed Dovid

---

[52] *Rashi, Bereishis* 28:17.
[53] *Rashi, Bereishis* 28:17, from *Bereishis Rabbah* 69:7.
[54] *Bereishis* 28:18–22.
[55] *Midrash Tehillim, Shocher Tov* 11.
[56] *II Shmuel* 17:1–2.

was asleep and vulnerable, and thus would have been susceptible to outside dangers, at least from a "natural" perspective.

Yet this *pasuk* is also a universal statement of *bitachon* in Hashem, that despite being beset by troubles, the Jew can still sleep soundly and securely, for he knows that Hashem is protecting him.

Most of all, the reference to sleep here in *Tehillim* 3 is astounding because it corresponds to the very start of *Parshas Vayeitzei*[57] where we find that Yaakov, never having slept for fourteen years while learning Torah in Yeshivas Shem V'Eiver,[58] unknowingly reached the site of the Beis HaMikdash and, of all things, went to sleep and experienced the famous God-given dream of "Jacob's Ladder." And when Yaakov awoke, it was with the realization that Hashem's Presence was closer than ever before, guarding him all evening and all his life. This recognition also prompted Yaakov to immediately daven to Hashem for *continued* support in the future.

Pasuk 7:

לֹא אִירָא מֵרִבְבוֹת עָם,
אֲשֶׁר סָבִיב שָׁתוּ עָלָי

**I fear not the tens of thousands of people
that all around are deployed against me.**

The Bedtime Prayer and *Tehillim* 3

Whether it be Avshalom's military forces deployed against Dovid[59] or the terrible dangers posed by Eisav and Lavan against Yaakov, this *pasuk* expresses that our heroic *tzaddikim* are unafraid, for they are confident that Hashem is with them.

---

[57] *Bereishis* 28:10–22.
[58] *Rashi, Bereishis* 28:11, from *Bereishis Rabbah* 68:11.
[59] *Malbim, Tehillim* 3:7.

In addition, continuing with the theme of sleep that began in *pasuk* 6, "רִבְבוֹת עָם" alludes to harmful spirits, known as *mazikin* or *sheidim*, that can attack and harm a person while asleep.[60] For this reason, Chazal instituted that each night we are to recite *Krias Shema Al HaMitah*, also known as the Bedtime Prayer, thereby ensuring that each Jew goes to sleep with words of Torah on his lips, and in that merit be protected while asleep.[61]

When considering *pesukim* 6 and 7, it should come as no surprise that Chazal incorporated *Tehillim* 3 into the nightly *Krias Shema Al HaMitah* prayer.

Additionally, as we go to sleep each night, our recitation of *Tehillim* 3 should cause us to reflect upon the holy dream that Hashem graced Yaakov Avinu with in *Parshas Vayeitzei*: a dream filled with angels and the blessings of Hashem, a dream that took place at the future site of the Beis HaMikdash. With proper focus, such beautiful thoughts can accompany us as we close our eyes and relinquish our mind and soul to Hashem each evening.

Ha'malach Ha'goel

The Bedtime Prayer also contains the famous *tefillah* known as *Ha'malach Ha'goel*:

הַמַּלְאָךְ הַגֹּאֵל אֹתִי מִכָּל רָע יְבָרֵךְ אֶת הַנְּעָרִים
וְיִקָּרֵא בָהֶם שְׁמִי, וְשֵׁם אֲבֹתַי אַבְרָהָם וְיִצְחָק,
וְיִדְגּוּ לָרֹב בְּקֶרֶב הָאָרֶץ

May the angel who redeems me from all evil bless the young men,
and may my name be declared upon them,
and the names of my forefathers Avraham and Yitzchak,
and like fish may they reproduce abundantly within the land.[62]

---

[60] E.g., *Rashi, Tehillim* 91:7.
[61] *Brachos* 5a.
[62] *Bereishis* 48:16.

PARSHAH & TEHILLIM HAND IN HAND

This poignant prayer, originally said by Yaakov Avinu as a blessing to his grandchildren Ephraim and Menashe the sons of Yosef, has become a fundamental bedtime *tefillah* recited by even the sleepiest of Jews before falling asleep. In addition, *Ha'malach Ha'goel* is a *pasuk* especially beloved by parents and children, who often sing it together as part of their nightly bedtime routine, creating cherished and holy memories from generation to generation.

Torah Twenty-Four Hours a Day/Seven Days a Week

Interestingly, in connection with Yaakov's dream of the ladder, the Torah states: "וַיִּיקַץ יַעֲקֹב מִשְּׁנָתוֹ – And Yaakov awoke from his sleep."[63] The *Baal Haturim* interprets this phrase to possess an additional meaning: that Yaakov awoke "מִמִּשְׁנָתוֹ – from his Torah learning," for his day was so filled with the study of Torah that even while he slept, his mind, heart, and soul continued learning even in his dreams.[64]

This was not only true of Yaakov Avinu but is true of every Jew: the Torah we learn each day is reviewed by our *neshamah* when we sleep (and some say that we are even *rewarded* for that subconscious sleep-learning). This is indeed a great opportunity and gift from Hashem. Yet it also contains a warning: if a Jew has not learned any Torah that day, then his soul has nothing productive to do when the body is asleep, and negative thoughts and dreams can potentially fill that void. For this reason, the Bedtime Prayer itself contains paragraphs and *pesukim* specifically designed to count as some last-second Torah learning before we fall asleep.

Waking Up with Hashem

Finally, a "good night's sleep" for a Jew means that he awakens invigorated not only physically but spiritually. Yaakov went to sleep

---

[63] *Bereishis* 28:16.

[64] *Baal Haturim, Bereishis* 28:16, from *Bereishis Rabbah* 69:7.

in danger and on the run. But when he awoke from his dream with the ladder and recalled that Hashem had promised to protect him, "His heart lifted his feet and it became easy to walk," for he trusted that he was under the guardianship of Hashem.[65]

While it is true that Yaakov had not experienced an ordinary dream but rather a prophecy, each of us can also awake reinvigorated every morning with a heartfelt *Modeh Ani*, thanking Hashem for our new and improved *neshamah*, confident that we too will be protected by Hashem in the day to come.

Importantly, one of the best ways to ensure that we wake up properly and fully recharged is to go to sleep properly. As Rav Shimshon Pincus said, we must "go to sleep like a Jew" by reciting *Krias Shema Al HaMitah*.

Pasuk 8:
קוּמָה ה'׳, הוֹשִׁיעֵנִי אֱ-לֹהַי,
כִּי הִכִּיתָ אֶת כָּל אֹיְבַי לֶחִי;
שִׁנֵּי רְשָׁעִים שִׁבַּרְתָּ
**Rise up Hashem, save me, my God,
for You struck all my enemies on the cheek;
the teeth of the wicked You broke.**

Amazingly, this *pasuk* is strongly associated with Yaakov Avinu. Specifically, this *pasuk* focuses on Hashem's dealings with Yaakov's enemies and the protection He had afforded Yaakov. Of course, this *pasuk* is applicable to us as well, for it describes our confidence in Hashem that He will continue to protect us in the future.

We will now analyze this *pasuk* in reverse order.

---

[65] *Rashi, Bereishis* 29:1, from *Bereishis Rabbah* 70:8.

Break His Teeth

"שִׁנֵּי רְשָׁעִים שִׁבַּרְתָּ – The teeth of the wicked You broke" is an explicit reference to the punishment of עֵשָׂו הָרָשָׁע, Eisav the Wicked. When Eisav confronted Yaakov in *Parshas Vayishlach*, the Torah tells us: "וַיָּרָץ עֵשָׂו לִקְרָאתוֹ וַיְחַבְּקֵהוּ, וַיִּפֹּל עַל צַוָּארָו וַיִּשָּׁקֵהוּ, וַיִּבְכּוּ" – Eisav ran toward him, and he embraced him, and fell upon his neck, and kissed him, and they wept."[66]

There is a discussion in Chazal about the sincerity of Eisav's kiss,[67] and even an opinion that Eisav tried to kill Yaakov at that moment by biting his neck.[68] The Midrash says that Hashem turned Yaakov's neck to marble to protect him, and that Eisav injured himself and broke his teeth in fulfillment of the *pasuk* "שִׁנֵּי רְשָׁעִים שִׁבַּרְתָּ".[69]

It should be noted that the concept of the "breaking of the teeth" reflects that Eisav was beyond reformation. Regarding another famous רָשָׁע, one of the "four sons" discussed in the Pesach Haggadah, Chazal recognize his wickedness and say "הַקְהֵה אֶת שִׁנָּיו – blunt his teeth," but do not *break* them, for he can still do *teshuvah*. Eisav, however, had his teeth *broken*, to show that there was no hope for him.

Kisses of the Enemy

"כִּי הִכִּיתָ אֶת כָּל אֹיְבַי לֶחִי – For You struck all my enemies on the cheek."

The enemy referenced here is Lavan HaRama'i. The Torah reveals that Lavan was a very big kisser, even of strangers, presumably on the cheek. In *Parshas Vayeitzei*, when Lavan and Yaakov first met and were essentially strangers, Lavan nonetheless hugged and kissed Yaakov,[70] and Chazal tell us that he was not showing sincere affection but was rather

---

[66] *Bereishis* 33:4.
[67] E.g., *Rashi, Bereishis* 33:4.
[68] *Rashi*, Bereishis 33:4.
[69] *Bereishis Rabbah* 78:9.
[70] *Bereishis* 29:13.

slyly searching for riches that Yaakov might have been carrying.[71] Years later, after Yaakov and his family secretly ran away from Lavan in an effort to return home to Yaakov's parents, Lavan caught up with them and stated that he was distraught because he was not given the opportunity to kiss his daughters and grandchildren goodbye.[72] Ultimately, the Torah tells us that he did kiss his family immediately before their two camps parted ways forever at the end of *Parshas Vayeitzei*.[73]

However, just prior to that final encounter, Hashem rebuked and threatened Lavan in a dream, instructing him to desist from causing any evil toward Yaakov – and not even to attempt to do good toward Yaakov,[74] for even Lavan the Wicked's "good" was evil in the eyes of Hashem.[75] As the *pasuk* in *Mishlei* (quoted by *Rashi* in his commentary on the prior *Parshah* of *Vayeitzei*[76]) so beautifully testifies: "נֶאֱמָנִים פִּצְעֵי אוֹהֵב; וְנַעְתָּרוֹת נְשִׁיקוֹת שׂוֹנֵא – Faithful are the wounds from a friend, but the numerous kisses of an enemy are deceitful"[77] – such kisses are at best an unwelcome overture and burden, and at worst are revolting and treacherous.

It is therefore befitting that the trickery of Lavan – who would lure his victims with disingenuous closeness and unwelcome kisses on the cheek – was punished by Hashem, *middah k'neged middah*, in the form of one final and conclusive rebuke tantamount to a proverbial "slap in the face" in poetic fulfillment on Yaakov Avinu's behalf of the promise of "כִּי הִכִּיתָ אֶת כָּל אֹיְבַי לֶחִי".

---

[71] *Rashi, Bereishis* 29:13, from *Bereishis Rabbah* 70:13.
[72] *Bereishis* 31:28.
[73] *Bereishis* 32:1.
[74] *Bereishis* 31:24.
[75] *Rashi, Bereishis* 31:24.
[76] *Rashi, Bereishis* 25:21.
[77] *Mishlei* 27:6.

Hashem, Please "Arise" and Redeem Us

On the phrase "קוּמָה ה', הוֹשִׁיעֵנִי אֱ-לֹהָי – Rise up Hashem, save me, my God," the *Midrash Tehillim*[78] says that this is the first of only five times in all of *Sefer Tehillim* in which Dovid HaMelech is "מְקִים" Hashem – beseeches Hashem to "rise up." Four times correspond to each of the four exiles, and the fifth corresponds to *Gog U'Magog*, the term given to the enemy and time period of Armageddon, which will be the final war to end all wars and bring Moshiach, and which will be a war fought by Bnei Yisrael against the Kingdom of Edom, descendants of Eisav, as well as the descendants of Yishmael.

There is a moment every single day in which we too can be "מְקִים" Hashem and implore Him to rise up and bring the *geulah* and Moshiach. And that special moment is very much intertwined with Yaakov Avinu as well, for we know from the upcoming *Parshas Vayishlach* that Yaakov is also named Yisrael,[79] and it is from Yaakov that the Jewish People derive the name of our nation, Bnei Yisrael. That special moment takes place immediately before we begin our *Shacharis Shemoneh Esrei*, which, according to *halachah*, must be connected to the blessing called *Ga'al Yisrael*, Redeemer of Yisrael.[80] The blessing of *Ga'al Yisrael* is as follows:

צוּר יִשְׂרָאֵל, קוּמָה בְּעֶזְרַת יִשְׂרָאֵל
Rock of **Yisrael**, **Arise** to the aid of **Yisrael**

וּפְדֵה כִנְאֻמֶךָ יְהוּדָה וְיִשְׂרָאֵל
and liberate, as You pledged/promised, Yehudah and **Yisrael**

גֹּאֲלֵנוּ ה' צְבָא-וֹת שְׁמוֹ קְדוֹשׁ יִשְׂרָאֵל.
Our Redeemer, Hashem, Master of Legions is His Name,
the Holy One of **Yisrael**.

---

[78] *Midrash Tehillim, Shocher Tov* 3.
[79] *Bereishis* 32:29 and 35:10.
[80] E.g., *Shulchan Aruch, Orach Chaim, siman* 111.

CHAPTER 7: VAYEITZEI & TEHILLIM 3

בָּרוּךְ אַתָּה ה' גָּאַל יִשְׂרָאֵל
Blessed are You, Hashem, Who redeemed **Yisrael**.

There we request of Hashem: קוּמָה – arise, and redeem us as You promised You would, while we mention יִשְׂרָאֵל five times and thereby call upon the merit of Yaakov Avinu with great intensity.

This is how *we* "arise" and enter our *Shemoneh Esrei* each and every day.

Pasuk 9:
לַה' הַיְשׁוּעָה;
עַל עַמְּךָ בִרְכָתֶךָ סֶּלָה
To Hashem is Salvation;
upon Your people is Your blessing, Selah.

The *Brachos* of Yitzchak to Yaakov to Us All

This *pasuk* not only concludes *Tehillim* 3 but also contains yet another direct connection to Yaakov Avinu. The *Baal Haturim*[81] writes that the word "בִרְכָתֶךָ" appears only two times in all of Tanach: here in *Tehillim* 3:9 and in *Parshas Toldos* when Yitzchak informed Eisav: "בָּא אָחִיךָ בְּמִרְמָה וַיִּקַּח בִּרְכָתֶךָ – Your brother [Yaakov] came with cleverness and took your blessings."[82] The *Baal Haturim* connects the two instances and says that it is from the *brachah* of Yitzchak to Yaakov that the *brachah* of "עַל עַמְּךָ בִרְכָתֶךָ סֶּלָה" flows to the sons of Yaakov and to all of Am Yisrael forever.

The Theme of *Yeshuah*

Building on the connection between Yitzchak and Yaakov, this *pasuk* also contains a hidden theme we have not yet discussed in this *kapitel*, nor in this *sefer*: the word "יְשׁוּעָה – salvation."

---

[81] *Baal Haturim, Bereishis* 27:35 and *Tehillim* 3:9.
[82] *Bereishis* 27:35, and *Rashi* there, from *Bereishis Rabbah* 67:4.

The word יְשׁוּעָה (*yeshuah*) is first mentioned earlier in *pasuk* 3 of *Tehillim* 3, in which the enemies of the *tzaddik* disparagingly proclaim "אֵין יְשׁוּעָתָה לּוֹ בֵא-לֹהִים סֶלָה" – There is no salvation for him from God, Selah." The root word of *yeshuah* is stated again in *pasuk* 8: "קוּמָה ה', הוֹשִׁיעֵנִי אֱ-לֹהַי" – Rise up Hashem, save me, my God," and yet a third time here in *pasuk* 9: "לַה' הַיְשׁוּעָה" – To Hashem is Salvation."

The progression is clear: first, in *pasuk* 3, the enemy criticizes and declares that there is no salvation for the *tzaddik*, whom they claim is undeserving and has been abandoned by Hashem. Then, in *pasuk* 8, the *tzaddik* turns to Hashem and davens for salvation, and immediately thereafter in *pasuk* 9 the *tzaddik* declares that Hashem's salvation will come – no, it has *already* come – for the *tzaddik* is so confident that Hashem's salvation is inevitable that he is able to transcend the difficulties of the present moment and elevate himself to a holier reality: that of "לַה' הַיְשׁוּעָה" – as if Hashem's salvation has already arrived!

Similarly, the *Haftarah* of *Parshas Vayeitzei* contains the powerful *yeshuah*-related statement: "וְאָנֹכִי ה' אֱ-לֹהֶיךָ מֵאֶרֶץ מִצְרָיִם; וֵא-לֹהִים זוּלָתִי לֹא תֵדָע, וּמוֹשִׁיעַ אַיִן בִּלְתִּי – I am Hashem, your God, since the land of Egypt; and you did not know a god other than Me, and there is no מוֹשִׁיעַ – no Savior – other than Me."[83]

The unique meaning and significance of the word *yeshuah* will be explored further in this *sefer*, including in the pages that immediately follow and in Chapter 10 on *Parshas Mikeitz* & *Tehillim* 40.

---

[83] *Hoshea* 13:4.

THE AVOS AND HASHEM AS *OZER, U'MOSHIA, U'MAGEN*

It cannot be overstated that יְשׁוּעָה (*yeshuah*) is a concept that expresses much more than just a generic act of salvation or rescue. יְשׁוּעָה has special meaning and significance. In the first *brachah* of *Shemoneh Esrei* we say "מֶלֶךְ עוֹזֵר וּמוֹשִׁיעַ וּמָגֵן." While this statement is first and foremost a praise of *Hashem* as our "King (מֶלֶךְ), Helper (עוֹזֵר), Savior (מוֹשִׁיעַ), and Shield (מָגֵן)," the *Iyun Tefillah*[84] explains that וּמָגֵן is a hidden reference to Avraham Avinu, מוֹשִׁיעַ is a hidden reference to Yitzchak Avinu, and עוֹזֵר is a hidden reference to Yaakov Avinu.[85]

The *Iyun Tefillah* expounds that מָגֵן refers to protection from Hashem in the form of a "Shield," meaning that Hashem preemptively protects the Jew from troubles and dangers like a shield in battle protects the soldier from dangers even *before* they strike, just as Hashem protected Avraham Avinu as his מָגֵן אַבְרָהָם.

עוֹזֵר (*ozer*) refers to Hashem as "Helper," meaning that the Jew must perform the necessary *hishtadlus*, effort of his own, after which Hashem

---

[84] *Iyun Tefillah, Siddur Otzar HaTefillah*.

[85] In addition, one cannot help but wonder whether the word מֶלֶךְ is a hidden reference to Dovid HaMelech, who is famously grouped together with Avraham, Yitzchak, and Yaakov to complete the אַרְבַּע רַגְלֵי הַמֶּרְכָּבָה, the four legs (wheels) of the Chariot of Hashem (e.g., *Malbim, Devarim* 33:13; *Ben Ish Chai, Drashos, Behaalosecha* 1). However, it is possible that the *Iyun Tefillah* intentionally omitted this insight based upon the Gemara in *Sanhedrin* 107a in which Dovid HaMelech attempted to earn the right to be expressly added to the first *brachah* of *Shemoneh Esrei* and was not successful. In addition, adding a reference to Dovid in the first blessing of *Shemoneh Esrei* would go beyond the intended scope of the *brachah*, which is aptly named "*Avos*" and specifically focuses on the Avos HaKedoshim.

will take over and accomplish the rest. An example of this is a Jew's battle against his *yetzer hara*, in which Chazal specifically tell us: "יִצְרוֹ שֶׁל אָדָם מִתְגַּבֵּר עָלָיו בְּכָל יוֹם וּמְבַקֵּשׁ לַהֲמִיתוֹ... וְאִלְמָלֵא הַקָּדוֹשׁ בָּרוּךְ הוּא שֶׁעוֹזֵר לוֹ אֵינוֹ יָכוֹל לוֹ – A person's evil inclination overpowers him every day, and if not for Hashem Who is עוֹזֵר לוֹ – assists him, he could not overcome it."[86] Although the thrust of this lesson is that Hashem's help is absolutely necessary, it implies that the Jew must also help himself by applying his best efforts to overcome the evil inclination on his own. The above corresponds perfectly to Yaakov Avinu, who was actively involved in addressing his challenges, and whose constant *hishtadlus* led to his God-given successes.

Finally, מוֹשִׁיעַ, which has the same *shoresh* as יְשׁוּעָה, corresponds to Yitzchak Avinu, who received "Salvation" from Hashem without any active contribution of his own, and, more specifically, because of his passivity. Examples of this *middah* are Yitzchak's willingness to literally be sacrificed at the *Akeidah*; his seeming indifference when his newly dug wells were clogged by wicked people multiple times and in multiple locations; and, upon realizing that he had bestowed his cherished *brachos* upon an unintended recipient, his immediate response was: "גַּם בָּרוּךְ יִהְיֶה – so shall he be blessed."[87] This submissiveness and purposeful inaction was not the result of indecisiveness or weakness but was rather the apex of self-control and trust in Hashem, thus activating God-given Salvation. This is the essence of מוֹשִׁיעַ, and this is the approach epitomized by Yitzchak Avinu.[88]

With this background, we can now more deeply appreciate the magnitude of the three-fold emphasis on the *shoresh* of the word "יְשׁוּעָה" in *Tehillim* 3. Here specifically, Dovid HaMelech and Yaakov Avinu were pleading to Hashem not simply for a complete salvation, but that such salvation should come entirely from Hashem, with nothing done, caused,

---

[86] *Kiddushin* 30b.
[87] *Bereishis* 27:33.
[88] יְשׁוּעָה was also an approach required of Yosef HaTzaddik, as we shall discuss in more detail in Chapter 10 of this *sefer* on *Parshas Mikeitz* & *Tehillim* 40.

CHAPTER 7: VAYEITZEI & TEHILLIM 3

or triggered by them – except their own *bitul*, inaction, and passivity, reflective of their complete confidence and *emunah* in Hashem.

Why *"Moshia"* When Yaakov (and Dovid) Are *"Ozer"*?

However, the above presents a difficulty because יְשׁוּעָה is the approach shown by Yitzchak and not by Yaakov or Dovid. Both Dovid and Yaakov were very much actively involved in all situations while simultaneously davening and relying on Hashem to assist as an עוֹזֵר, not to unilaterally save them as a מוֹשִׁיעַ.

To deepen the question, Yaakov's active approach of עוֹזֵר is particularly evident throughout *Parshas Vayeitzei*:

- After awakening from the dream with the ladder and having received Hashem's blessing, Yaakov volunteered to make a *neder* to Hashem, thus undertaking an additional and unsolicited arrangement with Hashem to help ensure his own protection. Moreover, this self-imposed vow involved voluntarily "giving back" certain things to Hashem such as promising to return to that very same spot to worship Hashem and to donate *maaser*, one-tenth of his earnings, for the sake of Hashem.[89]

- Himself a stranger in a new land, and without truly knowing his surroundings, whom he was dealing with, or waiting for others per the local custom, Yaakov single-handedly and publicly removed a giant boulder from atop a well of water to assist some strangers and to aid Rochel in watering Lavan's flock.[90]

- Yaakov proactively attempted to thwart any plans by Lavan to rob him of his intended bride, Rochel, by giving her the *simanim*, special "signs" by which to corroborate her identity.[91]

---

[89] *Bereishis* 28:20–22.
[90] *Bereishis* 29:10.
[91] *Rashi, Beresishis* 29:25.

- Yaakov actively and strenuously worked for Lavan for seven years, then another seven years, and then another six years, all with faithfulness and honesty, never taking a day off[92] and never relying on others.[93]
- Yaakov innovated and carved the checkered rods that he used to stimulate the birth of a speckled flock, which would become all his own and earn him great wealth.[94]
- Even though Hashem had already given Yaakov a prophecy to leave, Yaakov still consulted with Rochel and Leah about whether to flee from Lavan's home without informing him.[95]
- During his final meeting with Lavan, although Yaakov surely knew that even the trickery of Lavan was all the *ratzon Hashem*, he nonetheless stood up for himself and confronted Lavan for all his improprieties over the years.[96]

These are just a few examples of Yaakov's approach of עוֹזֵר *(ozer)*, the principle that Hashem helps those, who in a positive and Torah-true way, help themselves.

Of course, Dovid HaMelech is also famous for his active and involved approach of *ozer* throughout his life, whether it be through prayer, politics, or through actively fighting many wars on behalf of Hashem and the Jewish People, including volunteering to fight the most intimidating of warriors, Golias, without any military training or armor and with only a simple slingshot as his weapon.

With this backdrop, we can now try to answer our question regarding why *Tehillim* 3 emphasizes the *middah* of יְשׁוּעָה when the more typical

---

[92] *Bereishis* 31:40.
[93] *Rashi, Bereishis* 30:30.
[94] *Bereishis* 30:37–38.
[95] *Bereishis* 31:4.
[96] *Bereishis* 31:36.

CHAPTER 7: VAYEITZEI & TEHILLIM 3

approach of both Dovid and Yaakov was not to connect to Hashem as מוֹשִׁיעַ but rather as עוֹזֵר.

On a simple level,[97] and on a level that could also apply to various facets of our own lives such as our davening and study of *Tehillim*, we can suggest that the specific terminology and meaning behind each of the words in the phrase "עוֹזֵר וּמוֹשִׁיעַ וּמָגֵן" come into play when these various terms are written together, in which case there is the need to define them with more precision in order to differentiate their meanings in context. However, when only one of the terms is written alone, such as the word יְשׁוּעָה in *Tehillim* 3, the word can have a more generic meaning that includes save, protect, help, rescue, etc.

However, a deeper answer is that here, in the context of *Tehillim* 3 in which Dovid HaMelech and Yaakov Avinu were each forced to flee from their homes due to mortal danger posed by their own flesh and blood, Dovid and Yaakov were so desperate and at such a loss as to what to do next, yet simultaneously were filled with such clear *bitachon* in Hashem, that each veered from his own personal norm of עוֹזֵר and begged Hashem for His complete and unassisted salvation – for יְשׁוּעָה. As the saying goes, "Desperate times call for desperate measures," and in this case desperate times called for *different* measures.

A third approach is based upon the *Malbim*[98] who explains that when Dovid requested and proclaimed "לַה' הַיְשׁוּעָה," he was not doing so on his own behalf (for which his approach of עוֹזֵר would have been expected), but rather on behalf of the Jewish People. The same can be said of Yaakov, who always looked beyond himself toward the ultimate goal of continuing the line of Avraham and Yitzchak and meriting to create a Jewish Nation.[99] Therefore, as emissaries of Klal Yisrael rather than as self-interested individuals, when circumstances required, Yaakov and Dovid extended

---

[97] Based upon the *sefer Beis Elokim, Shaar HaTefillah, perek* 8.
[98] *Malbim, Tehillim* 3:9.
[99] E.g., *Rashi, Bereishis* 29:21.

beyond their personal approaches of עוֹזֵר and sought from Hashem what appears to be the "easier" – yet perhaps most miraculous – of the approaches: that of Hashem as מוֹשִׁיעַ, bringing salvation entirely by Himself, without any human intervention.

As an additional approach, we can suggest that Yaakov Avinu and Dovid HaMelech, who in *Tehillim* 3 share the same experiences of plight and flight, were reaching beyond their traditional approach and connecting to their shared "*Av*," their shared father and forefather (respectively) – Yitzchak Avinu, whose merit they so desperately needed and whom they so desperately missed. In fact, the Torah records that Lavan himself recognized this yearning in Yaakov and stated: "וְעַתָּה הָלֹךְ הָלַכְתָּ, כִּי נִכְסֹף נִכְסַפְתָּה לְבֵית אָבִיךָ – And now you have left me because you have greatly longed for the house of your father."[100] As such, both Yaakov and Dovid yearned specifically to be the beneficiaries of the special *middah* of Yitzchak, which was also so intimately intertwined with the *middah* of Hashem: that of מוֹשִׁיעַ.

Finally, in a similar, albeit less emotional manner, we can say that in truth Yaakov's standard approach of עוֹזֵר was not at odds with or mutually exclusive of Yitzchak's מוֹשִׁיעַ approach at all. In fact, Yaakov's response to Lavan included his taking an oath and swearing specifically "בְּפַחַד אָבִיו יִצְחָק – by the fear of his father Yitzchak."[101] Yaakov appreciated, built upon, and synthesized Yitzchak's and Avraham's approaches to create his own perfect combination of the two. Thus, for Yaakov to call upon Hashem's *middah* of מוֹשִׁיעַ by channeling Yitzchak's approach of מוֹשִׁיעַ is to simply compartmentalize one of the three main approaches of the Avos HaKedoshim that Yaakov already possessed, and which was always in his arsenal of prayers waiting for the right opportunity to be released:

"...יְשׁוּעָתָה לּוֹ בֵא-לֹהִים... הוֹשִׁיעֵנִי אֱ-לֹהַי... לַה' הַיְשׁוּעָה!"

---

[100] *Bereishis* 31:30.
[101] *Bereishis* 31:53.

CHAPTER 8

PARSHAS VAYISHLACH & TEHILLIM 140

פָּרָשַׁת וַיִּשְׁלַח / תְּהִלִּים קמ

TEHILLIM 140 — תְּהִלִּים קמ

1	For the conductor, a psalm by Dovid.	לַמְנַצֵּחַ מִזְמוֹר לְדָוִד.	א
2	Free me, Hashem, from the man who is wicked; from the man of violence protect me.	חַלְּצֵנִי ה' מֵאָדָם רָע; מֵאִישׁ חֲמָסִים תִּנְצְרֵנִי.	ב
3	Who devise evil in their heart, who every day assemble for wars.	אֲשֶׁר חָשְׁבוּ רָעוֹת בְּלֵב; כָּל יוֹם יָגוּרוּ מִלְחָמוֹת.	ג
4	They have sharpened their tongue like a serpent; the venom of a spider is under their lips, Selah.	שָׁנֲנוּ לְשׁוֹנָם כְּמוֹ נָחָשׁ; חֲמַת עַכְשׁוּב תַּחַת שְׂפָתֵימוֹ סֶלָה.	ד
5	Guard me, Hashem, from the hands of the wicked one, from the man of violence protect me; who have contrived to trip up my steps.	שָׁמְרֵנִי ה' מִידֵי רָשָׁע, מֵאִישׁ חֲמָסִים תִּנְצְרֵנִי; אֲשֶׁר חָשְׁבוּ לִדְחוֹת פְּעָמָי.	ה
6	Hidden have the arrogant a snare for me and ropes, they spread a net near my footpath; traps they set for me, Selah.	טָמְנוּ גֵאִים פַּח לִי וַחֲבָלִים, פָּרְשׂוּ רֶשֶׁת לְיַד מַעְגָּל; מֹקְשִׁים שָׁתוּ לִי סֶלָה.	ו

7	I have said to Hashem: My God You are! Give ear, Hashem, to the sound of my pleading.	אָמַרְתִּי לַה': אֵ-לִי אָתָּה; הַאֲזִינָה ה' קוֹל תַּחֲנוּנָי. ז
8	Elokim, my Lord, might of my salvation, You protected my head on the day of armed battle.	יֱהוִ-ה, אֲדֹ-נָי, עֹז יְשׁוּעָתִי; סַכֹּתָה לְרֹאשִׁי בְּיוֹם נָשֶׁק. ח
9	Grant not, Hashem, the desires of the wicked one; to his conspiracy do not grant fruition, for them to be exalted, Selah.	אַל תִּתֵּן, ה', מַאֲוַיֵּי רָשָׁע; זְמָמוֹ אַל תָּפֵק, יָרוּמוּ סֶלָה. ט
10	As for the head of my besiegers, let the mischief of their own lips bury them.	רֹאשׁ מְסִבָּי, עֲמַל שְׂפָתֵימוֹ יְכַסֵּימוֹ. י
11	Let descend upon them burning coals; into the fire let it [their own mischief] cast them down, into deep pits never to rise again.	יִמּוֹטוּ עֲלֵיהֶם גֶּחָלִים; בָּאֵשׁ יַפִּלֵם, בְּמַהֲמֹרוֹת בַּל יָקוּמוּ. יא
12	The man of slander, let him not be established on earth; the man of violence who is evil, may he be hunted until he is overthrown.	אִישׁ לָשׁוֹן, בַּל יִכּוֹן בָּאָרֶץ; אִישׁ חָמָס רָע, יְצוּדֶנּוּ לְמַדְחֵפֹת. יב
13	I know that Hashem will judge [favorably] the poor, the judgment of the destitute.	יָדַעְתִּי כִּי יַעֲשֶׂה ה' דִּין עָנִי, מִשְׁפַּט אֶבְיֹנִים. יג
14	Only the righteous will give thanks to Your Name; dwell will the upright in Your Presence.	אַךְ צַדִּיקִים יוֹדוּ לִשְׁמֶךָ; יֵשְׁבוּ יְשָׁרִים אֶת פָּנֶיךָ. יד

INTRODUCTION:
A PLEA FOR VICTORY
WHILE ON THE BRINK OF BATTLE

Tehillim 140 is intense. It is a heartfelt, even frightened plea to Hashem by one who is on the brink of battle, anticipating mortal combat against true evil. It is a plea for safety. It is a plea for victory – because sometimes terrible battles must be fought for the greater good.

It is not clear when Dovid HaMelech composed this *kapitel Tehillim*, but it appears to have been before he was king,[1] while he was still a youth, and certainly before he had an army at his disposal. The fear is not theoretical. The fear is real and personal. Yet, the fear gives rise to even greater closeness to Hashem.

As we shall see, the precision of *Tehillim* 140 in its correspondence to *Parshas Vayishlach* is reminiscent of a skilled archer's arrow hitting its target.

Parshas Vayishlach recounts the struggles, and even fears, of Yaakov Avinu and his young family as they face numerous mortal dangers. The dangers of *Parshas Vayishlach* include escaping the clutches of Lavan HaRama'i, Yaakov wrestling with the *Sar shel Eisav* (the Ministering Angel of Eisav/Edom), the sons of Yaakov waging war against the entire city of Shechem, and amidst it all, Yaakov and family coming face to face with Eisav HaRasha storming forth with four hundred warriors intent on battling Yaakov and killing him, his wives, and his children.

Paralleling the *Parshah*, the *pesukim* of *Tehillim* 140 recount Yaakov's fear, his concern for the lives of his family, his undertaking to appease

---

[1] *Ibn Ezra, Tehillim* 140:2.

PARSHAH & TEHILLIM HAND IN HAND

Eisav, his beseeching Hashem with prayer, and as a last resort, the possibility of having to fight Eisav to the death.

Tehillim 140 refers to a vast array of evildoers: the wicked man; the man of violence; the deviser of evil schemes in his heart; those who assemble for war; those with sharpened tongues like a serpent; those with the mouth of a spider dripping with venom; the arrogant; those engaged in armed battle; the wicked yet again; the conspirator; the besieger; the mischievous; the slanderer; and the man of violence who is evil personified.

Weave all this into a single terrifying blend, and the product is Eisav HaRasha and his descendants: Edom, Amalek, the Greek Empire, the Roman Empire, and Nazi Germany (*yemach shemam*). This is whom Yaakov wrestled with in the form of an angel, and this is whom Yaakov confronted in the form of his evil brother. This is the target of the archer's arrow in *Tehillim* 140, and this is the target of our *tefillos* in this *kapitel Tehillim* and beyond.

THE MANY CONNECTIONS BETWEEN PARSHAS VAYISHLACH & TEHILLIM 140

Pasuk 1:

לַמְנַצֵּחַ מִזְמוֹר לְדָוִד

For the conductor, a psalm by Dovid.

Yaakov's Victories Are for All Time

"לַמְנַצֵּחַ" means "for the conductor," the person whom Dovid envisioned would ultimately lead the recitation of this *kapitel Tehillim* in the Beis HaMikdash. Yet it also refers to the "מְנַצֵּחַ," the "victor" – the victor who is young Dovid, and the victor who is Dovid HaMelech; the victor who is Yaakov Avinu, and the victor who is elevated to the name Yisrael; the victor who is Am Yisrael as individuals, and the victor who is Am Yisrael as a nation.

In *Parshas Vayishlach* we focus on Yaakov Avinu who, despite the dangers and fears, relied on Hashem and was able to accomplish so much and vanquish so many. On the heels of having overcome Lavan HaRama'i, Yaakov was able to defeat the *Sar shel Eisav*, to avoid a battle to the death with Eisav himself, to absorb the fact that two of his sons destroyed the entire city of Shechem in order to avenge their sister's honor, and to defeat the nation of Emor with his sword and bow.[2] Particularly timeless was Yaakov's fight with the *Sar shel Eisav*, which possesses protective effects for the Jewish People that will last until the arrival of Moshiach. Indeed, the opening word "לַמְנַצֵּחַ" signifies Yaakov's many vital "victories" in *Parshas Vayishlach*.

Just as importantly, as we recite *Tehillim* 140 and learn through *Parshas Vayishlach*, "לַמְנַצֵּחַ" reorients us to the true "Conductor" responsible for orchestrating all those victories: our beloved Hashem.

Pasuk 2:
חַלְּצֵנִי ה' מֵאָדָם רָע;

מֵאִישׁ חֲמָסִים תִּנְצְרֵנִי

**Free me, Hashem, from the man who is wicked;
from the man of violence protect me.**

Eisav Is Pure Death

*T*ehillim 140 is all about the dangers and traps of the "אָדָם רָע – the evil man," and the "אִישׁ חֲמָסִים – the man of violence." Who is this man? The *Midrash Tehillim* states directly that Dovid's prayer of "'חַלְּצֵנִי ה," in

---

[2] *Rashi, Bereishis* 48:22, from *Bereishis Rabbah* 80:10.

which he begged Hashem to please "release me from the evil man and the man of violence," is indeed specifically referring to Eisav HaRasha, the first and primary antagonist in *Parshas Vayishlach*.[3]

Though Yaakov Avinu sent messengers, even angels, "לִמְצֹא חֵן בְּעֵינֶיךָ – to find favor in your eyes"[4] and to make peace, Eisav instead set out to attack Yaakov with four hundred warriors, causing Yaakov to fear that a battle was inevitable and that his family would be in mortal danger.[5] The *Midrash Tehillim* continues: "What is Eisav's evil? מָוֶת – death. Thus said Hashem: When I redeem you, I redeem you from death… Behold, death is Eisav HaRasha. Therefore he [Dovid] said: 'חַלְּצֵנִי ה' מֵאָדָם רָע' and so too did Yaakov. For Yaakov also davened: 'הַצִּילֵנִי נָא מִיַּד אָחִי מִיַּד עֵשָׂו – Rescue me, please, from the hand of my brother, from the hand of Eisav.'"[6]

Such is the tone set by the *Midrash Tehillim*: Eisav is the enemy and Eisav is spiritual and physical death. So many faces of death require the combined forces, merits, and prayers of a Dovid and a Yaakov to fight them.

Nonetheless, we have unfortunately seen all too well how Eisav's evil has continued to infiltrate and manifest itself throughout history, especially over the course of these two thousand years of *Galus Edom* in which we remain exiled by and living among Eisav's descendants. As such, we too need the power and protection contained in *pasuk* 2.

Pasuk 3:
אֲשֶׁר חָשְׁבוּ רָעוֹת בְּלֵב;
כָּל יוֹם יָגוּרוּ מִלְחָמוֹת
Who devise evil in their heart,
who every day assemble for wars.

---

[3] *Midrash Tehillim, Shocher Tov* 140.
[4] *Bereishis* 32:6.
[5] *Bereishis* 32:7–9.
[6] *Bereishis* 32:12.

CHAPTER 8: VAYISHLACH & TEHILLIM 140

Eisav's Heart Beats Only Evil and War

Eisav's heart is mentioned only once in the Torah, in *Parshas Toldos*: "וַיֹּאמֶר עֵשָׂו בְּלִבּוֹ, יִקְרְבוּ יְמֵי אֵבֶל אָבִי, וְאַהַרְגָה אֶת יַעֲקֹב אָחִי" – And Eisav said in his heart: May the days of mourning for my father draw near, then I will kill my brother Yaakov."[7] Apparently Eisav does have a heart… but it is a heart filled with "רָעוֹת בְּלֵב" – evil thoughts, even the psychotic thought of wishing for his father's death so that he would be able to carry out the murder of his own brother!

The foregoing evil desire nearly came to fruition in *Parshas Vayishlach*. Despite Yitzchak still being alive, Eisav could not resist a confrontation and set out to kill Yaakov along with what was essentially an army of four hundred men in fulfillment of "כָּל יוֹם יָגוּרוּ מִלְחָמוֹת" – who every day assemble for wars."

Amazingly, in the fateful moment when Eisav and Yaakov could have clashed, instead Eisav's cold heart thawed, if only for a moment. The Torah states: "וַיָּרָץ עֵשָׂו לִקְרָאתוֹ וַיְחַבְּקֵהוּ, וַיִּפֹּל עַל צַוָּארָו וַיִּשָּׁקֵהוּ; וַיִּבְכּוּ" – Eisav ran toward him, and he embraced him, and he fell upon his neck, and kissed him; and they wept."[8] Some commentators say that Eisav actually tried biting and killing Yaakov, and that Eisav's cry was one of pain when his teeth were broken as a result of the failed bite.[9] Others say that Eisav kissed Yaakov, but "not with all his heart."[10]

A third line of commentators say that although it is an indisputable fact that Eisav hated Yaakov, Eisav's mercy was warmed at that time and, shockingly, "He kissed him with all of his heart." However, even this last opinion emphasizes that it was only a momentary aberration, and that "עֵשָׂו שׂוֹנֵא לְיַעֲקֹב" – Eisav will always hate Yaakov.[11]

---

[7] *Bereishis* 27:41.
[8] *Bereishis* 33:4.
[9] *Bereishis Rabbah*, *Vayishlach* 78:9.
[10] *Rashi*, *Bereishis* 33:4, from *Sifrei, Bamidbar* 69.
[11] *Rashi*, *Bereishis* 33:4, from *Sifrei, Bamidbar* 69.

That Yaakov was able to penetrate Eisav's heart for even just a moment is more of a tribute to Yaakov, and to Hashem, than a tribute to Eisav, whose heart contained "רָעוֹת בְּלֵב" and beat to the haunting rhythm of evil and war.

The Destruction of Shechem in Eisav-Like Fashion

Of course, *Parshas Vayishlach* is marked, or some might say marred, by an actual episode of "יָגוּרוּ מִלְחָמוֹת" a full-fledged war.[12] This was not a war initiated by *reshaim* but rather by two of the sons of Yaakov Avinu, Shimon and Levi. Fueled by their desire to avenge the misdeeds of Shechem ben Chamor who took advantage of their sister Dinah, all the sons of Yaakov first convinced the males in the city of Shechem to have themselves circumcised. Three days later, when the men of Shechem were in their most weakened state, Shimon and Levi furtively attacked the city and killed every single one of the men, and thereafter the other brothers plundered the city and captured its surviving residents, essentially conquering the entire city. This was done without the prior knowledge and consent of their father Yaakov, who was much aggrieved and rebuked Shimon and Levi. Yet, in *Parshas Vayishlach* at least, it is Shimon and Levi who have the last word, stating: "הַכְזוֹנָה יַעֲשֶׂה אֶת אֲחוֹתֵנוּ – Should our sister be treated like a harlot?"[13]

However, decades later as part of Yaakov's deathbed blessings to his sons, Yaakov once again admonished Shimon and Levi, and at that time he had the final and only word. What was Yaakov's message? "שִׁמְעוֹן וְלֵוִי אַחִים כְּלֵי חָמָס מְכֵרֹתֵיהֶם – Shimon and Levi are brothers, stolen tools are their weapons."[14] *Rashi* explains that Yaakov was declaring that they were more than just "brothers;" they were of "one mind" when they destroyed the city

---

[12] *Bereishis, Perek* 34.
[13] *Bereishis* 34:31.
[14] *Bereishis* 49:5.

of Shechem as well as when they attempted to murder Yosef.[15] As for the meaning of "stolen tools are their weapons," these words refer to the type of misbehavior and "craft" Shimon and Levi demonstrated in Shechem and with Yosef. Yaakov stated in disapproval that these tools were "stolen" from none other than Eisav, who lived by the sword[16] and whose hands were used for murder.

Thus, the real reason Yaakov chastised and criticized Shimon and Levi was because their conduct was modeled after Eisav HaRasha himself. This was conduct that reflected a certain "חָשְׁבוּ רָעוֹת בְּלֵב," premeditated evil in their hearts to coordinate such a precise attack and being able to "יָגוּרוּ מִלְחָמוֹת" and assemble for war. Because of the similarities to Eisav, Yaakov particularly abhorred this behavior and would not tolerate it, especially from his own precious sons who were destined to be part of the establishment of the fledgling Jewish Nation, and whose *middos* needed to be refined to the highest degree and thus become the polar opposite of Eisav.

Eisav Followed by a Long Line of Jewish Foes

It must be noted that while *pasuk* 2 speaks of the individual, *pasuk* 3 switches to *lashon rabim*, the plural form, in describing a *multitude* of evildoers; such shifting back-and-forth between singular and plural continues throughout the *kapitel*. Indeed, the commentators explain that this *kapitel* describes not just the plight of Yaakov, but the plight of the Jewish People in general throughout the centuries and throughout each *galus*.

The *Baal Haturim*[17] draws parallels between Yaakov's confrontation with Eisav and Dovid's fight against Golias, and teaches that it was

---

[15] *Rashi, Bereishis* 49:5.

[16] *Rashi, Bereishis* 49:5, from *Midrash Tanchuma*, Vayishlach 9; *Bereishis Rabbah* 99:6.

[17] *Baal Haturim, Bereishis* 32:12.

specifically the merit of Yaakov that protected Dovid from Golias. The *Baal Haturim* draws further connections throughout history, even to the wicked Haman of the Purim story, who was himself a direct descendant of Eisav through Amalek. There the *Baal Haturim* notes that in the famous plea of Yaakov to Hashem: "הַצִּילֵנִי נָא מִיַּד אָחִי מִיַּד עֵשָׂו – Save me from the hand of my brother, from the hand of Eisav,"[18] the first letters of Yaakov's statement "הַצִּילֵנִי נָא מִיַּד," contain the letters that spell out "הָמָן."

Thus, the sudden transitions in *Tehillim* 140 to and from the singular and the plural in describing evil and evildoers indicate that Eisav's deadly trait of "כָּל יוֹם יָגוּרוּ מִלְחָמוֹת – who every day assemble for wars," extended far beyond just himself and was clearly passed down to his *descendants*, the original Edom, Amalek, the Greek Empire, the Roman Empire, and even Nazi Germany (*yemach shemam*), whose nature it is to mercilessly attack, plunder, and slaughter.

Pasuk 4:
שָׁנְנוּ לְשׁוֹנָם כְּמוֹ נָחָשׁ;
חֲמַת עַכְשׁוּב תַּחַת שְׂפָתֵימוֹ סֶלָה
They have sharpened their tongue like a serpent;
the venom of a spider is under their lips, Selah.

Wickedness Like the Original Serpent

That Eisav and *reshaim* like him are "כְּמוֹ נָחָשׁ," like a serpent and snake, is not only appropriate in an animalistic and derogatory sense, but is even more appropriate when we think of the original נָחָשׁ of *Parshas Bereishis*. The Serpent whose "sharpened tongue" and wicked intentions caused Chavah and Adam to eat from the Tree of Knowledge of Good and Evil, and who brought sin, suffering, and death into Creation, thereby made it possible for someone as nefarious as Eisav to prosper in this now-

---

[18] *Bereishis* 32:12.

CHAPTER 8: VAYISHLACH & TEHILLIM 140

adulterated world. In other words, Eisav was not just a random wicked man. Eisav, and those like him, perpetuate the selfishness, lust, destruction, and death of the original Serpent. That's how evil he and they truly are.

Fear of Spiders

The comparison of Eisav and *reshaim* to an "עַכָּשׁוּב – spider," is very interesting, as spiders are not commonly referenced in Tanach or Chazal. Clearly, the lies and deceit spun by *reshaim* can be compared to a spider's web: intricate, entangling, and deadly. The *Yalkut Shimoni* teaches that the spider is the most hated of the creeping creatures,[19] and even to this day, arachnophobia is consistently ranked among the top listed fears worldwide. Rav Moshe Feinstein[20] rules that if a bug such as a spider is disturbing a weekday meal, it is permissible to kill it; however, says Rav Moshe based on the *Ohr Hachaim Hakadosh's* approach to an *ir ha'nidachas*, a wayward city,[21] it must be done in a manner that is without cruelty, and, if possible, not directly by hand but rather indirectly so that the Jew does not become insensitive to killing even when permitted.

May we merit to see the day that the spidery Eisav and his evil descendants finally be dealt with, in a proper manner, once and for all.

Dovid HaMelech's Connection to Spiders

We must also note that while the mention of spiders in *Tehillim* is extraordinarily rare, Dovid HaMelech had a personal and pivotal experience with spiders. The *Devash Lefi*[22] cites a teaching of Chazal that years before he was to become king, as a young shepherd Dovid took notice of a spider spinning a web, and while he appreciated its diligence,

---

[19] *Yalkut Shimoni, Mishlei* 30, *siman* 964.
[20] *Igros Moshe, Choshen Mishpat, chelek* 2, *siman* 47, #1.
[21] *Ohr Hachaim, Devarim* 13:18.
[22] *Devash Lefi, Os Beis.*

he also questioned Hashem's purpose in creating spiders at all. Hashem responded that one day Dovid would come to understand. Years later, when running for his life from Shaul HaMelech's army, Dovid hid in a remote cave but was in jeopardy of being discovered. Suddenly, a spider appeared and quickly wove a giant web, which not only served as a perfect roadblock from Dovid's foes but also gave the impression that no human had traversed the cave in quite some time. Upon investigating the cave, Shaul's soldiers saw the web, naturally assumed that no one could be hiding behind it, and gave up their search. It is for this reason that even to this day, some Jews are careful not to kill spiders, instead opting to catch them and gently remove them from their homes.

Of course, just as Dovid came to understand that even spiders have a God-given purpose, we too must recognize that the wicked, likened to a dangerous and venomous spider, also serve a God-given purpose which may include testing our faith in Hashem and/or providing us with a stark contrast to the greatness of the righteous, until ultimately all wickedness will be eradicated in the time of Moshiach.

Pasuk 5:

שָׁמְרֵנִי ה' מִידֵי רָשָׁע,
מֵאִישׁ חֲמָסִים תִּנְצְרֵנִי;
אֲשֶׁר חָשְׁבוּ לִדְחוֹת פְּעָמָי

**Guard me, Hashem, from the hands of the wicked one,
from the man of violence protect me;
who have contrived to trip up my steps.**

Pasuk 6:

טָמְנוּ גֵאִים פַּח לִי וַחֲבָלִים,
פָּרְשׂוּ רֶשֶׁת לְיַד מַעְגָּל;
מֹקְשִׁים שָׁתוּ לִי סֶלָה

> **Hidden have the arrogant a snare for me and ropes,**
> **they spread a net near my footpath;**
> **traps they set for me, Selah.**

The Hands of Eisav

The reference to "hands of the wicked one" in the expression "שָׁמְרֵנִי ה' מִידֵי רָשָׁע" is surely an allusion to Eisav, about whom the Torah says in *Parshas Toldos*: "וְהַיָּדַיִם יְדֵי עֵשָׂו" – And the hands are the hands of Eisav,"[23] which has become the expression of Eisav and Edom's bloodthirsty and violent nature. In *Parshas Vayishlach* as well, Yaakov's prayer includes references to the brutal hands of Eisav in the phrase "הַצִּילֵנִי נָא מִיַּד אָחִי מִיַּד עֵשָׂו, כִּי יָרֵא אָנֹכִי אֹתוֹ פֶּן יָבוֹא וְהִכַּנִי אֵם עַל בָּנִים" – Save me from the hand of my brother, from the hand of Eisav, for I fear him, lest he come and strike me, mother and children."[24]

Eisav and Yishmael: Each Is the Anti-*Yedid*

We must also point out that both of the above descriptions in the Torah describing Eisav contain a *double* mention of the *shoresh* of the word "יָד," which is significant and confusing, since each of the dual references to יָד can be combined to form the word "יְדִיד – beloved," a reference to the honored title of "יְדִיד ה' – beloved of Hashem."[25]

The Torah uses the precious description of "יְדִיד ה'" explicitly only once, in reference to the status of Yaakov and Rochel's beloved son Binyamin as an expression of the immense love that Hashem had for Binyamin and his Tribe.[26]

---

[23] *Bereishis* 27:21.
[24] *Bereishis* 32:12.
[25] *Devarim* 33:12.
[26] *Devarim* 33:12.

By extension, the exalted status of יְדִיד ה' pertains to each and every one of us as well; we as Jews are each a *yedid* of Hashem, His friend and His beloved.[27]

Thus, to find such references to the double יָד hinting to יְדִיד in connection with *Eisav HaRasha* seems completely incongruous. However, the lesson is clear: Eisav is the "anti-*yedid!*" His violence and sins, with which he and his descendants have reaped so much terrible and terrifying success throughout the millennia, exist to test our *bitachon* in Hashem.

Frighteningly, the same "anti-*yedidus*" can be said about Yishmael and his offspring, of whom the Torah also uses the double יָד and states: "וְהוּא יִהְיֶה פֶּרֶא אָדָם; יָדוֹ בַכֹּל וְיַד כֹּל בּוֹ – And he will be a wild-man; his hand will be against everything, and everyone's hand will be against him."[28]

When Eisav and Yishmael *chas v'shalom* strike, we have a decision to make. Will we allow their atrocities to undermine our feelings of *yedidus* from and with Hashem, or will we trust in Hashem and continue to feel His *yedidus* despite the *rishus* and bloodshed of the "יָדַיִם יְדֵי עֵשָׂו" and the "יָדוֹ בַכֹּל" of Yishmael?

Astoundingly, Jewish history has shown time and time again that Am Yisrael will feel Hashem's *yedidus* even more strongly *because of* Eisav's and Yishmael's anti-*yedidus*.

To Trap and Trip Up the *Tzaddik*

The phrase "אֲשֶׁר חָשְׁבוּ לִדְחוֹת פְּעָמָי" in *pasuk* 5 describing the *reshaim* who "contrive to trip up my steps" and the description in *pasuk* 6 of snares, ropes, and traps to catch and harm the tzaddik are particularly remarkable in connection with *Parshas Vayishlach*.

After Eisav and Yaakov seemed to have reconciled, Eisav insisted upon accompanying Yaakov and his family on the road, while Yaakov desired that Eisav go his separate way, still fearful that Eisav might secretly have

---

[27] E.g., *Menachos* 53a.
[28] *Bereishis* 16:12.

CHAPTER 8: VAYISHLACH & TEHILLIM 140

had nefarious plans to "trip up Yaakov's steps" and harm him and/or his family as they traveled. First, Eisav said "נִסְעָה וְנֵלֵכָה; וְאֵלְכָה לְנֶגְדֶּךָ" – Travel on and let us go; I will proceed alongside you."[29] Yaakov responded that his children, flocks, and cattle cannot be driven too hard, and that Eisav should travel ahead while Yaakov would move at a slower pace appropriate for his large clan.[30] Eisav continued to press Yaakov and offered to at least assign some of his men to accompany Yaakov on the road, which made Yaakov no less wary until Eisav finally relented after Yaakov again declined his allegedly kind offer.[31] As *Rashi* tells us, Yaakov was concerned that Eisav still intended to do him harm.[32]

Whether directly through violence or indirectly by pushing Yaakov's caravan beyond their capabilities, Yaakov sensed that the wicked Eisav "חָשְׁבוּ לִדְחוֹת פְּעָמָי" and intended to trap, ensnare, and harm Yaakov and family as they traveled.

Yaakov's Connection to *Tefillas Haderech*

The above *pesukim* and explanations are also part of the reason that Yaakov Avinu is connected to *Tefillas Haderech*, the Traveler's Prayer.

It is well known that Hashem provided Yaakov with angels to accompany him during his journeys: one set of angels when he traveled within Eretz Yisrael, and another set of angels when he traveled outside of Eretz Yisrael.[33] In addition, at the start of *Parshas Vayeitzei*, Yaakov was blessed with *kefitzas haderech* in which the earth miraculously contracted for him making his journey significantly shorter and faster.[34]

---

[29] *Bereishis* 33:12.
[30] *Bereishis* 33:13–14.
[31] *Bereishis* 33:15.
[32] Rashi, *Bereishis* 33:14, from *Avodah Zarah* 25b.
[33] Rashi, *Bereishis* 28:12, from *Bereishis Rabbah* 68:12; and Rashi, *Bereishis* 32:3, from *Midrash Tanchuma*, *Vayishlach* 3.
[34] Rashi, *Bereishis* 28:11, from *Chullin* 91b.

PARSHAH & TEHILLIM HAND IN HAND

It is among these reasons that *Tefillas Haderech*, which is supplemented with additional *pesukim* of protection for travelers, includes the following *pesukim* from the Torah originally said by/about Yaakov Avinu himself:

וְיַעֲקֹב הָלַךְ לְדַרְכּוֹ, וַיִּפְגְּעוּ בוֹ מַלְאֲכֵי אֱ-לֹהִים.
וַיֹּאמֶר יַעֲקֹב כַּאֲשֶׁר רָאָם, מַחֲנֵה אֱ-לֹהִים זֶה;
וַיִּקְרָא שֵׁם הַמָּקוֹם הַהוּא מַחֲנָיִם.

And Yaakov traveled on his way and was met by angels of God. And Yaakov said when he saw them: "A camp that is Godly is this." So he called the name of the place Machanayim.[35]

הַמַּלְאָךְ הַגֹּאֵל אֹתִי מִכָּל רָע, יְבָרֵךְ אֶת הַנְּעָרִים,
וְיִקָּרֵא בָהֶם שְׁמִי, וְשֵׁם אֲבֹתַי אַבְרָהָם וְיִצְחָק; וְיִדְגּוּ לָרֹב בְּקֶרֶב הָאָרֶץ.

May the angel who redeems me from all evil bless the young boys, and declared upon them may my name be, and the names of my forefathers Avraham and Yitzchak, and like fish may they proliferate abundantly within the land.[36]

לִישׁוּעָתְךָ קִוִּיתִי ה'.
For Your salvation do I yearn, Hashem.[37]

When we travel and recite *Tefillas Haderech* together with the above accompanying *pesukim*, this can trigger great merit and safety. Incredibly, the same protection that Yaakov and family received from Hashem in avoiding a conflict with Eisav while traveling on the road can be bestowed upon us as we travel, even thousands of years later.

Taryag Mitzvos Shamarti

Ultimately, everything hinges upon Hashem and His protection, as we see in *pasuk* 5, which begins with the straightforward request: "שָׁמְרֵנִי ה'" – Guard me, Hashem."

---

[35] *Parshas Vayishlach, Bereishis* 32:2–3.
[36] *Parshas Vayechi, Bereishis* 48:16.
[37] *Parshas Vayechi, Bereishis* 49:18.

Moreover, in these words we find a parallel to Yaakov's famous opening words to Eisav in *Parshas Vayishlach*: "עִם לָבָן גַּרְתִּי – I have lived with Lavan,"[38] which contained the deeper message of "I have dwelt with Lavan HaRasha, an evildoer just like you, Eisav, and yet וְתַרְיַ"ג מִצְוֹת שָׁמַרְתִּי – I have guarded/kept all 613 mitzvos and did not emulate Lavan's evil actions."[39] As a result, Yaakov was emphasizing to Eisav – even warning him and perhaps even threatening him – that he, Yaakov, was confident that he would receive the protections inherent in "שָׁמְרֵנִי ה'."

While everything boils down to Hashem and His protection, the best way to merit such protection is to observe Hashem's Torah and mitzvos. As the expression goes: "More than the Jews have kept Shabbos, Shabbos has kept the Jews." This is true not only of שְׁמִירַת שַׁבָּת, but of *all* Hashem's commandments: each and every sincerely performed mitzvah provides a שְׁמִירָה, a protection, bestowed by Hashem.

In short, one of the key formulas for receiving "שָׁמְרֵנִי ה'," is living a life of "וְתַרְיַ"ג מִצְוֹת שָׁמַרְתִּי."

Pasuk 6:
טָמְנוּ גֵאִים פַּח לִי
Hidden have the arrogant a snare for me.

Arrogant Antoninus and Proud Rabbi Yehudah HaNasi

The word "גֵאִים" has particular relevance to Yaakov and Eisav and their progeny. When Rivkah was prophetically informed that her difficult pregnancy was due to her having twins, the *pasuk* describes the future conflicts that the children will have with one another and states: "שְׁנֵי גיים בְּבִטְנֵךְ וּשְׁנֵי לְאֻמִּים מִמֵּעַיִךְ יִפָּרֵדוּ; וּלְאֹם מִלְאֹם יֶאֱמָץ וְרַב יַעֲבֹד צָעִיר" – Two nations are in your womb, and two regimes from your insides will be

---

[38] *Bereishis* 32:5.
[39] Rashi, *Bereishis* 32:5.

separated; and one regime will become strong through the other regime, and the elder shall serve the younger."[40]

On the word "גיים," *Rashi* says that the written word is spelled "גיים," which means "proud ones." The proud ones were destined to be Antoninus whi was a Roman emperor and descendant of Eisav, and Rabbi Yehudah HaNasi (also known as Rebbi) who was a descendant of Yaakov, both of whom were of the ancestry of Rivkah and who were so wealthy that they could afford to have seasonal produce such as radishes and lettuce on their tables all year round.[41]

Nonetheless, for Antoninus and similar Romans, the wealth was a "פַּח – snare" for them and contributed to their being גֵאִים in the form of arrogance and opulence used to fatten only themselves. On the other hand, for Rebbi and similar Jews, the wealth was a *brachah*, as it contributed to their being גֵאִים in the form of their proud performance of mitzvos, such as feeding *talmidei chachamim* and graciously bestowing *hachnasas orchim* upon those in need.[42]

Pasuk 7:
אָמַרְתִּי לַה': אֵ-לִי אָתָּה;

הַאֲזִינָה ה' קוֹל תַּחֲנוּנָי

I have said to Hashem: My God You are!
Give ear, Hashem, to the sound of my pleading.

The Power and Style of Prayer

Here we have the first sign of real optimism in *Tehillim* 140, as there is a three-fold mention of Names of God: twice "י-ה-ו-ה," the Name which indicates Divine mercy, and the Name "אֵ-ל," which represents

---

[40] *Bereishis* 25:23.
[41] *Rashi, Bereishis* 25:23, from *Avodah Zarah* 11a.
[42] *Tosafos, Avodah Zarah* 11a.

CHAPTER 8: VAYISHLACH & TEHILLIM 140

Hashem's combining *chozek* (power) with *chessed* by being powerful in/with kindness.[43]

We find the Name אֵ-ל used often in davening. For example, in the first of the daily *Hallelukah*s we say: "אַשְׁרֵי שֶׁאֵ-ל יַעֲקֹב בְּעֶזְרוֹ; שִׂבְרוֹ עַל ה' אֱ-לֹהָיו – Praiseworthy is he who the אֵ-ל – God of Yaakov is his help; whose hope is in Hashem his God."[44] This *pasuk* associates the Name אֵ-ל with Yaakov Avinu and also contains a three-fold mention of different names of God, making it a very powerful *pasuk* and one similar to *pasuk* 7 of *Tehillim* 140.

Most importantly, *pasuk* 7 contains the word "קוֹל – voice," which calls upon the power of Yaakov in prayer: "הַקֹּל קוֹל יַעֲקֹב – the voice is the voice of Yaakov,"[45] protecting against the violence of "הַיָּדַיִם יְדֵי עֵשָׂו – the hands are the hands of Eisav."[46]

In addition, the word "הַאֲזִינָה – give ear" said in reference to Hashem is not a poetic personification but rather a vital lesson in the approach to proper prayer.

Many wonder: Why do we have to daven in the first place? After all, Hashem knows our thoughts, wants, and needs even better than we do, so why ask at all? If He wants to give, He will give!

Rav Shimshon Pincus[47] explains that at times Hashem makes Himself as if He has ears. He expects to "hear" the Jew articulate and verbalize his prayer aloud using his קוֹל, his voice, as Dovid HaMelech famously stated: "אֲדֹנָ-י שִׁמְעָה בְקוֹלִי, תִּהְיֶינָה אָזְנֶיךָ קַשֻּׁבוֹת לְקוֹל תַּחֲנוּנָי – Hashem, listen to my *voice*, please let *Your ears* be attentive to the *voice* of my supplication."[48] Why does Hashem do this? So that we must daven; so that we must

---

[43] E.g., *Shabbos Malkesa*, p. 21. See also *Ohev Yisroel, Tzav* 2:2; *Kedushas Levi, Parshas Vayakhel*.
[44] *Tehillim* 146:5.
[45] *Bereishis* 27:21.
[46] *Bereishis* 27:21.
[47] *She'arim Be'Tefillah*, p. 30.
[48] *Tehillim* 130:2.

literally speak to Hashem and thereby forge a real relationship with Him. For Hashem *wants* us to daven, to reach out, to connect to Him. More than just *knowing* the desires of our heart, Hashem wants to "hear" our prayers, our voice, our needs, our love.

And so, the exact same concept is expressed here in *Tehillim* 140:7: "הַאֲזִינָה ה' קוֹל תַּחֲנוּנָי – Give ear, Hashem, to the sound/voice of my pleading," as the *mispallel* davens aloud, confident that Hashem will hear and answer.

Therefore, we too must ensure that when we daven, we add our *own* קוֹל, our *own* voice, feelings, and desire for closeness to Hashem to the already constant symphony of the קֹל קוֹל יַעֲקֹב of Yaakov Avinu, Dovid HaMelech, and the Jewish People.

Pasuk 8:
יֱהֹוִ-ה, אֲדֹ-נָי, עֹז יְשׁוּעָתִי;
סַכֹּתָה לְרֹאשִׁי בְּיוֹם נָשֶׁק

**Elokim, my Lord, might of my salvation,
You protected my head on the day of armed battle.**

A Chanukah Connection

The words "עֹז יְשׁוּעָתִי" mirror the opening line of the famous "מָעוֹז צוּר יְשׁוּעָתִי" prayer sung by Jewish families worldwide as they stand in front of the lit Chanukah candles. Chanukah coincides each year around the time of *Parshas Vayishlach*. Chanukah is a celebration of the victory of the Maccabim and their "יוֹם נָשֶׁק – day/period of armed battle" against the wicked and mighty Greek army. Chanukah is the time of both Hashem's revealed and hidden miracles that enabled Am Yisrael to achieve the lofty status of "the strong delivered into the hands of the weak, the many into the hands of the few, the impure into the hands of the pure, the *reshaim* into the hands of *tzaddikim*, and the vicious sinners into the hands of the diligent students of Torah."⁴⁹ Chanukah symbolizes the quintessential battle of light versus darkness, Torah versus so-called enlightenment, and Jew versus Greek in continuation of the battle that started with Yaakov Avinu versus Eisav HaRasha who was the forefather of Yavan and the Greek Empire.

Yaakov's Connection to Sukkos

The phrase "סַכֹּתָה לְרֹאשִׁי בְּיוֹם נָשֶׁק – You protected my head on the day of armed battle" is very much connected to Yaakov Avinu as well, for "סַכֹּתָה" is a reference to the Jewish holiday of Sukkos, the holiday of Yaakov (while Pesach corresponds to Avraham, and Shavuos corresponds to Yitzchak).⁵⁰

Like a sukkah that serves as a physical shield protecting its occupants from the elements as well as functioning as the spiritual shield of the Clouds of Glory,⁵¹ so too in *Parshas Vayishlach* Hashem protected Yaakov by enabling him to avoid an armed conflict with Eisav. Remarkably, after the Torah tells us that Eisav parted ways from Yaakov and went to Seir, the Torah describes where Yaakov went and what he did: "וְיַעֲקֹב נָסַע סֻכֹּתָה וַיִּבֶן לוֹ בָּיִת וּלְמִקְנֵהוּ עָשָׂה סֻכֹּת; עַל כֵּן קָרָא שֵׁם הַמָּקוֹם סֻכּוֹת" – Then Yaakov journeyed to Sukkos and built himself a house; and for his livestock he made sukkos (shelters); therefore he called the name of the place Sukkos."⁵² From here Chazal derive that of all the *Shalosh Regalim*, it is the holiday of Sukkos that most directly corresponds to Yaakov.

The Day of the Kiss

There is also a beautiful *Talmud Yerushalmi* that explains "נָשֶׁק" as having an entirely different and even deeper meaning than that of

---

⁴⁹ From *Al HaNissim*.
⁵⁰ *Tur, Orach Chaim* 417.
⁵¹ *Sukkah* 11b.
⁵² *Bereishis* 33:17.

"armed battle." "נָשָׁק" refers to "נְשִׁיקָה – a kiss."[53]

In reference to the phrase "סֻכֹּתָה לְרֹאשִׁי בְּיוֹם נָשֶׁק," the *Yerushalmi* explains that Hashem protects the Jew ",בְּיוֹם שֶׁשְּׁנֵי עוֹלָמוֹת נוֹשְׁקִין זֶה אֶת זֶה, הָעוֹלָם הַזֶּה יוֹצֵא וְהָעוֹלָם הַבָּא נִכְנָס – on the day that the two worlds kiss one another; when this world exits and the World to Come enters," which can be understood as referring to the day of death.

However, Rav Shimshon Pincus explains that "the day that the two worlds kiss one another" can also refer to the "world" of the *Yamim Noraim*. These Days of Awe are heavenly days, but they are days which, with the conclusion of Sukkos, will soon "kiss" and merge with the so-called "real world" of the ordinary non-holiday days of *chol*. Such a sudden transition can pose a great danger to the Jew, requiring extra protection and shielding. This, says Rav Pincus, is the function of Sukkos. Sukkos is not simply the end of the *Yamim Noraim*. Rather, the holiday of Sukkos serves as a vital bridge and transition period of "סֻכֹּתָה לְרֹאשִׁי," which literally and spiritually provides a protective sukkah above our רֹאשׁ, our head, and in many ways helps us transcend even above and beyond רֹאשׁ הַשָּׁנָה and the *Yamim Noraim*, thereby preparing us for the "ordinary" days that start on "the day of the kiss" when the two "worlds" of *kodesh* and *chol* inevitably intertwine.[54]

Incredibly, in the context of Yaakov and his encounter with Eisav, we can explain the dual understandings of the "day of armed battle" and "day of the kiss" in combination with one another; they refer to that fateful moment in which Yaakov saw the hostile Eisav aggressively running at him to wage war but instead Eisav embraced Yaakov, fell upon his neck, and "וַיִּשָּׁקֵהוּ – and he kissed him"[55] and they cried. After this, Yaakov safely traveled to a place he called Sukkos, all in fulfillment of "סֻכֹּתָה לְרֹאשִׁי בְּיוֹם נָשֶׁק" which now reverberates with the praise: Hashem,

---

[53] *Yerushalmi, Yevamos* 15:12.
[54] *Sichos Rav Shimshon Pincus – Sukkos*, p. 10.
[55] *Bereishis* 33:4.

You protected my head on the day of armed battle and transformed it into the peaceful day of the kiss.

Pasuk 9:
אַל תִּתֵּן, ה', מַאֲוַיֵּי רָשָׁע;
זְמָמוֹ אַל תָּפֵק, יָרוּמוּ סֶלָה.

**Grant not, Hashem, the desires of the wicked one;
to his conspiracy do not grant fruition,
for them to be exalted, Selah.**

A Plea That Hashem Not Listen to the Wicked

The Gemara[56] cites this entire *pasuk* as a harrowing statement by Yaakov about Eisav and his deadly progeny, expounding as follows: "רִבּוֹנוֹ שֶׁל עוֹלָם: אַל תִּתֵּן לְעֵשָׂו הָרָשָׁע תַּאֲוַת לִבּוֹ..." – Master of the Universe, do not grant the wicked Eisav the desires of his heart, since what he really wishes is to destroy me and my offspring. זְמָמוֹ אַל תָּפֵק – Do not listen to his conspiracy, and do not remove the נֶזֶם, muzzle, from *Germanyah shel Edom*, i.e., Germany, שֶׁאִלְמָלֵי הֵן יוֹצְאִין, מַחֲרִיבִין כָּל הָעוֹלָם כּוּלּוֹ – for if they would go forth, they would destroy the entire world."

As we now sadly know in hindsight, this was clearly a prayer and prophecy applicable to the horrors perpetrated by Nazi Germany *yemach shemam*. May there never be revealed a more haunting Gemara than this.

Would Hashem Ever Side with Evil?

This thought-provoking and perhaps disturbing *pasuk* implores Hashem not to allow the wicked to succeed. Worse (as we shall see below), this *pasuk* may be understood as carrying within it the implication that Hashem might otherwise actually side with the *rasha* by granting his wicked wishes. Is this possible?

---

[56] *Megillah* 6a–b.

In the context of Yaakov's meeting with Eisav in *Parshas Vayishlach*, we do find that Yaakov was afraid and even concerned about Eisav's merit earned by fulfilling the mitzvah of *kibbud av*, honoring their father Yitzchak, while in contrast Yaakov was away from home for twenty-two years unable to perform such active honor toward his parents (albeit *because* of Eisav). In addition, it is possible that Yaakov was concerned that the blessings that Yitzchak bestowed upon Eisav might serve as a *zechus* for Eisav.

Most troubling of all is that *Rashi* on this *pasuk* interprets "מְאוֹיְבֵי רֶשַׁע" in this context as "Amalek HaRasha," Eisav's most evil of descendants, which should send shivers down one's spine.

What is the *hava amina*?[57] How could this *kapitel* even allude to the possibility that Hashem might ever side with such terrible *reshaim* as Eisav and Amalek, let alone *reshaim* of any type?

Hashem is pure good; He never sides with the wicked even when it may appear that He is allowing them to succeed. As Dovid HaMelech powerfully proclaimed: "כִּי לֹא אֵ-ל חָפֵץ רֶשַׁע אָתָּה; לֹא יְגֻרְךָ רָע" – For You are not a God Who desires wickedness; no evil dwells with You!"[58]

Furthermore, even the apparent successes of the wicked are cloaked with Divine mercy and may occur for a myriad of hidden reasons including in order to more thoroughly punish the wicked in the end, to test Hashem's righteous ones, to serve as a *kaparah* for Hashem's righteous ones, to magnify a future *Kiddush HaShem*, and/or for a different and deeper purpose that is entirely concealed from us.

Regardless of what transpires, Hashem is pure good, His actions are pure good, and He is never, ever, on the side of evil or the wicked.

---

[57] "*Hava amina*" is a Talmudic expression that means "original assumption."
[58] *Tehillim* 5:5.

Pasuk 10:
רֹאשׁ מְסִבָּי,
עֲמַל שְׂפָתֵימוֹ יְכַסֵּימוֹ

**As for the head of my besiegers,
let the mischief of their own lips bury them.**

Eisav's Death by Decapitation

Amazingly, this *pasuk* literally describes Eisav's death. The Gemara[59] recounts that Yaakov had passed away and his body was being escorted to Eretz Yisrael by Yosef and his brothers. They were accompanied by the leaders of Egypt (other than Pharaoh) and the kings of the primary nations of the world who each wished to honor both the deceased Yaakov as well as his son Yosef the Viceroy of Egypt who had saved their lives and the lives of their nations during the earlier years of famine.

When the funeral procession reached the intended burial place of Me'aras Hamachpeilah, Eisav appeared and created obstacles to prevent them from moving forward. Eisav announced that the cave, located in Kiryas Arba, the "City of Four" in Chevron, was aptly named because it was destined to be the burial place of four pairs of people, and four pairs only. Already buried there were Adam and Chavah, Avraham and Sarah, Yitzchak and Rivkah, and Yaakov's wife Leah. Only one burial plot remained. Eisav argued that Yaakov had already used his allotted spot by burying Leah, and that the remaining space was designated for Eisav, not for Yaakov.

A discussion ensued in which the sons of Yaakov explained that Eisav's selling of the birthright included not only his double portion as a firstborn, but also his entire portion as a son – including the burial plot. This was a position with which Eisav insincerely but no less vehemently

---

[59] *Sotah* 13a.

disagreed. The sons of Yaakov pointed to Yaakov's dying declaration in which Yaakov specifically commanded his sons to bury him in Me'aras Hamachpeilah. Chazal also reveal to us that Eisav's claim was baseless, for Yaakov had previously purchased Me'aras Hamachpeilah from Eisav after Yitzchak's death in exchange for a heap of gold and silver he had amassed from his dealings with Lavan and of which Yaakov wanted to rid himself.[60]

Nevertheless, in a ploy to further delay Yaakov's funeral, Eisav argued that if Yaakov had bought the cave from him, the sale should be proven by displaying the deed of sale. Although the deed was in Egypt and would take time to retrieve while Yaakov awaited burial, Eisav insisted that the deed be brought. The brothers sent Naftali, who was swift as a deer, to run to Egypt and bring back the deed. In the meantime, Yaakov's grandson, Chushim the son of Dan, who was hard of hearing and thus had been unaware of these events, inquired as to the reason for the delay. When it was explained to him that the wicked Eisav was obstructing the burial, Chushim proclaimed: "Until Naftali comes back from Egypt, will my grandfather be lying here in disgrace?" Chushim picked up a staff and hit Eisav in the head, killing him.[61] There is even an opinion that Chushim took a sword and cut off Eisav's head after which the head rolled into Me'aras Hamachpeilah and was forever entombed there, separate from the rest of Eisav's body.[62]

While the Gemara[63] explicitly connects the above episode to *Tehillim* 58:11, the *pasuk* here in *Tehillim* 140:10 is also a perfect summary of the above events: "רֹאשׁ מְסִבָּי, עֲמַל שְׂפָתֵימוֹ יְכַסֵּימוֹ – As for the head of my besiegers, let the mischief of their own lips bury them." Eisav laid siege upon Yaakov's funeral, and with mischievous lips made a false claim over

---

[60] Rashi, Bereishis 50:5, from *Midrash Tanchuma, Vayechi* 6.
[61] *Sotah* 13a.
[62] *Targum Yonasan Ben Uziel, Bereishis* 50:13.
[63] *Sotah* 13a.

the burial place; but all this led to his *own* death by decapitation. The above is clearly a parallel of pure precision.

Pasuk 11:
יִמּוֹטוּ עֲלֵיהֶם גֶּחָלִים;
בָּאֵשׁ יַפִּלֵם,
בְּמַהֲמֹרוֹת בַּל יָקוּמוּ

**Let descend upon them burning coals;
into the fire let it [their own mischief] cast them down,
into deep pits never to rise again.**

May the *Reshaim* Suffer in Gehinnom Forever

This *pasuk* begins with a request for Hashem to rain down fire and brimstone on the *reshaim* in the form of "burning coals" and to thus destroy them in the manner reminiscent of that of Sedom and Amorah, history's most wicked cities.[64] This *pasuk* also contains a vivid request for the *reshaim* to be "cast down into deep pits," which *Rashi* says is an expression of punishment in Gehinnom.[65]

However, the addition of the expression "בַּל יָקוּמוּ – never to rise again" takes the request to the furthest degree. Ordinarily, Gehinnom serves as a temporary purgatory for souls to suffer as an atonement for their sins in order to reach a state of purification before these souls are relocated to a place befitting each one, on its level, in the World to Come. Here, however, the request is "בַּל יָקוּמוּ," that they never rise again – not just in this world but even in the next world – thus losing their entire *chelek l'Olam Haba*. Amazingly, there is a *Midrash Tanchuma* that indicates Eisav HaRasha will suffer such a fate.[66]

---

[64] *Bereishis* 19:24; *Tehillim* 11:6.
[65] *Rashi, Tehillim* 140:11.
[66] *Midrash Tanchuma, Tzav* 2.

Ultimately, punishment is the realm of Hashem, but here the *kapitel* reminds us that we must hope and pray that Hashem punish, forever and to the fullest extent, Eisav's evil descendants such as Amalek and Nazi Germany, as well as Yishmael's evil descendants such as Arab terrorists and those who proliferate such wicked ideologies, *yemach shemam v'zichram*.

In contrast, regarding the Jewish People, Chazal tell us:[67] "כָּל יִשְׂרָאֵל יֵשׁ לָהֶם חֵלֶק לְעוֹלָם הַבָּא שֶׁנֶּאֱמַר וְעַמֵּךְ כֻּלָּם צַדִּיקִים לְעוֹלָם יִירְשׁוּ אָרֶץ נֵצֶר מַטָּעַי מַעֲשֵׂה יָדַי לְהִתְפָּאֵר – All Yisrael have a share in the World to Come, as it is stated:[68] 'And Your people are all righteous. They shall inherit the land forever. They are the branch of My planting, the work of My hands, in which I take pride.'" How fortunate we are that we merit the blessings and goodness of Yiddishkeit in this temporary world and are simultaneously earning our own place in the World to Come for all eternity.

Pasuk 12:
אִישׁ לָשׁוֹן, בַּל יִכּוֹן בָּאָרֶץ;
אִישׁ חָמָס רָע,
יְצוּדֶנּוּ לְמַדְחֵפֹת

**The man of slander, let him not be established on earth;
the man of violence who is evil,
may he be hunted until he is overthrown.**

Let the Hunter Become the Hunted

This *pasuk* as well is clearly a befitting protective prayer against Eisav HaRasha, who is the "man of slander" and the "man of violence who is evil," a connection explicitly confirmed by *Rashi*.[69] As such, we can add

---

[67] *Sanhedrin* 90a.
[68] *Yeshayahu* 60:21.
[69] *Rashi, Tehillim* 140:12.

the following: Eisav, upon whom his father bestowed the blessings of אַרְצִיּוּת, earthiness and *gashmius*, of him this *pasuk* declares: "בַּל יִכּוֹן בָּאָרֶץ – let him *not* be established on earth;" let his blessing of אַרְצִיּוּת never come to fruition.

Most magnificent of all is the use of the word "יְצוּדֶנּוּ" which contains the plea that Eisav be "hunted" and overthrown. For Eisav was a hunter: a hunter and killer with weapons and also a hunter, trapper, and deceiver with words. These various types of hunting and trapping with his treacherous tongue and propensity toward violence made him infamous. All this evil is intertwined with his ability of "צַיִד," his skill as a hunter.

In *Parshas Toldos* the Torah twice describes Eisav by using the word צַיִד: "עֵשָׂו אִישׁ יֹדֵעַ צַיִד, אִישׁ שָׂדֶה" – Eisav was a man with knowledge of hunting, a man of the field,"[70] and "כִּי צַיִד בְּפִיו" – For trapping/hunting was in his mouth."[71] *Rashi* explains that Eisav knew how to use words to ensnare and deceive even his holy father Yitzchak by asking insincere questions to feign righteousness, and that Eisav was a "man of the field" who hunted with weapons.[72] *Rashi* also tells us that he used these skills to perform terrible acts of evil, including to lure married women away from their husbands[73] and even for murder.[74]

Tehillim 140, the *kapitel* connected to *Parshas Vayishlach* and its "Eisav versus Yaakov" message, contains a *pasuk* in which the *tzaddik* requests that the wicked hunter *himself* become the hunted. In fact, on the word "יְצוּדֶנּוּ," *Rashi* says that the very same acts of evil the wicked perform against others will return to hunt down, ensnare, and punish those same *reshaim* who perpetrated such evil.[75] This request for the hunter to become the hunted is clearly a prayer for perfect retribution, as only Hashem can

---

[70] *Bereishis* 25:27.
[71] *Bereishis* 25:28.
[72] *Rashi, Bereishis* 25:27.
[73] *Rashi, Bereishis* 26:34.
[74] *Rashi, Bereishis* 25:29.
[75] *Rashi, Tehillim* 140:12.

orchestrate.

Pasuk 13:
יָדַעְתִּי כִּי יַעֲשֶׂה ה' דִּין עָנִי,
מִשְׁפַּט אֶבְיֹנִים
**I know that Hashem will judge [favorably] the poor,
the judgment of the destitute.**

Katonti Mikol Ha'chassadim: Yaakov's Immense Humbleness

Yaakov Avinu knew what it is was like to be poor. When fleeing from Eisav in *Parshas Vayeitzei*, Yaakov allowed himself to be stripped of nearly all his possessions by Eisav's son Elifaz and to be left with only his walking-staff, so impoverished that he had a halachic status of a dead man.[76] As a result, we are told later in *Parshas Vayeitzei* that Yaakov cried upon meeting Rochel Imeinu for the first time because he was emptyhanded and unable to grant her gifts, and was further saddened by the memory of his family's servant Eliezer who had previously showered Rivkah Imeinu with gifts on Yitzchak's behalf when he had encountered Rivkah, Rochel's aunt, for the first time.[77] In addition, for the initial fourteen years that Yaakov worked for Lavan, Yaakov's earnings remained in Lavan's hands, leaving Yaakov feeling inadequate because he was unable to directly provide for his own family.[78]

However, in *Parshas Vayishlach* after Yaakov had been blessed with a flourishing family and financial status, he nonetheless uttered the famous prayer to Hashem: "קָטֹנְתִּי מִכֹּל הַחֲסָדִים וּמִכָּל הָאֱמֶת אֲשֶׁר עָשִׂיתָ אֶת עַבְדֶּךָ; כִּי בְמַקְלִי עָבַרְתִּי אֶת הַיַּרְדֵּן הַזֶּה וְעַתָּה הָיִיתִי לִשְׁנֵי מַחֲנוֹת — I have been diminished by all the

---

[76] *Rashi, Bereishis* 29:11; *Nedarim* 64b.
[77] *Rashi, Bereishis* 29:11, from *Bereishis Rabbah* 70:12.
[78] *Bereishis* 30:30, and *Rashi* there.

CHAPTER 8: VAYISHLACH & TEHILLIM 140

kindness and by all the truth that You have done Your servant; for with [only] my staff I crossed this Jordan, and now have become two camps."[79]

This statement raises an important question: Why would Yaakov declare himself "diminished" when proclaiming and recognizing how much Hashem has allowed him to prosper?

Focusing on the words קָטֹנְתִּי מִכֹּל הַחֲסָדִים, *Rashi* explains that Yaakov was concerned that his merits may have been reduced by the kindness and truth Hashem had shown him, and that as a result he might be susceptible to harm by Eisav.[80] Of course, Yaakov's sincere statement reveals his true modesty: he never felt he had "earned" anything on his own, nor that he "deserved" anything, but rather viewed all that he had as a *matnas chinam* – a free gift from Hashem. Such is the way of the true *tzaddik*.

Similarly, we are taught that Moshe Rabbeinu revealed this perspective at the start of *Parshas Va'eschanan*, where he utilizes the term "*Va'eschanan*"[81] (from the *shoresh* of "*chinam* – free") in describing his pleading with Hashem rather than a more customary term such as "*va'espallel*" (from the *shoresh* of "*tefillah*"). *Rashi* tells us that Moshe was asking Hashem to let him enter Eretz Yisrael – but not because of his virtues or piety but simply as a *matnas chinam*. Although *tzaddikim* could theoretically request reward as compensation for their good deeds, they only ask for free gifts from Hashem; for in their modesty, they truly feel that their deeds do not merit reward.[82]

Indeed, Yaakov Avinu's statement of קָטֹנְתִּי מִכֹּל הַחֲסָדִים was a sincere expression of humility. His own wealth, family, and righteousness notwithstanding, he saw himself as impoverished and undeserving of all he possessed and had become.

In fact, Yaakov's humility was so genuine that he even viewed his own primary characteristic and focus in *avodas Hashem*, that of אֱמֶת, as a God-

---

[79] *Bereishis* 32:11.
[80] *Rashi, Bereishis* 32:11, from *Taanis* 20b.
[81] *Devarim* 3:23.
[82] *Rashi, Devarim* 3:23.

given gift. For Yaakov stated "קָטֹנְתִּי... וּמִכָּל הָאֱמֶת," and in doing so gratefully acknowledged that his having received Hashem's *emes* – even in the form of repayment for his efforts in performing righteous deeds of *emes* – was in Yaakov's view undeserved. The man of *emes* attributed every ounce of that *emes* only to the grace of Hashem. So astounding was Yaakov's humility.

Therefore, as a parallel to all the above, *pasuk* 13 of *Tehillim* 140 states: "יָדַעְתִּי כִּי יַעֲשֶׂה ה' דִּין עָנִי, מִשְׁפַּט אֶבְיֹנִים" – I know that Hashem will judge [favorably] the poor, the justice of the destitute," which contains sentiments very much applicable to Yaakov in relation to his self-perception. For Yaakov saw himself through the humblest of lenses, poor and undeserving, despite his righteousness and greatness.

Pasuk 14:
אַךְ צַדִּיקִים יוֹדוּ לִשְׁמֶךָ;
יֵשְׁבוּ יְשָׁרִים אֶת פָּנֶיךָ

**Only the righteous will give thanks to Your Name;
dwell will the upright in Your Presence.**

A Befitting Conclusion to Yaakov in *Parshas Vayishlach*

This concluding *pasuk* contains so much and requires a more detailed breakdown to properly explain its many connections to Yaakov Avinu and *Parshas Vayishlach*.

For starters, "צַדִּיקִים" here refers to Yaakov, to his children,[83] and to his extended family – all of us, all of Klal Yisrael. As noted in connection with *pasuk* 11 above, "וְעַמֵּךְ כֻּלָּם צַדִּיקִים" – Your people [Hashem], are all righteous."[84]

---

[83] E.g., *Rashi, Bereishis* 35:22.
[84] *Yeshayahu* 60:21.

CHAPTER 8: VAYISHLACH & TEHILLIM 140

The Wounded *Tzaddik* Is Still a *Tzaddik*

The phrase "אַךְ צַדִּיקִים" means "only the righteous" or "however, the righteous." Yet we also find the word אַךְ to be understood by Chazal in a different and more creative way. In *Parshas Noach* the Torah uses the expression "אַךְ נֹחַ – only Noach,"[85] but Chazal say that this expression means that Noach was coughing and retching blood due to the toil and troubles of caring for all the animals on the Ark,[86] or even that he was attacked by a lion and was gravely wounded.[87] In any case, the word "אַךְ" connotes being minimized, impaired, even injured. Thus, here the phrase "אַךְ צַדִּיקִים" tells us about the righteous in general: even if they are "אַךְ" and diminished, weakened, or harmed by the *reshaim*, they nonetheless remain צַדִּיקִים.

Perhaps more than anyone else, Yaakov Avinu exemplified this characteristic, as his spiritual and physical battles were continuous, and in *Parshas Vayishlach* he was even bodily injured by the *Sar shel Eisav* who dislocated Yaakov's thighbone,[88] leaving him limping and temporarily crippled.[89] Nevertheless, "אַךְ צַדִּיקִים יוֹדוּ לִשְׁמֶךָ" – like all true *tzaddikim*, he, they, and even we, will continue to give thanks to Hashem's Name no matter the challenges and circumstances.

The Warriors Who Fight For and Praise Hashem

The phrase "יוֹדוּ לִשְׁמֶךָ," that *tzaddikim* will "give thanks and/or acknowledge Your Name," is very poignant here, for Chazal tell us that Yaakov's confrontation with Eisav did not end in *Parshas Vayishlach*, or even in *Parshas Vayechi* with Eisav's beheading and Yaakov's burial. Their confrontation transcended their lifetimes and continues to this very

---

[85] *Bereishis* 7:23.
[86] Rashi, *Bereishis* 7:23, from *Sanhedrin* 108b.
[87] Rashi, *Bereishis* 7:23, from *Midrash Tanchuma, Noach* 9.
[88] *Bereishis* 32:26.
[89] *Bereishis* 32:32.

day with the battle between good and evil and with the battle between the Jewish People and this *galus* of Edom/Eisav. However, one day, perhaps even *today* with the coming of Moshiach,[90] this conflict will come to a dazzling conclusion and culminate in a *Kiddush Shem Shamayim* – sanctification of the Name of Heaven – of the highest degree and entirely "לִשְׁמֶךָ".

In fact, it will be Yaakov, through his courageous descendants, who will be the warriors surging forth in battle and opposing Eisav and his descendants on Eisav's home turf of Har Seir just as Yaakov alluded to Eisav in *Parshas Vayishlach*.[91]

In addition, we read in the *Haftarah* of *Parshas Vayishlach*, which describes the days immediately preceding the arrival of Moshiach, the following stirring words: "וְעָלוּ מוֹשִׁעִים בְּהַר צִיּוֹן לִשְׁפֹּט אֶת הַר עֵשָׂו, וְהָיְתָה לַה' הַמְּלוּכָה – And the saviors will ascend on Har Tzion to judge the mountain of Eisav, and kingship shall be Hashem's."[92]

Moreover, this above *pasuk* in Ovadyah is one we say every day at the conclusion of the *Az Yashir tefillah*, where it is followed by the *pasuk*: "וְהָיָה ה' לְמֶלֶךְ עַל כָּל הָאָרֶץ; בַּיּוֹם הַהוּא יִהְיֶה ה' אֶחָד וּשְׁמוֹ אֶחָד" – Then will Hashem be King over all the world; on that day shall Hashem be One and His Name shall be One."[93] At that time, all of mankind will recognize Hashem and will willingly "יוֹדוּ לִשְׁמֶךָ," praise Hashem's Name in an everlasting *Kiddush HaShem*.

May we too be counted among those מוֹשִׁעִים, warrior-saviors, and be brave enough and righteous enough to battle Eisav's descendants to help usher in that glorious time when Hashem will be recognized and praised by all.

---

[90] E.g., *Tehillim* 95:7, and *Sanhedrin* 98a.
[91] *Rashi, Bereishis* 37:14, from *Bereishis Rabbah* 78:14.
[92] *Ovadyah* 1:21.
[93] *Zechariah* 14:9.

CHAPTER 8: VAYISHLACH & TEHILLIM 140

The Dwellings of the Upright in Both Worlds

The latter half of *pasuk* 14 begins with the phrase "יֵשְׁבוּ יְשָׁרִים – dwell will the upright." As we have noted many times, "יְשָׁרִים" is a reference to all three of the Avos – Avraham, Yitzchak, and Yaakov.

That the word "יֵשְׁבוּ" is mentioned here must be noted because it shares the same *shoresh* as the word "וַיֵּשֶׁב,"[94] thus serving as the perfect bridge to the next *Parshah* of *Parshas Vayeishev*, which continues to follow the life of the יְשָׁרִים – Yaakov and his sons, as well as Yitzchak.[95]

In addition, *Parshas Vayeishev* opens with Chazal telling us that Yaakov longed for Hashem to transform and improve his life, thus allowing him "לֵישֵׁב בְּשַׁלְוָה – to dwell in tranquility." However, Hashem refused, explaining that it is enough that the World to Come awaits the *tzaddik*,[96] and at which point Hashem immediately introduced Yaakov's travails revolving around Yosef.

Finally, the expression "יֵשְׁבוּ יְשָׁרִים" also refers to that future time when each righteous Jew will indeed dwell in tranquility in the World to Come, thanks to the great toil and effort they exerted while alive in this world. It is a glorious and holy time described by the Gemara as one in which 'צַדִּיקִים יוֹשְׁבִין וְעַטְרוֹתֵיהֶם בְּרָאשֵׁיהֶם וְנֶהֱנִים מִזִּיו הַשְּׁכִינָה – The righteous will be יוֹשְׁבִין – dwelling with crowns upon their heads, enjoying the radiance of the Divine Presence."[97]

From Facing Evil to Face-to-Face with Hashem

"אֶת פָּנֶיךָ – Your Presence" or literally "Your face" in reference to Hashem is the dream of every *tzaddik*: to know Hashem, to be close to Hashem.

---

[94] *Bereishis* 37:1.
[95] See *Rashi, Bereishis* 37:33.
[96] *Rashi, Bereishis* 37:2, from *Tanchuma Yashan, Mevo*, ms. 3, 13; see also *Bereishis Rabbah* 84:3.
[97] *Brachos* 17a.

This is especially true of a *tzaddik* like Yaakov Avinu, who in *Parshas Vayishlach* saw the exact opposite. Yaakov had come face-to-face with the terrible presence of the *Sar shel Eisav*/Edom, of whom Yaakov said: "וַיִּקְרָא יַעֲקֹב שֵׁם הַמָּקוֹם פְּנִיאֵל, כִּי רָאִיתִי אֱלֹהִים פָּנִים אֶל פָּנִים וַתִּנָּצֵל נַפְשִׁי" – And Yaakov called the name of the place Peniel, 'For I have seen this Divine being [the angel] face-to-face, yet my soul was spared.'"[98]

In addition, during the confrontation between Yaakov and Eisav in *Parshas Vayishlach*, Yaakov made mention of Eisav's face and stated: "כִּי עַל כֵּן רָאִיתִי פָנֶיךָ כִּרְאֹת פְּנֵי אֱלֹהִים, וַתִּרְצֵנִי" – For therefore I have seen your face, which is like seeing the face of a Divine being, and you have been appeased by me."[99]

After having seen such faces of evil and death, one can only imagine how much Yaakov Avinu must have yearned to see only "אֶת פָּנֶיךָ," Hashem's face, and how much he must have cherished those moments of prophesy, *ruach hakodesh*, and *tefillah*, longing to be with Hashem's Presence always.

Such is a lofty goal for each of us, yet Chazal tell us that each *Shemoneh Esrei* we daven is actually a face-to-face interaction with Hashem, one in which we are עוֹמֵד לִפְנֵי הַמֶּלֶךְ, standing before the King, Who is actually so very close that we can and must whisper our prayers to Him.[100] Therefore, we must truly cherish each and every moment of davening and *deveikus*, and try to connect to Hashem with the sincerity and closeness that Hashem deserves. In doing so, may we ourselves be the fulfillment of this closing *pasuk* that Dovid HaMelech and Yaakov Avinu held so dear: "אַךְ צַדִּיקִים יוֹדוּ לִשְׁמֶךָ; יֵשְׁבוּ יְשָׁרִים אֶת פָּנֶיךָ."

---

[98] *Bereishis* 32:31.
[99] *Bereishis* 33:10.
[100] *Brachos* 33a; *Shulchan Aruch, Orach Chaim* 98:1.

CHAPTER 8: VAYISHLACH & TEHILLIM 140

ERADICATING THE EISAV AND EVIL THAT LURKS WITHIN

There are many variations of a famous story of a Chassidic Rebbe who once told his *talmid* (or *chazzan*, or even his entire congregation) that the solution to all problems can be found by properly davening the words "אָנָּא ה' – Please, Hashem," during *Hallel*. The willing chassid went and fervently davened: "אָנָּא ה' הוֹשִׁיעָה נָּא; אָנָּא ה' הַצְלִיחָה נָּא – Please, Hashem, save now! Please, Hashem, bring success now!"[101] but ultimately returned to his Rebbe forlorn, respectfully saying that the Rebbe's sage advice had failed. The Rebbe responded that he had intentionally left it to the chassid to try and decipher the lesson on his own, and the *talmid* had misunderstood. In actuality, the Rebbe was referring to a completely different אָנָּא ה', one that appears earlier in *Hallel*, that of "אָנָּה ה' כִּי אֲנִי עַבְדֶּךָ – Please, Hashem, for I am Your servant!"[102]

This story's powerful messages of selflessness and subservience to Hashem absolutely ring true. Yet, there is another אָנָּא ה', one that appears even earlier in *Hallel*, which for some may be the most applicable and important אָנָּא ה' of them all: "אָנָּה ה' מַלְּטָה נַפְשִׁי – Please, Hashem, save my soul!"[103]

As discussed throughout this chapter, *Tehillim* 140 is very much about protection from dangers and opposition posed by external forces and enemies, whether they be Doeg and Shaul in the life of Dovid HaMelech,[104] Eisav and Lavan in the life of Yaakov Avinu, and even

---

[101] *Tehillim* 118:25.
[102] *Tehillim* 116:16.
[103] *Tehillim* 116:4.
[104] E.g., *Radak, Tehillim* 140:1.

protection from *rishus* and *reshaim* who have arisen in the past and might yet arise in every generation until Moshiach.

However, as one recites *Tehillim* 140, one cannot help but sense that there is an additional layer to this *kapitel*. We see here the message of protection from *internal* drives, difficulties, and dangers, as if to say that the dual intent of statements in *Tehillim* 140 such as "חַלְּצֵנִי ה' מֵאָדָם רָע; מֵאִישׁ חֲמָסִים תִּנְצְרֵנִי – Free me, Hashem, from the man who is wicked; from the man of violence protect me,"[105] also includes a request by Dovid to be rescued and protected from the רָע and other negative *middos* latent within himself. This, then, would be an identical plea to that of "אָנָּה ה' מַלְּטָה נַפְשִׁי – Please, Hashem, save my soul!" Save my soul from the danger of others! Save my soul from the danger of myself!

The Midrash[106] explains that Eisav was not the only child described as אַדְמוֹנִי, ruddy,[107] which foretold that he would be a *shofeich damim*, spiller of blood. For Dovid, too, is referred to as אַדְמוֹנִי as the *pasuk* says: "וַיִּשְׁלַח וַיְבִיאֵהוּ וְהוּא אַדְמוֹנִי – [Shmuel] sent for him [Dovid] and they brought him, and he was ruddy."[108] Upon seeing Dovid, Shmuel "נִתְיָרֵא וְאָמַר אַף זֶה שׁוֹפֵךְ דָּמִים כְּעֵשָׂו – became frightened and said: 'This one, too, shall be a spiller of blood like Eisav.'" Hashem then responded: "עִם יְפֵה עֵינָיִם,"[109] indicating that Dovid possessed "beautiful eyes," which meant that "עֵשָׂו מִדַּעַת עַצְמוֹ הוּא הוֹרֵג, אֲבָל זֶה מִדַּעַת סַנְהֶדְרִין הוּא הוֹרֵג – Eisav killed on his own whim, while this one [Dovid] would kill with the counsel of the Sanhedrin," the Jewish High Court referred to as the "eyes of the congregation."[110] Thus, while Dovid was able to properly channel his bloody nature toward the service of Hashem, he was born with certain natural tendencies similar to those of Eisav.

---

[105] *Tehillim* 140:2.
[106] *Bereishis Rabbah* 63:8.
[107] *Bereishis* 25:25.
[108] *I Shmuel* 16:12.
[109] *I Shmuel* 16:12.
[110] E.g., *Bamidbar* 15:24.

CHAPTER 8: VAYISHLACH & TEHILLIM 140

The *sefer Bilvavi Mishkan Evneh*[111] teaches that every single element of the Torah is connected to and has a place in the soul of every person. Thus, for example, every person has an aspect of Avraham Avinu, Yitzchak Avinu, and Yaakov Avinu inside himself. However, the opposite is also true. Every person has within him an aspect of Lavan, Pharaoh, Bilaam, etc., and Eisav as well. If they are in the Torah, then they are in us. This does not simply mean that we learn from them and about them in the Torah. It means that Avraham is a power of purity that exists in every soul, as are all the Avos, Imahos, Moshe Rabbeinu, Aharon HaKohen, etc., and these powerful and positive connections need to be constantly nurtured. However, each of the evildoers in the Torah are also a power of impurity found inside every soul, and while these evildoers have lived and died, the imprint they left upon future souls lives on, in varying degrees, in each person and in each *neshamah*, and needs to be constantly battled.[112]

Each day in *Pesukei D'Zimra* we daven: "וְאַל יִשְׁלֹט בָּנוּ יֵצֶר הָרָע. וְהַרְחִיקֵנוּ מֵאָדָם רָע וּמֵחָבֵר רָע. וְדַבְּקֵנוּ בְּיֵצֶר הַטּוֹב וּבְמַעֲשִׂים טוֹבִים וְכוֹף אֶת יִצְרֵנוּ לְהִשְׁתַּעְבֶּד לָךְ – Let not the evil inclination rule over us. Distance us from an evil person and from an evil companion. Attach us to the good inclination and to good deeds and compel our evil inclination to be subservient to You." The basic intent behind this request for protection from מֵאָדָם רָע וּמֵחָבֵר רָע refers to outsiders who might try to harm us or influence us negatively. However, on a deeper level, it refers to *us* – we daven that *we* not be guilty of becoming an evil person or evil friend; not to others, and not to ourselves! This sentiment is reinforced by the fact that the words מֵאָדָם רָע וּמֵחָבֵר רָע are surrounded by prayers relating to our own internal evil inclination and good inclination.

Yaakov, too, in *Parshas Vayishlach* underwent unique experiences relating to his past and to his innermost *middos*. For example, Yaakov had

---

[111] *Bilvavi Mishkan Evneh, Chelek aleph, perek* 69.
[112] *Bilvavi Mishkan Evneh, Chelek aleph, perek* 70.

his name changed from Yaakov to Yisrael, first by the *Sar shel Eisav*[113] and later by Hashem Himself.[114] In these instances, Chazal explain that the name Yaakov connotes "בְּעָקְבָה וּרְמִיָּה – treachery and deceit,"[115] and "בְּמַאֲרָב וְעָקְבָה – stealth and treachery"[116] but that he will no longer be associated with such negative traits and instead be known as "Yisrael," connoting authority and nobility,[117] traits reflective of Yaakov's inner enhancement and wholeness – *sheleimus*.

The episode and lesson gleaned from Yaakov's response during his confrontation with Eisav in *Parshas Vayishlach* contains great encouragement for Klal Yisrael. Eisav and his army of four hundred men set out for war against Yaakov, and Yaakov was fully prepared to engage in battle against them.[118] Nonetheless, when Eisav ran directly at Yaakov clearly to attack, grabbed him in a bear hug, and even tried to bite his neck and kill him, Yaakov did not actually defend himself, and certainly did not attack first. What would *we* do in such a situation? Had we not been paralyzed with fear, we certainly would have tried to protect ourselves, to stave off the attack, even to stab Eisav at the last second. Or better yet, while Eisav was still at a distance, perhaps we would take a bow and arrow and shoot him from afar. But Yaakov did none of that. He did not resort to violence. Yaakov passively allowed the situation to unfold even at the expense of his vulnerability, and in so doing, he refrained from engaging in any Eisav-like tendencies of violence.

This boundless self-control and reliance on the peaceful and faith-filled קֹל קוֹל יַעֲקֹב astounds us. Yaakov refused to become ensnared by the vicious and war-filled יָדַיִם יְדֵי עֵשָׂו, a violent trap into which Yaakov's sons Shimon and Levi would fall prey in *Parshas Vayishlach* when they displayed

---

[113] *Bereishis* 32:29.
[114] *Bereishis* 35:10.
[115] *Rashi, Bereishis* 32:29.
[116] *Rashi, Bereishis* 35:10.
[117] *Rashi, Bereishis* 35:10, from *Chullin* 92a.
[118] *Rashi, Bereishis* 32:9 and 33:3.

Eisav-like behavior in wiping out the City of Shechem, much to the disappointment of their father (as discussed above).[119]

Furthermore, thanks to Yaakov's passive reaction to Eisav, they were spared from Rivkah's prophetic fear and concern of "לָמָה אֶשְׁכַּל גַּם שְׁנֵיכֶם יוֹם אֶחָד – Why should I be bereaved of both of you on the same day,"[120] which foretold that her two sons would die (or at least be buried), at the same time. Had Yaakov attacked Eisav or even struck first in self-defense, Yaakov's death blow to Eisav would have inevitably resulted in Yaakov's own death as well. It is specifically because Yaakov refused to engage in any Eisav-like behaviors that he and his family survived the encounter with Eisav unscathed.

In addition, Yaakov had to overcome a self-inflicted *spiritual* trauma of sorts, as he worried: "קָטֹנְתִּי מִכֹּל הַחֲסָדִים וּמִכָּל הָאֱמֶת אֲשֶׁר עָשִׂיתָ אֶת עַבְדֶּךָ – I have been diminished by all the kindness and by all the truth that You have done Your servant."[121] As *Rashi* explains, Yaakov was worried that perhaps his merits had been reduced due to all the kindness and truth shown him by Hashem.[122] Furthermore, Yaakov was afraid that since the time of Hashem's initial promises of protection many years earlier, perhaps "נִתְלַכְלַכְתִּי בְּחֵטְא – I have become soiled with sin,"[123] or as the Gemara famously states: "שֶׁמָּא יִגְרוֹם הַחֵטְא – perhaps transgression will cause" Hashem to revoke His promise of protection and thus render Yaakov susceptible to falling into the hands of the wicked Eisav.[124] These were extreme worries, but real worries that burdened Yaakov. Although the common explanation is that these concerns were a result of Yaakov's profound humility, these same concerns were self-imposed, even self-inflicted, and thus needed to be overcome.

---

[119] *Rashi, Bereishis* 49:5, from *Bereishis Rabbah* 99:6.
[120] *Bereishis* 27:45.
[121] *Bereishis* 32:11.
[122] *Rashi, Bereishis* 32:11, from *Taanis* 20b and *Shabbos* 32a.
[123] *Rashi, Bereishis* 32:11, from *Midrash Tanchuma, Beshalach* 28.
[124] *Brachos* 4a. See also *Rashi, Bereishis* 32:11.

Finally, the last forty-three *pesukim* of *Parshas Vayishlach*[125] contain a somewhat lengthy description of the family and lineage of Eisav, designed not to praise Eisav but rather to inform us that his descendants were all wicked and all *mamzeirim* (the issue of adulterous or incestuous unions),[126] and that they were never treasured or held in any esteem by Hashem.[127] Therefore, in the spirit of the lesson of the *Bilvavi Mishkan Evneh* cited above, as we *lein* and learn those *pesukim*, it behooves us to take steps to cleanse and purify ourselves from any speck of Eisav that may be lurking inside ourselves.

Similarly, before we step out of every *Shemoneh Esrei*, we say the words:

אֱלֹהַי נְצוֹר לְשׁוֹנִי מֵרָע וּשְׂפָתַי מִדַּבֵּר מִרְמָה. וְלִמְקַלְלַי נַפְשִׁי תִדּוֹם וְנַפְשִׁי כֶּעָפָר לַכֹּל תִּהְיֶה... וְכֹל הַחוֹשְׁבִים עָלַי רָעָה מְהֵרָה הָפֵר עֲצָתָם וְקַלְקֵל מַחֲשַׁבְתָּם – My God, guard my tongue from evil and my lips from speaking deceitfully. To those who curse me, let my soul be silent; and let my soul be like dust to everyone… As for all those who design evil against me, speedily nullify their counsel and disrupt their design.

This is a very powerful and very personal prayer. It has been suggested that this entire declaration, even the protection against the וְלִמְקַלְלַי and the וְכֹל הַחוֹשְׁבִים עָלַי רָעָה, are not simply intended as protection from third parties, but also protection against "כֹּל – *all*," including even the mispallel himself, lest he be capable and culpable of self-injury due to his own flawed *middos* and self-destructive thoughts and actions.

In a similar vein, it is remarkable that in the entirety of the weekday *Shemoneh Esrei* which we daven in *lashon rabim* on behalf of not only ourselves but all Jews, the *shoresh* of the word "רָע" does not appear even a single time. Yet, in the above concluding passage of *Elokai Netzor*, which is said in singular as a unique prayer on our own behalf, the *shoresh*

---

[125] *Bereishis, Perek* 36.
[126] *Rashi, Bereishis* 36:2, *Bereishis Rabbah* 82:15.
[127] *Rashi, Bereishis* 37:1.

רָע appears not once but twice. Sadly, we can be our own worst enemy; therefore, we daven against this insidious and self-destructive behavior and privately ask Hashem: Please save me from myself! It is a prayer that echoes: "אָנָּה ה' מַלְּטָה נַפְשִׁי – Please, Hashem, save my soul!" Please, Hashem, save my soul from me!

Thus, in general and especially in the context of *Parshas Vayishlach*, *Tehillim* 140's opening statement of "חַלְּצֵנִי ה' מֵאָדָם רָע – Free me, Hashem, from the man who is wicked" contains an additional, even deeper message: "Hashem, please free me from me." Free me so that I should not be wicked. Free me so that I should not consider myself as wicked. Free me from that last little wicked trace of Eisav lurking inside of me.

And instead, fulfill in us *Tehillim* 140's glorious concluding *pasuk*: "אַךְ צַדִּיקִים יוֹדוּ לִשְׁמֶךָ; יֵשְׁבוּ יְשָׁרִים אֶת פָּנֶיךָ – Only the righteous will give thanks to Your Name; dwell will the upright in Your Presence," and please, Hashem, give each of us the strength to consider ourselves to be counted among the righteous, and so may it truly be, *Amen*.

CHAPTER 9

PARSHAS VAYEISHEV & TEHILLIM 112

פָּרָשַׁת וַיֵּשֶׁב / תְּהִלִּים קיב

תְּהִלִּים קיב — TEHILLIM 112

1	Halleluy-ah! Praiseworthy is the man who fears Hashem, who His commandments he desires greatly.	הַלְלוּיָ-הּ! אַשְׁרֵי אִישׁ יָרֵא אֶת ה', בְּמִצְוֹתָיו חָפֵץ מְאֹד.	א
2	Mighty in the land will be his offspring, a generation of the upright who will be blessed.	גִּבּוֹר בָּאָרֶץ יִהְיֶה זַרְעוֹ; דּוֹר יְשָׁרִים יְבֹרָךְ.	ב
3	Wealth and riches are in his house, and his righteousness endures forever.	הוֹן וָעֹשֶׁר בְּבֵיתוֹ; וְצִדְקָתוֹ עֹמֶדֶת לָעַד.	ג
4	Shine even in darkness does a light for the upright; He is gracious, compassionate, and righteous.	זָרַח בַּחֹשֶׁךְ אוֹר לַיְשָׁרִים; חַנּוּן וְרַחוּם וְצַדִּיק.	ד
5	Good is the man who is gracious and makes loans; who conducts his affairs with justice.	טוֹב אִישׁ חוֹנֵן וּמַלְוֶה; יְכַלְכֵּל דְּבָרָיו בְּמִשְׁפָּט.	ה

CHAPTER 9: VAYEISHEV & TEHILLIM 112

6	For never will he falter; a remembrance everlasting, he will remain the righteous man.	ו	כִּי לְעוֹלָם לֹא יִמּוֹט; לְזֵכֶר עוֹלָם יִהְיֶה צַדִּיק.
7	Of tidings that are evil, he will have no fear; firm is his heart, trusting in Hashem.	ז	מִשְּׁמוּעָה רָעָה לֹא יִירָא; נָכוֹן לִבּוֹ בָּטֻחַ בַּה'.
8	Steadfast is his heart, he will not fear; until he can look [calmly] at his tormentors.	ח	סָמוּךְ לִבּוֹ לֹא יִירָא; עַד אֲשֶׁר יִרְאֶה בְצָרָיו.
9	He distributed widely by giving to the destitute, his righteousness endures forever; his pride will be exalted with glory.	ט	פִּזַּר נָתַן לָאֶבְיוֹנִים, צִדְקָתוֹ עֹמֶדֶת לָעַד; קַרְנוֹ תָּרוּם בְּכָבוֹד.
10	The wicked man will see this and be angered, his teeth he will gnash and melt away; the ambition of the wicked will perish.	י	רָשָׁע יִרְאֶה וְכָעָס, שִׁנָּיו יַחֲרֹק וְנָמָס; תַּאֲוַת רְשָׁעִים תֹּאבֵד.

PARSHAH & TEHILLIM HAND IN HAND

INTRODUCTION: YAAKOV AND HIS SONS AROUND THE SHABBOS TABLE

"אַבְרָהָם יָגֵל, יִצְחָק יְרַנֵּן, יַעֲקֹב וּבָנָיו יָנוּחוּ בוֹ – Avraham would rejoice, Yitzchak would exult, Yaakov and his sons would rest on it." This famous sentence from the Shabbos *Minchah Shemoneh Esrei* provides us with a beautiful description of the Avos HaKedoshim and their observance of Shabbos and continues: "מְנוּחַת אַהֲבָה וּנְדָבָה..." – A rest of love and magnanimity, a rest of truth and faith, a rest of peace, שַׁלְוָה – serenity, tranquility, and security, a perfect rest that You desire. May Your children recognize and know that from You is their rest, and through their rest they will sanctify Your Name."[1]

In particular, the words יַעֲקֹב וּבָנָיו יָנוּחוּ בוֹ, which describe Yaakov Avinu and his twelve sons delighting in the serenity of Shabbos, conjure up further images of Yaakov's family sitting around the Shabbos table together, bonding, eating, singing, talking in Torah, and enjoying the *kedushah* of Shabbos.

These images are especially poignant since we often think of Yaakov's family life as being beset by constant turmoil. First, Lavan's treacherous presence was always lurking, then competition and even heartbreak between his wives, followed by sons overstepping boundaries, a daughter who was taken advantage of by a stranger, Eisav's terrifying presence even from afar and then suddenly face-to-face, Rochel Imeinu's tragic passing, and of course, the brothers' jealousy and hatred of Yosef. This hatred began in *Parshas Vayeishev* where the Torah recounts the story of the

---

[1] Translation from ArtScroll Shabbos and Yom Tov Siddur.

CHAPTER 9: VAYEISHEV & TEHILLIM 112

brothers' sale of Yosef as a slave to Egypt, which resulted in Yosef's family presuming him dead.

Parshas Vayeishev begins with Chazal[2] revealing to us that Yaakov implored Hashem to finally permit him לֵישֵׁב בְּשַׁלְוָה, to permanently dwell in tranquility. Yet Hashem answered with an emphatic "No," explaining that Yaakov's *tzaros* and troubles had not reached their end, for Yaakov was a *tzaddik*. There can be no perpetual rest for a *tzaddik* while he yet lives on this earth because a *tzaddik* is destined to instead rest eternally in an exalted place in the World to Come. And with this Godly declaration the ordeal of Yosef began, marking perhaps Yaakov's most severe *tzarah*: the loss of Yaakov's most beloved son, born to Yaakov's most beloved wife, Rochel – a son who will be thought dead for twenty-two mournful years, and secretly all at the hand of his very own brothers.

Yet despite all the above, Yaakov and his sons and family did live in harmony in the period between the end of *Parshas Vayishlach* and the start of *Parshas Vayeishev*. Yosef was sold at the age of seventeen, and Yaakov had returned home to Yitzchak when Yosef was approximately eight years old. Therefore, for approximately nine years the budding family of Yaakov with its young sons and brothers were together at home and in harmony in fulfillment of the beautiful phrase יַעֲקֹב וּבָנָיו יָנוּחוּ בוֹ.

Indeed, the first three *pesukim* of *Tehillim* 112 describe from the perspective of Yaakov Avinu that special bubble of time of שַׁלְוָה in the family life of Yaakov:

Tehillim 112

Pasuk 1:
אַשְׁרֵי אִישׁ יָרֵא אֶת ה',
בְּמִצְוֹתָיו חָפֵץ מְאֹד

---

[2] *Rashi, Bereishis* 37:2, from *Tanchuma Yashan, Mevo*, ms. 3, 13; see also *Bereishis Rabbah* 84:3.

Praiseworthy is the man who fears Hashem,
who His commandments he desires greatly.

Pasuk 2:

גִּבּוֹר בָּאָרֶץ יִהְיֶה זַרְעוֹ;

דּוֹר יְשָׁרִים יְבֹרָךְ

Mighty in the land will be his offspring,
a generation of the upright who יְבֹרָךְ – will be blessed.

Pasuk 3:

הוֹן וָעֹשֶׁר בְּבֵיתוֹ;

וְצִדְקָתוֹ עֹמֶדֶת לָעַד

Wealth and riches are in his house,
and his righteousness endures forever.

Amazingly, the image described in the opening paragraph of this chapter, that of Yaakov Avinu's Shabbos table bedecked by his sons, wives, and family, is in fact noted as such in the *Mesorah* commentary,[3] which cites the matching use of the word "יְבֹרָךְ" both here in *Tehillim* 112:2 and later in *Tehillim* 128:4 as a link between the two *kapitelach*. There, the *Mesorah* commentary explains that *Tehillim* 128 contains a set of *pesukim* that explicitly describes the hard-working and righteous Jewish father and his home, the focal point of which is his family gathered around the table in harmony.

Tehillim 128 begins as follows:

Tehillim 128

Pasuk 1:

שִׁיר הַמַּעֲלוֹת: אַשְׁרֵי כָּל

יְרֵא ה', הַהֹלֵךְ בִּדְרָכָיו

---

[3] E.g, see *Mikraos Gedolos Tehillim* on *Tehillim* 112.

A song of ascents: Praiseworthy is each
man who fears Hashem, who walks in His paths.

Pasuk 2:

יְגִיעַ כַּפֶּיךָ כִּי תֹאכֵל,
אַשְׁרֶיךָ וְטוֹב לָךְ

When you eat the labor of your hands,
you are praiseworthy and good is with you.

Pasuk 3:

אֶשְׁתְּךָ כְּגֶפֶן פֹּרִיָּה בְּיַרְכְּתֵי בֵיתֶךָ,
בָּנֶיךָ כִּשְׁתִלֵי זֵיתִים סָבִיב לְשֻׁלְחָנֶךָ

Your wife will be like a fruitful vine
in the inner chambers of your home;
your children like olive shoots
surrounding your table.

Pasuk 4:

הִנֵּה כִי כֵן יְבֹרַךְ גָּבֶר יְרֵא ה'

Behold! For so יְבֹרַךְ – will be blessed,
the man who fears God.

These two sets of *pesukim* in *Tehillim* 112 and 128 closely parallel one another in painting a beautiful picture of the classic Jewish home as blessed – "יְבֹרַךְ." This, combined with *Tehillim* 112's intimate connection to *Parshas Vayeishev*, provides a glimpse of *Yaakov Avinu's* home and Shabbos table. They are a poignant and all too rare glimpse of יַעֲקֹב וּבָנָיו יָנוּחוּ בוֹ and must be cherished as such.

However, just as the story of *Parshas Vayeishev* suddenly shifts from the sacred and serene home of Yaakov to the infighting and jealousy of the brothers who would fake Yosef's death and sell him to strangers hoping to rid themselves of him forever, our *Tehillim* 112 also takes a radical shift.

It transitions from describing the tranquil and prosperous Jewish home to the subject of fears and challenges. These are fears and challenges which, as we will discuss in more detail in this chapter, parallel unique aspects of the Yaakov-Yosef story including Yaakov's reaction to hearing of Yosef's death as well as Yosef's rising to a position of political power in Egypt. This position enabled him to protect and preserve his beloved family from afar, and to be *Mekadeish Shem Shamayim* – to sanctify the Name of Heaven – in the process.

We all know of Yosef's many accomplishments in Egypt despite the incomprehensible challenges. From where did Yosef get such *koach*, such strength? Yosef's fortitude clearly came, at least in great part, from those nine years of tranquility at home where he learned Torah with his father and lived with his dear brothers during those peaceful and precious youthful years of יַעֲקֹב וּבָנָיו יָנוּחוּ בוֹ, in which every day must have had a Shabbos-like quality to it.

Over the years, I have often wondered why we say this most moving of phrases, "אַבְרָהָם יָגֵל, יִצְחָק יְרַנֵּן, יַעֲקֹב וּבָנָיו יָנוּחוּ בוֹ," only toward the end of Shabbos during *Minchah* and not at the very *start* of Shabbos.

Perhaps we can answer that while we all wish for a Shabbos table that mirrors that of the Avos, for many of us the Shabbos *seudos* as beautiful as they are do not always turn out exactly as we planned – a spilled glass, a broken plate, misbehaving children, hurt feelings. As such, to begin Shabbos with the lofty image of the Shabbos experience of the Avos might lead to disappointment.

However, at *Minchah*, as Shabbos will soon be coming to an end and as the feelings of nostalgia for Shabbos begin to take hold, the image of the Shabbos of Avraham, Yitzchak, and Yaakov with his twelve sons instills within us a yearning to improve and a strong desire to at least try and make *next* week's Shabbos a bit more holy and a bit more special.

Or better yet as my wife so tenderly added, it reminds us that the *present* Shabbos, which at *Minchah* time is slowly slipping from our grasp, was and is – even with all its challenges – a great gift from Hashem to be cherished and valued, especially as the last seconds of Shabbos tick away.

Therefore, as we approach *Parshas Vayeishev* and intertwine it with *Tehillim* 112, let us make sure that we sit בְּשַׁלְוָה at our Shabbos table this week and every week, treasuring our precious family, our precious spouse, our precious children, our precious parents, our precious health, our precious safe surroundings, our precious Am Yisrael, and our precious *Shabbos Kodesh*, proud of the fact that we are indeed the present-day continuation of יַעֲקֹב וּבָנָיו יָנוּחוּ בוֹ.

THE MANY CONNECTIONS BETWEEN PARSHAS VAYEISHEV & TEHILLIM 112

The commentators on *Tehillim* 112 do not provide any real indication of what inspired Dovid HaMelech to compose this *kapitel* or when it was written. However, we do know that on a basic level, *Tehillim* 112 describes not the "everyman" (i.e., the average person), or even the "every Jew," but rather the "every *tzaddik*" (which is itself a contradiction in terms, as there is nothing "every" or typical about a *tzaddik*).

However, when *Tehillim* 112 is studied through the prism of *Parshas Vayeishev* and the events of Yaakov and Yosef within the *Parshah*, this *kapitel* provides us with an additional, and even closer, connection to both the *Parshah* and to the *tzaddikim* discussed within it.

Pasuk 1:
הַלְלוּיָ-הּ! אַשְׁרֵי אִישׁ יָרֵא אֶת ה',
בְּמִצְוֹתָיו חָפֵץ מְאֹד
Halleluy-ah! Praiseworthy is the man who fears Hashem, who His commandments he desires greatly.

The Jewish Father

As noted in the Introduction to this chapter, this *kapitel* begins with a description of the righteous Jewish man, and as we shall see not only in this first *pasuk* but in the following two *pesukim* as well, this *kapitel* specifically describes the quintessential Jewish father.

As such, this *pasuk* speaks of Yaakov Avinu, father of Yosef and his brothers. He was the first father among the Avos to merit having only righteous children. Indeed, Yaakov was the father who gave rise to the *family* known as Bnei Yisrael, and to the entire *nation* of Klal Yisrael.

Yosef, too, would go on to become a father to Ephraim and Menasheh, who would be blessed by Hashem to join with the sons of Yaakov to form the *Shivtei Kah*, the Twelve Tribes of Hashem, replacing Levi and Yosef in the count of twelve. As such, Yosef would also rise from the level of a son and tribe founder to the level of a father and tribe "creator," just like Yaakov.[4]

The Desire for Mitzvos

This *pasuk* further applies to Yaakov, who previously in *Parshas Vayishlach* exemplified "בְּמִצְוֹתָיו חָפֵץ מְאֹד" when he took great pride in his love of mitzvos by boldly reintroducing himself to Eisav with the statement and threat of "עִם לָבָן גַּרְתִּי וְתַרְיַ"ג מִצְוֹת שָׁמַרְתִּי" – Even when I lived with Lavan, I kept all 613 commandments and did not emulate his evil

---

[4] E.g., *Ohr Hachaim*, *Bereishis* 48:6.

actions."[5] Clearly, Yaakov displayed confidence that the power of mitzvos would both intimidate Eisav and protect himself and his family.

The Torah tells us that Yosef was also careful to observe the mitzvos even from the time of his youth and was also concerned about the mitzvah observance of his brothers. Despite the risk of bringing their ire upon himself, it was solely because Yosef cared for the spiritual wellbeing of his brothers[6] that Yosef monitored their behavior and reported to Yaakov Avinu any seeming misconduct.[7]

It should be noted that the *pasuk's* phraseology is precise: the words "בְּמִצְוֹתָיו חָפֵץ מְאֹד," refer to "חָפֵץ" and "desire" for mitzvos but do not necessarily refer to the *performance* of the mitzvos. We must recall that for many years, Yaakov was away from his parents and outside of Eretz Yisrael, unable to actively fulfill many of the 613 mitzvos. Yosef as well found himself in this predicament. However, the Chasam Sofer explains that both Yaakov and Yosef possessed such a sincere and strong desire (חָפֵץ) for mitzvos, and so greatly waited with yearning (שָׁמַרְתִּי) to fulfill the mitzvos, that it was considered by Hashem as if they had performed them.[8]

Fortunately, most of us are blessed to live in a country in which we have the right to perform mitzvos freely. Nevertheless, on occasion we may yearn to do a mitzvah but not have the opportunity to fulfill it. Alternatively, we might perform the mitzvah in a less-than-optimal manner, perhaps without the required *kavanah* or focus. While the actual performance of mitzvos is certainly of primary importance, the חָפֵץ, desire, is a powerful element as well, so much so that the proper חָפֵץ for the mitzvah can cause Hashem to consider the mitzvah to have been completed even when the actual performance of the mitzvah was

---

[5] *Rashi, Bereishis* 32:5.
[6] E.g., *Yareiach LaMoadim, Chanukah* pp. 531–32, citing *Chochmah U'Mussar* of the Alter of Kelm.
[7] *Bereishis* 37:2.
[8] *Chasam Sofer, Bereishis* 32:5.

incomplete, hampered, or even entirely prevented from having been performed.

A True Man Fears Only Hashem

Furthermore, although in the prior *Parshah* of *Vayishlach* Yaakov stated regarding the wicked Eisav: "כִּי יָרֵא אָנֹכִי אֹתוֹ – For I fear him,"[9] *Tehillim* 112 as applied to Yaakov now refers to him as having risen to the most elevated of levels, that of a "יָרֵא אֶת ה'," one who fears Hashem and only Hashem.

The *Radak* explains that fear of Hashem is particularly important in ensuring that the Jew not only serves Hashem while in the public eye, but also ensures that his service of Hashem will take place behind closed doors where no one else besides Hashem can see.[10]

Yaakov's attribute of "אַשְׁרֵי אִישׁ יָרֵא אֶת ה'" was also conveyed to, and very much ingrained in, Yosef. One cannot begin to imagine the loneliness and desire for companionship that the young Yosef must have felt when he was betrayed by his brothers and all alone in a foreign country. In addition, in *Parshas Vayeishev* the Torah and Chazal go into great detail to reveal to us the frequency and nature of the overtures and temptations of the wife of Potiphar toward Yosef.[11] Yet, Yosef's ability to overcome that *yetzer hara* – particularly in a private setting in which both participants had a mutual self-interest in keeping their actions hidden from other people – stemmed from Yosef's respect for and practice of the *middah* of "יָרֵא אֶת ה'." For while no human eye might be present to witness his actions, Yosef's *yiras Shamayim* provided him with a constant reminder that Hashem was there with him always.

In addition, the concept of having the willpower to resist the *yetzer hara* when it is at its strongest is derived from the use of the word "אִישׁ," as the

---

[9] *Bereishis* 32:12.
[10] *Radak, Tehillim* 112:1.
[11] See *Rashi* and other commentaries on *Bereishis* 39:7–20.

Gemara[12] teaches based on *pasuk* 1 here: "אַשְׁרֵי מִי שֶׁעוֹשֶׂה תְּשׁוּבָה כְּשֶׁהוּא אִישׁ" – Praiseworthy is the one who repents when he is a man," i.e., when he still has the vigor and temptations of a younger man and not simply in his old age when these desires tend to fade naturally. This is particularly true of Yosef, who was in the physical prime of his life when Potiphar's wife tried to seduce him. In fact, after being rejected by Yosef once and for all, Potiphar's wife refers to Yosef not only as an "עִבְרִי" but as an "אִישׁ עִבְרִי"[13] in astonished, and disappointed, recognition of his self-control.

Indeed, of both Yaakov and Yosef we can declare with certainty: "אַשְׁרֵי אִישׁ יָרֵא אֶת ה'".

These Are the Offspring of Yaakov: Yosef

It is the above types of parallels between Yaakov and Yosef that are alluded to in the opening words of *Parshas Vayeishev*: "אֵלֶּה תֹּלְדוֹת יַעֲקֹב, יוֹסֵף – These are the offspring of Yaakov: Yosef."[14] *Rashi* explains that Yosef was Yaakov's favorite child, in part because the two would be confronted with identical challenges and enemies in the form of brothers who hated them and tried to kill them.[15]

However, as we now see from this opening *pasuk* of *Tehillim* 112, Yaakov and Yosef also shared identical positive attributes and experiences: they both shared a fear of Hashem and a tremendous desire for mitzvos, no matter how difficult the circumstances or formidable the barriers.

In addition, Yaakov and Yosef were *chavrusas*, with Yaakov transmitting to Yosef the Torah and life lessons he had learned in Yeshivas Shem V'Eiver.[16] These were lessons that Yaakov made sure to internalize before he was to be separated from his family and outside of Eretz Yisrael

---

[12] *Avodah Zarah* 19a.
[13] *Bereishis* 39:14.
[14] *Bereishis*, 37:2.
[15] *Rashi, Bereishis* 37:2, from *Bereishis Rabbah* 84:6.
[16] *Rashi, Bereishis* 37:3, from *Bereishis Rabbah* 84:8.

for twenty-two years, and lessons that Yosef would need when he would experience much of the same during his own exile of twenty-two years designed by Hashem to parallel Yaakov's.

As individuals and as a unit, Yaakov and Yosef epitomized "אַשְׁרֵי אִישׁ יָרֵא אֶת ה', בְּמִצְוֹתָיו חָפֵץ מְאֹד".

Pasuk 2:
גִּבּוֹר בָּאָרֶץ יִהְיֶה זַרְעוֹ; דּוֹר יְשָׁרִים יְבֹרָךְ

Mighty in the land will be his offspring, a generation of the upright who will be blessed.

The Mighty Yaakov and Sons

The *Midrash Tehillim*[17] delves into this *pasuk* and explains as follows: "גִּבּוֹר בָּאָרֶץ יִהְיֶה זַרְעוֹ" refers to Yaakov Avinu, as we see in the *Navi Yeshayahu*: "וְאַתָּה יִשְׂרָאֵל עַבְדִּי, יַעֲקֹב אֲשֶׁר בְּחַרְתִּיךָ; זֶרַע אַבְרָהָם אֹהֲבִי" – And you, Yisrael My servant, Yaakov whom I have chosen; the offspring of Avraham, who loved Me."[18] What was Yaakov's *gevurah* and strength? That he took hold of the Angel [the *Sar shel Eisav*], and conquered him on the earth, as it says in the *Navi Hoshea*: "וַיָּשַׂר אֶל מַלְאָךְ וַיֻּכָל" – And he strove with an angel and prevailed."[19]

In addition, among the Avos, it was Yaakov, and only Yaakov, who merited having a "דּוֹר יְשָׁרִים יְבֹרָךְ" – righteous and blessed children, as the Torah states in *Parshas Vayechi*: "כָּל אֵלֶּה שִׁבְטֵי יִשְׂרָאֵל, שְׁנֵים עָשָׂר" – All these are the tribes of Yisrael – twelve,"[20] thereby equating, praising, and memorializing their individual and collective *tzidkus*.

---

[17] *Midrash Tehillim, Shocher Tov,* 112.
[18] *Yeshayahu* 41:8.
[19] *Hoshea* 12:5.
[20] *Bereishis* 49:28.

The Sons of Yaakov: The First Mighty and Upright "Generation"

This *pasuk* also directly describes the sons of Yaakov, who were גִּבּוֹרִים and יְשָׁרִים not only as a reward to Yaakov, but as a natural outgrowth of Yaakov himself. As Rav Chayun explains here, children simply watch their father and follow in his pious ways.[21]

Each was a "גִּבּוֹר," as *Rashi* specifically describes in *Parshas Mikeitz*. *Rashi* explains that the first time the brothers went down to Mitzrayim they did so covertly so that people should not recognize them as brothers. For Yaakov had commanded them to enter the city each one through his own entrance and not as a group because all of them were handsome and "וְכֻלָּם גִּבּוֹרִים" – all of them were mighty." Thus, their entrance together would have attracted too much attention, and even possibly engendered an *ayin hara*, evil eye, from jealous onlookers.[22]

They were also "יְשָׁרִים," for they were the children, grandchildren, and great-grandchildren of Yaakov, Yitzchak, and Avraham, who are known as the original "יְשָׁרִים."

In addition, the expression "דּוֹר יְשָׁרִים – a generation of the upright," is particularly poignant here because until Yaakov's sons were born, the יְשָׁרִים who existed were only *individuals* (albeit the Avos HaKedoshim). However, the sons of Yaakov were an ensemble of twelve, then seventy, and, ultimately, millions. The sons of Yaakov represented the first true "דּוֹר – *generation*" of יְשָׁרִים in the broadest sense of the word.

Pasuk 3:
הוֹן וָעֹשֶׁר בְּבֵיתוֹ;
וְצִדְקָתוֹ עֹמֶדֶת לָעַד

---

[21] Rav Chayun, as cited in *Me'am Lo'ez, Tehillim* 112:2.
[22] *Rashi, Bereishis* 42:5, from *Midrash Tanchuma, Vayeishev* 8, and *Bereishis Rabbah* 91:6.

Wealth and riches are in his house, and his righteousness endures forever.

Yaakov: From Rags to Riches, He Remained Reserved

The Torah reveals that Hashem blessed Avraham and Yitzchak with great wealth. Yaakov, too, although having arrived at the home of Lavan completely impoverished,[23] amassed great wealth in his last six years with Lavan.[24] Yaakov cherished all that he owned, even placing himself in harm's way to recover *pachim ketanim*, small jars of low value,[25] because Yaakov truly understood that every *shekel* had come to him directly from Hashem. Lest one think that Yaakov had to relinquish a significant portion of his possessions in appeasing Eisav in *Parshas Vayishlach*, Chazal tell us that Yaakov lost nothing from these lavish gifts, as they were either a mirage or miraculously returned to him such that Yaakov escaped Eisav unscathed physically and שָׁלֵם בְּמָמוֹנוֹ, intact and complete financially.[26]

It must be noted, however, that *Tehillim* 112:3 specifically states that wealth and riches are "בְּבֵיתוֹ – in his house," indicating that despite Yaakov's wealth, he remained reserved and modest, keeping his wealth private and "inside his home," neither flaunting it nor using it in a manner that could arouse jealousy or cause others to feel insecure or inferior. For example, in *Parshas Mikeitz* Yaakov initially sent ten of his sons to Egypt during the famine to buy food even though they still had adequate supplies. He did this so as not to draw undue attention to his successful financial status while all the world around him was crumbling from the years of famine.[27]

---

[23] *Rashi, Bereishis* 29:11.
[24] *Bereishis* 30:43.
[25] *Rashi, Bereishis* 32:25.
[26] *Rashi, Bereishis* 33:18, from *Shabbos* 33b.
[27] *Rashi, Bereishis* 42:1, from *Taanis* 10b.

Homeless, Yosef Created a Home for Others

Although Yosef was cast away by his brothers and initially destitute and homeless, alone and far away from his family and home for many years, nonetheless the *pasuk* of "הוֹן וָעֹשֶׁר בְּבֵיתוֹ; וְצִדְקָתוֹ עֹמֶדֶת לָעַד" aptly describes Yosef and his influence on the homes and dwelling places of others who were in need throughout *Parshas Vayeishev*.

After Potiphar purchased Yosef, Yosef was blessed with success and was put in charge of Potiphar's household and business matters. As a result, all that Potiphar owned began to flourish: "וַיְבָרֶךְ ה' אֶת בֵּית הַמִּצְרִי בִּגְלַל יוֹסֵף; וַיְהִי בִּרְכַּת ה' בְּכָל אֲשֶׁר יֶשׁ לוֹ בַּבַּיִת וּבַשָּׂדֶה – Hashem blessed the Egyptian's house because of Yosef, and Hashem's blessing was in all that he had, in the house and in the field."[28] Because of the *tzidkus* of Yosef, even the immoral Potiphar was the beneficiary of "יְבָרֵךְ. הוֹן וָעֹשֶׁר בְּבֵיתוֹ – he was blessed, with wealth and riches in his house."

It is interesting to note that in this small section describing Yosef's arrival and role in the life of Potiphar, the *shoresh* of the word "בַּיִת" appears not once but five times in the span of only six *pesukim*,[29] as if to emphasize that Yosef helped transform not only Potiphar's business endeavors, but also helped transform his house into a real home (albeit temporarily).

In addition, the next section of *Parshas Vayeishev* revolves around the inappropriate overtures of Potiphar's wife toward Yosef.[30] There the *shoresh* of "בַּיִת" appears not once but seven additional times, including twice as part of Yosef's plea for loyalty and his refusal to betray his master.[31] Indeed, among Yosef's many reasons for resisting temptation can be counted the respect, care, and concern Yosef had for Potiphar's home and family life.

---

[28] *Bereishis* 39:5.
[29] *Bereishis* 39:1–6.
[30] *Bereishis* 39:7–19.
[31] *Bereishis* 39:8–9.

Finally, after being wrongfully accused and thrown into the "בֵּית הַסֹּהַר" which refers to "prison," but which literally means "house of imprisonment," Yosef had similar success even there. He was quickly put in charge of running the prison and caring for the other prisoners. Ultimately, Yosef was appointed to care for Pharaoh's *Sar HaMashkim* and *Sar HaOfim*, the royal cupbearer and royal baker who were important members of the king's court and whom Hashem would eventually use as messengers to free Yosef from prison. In the four introductory *pesukim* of Yosef's arrival, the words "בֵּית הַסֹּהַר" are written a total of six times.[32] While בֵּית הַסֹּהַר, prison, is ordinarily the furthest thing from one's own true home, the recurrence of the word "בַּיִת" in this context once again emphasizes that Yosef's presence brought a certain order, comfort, and kindness to his environment and everyone in it, so much so that even the lowly prison was transformed by Yosef into a "בַּיִת – a home" of sorts for its inmates.

Yosef HaTzaddik: *Tzaddik Yesod Ha'olam*

This *pasuk* is the first of four times in *Tehillim* 112 in which the *shoresh* of the term "צַדִּיק," righteous person, is used.[33]

All the Avos were certainly the highest level of *tzaddikim*. In addition, one who studies *Parshas Vayeishev* will find the theme of *tzidkus* permeates the *Parshah*. For example, *Rashi's* commentary utilizes the term צַדִּיק to describe many different people: Yaakov Avinu,[34] Yehudah,[35] and Yehudah's sons Peretz and Zarach.[36] Of course, the lineage of Yaakov through Yehudah and Peretz will ultimately give rise to the *Melech HaMoshiach* who is also referred to as "*Moshiach Tzidkeinu* – Moshiach, our righteous one/our *tzaddik*."

---

[32] *Bereishis* 39:20–23.
[33] See *Tehillim* 112, *pesukim* 3, 4, 6, and 9.
[34] *Rashi, Bereishis* 37:2.
[35] *Rashi, Bereishis* 38:18.
[36] *Rashi, Bereishis* 38: 27.

Nevertheless, while there have been multitudes of *tzaddikim* throughout Jewish history as described in Tanach, portrayed in the Gemara, reflected in our Rishonim throughout the centuries that followed, and even new *tzaddikim* in our time, it is actually Yosef who is given the prestigious title of "Yosef HaTzaddik – Yosef the Righteous."[37] While this is not the place for a comprehensive explanation of Yosef's righteousness, the *Parshas Vayeishev & Tehillim* 112 connection requires us to at least note some of the basics, as follows:

- A true *tzaddik* seeks *deveikus* – to cleave and connect with Hashem – as well as to emulate Hashem and to sanctify the Name of Hashem; Hashem Who Himself is referred to in the Torah as *Tzaddik*, e.g., "צַדִּיק וְיָשָׁר הוּא – Righteous and straight is He."[38] In such a manner did Yosef conduct himself even during his time in Potiphar's service and throughout the remainder of his life, so much so that even someone as spiritually impure as Potiphar was able to see and appreciate Yosef's holiness and *deveikus*: "וַיַּרְא אֲדֹנָיו כִּי ה' אִתּוֹ; וְכֹל אֲשֶׁר הוּא עֹשֶׂה ה' מַצְלִיחַ בְּיָדוֹ – And his [Yosef's] master saw that Hashem was with him; and all that he would do Hashem would make successful in his hand."[39] *Rashi* explains that Yosef would always refer to Hashem in conversation and would attribute each of his successes to Hashem.[40] Others say that Yosef davened constantly, even while engaged in work.[41] This conduct enabled Yosef to continuously remain *davuk* to Hashem and made a genuine impression on those around him, resulting in a constant *Kiddush Shem Shamayim*.

---

[37] E.g., *Yoma* 35b.
[38] *Devarim* 32:4.
[39] *Bereishis* 39:3.
[40] *Rashi, Bereishis* 39:3, from *Midrash Tanchuma, Vayeishev* 8.
[41] *Bereishis Rabbah* 86:5 and the *Maharzav* there.

- The *pasuk* in *Mishlei* states "וְצַדִּיק יְסוֹד עוֹלָם – And the righteous is the *yesod*, foundation, of the world."[42] Based upon this *pasuk*, the Kabbalists teach that the *middah* of Yosef HaTzaddik is the *middah* of *Yesod*, which relates to the sanctity of the *bris milah* that Yosef faithfully preserved when he resisted the temptations of Potiphar's wife.

- The *tzaddik* and the *middah* of *Yesod* is also described as: "כִּי כֹל בַּשָּׁמַיִם וּבָאָרֶץ – For all that is in heaven and earth,"[43] meaning that the true *tzaddik* is able to bridge and even combine the spiritual and the physical, while also inspiring others to do the same. This we find epitomized by Yosef HaTzaddik, who spent so many years as viceroy to Pharaoh, involved in politics and business, and yet sustained the entire world while making a *Kiddush HaShem* in all his actions, so much so that at Yaakov's funeral all the world's kings and princes laid down their swords to pay homage upon seeing the crown of Yosef who had saved their very lives years earlier during the famine.[44] Even steeped within Mitzrayim, the most depraved of lands, Yosef was able to connect heaven and earth by spreading the sanctity of Hashem and the Jewish People throughout the world.

As such, it is apropos that *Tehillim* 112 contains such a strong emphasis on the word "צַדִּיק" and does so starting with *pasuk* 3 as it begins to transition its focus from Yaakov Avinu to Yosef HaTzaddik for the remainder of the *kapitel*.

---

[42] *Mishlei* 10:25.
[43] *I Divrei HaYamim* 29:11.
[44] *Rashi, Bereishis* 50:10, from *Sotah* 13a.

CHAPTER 9: VAYEISHEV & TEHILLIM 112

Pasuk 4:
זָרַח בַּחֹשֶׁךְ אוֹר לַיְשָׁרִים;
חַנּוּן וְרַחוּם וְצַדִּיק

**Shine even in darkness does a light for the upright;
He is gracious, compassionate, and righteous.**

Zarach and Yosef: Seeing Light Amidst the Darkness

We would be remiss not to point out that the word "זָרַח" used here also appears in *Parshas Vayeishev*, for the two sons born to Yehudah and Tamar are named Peretz and Zarach.[45] Furthermore, the entire phrase "זָרַח בַּחֹשֶׁךְ אוֹר לַיְשָׁרִים" is very fitting for Zarach, for he was the child who first began to emerge from the womb, yet it was his twin brother Peretz who ultimately breached forth and was born first. As a result, it was Peretz, not Zarach, who became the *bechor* and merited to be the forefather of the Davidic Dynasty from whom Moshiach ben Dovid will come. Nonetheless, Zarach did not turn jealous or succumb to despair, but rather epitomized "זָרַח בַּחֹשֶׁךְ אוֹר לַיְשָׁרִים," for he continued to "זָרַח...אוֹר – shine... light," even amidst the potential "חֹשֶׁךְ – darkness" of lost merits and prestige, and he continued to be counted among the "יְשָׁרִים – upright," as both he and his brother were *geborim* and *tzaddikim* just like their father, Yehudah.[46]

In addition, the lesson of "זָרַח בַּחֹשֶׁךְ אוֹר לַיְשָׁרִים" is applicable to Yosef throughout *Parshas Vayeishev*. Whether it be dutifully obeying his father's request to travel to Shechem and check on his brothers despite their hatred and the danger this posed, or his optimistic attitude and ability to radiate trust in Hashem in the house of Potiphar and even after being wrongfully imprisoned, Yosef always saw the light amidst the darkness. In fact, this lesson is subtly yet firmly established in the early stages of

---

[45] *Bereishis* 38:29–30.
[46] *Rashi, Bereishis* 38:17, from *Bereishis Rabbah* 85:9.

Yosef's saga, when in *Parshas Vayeishev* the Torah informs us that the caravan to which Yosef was sold by his brothers was carrying not the usual foul-smelling petroleum and resin, but rather sweet-smelling spices.[47] *Rashi* explains that the sweet smell was a reward to Yosef the "*tzaddik*."[48] However, many question the value of this reward, since a sweeter smell could hardly make up for the horrific treatment Yosef was forced to endure at the hands of his brothers and captors, having been nearly murdered, then left to die in a pit, and then sold to non-Jewish merchants. My *rebbi*, Rabbi Shmuel Brazil, explained that the sweet smell was indeed a gift; it was a small sign from Hashem that He had not abandoned Yosef. It was a subtle reminder to Yosef that in the difficult days to come he should always look to find that little bit of light, even amidst the blackest darkness, for Hashem would always provide a light and be his "זָרַח בַּחֹשֶׁךְ אוֹר לַיְשָׁרִים." As Rav Shimshon Pincus might say, it was "a wink from Hashem." And Yosef saw it!

Flashes of Chanukah

Once again, we find the *Parshas HaShavua* intertwined with references to the holiday of Chanukah, which often coincides with *Parshas Vayeishev* and its surrounding *parshiyos*. Chanukah, in which the חֹשֶׁךְ, the darkness of Yavan embodied in the Greek descendants of Eisav, was dispelled by the miracles of the אוֹר, the light of the Menorah, Torah, and Hashem, Who is referred to "ה' אוֹרִי וְיִשְׁעִי" — Hashem is my light and my salvation."[49]

Furthermore, the connections between Chanukah and *Parshas Vayeishev* abound. For example, the Greeks sought to eradicate the mitzvah of *bris milah*, which as noted above is the mitzvah corresponding to the *middah* of *Yesod* and a primary *middah* of Yosef HaTzaddik. Of

---

[47] *Bereishis 37:25.*
[48] *Rashi, Bereishis 37:25, from Bereishis Rabbah 84:17.*
[49] *Tehillim 27:1.*

course, the military victory of Chanukah was led by none other than Yehudah HaMaccabi, who shared the same name as one of Yosef's older brothers: Yehudah the son of Yaakov who played a prominent role in the selling of Yosef HaTzaddik, as well as in the episode with Tamar from which the ultimate savior of the Jewish People, *Moshiach Tzidkeinu*, will descend.

In conclusion, according to the *Bas Ayin*, "זָרַח בַּחֹשֶׁךְ אוֹר לַיְשָׁרִים" expresses that for those Jews who are *yesharim* (upright), light shines amidst the darkness; it is the *yesharim*, specifically, who can perceive the light within the darkness.[50]

This remarkable ability to see the light from within the darkness is ultimately the theme of the Yaakov-Yosef story, the Yehudah-Tamar story, the Chanukah story, and the grand theme of our lives in *galus* as we eagerly await the coming of *Moshiach Tzidkeinu*.

Chanukah and the Mystical Number Thirteen

The expression "חַנּוּן וְרַחוּם וְצַדִּיק" – He [Hashem] is gracious, compassionate, and righteous," is a powerful one, as "חַנּוּן וְרַחוּם" are two of the "שְׁלֹשׁ עֶשְׂרֵה מִדּוֹת הָרַחֲמִים" – Thirteen Middos of Divine Mercy,"[51] which also correspond to the "שְׁלֹשׁ עֶשְׂרֵה מִדּוֹת שֶׁהַתּוֹרָה נִדְרֶשֶׁת בָּהֶן" – Thirteen Middos Upon Which the Torah is Expounded."[52]

These two sets of Thirteen Middos interlace twenty-six ways for us to connect to Hashem, Whose Name י-ה-ו-ה in *gematria* is twenty-six. Each of these Middos teach us how to become a *tzaddik* and how to emulate Hashem who is the Ultimate *Tzaddik*.

It is for this reason that in the period preceding the miracles of Chanukah, the evil Greek Empire sought to attack the Jewish People

---

[50] *Bas Ayin*, as cited in *Me'am Lo'ez*, *Tehillim* 112:4.
[51] *Shemos* 34:6–7.
[52] *Beraisa* of Rabbi Yishmael, introduction to the *Sifra*; see also the *Korbanos* section of the daily *Shacharis* prayer.

through "וּפָרְצוּ חוֹמוֹת מִגְדָּלַי,"[53] making exactly thirteen "breaches in the walls and towers" comprising the borders of the Beis HaMikdash. The Greek army specifically made breaches in the *soreg*, which marked the boundary beyond which a non-Jew was forbidden to cross. This was all part of a two-pronged strike to undermine the twenty-six connections of the Jewish People to Hashem's Torah. Specifically, the Greeks attacked the Thirteen Middos Upon Which the Torah is Expounded and the Thirteen Middos HaRachamim that express Hashem's boundless mercy toward us.

Of course, our Hashem, the "חַנּוּן וְרַחוּם וְצַדִּיק," ensured that we prevailed.

Pasuk 5:
טוֹב אִישׁ חוֹנֵן וּמַלְוֶה; יְכַלְכֵּל דְּבָרָיו בְּמִשְׁפָּט

Good is the man who is gracious and makes loans; who conducts his affairs with justice.

Yosef's Successes in Egypt: Due to *Chein*

This *pasuk* applies beautifully to Yosef in Egypt. Yosef was the "אִישׁ חוֹנֵן – the man who is gracious," who possessed a God-given חֵן (*chein*), grace and favor in the eyes of others. This is stated by the Torah in connection with Potiphar: "וַיִּמְצָא יוֹסֵף חֵן בְּעֵינָיו – And Yosef found favor in his eyes"[54] and in connection with the prison warden: "וַיִּתֵּן חִנּוֹ בְּעֵינֵי שַׂר בֵּית הַסֹּהַר – And Hashem granted him grace in the eyes of the prison warden."[55] Yosef's grace appears in many other places as well[56] and would seem to be a quality passed on to him by his great-grandfather Avraham

---

[53] From the Chanukah *tefillah Maoz Tzur*.
[54] *Bereishis* 39:4.
[55] *Bereishis* 39:21.
[56] E.g., *Rashi* to *Bereishis* 49:22 in which Yosef is described as "בֵּן חֵן – son of grace."

Avinu, of whom the *pasuk* says: "יְפָיְפִיתָ מִבְּנֵי אָדָם, הוּצַק חֵן בְּשִׂפְתוֹתֶיךָ" – You are more beautiful than other men, חֵן, grace, flows from your lips."[57]

In addition, the *Haftarah* for Shabbos Chanukah, often read on *Parshas Vayeishev*, concludes with the powerful declaration: "חֵן חֵן לָהּ – Grace, grace unto her,"[58] in reference to Am Yisrael's salvation from *galus*, further reinforcing the prominence of the role of *chein* throughout Jewish history.

Yosef as Provider to All

The word "וּמַלְוֵה – who loans," alludes to the many financial credits and advances that Yosef granted to the Egyptians during the years of famine.[59]

The word "יְכַלְכֵּל" refers to the sustenance and special treatment that Yosef was able to provide to his family during the famine, as the Torah states: "וַיְכַלְכֵּל יוֹסֵף אֶת אָבִיו וְאֶת אֶחָיו וְאֵת כָּל בֵּית אָבִיו, לֶחֶם לְפִי הַטָּף – Yosef sustained his father and his brothers and all his father's household with food according to the children."[60] Of course, Yosef was also the provider for all of Egypt as well as to the world at large throughout the years of famine.

Amazingly, although the Egyptian populace would be uprooted and slowly enslaved by Yosef into the servitude of Pharaoh, Chazal reveal that the Egyptians nonetheless had tremendous *hakaras hatov* toward Yosef and fondly referred to him by the prestigious title of "כַּלְכֹּל – Sustainer of All" because he literally kept them alive by providing for them during the years of famine.[61]

---

[57] *Tehillim* 45:3. See Chapter 5, *Parshas Chayei Sarah* & *Tehillim* 45 for a detailed discussion of Avraham's *chein*.
[58] *Zechariah* 4:7.
[59] *Bereishis* 47:13–26.
[60] *Bereishis* 47:12.
[61] *Pirkei D'Rabi Eliezer, perek* 39.

PARSHAH & TEHILLIM HAND IN HAND

A Tribute to the Jewish Wife

The Introduction to this chapter revolves around the theme of "אַבְרָהָם יָגֵל, יִצְחָק יְרַנֵּן, יַעֲקֹב וּבָנָיו יָנוּחוּ בוֹ – Avraham would rejoice, Yitzchak would exult, Yaakov and his sons would rest on it" as it paints a picture of a Shabbos table that is male-centered. Yet even in this *Parsha* that focuses on men such as Yaakov, Yosef, and Yehudah, the women in their lives play a pivotal role.

For example, we see this in Yosef's second dream about the sun, moon, and eleven stars bowing down to Yosef. Yaakov attempted to deflect the anger cast upon Yosef because of this dream by disproving the accuracy of the dream. Yaakov did so by stating that it was impossible for the moon – which symbolized Yosef's mother – to bow down to him, for she had already died.[62] There, Yaakov made mention of his beloved Rochel Imeinu, whom he loved and missed so dearly, and whose remembrance and loss should have triggered feelings of mercy and patience from the brothers toward Yosef.

In addition, in helping us understand why Yaakov loved and favored Yosef among all his brothers, the *Zohar Hakadosh* poignantly states:

כֵּיוָן דְּחָמָא לְיוֹסֵף וְהֲוָה קָאִים קַמֵּיהּ, כַּד יַעֲקֹב מִסְתַּכֵּל בְּיוֹסֵף הֲוָה אִשְׁתְּלִים בְּנַפְשֵׁיהּ כְּאִילּוּ חָמָא לְאִמֵּיהּ דְיוֹסֵף, דְּשַׁפִּירוּ דְיוֹסֵף דָּמֵי לְשַׁפִּירוּ דְרָחֵל. וְהֲוָה דָּמֵי בְּגַרְמֵיהּ כְּמָה דְּלָא אַעֲבַר עֲלֵיהּ צַעֲרָא בְּיוֹמוֹי – When Yaakov would beckon Yosef, and Yosef would stand before him, when Yaakov would look at Yosef, Yaakov's soul would once again become complete/at peace, as if Yaakov were looking at the mother of Yosef because the beauty of Yosef was like the beauty of Rochel. And because of Yosef, it was as if Yaakov had never experienced in all his days [the] pain [of losing Rochel].[63]

---

[62] *Rashi, Bereishis* 37:10.
[63] *Zohar Hakadosh* 1:216b.

CHAPTER 9: VAYEISHEV & TEHILLIM 112

Other women in *Parshas Vayeishev* were also crucial to the Torah's events. We read of Tamar, who played a complex and important role in becoming the wife of Yehudah, and *lehavdil*, we read of the wife of Potiphar playing a prominent role in testing Yosef and impacting his life.

Finally, the *Sefer Chassidim* teaches that because Yehudah spearheaded the sale of Yosef and thus caused Yosef to remain unmarried until the age of thirty, Yehudah was punished as was his descendant Dovid HaMelech who did not reign until he reached the age of thirty.[64]

As a result, it is fitting that Chazal see in *pasuk* 5 of *Tehillim* 112 a resounding lesson of commitment on behalf of the Jewish husband to his wife. The Gemara[65] inquires: What is the meaning and lesson of the *pasuk* "טוֹב אִישׁ חוֹנֵן וּמַלְוֶה; יְכַלְכֵּל דְּבָרָיו בְּמִשְׁפָּט" – Good is the man who is gracious and makes loans; who conducts his affairs with justice." It teaches that "לְעוֹלָם יֹאכַל אָדָם וְיִשְׁתֶּה פָּחוֹת מִמַּה שֶּׁיֵּשׁ לוֹ, וְיִלְבַּשׁ וְיִתְכַּסֶּה בְּמָה שֶּׁיֵּשׁ לוֹ, וִיכַבֵּד אִשְׁתּוֹ וּבָנָיו יוֹתֵר מִמַּה שֶּׁיֵּשׁ לוֹ, שֶׁהֵם תְּלוּיִין בּוֹ וְהוּא תָּלוּי בְּמִי שֶׁאָמַר וְהָיָה הָעוֹלָם" – A man should always eat and drink less than what is within his means, he should dress and cover himself in accordance with his means, and he should honor his wife and children with more than what is within his means, as they are dependent on him and he is dependent on the One Who spoke and the world was created."

Rashi further emphasizes the importance of taking care of one's wife in a manner even beyond one's means.[66] For indeed, one's wife is the עֲקֶרֶת הַבַּיִת – the עִיקָר – the most precious, and the essence of the Jewish home, and must therefore be treated in a manner that goes above and beyond![67] Such behavior is the true sign of a "אִישׁ טוֹב – a good man."

---

[64] *Sefer Chassidim*, siman 504.
[65] *Chullin* 84b.
[66] *Rashi, Chullin* 84b.
[67] Based upon *Bamidbar Rabbah* 14:8.

Pasuk 6:
כִּי לְעוֹלָם לֹא יִמּוֹט;
לְזֵכֶר עוֹלָם יִהְיֶה צַדִּיק
**For never will he falter;
a remembrance everlasting,
he will remain the righteous man.**

Other Famous References to the *Tzaddik*

Continuing with the life of Yosef HaTzaddik, this *pasuk* alludes to two of the most famous *tzaddik*-related references (which, not coincidentally, are also contrasted with that of the tzaddik's antithesis: the *rasha*):

1. "כִּי לְעוֹלָם לֹא יִמּוֹט – For never will he falter," echoes the *pasuk* in *Mishlei*: "כִּי שֶׁבַע יִפּוֹל צַדִּיק וָקָם; וּרְשָׁעִים יִכָּשְׁלוּ בְרָעָה – For the righteous man will fall seven times and rise up again; but the wicked stumble in evil."[68] The *tzaddik* may fall repeatedly, yet each time the *tzaddik* will rise stronger than ever. On Yosef's level, he might be considered to have fallen at times: in his interactions with his brothers, with the wife of Potiphar when he went "לַעֲשׂוֹת מְלַאכְתּוֹ,"[69] and in prison in asking the *Sar HaMashkim* to remember and rescue him.[70] Yet amidst all this, Yosef remained a *tzaddik*. For example, Chazal teach that on the heels of Yosef's imprisonment, Hashem made sure to turn Egypt's attention to even fresher news of the scandal of the *Sar HaMashkim* and the *Sar HaOfim*. Why? *Rashi* explains that this was "so that Yosef 'הַצַּדִּיק' should not be the topic of conversation" and gossip in Egypt.[71] The wicked will fall and

---

[68] *Mishlei 24:16.*
[69] *Rashi, Bereishis 39:11, from Sotah 36b.*
[70] *Rashi, Bereishis 40:23, from Bereishis Rabbah 89:3.*
[71] *Rashi, Bereishis 40:1, from Bereishis Rabbah 88:1.*

stay down. A *tzaddik* may fall and fall, but if he gets up again, he remains a *tzaddik*. Moreover, as Rav Hutner would emphasize, a *tzaddik* is a *tzaddik* not *despite* his failures and falls, but *because* of them.[72]

2. "לְזֵכֶר עוֹלָם יִהְיֶה צַדִּיק" – A remembrance everlasting, he will remain the righteous man," echoes the *pasuk* in *Mishlei* which states: "זֵכֶר צַדִּיק לִבְרָכָה; וְשֵׁם רְשָׁעִים יִרְקָב" – The memory of the righteous shall be for a blessing; but the name of the wicked shall rot."[73] It is because of this *pasuk* that there is a Jewish tradition to say זֵכֶר צַדִּיק לִבְרָכָה when mentioning the name of a righteous deceased Jew. In contrast, for the most terrible of *reshaim*, such as the Nazis, we have the custom to say "יִמַּח שְׁמָם וְזִכְרָם" – may their name and memory be *erased*."

Thus, *pasuk* 6 is not only a tribute to Yosef HaTzaddik alone, but rather contains fundamental lessons in defining a *tzaddik* and why we must treasure them throughout their life struggles and beyond.

Pasuk 7:
מִשְּׁמוּעָה רָעָה לֹא יִירָא;
נָכוֹן לִבּוֹ בָּטֻחַ בַּה'
**Of tidings that are evil, he will have no fear;
firm is his heart, trusting in Hashem.**

Tales of Terrible and Tearful Tidings

If ever there was a *Parshah* filled with "שְׁמוּעָה רָעָה – evil tidings" and bad news, *Parshas Vayeishev* is certainly the one. From the perspective of the brothers, Yosef's dreams of sovereignty over them caused unease

---

[72] *Pachad Yitzchak, Igros U'Kesavim, egeres* 128.
[73] *Mishlei* 10:7.

and concern, leading to jealousy and hatred.[74] Reuven returned to the pit to rescue Yosef only to be shocked and dismayed to find Yosef no longer there, having been sold.[75] Yehudah's two sons died[76] and he was later informed that his daughter-in-law had been unfaithful.[77] These were all terrible blows. Even more shocking, after Yehudah decreed that Tamar be sentenced to death,[78] he learned that he himself was responsible.[79] Additionally, we cannot forget that the wife of Potiphar falsely and publicly accused Yosef of improprieties, leading to his false imprisonment.[80] Yet the worst and certainly the most prominent "שְׁמוּעָה רָעָה" was the news of Yosef's alleged death.[81]

Yaakov's Reaction to Yosef's "Death"

Indeed, based upon the Torah's description, emphasis, and the parties involved, the worst "שְׁמוּעָה רָעָה" of all was when Yaakov was told the terrible news that his son Yosef had been killed. The Torah tells us that Yaakov mourned for Yosef constantly and refused to be consoled,[82] and that Yaakov even lamented that he "will go down to the grave mourning his son."[83]

At first glance, this reaction seems to contradict the expression of "מִשְּׁמוּעָה רָעָה לֹא יִירָא," which teaches that a *tzaddik* will not fear evil tidings due to his faith in Hashem.

---

[74] *Bereishis* 37:5, 8, and 11.
[75] *Bereishis* 37:29.
[76] *Bereishis* 38:7 and 10.
[77] *Bereishis* 38:24.
[78] *Bereishis* 38:24.
[79] *Bereishis* 38:26.
[80] *Bereishis* 39:20.
[81] *Bereishis* 37:32-35.
[82] *Bereishis* 37:34–35.
[83] *Bereishis* 37:35.

The *Me'am Lo'ez*[84] addresses this contradiction by explaining that the *tzaddik* is only impervious to bad news when the news relates to something other than his own "*sheleimus*," his own "completion and perfection in service of Hashem." However, concern for one's own *sheleimus* and spiritual wellbeing would indeed be grounds for fear of evil tidings.

Based on this we can more deeply understand Yaakov's heartbroken and inconsolable reaction, for Chazal tell us that Yaakov associated Yosef's "death" with Yaakov's own spiritual failure. Hashem had previously transmitted a promise to Yaakov that if he would be outlived by all his sons, he would not go to Gehinnom.[85] However, the premature death of Yosef signified a failure in Yaakov's *sheleimus* requiring punishment and atonement. As such, Yaakov's reaction to hearing that Yosef had died was not indicative of a lack of faith, but rather was indicative of his yearning to be *shaleim* and close to Hashem always, and as such, his devastated reaction was justified under these circumstances.

Yosef's Reaction to Dire Warnings

It is also interesting to note that toward the start of *Parshas Vayeishev*, Yosef was told of a "שְׁמוּעָה רָעָה" in the form of a warning given to him by a man whom he had met in the field, a man whom Chazal identify as the *malach* Gavriel.[86] Gavriel warned Yosef that his brothers had disassociated themselves from him and thus no longer considered Yosef to be one of the twelve brothers.[87] Worse, warned Gavriel, they were plotting against him and even searching for legal pretexts and grounds in *halachah* to put Yosef to death.[88]

How did Yosef react? It seems that he was "not *mekabel*" and did not take those dire warnings to heart. Was he oblivious? Was he naive? Was

---

[84] *Me'am Lo'ez, Tehillim* 112:7.
[85] Rashi, *Bereishis* 37:35, from *Midrash Tanchuma, Vayigash* 9.
[86] Rashi, *Bereishis* 37:15, from *Midrash Tanchuma, Vayeishev* 2.
[87] Rashi, *Bereishis* 37:17.
[88] Rashi, *Bereishis* 37:17.

he hopeful? Perhaps he was just epitomizing this very *pasuk*: "מִשְּׁמוּעָה רָעָה לֹא יִירָא; נָכוֹן לִבּוֹ בָּטֻחַ בַּה'."

Pasuk 8:
סָמוּךְ לִבּוֹ לֹא יִירָא;
עַד אֲשֶׁר יִרְאֶה בְצָרָיו
Steadfast is his heart, he will not fear;
until he can look [calmly] at his tormentors.

Yosef's Apparent Death: Fearless Toward Man, but Fearful of God

As discussed in Chapter 7 (*Parshas Vayeitzei* & *Tehillim* 3), "צָרָיו" in the form of "his tormentors" and "his problems" is the term used by Chazal to describe all the צָרוֹת and challenges with which Hashem tested Yaakov throughout his life. In addition, these same tests would ultimately be mirrored in those of Yosef.[89]

Here the *pasuk* states that the *tzaddik* is "סָמוּךְ לִבּוֹ," reliant upon Hashem, and "לֹא יִירָא," not afraid of anyone *but* Hashem. In fact, the *tzaddik* can look his tormentors steadily in the eye without fear and can even calmly enjoy watching their downfall.[90]

The commentators such as the *Radak* and Rav Chayun on *pasuk* 8 emphasize that the lack of fear toward man is a particularly relevant point regarding Yaakov's brokenhearted reaction to Yosef's alleged death. Based on the evidence presented to him, Yaakov deduced and then declared: "חַיָּה רָעָה אֲכָלָתְהוּ; טָרֹף טֹרַף יוֹסֵף – An evil beast devoured him! Yosef has surely been torn to pieces."[91] Based on the *Ohr Hachaim Hakadosh*,[92] from Yaakov's perspective this was the most disturbing type

---

[89] *Rashi, Bereishis 37:2, from Bereishis Rabbah 84:6.*
[90] *Radak, Tehillim 112:8.*
[91] *Bereishis 37:33.*
[92] *Ohr Hachaim, Bereishis 37:33. See also Alshich, Megillas Esther 8:17.*

of death possible, for had Yosef been killed by the hands of man it would have meant that man's power of free choice could have intervened, and thus Yosef's death would not necessarily reflect negatively on his spiritual level. However, if a wild animal killed him, that would mean that there was no human intervention and thus it was Hashem Himself Who caused Yosef's untimely and gruesome death, presumably as a punishment for a lack of spiritual elevation and purity that was required of him. Thus, while Yaakov no longer feared man, he was fearful of Divine retribution. Yaakov perceived direct Divine retribution as the true and sole cause of Yosef's supposed demise. Such a thought is indeed frightening.

Is It Fitting to Feel Fear?

In this relatively short *kapitel* consisting of only ten *pesukim*, *Tehillim* 112 mentions the *shoresh* of יִרְאָה, fear, three times: fear of Hashem in *pasuk* 1, no fear of tragic news in *pasuk* 7, and here in *pasuk* 8, no fear of anyone or anything other than Hashem.

However, especially considering *Tehillim* 112's connection to Yaakov Avinu, *pasuk* 8's declaration of lack of fear for anyone but Hashem raises an important question because we do indeed find instances in which the Torah tells us that Yaakov was afraid.

For example, in *Parshas Vayishlach* when Yaakov became aware of an impending attack by Eisav and his army of four hundred men, the Torah testifies: "וַיִּירָא יַעֲקֹב מְאֹד – And Yaakov became very frightened,"[93] upon which *Rashi* comments that Yaakov was afraid he would be killed.[94] A few *pesukim* later Yaakov expresses his fears in prayer: "הַצִּילֵנִי נָא מִיַּד אָחִי מִיַּד עֵשָׂו; כִּי יָרֵא אָנֹכִי אֹתוֹ פֶּן יָבוֹא וְהִכַּנִי אֵם עַל בָּנִים – Rescue me, please, from the hand of my brother, from the hand of Eisav, for I fear him, lest he come and strike me, mother and children."[95]

---

[93] *Bereishis* 32:8.
[94] *Rashi, Bereishis* 32:8, from *Bereishis Rabbah* 76:2.
[95] *Bereishis* 32:12.

Rav Shimon Schwab addresses this seeming contradiction.[96] To begin his explanation, Rav Schwab explains that although the Gemara states that fear is a sign of a sinner,[97] it cannot be suggested that Yaakov was afraid because he had sinned and had thus become vulnerable or worthy of punishment because in Yaakov's prayer he states: "כִּי יָרֵא אָנֹכִי אֹתוֹ – for I fear *him*," indicating that Yaakov was afraid of Eisav HaRasha specifically.

Rav Schwab continues that, in truth, it is the nature of a person to be afraid of danger, and that includes even *tzaddikim*, who are not immune from such instinctive human reactions. The difference is that *tzaddikim* channel their fear. They pour out their prayers to Hashem asking to be saved, and following such prayers, their hearts promptly become secure and confident that Hashem has heard their voice. From that moment onward, they do not feel even the slightest inkling of fear.

We find this approach again in the words of Dovid HaMelech, who davened: "רְפָאֵנִי ה' כִּי נִבְהֲלוּ עֲצָמָי" – Heal me Hashem, for shudder with terror do my bones,"[98] but who then promptly declared: "סוּרוּ מִמֶּנִּי כָּל פֹּעֲלֵי אָוֶן, כִּי שָׁמַע ה' קוֹל בִּכְיִי – Depart from me all doers of evil, for Hashem has heard the sound of my weeping,"[99] and "שָׁמַע ה' תְּחִנָּתִי; ה' תְּפִלָּתִי יִקָּח" – Hashem has heard my plea, Hashem my prayer will accept."[100] So powerfully cathartic are these statements that they were codified as part of our daily *Tachanun* prayer, during which we are simultaneously at our most vulnerable and at our most protected.

Therefore, before and even during Yaakov's prayer, he was indeed afraid of Eisav and afraid that he might be killed. However, after his *tefillos*, Yaakov had complete trust in Hashem. The proof is that Yaakov subsequently left his family and went out alone at night to retrieve his

---

[96] *Maayan Beis Hashoeivah*, p. 83.
[97] *Brachos* 60a.
[98] *Tehillim* 6:3.
[99] *Tehillim* 6:9.
[100] *Tehillim* 6:10.

pachim ketanim, small jars,[101] and even wrestled with the *Sar shel Eisav*[102] – yet we do not find in either situation that Yaakov experienced any fear. Instead, Yaakov calmly prepared himself for his encounter with Eisav, and, concludes Rav Schwab, "His heart was steadfast within him in *bitachon* in Hashem," thereby paraphrasing the prior *pasuk* of *Tehillim* 112:7: "נָכוֹן לִבּוֹ בָּטֻחַ בַּה׳."

Pasuk 9:
פִּזַּר נָתַן לָאֶבְיוֹנִים,
צִדְקָתוֹ עֹמֶדֶת לָעַד;
קַרְנוֹ תָּרוּם בְּכָבוֹד

**He distributed widely by giving to the destitute,
his righteousness endures forever;
his pride will be exalted with glory.**

Yosef's Rise to Power in Egypt

Pasuk 9 contains numerous important elements connected to *Parshas Vayeishev* that we will analyze in separate subchapters. However, even the basic explanation of *pasuk* 9 is a tailor-made description of Yosef's rise to power in Egypt, as follows:

- "פִּזַּר נָתַן לָאֶבְיוֹנִים" – he distributed food to the poor and starving throughout the world during the seven years of famine;

- "צִדְקָתוֹ עֹמֶדֶת לָעַד" – he remained Yosef HaTzaddik, the quintessential "*tzaddik*" of Am Yisrael forever;[103] and

- "קַרְנוֹ תָּרוּם בְּכָבוֹד" – "His pride was exalted with glory" when he was suddenly elevated from lowly prisoner to Viceroy of Egypt,

---

[101] *Rashi, Bereishis* 32:25, from *Chullin* 91a.
[102] *Rashi, Bereishis* 32:25, from *Bereishis Rabbah* 77:3.
[103] *Rashi, Shemos* 1:5.

second only to Pharaoh; but in reality Yosef controlled the country and the known world, as even Pharaoh complimented and exalted Yosef by publicly declaring: "אֵין נָבוֹן וְחָכָם כָּמוֹךָ – there is no one as wise and understanding as you [Yosef],"[104] deferring to Yosef in all government matters.

In addition, the *Zohar Hakadosh*[105] connects the phrase "פִּזַּר נָתַן לָאֶבְיוֹנִים" with the phrase in *Mishlei*, "יֵשׁ מְפַזֵּר וְנוֹסָף עוֹד – There are those who distribute, yet increase more."[106] The *Zohar* expounds that proper "distribution" is giving to the poor, while the resultant (and counterintuitive) expression of "increase more" refers to even more wealth and more life for the giver, and not diminution, dearth, or death. Amazingly, the *Zohar* continues to explain that technically the proper phraseology in *Mishlei* should have been: "יֵשׁ מְפַזֵּר וְיוֹסֵף עוֹד," with the sudden insertion of the word "יוֹסֵף" certainly an additional hint to the achievements and mitzvos of Yosef in his role as Egyptian Viceroy.

The *Aleph-Beis* Connection

The *Radak* points out that *Tehillim* 12 is actually written in *aleph-beis* format, with each phrase beginning with a letter of the Hebrew alphabet in order from *aleph* to *tav*.[107]

This hints to the fact that Yosef utilized the Hebrew language to his advantage in Egypt. Egyptian law required that the Pharaoh be fluent in all seventy of the world's languages, and the Pharaoh who reigned in the time of Yosef was indeed fluent, but with one exception: he did not know *lashon hakodesh*, the holy Hebrew language. This flaw would have disqualified him from rulership.[108] Of course, Yosef was expert in *lashon*

---

[104] *Bereishis* 41:39.
[105] *Zohar Hakadosh* 3:153b.
[106] *Mishlei* 11:24.
[107] *Radak, Tehillim* 112:1.
[108] *Sotah* 36b.

hakodesh, and the angel Gavriel taught him all the other languages as well. As a result, Yosef was even more qualified to rule than Pharaoh was. Knowing this, Yosef kept Pharaoh in line when necessary by threatening to reveal his ignorance of Hebrew in times of need.[109] Thus, it was the Hebrew alphabet that was the mechanism used by Hashem to shield Yosef. As such, *Tehillim* 112 is particularly arranged with the Hebrew alphabet from *aleph* to *tav* in special recognition of the protection and power that *lashon hakodesh* provided Yosef.

The Coat of Many Colors

The famous "coat of many colors" that Yaakov gave to Yosef to symbolize his love for him above and beyond his other sons is called the "כְּתֹנֶת פַּסִּים," which literally means a "fine tunic of wool."[110] *Rashi* tells us that פַּסִּים is also an acronym that alludes to all of Yosef's troubles: he was sold to פּוֹטִיפַר (פ), to the סוֹחֲרִים (ס), to the יִשְׁמְעֵאלִים (י), and to the מִדְיָנִים (מ).[111]

B'ezras Hashem, we can add an additional layer to the above. If we look at *Tehillim* 112's *aleph-beis* phraseology and we take the י from יְכַלְכֵּל in *pasuk* 5, the כ from כִּי that starts *pasuk* 6, the מ from מִשְּׁמוּעָה that starts *pasuk* 7, the ס from סָמוּךְ that starts *pasuk* 8, and the פ from פִּזַּר that starts *pasuk* 9, we have a combination of letters that spell out "כ פַּסִּים."

The Seductiveness of Potiphar's Wife and its Impact

The word "פִּזַּר – distributed widely" is clearly a reference to Yosef's masterful worldwide allocation of food during the years of famine. It also alludes to the extent of the seductiveness of the wife of Potiphar and her long-lasting impact.

---

[109] *Rashi, Bereishis* 50:6, from *Sotah* 36b.
[110] *Bereishis* 37:3.
[111] *Rashi, Bereishis* 37:3, from *Bereishis Rabbah* 84:4.

The Torah tells us that the wife of Potiphar cast her eyes upon Yosef and attempted to seduce him day after day.[112] Yosef's response was always a reasoned, forceful, and respectful rejection[113] introduced by the Torah with the word "וַיְמָאֵן – And he refused."[114] Such refusal is made even more emphatic by the *trop* that accompanies it, i.e., the melodious and resounding musical note called a "*shalsheles*," which is actually a threefold repetition of a different musical note known as the "פָּזֵר."[115]

Nevertheless, despite the admirable, even supernatural, and vehement refusal by Yosef alluded to in the above "פָּזֵר" / "פָּזֵר" connection, the repercussions of this experience were far worse than even the years of imprisonment Yosef had to endure.

In Yaakov's final blessing to Yosef in *Parshas Vayechi*, Yaakov states: "וַתֵּשֶׁב בְּאֵיתָן קַשְׁתּוֹ, וַיָּפֹזּוּ זְרֹעֵי יָדָיו" – But his bow was firmly emplaced and his arms were gilded."[116] There, *Rashi* explains that "his bow was firmly emplaced" refers to Yosef's suppressing his physical urge at the main and final incident involving the wife of Potiphar,[117] and that "וַיָּפֹזּוּ זְרֹעֵי יָדָיו – his arms were gilded" really means that his arms dispersed seed, which Chazal reveal is an indication that seed went out from between the fingers of Yosef's hands. Yosef suppressed his physical desire by painfully digging his fingertips into the ground and leaning on them, and his seed was miraculously released from between his fingers.[118]

Chazal tell us that this incident not only shows us the extent of Yosef's ordeal and self-control, but that this incident also negatively impacted Yosef's status as an *Av*, a "father." For sadly, a total of twelve tribes were intended to have been born from Yosef, but the potential for ten of them

---

[112] E.g., *Bereishis* 39:7 and 39:10.
[113] *Bereishis* 39:8–9.
[114] *Bereishis* 39:8.
[115] *Sefer Vayehi Yadav Emunah*, p. 17.
[116] *Bereishis* 49:24.
[117] *Bereishis* 39:11–20.
[118] *Rashi*, *Bereishis* 49:24, from *Sotah* 36b and *Rashi* there.

was dispersed and wasted from his ten fingers during this episode, leaving Yosef with the potential for only two remaining sons, Ephraim and Menasheh.[119]

It is amazing that this event is hinted to in *Tehillim* 112:9 in the word "פִּזַּר," which means to "disburse, expend, and disseminate," and which is an allusion to the expression "וַיִּפֹּזּוּ זְרֹעֵי," which contains the sounds and letters of "פִּזַּר" and "פִּזַּר."

Yosef and Moshiach Ben Yosef's Power to Defeat Edom

The phrase "קַרְנוֹ תָּרוּם בְּכָבוֹד" – his pride will be exalted with glory," is also very much connected to Yosef. The word "קֶרֶן" means "pride" as well as "horn," for an animal's horns are its greatest pride. Yosef is often likened to a powerful ox, proudly crowned with thick and strong horns. For example, at the end of the Torah in Moshe Rabbeinu's final blessing to the Tribe of Yosef he includes the following statement: "בְּכוֹר שׁוֹרוֹ הָדָר לוֹ, וְקַרְנֵי רְאֵם קַרְנָיו, בָּהֶם עַמִּים יְנַגַּח יַחְדָּו אַפְסֵי אָרֶץ – His firstborn ox, majesty is his, and his horns are the horns of the *re'eim*, with them he will gore all of the nations even to the ends of the earth."[120]

It is these mighty qualities possessed by Yosef HaTzaddik and his descendants that enable them to be the nemesis of and antidote to Eisav HaRasha and his descendants, the nation of Edom, both throughout the ages as well as in our current and final *galus* before Moshiach. We first learn of this when, immediately after Yosef was born, Yaakov sought to finally leave Lavan after twenty years because he felt instantly ready to confront Eisav.[121] Even with Yosef as only a seemingly vulnerable infant, Yaakov perceived his birth, which also marked the first birth of a son of

---

[119] *Sotah* 36b; see also e.g., *Tikkunei Zohar* 110a; *Be'er Mayim Chaim, Bereishis* 48:5.
[120] *Devarim* 33:17.
[121] *Bereishis* 30:25.

Rochel Imeinu, as the start of the fulfillment of the crucial and much yearned for prophecy of "וְהָיָה בֵית יַעֲקֹב אֵשׁ וּבֵית יוֹסֵף לֶהָבָה, וּבֵית עֵשָׂו לְקַשׁ – And the House of Yaakov will be a fire and the House of Yosef will be a flame, and the House of Eisav will be straw."[122] As *Rashi*[123] explains, fire without flame does not have an effect from a long distance. However, once Yosef – the far-reaching flame – was born, Yaakov felt assured he would have Hashem's protection against Eisav and immediately wished to return to Eretz Canaan even though he would be forced to face Eisav, with the likelihood of a conflict high if not inevitable.

Although the struggle between the descendants of Yaakov and Eisav has continued for more than two thousand years, Chazal[124] tell us that if the War of *Gog U'Magog*, Armageddon, should happen in the days leading up to the Messianic Era,[125] there will be a great warrior who will descend from the lineage of Yosef, known as Moshiach ben Yosef. This Moshiach will lead the Jewish People in battle against the sons of Eisav and the rest of the world who rise against Am Yisrael. The tradition is that Moshiach ben Yosef will win many wars but will ultimately be killed in battle, setting the stage for Moshiach ben Dovid of the Davidic Dynasty to lead the Jewish People to total victory and usher in the Era of Moshiach when we will all return to Eretz Yisrael, the Beis HaMikdash will be rebuilt, the righteous and worthy dead will be resurrected, and all the world will live in peace under the Kingship of Hashem forever.

In this context, the *Eitz Yosef*[126] teaches something crucial. In the *brachah* of *Shemoneh Esrei* known as *Es Tzemach Dovid* in which we daven to Hashem to bring Moshiach ben Dovid and restore the Davidic

---

[122] *Ovadyah* 1:18.
[123] *Rashi, Bereishis* 30:25, from *Bereishis Rabbah* 73:7 and *Bava Basra* 123b.
[124] E.g., *Sukkah* 52a-b.
[125] As noted earlier in this *sefer*, the War of *Gog U'Magog*, Armageddon, is *not* inevitable and can be avoided. If Klal Yisrael bring the Era of Moshiach due to our *merits*, Moshiach will arrive in a peaceful and miraculous manner (e.g., *Sanhedrin* 98a; *Ohr Hachaim, Devarim* 24:17).
[126] *Eitz Yosef, Siddur Otzar HaTefillah* – *brachah* of *Es Tzemach Dovid*.

Dynasty, the phrase "וְקַרְנוֹ תָּרוּם בִּישׁוּעָתֶךָ" – and his קֶרֶן – pride/horn, shall be exalted with Your salvation," is also a hidden reference to Moshiach ben Yosef, who possesses the Yosef-like quality of the קֶרֶן, and for whom we must daven as we say these words. Pleads the *Eitz Yosef*, these heartfelt *tefillos* for Moshiach ben Yosef have the potential to change his fate so that he will be spared by Hashem in the terrible war of *Gog U'Magog*. We can, and we must, help ensure that he not die but rather live, by virtue of the power of this prayer.

Incredibly, *Tehillim* 112, which is the product of Dovid HaMelech's *ruach hakodesh* about the tribulations of Yosef HaTzaddik in *Parshas Vayeishev*, contains within the succinct phrase of "קַרְנוֹ תָּרוּם בְּכָבוֹד," allusions to all the above.

Care for *Kavod* and Avoiding Embarrassment

As noted above, the phrase "קַרְנוֹ תָּרוּם בְּכָבוֹד" – his pride will be exalted with glory," proclaimed by Dovid HaMelech in Tehillim 112 bears an obvious similarity to the expression of "וְקַרְנוֹ תָּרוּם בִּישׁוּעָתֶךָ," which is a key element of the *brachah* of *Es Tzemach Dovid* in which we daven for the scion of Dovid to lead us in the Era of Moshiach. As such, the expression "קַרְנוֹ תָּרוּם בְּכָבוֹד" is very much connected to the forefather whom both Dovid HaMelech and the *Melech HaMoshiach* share: Yehudah ben Yaakov. Yehudah's relationship with Tamar in *Parshas Vayeishev* brought forth their son Peretz from whom the glorious Davidic Dynasty will be traced all the way to Moshiach ben Dovid.[127] We reference this heritage as we daven each Friday night in *Lecha Dodi*: "עַל יַד אִישׁ בֶּן פַּרְצִי – Through the man descended from Peretz," in reference to Moshiach.

In addition, the word "כָּבוֹד" is often translated as "honor," and its antonym is disgrace and embarrassment, concepts that are very much connected to the story of Yehudah and Tamar in *Parshas Vayeishev*.[128]

---

[127] *Bereishis Rabbah* 85:1.
[128] *Bereishis* 38.

Initially, Yehudah was very concerned about his own כָּבוֹד. When he was unable to locate and pay the apparent harlot to whom he owed money, he stated: "תִּקַּח לָהּ פֶּן נִהְיֶה לָבוּז – Let her take for herself [his collateral], lest we become a laughingstock,"[129] about which *Rashi* explains that Yehudah was afraid his actions would become publicized "וְיִהְיֶה גְּנַאי – and it will be a disgrace" for him.[130]

Tamar's response is a study in contrast. Although Tamar was on the verge of receiving the capital punishment of *sereifah*, burning, for alleged infidelity, she was extremely sensitive to Yehudah's כָּבוֹד. Tamar refused to risk embarrassing Yehudah in any way. Her unwillingness to expose Yehudah as the father of her unborn child is the source for Chazal's famous statement: "נוֹחַ לוֹ לְאָדָם שֶׁיַּפִּיל עַצְמוֹ לְתוֹךְ כִּבְשַׁן הָאֵשׁ וְאַל יַלְבִּין פְּנֵי חֲבֵירוֹ בָּרַבִּים – It is preferable for a person to throw himself into a fiery furnace and not make his friend's face pale in public,"[131] i.e., not publicly embarrass another.

Tamar was sensitive to Yehudah's כָּבוֹד, and ultimately Yehudah, too, was able to set aside his own כָּבוֹד and admit both that he was the father and that Tamar's actions were justified, thereby saving mother and child from death. As a result, the line of Moshiach was fittingly established through them – Moshiach, who will serve as Hashem's trusted emissary in bringing the entire world to the highest level of כְּבוֹד שָׁמַיִם, honor of Heaven.

Pasuk 10:
רָשָׁע יִרְאֶה וְכָעָס,
שִׁנָּיו יַחֲרֹק וְנָמָס;
תַּאֲוַת רְשָׁעִים תֹּאבֵד

---

[129] *Bereishis* 38:23.
[130] *Rashi, Bereishis* 38:23.
[131] *Sotah* 10b.

The wicked man will see this and be angered, his teeth he will gnash and melt away; the ambition of the wicked will perish.

Our Modern-Day Revenge

While we believe that Moshiach can come at any moment, at which time *pasuk* 10 will come to fruition in all its miraculous Messianic glory, in truth *pasuk* 10 has and does come to fruition even today from within this prolonged and terrible exile.

For while Moshiach will bring the ultimate and everlasting revenge upon evil and the evildoers, our day-in and day-out lives as religious Jews are also a form of revenge upon the wicked.

When the evil Eisav, Yishmael, Lavan, and their wicked descendants – who all sought to eradicate the Torah way of life even in its infancy – see us, our families, our Shabbos, our Yom Tov, our Torah, our mitzvos, and our *simchas ha'chaim* and joy in living a Torah-true way of life, this too leads to the fulfillment of this concluding *pasuk* of *Tehillim* 112: "The wicked man will see this and be angered, his teeth he will gnash and melt away; the ambition of the wicked will perish."

In addition, the Torah life that we embody not only exacts revenge on the wicked but can even inspire them to repent, as the *pasuk* states: "תַּאֲוַת רְשָׁעִים תֹּאבֵד – the ambition [and base desires] of the wicked will perish," but not necessarily that the wicked themselves will perish. When they see us and are heartened by our example, they too can be instilled with a yearning to improve and may yet transform themselves and deserve to survive.[132]

For we and our precious families are indeed the present-day continuation of "אַבְרָהָם יָגֵל, יִצְחָק יְרַנֵּן, יַעֲקֹב וּבָנָיו יָנוּחוּ בוֹ" and will faithfully

---

[132] E.g., *Tehillim* 104:35, and *Brachos* 10a.

remain so until the coming of *Moshiach Tzidkeinu, b'miheirah b'yameinu, Amen*!

CHAPTER 10

PARSHAS MIKEITZ & TEHILLIM 40

פָּרָשַׁת מִקֵּץ / תְּהִלִּים מ

TEHILLIM 40 — תְּהִלִּים מ

1 For the conductor, by Dovid, a psalm.	א לַמְנַצֵּחַ לְדָוִד מִזְמוֹר.
2 I have placed great hope in Hashem; He inclined to me and heard my cry.	ב קַוֹּה קִוִּיתִי ה'; וַיֵּט אֵלַי וַיִּשְׁמַע שַׁוְעָתִי.
3 He raised me from the pit of raging waters, from mud which is slimy; He set my feet upon a rock, firmly establishing my steps.	ג וַיַּעֲלֵנִי מִבּוֹר שָׁאוֹן, מִטִּיט הַיָּוֵן; וַיָּקֶם עַל סֶלַע רַגְלַי, כּוֹנֵן אֲשֻׁרָי.
4 And He put into my mouth a new song, a praise to our Elokim;[1] the multitudes will see, and they will be awed, and they will trust in Hashem.	ד וַיִּתֵּן בְּפִי שִׁיר חָדָשׁ, תְּהִלָּה לֵא-לֹהֵינוּ; יִרְאוּ רַבִּים וְיִירָאוּ, וְיִבְטְחוּ בַּה'.

---

[1] For purposes of this Chapter 10, the translation "Elokim" is used rather than "God."

5	Praiseworthy is the man who has made Hashem his trust, and turned not to the arrogant and to strayers after falsehood.	אַשְׁרֵי הַגֶּבֶר אֲשֶׁר שָׂם ה' מִבְטַחוֹ, וְלֹא פָנָה אֶל רְהָבִים וְשָׂטֵי כָזָב.	ה
6	Much have You done, You Hashem, my Elokim, Your wonders and Your thoughts are for us, none can compare to You; were I to relate or speak of them, they are too overwhelming to count.	רַבּוֹת עָשִׂיתָ, אַתָּה ה', אֱ-לֹהַי, נִפְלְאֹתֶיךָ וּמַחְשְׁבֹתֶיךָ אֵלֵינוּ, אֵין עֲרֹךְ אֵלֶיךָ; אַגִּידָה וַאֲדַבֵּרָה, עָצְמוּ מִסַּפֵּר.	ו
7	Sacrifice and meal-offering You desired not, but ears You opened for me; burnt-offering and sin-offering You did not request.	זֶבַח וּמִנְחָה לֹא חָפַצְתָּ, אָזְנַיִם כָּרִיתָ לִּי; עוֹלָה וַחֲטָאָה לֹא שָׁאָלְתָּ.	ז
8	Then I said, 'Behold have I come with the Scroll of the Book that is written for me!'	אָז אָמַרְתִּי, הִנֵּה בָאתִי בִּמְגִלַּת סֵפֶר כָּתוּב עָלָי.	ח
9	To fulfill Your will, my Elokim, do I desire, and Your Torah is in my innermost parts.	לַעֲשׂוֹת רְצוֹנְךָ אֱ-לֹהַי חָפָצְתִּי; וְתוֹרָתְךָ בְּתוֹךְ מֵעָי.	ט
10	I proclaimed Your righteousness in a vast assembly, behold my lips will not restrain; Hashem, You know it.	בִּשַּׂרְתִּי צֶדֶק בְּקָהָל רָב, הִנֵּה שְׂפָתַי לֹא אֶכְלָא; ה', אַתָּה יָדָעְתָּ.	י
11	Your righteousness I have not concealed within my heart, of Your faithfulness and Your salvation have I spoken; I have not concealed Your kindness and Your truth from the vast assembly.	צִדְקָתְךָ לֹא כִסִּיתִי בְּתוֹךְ לִבִּי, אֱמוּנָתְךָ וּתְשׁוּעָתְךָ אָמָרְתִּי; לֹא כִחַדְתִּי חַסְדְּךָ וַאֲמִתְּךָ לְקָהָל רָב.	יא

CHAPTER 10: MIKEITZ & TEHILLIM 40

12 You, Hashem, do not withhold Your mercy from me; may Your kindness and Your truth always protect me.

13 For encircled me have innumerable evils, overtaken me have my sins and I am unable to see; they have become more numerous than the hairs on my head, and my courage has abandoned me.

14 May it be Your will, Hashem, to rescue me; Hashem, to my assistance hasten.

15 May they be put to shame and disgrace, all together, those who seek my soul to put an end to it; may they draw back and be humiliated, those who desire my misfortune.

16 May they be desolate because of their shaming, those who say about me "Aha! Aha!"

17 May they rejoice and be glad in You, all who seek You; may they say always, "Be magnified, Hashem,"

יב אַתָּה ה' לֹא תִכְלָא רַחֲמֶיךָ מִמֶּנִּי; חַסְדְּךָ וַאֲמִתְּךָ תָּמִיד יִצְּרוּנִי.

יג כִּי אָפְפוּ עָלַי רָעוֹת עַד אֵין מִסְפָּר, הִשִּׂיגוּנִי עֲוֺנֹתַי וְלֹא יָכֹלְתִּי לִרְאוֹת; עָצְמוּ מִשַּׂעֲרוֹת רֹאשִׁי וְלִבִּי עֲזָבָנִי.

יד רְצֵה ה' לְהַצִּילֵנִי; ה', לְעֶזְרָתִי חוּשָׁה.

טו יֵבֹשׁוּ וְיַחְפְּרוּ יַחַד מְבַקְשֵׁי נַפְשִׁי לִסְפּוֹתָהּ; יִסֹּגוּ אָחוֹר וְיִכָּלְמוּ חֲפֵצֵי רָעָתִי.

טז יָשֹׁמּוּ עַל עֵקֶב בָּשְׁתָּם, הָאֹמְרִים לִי הֶאָח הֶאָח.

יז יָשִׂישׂוּ וְיִשְׂמְחוּ בְּךָ כָּל מְבַקְשֶׁיךָ; יֹאמְרוּ תָמִיד יִגְדַּל ה', אֹהֲבֵי תְּשׁוּעָתֶךָ.

those who love Your salvation.

18 As for me, I am poor and destitute, the Lord will think of me; my help and my rescuer You are, my Elokim, do not delay.

יח וַאֲנִי עָנִי וְאֶבְיוֹן, אֲדֹנָ-י יַחֲשָׁב לִי; עֶזְרָתִי וּמְפַלְטִי אַתָּה, אֱ-לֹהַי אַל תְּאַחַר.

INTRODUCTION: PLACE YOUR HOPE IN HASHEM, AND ONLY HASHEM

The commentators on *Tehillim* 40 provide various contexts for this *kapitel*. *Rashi* explains *Tehillim* 40 as applicable to the time of Moshe Rabbeinu and the Jewish People during *Yetzias Mitzrayim*, *Krias Yam Suf*, and Hashem's giving of the Torah on Har Sinai. The *Radak* explains that this *kapitel* is the third successive *kapitel* in which Dovid himself suffered from illness. Here in *Tehillim* 40, we see Dovid beset by physical pain so severe that he davens that Hashem not leave him for dead and continues by praising Hashem for having healed him. Others view this *kapitel* as an attempt by Dovid to strengthen the Jews of his time and in the future – those people whose spirits are crushed and who worry about how they will ever deserve "יְשׁוּעָה – salvation" when they feel as though they do not have any merits to protect them.[2]

No matter the approach, the common denominator is the opening message of *Tehillim* 40: "קַוֹּה קִוִּיתִי ה'" – I have placed great hope in Hashem.

---

[2] E.g., *Baal Bris Avraham*, as cited in *Me'am Lo'ez*, *Tehillim* 40.

CHAPTER 10: MIKEITZ & TEHILLIM 40

It must be noted that the double expression of "קַוֹּה קִוִּיתִי" expresses *continuous* hope. And how and where should that hope be directed? Dovid HaMelech teaches us to hope and yearn not for the solution or resolution, but in *Hashem* – "'קַוֹּה קִוִּיתִי ה." The focal point must be Hashem and our connection to Him.

The *Alshich Hakadosh*[3] elaborates by drawing from the experience of Yitzchak and Rivkah when they desperately davened for a child in *Parshas Toldos*. The Torah tells us: "'וַיֶּעְתַּר יִצְחָק לַה... וַיֵּעָתֶר לוֹ ה – Yitzchak entreated Hashem… and Hashem allowed Himself to be entreated."[4] The *Alshich* brings a powerful parable of a father and son who were separated from one another by a thick wall. Frantic to see his father, the son began digging and clawing at the wall. Determined to see his son, the father also began scraping and hollowing out his side of the wall in a desperate attempt to reunite. So too, Yitzchak's davening described as "עָתַר," which connotes "digging" and "burrowing" functioned as a spiritual form of excavating a barrier in order to request of and draw close to Hashem. Incredibly, this was not a one-way endeavor. Hashem was simultaneously involved in extracting the blockage from *His* side as well, to expedite His availability to Yitzchak and speed his "יְשׁוּעָה."

The *Alshich* sees a parallel to the above in Dovid HaMelech's writing of *Tehilllim* and service of Hashem in general. Dovid HaMelech prepared himself each evening to merit *ruach hakodesh*, while Hashem would assist by sending the Northern Wind into Dovid's bed chambers and miraculously activating the strings of Dovid's harp, thereby rousing Dovid to *avodas Hashem* each night. Per the *Alshich*, this is the meaning of "'קַוֹּה קִוִּיתִי ה." Hashem is קַוֹּה, hoping for us to reach out to Him while He simultaneously helps us. And 'קִוִּיתִי ה, we too must hope and place our sincere trust in Hashem, inspired by the knowledge that Hashem is

---

[3] *Alshich*, as cited in *Me'am Lo'ez*, *Tehillim* 40:2.
[4] *Bereishis* 25:21.

Yosef's Prolonged Imprisonment

The primary connection between *Parshas Mikeitz* and *Tehillim* 40 is *pasuk* 5 of the *kapitel*: "אַשְׁרֵי הַגֶּבֶר אֲשֶׁר שָׂם ה' מִבְטַחוֹ, וְלֹא פָנָה אֶל רְהָבִים..." – Praiseworthy is the man who has made Hashem his trust, and turned not to the arrogant...," which is famously brought by *Rashi* at the end of *Parshas Vayeishev*.[5] *Rashi* explains that after having interpreted the dreams of Pharaoh's *Sar HaMashkim* and *Sar HaOfim* who were with him in prison, Yosef did not properly fulfill the dictates of this *pasuk* when he asked the *Sar HaMashkim*, whom Yosef foresaw would soon be released from prison and returned to his position of power, to remember him and help free him from prison. Yosef should not have placed his hope and faith in an Egyptian man whose nation is referred to as "רְהָבִים – arrogant;"[6] rather, Yosef should have relied entirely on Hashem for his salvation. As a result, Hashem kept Yosef in prison for an additional two years.

Essentially, Yosef's dependence on the *Sar HaMashkim* showed, if only in that one fateful moment, a lack of "שָׂם ה' מִבְטַחוֹ" and a lack of "קַוֹּה קִוִּיתִי ה':" a lack of hope and trust in the יְשׁוּעָה coming from Hashem and only Hashem.

What Did Yosef Do Wrong?

Of course, many wonder: What did Yosef do wrong? After all, isn't asking a person to remember him in the future and to help him – especially in such dire circumstances – merely common *hishtadlus*, effort, typically required of every Jew? The question is a strong one.

A common answer is that there are two elements to "אַשְׁרֵי הַגֶּבֶר אֲשֶׁר שָׂם ה' מִבְטַחוֹ, וְלֹא פָנָה אֶל רְהָבִים." Yosef did possess the first element of "שָׂם ה'

---

[5] *Rashi, Bereishis* 40:23, from *Bereishis Rabbah* 89:3.
[6] E.g., *Yeshayahu* 30:7.

מִבְטַחוֹ‎," as he had full and proper trust in Hashem and could thus faithfully turn to others whom he recognized were specifically placed around him by Hashem for assistance. However, Yosef's error was to whom he had turned. He turned to one of the רְהָבִים, arrogant and haughty Egyptians, and doing so was beneath him. *Hishtadlus* must always be in the proper measure and in a proper manner. Turning to the debased *Sar HaMashkim* was not appropriate for one such as Yosef HaTzaddik.

Hashem's, and Only Hashem's, Salvation

However, a more astounding answer is based on a *yesod* we discussed in Chapter 7 (*Parshas Vayeitzei* & *Tehillim* 3). In the first *brachah* of *Shemoneh Esrei*, we say the words "מֶלֶךְ עוֹזֵר וּמוֹשִׁיעַ וּמָגֵן – King, Helper, Savior, and Shield," which are praises directed primarily toward Hashem. Yet in addition, the *Iyun Tefillah*[7] explains that עוֹזֵר is a hidden reference to Yaakov Avinu; מוֹשִׁיעַ is a hidden reference to Yitzchak Avinu; and מָגֵן is a hidden reference to Avraham Avinu. מָגֵן refers to protection from Hashem using His *middah* of Shield, for just as in battle a shield protects the warrior from sword, spear, and arrow before they can harm him, so too Hashem shielded Avraham from harm's way. עוֹזֵר refers to Hashem as Helper, meaning that the Jew must perform the necessary *hishtadlus* and effort on his own and thereafter Hashem will perform the rest. This corresponds to Yaakov Avinu and his approach of "partnering" (so to speak) with Hashem whenever Hashem sent challenges his way.

Finally, and most relevant to Yosef, is the word מוֹשִׁיעַ, which refers to Hashem as Savior and corresponds to Yitzchak Avinu, who received יְשׁוּעָה from Hashem without any active contribution of his own. Moreover, Yitzchak was saved specifically because of such passivity. Yitzchak, who mirrored Hashem's *middah* of *gevurah*, the characteristic of might and strength, was faced with challenges that required the opposite response. His challenges required not responses of power or fury, but rather a *bitul*,

---

[7] *Iyun Tefillah, Siddur Otzar HaTefillah* – *brachah* of Avos.

a self-nullification and subservience to the desire of Hashem even if this meant allowing himself to be bound and slaughtered as a sacrifice to God at the *Akeidah*. Such *bitul* was not a sign of weakness but rather required great spiritual power and strength to remove his own self-interests from the equation and to fully give himself over to the *ratzon Hashem*, the desire of God. This was especially difficult for Yitzchak Avinu, who was blessed with the power of *gevurah* but had to refrain from wielding the power and proactivity that *gevurah* commands. As Rav Shimshon Pincus[8] explains, Yitzchak's *gevurah* was manifest not in feats of strength like Yaakov nor in victories in battle like Avraham, but rather in his self-restraint and passivity, which was the fulfillment of the *middah* of *gevurah* as described in *Pirkei Avos*: "אֵיזֶהוּ גִבּוֹר, הַכּוֹבֵשׁ אֶת יִצְרוֹ – Who is the mighty one? One who can conquer his personal inclination."[9]

To be clear, mankind's standard approach to challenges using the method of מוֹשִׁיעַ is exceedingly rare and is reserved for only a select few *tzaddikim*. עוֹזֵר and its required *hishtadlus* is the norm, as well as מָגֵן; for Hashem is constantly shielding us from harm more than we will ever know.

However, like Yitzchak Avinu, Yosef HaTzaddik was one of the select few that Hashem tested and expected to rise to the mode of מוֹשִׁיעַ in the face of Hashem's challenges; to refrain from *hishtadlus* and to allow Hashem to bring the entirety of the salvation Himself. This is why with regard to Yosef in prison, Chazal call attention to our *pasuk* in *Tehillim* 40:5: "אַשְׁרֵי הַגֶּבֶר אֲשֶׁר שָׂם ה' מִבְטַחוֹ." Yosef needed to trust Hashem and to do nothing more. When Yosef injected himself into the situation and made his own independent *hishtadlus*, even by simply asking the *Sar HaMashkim* to remember him as an ordinary person might so request, this

---

[8] *Nefesh Shimshon: Siddur HaTefillah*, p. 389.
[9] *Pirkei Avos* 4:1.

resulted in two additional years in prison[10] because Yosef, on his level, was supposed to rely completely on Hashem to be his מוֹשִׁיעַ.

In other words, borrowing from the terminology of *Tehillim* 40, Yosef was expected to exemplify "קַוֹּה קִוִּיתִי ה'" and "שָׂם ה' מִבְטַחוֹ". Yosef's test was to demonstrate complete hope and faith in Hashem alone – not in the *Sar HaMashkim*, not even in himself and his own *hishtadlus*, but only in Hashem.

Other Examples of Yosef's "*Moshia*" Missteps

It should be noted that in the prior *Parshah* of *Vayeishev*, each time Yosef actively involved himself or asserted himself, trouble ensued. He actively informed his father of perceived wrongdoings by his brothers, garnering their hatred. He voluntarily shared his dreams with others, which earned him the rebuke of his father and further jealousy and hatred from his brothers. Although a man/angel warned him that his brothers were looking to kill him, he decided to ignore the warnings and went to seek out his brothers, falling right into their trap. He proactively "went to do his work" and was lured by the wife of Potiphar. Yosef took the liberty of asking the *Sar HaMashkim* to remember him, leading to a longer imprisonment. From these incidents, we clearly see that Yosef's essence required passivity by relying on Hashem's desires and decisions to dictate his experiences, rather than those of his own.

Recap and Digging Deeper

To summarize, the statement in *pasuk* 5 of *Tehillim* 40 "אַשְׁרֵי הַגֶּבֶר אֲשֶׁר שָׂם ה' מִבְטַחוֹ, וְלֹא פָנָה אֶל רְהָבִים" describes where Yosef erred at the end of *Parshas Vayeishev*, and the statement in *pasuk* 2 of *Tehillim* 40 "קַוֹּה קִוִּיתִי ה'," describes Hashem's expectations for Yosef and how he corrected his error at the start of *Parshas Mikeitz*.

---

[10] The same conclusion is drawn by Rav Moshe Feinstein in *Darash Moshe*, *Parshas Vayeishev*, pp. 29–30.

Considering this understanding, we now have a deeper appreciation of the *Alshich*'s connection of the phrase "'קַוֹּה קִוִּיתִי ה'" to Yitzchak Avinu. Yitzchak and Yosef shared this virtually unique approach of having to deal with challenges in a passive manner in the form of מוֹשִׁיעַ, faithfully and devotedly awaiting Hashem's יְשׁוּעָה. And although the *Alshich*'s description of desperate digging, clawing, and scraping gives the impression of *hishtadlus*, in reality the only *hishtadlus* that Yitzchak had done was exerting himself in prayer: "וַיֶּעְתַּר יִצְחָק לַה'." Yitzchak entreated Hashem, which *is* considered a form of *hishtadlus* by most but in actuality is a pure expression of nothing else other than קַוֹּה קִוִּיתִי ה'. Clearly, heartfelt prayer is a manifestation of one's hope in Hashem alone.

Establishing the Yitzchak-Yosef Connection to "Elokim"

Another important Yitzchak-Yosef connection throughout *Parshas Mikeitz* and *Tehillim* 40 is the use of the Name "אֱ-לֹהִים," the Divine Name of *middas ha'din*, strict judgment, which is a main characteristic of Yitzchak Avinu's service of Hashem. Even as Yosef prepared to hear Pharaoh's dreams and to interpret them, Yosef's first words were "בִּלְעָדָי; אֱ-לֹהִים יַעֲנֶה אֶת שְׁלוֹם פַּרְעֹה – This is beyond me. אֱ-לֹהִים will respond to Pharaoh's welfare."[11]

In fact, when Yosef interpreted the dreams and provided Pharaoh with advice about surviving the inevitable famine, Yosef repeated the Name אֱ-לֹהִים four times[12] and even inspired Pharaoh to himself use the Name אֱ-לֹהִים twice more,[13] including acknowledging the holy "רוּחַ אֱלֹהִים – spirit of Elokim" that rested within Yosef.[14]

---

[11] *Bereishis* 41:16.
[12] *Bereishis* 41:25, 28, and 32.
[13] *Bereishis* 41:38–39.
[14] *Rashi* and *Targum Onkelos*, *Bereishis* 41:38.

The emphasis on the Name אֱ-לֹהִים is indicative of Yosef's new understanding that all the seemingly tragic events he had experienced and all that was yet to occur were results of Hashem's Yitzchak-like approach of אֱ-לֹהִים and מוֹשִׁיעַ in his own life.

Furthermore, Yosef's highlighting of the Name אֱ-לֹהִים represents his willingness to be *matzdik* the *din*, to justify and accept the strict judgment that Hashem decreed upon him, without any reservations or regrets. This also signifies a total *bitul* to Hashem's *ratzon* as מוֹשִׁיעַ.

As we shall see and analyze below, the *shoresh* of the Name אֱ-לֹהִים appears numerous times in *Tehillim* 40 as does the description of Hashem as מוֹשִׁיעַ. This is further evidence of the above motif and approach.

ADDITIONAL YITZCHAK-YOSEF & MOSHIA-ELOKIM CONNECTIONS IN PARSHAS MIKEITZ & TEHILLIM 40

The themes analyzed in the above Introduction that focuses on *pasuk* 2 and *pasuk* 5 of *Tehillim* 40 and the Name אֱ-לֹהִים are also evident throughout the entirety of *Tehillim* 40. Here we find numerous allusions to Yosef trusting in God and remaining passive while God, specifically in His capacity as "אֱ-לֹהִים," single-handedly brings the salvation as מוֹשִׁיעַ.

Pasuk 2:
קַוֹּה קִוִּיתִי ה';

וַיֵּט אֵלַי וַיִּשְׁמַע שַׁוְעָתִי

I have placed great hope in Hashem;
He inclined to me and heard my cry.

See the Introduction to this chapter for the primary explanation of why this *pasuk* is such a fundamental element of the connection between Tehillim 40, *Parshas Mikeitz*, and the tests that Yosef endured in prison.

Pasuk 3:
וַיַּעֲלֵנִי מִבּוֹר שָׁאוֹן,
מִטִּיט הַיָּוֵן
He raised me from the pit of raging waters,
from mud which is slimy.

Yosef's Release from Prison

The phrase "וַיַּעֲלֵנִי מִבּוֹר – He [Hashem] raised me from the pit" refers to Yosef's release from prison in *Parshas Mikeitz*. The Torah describes the prison as a בּוֹר and states: "וַיְרִיצֻהוּ מִן הַבּוֹר – And they rushed him from the pit."[15] *Rashi* explains that this pit was an underground prison.[16]

In addition, the reference to "שָׁאוֹן – raging waters," is a reference to the *Sar HaMashkim*, whose job it was to provide drinks and beverages to hydrate and entertain Pharaoh, but whose involvement in Yosef's life submerged Yosef deeper into the proverbial raging waters of the prison that engulfed him.

However, the most vital element here is the word "וַיַּעֲלֵנִי – He [Hashem] raised me," which expresses recognition that it was Hashem Who freed Yosef, with no credit attributed to the *Sar HaMashkim*, Pharaoh, or to Yosef himself, but rather only to Hashem as מוֹשִׁיעַ.

---

[15] *Bereishis* 41:14.

[16] *Rashi, Bereishis* 41:14.

Pasuk 4:

וַיִּתֵּן בְּפִי שִׁיר חָדָשׁ,
תְּהִלָּה לֵא-לֹהֵינוּ;
יִרְאוּ רַבִּים וְיִירָאוּ,
וְיִבְטְחוּ בַּה'

**And He put into my mouth a new song,
a praise to our Elokim;
the multitudes will see, and they will be awed,
and they will trust in Hashem.**

The "New Song" of Yosef

This *pasuk* tracks the Introduction to this chapter beautifully: even a "new song from my mouth" is not mine at all but rather was "placed there" by God, Who is referred to specifically as "אֱ-לֹהֵינוּ" – the Name of *middas ha'din* as discussed above.

Furthermore, this new song triggered "יִרְאוּ רַבִּים וְיִירָאוּ" – a reaction by the Egyptian masses of יִרְאָה, awe, and also "fear" of God as אֱ-לֹהִים, who had just revealed to Yosef the frightening prophecy of the impending seven years of famine that would ravage Egypt and the world. As discussed,[17] אֱ-לֹהִים as well as יִרְאָה are quintessential elements of Yitzchak Avinu's characteristics and approach to service of Hashem, which Yosef HaTzaddik was expected to emulate.

What was the result? "וְיִבְטְחוּ בַּה'" – they will trust in Hashem," which, as noted above, is the essential element that enables one to come to *bitul* and relinquish control to God. This was the *bitul* required of Yosef, just as it was required of and fully attained by Yitzchak, and was ultimately fully attained by Yosef as well. In addition, we must remember that the Divine Name present in the phrase "וְיִבְטְחוּ בַּה'" is actually "י-ה-ו-ה," teaching us

---

[17] E.g., see Introduction to Chapter 6, *Parshas Toldos* & *Tehillim* 36.

that such *bitul* is the gateway to yet another exalted level of *brachah* and *avodah*: Hashem's *middas ha'rachamim*, Divine mercy.

Indeed, Yosef's proverbial "שִׁיר חָדָשׁ – new song" describes his new attitude and approach: a Yitzchak-like attitude and approach that was not only the key to Yosef's salvation, but also inspired non-Jew and Jew alike to recognize and serve Hashem in His dual capacity as אֱ-לֹהִים and as י-ה-ו-ה.

Pasuk 5:
אַשְׁרֵי הַגֶּבֶר אֲשֶׁר שָׂם ה' מִבְטַחוֹ,
וְלֹא פָנָה אֶל רְהָבִים וְשָׂטֵי כָזָב

Praiseworthy is the man who has made Hashem his trust, and turned not to the arrogant and to strayers after falsehood.

Yosef's Mistaken Reliance on the *Sar HaMashkim*

See the Introduction to this chapter for a more detailed analysis of this *pasuk*, which Chazal reveal contains the primary connection between *Tehillim* 40 and *Parshas Mikeitz*.

In short, *Rashi* at the end of *Parshas Vayeishev*[18] explains that Yosef should never have placed his hope for release from prison into the unholy hands of the *Sar HaMashkim*, an Egyptian whose nation is referred to as "רְהָבִים – arrogant."[19] Instead, Yosef should have relied entirely on Hashem for his salvation and placed his trust in Hashem and only Hashem, in fulfillment of the holy directive to "שָׂם ה' מִבְטַחוֹ" and rely upon Hashem as his מוֹשִׁיעַ.

---

[18] *Rashi, Bereishis* 40:23, from *Bereishis Rabbah* 89:3.
[19] E.g., *Yeshayahu* 30:7.

Pasuk 6:

רַבּוֹת עָשִׂיתָ, אַתָּה ה׳, אֱ-לֹהַי,
נִפְלְאֹתֶיךָ וּמַחְשְׁבֹתֶיךָ אֵלֵינוּ,
אֵין עֲרֹךְ אֵלֶיךָ;
אַגִּידָה וַאֲדַבֵּרָה,
עָצְמוּ מִסַּפֵּר

**Much have You done, You Hashem, my Elokim,
Your wonders and Your thoughts are for us,
none can compare to You;
were I to relate or speak of them,
they are too overwhelming to count.**

Our Own Personal Elokim

Here, with the phrase "אַתָּה ה׳, אֱ-לֹהַי" – You Hashem, my Elokim," there is a continued emphasis on the Name אֱ-לֹהִים and the *middas ha'din*, while conveying that it is God Who controls and accomplishes wonders and directs nature, as opposed to crediting the actions of the individual person. However, the Name of *middas ha'din* is tempered through a number of more personal and gentle expressions. For example, the Name י-ה-ו-ה is also used, indicating Divine mercy, and even the Name אֱ-לֹהִים itself is softened with the expression of "אֱ-לֹהַי," which connotes "My own personal Elokim." Finally, the inclusion of the word "אַתָּה – You," is a powerfully direct and intimate way of addressing Hashem.

Of Wonders and Wisdom

It must also be noted that this *pasuk* ends with the words: "נִפְלְאֹתֶיךָ וּמַחְשְׁבֹתֶיךָ אֵלֵינוּ, אֵין עֲרֹךְ אֵלֶיךָ; אַגִּידָה וַאֲדַבֵּרָה, עָצְמוּ מִסַּפֵּר" – Your wonders and Your thoughts are for us; none can compare to You; were I to relate or speak of them, they are too overwhelming to count." This is a glowing tribute to Hashem's unfathomable *chochmah*, wisdom. Of course,

Hashem's wisdom is clearly revealed in the original Creation and in His daily re-creation of the world. Yet Hashem's wisdom is no less evident from a small-scale perspective such as in the way Hashem directed the course of events between Yosef and his brothers. Here, each word and action over the course of decades finally clicks into place, fitting perfectly and forming a unified and majestic picture. From our perspective, seeing Hashem's precision should inspire us toward awe and fear of Him as well as *bitul* to Him. Truly, as we observe all His wonders, from global to personal, we are amazed.

In a similar vein, the *Haftarah* to *Parshas Mikeitz*[20] contains Shlomo HaMelech's first experience with his newly received God-given power of חָכְמָה, for which he would become known as "וַיֶּחְכַּם מִכָּל הָאָדָם – the wisest of all men."[21] Yet how is such wisdom ultimately described in the penultimate *pasuk* of the *Haftarah*? It is described as "חָכְמַת אֱ-לֹהִים – the wisdom of *God*," *not* the wisdom of Shlomo. Furthermore, it was specifically the wisdom of God through the conduit of the Name "אֱ-לֹהִים" that required of Shlomo a complete *bitul* toward the *middas ha'din* of אֱ-לֹהִים in order for him to utilize that wisdom properly.

With that, the "חוּט הַמְשֻׁלָּשׁ – the threefold cord,"[22] of the *Parshah*, *Haftarah*, and *Tehillim* intertwine in recognition of the חָכְמַת אֱ-לֹהִים to create a powerful triumvirate of Tanach (*Torah, Neviim,* and *Kesuvim*) that is rock-solid and "לֹא בִמְהֵרָה יִנָּתֵק – cannot be quickly broken."[23]

Pasuk 7:
זֶבַח וּמִנְחָה לֹא חָפַצְתָּ,
אָזְנַיִם כָּרִיתָ לִּי;
עוֹלָה וַחֲטָאָה לֹא שָׁאָלְתָּ

---

[20] *I Melachim* 3:15–4:1.
[21] *I Melachim* 5:11.
[22] *Koheles* 4:12.
[23] *Koheles* 4:12.

CHAPTER 10: MIKEITZ & TEHILLIM 40

**Sacrifice and meal-offering You desired not,
but ears You opened for me;
burnt-offering and sin-offering You did not request.**

Hashem Wants to Hear Our *Tefillos*

The message here is much more than "Hashem does not desire sacrificial offerings brought in an insincere and hypocritical manner." Rather, even sincerely brought *korbanos* are not requested in this context, for, consistent with our ongoing theme, God is not looking for the active involvement of the Jew at all, but rather *bitul* to His will.

There is one exception, however: Hashem desires our prayers. The meaning conveyed by "אָזְנַיִם כָּרִיתָ לִּי – but ears You opened for me" is an expression of Hashem's desire to listen to our *tefillos*. Indeed, Hashem wants us to trust in Him and daven. When we do so, Hashem intervenes on our behalf as our מוֹשִׁיעַ.[24]

Pasuk 9:
לַעֲשׂוֹת רְצוֹנְךָ אֱ-לֹהַי חָפָצְתִּי
To fulfill Your will, my Elokim, do I desire.

Bitul to Hashem with Heartfelt Love

Again, the use of the Name "אֱ-לֹהִים" is an expression of *bitul* to the *middas ha'din*, a proud proclamation: Whatever Your Will may be, I will do it, even if my "doing" Your Will requires that I defer to You completely and refrain from taking action.

Furthermore, as we saw in *pasuk* 6, the Name of the *middas ha'din* used here is not "אֱ-לֹהִים," but rather "אֱ-לֹהַי," which connotes "*My* אֱ-לֹהִים" in a loving expression of *bitul* and personal closeness even to the daunting

---

[24] See also Chapter 8, *Parshas Vayishlach* & *Tehillim* 140, at *pasuk* 7 for a detailed discussion on the unusual expression of Hashem having "ears."

middas ha'din. This intimate and heartfelt expression is further punctuated by the accompanying powerful words: "לַעֲשׂוֹת רְצוֹנְךָ חָפָצְתִּי," which is a sincere statement that our truest desire is to fulfill *Hashem's* desire.

Pasuk 11:
אֱמוּנָתְךָ וּתְשׁוּעָתְךָ אָמָרְתִּי
Of Your faithfulness and Your salvation have I spoken.

Mutual Faith That Hashem Will Save

This is a declaration of mutual אֱמוּנָה, faithfulness, between Hashem and man. We declare our faith that You, Hashem, will be faithful toward us. This is consistent with the parable of the *Alshich Hakadosh* discussed in the Introduction to this chapter, in which both man and Hashem attempt to reach one another, each simultaneously yearning to break through the barriers separating them.

In addition, the word "תְּשׁוּעָתְךָ," is an explicit request for Hashem to engage with us as מוֹשִׁיעַ; we desire that Hashem alone act, accomplish, and bring the יְשׁוּעָה that each Jew so desperately needs.

Pasuk 17:
יָשִׂישׂוּ וְיִשְׂמְחוּ בְּךָ כָּל מְבַקְשֶׁיךָ;
יֹאמְרוּ תָמִיד יִגְדַּל ה', אֹהֲבֵי תְּשׁוּעָתֶךָ
May they rejoice and be glad in You, all who seek You;
may they say always, 'Be magnified, Hashem,'
those who love Your salvation.

The *Simchah* of Salvation

This *pasuk* is a celebratory one now and for the future as it contains the promise that all those who search for Hashem and wish to magnify Hashem's glory will surely find Him and experience great joy.

Of course, the final word, "תְּשׁוּעָתֶךָ," is yet another explicit reference to the recurring theme of Hashem as the sole מוֹשִׁיעַ Who will bring us both personal salvation and national salvation.

Pasuk 18:
וַאֲנִי עָנִי וְאֶבְיוֹן,
אֲדֹנָ-י יַחֲשָׁב לִי;
עֶזְרָתִי וּמְפַלְטִי אַתָּה,
אֱ-לֹהַי אַל תְּאַחַר.

As for me, I am poor and destitute,
the Lord will think of me;
my help and my rescuer You are,
my Elokim, do not delay.

Though Destitute, *Din* Will Deliver Without Delay

This concluding *pasuk* in *Tehillim* 40 contains an acknowledgment of the speaker's limitations and frailty, as he realizes that he must at the same time feel impoverished and incapable of independent success but hopeful that Hashem will think of him, help him, and deliver him.

This recognition culminates in the poignant request: "אֱ-לֹהַי אַל תְּאַחַר – My own personal אֱ-לֹהִים, my אֱ-לֹהַי, please do not delay." Here, Dovid HaMelech directly addresses the *middas ha'din*, Yitzchak Avinu's characteristic that Yosef, too, was expected to embody. Completely reliant, Dovid begs the *middas ha'din* to refrain from prolonging the much needed salvation, which only Hashem can properly bestow in His role as מוֹשִׁיעַ.

Culmination of the Yitzchak-Yosef & Elokim-*Moshia* Connections

Indeed, the Yitzchak-Yosef connection to אֱ-לֹהִים and מוֹשִׁיעַ are undeniably emphasized throughout *Tehillim* 40.

May Hashem bless us to be sensitive to these words and messages and to internalize them in our prayers and daily conduct. In doing so, may we merit to transcend the need for *middas ha'rachamim* altogether, such that even God as revealed to us through the Name אֱ-לֹהִים and *middas ha'din* will allow Himself to approach us only with *rachamim*,[25] granting us all the ultimate מוֹשִׁיעַ in the form of *Moshiach Tzidkeinu, b'miheirah b'yameinu*.

ADDITIONAL CONNECTIONS BETWEEN PARSHAS MIKEITZ & TEHILLIM 40

Pasuk 3:

וַיַּעֲלֵנִי מִבּוֹר שָׁאוֹן, מִטִּיט הַיָּוֵן

He raised me from the pit of raging waters, from mud which is slimy.

Torah's Study and Wisdom Saves from Gehinnom

From this *pasuk* the *Zohar Hakadosh*[26] derives the importance of learning Torah and never abandoning it in order to avoid the fate of Gehinnom, called the "בּוֹר שָׁאוֹן, טִיט הַיָּוֵן" – pit of raging waters and slimy

---

[25] E.g., *Rashi, Shemos* 15:6, from *Mechilta*.
[26] *Zohar Hakadosh* 1:185a.

CHAPTER 10: MIKEITZ & TEHILLIM 40

mud."[27] In the context of discussing one who does not learn Torah and allows himself to become soiled in the filth of sin, the *Zohar* brings the *pasuk* from *Parshas Vayeishev* that describes Yosef's brothers initially throwing him into a pit: "וַיִּקָּחֻהוּ וַיַּשְׁלִכוּ אֹתוֹ הַבֹּרָה,"[28] which in more general terms refers to the "pit" of Gehinnom into which a person may be cast by Hashem. Why does the person deserve such a terrible fate? Because just as with regard to Yosef and his brothers the Torah tells us "וְהַבּוֹר רֵק, אֵין בּוֹ מָיִם – the pit was empty, there was no water in it," so too says the *Zohar* such a person himself lacks any Torah whatsoever (and, we can add, perhaps there are even "snakes and scorpions" lurking within him).[29]

Instead, like Yosef, we must strive to be "נָבוֹן וְחָכָם – wise and understanding"[30] and toil in Hashem's Torah. In addition, the above *Zohar* concludes with the eerily similar warning of Yirmiyahu HaNavi:[31] "מִי הָאִישׁ הֶחָכָם וְיָבֵן אֶת זֹאת – Who is the man who is wise that he may understand this?" as certainly Yosef HaTzaddik understood. "עַל מָה אָבְדָה הָאָרֶץ – Why was the land [and/or eternal life] lost?" Hashem says: "עַל עָזְבָם אֶת תּוֹרָתִי – Because they have forsaken My Torah."

A Spark of Chanukah

*P*asuk 3 contains a request to be saved "מִטִּיט הַיָּוֵן – from mud which is slimy," but the unusual word "יָוֵן" is also a hidden reference to salvation from יָוָן, the Greek Empire. This was an empire that so terribly oppressed the Jewish People and whose goal it was to sully and muddy the Torah by trapping Jews in the quicksand of Hellenism, but thankfully Galus Yavan culminated in the miracles of Chanukah, the Yom Tov that coincides with *Parshas Mikeitz*.

---

[27] *Tehillim* 40:3.
[28] *Bereishis* 37:24.
[29] Based on *Rashi, Bereishis* 37:24.
[30] *Bereishis* 41:39.
[31] *Yirmiyahu* 9:11–12.

Pasuk 3:
כּוֹנֵן אֲשֻׁרָי
[Hashem] firmly establishing my steps.

Footsteps Ascending the Steps to Pharaoh's Throne

Rashi[32] explains "כּוֹנֵן אֲשֻׁרָי" to mean that Hashem established and prepared Dovid's footsteps. As such, this phrase is a recognition by Dovid HaMelech that Hashem guided his comings and goings both in his daily life and during wartime, protecting his every stride and every action always.

On a deeper level, the Midrash[33] explains this *pasuk* in the context of *Yetzias Mitzrayim* by interpreting this phrase as referring to the feet of Bnei Yisrael crossing the Yam Suf on dry land, where vast waters had been surging just moments prior. Thus, these words are immediately followed by the words in *pasuk* 4: "וַיִּתֵּן בְּפִי שִׁיר חָדָשׁ" – And He put into my mouth a new song," which refers to the famed song of "*Az Yashir*" sung by Moshe and Bnei Yisrael upon being saved by Hashem at *Krias Yam Suf*, due in part to the merit of Yosef HaTzaddik.[34]

However, regarding Yosef and *Parshas Mikeitz*, my son, Chaim Zev, immediately recognized a parallel between the emphasis on steps in "כּוֹנֵן אֲשֻׁרָי" and a teaching from Chazal describing Yosef HaTzaddik and his "footsteps" ascending the stone "steps" leading directly to the throne of Pharaoh. Indeed, the Midrash[35] reveals the following:

> The throne upon which Pharaoh sat was covered with gold and with silver and with onyx stones, and there were to it seventy steps. It

---

[32] *Rashi, Tehillim* 40:3.
[33] *Shemos Rabbah* 23:12.
[34] *Bereishis Rabbah* 87:8. See also *Tehillim* 40:4 as studied later in this *sefer*.
[35] *Midrash Sefer HaYashar, Bereishis, Mikeitz* 4. English translation attributed to *Sefer HaYashar*, translated by Edward B.M. Browne, New York, 1876, with some modifications by the author of this *sefer*.

CHAPTER 10: MIKEITZ & TEHILLIM 40

was the rule in all the land of Egypt that when a man came to speak to Pharaoh, if he was a prince or one highly esteemed by Pharaoh, that he ascended toward Pharaoh up to the thirty-first step, and Pharaoh would descend to the thirty-sixth step and speak to him. And if he was of the common people, he ascended to the third step, and Pharaoh descended all the way down to the fourth step and spoke unto him. It was further their rule that every man who understood and could speak the seventy languages would scale the seventy steps, and while ascending he would speak [each language] until he reached Pharaoh. And any man that knew not all the seventy languages was permitted to ascend the steps according to the number of his languages. It was also a law in Egypt in those days that no man could be king over them unless he knew the seventy languages. When Yosef first appeared before Pharaoh he bowed down before him to the ground, and he ascended three steps, and Pharaoh sat down on the fourth step and he spoke to Yosef saying, "I have dreamed a dream, and no one can interpret it correctly." Yosef answered Pharaoh saying, "Let the king relate his dream which he has dreamed, but certainly its interpretation is with Elokim." And [after Yosef interpreted Pharaoh's dreams and was on the brink of being elevated to Viceroy] all the princes answered to Pharaoh saying, "And is it not written in the laws of Egypt, which should not be violated, that no man shall be Pharaoh of Egypt, nor second to Pharaoh, unless he knows all the languages of the sons of man? And now, my lord and king, this Hebrew man speaks only the Hebrew language, and how can he be second to Pharaoh, he who does not even know our language?" On that night Hashem sent an angel from among the angels that minister to Him, and he came to the land of Egypt to Yosef, and the angel stood before Yosef... and the angel woke him up from his sleep. Yosef arose and stood upon his feet and behold an angel of the Lord was standing before him. And the angel of the Lord spoke to Yosef, and he taught him all the languages of the sons of man on that night, and he called his name יְהוֹסֵף (e.g., see *Tehillim* 81:6), and the angel of the Lord left him, and Yosef returned to his bed and was greatly astonished at the vision which he had seen. In the morning Pharaoh sent for Yosef, and the servants of Pharaoh went and brought Yosef before Pharaoh. And Pharaoh sent for all his princes and servants who were to sit before Pharaoh, and [in their presence] Yosef ascended the steps of the throne of Pharaoh while he spoke to Pharaoh in all of the languages, speaking to the king as he was going up, until he reached Pharaoh on the seventieth step, and he sat down before Pharaoh. And Pharaoh rejoiced greatly over Yosef, and all of Pharaoh's princes also rejoiced exceedingly with their king on hearing the words of Yosef. And it seemed good in the eyes of Pharaoh and his princes to appoint Yosef second to Pharaoh, over the whole land of Egypt.

Indeed, Hashem certainly fulfilled "כּוֹנֵן אֲשֻׁרָי" in protecting Yosef and enabling his footsteps to ascend each one of the royal steps all the way to Pharaoh's throne, thereby ensuring Yosef's rise to worldwide renown while still serving as a source of pride and salvation for Yaakov and his family.

Pasuk 4:
וַיִּתֵּן בְּפִי שִׁיר חָדָשׁ,
תְּהִלָּה לֵא-לֹהֵינוּ
And He put into my mouth a new song,
a praise to our Elokim.

Songs Amidst the Sorrow

At first glance there would seem to be little opportunity or desire to sing "a new song" in these tragic *parshiyos* revolving around Yosef.

Yet, in *Parshas Mikeitz* after Yaakov worriedly realized he had no choice but to send his sons back to Mitzrayim along with Binyamin in order to free Shimon and to obtain food for their family, Yaakov sent a variety of gifts to the Egyptian Viceroy and said: "קְחוּ מִזִּמְרַת הָאָרֶץ – Take of the land's glory,"[36] which literally means "Take from the *song* of the land!"

Rashi quotes *Targum Onkelos* who explains that "מִזִּמְרַת הָאָרֶץ" means "from that which is most praiseworthy in the land," and adds that the produce of the land of Israel is so special that everyone sings about it.[37] Thus, in addition to Yaakov inspiring his own family to think of songs of Israel and salvation, the implication is that Yaakov hoped that the produce of Eretz Yisrael would also inspire the Viceroy of Egypt to sing and be gladdened and pacified, and thereby act mercifully and compassionately toward the sons of Yaakov.

Furthermore, Chazal[38] tell us of Yaakov's granddaughter, Serach bas Asher, who would gently sing to Yaakov the lullaby of "עוֹד יוֹסֵף חַי – Yosef is still alive" to soothe Yaakov amidst his despair. Serach's singing also prepared the elderly Yaakov to ultimately receive the thrilling yet shocking news that Yosef was indeed still alive with the composure necessary for someone of Yaakov's advanced age.

That these songs of the "שִׁיר חָדָשׁ" are also tied to the Name אֱ-לֹהִים – "תְּהִלָּה לֵא-לֹהֵינוּ" – is most appropriate, for as noted above these were songs sung in the context of the danger and despair indicative of the *middas ha'din*. In addition, these songs emphasize being *matzdik* the *din*, coping while trusting that Hashem's designs are for the best.

The lesson is clear: Even amidst God's strict judgment, the Jewish soul can always find a way to sing.

---

[36] *Bereishis* 43:11.

[37] *Rashi* and *Targum Onkelos*, *Bereishis* 43:11, from *Bereishis Rabbah* 91:11.

[38] E.g., *Targum Yonasan*, *Bereishis* 46:17; *Midrash Sefer HaYashar*, *Bereishis*, *Vayigash* 9.

PARSHAH & TEHILLIM HAND IN HAND

Az Yashir in the Merit of Yosef

Rashi explains that the "שִׁיר חָדָשׁ" refers to the שִׁירַת הַיָּם,[39] also known as אָז יָשִׁיר, which Moshe and Bnei Yisrael sang after Hashem saved them by performing the miracle of *Krias Yam Suf* in which He simultaneously drowned the mighty Egyptian army on the seventh day following *Yetzias Mitzrayim*.

The connection to Yosef is clear. Chazal tell us: "בִּזְכוּת עַצְמוֹתָיו שֶׁל יוֹסֵף נִקְרַע הַיָּם לְיִשְׂרָאֵל – In the merit of the bones of Yosef, the sea split for Yisrael,"[40] as the *pasuk* says: "הַיָּם רָאָה וַיָּנֹס – The sea saw and fled."[41] Similarly, of Yosef in the context of the wife of Potiphar the Torah states: "וַיַּעֲזֹב בִּגְדוֹ בְּיָדָהּ וַיָּנָס וַיֵּצֵא הַחוּצָה" – And he left his garment in her hand and he fled and went outside."[42]

Adding a layer to this Chazal, my *rebbi*, Rabbi Shmuel Brazil, explained that the sea was reluctant to split, arguing that doing so would be contrary to the very nature with which Hashem bestowed it. However, when the sea saw the coffin of Yosef and recalled how Yosef overcame human nature in resisting the temptations of the wife of Potiphar, the sea acquiesced and changed its own nature as well, immediately splitting for the sake of Yosef's relatives, Bnei Yisrael.

As such, the "שִׁיר חָדָשׁ" of אָז יָשִׁיר was triggered by the merit of Yosef.

Pasuk 7:
זֶבַח וּמִנְחָה לֹא חָפַצְתָּ,
אָזְנַיִם כָּרִיתָ לִּי;
עוֹלָה וַחֲטָאָה
לֹא שָׁאָלְתָּ

---

[39] *Rashi, Tehillim* 40:4.
[40] *Bereishis Rabbah* 87:8.
[41] *Tehillim* 114:3.
[42] *Bereishis* 39:13.

Sacrifice and meal-offering You desired not, but ears You opened for me; burnt-offering and sin-offering You did not request.

The Attribute of Sincere Tribute

"עוֹלָה וַחֲטָאָה לֹא שָׁאָלְתָּ" and "זֶבַח וּמִנְחָה לֹא חָפַצְתָּ" echo the famous concept found throughout *Neviim* and *Kesuvim*: Hashem does not desire *korbanos* per se; rather, Hashem desires that our religious observance and service be performed with sincerity.[43]

While "מִנְחָה" here refers to a consecrated meal-offering or flour-offering, this word can also more generally refer to a "tribute." For example, in *Parshas Vayishlach* the Torah uses the word מִנְחָה four times[44] in describing the tribute that Yaakov sent Eisav to appease him.[45]

Similarly, in *Parshas Mikeitz*, once Yaakov reconciled himself to the terrifying fact that he had no choice but to send his remaining sons down to Mitzrayim, including his precious Binyamin, to confront the Viceroy who had already imprisoned Shimon and accused them all of being spies, Yaakov immediately started searching for a solution in order to protect his sons and placate the Viceroy.[46] What was Yaakov's first reaction? He told his sons to bring a מִנְחָה and said: "אִם כֵּן אֵפוֹא זֹאת עֲשׂוּ, קְחוּ מִזִּמְרַת הָאָרֶץ בִּכְלֵיכֶם, וְהוֹרִידוּ לָאִישׁ מִנְחָה – If it must be so, do this: take of the land's glory in your vessels and bring it down to the man as a מִנְחָה – as a tribute."[47]

In addition, when Yaakov's sons stood fearfully in the inner chambers of the Viceroy's home awaiting his arrival, what did they do? The Torah states: "וַיָּכִינוּ אֶת הַמִּנְחָה עַד בּוֹא יוֹסֵף" – They prepared the מִנְחָה, the tribute,

---

[43] E.g., *Yirmiyahu* 7:22–23, and *Tehillim* 50:8-14.
[44] *Bereishis* 32:14, 32:19, 32:22, and 33:10.
[45] Rashi, *Bereishis* 32:9.
[46] Rashi, *Bereishis* 43:11.
[47] *Bereishis* 43:11.

until Yosef came."[48] *Rashi* says that they continued to beautify the tribute by decorating it with pretty vessels.[49] The Torah then describes the actual presentation of the מִנְחָה to the Viceroy: "וַיָּבֹא יוֹסֵף הַבַּיְתָה וַיָּבִיאוּ לוֹ אֶת הַמִּנְחָה אֲשֶׁר בְּיָדָם הַבָּיְתָה – And Yosef returned home and they brought him the tribute that was in their hands, into the house."[50]

As shown above, a מִנְחָה in the form of a tribute, despite seeming to be a trivial element of the story, is prominently featured in the Torah's narrative. Unlike the insincere מִנְחָה described in *Tehillim* 40:7, *Parshas Mikeitz* features an important מִנְחָה insofar as it was sincerely devised by Yaakov and painstakingly delivered and prepared by his sons to properly honor the Egyptian Viceroy who held their lives in his hands.

How much more so must *our* daily sacrifices, tributes, *tefillos*, and requests be sincerely bestowed upon Hashem.[51]

Yosef's Skill of Listening

"אָזְנַיִם כָּרִיתָ לִּי – Ears You opened for me" is an intriguing expression, as it is a personification of Hashem listening to Dovid, to Yosef, and to every Jew.

However, in the context of *Parshas Mikeitz* this description has additional significance. For in Pharaoh's very first statement to Yosef he said: "I dreamt a dream but there is no one who can interpret it. But I have heard it said תִּשְׁמַע חֲלוֹם – that you hear a dream, to interpret it."[52] Pharaoh was acknowledging Yosef's reputation and skillfulness at listening to others and caring for them and their plights. Because of his listening and sensitivity, Yosef had the ability to understand and comprehend the hidden meaning of their dreams.[53]

---

[48] *Bereishis* 43:25.
[49] *Rashi, Bereishis* 43:25.
[50] *Bereishis* 43:26.
[51] See also *Tehillim* 20 for references to Yaakov and מִנְחָה.
[52] *Bereishis* 41:15.
[53] Based on *Rashi, Bereishis* 41:15.

Thus, the phrase "אָזְנַיִם כָּרִיתָ לִּי" need not only mean that Hashem listened to Yosef's (and Dovid's, and our own) prayers. It also refers specifically to Hashem Who bestowed upon *Yosef* the ability to listen. It is as if Yosef is recognizing and declaring: "Hashem, אָזְנַיִם כָּרִיתָ לִּי – my ears You opened for *me*" in blessing me with the ability to listen and to truly hear others who are in need and thereafter to discern how best to help them.

Pasuk 8:
אָז אָמַרְתִּי, הִנֵּה בָאתִי בִּמְגִלַּת סֵפֶר כָּתוּב עָלָי
Then I said, "Behold have I come with the *Megillas Sefer* – the Scroll of the Book – that is written for me!"

The Mysterious "*Megillos*" of Mitzrayim

In their commentaries on this *pasuk*, *Rashi* and the *Radak* teach that *Megillas Sefer* is simply a reference to the *Torah She'bichsav*, the Written Torah that guides each Jew, while the *Seforno* learns that it refers to the two personal *Sifrei Torah* a Jewish king is required to have written for himself: one to remain at home and the other to accompany him wherever he would go. Nonetheless, the expression *Megillas Sefer* is certainly mysterious and requires further exploration.

The Midrash tells us that while enslaved in Mitzrayim, the Jewish People had in their hands *megillos* – written scrolls that they would learn and delight in each Shabbos day, the one day each week that they had respite from their forced labor. The content of these *megillos* emphasized that Hashem would eventually redeem them from slavery, which strengthened and encouraged them during their subjugation.[54]

---

[54] *Shemos Rabbah* 5:18.

The *Maharzav* on the Midrash says that these *megillos* were comprised of all of *Sefer Bereishis*, and specifically the stories of Adam, Noach, the *Mabul*, the *Dor Haflagah*, and the Avos HaKedoshim, as well as all the prophecies and promises that the Avos received from Hashem.

Rav Yaakov Kamenetsky[55] suggests that the *Megillas Sefer* was comprised of *Sefer Iyov* and *Tehillim* 90 through 100, whose original authorship is attributed to Moshe Rabbeinu and included the *kapitel* of מִזְמוֹר שִׁיר לְיוֹם הַשַּׁבָּת,[56] which was especially appropriate for Shabbos study. Additionally, these specific writings focus on the enigmatic theme of "צַדִּיק וְרַע לוֹ, רָשָׁע וְטוֹב לוֹ – righteous people upon whom evil befalls, and wicked people who receive good."[57] Moshe knew this was exactly what the Jews suffering in slavery in Egypt needed to hear and internalize in order to withstand their daily toil and tortures.

While interesting, the above begs the question: what is the connection between *Megillas Sefer*, and especially its partial authorship by Moshe Rabbeinu, and *Tehillim* 40 and Yosef HaTzaddik?

Pirkei D'Rabi Eliezer[58] explains that Hashem first appeared to Moshe specifically in a burning bush because the Jewish People possess the flame of Yosef, as it says in the *Navi Ovadyah*: "וְהָיָה בֵית יַעֲקֹב אֵשׁ וּבֵית יוֹסֵף לֶהָבָה, וּבֵית עֵשָׂו לְקַשׁ – And the House of Yaakov will be a fire, and the House of Yosef will be a flame, and the House of Eisav will be straw"[59] and flammable thorns and thistles, just like a bush.

Later, toward the conclusion of the Torah when Moshe blessed the Tribe of Yosef at the end of his life, Moshe made an unexpected and seemingly unconnected reference to the *sneh*, the burning bush, where Hashem first revealed Himself to Moshe, and stated: "וּרְצוֹן שֹׁכְנִי סְנֶה; תָּבוֹאתָה לְרֹאשׁ יוֹסֵף – And the desire of Him that dwelt in the bush; let the

---

[55] *Emes L'Yaakov, Shemos* 5:9.
[56] *Tehillim* 92.
[57] E.g., *Brachos* 7a.
[58] *Pirkei D'Rabi Eliezer, perek* 39.
[59] *Ovadyah* 1:18.

blessing come upon the head of Yosef."⁶⁰ This association requires explanation.

Rabbi Shlomo Horwitz of Baltimore explained that Moshe himself must surely have been inspired by Yosef, for just as Moshe had grown up separated from family and in the palace of Pharaoh, prior to Moshe it was Yosef who had undergone a similar experience. More importantly, just as Yosef remained a *tzaddik* despite his environment, so too Moshe Rabbeinu took strength from Yosef and their shared experience in order to remain steadfast in his own *tzidkus*. As such, Moshe's final blessing to the Tribe of Yosef included a reference to the *sneh* in recognition of the crucial impact that Yosef's story had on the formative years of Moshe's life.

In light of the above, although Moshe is often credited as the one who provided, or at least contributed to a portion of, the "מְגִלַּת סֵפֶר" upon which the Jewish People relied so heavily in their time of enslavement, the additional words "כָּתוּב עָלָי" on a deeper level can refer to *Yosef*, who was a role model to a young Moshe in Egypt. In other words, it is as if Yosef is recognizing and declaring that the מְגִלַּת סֵפֶר was כָּתוּב עָלָי, i.e., written by Moshe amidst inspiration from *me*!

Pasuk 9:
וְתוֹרָתְךָ בְּתוֹךְ מֵעָי
And Your Torah is in my innermost parts.

Torah from One's Essence

Chazal tell us that the Avos, Yosef, and his brothers kept the entire Torah long before the Torah was formally gifted by Hashem to the Jewish People on Har Sinai. For example, the Avos kept Pesach centuries before *Yetzias Mitzrayim*.⁶¹

---

⁶⁰ *Devarim* 33:16.
⁶¹ E.g., *Rashi*, *Bereishis* 18:10 in connection with Avraham, and *Rashi*, *Bereishis* 27:9 in connection with Yitzchak.

Another example is found in *Parshas Mikeitz* in the context of Yosef as Viceroy having invited the sons of Yaakov to dine with him. On the phrase "וְהָכֵן וּטְבֹחַ טֶבַח" – slaughter and prepare the meat,"[62] the Gemara says that Yosef instructed that the meat be properly *shechted* for himself and his brothers.[63]

Yet another example in *Parshas Mikeitz* concerns Yosef cutting his hair before appearing before Pharaoh for the first time. Many commentators ask how Yosef could do so when the Gemara[64] says that Yosef was freed from prison on the day of Rosh Hashanah, a day on which haircuts are forbidden. However, because he was going to stand before Pharaoh, a non-Jewish king who wielded the power to execute him and who would have felt disrespected if Yosef appeared before him disheveled, Yosef analyzed his predicament in a halachic manner and concluded that he was not obligated to sacrifice his life, or even risk jeopardizing his life, in such a situation.

Indeed, Torah and mitzvos were intrinsically a part of Yosef and the Avos. Similar to Chazal's explanation that Avraham knew the Torah because his *kelayos*, kidneys, were like two wise men who taught Torah to him,[65] so too *pasuk* 9 here beautifully attests: "וְתוֹרָתְךָ בְּתוֹךְ מֵעָי" – Your Torah is in my innermost parts." For Yosef and the Avos, the Torah was not yet fully codified or available from the outside to be studied and absorbed in their hearts and minds in the way we strive to acquire Torah. Instead, they intuited the teachings of the Torah, discovering its laws from within the very fiber of their being. Torah was inherently part of their essence.

---

[62] *Bereishis* 43:16.
[63] *Chullin* 85a.
[64] *Rosh Hashanah* 10b.
[65] *Avos D'Rabi Nosson, perek* 33.

Pasuk 10:
בִּשַּׂרְתִּי צֶדֶק בְּקָהָל רָב,
הִנֵּה שְׂפָתַי לֹא אֶכְלָא;
ה׳, אַתָּה יָדָעְתָּ
**I proclaimed Your righteousness in a vast assembly,
behold my lips will not restrain;
Hashem, You know it.**

Recognizing Miracles of All Types

The commentators on *Tehillim* explain that "בִּשַּׂרְתִּי צֶדֶק בְּקָהָל רָב" requires crediting Hashem in a public setting, not just privately.[66] The most prominent example of this is the *hodaah*, thanksgiving, requirement incumbent upon Jews saved from one of the following life-threatening situations, which are considered to be *nissim geluyim*, revealed miracles: crossing a desert, navigating an ocean, healing from illness, and release from prison,[67] the latter of which applied to Yosef in *Parshas Mikeitz*.

In addition, the phrase "שְׂפָתַי לֹא אֶכְלָא; ה׳, אַתָּה יָדָעְתָּ" refers to the Jew's unrestrained and unlimited praise of Hashem, the consistency and magnitude of which only Hashem knows and which applies to the personal prayers of those who experience *nissim nistarim*, hidden miracles. Yosef as well was very attuned to hidden miracles in these *Parshiyos Hashavua*, constantly acknowledging the *Yad Hashem*, the Hand of God, in everything that he experienced,[68] especially as he saw the fulfillment of his dreams and the repentance of his brothers beginning to materialize in *Parshas Mikeitz* and culminating in next week's *Parshah*, *Vayigash*.

---

[66] E.g., *Radak, Tehillim* 40:10.
[67] *Brachos* 54b.
[68] E.g., *Bereishis* 41:16, and *Rashi, Bereishis* 39:3, from *Midrash Tanchuma, Vayeishev* 8.

The "World of Prayer"

As discussed in the previous chapter, the Midrash teaches that Yosef constantly acknowledged Hashem, either praising Hashem to others and/or davening to Hashem at all times.[69] As such, the expression "הִנֵּה שְׂפָתַי לֹא אֶכְלָא; ה', אַתָּה יָדָעְתָּ – Behold my lips will not restrain; Hashem, You know it," is most apropos to Yosef. Yosef did not just recognize Hashem's miracles; he actively and constantly acknowledged them, thus meriting to receive more and more by virtue of his holy lips continuously engaged in prayer and thanksgiving to Hashem.

As the *Bilvavi Mishkan Evneh*[70] emphasizes, each Jew can and should enter the profound world of the *Olam Shel Tefillah*, the World of Prayer. This is a vibrant spiritual world in which the Jew does not simply daven three times a day along with occasional *brachos* on food, etc.; it is an exciting new form of existence, a new way of life, in which our every action and activity is preempted by a *tefillah* to Hashem for assistance and success. Yosef HaTzaddik lived this way. Dovid HaMelech also lived this way, having proclaimed about himself: "וַאֲנִי תְפִלָּה – And I am prayer!"[71]

We can, and must, begin to live in such a wonderous world as well.

Haunting References to the Sons of Yaakov

Pasuk 10 and *Pasuk* 11 both contain the expression "קָהָל רָב – in a vast assembly."

Such terminology means more than just a nameless large crowd; it is a reference to the twelve sons of Yaakov – Yosef and his brothers – who would ultimately give rise to the vast assembly of the Twelve Tribes of the Jewish People, sometimes referred to as "קְהַל עֲדַת יִשְׂרָאֵל – the assembly of the Congregation of Yisrael."[72]

---

[69] *Bereishis Rabbah* 86:5 and *Maharzav* there.
[70] *Bilvavi Mishkan Evneh, chelek aleph, perek* 129.
[71] *Tehillim* 109:4.
[72] E.g., *Shemos* 12:6.

CHAPTER 10: MIKEITZ & TEHILLIM 40

Furthermore, the Gemara[73] discusses that every *shevet* among the Twelve Tribes, in addition to being part of the broader Jewish People, is also considered a "קָהָל" unto itself. Although Hashem promised Yaakov in *Parshas Vayishlach*: "גּוֹי וּקְהַל גּוֹיִם יִהְיֶה מִמֶּךָּ" – A nation and an assembly of nations shall descend from you,"[74] only one additional child, Binyamin, would thereafter be born to Yaakov, from whom the Tribe of Binyamin would directly emerge. As such, says the Gemara, we see from here that even a single tribe is considered a "קָהָל."

Moreover, the two references to "קָהָל" in *pesukim* 10 and 11 both use the expression "קָהָל רָב." The word "רָב" not only means "vast" and "great" but also means "fight," for example "רַבְתָּ אֶת רִיבָם" – [Hashem] You fought their fight."[75] This consistent combination of the words "קָהָל רָב" in *Tehillim* 40 and its connotation of "an assembly that fights" alludes to the hostile attitude that the brothers had toward Yosef, which reared its ugly head in *Parshas Vayeishev* when the brothers almost succeeded in killing Yosef before Yosef was sold into slavery.

Yes, the sons of Yaakov were a "קָהָל רָב" in all senses of the expression: they would become a vast collective of the Jewish People; they each had a status of a "קָהָל" in and of themselves; and they each were involved in a terrible "רָב" when fighting to eliminate Yosef. This antagonistic nature would prove to have both immediate and long-term negative repercussions, including the secession of the Ten Tribes from the greater nation as well as the *Asarah Harugei Malchus*, the Ten Martyrs, whose lives would be taken as an atonement for the selling of none other than Yosef.[76]

In light of the above, we must pause to contemplate the fact that the expression "קָהָל רָב" appears twice in *Tehillim* 40, the *kapitel* that parallels *Parshas Mikeitz* in which the brothers of Yosef would be forced to truly

---

[73] *Pesachim* 80a.
[74] *Bereishis* 35:11.
[75] From the *tefillah Bimei Matisyahu* said throughout Chanukah.
[76] E.g., see the Yom Kippur *Mussaf Shemoneh Esrei*.

commence the *teshuvah* process for the sale of Yosef. This is especially haunting when one examines the full context of both the simple and deeper meaning of *pesukim* 10 and 11, as discussed in this chapter. These *pesukim* teach us to draw ever closer to Hashem and one another, and not, *chas veshalom*, tear ourselves away from either or both.

Pasuk 11:
צִדְקָתְךָ לֹא כִסִּיתִי בְּתוֹךְ לִבִּי,
אֱמוּנָתְךָ וּתְשׁוּעָתְךָ אָמָרְתִּי;
לֹא כִחַדְתִּי חַסְדְּךָ וַאֲמִתְּךָ לְקָהָל רָב

Your righteousness I have not concealed within my heart, of Your faithfulness and Your salvation have I spoken; I have not concealed Your kindness and Your truth from the vast assembly.

Zechus Avos

This *pasuk* is a detailed declaration that all good and salvation comes from Hashem, which seems obvious but is all too often entirely overlooked. As such, this *pasuk's* pronouncement is refreshing and inspiring.

In addition, within this declaration we find many key terms, especially those that reference the Avos and Yosef, and in doing so this *pasuk* calls upon the *zechus Avos*, the merit of our Forefathers, further inspiring and protecting us:

- "צִדְקָתְךָ" is a reference to Yosef הַצַּדִּיק.
- "וּתְשׁוּעָתְךָ" is a reference to Yitzchak Avinu, who represents the *middah* of יְשׁוּעָה, and as discussed at length throughout this chapter is also a reference to Yosef who was similarly required to emulate the *middah* of יְשׁוּעָה.
- "חַסְדְּךָ" is a reference to Avraham Avinu, who was the embodiment of the *middah* of חֶסֶד.

- "וַאֲמִתְּךָ" is a reference to Yaakov Avinu, who was the embodiment of the *middah* of אֱמֶת.

Thus in *pasuk* 11, amidst our focus on and praise of Hashem, we also learn from and lean on our Forefathers as part of the continued bolstering of "אֱמוּנָתְךָ," our faith in You, Hashem.

The Ultimate Coverup

While declaring that righteousness, faithfulness, salvation, kindness, and truth are all unquestionably and unabashedly direct gifts from Hashem, this *pasuk* also contains an unusual double emphasis on the concept of not concealing and not hiding with the phrases "לֹא כִסִּיתִי" and "לֹא כִחַדְתִּי."

Amazingly, however, if there was ever a *Parshah* filled with disguise and concealment, it is *Parshas Mikeitz*! The Torah states that Yosef hid his identity from this brothers: "וַיַּרְא יוֹסֵף אֶת אֶחָיו וַיַּכִּרֵם; וַיִּתְנַכֵּר אֲלֵיהֶם וַיְדַבֵּר אִתָּם קָשׁוֹת – Yosef saw his brothers and he recognized them, but he acted like a stranger toward them and spoke with them harshly."[77] The Torah even repeats Yosef's deception in the very next *pasuk* and then recounts how he accused his brothers of being secret spies probing for weaknesses in Egypt's defenses in the hope of conquering the land.[78] Without listing the many examples found in the Torah and Chazal, suffice it to say that the entire *Parshas Mikeitz* and start of *Parshas Vayigash* revolve around Yosef's clandestine machinations and manipulations of his brothers; in this sense, these *Parshiyos* are predicated entirely upon acts of "כִסִּיתִי" and "כִחַדְתִּי."

Indeed, while Dovid in *Tehillim* 40:11 declares that he will never cover up Hashem's greatness, Yosef HaTzaddik engaged in one of the Torah's most elaborate cover-ups in keeping his identity secret from his own brothers.

---

[77] *Bereishis* 42:7.
[78] *Bereishis* 42:9–10.

However, Yosef's actions concealed for the purpose of revealing. Whether it was in helping to ensure that his God-given dreams were fulfilled or in giving his brothers the opportunity to do a complete and sincere *teshuvah* for their cruel mistreatment of him twenty-two years earlier, and even in giving his brothers the opportunity to do a complete *teshuvah* for the insensitivity that they showed toward their father Yaakov and for the suffering they caused him,[79] each of Yosef's many hidden actions were acts of purity and selflessness, focused solely on repairing wrongdoings and thereby revealing the greatness of Hashem in its many forms.

Pasuk 12:

אַתָּה ה' לֹא תִכְלָא רַחֲמֶיךָ מִמֶּנִּי;
חַסְדְּךָ וַאֲמִתְּךָ תָּמִיד יִצְּרוּנִי

**You, Hashem, do not withhold Your mercy from me;
may Your kindness and Your truth always protect me.**

Pasuk 13:

כִּי אָפְפוּ עָלַי רָעוֹת עַד אֵין מִסְפָּר,
הִשִּׂיגוּנִי עֲוֹנֹתַי וְלֹא יָכֹלְתִּי לִרְאוֹת;
עָצְמוּ מִשַּׂעֲרוֹת רֹאשִׁי וְלִבִּי עֲזָבָנִי

**For encircled me have innumerable evils,
overtaken me have my sins and I am unable to see;
they have become more numerous than the hairs on my
head, and my courage has abandoned me.**

---

[79] E.g., *Darchei Noam* of Slonim, *Vayigash* 2002.

Pasuk 14:
רְצֵה ה' לְהַצִּילֵנִי;
ה', לְעֶזְרָתִי חוּשָׁה
**May it be Your will, Hashem, to rescue me;
Hashem, to my assistance hasten.**

We Always Need Hashem, and Must Always Ask For More

Pesukim 12, 13, and 14 contain a unified declaration that although enemies and evil may always encircle the Jew (*pasuk* 13), we trust and affirmatively state that Hashem will not abandon the Jew but rather protect him with His *rachamim*, *chessed*, and *emes* (*pasuk* 12). Moreover, we know and ask: "רְצֵה ה' לְהַצִּילֵנִי; ה', לְעֶזְרָתִי חוּשָׁה" – that Hashem desire us, save us, and even rush to our assistance (*pasuk* 14).

The above also conveys the fundamental concept that a Jew can never become complacent and expect life to proceed smoothly on its own. Rather, we are in constant need of Hashem's protection and must always daven to Him. Moreover, as Rav Shimshon Pincus often emphasized, even when things are going *well*, we must still daven to Hashem and ask Him for additional blessing and goodness, as there is no limit to Hashem's capabilities and kindness.

In fact, Rav Pincus derived this *yesod* from none other than Yaakov's wife Leah when she gave birth to Yosef's eldest brothers in *Parshas Toldos*. When Reuven, Shimon, and Levi were born, each time Leah asked Hashem for more blessings and more closeness to Yaakov.[80] However, after she gave birth to her fourth son, Yehudah, she only declared: "הַפַּעַם אוֹדֶה אֶת ה'" – This time I will give thanks to Hashem."[81] Although she gave Hashem a grand "Thank You," because she did not ask Hashem for

---

[80] *Bereishis* 29:32–34.
[81] *Bereishis* 29:35.

even more blessings, she did not receive them. Leah's greatest blessings came to a halt, as the Torah then immediately states: "וַתַּעֲמֹד מִלֶּדֶת – then she stopped giving birth."[82] This should inspire *us* to always ask Hashem for more.

Yosef and His Hair

Tehillim 40's reference in *pasuk* 13 to evils that "עָצְמוּ מִשַּׂעֲרוֹת רֹאשִׁי – have become more numerous than the hairs on my head," is particularly relevant to Yosef, for not once but twice did Yosef's focus on his hair trigger problems for him.

First, at the start of *Parshas Vayeishev* the Torah describes Yosef as "וְהוּא נַעַר – He was a youth,"[83] which *Rashi* says implies that he would act immaturely, fixing his hair and grooming his eyes to look attractive.[84] These are acts that bespeak a focus atypical, even unbecoming, of a pious son of Yaakov Avinu.

Later in that same *Parshah*, the Torah tells us that Yosef was handsome, and *Rashi* explains that once Yosef saw himself elevated to a position of authority in the house of Potiphar, he began to eat and drink and curl his hair. This prompted Hashem to judge Yosef's actions critically, for such actions are incongruous for a son aware that his father was mourning for him at that very moment. As a result, Hashem used Yosef's appearance to attract and provoke the wife of Potiphar to cast her eyes upon him and to challenge his morals.[85]

That *Tehillim* 40 contains a reference to hair at all, much less that it uses hair as an analogy for enemies and dangers, presents a surprising yet powerful image upon which to reflect.

---

[82] *Bereishis* 29:35.
[83] *Bereishis* 37:2.
[84] *Rashi, Bereishis* 37:2, from *Bereishis Rabbah* 84:7.
[85] *Rashi, Bereishis* 39:6, from *Midrash Tanchuma, Vayeishev* 8.

CHAPTER 10: MIKEITZ & TEHILLIM 40

Pasuk 15:
יֵבֹשׁוּ וְיַחְפְּרוּ יַחַד מְבַקְשֵׁי נַפְשִׁי לִסְפּוֹתָהּ;
יִסֹּגוּ אָחוֹר וְיִכָּלְמוּ חֲפֵצֵי רָעָתִי
**May they be put to shame and disgrace, all together,
those who seek my soul to put an end to it;
may they draw back and be humiliated,
those who desire my misfortune.**

The Reaction of the Brothers

This *pasuk* literally contains a description of the reaction of Yosef's brothers when he revealed his true identity to them in the upcoming *Parshah* of *Vayigash*. The Torah tells us: "וַיֹּאמֶר יוֹסֵף אֶל אֶחָיו אֲנִי יוֹסֵף, הַעוֹד אָבִי חָי; וְלֹא יָכְלוּ אֶחָיו לַעֲנוֹת אֹתוֹ כִּי נִבְהֲלוּ מִפָּנָיו – And Yosef said to his brothers, 'I am Yosef. Is my father still alive?' But his brothers could not answer him because they were left disconcerted before him."[86] *Rashi* explains that the brothers couldn't answer "מִפְּנֵי הַבּוּשָׁה," because they were too ashamed about what they had done to him,[87] as in the expression "יֵבֹשׁוּ וְיַחְפְּרוּ יַחַד" meaning collective embarrassment and shame.

Furthermore, in the next *pasuk* Yosef responds: "גְּשׁוּ נָא אֵלַי – Come close to me, please"[88] and thus spoke more gently to them to reduce their embarrassment. Why did he beckon them to come closer? *Rashi* explains that this was because Yosef saw them "נְסוֹגִים לְאָחוֹר – backing away in shame," which is identical to the expression "יִסֹּגוּ אָחוֹר."

The Attempted Murder of Yosef

It should be noted that the word "לִסְפּוֹתָהּ – to put an end to" used here in *pasuk* 15 is an unusual, even strange, choice of terminology to describe killing someone.

---

[86] *Bereishis* 45:3.
[87] *Rashi*, *Bereishis* 45:3, from *Midrash Tanchuma*, *Mikeitz* 5.
[88] *Bereishis* 45:4.

Amazingly, however, if you take the letter י from the end of the word "נַפְשִׁי" which immediately precedes the word "לְסִפּוֹתָה," and if you take the first four letters from the word "לְסִפּוֹתָה" itself, these letters spell out the word "לְיוֹסֵף – to Yosef," a hidden but now clear indication that the murderous phrase of "נַפְשִׁי לְסִפּוֹתָה" applies "to Yosef," the victim at the hand of his brothers who tried to "put an end to him" in *Parshas Vayeishev*.

Pasuk 16:
יָשֹׁמּוּ עַל עֵקֶב בָּשְׁתָּם,
הָאֹמְרִים לִי הֶאָח הֶאָח

**May they be desolate because of their shaming,
those who say about me "Aha! Aha!"**

Yosef's Final Rebuke of His Brothers

There is much to learn from this *pasuk* when viewed from the lens of *Parshas Mikeitz* and the story of Yosef. For, as mentioned in *pasuk* 15, Yosef's brothers were embarrassed when he revealed his identity; consequently, the use of the word "בָּשְׁתָּם" here in *pasuk* 16 certainly applies to the brothers.

Additionally, the brothers were even more embarrassed when Yosef confronted them with the words "אֲנִי יוֹסֵף, הַעוֹד אָבִי חָי" – I am Yosef. Is my father still alive?"[89] as if to say to them: "How dare you that you did not take into account how our father Yaakov would react to my alleged death! It is a wonder that you did not kill him from shock: I am Yosef, and you are fortunate that my father is still alive and that you did not indirectly kill him!" Therefore, "יָשֹׁמּוּ עַל עֵקֶב בָּשְׁתָּם" can also mean that the brothers were utterly embarrassed "עַל עֵקֶב," due to the rebuke they received from Yosef

---

[89] *Bereishis* 45:3.

for the lack of sensitivity they showed toward their father יַעֲקֹב, whose very name is derived from the word "עָקֵב."[90]

Furthermore, in the very next *pasuk* Yosef states: "אֲנִי יוֹסֵף אֲחִיכֶם, אֲשֶׁר מְכַרְתֶּם אֹתִי מִצְרָיְמָה – I am Yosef, your brother, whom you sold to Egypt,"[91] which seems to include an obvious and unnecessary statement by Yosef that they are "אַחִים – brothers."

Incredibly, *Tehillim* 40:16 contains another unusual phrase: "הָאֹמְרִים לִי הֶאָח הֶאָח – those who say about me 'Aha! Aha!'" However, we can interpret this phrase in an entirely different manner by understanding it as an intense, powerful challenge from Yosef to his brothers: "הָאֹמְרִים לִי הֶאָח הֶאָח – you who questioned and challenged regarding me: הֶאָח הֶאָח – are you my אָח, are you really my brother?" As such, this was a strong message of *mussar* from Yosef that he was not treated like a brother at all. He was rejected, disowned, almost killed, and actually sold by his own flesh and blood – certainly not shown the compassion and mercy a brother deserves – all of which adds a powerful additional layer of rebuke from Yosef to his siblings when he revealed himself as "אֲנִי יוֹסֵף אֲחִיכֶם – I am Yosef your brother."

As a final note, it must be made abundantly clear that Yosef's machinations and even embarrassment of his brothers was not a product of a thirst for revenge, nor was it personal in any way. As noted in Chapter 9, Yosef always retained the spiritual wellbeing of his brothers foremost on his mind.[92] Rather, Yosef HaTzaddik caused to unfold situations that enabled the brothers to be tested in a manner similar to the one in which they had failed with Yosef twenty-two years earlier, all in a way that enabled the brothers to achieve a *tikkun* and repair their misdeeds by doing a full-fledged *teshuvah*.

---

[90] *Bereishis* 25:26.
[91] *Bereishis* 45:4.
[92] *Yareiach LaMoadim, Chanukah* pp. 531–32, citing *Chochmah U'Mussar* of the Alter of Kelm.

Pasuk 18:
עֶזְרָתִי וּמְפַלְטִי אַתָּה,
אֱ-לֹהַי אַל תְּאַחַר
My help and my rescuer You are,
my Elokim, do not delay.

No Delays

This closing phrase of *Tehillim* 40, in which we ask Hashem to rescue us immediately, ends the *kapitel* on a high note of enthusiasm and urgency. Remarkably, this high note is not simply designed for the ordinary reciter of this *kapitel Tehillim*, but rather is especially poignant for those focused on intertwining *Tehillim* with the *Parshah*. Indeed, this closing phrase alludes to the impending reunion of Yosef with his precious father and family soon to take place in the upcoming *Parshas Vayigash*.

There, Yosef commands his brothers: "מַהֲרוּ וַעֲלוּ אֶל אָבִי וַאֲמַרְתֶּם אֵלָיו: כֹּה אָמַר בִּנְךָ יוֹסֵף, שָׂמַנִי אֱ-לֹהִים לְאָדוֹן לְכָל מִצְרָיִם, רְדָה אֵלַי אַל תַּעֲמֹד – Hurry, and go up to my father and say to him: 'So said your son Yosef: God has set me as a master to all Egypt. Come down to me; do not delay.'"[93] This *pasuk* twice emphasizes to "hurry" and "not delay." Thereafter, Yosef reiterates: "וּמִהַרְתֶּם וְהוֹרַדְתֶּם אֶת אָבִי הֵנָּה – You must hurry, and bring my father down here."[94] Finally, Yosef tells his brothers "אַל תִּרְגְּזוּ בַּדָּרֶךְ – Do not become agitated on the way,"[95] which the Gemara reveals was a reference to Yosef instructing his brothers to refrain even from immersing themselves in holy matters of *halachah*, for such Torah discussions might distract them and slow them down on their journey.[96] So great was Yosef's sense of urgency for the brothers to return home to Yaakov with the unimaginably great news that Yosef was alive and well!

---

[93] *Bereishis* 45:9.
[94] *Bereishis* 45:13.
[95] *Bereishis* 45:24.
[96] *Rashi, Bereishis* 45:24, from *Taanis* 10b; see also *Nachalas Yaakov*.

Thus, the above expressions and concepts parallel the closing words of *Tehillim* 40: "אַל תְּאַחַר – do not delay," in anticipation of the excitement that is yet to come in the next *Parshah*.

May we, and all Klal Yisrael, be *zocheh* to witness the ultimate revelation of "אֱ-לֹהַי אַל תְּאַחַר – My God, do not delay" with the coming of *Moshiach Tzidkeinu* speedily in our days, *b'miheirah b'yameinu*, *Amen*!

CHAPTER 11

PARSHAS VAYIGASH & TEHILLIM 48

פָּרָשַׁת וַיִּגַּשׁ / תְּהִלִּים מח

TEHILLIM 48 – תְּהִלִּים מח

1	A song, a psalm, by the sons of Korach.	שִׁיר מִזְמוֹר לִבְנֵי קֹרַח.	א
2	Great is Hashem and much praised, in the City of our God, His Mountain of Holiness.	גָּדוֹל ה' וּמְהֻלָּל מְאֹד, בְּעִיר אֱ-לֹהֵינוּ, הַר קָדְשׁוֹ.	ב
3	Fairest of sites, joy of all the earth, Mount Tzion, by the northern side of the City of the great King.	יְפֵה נוֹף, מְשׂוֹשׂ כָּל הָאָרֶץ, הַר צִיּוֹן, יַרְכְּתֵי צָפוֹן, קִרְיַת מֶלֶךְ רָב.	ג
4	God in the City's palaces is known as the Stronghold.	אֱ-לֹהִים בְּאַרְמְנוֹתֶיהָ נוֹדַע לְמִשְׂגָּב.	ד
5	For behold the kings assembled, they came together.	כִּי הִנֵּה הַמְּלָכִים נוֹעֲדוּ, עָבְרוּ יַחְדָּו.	ה
6	They saw and indeed were astounded, they were confounded and fled in haste.	הֵמָּה רָאוּ כֵּן תָּמָהוּ, נִבְהֲלוּ נֶחְפָּזוּ.	ו

CHAPTER 11: VAYIGASH & TEHILLIM 48

7	Trembling gripped them there, convulsions like a woman in birth travail.	רְעָדָה אֲחָזָתַם שָׁם, חִיל כַּיּוֹלֵדָה.	ז
8	With a wind from the east, You smashed the ships of Tarshish.	בְּרוּחַ קָדִים, תְּשַׁבֵּר אֳנִיּוֹת תַּרְשִׁישׁ.	ח
9	As we heard, so we saw in the City of Hashem, Master of Legions, in the City of our God, may God establish it to eternity, Selah!	כַּאֲשֶׁר שָׁמַעְנוּ כֵּן רָאִינוּ בְּעִיר ה' צְבָא-וֹת, בְּעִיר אֱ-לֹהֵינוּ, אֱ-לֹהִים יְכוֹנְנֶהָ עַד עוֹלָם סֶלָה.	ט
10	We hoped, God, for Your kindness in the midst of Your Sanctuary.	דִּמִּינוּ, אֱ-לֹהִים, חַסְדֶּךָ בְּקֶרֶב הֵיכָלֶךָ.	י
11	Like Your Name, God, so is Your praise to the ends of the earth; righteousness fills Your right hand.	כְּשִׁמְךָ, אֱ-לֹהִים, כֵּן תְּהִלָּתְךָ עַל קַצְוֵי אֶרֶץ; צֶדֶק מָלְאָה יְמִינֶךָ.	יא
12	May gladdened be Mount Tzion, rejoice the daughters of Yehudah, because of Your judgments.	יִשְׂמַח הַר צִיּוֹן, תָּגֵלְנָה בְּנוֹת יְהוּדָה, לְמַעַן מִשְׁפָּטֶיךָ.	יב
13	Walk throughout Tzion and encircle her, count her towers.	סֹבּוּ צִיּוֹן וְהַקִּיפוּהָ, סִפְרוּ מִגְדָּלֶיהָ.	יג
14	Mark well in your hearts her ramparts, raise up her palaces, so that you may retell it to the succeeding generation.	שִׁיתוּ לִבְּכֶם לְחֵילָה, פַּסְּגוּ אַרְמְנוֹתֶיהָ, לְמַעַן תְּסַפְּרוּ לְדוֹר אַחֲרוֹן.	יד
15	For this is God, our God, forever and ever; He will guide us eternally.	כִּי זֶה אֱ-לֹהִים, אֱ-לֹהֵינוּ עוֹלָם וָעֶד; הוּא יְנַהֲגֵנוּ עַל-מוּת.	טו

INTRODUCTION: THE UNITY OF YERUSHALAYIM AND YAAKOV & SONS: *YACHDAV*

On its surface, *Tehillim* 48 focuses on the beauty and holiness of Yerushalayim and the Beis HaMikdash. However, *Tehillim* 48 also contains within it many hidden references to the events of *Parshas Vayigash*, including the climactic confrontation between Yehudah and Yosef, Yosef's revelation of his identity to his brothers and father, Yaakov's reaction to the news that Yosef is alive and well, and the resultant relocation to Egypt by Yaakov and his entire family at Yosef's request.

The *Sfas Emes*[1] explains that *Parshas Vayigash* is a *Parshah* of *shalom* and *achdus*, peace and unity, as ultimately true comradery and harmony are formed among all twelve of the sons of Yaakov. Similarly, Yerushalayim and the Beis HaMikdash would eventually become the primary locations of *shalom* and *achdus* on earth, as Dovid HaMelech famously declared: "יְרוּשָׁלַיִם הַבְּנוּיָה: כְּעִיר שֶׁחֻבְּרָה לָּהּ יַחְדָּו – Yerushalayim built up: the City that unites us all together."[2]

In both such instances, how was that peace and unity achieved? According to the *Sfas Emes*, it depended upon connection to the "*Daas Elyon* – Knowledge of the Supreme One." In Kabbalistic thought, *Daas Elyon* refers to the "Higher Understanding," the God-like perspective from which the realm of *ruchniyus* is perceived as reality, and from which the Jew can directly connect to the *Ratzon Hashem* – the Will of Hashem.

---

[1] *Sfas Emes, Vayigash* 5647.
[2] *Tehillim* 122:3.

CHAPTER 11: VAYIGASH & TEHILLIM 48

When the Will of Hashem is revealed and internalized, differences and disagreements between Jews cease to matter, and all unite "יַחְדָּו" under the common goal of fulfilling Hashem's Will. The *Sfas Emes* says that the *Daas Elyon* was revealed to the family of Yaakov in *Parshas Vayigash*, and that later in history all Klal Yisrael merited to see and experience firsthand the *Daas Elyon* in the Beis HaMikdash.

As such, we can now more deeply appreciate the connection between *Parshas Vayigash* and *Tehillim* 48. *Parshas Vayigash* is a *Parshah* of unity and "יַחְדָּו" in which the sons of Yaakov reunited in the manner described in *Tehillim* 48 as "כִּי הִנֵּה הַמְּלָכִים נוֹעֲדוּ, עָבְרוּ יַחְדָּו – For behold the kings assembled, they came together,"[3] just as *Tehillim* 48 so vividly describes Am Yisrael's meriting to experience the blessing of true "יַחְדָּו" in the Beis HaMikdash under the proud banner of "כְּעִיר יְרוּשָׁלַיִם הַבְּנוּיָה: שֶׁחֻבְּרָה לָּהּ יַחְדָּו."

In addition, explains the *Sfas Emes*, even after the destruction of the Beis HaMikdash the Jewish People continue to encounter, experience, and enjoy the *Daas Elyon* through a different medium – the holiness of *Shabbos Kodesh*, the day designed for us to simply stop and reattach ourselves to the Will of Hashem. Therefore, as we delve into the study of *Tehillim* 48 and the *Parshas HaShavua* of Shabbos *Parshas Vayigash*, may we merit to discover the *Daas Elyon* in the intertwining of *Tehillim* 48, *Parshas Vayigash*, and *Shabbos Kodesh*; and may the *Daas Elyon* inspire us and unite us with Hashem and with each other, blessing us with the *shalom* and *achdus* of "יַחְדָּו" that we so desperately desire.

---

[3] *Tehillim* 48:5.

THE MANY CONNECTIONS BETWEEN PARSHAS VAYIGASH & TEHILLIM 48

Pasuk 1:

שִׁיר מִזְמוֹר לִבְנֵי קֹרַח

A song, a psalm, by the sons of Korach.

Sons of Korach and Sons of Yaakov

At first glance the sons of Korach seem to have nothing to do with *Parshas Vayigash*. After all, Korach appears much later in the Torah in the time of *Yetzias Mitzrayim* and the *Dor Hamidbar* of *Sefer Bamidbar*.[4] Furthermore, unlike Yaakov, Korach revealed himself to be a *rasha* who negatively impacted his family and neighbors, and even caused their deaths.

However, the connection between Yaakov and Korach becomes clear when we look more closely at Korach's sons. Their father was a wicked man who thirsted for power and revolted against Aharon HaKohen and Moshe Rabbeinu by challenging their leadership, and in so doing had the audacity to challenge even *Hashem*. In the end, Korach was killed by Hashem, and his entire family was caught in the retribution, swallowed by the earth and cast into the depths of Gehinnom. However, Chazal tell us that during their descent into Gehinnom, the children of Korach developed thoughts of *teshuvah* in their hearts, and even sang *shirah* to Hashem as they were plummeting. As a result, Hashem spared them by creating a little "bubble" of sorts that suspended them and protected them from falling into

---

[4] *Bamidbar, Perek* 16.

CHAPTER 11: VAYIGASH & TEHILLIM 48

Gehinnom. Ultimately, Hashem transported them back to the land of the living and reintegrated them into the Jewish People.[5]

Parshas Vayigash as well focuses on children: the twelve sons of the righteous Yaakov Avinu, who at that time were also on the verge of sinking into the depths of Gehinnom. Yehudah had already put his *Olam Hazeh* and *Olam Haba* in jeopardy when he promised to take responsibility for the safety of Binyamin,[6] and all eleven brothers found themselves on the verge of war with the Viceroy of Egypt[7] whom they did not yet know was their very own brother Yosef, the same Yosef whom they had sold into servitude and was presumed to be a slave, assimilated, or dead. In addition, their father Yaakov had already resigned himself to punishment in Gehinnom due to the alleged death of Yosef[8] and was terribly worried for the lives of the imprisoned Shimon, for his beloved Binyamin, and for all his remaining children.

Moreover, as Yehudah aggressively approached the Egyptian Viceroy at the start of *Vayigash*, he threatened to kill Pharaoh, to initiate a bloody war against Egypt, and even directly threatened the life of the Viceroy who was actually Yosef in disguise.[9] Imagine what Yaakov would have thought about his own already doomed status had his sons truly waged war against Egypt in what would have been an accidental civil war against their own brother Yosef, and suffered familial casualties on both sides! The predicament of the sons of Yaakov at the start of *Parshas Vayigash* is truly frightening.

But like the sons of Korach, all twelve of the sons of Yaakov instead found themselves in a situation arranged by Hashem in which there was still time to avoid bloodshed and still time to do *teshuvah*. And *teshuvah*

---

[5] *Rashi, Bamidbar* 26:11, from *Sanhedrin* 110a.
[6] *Rashi, Bereishis* 44:32, from *Tanchuma Yashan, Vayigash* 4.
[7] *Rashi, Bereishis* 44:18, from *Bereishis Rabbah* 93:6.
[8] *Rashi, Bereishis* 37:35, from *Midrash Tanchuma, Vayigash* 9.
[9] *Rashi, Bereishis* 44:18, from *Bereishis Rabbah* 93:6.

they did, thanks to many Godly machinations coupled with their own power of free choice involved in their reconciliation with Yosef.

Not only do the above accounts of the *bnei Korach* and *bnei Yaakov* parallel one another, it could very well be that the sons of Korach, who had no doubt studied the Torah's accounts and lessons regarding the sons of Yaakov – and perhaps even heard first or second-hand accounts thereof – were inspired by the sons of Yaakov to repent as they descended into Gehinnom, never relinquishing their faith in Hashem even at the last moment and in the seemingly most hopeless of situations.

Korach's Redemption

It should also be noted that in *Parshas Vayechi* when Yaakov blessed his son Levi, Yaakov specifically davened that his own name not be associated with Korach's evil uprising against Moshe and Aharon in the Torah. However, in other instances in which Korach and his family are mentioned in a praiseworthy manner such as with regard to the *duchan* service (the platform upon which the families of Levi stood to sing as part of the services in the Beis HaMikdash), Yaakov is clearly associated with the family of Korach.[10] So too here in *Tehillim* 48, Yaakov and his family reconnect with Korach and his family in the positive context of repentance and never-ending faith in Hashem, as encapsulated by Dovid HaMelech's Divinely inspired words.

Therefore, due to the interplay between *Parshas Vayigash* and *Tehillim* 48:1 that associates Yaakov and his sons with Korach and his sons in a positive manner, *Tehillim* 48 stands as a symbol of *redemption* for Korach himself.

Indeed, the *Shelah Hakadosh*[11] reveals that in the "end," i.e., in the future time of Moshiach, even Korach will be reintegrated into Klal Yisrael, as alluded to in the well-known phrase said each Shabbos and

---

[10] *Rashi, Bereishis* 49:6, from *Bereishis Rabbah* 98:5.

[11] *Shenei Luchos HaBris, Torah She'bichsav.*

Yom Tov: "צַדִּיק כַּתָּמָר יִפְרָח – A righteous man like a date palm will flourish,"[12] whose "end" letters spell out the name "קֹרַח."

We should also add that in the phrase "צַדִּיק כַּתָּמָר יִפְרָח," the word "צַדִּיק" hints to Yosef HaTzaddik, while "תָּמָר" is also the name of the famed wife of Yehudah ben Yaakov, from whose union Moshiach ben Dovid will be a descendent. All this further hints to the fact that the sons of Yaakov were not only an inspiration to the sons of Korach, but also were an inspiration to Korach himself, ultimately motivating him to "יִפְרָח – sprout" once again even from the depths of Gehinnom, renewed and purified in the time of Moshiach.

Pasuk 2:
גָּדוֹל ה' וּמְהֻלָּל מְאֹד,
בְּעִיר אֱ-לֹהֵינוּ, הַר קָדְשׁוֹ
Great is Hashem and much praised,
in the City of our God, His Mountain of Holiness.

Experience Yerushalayim and the Beis HaMikdash

This *pasuk* contains references to Yerushalayim: "עִיר אֱ-לֹהֵינוּ – the City of our God," and to the holy site of the Beis HaMikdash: "הַר קָדְשׁוֹ – Hashem's Mountain of Holiness." In fact, this *pasuk* begins a uniquely beautiful assortment of such descriptions that extend throughout the entirety of the *kapitel*:

- *Pasuk 3*: "יְפֵה נוֹף, מְשׂוֹשׂ כָּל הָאָרֶץ, הַר צִיּוֹן, יַרְכְּתֵי צָפוֹן, קִרְיַת מֶלֶךְ רָב – Fairest of sites, joy of all the earth, Mount Tzion, by the northern side of the City of the great King."
- *Pasuk 4*: "אֱ-לֹהִים בְּאַרְמְנוֹתֶיהָ נוֹדַע לְמִשְׂגָּב – God in the City's palaces is known as the Stronghold."

---

[12] *Tehillim* 92:13.

- *Pasuk* 9: "כַּאֲשֶׁר שָׁמַעְנוּ כֵּן רָאִינוּ בְּעִיר ה' צְבָא-וֹת, בְּעִיר אֱ-לֹהֵינוּ, אֱ-לֹהִים יְכוֹנְנֶהָ עַד עוֹלָם סֶלָה – As we heard, so we saw in the City of Hashem, Master of Legions, in the City of our God, may God establish it to eternity, Selah!"

- *Pasuk* 10: "דִּמִּינוּ, אֱ-לֹהִים, חַסְדֶּךָ בְּקֶרֶב הֵיכָלֶךָ – We hoped, God, for Your kindness in the midst of Your Sanctuary."

- *Pasuk* 12: "יִשְׂמַח הַר צִיּוֹן, תָּגֵלְנָה בְּנוֹת יְהוּדָה, לְמַעַן מִשְׁפָּטֶיךָ – May gladdened be Mount Tzion, rejoice the daughters of Yehudah, because of Your judgments."

- *Pasuk* 13: "סֹבּוּ צִיּוֹן וְהַקִּיפוּהָ, סִפְרוּ מִגְדָּלֶיהָ – Walk throughout Tzion and encircle her, count her towers."

- *Pasuk* 14: "שִׁיתוּ לִבְּכֶם לְחֵילָה, פַּסְּגוּ אַרְמְנוֹתֶיהָ, לְמַעַן תְּסַפְּרוּ לְדוֹר אַחֲרוֹן – Mark well in your hearts her ramparts, raise up her palaces, so that you may retell it to the succeeding generation."

One who focuses on these evocative *pesukim* while reciting *Tehillim* 48 can almost feel the stones of Yerushalayim's streets under his feet. It is as if this *kapitel* takes us on a tour of Jerusalem: "Fairest of sites, joy of all the earth… Walk throughout Tzion and encircle her, count her towers… Mark well in your hearts… so that you may retell it to the succeeding generation."

Yet the tour is not just of the City and its palaces and fortresses, but even to the ancient holy site of Har Tzion – the Beis HaMikdash and its *Heichal* and Sanctuary – the place where our ancestors experienced the ultimate *deveikus* with Hashem, the place where *ruach hakodesh* was absorbed, and the place where "by the northern side" *korbanos* were offered and atonement for sin was achieved. *Tehillim* 48 transports us back in time to our Nation's glorious past.

Tehillim 48 also propels us into the future. It transports us to the place we longingly face during every *Shemoneh Esrei*, and to the time that we all dream of witnessing with our own eyes. This *kapitel* transports us to "יְרוּשָׁלַיִם הַבְּנוּיָה – Jerusalem Rebuilt" in all its holiness and grandeur,

Yerushalayim: the place where we can truly become "וְיַחְדָּו" – one with each other and one with Hashem.[13]

Our Monday Morning Tour of Yerushalayim

It must be noted that *Tehillim* 48 is incorporated into our weekly davening as a *Shir Shel Yom*, Song of the Day, that the Leviim (including the family of Korach) would sing in the Beis HaMikdash. To which day of the week does *Tehillim* 48 correspond? Surprisingly, the answer is Monday.[14]

Monday? A day so far away from Shabbos? A day of *din* and strict judgment?[15] A day that starts the grueling work week? A day dreaded by laborers and students, young and old?

Yes. Exactly! The message is a vital one: before we run to start the work week and perform our necessary *hishtadlus*, we must first become properly oriented to what really matters, to what a Jew truly hopes for. Wherever we are and whatever we are going to do in the days ahead, our first step is to take a tour of Yerushalayim through the *Shir Shel Yom*. We even teleport our minds and hearts to the Beis HaMikdash to reorient ourselves.

This is how we must leave shul every Monday morning: longing for Yerushalayim and for the rebuilding of the Third Beis HaMikdash; longing for the ultimate closeness to Hashem.

With this mindset borne from the "experience" of our Monday morning tour of Yerushalayim, we can then confidently trust that our week will be filled with actions and intentions that bring *Moshiach Tzidkeinu* closer each day.

---

[13] See the Introduction to this chapter; see also *Tehillim* 122:3 and *Tehillim* 48:5.
[14] *Rosh Hashanah* 31a.
[15] *Shabbos* 129b.

The Yosef-Binyamin Yearning for Yerushalayim

In addition to the approach of the *Sfas Emes* discussed in the Introduction to this chapter, there are several additional connections between *Tehillim* 48's emphasis on Yerushalayim and the Beis HaMikdash, and its association with *Parshas Vayigash*.

At first glance, the connection is not abundantly clear. After all, most of *Parshas Vayigash* takes place not in Eretz Yisrael but in Mitzrayim and revolves around the Jewish People leaving Israel for Egypt. Furthermore, Yerushalayim certainly had not yet taken center stage as the holiest city of the Jews, and the Beis HaMikdash would not be built until the generation of Shlomo HaMelech approximately seven hundred years later.

Nevertheless, *Parshas Vayigash* recounts the dramatic reuniting of Yosef and his brothers, which includes the most poignant of scenes: the reunion of Rochel Imeinu's two sons, the dear brothers Yosef and Binyamin. They met, they hugged, and they cried. And we cry with them.

But why exactly did they cry? The Torah describes their reunion vividly: "וַיִּפֹּל עַל צַוְּארֵי בִנְיָמִן אָחִיו וַיֵּבְךְּ; וּבִנְיָמִן בָּכָה עַל צַוָּארָיו" – And he [Yosef] fell upon his brother Binyamin's neck and cried; and Binyamin cried upon his [Yosef's] neck."[16] Did they cry out of joy? Did they cry out of sadness? Did they cry for the twenty-two years they lost? Did they cry for their father, Yaakov? Did they cry for their mother, Rochel?

No! Chazal tell us that in that moment they cried for the Beis HaMikdash. They cried for the Beis HaMikdash still yet to be built in the then distant future and that was destined to be destroyed. In Tanach, the word "צַוָּאר – neck," alludes to the Beis HaMikdash.[17] Thus, *Rashi* explains that when Yosef fell upon his brother Binyamin's neck and cried, Yosef was crying over the two holy Temples, the two *Batei Mikdash*, that were destined to be located in land bestowed by Hashem to the Tribe of Binyamin hundreds of years later, and which in the end would both be

---

[16] *Bereishis* 45:14.

[17] E.g., *Rashi, Devarim* 33:12; *Rashi, Shir HaShirim* 7:5.

destroyed. Furthermore, *Rashi* explains that when Binyamin fell upon Yosef's neck and cried, he was crying over the future Mishkan Shiloh, an interim site treated as a Beis HaMikdash destined to be located in the portion of Yosef through the Tribe of Ephraim, and which was also going to be destroyed.[18]

Yosef and Binyamin did not cry for themselves, nor did they even cry for the individual suffering of one another. They cried for Hashem's Beis HaMikdash.

It is also striking that they did not cry for their own suffering and loss when *their* Beis HaMikdash would be destroyed; they cried for the loss and suffering that the *other* was going to endure. And, by extension, they cried for the loss of all Jews everywhere in all generations, a *middah* reminiscent of that of their mother Rochel Imeinu, who continuously cries for all Jews in exile, as Yirmiyahu HaNavi bewails: "רָחֵל מְבַכָּה עַל בָּנֶיהָ – Rochel cries for her children [the Jewish People]."[19] Furthermore, in displaying an unprecedented love for the Beis HaMikdash, Yosef and Binyamin also displayed *ahavas chinam*, unsolicited and unqualified love for "the other." In this way, they once again emulated their mother Rochel, who displayed the ultimate *ahavas chinam* when she gave the *simanim*, signs, to her sister Leah,[20] thereby enabling Leah's marriage to Rochel's beloved Yaakov and jeopardizing Rochel's own marriage to him.

Such behavior may seem even supernatural, but such behavior is vital to the Redemption, as *ahavas chinam* is the pathway to the *tikkun* for the *sinas chinam*, baseless hatred, that was the underlying cause of the destruction of Second Beis HaMikdash and, sadly, remains the underlying cause of our current *Galus Edom* today.[21]

This love for the Beis HaMikdash as well as this unconditional, selfless love for one's fellow Jew that is so fundamental to our meriting the

---

[18] *Rashi, Bereishis* 45:14, from *Bereishis Rabbah* 93:13 and *Megillah* 16b.
[19] *Yirmiyahu* 31:14.
[20] *Rashi, Bereishis* 29:25, from *Megillah* 13b.
[21] E.g., *Yoma* 9b.

rebuilding of the *Third* Beis HaMikdash is what so deeply connects the Yerushalayim/Beis HaMikdash emphasis in *Tehillim* 48 to *Parshas Vayigash*.

Berlin Is Not Yerushalayim

We would be remiss not to address an additional connection: the fact that in *Parshas Vayigash* the family of Yaakov *left* Eretz Yisrael and went down to Mitzrayim (albeit with Hashem's permission).[22] Doing so started a process that would ultimately lead to the enslavement of the Jewish People in Egypt for 210 years. But it would also lead to many of the greatest moments in history: the fulfillment of Hashem's prophetic promises to Avraham at the *Bris Bein Habesarim*, the powerful Ten Plagues, the grand Exodus from Egypt, the incredible Splitting of the Sea of Reeds, Hashem's graciousness in giving the Torah to the Jewish People on Har Sinai, and then – after forty miraculous years in the Sinai Desert – the Jewish People's all-important conquering of Eretz Yisrael and the building of the holy Beis HaMikdash. All the above are vital pieces of Hashem's master plan that continues to this very day.

While the descent to Egypt in *Parshas Vayigash* would initially usher in a time of unprecedented prosperity for the rapidly increasing family of Yaakov, the very last *pasuk* in *Vayigash* states: "וַיֵּשֶׁב יִשְׂרָאֵל בְּאֶרֶץ מִצְרַיִם, בְּאֶרֶץ גֹּשֶׁן; וַיֵּאָחֲזוּ בָהּ, וַיִּפְרוּ וַיִּרְבּוּ מְאֹד – Thus Yisrael settled in the land of Egypt, in the land of Goshen; they took holdings in it and they were fruitful and multiplied greatly."[23] On the phrase "וַיֵּאָחֲזוּ בָהּ – they took holdings in it," *Rashi* describes that they bought houses and estates and formed land holdings in Egypt.

However, Rav Shimshon Rafael Hirsch[24] explains that "וַיֵּאָחֲזוּ בָהּ" means something different, something troubling. They felt comfortable in

---

[22] *Bereishis* 46:3.
[23] *Bereishis* 47:27.
[24] The Hirsch Chumash, *Bereishis* 47:27.

CHAPTER 11: VAYIGASH & TEHILLIM 48

Egypt. They felt like they belonged. They took possession of their own lands and may have been content to remain there forever. Therein lies the flaw, the danger. This is why *Parshiyos Vayigash* and *Vayechi* are uncharacteristically סְתוּמָה, closed off in the Torah without the usual number of blank spaces to separate and distinguish them: to reflect that "נִסְתְּמוּ עֵינֵיהֶם וְלִבָּם שֶׁל יִשְׂרָאֵל – closed were the eyes and hearts of Am Yisrael"[25] in a spiritual manner, and that the suffering and enslavement had commenced. For once the family of Yaakov entrenched themselves comfortably in Egypt, the *galus* and enslavement instantly began, even if only subconsciously.

We can add that the above criticism of the mindset and behavior of "וַיֹּאחֲזוּ בָהּ" is even alluded to in the expression in *Tehillim* 48:7: "רְעָדָה אֲחָזָתַם שָׁם – trembling grabbed hold of them there," as the words "וַיֹּאחֲזוּ" and "אֲחָזָתַם" share the same *shoresh*. As Rabbi Meir Simchah of Dvinsk so ominously forewarned of the German Jewry of his time: "They think that Berlin is Jerusalem... from there will go forth a great storm that will uproot them."[26] When the Jew believes he is taking hold of a foreign land and begins to integrate himself there, eventually fear will take hold of him, and what was thought to be solid and stable will be uprooted, as was the case in Nazi Germany, *yemach shemam*, in which "וַיֹּאחֲזוּ בָהּ" turned into the nightmare of "רְעָדָה אֲחָזָתַם שָׁם."

Therefore, in tandem with *Parshas Vayigash* in which Yaakov and his entire family would leave Eretz Yisrael for Mitzrayim and remain there, initially thrive there, and become content there, comes the corresponding *Tehillim* 48 to emphasize the beauty and glory not of Egypt or any other land but only of *Yerushalayim*, "עִיר אֱ-לֹהֵינוּ," the City of our God and the location of "הַר קָדְשׁוֹ," the holy Beis HaMikdash. *Tehillim* 48 describes the one and only setting in which a Jew should ever feel completely at home.

---

[25] *Rashi, Bereishis* 47:28.
[26] *Meshech Chochmah, Vayikra* 26:44.

By no coincidence, these vital sentiments are also echoed by the *Haftarah* of *Parshas Vayigash*, which concludes with three *pesukim* revolving around Hashem's future closeness to the Jewish People in His Sanctuary that is the Beis HaMikdash:[27]

וְנָתַתִּי אֶת מִקְדָּשִׁי בְּתוֹכָם לְעוֹלָם...
...and I shall place My Sanctuary among them forever.

וְהָיָה מִשְׁכָּנִי עֲלֵיהֶם וְהָיִיתִי לָהֶם לֵא-לֹהִים; וְהֵמָּה יִהְיוּ לִי לְעָם
My dwelling place will be on them, and I will be for them a God; and they will be to Me a People.

וְיָדְעוּ הַגּוֹיִם כִּי אֲנִי ה' מְקַדֵּשׁ אֶת יִשְׂרָאֵל; בִּהְיוֹת מִקְדָּשִׁי בְּתוֹכָם לְעוֹלָם
Then the nations will know that I am Hashem, Who sanctifies Yisrael; when My Sanctuary is among them forever.

While *Parshas Vayigash* temporarily drew Bnei Yisrael away from the Holy Land, *Tehillim* 48 and the *Haftarah* remind us where our heart is and for what our soul truly yearns: Yerushalayim and the rebuilding of the Beis HaMikdash!

The Monday *Shir Shel Yom* and Yosef

There is another layer of connection between *Tehillim* 48 as the *Shir Shel Yom* for Monday and *Parshas Vayigash's* central focus: Yosef HaTzaddik.

The Gemara states that the reason *Tehillim* 48 is the *Shir Shel Yom* for Monday is because *pasuk* 2 contains the proclamation: "גָּדוֹל ה' וּמְהֻלָּל מְאֹד – Great is Hashem and much praised," which is a reference to the fact that on the second day of Creation "חִלֵּק מַעֲשָׂיו וּמָלַךְ עֲלֵיהֶן – Hashem separated His works and ruled over them,"[28] dividing between the upper *rakia* (firmament/waters), and the lower rakia. At that point in time Hashem elevated Himself and sat high above in the upper realms.[29]

---

[27] *Yechezkel* 37:26–28.
[28] *Rosh Hashanah* 31a.
[29] *Rashi, Rosh Hashanah* 31a.

CHAPTER 11: VAYIGASH & TEHILLIM 48

Such a phenomenon – the distinction and divide between upper and lower, holy and mundane, and closeness to Hashem and distance from Hashem – is tailor-made for Yosef, whose very essence assists the Jewish People in bridging these gaps. As we discussed in Chapter 9 of this *sefer*, Yosef is referred to as "HaTzaddik" and represents the *middah* of *Yesod*, which is cryptically described as: "כִּי כֹל בַּשָּׁמַיִם וּבָאָרֶץ – For all that is in heaven and earth."[30] Indeed, the true *tzaddik* such as Yosef HaTzaddik is able to bridge and even recombine heaven and earth as well as the upper *rakia* and the lower *rakia*, while simultaneously inspiring others to do the same by coalescing the spiritual and the physical into one holistic unit fused with *ruchniyus* and holiness dedicated to service of Hashem.

Pasuk 3:
יְפֵה נוֹף, מְשׂוֹשׂ כָּל הָאָרֶץ, הַר צִיּוֹן,
יַרְכְּתֵי צָפוֹן, קִרְיַת מֶלֶךְ רָב
Fairest of sites, joy of all the earth, Mount Tzion,
by the northern side of the City of the great King.

Fairest of Sites: References to Yosef

In the words "יְפֵה נוֹף – Fairest of sites," which describes Yerushalayim and the Beis HaMikdash, we find an additional allusion to Yosef, who was himself described by the Torah as being "יְפֵה תֹאַר וִיפֵה מַרְאֶה – Beautiful in form and fair to look upon."[31] In fact, the *Zohar Hakadosh* states this precisely: "יְפֵה נוֹף דָּא אִיהוּ יוֹסֵף הַצַּדִּיק דִּכְתִיב בֵּיהּ וַיְהִי יוֹסֵף יְפֵה תֹאַר וִיפֵה מַרְאֶה – Fairest of sites: this is Yosef HaTzaddik, of whom the *pasuk* states 'And it was that Yosef was beautiful in form and fair to look upon.'"[32]

---

[30] *I Divrei HaYamim* 29:11.
[31] *Bereishis* 39:6.
[32] *Zohar Hakadosh* 1:206b.

In addition, there are other linguistic connections to be found. The words "יוֹסֵף" and "יְפֵה נוֹף" have a similar ring to them. Upon closer examination, the letters of the words "יְפֵה נוֹף" contain the same letters as the name יוֹסֵף (י, ו, ף), except that in יְפֵה נוֹף there is no ס. However, ס has a *gematria* of 60, and 61 with the *kollel* (the letter itself).[33] Amazingly, the phrase יְפֵה נוֹף contains the extraneous non-יוֹסֵף letters of ה and נ, and together with the ו from the immediately prior word "קָדְשׁוֹ" combine in *gematria* to the number 61, which covers the shortfall of the missing ס plus the *kollel* for יוֹסֵף. Stated differently, the *gematria* of Yosef with the *kollel* is 157, and the *gematria* of "...וֹ...יְפֵה נוֹ..." is also 157. This is yet another illustration of how both the revealed and hidden aspects of Yerushalayim and Yosef are so very intricately intertwined.

Furthermore, the above connection to the word "קָדְשׁוֹ," which refers to Hashem's holiness, reveals that the beauty of Yerushalayim and the beauty of Yosef were not relegated to physical appearance alone, but rather their physical beauty was a result of an inner spiritual beauty born of *kedushah* and connection to Hashem.

Regardless of these additional links and layers, the overarching message is clear: just as Yerushalayim is the fairest and most holy of all cities, so too was Yosef HaTzaddik the fairest and holiest of all the sons of Yaakov.

Beis HaMikdash: *Teshuvah* and Joy to All

Rashi[34] on the words "מְשׂוֹשׂ כָּל הָאָרֶץ, הַר צִיּוֹן, יַרְכְּתֵי צָפוֹן" explains that Har Tzion refers to the Beis HaMikdash. *Rashi* then states that Har Tzion was such a "joy to all of the earth" because it was a place of *kaparah* and forgiveness through *korbanos* and through the personal *teshuvah* process that accompanied these animal sacrifices. In fact, the reference to

---

[33] Regarding the use and importance of the *"kollel"* in *gematria*, see e.g., *Shabbos Malkesa*, pp. 23–25.
[34] *Rashi, Tehillim* 48:3.

the "northern side" refers to the northern part of the Temple Courtyard, where the ritual slaughtering of atonement offerings took place.

In addition, the Beis HaMikdash was a place of atonement for Jew and non-Jew alike, and as such, it was the "מְשׂוֹשׂ כָּל הָאָרֶץ" – source of joy for *all* of the lands and nations. For example, the Gemara tells us that the bulls sacrificed on Sukkos number seventy in total, corresponding to the seventy nations of the world who were protected through the merit of these sacrifices.[35] Chazal also teach that if the destroyers of the Beis HaMikdash had only known how much the Beis HaMikdash protected them, they never would have sought to desecrate or destroy it.[36] In addition, the *pasuk* in the *Navi Yeshayahu* famously states of the universality of the Beis HaMikdash as the place of forgiveness:

> וַהֲבִיאוֹתִים אֶל הַר קָדְשִׁי וְשִׂמַּחְתִּים בְּבֵית תְּפִלָּתִי, עוֹלֹתֵיהֶם וְזִבְחֵיהֶם לְרָצוֹן עַל מִזְבְּחִי, כִּי בֵיתִי בֵּית תְּפִלָּה יִקָּרֵא לְכָל הָעַמִּים – And I will bring them to My holy mountain and will gladden them in My House of Prayer; their elevation offerings and feast offerings will find favor on My Altar, for My House will be called a 'House of Prayer' for all of the nations.[37]

For Yosef, his brothers, and their father Yaakov, *Parshas Vayigash* centers around the *teshuvah* process as well. Moreover, here *teshuvah*, which is commonly translated as "repentance," additionally refers to the act of "returning" to one another and reuniting, as the word תְּשׁוּבָה is rooted in the word שָׁב, meaning "to return." Both the repentance and the returning brought deep *simchah* and joy, forms of "מָשׂוֹשׂ" that can hardly be matched.

---

[35] *Sukkah* 55b.
[36] E.g., *Midrash Tanchuma, Mikeitz* 2.
[37] *Yeshayahu* 56:7.

PARSHAH & TEHILLIM HAND IN HAND

The Immeasurable Joy of Yaakov and of Our Kings

The use of the word "רַב" in the phrase "קִרְיַת מֶלֶךְ רָב" – the City of the great King," corresponds to the famous words proclaimed by Yaakov in *Parshas Vayigash* that also included Yaakov's use of the word "רַב" upon hearing, and actually believing, the incredible news that indeed Yosef was alive! Yaakov declared: "רַב, עוֹד יוֹסֵף בְּנִי חָי – There is much! My son Yosef still lives."[38]

Rashi explains that while רַב typically means "much" or "great," in the context of Yaakov and Yosef it refers specifically to an abundance of joy and gladness[39] and in that regard, also ties in beautifully to the accompanying phrase of "מְשׂוֹשׂ כָּל הָאָרֶץ." It was the universal yet profound gladness of a father who discovered that his beloved child was not dead but rather alive, combined with a unique gladness augmented exponentially by virtue of it being the gladness of a *tzaddik* such as Yaakov in response to the *spiritual* success of a *tzaddik* such as Yosef. Such joy is immeasurable.

The same can be said of the expression "מֶלֶךְ רָב" in *Tehillim* 48. Whether it refers to Dovid HaMelech,[40] the *Melech HaMoshiach*,[41] or even more so to our *Melech Malchei HaMelachim Hakadosh Baruch Hu*, the greatness of each does not result in rulership through fear or an iron fist, but rather through rulership accompanied by abundant joy and gladness among Am Yisrael. It is joy of a magnitude so "רַב" – so vast and great, that it is beyond human comprehension.

Pasuk 4:
אֱ-לֹהִים בְּאַרְמְנוֹתֶיהָ נוֹדַע לְמִשְׂגָּב
God in the City's palaces is known as the Stronghold.

---

[38] *Bereishis 45:28.*
[39] *Rashi, Bereishis 45:28*
[40] *Ibn Ezra; Radak.*
[41] *Radak.*

CHAPTER 11: VAYIGASH & TEHILLIM 48

Hashem Is Our Stronghold

This *pasuk* as well is linked to the story of *Parshas Vayigash*. Here, Hashem is described as "מִשְׂגָּב – the Stronghold" to Whom we flee for safety and protection. This concept is often associated specifically with Yaakov Avinu. For example, in a pasuk from *Tehillim* that is also woven into many places in our daily davening, Dovid HaMelech states: "ה׳ צְבָא-וֹת עִמָּנוּ; מִשְׂגָּב לָנוּ אֱ-לֹהֵי יַעֲקֹב סֶלָה – Hashem, Master of Legions, is with us; a Stronghold for us is the God of Yaakov, Selah!"[42] Furthermore, in the *Selichos* prayers we state "עֲנֵנוּ מִשְׂגַּב אִמָּהוֹת עֲנֵנוּ – Answer us, Stronghold of the Matriarchs, answer us," as we call upon the merit of the four Imahos all of whom were righteous women lovingly linked to Yaakov Avinu: his wife Rochel, his wife Leah, his mother Rivkah, and his grandmother Sarah!

The use of the word "בְּאַרְמְנוֹתֶיהָ" here (along with the additional reference to "palaces" in *pasuk* 14) reveals an important principle. While luxurious palaces are different from and usually much more vulnerable than a stronghold such as a castle or fort, when *Hashem* is one's Stronghold, any and every site becomes fortified no matter what it is and where it is located, as famously expressed by Dovid HaMelech in the words "שַׁלְוָה בְּאַרְמְנוֹתָיִךְ – tranquility in your palaces."[43]

This was always the approach of Yaakov Avinu. Even as he was confronted by the terrifying foes such as Lavan and Eisav, he made sure to always stay connected to Hashem. And thereafter, Hashem reciprocated by becoming Yaakov's Stronghold: his "מִשְׂגָּב לָנוּ אֱ-לֹהֵי יַעֲקֹב."

The same is true of Yerushalayim and of all Jewish communities – both those within Israel and worldwide. Especially in these trying times, the more we place our trust in Hashem, the more Hashem in turn protects us

---

[42] *Tehillim* 46:8.
[43] *Tehillim* 122:7.

Pasuk 5:
כִּי הִנֵּה הַמְּלָכִים נוֹעֲדוּ, עָבְרוּ יַחְדָּו
For behold the kings assembled, they came together.

When the Kings Clash and Then Reconcile

In what is perhaps the most pivotal connection between *Tehillim* 48 and *Parshas Vayigash*, Chazal reveal to us that the *Parshah's* opening phrase: "וַיִּגַּשׁ אֵלָיו יְהוּדָה – And Yehudah approached him [Yosef]"[44] corresponds to the *pasuk* "כִּי הִנֵּה הַמְּלָכִים נוֹעֲדוּ, עָבְרוּ יַחְדָּו," which refers to the confrontation between the two kings, Yehudah and Yosef at the start of *Parshas Vayigash* in which they clashed, burned with anger, and nearly attacked one another.[45]

It is known that Yehudah and Yosef are each referred to as kings: Yosef was the Viceroy of Egypt, and Yehudah was the leader of the brothers and destined to become the forefather of Jewish Kingship.

Indeed, the Davidic Dynasty that began with Dovid HaMelech and continued through his son Shlomo HaMelech as the main kingship of the Jewish People passed from father to son for generations, is traced back to Yehudah as its progenitor by Divine design. The *Melech HaMoshiach* will also be from the Davidic Dynasty, as we say daily in the *brachah* of *V'LiYerushalayim* in *Shemoneh Esrei*: "וְכִסֵּא דָוִד מְהֵרָה לְתוֹכָהּ תָּכִין" – And the throne of Dovid, speedily within it [Yerushalayim] may You establish." This *brachah* is then immediately followed by the *brachah* of *Es Tzemach Dovid*, a blessing focused entirely on the reestablishment of the Davidic reign.

---

[44] *Bereishis* 44:18.

[45] *Yalkut Shimoni, Bereishis* 150.

CHAPTER 11: VAYIGASH & TEHILLIM 48

Yosef too contained royalty in his blood as the very first Jewish king, Shaul HaMelech, was from the Tribe of Binyamin. Additionally, at various times in Jewish history kings rose from the Tribe of Ephraim, one of two tribal offshoots of Yosef (along with the Tribe of Menashe).

The *Haftarah* to *Parshas Vayigash*[46] focuses on reuniting the divided kingdoms of Yehudah and Yosef in the time of Moshiach and states:

קַח לְךָ עֵץ אֶחָד וּכְתֹב עָלָיו לִיהוּדָה וְלִבְנֵי יִשְׂרָאֵל חֲבֵרָו; וּלְקַח עֵץ אֶחָד וּכְתוֹב עָלָיו לְיוֹסֵף עֵץ אֶפְרַיִם וְכָל בֵּית יִשְׂרָאֵל חֲבֵרָו – Take for yourself one branch and write upon it: for Yehudah and the children of Israel his companions; then take another branch and write upon it: for Yosef, the branch of Ephraim and all of the house of Israel and his companions.[47]

The *Haftarah* continues: "אֶחָד אֶל אֶחָד, לְךָ לְעֵץ אֶחָד; וְהָיוּ לַאֲחָדִים וְקָרַב אֹתָם בְּיָדֶךָ – One to another, for yourself into one branch; and they will become united and join them together in your hand."[48] Thereafter, the *Haftarah* describes that once the Nation is reunited, Hashem will ensure that a scion of Dovid HaMelech will ultimately be the one to rule over all. Then the Jewish People will return to the land of Eretz Yisrael given by Hashem to none other than "לְעַבְדִּי, לְיַעֲקֹב – to My servant, to Yaakov."[49]

Indeed, the confrontation between Yehudah and Yosef at the start of *Parshas Vayigash* foreshadows the many internal rifts and divides that have befallen Am Yisrael throughout Jewish history. More importantly however, the *Parshah's* peaceful outcome between Yosef, Yehudah, and all the brothers, as well as the *Haftarah's* poignant prophecy of peace, foreshadow the future promise of "יַחְדָּו," togetherness and *achdus* among Am Yisrael.

---

[46] *Yechezkel, Perek* 37.
[47] *Yechezkel* 37:16.
[48] *Yechezkel* 37:17.
[49] *Yechezkel* 37:24–25.

In addition, when we finally merit the time of *Yemos HaMoshiach*, we will witness the sacred collaboration between Moshiach ben Yosef and Moshiach ben Dovid during which the latter, the *Melech HaMoshiach* as Hashem's holy representative here on earth, will reunite the Jewish People and rightfully reclaim the Davidic throne, forever transforming the hostile and warlike "כִּי הִנֵּה הַמְּלָכִים נוֹעֲדוּ, עָבְרוּ יַחְדָּו," into the tranquil and peaceful "יְרוּשָׁלַיִם הַבְּנוּיָה: כְּעִיר שֶׁחֻבְּרָה לָּהּ יַחְדָּו."

Pasuk 6:

הֵמָּה רָאוּ כֵּן תָּמָהוּ,
נִבְהֲלוּ נֶחְפָּזוּ

**They saw and indeed were astounded,
they were confounded and fled in haste.**

The Reaction of the Brothers to Yosef's Reveal

Similar to the discussion in Chapter 10 in connection with *Parshas Mikeitz* and *Tehillim* 40:15, Chazal[50] teach that this *pasuk* is literally a detailed description of the reaction of Yosef's brothers when he revealed his true identity to them in *Parshas Vayigash*.

There, the Torah so vividly recounts what transpired and states: "וַיֹּאמֶר יוֹסֵף אֶל אֶחָיו אֲנִי יוֹסֵף, הַעוֹד אָבִי חָי; וְלֹא יָכְלוּ אֶחָיו לַעֲנוֹת אֹתוֹ כִּי נִבְהֲלוּ מִפָּנָיו" – And Yosef said to his brothers, 'I am Yosef. Is my father still alive?' However, his brothers could not answer him because they were נִבְהֲלוּ – disconcerted before him."[51] The use of the word "נִבְהֲלוּ" specifically ties into the expression of "הֵמָּה רָאוּ כֵּן תָּמָהוּ, נִבְהֲלוּ," and alludes to the realization of Yosef's brothers that they were suddenly standing at the mercy of the one sibling they had betrayed, resulting in their astonishment and perhaps even fear.

---

[50] *Yalkut Shimoni, Bereishis* 150.
[51] *Bereishis* 45:3.

Furthermore, in the Torah's very next *pasuk* Yosef says to them "גְּשׁוּ נָא אֵלַי – Come close to me please,"[52] thereby speaking to them in a gentler manner. Chazal explain that Yosef intentionally changed his tone because he saw them retreating in shame.[53] As such, the above ties into the expression of "נֶחְפָּזוּ – fled in haste," alluding to the brothers' initial attempt to run away from Yosef.

Pasuk 7:
רְעָדָה אֲחָזָתַם שָׁם,
חִיל כַּיּוֹלֵדָה
**Trembling gripped them there,
convulsions like a woman in birth travail.**

Yosef's Visceral Reaction That Could Not Be Held Back

This *pasuk* describes Yosef's emotional reaction to Yehudah's plea at the start of *Parshas Vayigash*, a reaction that resulted in Yosef having no choice but to reveal his identity to his brothers.

It began with "וְלֹא יָכֹל יוֹסֵף לְהִתְאַפֵּק – Yosef was unable to hold back"[54] insofar as he was unable to suppress his feelings. As a result, "וַיִּתֵּן אֶת קֹלוֹ בִּבְכִי – His voice burst forth with crying"[55] that was so intense that it was heard beyond his home and even echoed throughout all of Egypt.[56]

The above descriptions by the Torah coupled with the words of *Tehillim* 48:7 enable us to envision and empathize with Yosef's visceral reaction as he was completely overtaken בִּבְכִי – with crying, רְעָדָה – trembling, and חִיל – convulsions, while at the same time he emotionally

---

[52] *Bereishis 45:4.*
[53] *Rashi, Bereishis 45:4.*
[54] *Bereishis 45:1.*
[55] *Bereishis 45:2.*
[56] *Bereishis 45:2.*

and tearfully hugged, kissed, and reconciled with his brothers who were extremely moved and cried as well.

The Loss of Rochel Looms Over All

In addition, the expression "חִיל כַּיּוֹלֵדָה – convulsions like a woman in birth travail" placed here by Dovid HaMelech in the context of *Parshas Vayigash* and the reuniting of the brothers brings to mind Rochel Imeinu's death while giving birth to Yaakov's youngest child, Binyamin. That such a thought is intertwined with the reunion of Rochel's sons Yosef and Binyamin poignantly reminds us that the loss of Rochel Imeinu loomed large over the lives of Yaakov and his family.

However, "חִיל כַּיּוֹלֵדָה" also reminds us that although a woman in labor may convulse and endure the most extreme pain, she will find her suffering worthwhile when it results in the birth of her child. So too, the initial losses and separations endured by Yosef and Binyamin, who were first bereft of their mother and later even lost each other for twenty-two long years, were followed by the epic moment in *Parshas Vayigash* when they reconnected with one another and reunited all the sons of Yaakov together with them.

Pasuk 8:
בְּרוּחַ קָדִים, תְּשַׁבֵּר אֳנִיּוֹת תַּרְשִׁישׁ
With a wind from the east,
You smashed the ships of Tarshish.

Yissachar and Zevulun

Tarshish was a major non-Jewish Mediterranean seaport with a powerful navy. As such, this *pasuk* is a general description of Hashem protecting Eretz Yisrael from invading fleets. However, ships were used not only for war, but also for commerce.

Thus, the reference to "אֳנִיּוֹת – ships" is particularly relevant to Yaakov's son Zevulun and family, who are mentioned in *Parshas*

Vayigash[57] and whom Yaakov blessed in next week's *Parshah*, *Vayechi*, as follows: "זְבוּלֻן לְחוֹף יַמִּים יִשְׁכֹּן; וְהוּא לְחוֹף אֳנִיּת" – Zevulun will dwell by the seashores. He will be at the ship's harbor."[58] This teaches that Zevulun will earn a living by conducting business at ports and on the seas.

This *brachah* also impacted Yaakov's son Yissachar and family who are also mentioned in *Parshas Vayigash*.[59] The Tribes of Yissachar and Zevulun merited a special symbiotic relationship in that the Tribe of Zevulun would engage in commerce and thereby provide financial support not only to themselves but also to the Tribe of Yissachar. The Tribe of Yissachar was then free to fully engage in the study of Torah without worry for their livelihood. Their Torah learning would also serve as a merit for Zevulun in return.[60]

Wishing to be Shipwrecked in Eretz Yisrael

Rav Chayun explains that this *pasuk* echoes statements made by non-Jewish businessmen who sailed to Eretz Yisrael. Upon beholding the beauty of the land, the holy sites, and the *kedushah* that is all so vividly described in *Tehillim* 48, they would lament their lot in life, wishing they had been born as Jews. So strong was their regret and desire that they would even wish that God would bring a powerful wind to smash their ships so that they would be forced to remain in Eretz Yisrael and make it their home.[61] Of course, even without being shipwrecked, in many instances these businessmen did indeed choose to convert to Judaism and leave their old lives behind.[62]

---

[57] *Bereishis* 46:14.
[58] *Bereishis* 49:13.
[59] *Bereishis* 46:13.
[60] *Rashi, Bereishis* 49:13, from *Midrash Rabbah* 99:9.
[61] Rav Chayun, as cited in *Me'am Lo'ez, Tehillim* 48:8.
[62] E.g., *Rashi, Devarim* 33:19, from *Sifrei, Devarim* 354.

This same type of *Kiddush HaShem* was exemplified by Yaakov, his sons, and their entire family, as all of Mitzrayim was enamored with them and came to respect them and that which they represented.[63]

Yaakov's Soul and Spiritual Status, Restored

Of course, the use of the word "רוּחַ" here in the phrase "בְּרוּחַ קָדִים" when intertwined with *Parshas Vayigash* expresses a powerful connection, for this word can mean much more than simply "wind." The word "רוּחַ" also connotes "spirit" and "soul."

The word רוּחַ applied to Yaakov in the crucial moment of his recognition that indeed Yosef was alive and had remained righteous in Egypt. For twenty-two years Yaakov had been in a constant state of mourning for Yosef, a state of mind that prevented him from attaining the level of joy required to be a vessel capable of being filled by the Divine Presence of Hashem. However, upon seeing the wagons sent by Yosef, which proved that Yosef was indeed alive and well both physically and spiritually, the Torah tells us: "וַתְּחִי רוּחַ יַעֲקֹב אֲבִיהֶם – Then the רוּחַ, spirit, of their father Yaakov was revived."[64] This meant that the *Shechinah* returned to Yaakov,[65] along with the overarching רוּחַ נְבוּאָה – spirit of prophecy that enabled him to receive direct communication from Hashem.[66]

Indeed, Yaakov's original spiritual status, his original "רוּחַ" of spirit and soul, was completely restored. This is alluded to in the expression of *pasuk* 8: "בְּרוּחַ קָדִים," which can connote the "soul/spirit of old/original" as "קָדִים" is from the same *shoresh* as "קֶדֶם" which means "of the past/days of old."[67]

---

[63] E.g., *Rashi, Bereishis* 50:14, from *Sotah* 13a.
[64] *Bereishis* 45:27.
[65] *Rashi, Bereishis* 45:27, from *Midrash Tanchuma, Vayeishev* 2.
[66] *Targum Onkelos, Bereishis* 45:27.
[67] E.g, *Eicha* 5:21.

Finally, the Midrash reveals that on an even deeper level the revivification of Yaakov's רוּחַ meant that Yaakov's very soul would be spared from ever having to suffer in Gehinnom, for Yosef was not dead but alive, and thus Yaakov's *sheleimus*, completion and perfection of the family unit, which was the barometer of his spiritual status, was reestablished.[68]

Pasuk 9:
כַּאֲשֶׁר שָׁמַעְנוּ כֵּן רָאִינוּ בְּעִיר ה' צְבָא-וֹת, בְּעִיר אֱ-לֹהֵינוּ, אֱ-לֹהִים יְכוֹנְנֶהָ עַד עוֹלָם סֶלָה
As we heard, so we saw in the City of Hashem, Master of Legions, in the City of our God, may God establish it to eternity, Selah!

To See It with Your Own Eyes

This *pasuk* describes first "hearing" about the magnificence of Yerushalayim and then actually "seeing" it all to be true: "כַּאֲשֶׁר שָׁמַעְנוּ כֵּן רָאִינוּ – As we heard, so we saw."

Interestingly, the same can be said of the Torah's emphasis in narrating the story of Yosef's reunion with his family.

First, Yehudah's pleas to the Viceroy begin with the phrase: "יְדַבֶּר נָא עַבְדְּךָ דָבָר בְּאָזְנֵי אֲדֹנִי – May your servant please speak a word in my lord's ears,"[69] meaning first please listen and thereafter take heed to "see" and understand what I will convey.

Later, when Yosef wept aloud as he revealed his identity, the Torah highlights the importance of hearing as it states: "וַיִּשְׁמְעוּ מִצְרַיִם, וַיִּשְׁמַע בֵּית פַּרְעֹה" – Egypt heard, and Pharaoh's household heard."[70] Afterwards, Yosef emphasized the importance of the brothers

---
[68] *Rashi, Bereishis* 37:35, from *Midrash Tanchuma, Vayigash* 9.
[69] *Bereishis* 44:18.
[70] *Bereishis* 45:2.

seeing his glorious position in Egypt with their own eyes in order to corroborate the veracity of the words and messages they were hearing from him, and he stated: "וְהִנֵּה עֵינֵיכֶם רֹאוֹת וְעֵינֵי אָחִי בִנְיָמִין, כִּי פִי הַמְדַבֵּר אֲלֵיכֶם – Behold, your eyes see, and the eyes of my brother Binyamin, that it is my mouth that is speaking to you."[71]

In addition, although the sons of Yaakov informed their father that Yosef was alive and conveyed Yosef's messages to him, Yaakov did not immediately "hear" and remained in disbelief.[72] It was not until "וַיַּרְא אֶת הָעֲגָלוֹת – And he [Yaakov] *saw* the wagons"[73] that he accepted that Yosef was alive and understood Yosef's message to him. Once Yaakov *saw*, he believed; and the *Shechinah* came back to him.

Finally, and perhaps most importantly, when Yosef went out to greet his father, the Torah describes their meeting from the perspective of seeing: "וַיֵּרָא אֵלָיו – And he [Yosef] *appeared* to him [Yaakov]."[74]

Thus, just like the general grandeur and glory of Yerushalayim, the grandeur and glory of Yosef sounded too good to be true, yet it all *was* true – and the brothers saw it with their own eyes.

So too, when we daven in *Shemoneh Esrei* for Hashem to return His Divine Presence to Yerushalayim, we say: "וְתֶחֱזֶינָה עֵינֵינוּ בְּשׁוּבְךָ לְצִיּוֹן בְּרַחֲמִים – May we see with our own eyes when You return to Tzion with mercy." We are requesting to see Hashem's salvation with our own eyes and to experience it in real time.

Moreover, we are asking to *merit* beholding Hashem's salvation with our own eyes, for to merit witnessing it first-hand is a sign that we are not just a bystander or blessed beneficiary of the Redemption, but rather an active *contributor* to the Redemption.

---

[71] *Bereishis* 45:12.
[72] *Bereishis* 45:26–27.
[73] *Bereishis* 45:27.
[74] *Bereishis* 46:29.

Pasuk 10:

דִּמִּינוּ, אֱ-לֹהִים,
חַסְדֶּךָ בְּקֶרֶב הֵיכָלֶךָ
**We hoped, God, for Your kindness
in the midst of Your Sanctuary.**

Goshen and the Ever-Available *Mikdash Me'at*

Rashi interprets this *pasuk* as an expression of the hopes and yearning of the Jew to see Hashem's kindness and salvation revealed specifically in "הֵיכָלֶךָ – in Hashem's Sanctuary,"[75] which is typically an expression used to describe the Beis HaMikdash.

As discussed above in *pasuk* 2, the initial embrace between Yosef and Binyamin in which they fell upon each other's "neck" expressed their yearning for the Beis HaMikdash and mourning of its loss, a loss which we feel so strongly even today. Of course, the intensity of such a yearning automatically expands beyond the individual person and specific place, and thus includes a longing for Hashem's kindness and salvation to emanate from the Beis HaMikdash and flow throughout Eretz Yisrael and all the world.

So, what are we to do now, in a world that currently lacks a Beis HaMikdash? We can follow the same approach that Yaakov took in *Parshas Vayigash*. Yaakov sent Yehudah down to Egypt to establish a house of study in the Egyptian city of Goshen from which all Torah instruction would flow to the generations of Bnei Yisrael who settled in Egypt.[76] Although there is no true "replacement" for the Beis HaMikdash, there is a concept of *Mikdash Me'at*, a mini-Beis HaMikdash in the form

---

[75] *Rashi, Tehillim* 48:10.
[76] *Rashi, Bereishis* 46:28, from *Midrash Tanchuma, Vayigash* 11, and *Bereishis Rabbah* 95:3.

of our shuls, yeshivas, and even our homes, which serve as a place of *kedushah*, kindness, and even salvation.[77]

As Dovid HaMelech stated so beautifully in *Tehillim* 27:4: "אַחַת שָׁאַלְתִּי מֵאֵת ה', אוֹתָהּ אֲבַקֵּשׁ: שִׁבְתִּי בְּבֵית ה' כָּל יְמֵי חַיַּי, לַחֲזוֹת בְּנֹעַם ה' וּלְבַקֵּר בְּהֵיכָלוֹ — One thing have I asked from Hashem, it I shall seek: would that I dwell in the House of Hashem all the days of my life, to behold the delight of Hashem and to visit בְּהֵיכָלוֹ – in His Sanctuary." Although a famous and fundamental *pasuk*, the commentators note that on a basic level Dovid's request never came to fruition, for the actual Beis HaMikdash was not built until *after* he died. Other commentators point out that Dovid's request was surely in vain because as a king, Dovid could not abandon his responsibilities to sit in the Beis HaMikdash all his life, even had such a place been available to him.

Nonetheless, a single answer makes all of this clear: the Beis HaMikdash is not just a location; it can be a state of mind. If we care enough to be connected to Hashem, then wherever we are, that place is a place of *kedushah*, kindness, and salvation. It is הֵיכָלֶךָ, Hashem's Sanctuary in the form of a *Mikdash Me'at*. This is what Dovid longed to create and experience, and in this regard he was successful. Wherever Dovid HaMelech went and whatever he did, he was with Hashem בְּהֵיכָלוֹ, in Hashem's Sanctuary.

Just as the sons of Yaakov built a *Mikdash Me'at* in Goshen hundreds of years prior to the First Beis HaMikdash, and just as Dovid HaMelech dwelt in a spiritual Beis HaMikdash that accompanied him always, the same can be true of us if only we would truly have such a desire.

---

[77] E.g., *Yechezkel* 11:16; *Kitzur Shulchan Aruch* 13.

Pasuk 11:

כְּשִׁמְךָ, אֱ-לֹהִים, כֵּן תְּהִלָּתְךָ עַל קַצְוֵי אֶרֶץ;
צֶדֶק מָלְאָה יְמִינֶךָ

Like Your Name, God, so is Your praise to the ends of the earth; righteousness fills Your right hand.

Reexamining the Emphasis on "Elokim"

This *pasuk* is puzzling in both style and content. It opens with the word "כְּשִׁמְךָ," which means "Your Name" and which typically refers to י-ה-ו-ה, the Name of Divine kindness and mercy. However, the *pasuk* instead applies the Name "אֱ-לֹהִים," which is the Name referring to strict judgment. Then the *pasuk* refers to "צֶדֶק," an ambiguous term. At times this term refers to *tzedakah* and charity, and as such is associated with kindness, mercy, and the Name י-ה-ו-ה. Yet this term may also refer to righteousness and even justice, which is associated with strict judgment and the Name אֱ-לֹהִים. Finally, the last word in the *pasuk* is "יְמִינֶךָ," referring to Hashem's right hand which symbolizes kindness and mercy associated with י-ה-ו-ה, not אֱ-לֹהִים. In short, the words and concepts contained in this *pasuk* seem to be meshing opposites, which certainly requires explanation.

As one studies and davens *Tehillim* 48, the Name "אֱ-לֹהִים" is clearly a main part of the rhythm and content of the *kapitel*. While *Tehillim* 48 is fifteen *pesukim* long, four of these *pesukim* contain the Name אֱ-לֹהִים at least once (*pesukim* 2, 4, 10, and 11), and two *pesukim* contain the Name אֱ-לֹהִים twice (*pesukim* 9 and 15), for a total of eight times in fifteen *pesukim*. This reflects a strong emphasis on the Divine Name of strict judgment and the concept of judgment generally.[78] While we have already focused on the Name אֱ-לֹהִים in Chapter 10 in the context of *Parshas*

---

[78] Note that the word "מִשְׁפָּטֶיךָ" is used in *pasuk* 12, which is also a term synonymous with אֱ-לֹהִים, and which further increases the connections to the theme of אֱ-לֹהִים.

Mikeitz & Tehillim 40,[79] the question remains: what can we learn from the repeated emphasis of the Name אֱ-לֹהִים here in the context of *Parshas Vayigash & Tehillim* 48?

In *Parshas Vayigash*, after Yosef and the brothers reunited, Yosef attempted to console them by directing his brothers to inform Yaakov of Yosef's prominence in Egypt and his desire that they relocate their family to join him there. In doing so, Yosef emphasized the Name אֱ-לֹהִים, using it four times in succession:

- "כִּי לְמִחְיָה שְׁלָחַנִי אֱ-לֹהִים לִפְנֵיכֶם" – For to support your life did Elokim send me ahead of you;"[80]
- "וַיִּשְׁלָחֵנִי אֱ-לֹהִים לִפְנֵיכֶם לָשׂוּם לָכֶם שְׁאֵרִית בָּאָרֶץ" – And Elokim has sent me ahead of you to ensure your survival in the land;"[81]
- "וְעַתָּה לֹא אַתֶּם שְׁלַחְתֶּם אֹתִי הֵנָּה, כִּי הָאֱ-לֹהִים" – And now, it was not you who sent me here, but rather Elokim;"[82] and
- "מַהֲרוּ וַעֲלוּ אֶל אָבִי, וַאֲמַרְתֶּם אֵלָיו כֹּה אָמַר בִּנְךָ יוֹסֵף, שָׂמַנִי אֱ-לֹהִים לְאָדוֹן לְכָל מִצְרָיִם; רְדָה אֵלַי אַל תַּעֲמֹד" – Hurry, and go up to my father and say to him: So said your son Yosef: Elokim has set me as a master to all Egypt. Come down to me, do not delay."[83]

In the *sefer Nachlas Tzvi*, Rabbi Gross examines the above *pesukim* in *Bereishis* 45 and questions Yosef's emphasis of the Name אֱ-לֹהִים in that context. Yosef should have used the Name י-ה-ו-ה there and not the Name

---

[79] In Chapter 10 we explained that the Name אֱ-לֹהִים is associated with Yitzchak Avinu as well as Yosef HaTzaddik, and is thus intertwined with total salvation from Hashem as the "מוֹשִׁיעַ," without any involvement on the part of the Jew. It also reflects the ability of the Jew to be *matzdik* the *din*, to acknowledge and accept the justice found within the judgment, strict as it may be. This understanding can also be used to explain the various references to the Name אֱ-לֹהִים in *Tehillim* 48 and *Parshas Vayigash*. However, we will now present an additional approach derived from the *sefer Nachlas Tzvi*.
[80] *Bereishis* 45:5.
[81] *Bereishis* 45:7.
[82] *Bereishis* 45:8.
[83] *Bereishis* 45:9.

אֱ-לֹהִים, especially when speaking to his beloved brothers and father, in order to arouse and proclaim the *chessed* and *rachamim* of Hashem that had suddenly become so very clear in Yosef's story. Rabbi Gross answers based on the famous Midrash that reveals that when God created the world, He initially wanted to create it with His attribute of *middas ha'din* but instead began Creation with His attribute of *middas ha'rachamim* in an effort to decrease Godly judgment, standards, and expectations; for without doing so the world would have been unable to endure.[84] This is seen from the fact that the Torah begins with the words "בְּרֵאשִׁית בָּרָא אֱ-לֹהִים אֵת הַשָּׁמַיִם וְאֵת הָאָרֶץ",[85] utilizing only the Name אֱ-לֹהִים, but later shifts to "בְּיוֹם עֲשׂוֹת ה-ו-ה-י אֱ-לֹהִים אֶרֶץ וְשָׁמָיִם",[86] using *both* Names of God: ה-ו-ה-י and אֱ-לֹהִים.

Nonetheless, says Rabbi Gross, although the *middas ha'din* was tempered by Hashem, He still used, and continues to use, the original and independent *middas ha'din* in His dealings with and expectations for *tzaddikim*. A primary example is Noach of whom the Torah states: "נֹחַ אִישׁ צַדִּיק תָּמִים הָיָה בְּדֹרֹתָיו; אֶת הָאֱ-לֹהִים הִתְהַלֶּךְ נֹחַ – Noach was a righteous man, perfect in his generations; Noach walked with Elokim,"[87] in which Noach is referred to as a *tzaddik* and the Name אֱ-לֹהִים is used. Similarly, the Name אֱ-לֹהִים was proclaimed by Yaakov Avinu when davening for his own safety from Lavan and Eisav: "אִם יִהְיֶה אֱ-לֹהִים עִמָּדִי – If Elokim will be with me."[88] Furthermore, Yaakov used the Name אֱ-לֹהִים *twice* when he blessed Yosef in *Parshas Vayechei*: "הָאֱ-לֹהִים אֲשֶׁר הִתְהַלְּכוּ אֲבֹתַי לְפָנָיו, אַבְרָהָם וְיִצְחָק, הָאֱ-לֹהִים הָרֹעֶה אֹתִי מֵעוֹדִי עַד הַיּוֹם הַזֶּה – The Elokim, before whom my forefathers Avraham and Yitzchak walked; the Elokim Who shepherds me from my inception until this day."[89]

---

[84] E.g., *Rashi* to *Bereishis* 1:1, from *Bereishis Rabbah* 12:15.
[85] *Bereishis* 1:1.
[86] *Bereishis* 2:4.
[87] *Bereishis* 6:9.
[88] *Bereishis* 28:20.
[89] *Bereishis* 48:15.

Rabbi Gross explains that Yaakov feared that perhaps Yosef had declined from his holy status as a *tzaddik*; after all, he had been alone in the impure environs of Egypt for twenty-two years. Yosef knew this as well; and therefore in a brilliant effort to immediately assuage Yaakov's worry, Yosef emphasized the Divine Name אֱ-לֹהִים in his words and messages to his brothers and to his father to show he was conducting himself *specifically* under the strict framework of אֱ-לֹהִים. Yosef communicated that, throughout his entire ordeal, he was scrutinized and held to the highest standard of the *middas ha'din* and nonetheless excelled in every area. This is the greatest proof that Yosef HaTzaddik maintained his status as a *tzaddik*, for *tzaddikim* conduct themselves in accordance with the highest standards even as they are examined by God Himself under the Name אֱ-לֹהִים.

Thus, *Tehillim* 48, which corresponds to *Parshas Vayigash* and its climactic reunion of Yosef and his family, so strongly and so appropriately emphasizes the Name אֱ-לֹהִים. *Tehillim* 48 contains the Name אֱ-לֹהִים interwoven throughout, just as Yosef's struggles and successes while alone in Egypt involved, and were predicated upon, the Name and strict standard of אֱ-לֹהִים interwoven throughout.

With this understanding from Rabbi Gross, we can now clarify the verbiage in *Tehillim* 48:11 and explain it as follows:

- "כְּשִׁמְךָ" – Like Your primary Name of י-ה-ו-ה,
- so, too, is even Your Name "אֱ-לֹהִים,"
- specifically for the *tzaddik*, who "תְּהִלָּתְךָ" – constantly praises You no matter the circumstances,
- and for the *tzaddik* who, as the term *tzaddik* connotes, is on the level of "עַל קַצְוֵי אֶרֶץ" – able to rise above the ends of the earth and simultaneously bridge heaven and earth,[90]

---

[90] *I Divrei HaYamim* 29:11.

- for such a person, "צֶדֶק" – even Your strict judgment and *middas ha'din* will be treated by the *tzaddik* as being *tzodeik* – justified and proper,
- and all this is exactly as if it were both emanating from and yet filling "יְמִינֶךָ" – Your right hand of Divine mercy.

Pasuk 12:
יִשְׂמַח הַר צִיּוֹן,
תָּגֵלְנָה בְּנוֹת יְהוּדָה,
לְמַעַן מִשְׁפָּטֶיךָ

**May gladdened be Mount Tzion,
rejoice the daughters of Yehudah,
because of Your judgments.**

Time for the Brothers to Celebrate

This *pasuk* references "בְּנוֹת יְהוּדָה – the daughters of Yehudah," and in so doing reminds us of Yehudah himself, Yehudah ben Yaakov. Yehudah was the leader of the brothers; Yehudah vied with Yosef for Jewish kingship; Yehudah advised that Yosef be sold rather than rescued or killed; and Yehudah confronted the Viceroy of Egypt at the start of *Parshas Vayigash* to protect Yosef's brother, Binyamin, from harm.

Therefore, it is Yehudah, individually, and as the representative of all the brothers, who is being told here:

- "בְּנוֹת יְהוּדָה," daughters of Yehudah, and Yehudah himself along with all his brothers and entire family of Yaakov,
- "יִשְׂמַח" and be happy,
- "תָּגֵלְנָה" and rejoice.
- Why? "לְמַעַן מִשְׁפָּטֶיךָ," because all that had happened with Yosef was Divinely inspired. This was all part of God's *mishpat*, Divine judgment, and was for the best.

While the brothers' betrayal of Yosef was certainly a difficult period for Yaakov and his family and one that involved a deluge of אֱ-לֹהִים and *middas ha'din*, it was all the plan of God and thus needed to be recognized and even celebrated joyously.

Pasuk 13:
סֹבּוּ צִיּוֹן וְהַקִּיפוּהָ, סִפְרוּ מִגְדָּלֶיהָ
**Walk throughout Tzion and encircle her,
count her towers.**

Pasuk 14:
שִׁיתוּ לִבְּכֶם לְחֵילָה,
פַּסְּגוּ אַרְמְנוֹתֶיהָ,
לְמַעַן תְּסַפְּרוּ לְדוֹר אַחֲרוֹן
**Mark well in your hearts her ramparts,
raise up her palaces,
so that you may retell it to the succeeding generation.**

Israel: Traveling To and Fro, To and Fro

These two colorful and descriptive *pesukim* are the epitome of the "tour" of Yerushalayim and Eretz Yisrael which we discussed earlier in this chapter (see *pasuk* 2). This is a tour that all Am Yisrael were able to take during the *Shalosh Regalim*, and a tour that each of us can still take every Monday morning through the *Shir Shel Yom*.

Ironically, however, in *Parshas Vayigash* the family of Yaakov *left* the holy land of Israel and instead visited and ultimately settled in the unfamiliar land of Egypt. This was a debased realm defined by idol worship, witchcraft, and immorality; a land whose unholy environs and inhabitants would contribute to Bnei Yisrael's enslavement and descent into the forty-ninth level of impurity until Hashem urgently redeemed them just before their spiritual status became irreparable.

Nonetheless, Bnei Yisrael's experience in Egypt was an investment – it was a יְרִידָה לְצֹרֶךְ עֲלִיָּה, a descent for the purpose of ascent that would eventually propel them to heights immeasurably greater than before.

Interestingly, the phrase "לְמַעַן תְּסַפְּרוּ – so that you may retell," contains a reference to the holiday of Pesach, which focuses on the Seder and the mitzvah of סִפּוּר יְצִיאַת מִצְרַיִם, the retelling of the story of the Exodus from Egypt. Furthermore, "סַפְּרוּ מִגְדָּלֶיהָ" and its reference to "counting," is not limited to counting physical towers. This is a directive to count toward גַּדְלוּת, toward towering greatness, in reference to *sefiras ha'omer* and Shavuos. Finally, "סֹבּוּ צִיּוֹן וְהַקִּיפוּהָ" contains references to the "encircling" of the sukkah which surrounds and envelops us on the holiday of Sukkos, and to the "walking" and "encircling" of both the *hoshanos* service on Sukkos and the joyous *hakafos* we dance together in circles around the Torah during the Simchas Torah celebrations.

These hidden references in *pesukim* 13 and 14 to the *Shalosh Regalim* – the Three Primary Festivals marked by Am Yisrael's pilgrimages to Yerushalayim and the Beis HaMikdash – are particularly important considering the connection to *Parshas Vayigash* in which Bnei Yisrael collectively *left* Eretz Yisrael and descended to Mitzrayim. It is these hidden references that continue to bind us to Eretz Yisrael even as we *lein* and learn about Yaakov's family leaving it.

In addition, Chazal tell us that the primary reason Yaakov and his family descended to Egypt at all was really threefold: to fulfill Hashem's plan of refinement of Bnei Yisrael in the furnace of slavery and to redeem them in miraculous fashion as celebrated and relived each Pesach; to grant Bnei Yisrael His greatest gift in the form of the Torah as celebrated and relived each Shavuos; and to protect Bnei Yisrael in the desert, in the Land of Israel, and throughout the many exiles that would follow, as celebrated and relived each Sukkos.

PARSHAH & TEHILLIM HAND IN HAND

The Continuity of the Jewish People Guaranteed

The expression "לְמַעַן תְּסַפְּרוּ לְדוֹר אַחֲרוֹן – So that you may retell it to the succeeding generation" is a beautiful expression of the Divinely promised everlasting nature of the Jewish People.[91] This is often described in the *seforim hakedoshim* as "נֵצַח יִשְׂרָאֵל לֹא יְשַׁקֵּר – The Eternal One of Israel [Hashem] does not lie,"[92] which is a dramatic expression of נִצְחִיּוּת, eternity, in the form of Hashem's promise that regardless of how horrific our enemies may act toward us, there will always be a "דוֹר אַחֲרוֹן" – not a *final* generation (*chas veshalom*) but a *next* generation of Jews to ensure the continuity of Bnei Yisrael. If there is a world, the Jewish People will always be in it.[93]

In addition, "לְמַעַן תְּסַפְּרוּ לְדוֹר אַחֲרוֹן" is reminiscent of the statement by Yaakov to his sons in next week's *Parshas Vayechi*: "הֵאָסְפוּ וְאַגִּידָה לָכֶם אֵת אֲשֶׁר יִקְרָא אֶתְכֶם בְּאַחֲרִית הַיָּמִים – Gather yourselves together and I will tell you what will befall you in the End of Days"[94] in an effort by Yaakov to reveal what will happen to Am Yisrael in the Era of Moshiach. Although Hashem did not allow Yaakov to reveal the timing and details of Moshiach, there is no doubt that the time of Moshiach will come, and Hashem's loyal Chosen Nation will be the treasured focal point of it all.

Pasuk 15:
כִּי זֶה אֱ-לֹהִים, אֱ-לֹהֵינוּ עוֹלָם וָעֶד;
הוּא יְנַהֲגֵנוּ עַל-מוּת

**For this is God, our God, forever and ever;
He will guide us eternally.**

---

[91] E.g., *Rashi, Bereishis* 15:10.
[92] *I Shmuel* 15:29.
[93] E.g., *Netzach Yisrael* of the *Maharal MePrague*.
[94] *Bereishis* 49:1.

CHAPTER 11: VAYIGASH & TEHILLIM 48

A Farewell Message of Parental Love and Care

Although "עַל-מוּת" means "forever" (i.e., transcending even death and/or in the World to Come), *Rashi* here says that "עַל-מוּת" bears a "child-like" connotation of Hashem guiding us slowly in the manner that a parent guides a young child: with patience, love, and compassion.[95]

Similarly, the *Radak* explains that Hashem will guide and care for the "younger," more recent generations who may not be as elevated as those of yesteryear, in the very same caring manner as He cared for previous generations who were on loftier levels.[96]

The *Degel Machaneh Ephraim* explains this comparison to a child as follows: when a child is first learning to walk, the parent walks with him and holds on to him. But as the child becomes more experienced, the parent begins to let go and to move further and further away, to allow the child more independence and opportunity to grow, despite the risks. So too is Hashem's approach with us. At first Hashem draws our heart to Him, but thereafter He may at times distance Himself from us to provide us with the opportunity to reconnect with Him independently through our own toil and efforts.

How poignant it is that *Tehillim* 48 concludes with messages of parental love and care, corresponding to *Parshas Vayigash* in which Yosef is reunified with his father and brothers – the *Parshah* when the family of Yaakov Avinu is finally able to enjoy a peaceful and loving life together, יַחְדָּו.

---

[95] *Rashi, Tehillim* 48:15.
[96] *Radak, Tehillim* 48:15.

CHAPTER 12

PARSHAS VAYECHI & TEHILLIM 41

פָּרְשַׁת וַיְחִי / תְּהִלִים מא

TEHILLIM 41 — תְּהִלִים מא

1	For the conductor, a psalm by Dovid.	א לַמְנַצֵּחַ מִזְמוֹר לְדָוִד.
2	Praiseworthy is one who contemplates the needy; on the day of evil, Hashem will rescue him.	ב אַשְׁרֵי מַשְׂכִּיל אֶל דָּל; בְּיוֹם רָעָה, יְמַלְּטֵהוּ ה'.
3	Hashem will preserve him and restore him to life, and he will be happy on earth; and You will not give him over to the desire of his enemies.	ג ה' יִשְׁמְרֵהוּ וִיחַיֵּהוּ, וְאֻשַּׁר בָּאָרֶץ; וְאַל תִּתְּנֵהוּ בְּנֶפֶשׁ אֹיְבָיו.
4	Hashem will support him on the bed of misery; even when all his restfulness You have upset by his illness.	ד ה' יִסְעָדֶנּוּ עַל עֶרֶשׂ דְּוָי; כָּל מִשְׁכָּבוֹ הָפַכְתָּ בְחָלְיוֹ.
5	As for me, I said: Hashem, show me grace; heal my soul for I have sinned against You.	ה אֲנִי אָמַרְתִּי: ה' חָנֵּנִי; רְפָאָה נַפְשִׁי כִּי חָטָאתִי לָךְ.

CHAPTER 12: VAYECHI & TEHILLIM 41

6	My enemies speak evil of me: "When will he die and his name perish?"	ו אוֹיְבַי יֹאמְרוּ רַע לִי; מָתַי יָמוּת וְאָבַד שְׁמוֹ.
7	And if one comes to visit, insincerely does he speak, his heart gathers evil for himself; upon going out he speaks it.	ז וְאִם בָּא לִרְאוֹת, שָׁוְא יְדַבֵּר, לִבּוֹ יִקְבָּץ אָוֶן לוֹ; יֵצֵא לַחוּץ יְדַבֵּר.
8	Together, against me whisper all my enemies; against me they plot my harm.	ח יַחַד עָלַי יִתְלַחֲשׁוּ כָּל שֹׂנְאָי; עָלַי יַחְשְׁבוּ רָעָה לִי.
9	"The result of his lawlessness is poured over him, and now that he lies [ill], no more will he rise!"	ט דְּבַר בְּלִיַּעַל יָצוּק בּוֹ; וַאֲשֶׁר שָׁכַב, לֹא יוֹסִיף לָקוּם.
10	Even my ally whom I trusted in, who ate my bread, has raised against me his heel.	י גַּם אִישׁ שְׁלוֹמִי אֲשֶׁר בָּטַחְתִּי בוֹ, אוֹכֵל לַחְמִי, הִגְדִּיל עָלַי עָקֵב.
11	But as for You, Hashem, show me favor and stand me up; then I shall repay them.	יא וְאַתָּה ה' חָנֵּנִי וַהֲקִימֵנִי; וַאֲשַׁלְּמָה לָהֶם.
12	By this I will know that You desire me; that You would not let my foe shout gleefully over me.	יב בְּזֹאת יָדַעְתִּי כִּי חָפַצְתָּ בִּי; כִּי לֹא יָרִיעַ אֹיְבִי עָלָי.
13	And I, because of my wholeheartedness, You have supported me, and You have stood me upright before You forever.	יג וַאֲנִי בְּתֻמִּי תָּמַכְתָּ בִּי, וַתַּצִּיבֵנִי לְפָנֶיךָ לְעוֹלָם.
14	Blessed is Hashem, the God of Yisrael, from all times past to all times to come, *Amen* and *Amen*!	יד בָּרוּךְ ה', אֱ-לֹהֵי יִשְׂרָאֵל, מֵהָעוֹלָם וְעַד הָעוֹלָם, אָמֵן וְאָמֵן.

INTRODUCTION: SICKNESS, DEATH, AND *OLAM HABA*

Tehillim 41's second *pasuk* begins with the words "אַשְׁרֵי מַשְׂכִּיל אֶל דָּל – Praiseworthy is the one who contemplates the needy." In the context of this *kapitel*, "מַשְׂכִּיל אֶל דָּל" does not refer to the more traditional understanding of one who assists the poor and impoverished from an economic perspective. Instead, these words are a praise of the person who is caring enough to visit the sick and dying,[1] and to sincerely strengthen and support them in their time of need.

As a result of such sensitivity, Hashem will fulfill the promise of "בְּיוֹם רָעָה יְמַלְּטֵהוּ ה'" – on the day of evil Hashem will rescue him," as well as bestow the rewards described in *pesukim* 3 and 4 to *both* the patient and the visitor. Specifically, in the merit of the visitor's care, concern, and accompanying prayers, the ill person may merit to be healed.[2] In addition, *middah k'neged middah*, Hashem will repay the visitor by healing him from any future illnesses and shielding him from life-threatening circumstances.[3]

Moreover, the *Zohar Hakadosh* cites the entirety of *pasuk* 2 as the basis for instructing that in end-of-life situations it is vital that the person who is sitting by the bedside, if possible, respectfully direct the fading patient to analyze his past sins and actions and to do *teshuvah* before Hashem. The visitor should stress that doing so will help save the soul of both the patient, as well as the visitor, from suffering in Gehinnom.[4]

---

[1] *Rashi* and *Radak*, *Tehillim* 41.
[2] *Radak*, *Tehillim* 41.
[3] *Rashi*, *Tehillim* 41.
[4] *Zohar Hakadosh* 2:250b.

CHAPTER 12: VAYECHI & TEHILLIM 41

Furthermore, since Hashem does not permit anyone to live forever, the promise of "וִיחַיֵּהוּ" in *pasuk* 3 is more than just an assurance of another few days or even years of life in this world. Rather, for both the believing patient and the compassionate visitor, "וִיחַיֵּהוּ" conveys that after their respective allotted time on this earth reaches its completion, Hashem will ensure that each will depart from this world with comfort and dignity to enter the everlasting spiritual life of Gan Eden and *Olam Haba*, the World to Come.

In *pesukim* 5 through 10, the *kapitel* shifts to Dovid HaMelech's personal description of his own sickbed and even his deathbed. He humbly acknowledges that his sickness is a result of his own sins and asks Hashem to heal him. Sadly, he describes that in this time of vulnerability, his enemies criticize him and hope for his death, his acquaintances visit him but lack sincerity, and even those whom he considered to be his truest friends seek to shatter him in his time of fragility.

Then, from *pasuk* 11 through the conclusion of the *kapitel*, Dovid prays and pleads that Hashem heal him and restore his strength so that he can overcome all his foes, who, considering Dovid's God-given kingship and toiled-for righteousness, are also the foes of Hashem.

Finally, in *pasuk* 13, Dovid's statement of "וַתַּצִּיבֵנִי לְפָנֶיךָ לְעוֹלָם" – You have stood me before You upright forever," is not a request for everlasting life in this world, for Dovid knew that even his own precious life would be limited to just seventy years. Instead, it is his personal request for continued, everlasting life in *Olam Haba*, like the expression of "וִיחַיֵּהוּ" discussed above, for indeed it is *Olam Haba* that is the ultimate goal of every Jew.

Thus, the parallels between *Tehillim* 41 and *Parshas Vayechi* are clear: the *Parshah* begins with the Torah telling us about Yaakov Avinu: "וַיִּקְרְבוּ יְמֵי יִשְׂרָאֵל לָמוּת – The time approached for Yisrael to die."[5] This prompted Yaakov to call for his powerful and well-connected son Yosef, who at

---

[5] *Bereishis* 47:29.

Yaakov's request, swore to ensure that Yaakov would be buried not in Egypt but rather in Eretz Yisrael together with his parents and grandparents in Me'aras Hamachpeilah. The Torah then teaches that Yaakov fell ill, and Yosef was informed and immediately ran to his side,[6] enabling Yaakov to bless Yosef and Yosef's two sons, Ephraim and Menasheh from his sickbed. Later, the Torah takes us to Yaakov's deathbed[7] and shares with us his parting blessings to each of his twelve sons before he passed from this world.

In continuation of the parallel, the *Haftarah* to *Parshas Vayechi* describes Dovid HaMelech on his deathbed, with his final instructions, blessings, and encouragement to his son Shlomo, who would succeed him as the next king of the Jewish People.[8]

Thus, as we analyze *Tehillim* 41 and its many connections to Yaakov Avinu and *Parshas Vayechi*, we must unfortunately focus on the serious topic of death. However, we must bear in mind the statement of the Gemara: "צַדִּיקִים שֶׁבְּמִיתָתָן נִקְרָאוּ חַיִּים – The righteous, even in death, are called living"[9] by virtue of their Torah, mitzvos, *maasim tovim*, children, and *talmidim*, all of which continue to have positive ripple effects throughout this world long after the *tzaddik* has departed. Additionally, as noted above, the ultimate destination of the *tzaddik* is *Olam Haba*, the place of sublime closeness to Hashem and the very purpose for which the Jewish soul was created. The *Mesillas Yesharim*[10] famously describes *Olam Haba* as the place "לְהִתְעַנֵּג עַל ה' וְלֵהָנוֹת מִזִּיו שְׁכִינָתוֹ – To experience [spiritual] joy with Hashem, and to receive [spiritual] pleasure from the radiance of His Divine Presence." *Olam Haba* is the ultimate, everlasting, and ever-expanding experience, described by Dovid HaMelech as

---

[6] *Bereishis* 48:1.
[7] *Bereishis* 49:1.
[8] *I Melachim* 2:1–12.
[9] *Brachos* 18a.
[10] *Mesillas Yesharim, perek aleph*.

"וַאֲנִי קִרְבַת אֱלֹהִים לִי טוֹב" – And as for me, closeness to Hashem is my ultimate good."[11]

Thus, although the fear of death is natural, and while we all hope to live long and healthy lives, for a Torah-true Jew death is not necessarily something to be feared or intentionally ignored. Rather, death is the entryway to everlasting joy and closeness to Hashem in the World to Come.

THE MANY CONNECTIONS BETWEEN PARSHAS VAYECHI & TEHILLIM 41

Pasuk 1:
לַמְנַצֵּחַ מִזְמוֹר לְדָוִד
For the conductor, a psalm by Dovid.

Joy In and With Hashem, Even in Illness

The Gemara teaches that the order of the expression "מִזְמוֹר לְדָוִד," first "a psalm/song" and then "by Dovid," indicates that when composing this *kapitel*, Dovid was not initially connected to the *Shechinah*. He had to sing a song to Hashem to instill spiritual joy within himself, and only thereafter was he blessed to have the *Shechinah* rest upon him and inspire him to compose *Tehillim* 41. As Chazal teach, the Divine Presence does not rest upon a person except amidst *simchah* and, in particular, amidst "דְּבַר שִׂמְחָה שֶׁל מִצְוָה," an atmosphere infused with the joy of fulfilling a commandment of Hashem.[12]

---

[11] *Tehillim* 73:28.
[12] *Pesachim* 117a.

While inspirational, the above has some surprising implications. First, due to his illness, Dovid HaMelech was not automatically brimming with happiness. Indeed, Dovid was a human being and had human responses to sickness. He needed to push himself, to inspire himself, to sing, and to focus on the joy of mitzvos and closeness to Hashem to proactively raise his spirits and transcend his discomfort and pain. This, in and of itself, is a powerful lesson, and a *chizuk* to us all.

In addition, Dovid's illness did not miraculously disappear after he sang. He remained stricken but elevated himself above and beyond the sickness; he was content despite his ongoing suffering. This, too, is an important lesson and inspiration to us all: we must strive to stay positive and *b'simchah*, and to connect to Hashem in times of difficulties, sickness, and even impending death. This is one of the ultimate signs of a *maamin ba'Hashem*, a true believer in God.

Rising To *Ruach Hakodesh* Amidst Illness

At the start of *Parshas Vayechi* when Yosef came to Yaakov to be *mevaker cholim*, the Torah tells us that Yaakov prostrated himself toward the head of the bed.[13] From this, Chazal learn that the *Shechinah* rests above the head of all Jews who are ill and thus Yaakov adjusted his position out of respect, not for Yosef but for the Divine Presence of Hashem.[14] When a Jew is sick, Hashem is not distant; He is closer than ever.

Nonetheless, the closeness that the ailing Dovid HaMelech experienced when composing the Divinely inspired *Tehillim* 41 was on an entirely different level – that of *ruach hakodesh*. Dovid was bestowed with having the Holy Spirit of Hashem dwell within him.

In fact, just as Dovid composed *Tehillim* 41 through *ruach hakodesh*, so too were Yaakov's blessings in *Parshas Vayechi* inspired by *ruach*

---

[13] *Bereishis* 47:31.
[14] *Rashi, Bereishis* 47:31, from *Shabbos* 12b.

hakodesh, as were Dovid's parting words to Shlomo in the *Haftarah* to *Parshas Vayechi*. To experience the incredible heights of *ruach hakodesh* even amidst sickness and/or impending death is truly an ultimate sign of a *maamin ba'Hashem* and is a transcendent level of spirituality that both Yaakov Avinu and Dovid HaMelech shared.

Focus on the Future Time, for a Great Future Awaits

Interestingly, the Gemara in *Pesachim* referenced above[15] also teaches that the expression "לַמְנַצֵּחַ" is an expression of "לֶעָתִיד לָבוֹא," which means not only "the future," but also refers to the "future time to come" of Moshiach and/or *Olam Haba*. This is further hinted to by the fact that the word לַמְנַצֵּחַ is connected to the *shoresh* of the word נֶצַח, meaning "forever," which alludes to the נִצְחִיּוּת and "eternal" nature of Moshiach and *Olam Haba*.

Thus, the word "לַמְנַצֵּחַ" in "לַמְנַצֵּחַ מִזְמוֹר לְדָוִד" is a truly important opening word to *Tehillim* 41, for it is a word that reminds us that death is not the end. There is a future even after death. This opening word reminds us that we must always strive to maintain our focus on the ultimate destination and goal: that of true נִצְחִיּוּת in the form of the eternity of Moshiach and *Olam Haba*.

Pasuk 2:
אַשְׁרֵי מַשְׂכִּיל אֶל דָּל;
בְּיוֹם רָעָה, יְמַלְּטֵהוּ ה'

**Praiseworthy is one who contemplates the needy;
on the day of evil, Hashem will rescue him.**

---

[15] *Pesachim* 117a.

PARSHAH & TEHILLIM HAND IN HAND

The Mitzvah of Visiting the Sick

As noted in the Introduction to this chapter and as is clear from the context of this *kapitel*, "דָּל" does not mean "poor" but rather "sick"[16] or "dying."[17] Both *Rashi* and *Radak* teach that the directive to be a "מַשְׂכִּיל," to be one who is thoughtful and considerate of the needs of others, is fulfilled by visiting the one who is suffering from illness or near to death – to be *mevaker cholim*.

The opening *pasuk* of *Parshas Vayechi* states: "וַיְהִי אַחֲרֵי הַדְּבָרִים הָאֵלֶּה וַיֹּאמֶר לְיוֹסֵף הִנֵּה אָבִיךָ חֹלֶה; וַיִּקַּח אֶת שְׁנֵי בָנָיו עִמּוֹ אֶת מְנַשֶּׁה וְאֶת אֶפְרָיִם – And it came to pass after these things, that one said to Yosef: 'Behold, your father is sick.' And he took with him his two sons, Menasheh and Ephraim."[18] Yosef immediately rushed to Yaakov's bedside and fulfilled the mitzvah of visiting the sick.

Doing so can be extremely uncomfortable at times, but as Chazal teach us in *Pirkei Avos*: "לְפוּם צַעֲרָא אַגְרָא – Commensurate with the difficulty is the reward."[19]

Intelligent Interactions with the Ill

The powerful words "אַשְׁרֵי מַשְׂכִּיל אֶל דָּל – Praiseworthy is one who contemplates the needy" convey that true *bikur cholim* requires one to be a "מַשְׂכִּיל" by using one's "שֵׂכֶל – intelligence" to give proper forethought and discern who is in need, as well as when and how to best assist the needy.

A similar word is used in *Parshas Vayechi* when Yaakov desired to bless Yosef's sons and crossed his hands to place his holier and more prestigious right hand on the younger Ephraim. The Torah states that

---

[16] *Rashi* and *Radak*, *Tehillim* 41.
[17] *Radak*, *Tehillim* 41.
[18] *Bereishis* 48:1.
[19] *Pirkei Avos* 6:26.

CHAPTER 12: VAYECHI & TEHILLIM 41

Yaakov "שִׂכֵּל אֶת יָדָיו,"[20] which according to *Rashi* means that Yaakov "made his hands wise, moving with intelligence and wisdom" and in deliberate fashion.[21] This same *shoresh* of שָׂכַל is used in both the *Parshah* and its corresponding *kapitel Tehillim*, but what is the connection?

My beloved daughter Sima explained the connection as follows: while the visitor of the sick must use his own שֵׂכֶל as noted above, this includes not allowing himself to be fooled by the physical fragility of the one whom he is visiting. Though infirm and confined to a sickbed, the one who is ill may still have his usual שֵׂכֶל and mental faculties, and as such will expect to be treated and spoken to with the same dignity one addresses any intelligent person. We see this through Yaakov Avinu, who though sick and near death, still maintained and used his intelligence to "שִׂכֵּל אֶת יָדָיו" with great understanding and acumen. When Yosef questioned the appropriateness of his actions, Yaakov stated: "יָדַעְתִּי בְנִי יָדַעְתִּי – I know, my son, I know"[22] exactly what I am doing, and I have full capacity to make prudent decisions for myself and for others. Therefore, a deeper lesson of "מַשְׂכִּיל אֶל דָּל" is that the visitor must use his own intelligence to ensure that he does not accidentally "insult the intelligence" of the one whom he is visiting.

Of course, not all ill people are fortunate enough to maintain their mental faculties. In such instances, the visitor must nonetheless act in accordance with the spirit of the famous Gemara: "הַלּוּחוֹת וְשִׁבְרֵי לוּחוֹת מוּנָּחִין בָּאָרוֹן – Both the whole Tablets and the broken Tablets were placed in the Aron HaBris," which teaches that a Torah scholar who has forgotten his Torah knowledge due to circumstances beyond his control such as illness should not be treated in a degrading manner but rather with respect and sanctity, for he is likened to the broken Tablets that were treated with the same respect as the whole Tablets.[23]

---

[20] *Bereishis* 48:14.
[21] *Rashi, Bereishis* 48:14.
[22] *Bereishis* 48:19.
[23] *Menachos* 99a.

Lessons for Life and Death

With regard to proper interactions with the sick and appropriate conduct in connection with end-of-life matters, *Parshas Vayechi* itself provides much insight, including the following collection of lessons:

- Yaakov realized that he was going to die, and that his lifespan would not reach the age of his forefathers.[24] This is reminiscent of the Midrash that one should prepare for death within the five-year period before and after the age of the demise of each of one's parents.[25] For example, Yitzchak Avinu had initially become concerned at the age of 123, for he thought he might only reach the age of his mother, Sarah, who died at the age of 127.[26]

- Yaakov waited until the end of his life to bless his sons as well as to rebuke them, a lesson later followed by Moshe Rabbeinu, Yehoshua bin Nun, Shmuel HaNavi, and Dovid HaMelech.[27] Chazal teach that there are four reasons why one should not rebuke except immediately before death: (1) so that one should not rebuke a person and then rebuke him again at a later date for the same matter, as repetitive rebuke may be taken less seriously, and rebuke is especially effective one time before death; (2) so that the recipient of the rebuke not be embarrassed each time he sees the one who gave him rebuke; (3) so that the recipient of the rebuke not harbor a grudge; and (4) parting on peaceful terms is of utmost importance and is more likely to occur in the setting of impending death.[28]

---

[24] *Rashi, Bereishis* 47:29, from *Bereishis Rabbah* 96:4.
[25] *Bereishis Rabbah* 65:12.
[26] *Rashi, Bereishis* 27:2.
[27] *Rashi, Devarim* 1:3.
[28] *Rashi, Devarim* 1:3, from *Sifrei, Devarim* 2.

- The *Shechinah* is present above the head of Jews who are sick.[29] In fact, quoting *pasuk* 4 of *Tehillim* 41, the *Zohar Hakadosh*[30] explains that sickness might manifest itself like a raging fire or like a storming sea in its attempts to burst forth beyond its bounds to spread throughout the body and devour one's soul, but that the *Shechinah* protects and supports the person's body and soul, creating a protective boundary between the sickness and the patient. Therefore, continues the *Zohar*, a visitor of the sick should be careful where he sits. When the patient is a *beinoni*, an average person, the visitor should not sit by the head of the sick person for the *Shechinah* is there, nor should the visitor sit by the feet of the sick person since the Angel of Death may be there. Moreover, when the patient is a *tzaddik*, the patient may be surrounded by the *Shechinah*, while if the patient is a *rasha* he may be surrounded by the Angel of Death. The implication is that in both such instances, the visitor should keep a safe distance from the patient.

- On Yaakov's words to Yosef: "וְעָשִׂיתָ עִמָּדִי חֶסֶד וֶאֱמֶת – and do kindness and truth with me,"[31] *Rashi* explains that kindness performed on behalf of the dead is "חֶסֶד שֶׁל אֱמֶת – kindness of truth," i.e., genuine kindness, because by definition the deceased cannot repay and reciprocate the kindness.[32]

- In *Parshas Vayechi*, Yaakov specifically asked not to be buried in Mitzrayim,[33] in part because of the importance of being buried in Israel. Since the dead who are buried outside of Israel will only live again at the time of *Techiyas Ha'meisim*, the Resurrection of the Dead, after first having to endure the pain of rolling through

---

[29] *Rashi, Bereishis* 47:31, from *Shabbos* 12b.
[30] *Zohar Hakadosh* 3:234b.
[31] *Bereishis* 47:29.
[32] *Rashi, Bereishis* 47:29, from *Bereishis Rabbah* 96:5.
[33] *Bereishis* 47:29.

tunnels in order to reach the Land of Israel, Yaakov made this request.[34]

- According to *Rashi*,[35] Yaakov's statement: "לִישׁוּעָתְךָ קִוִּיתִי ה'" – For Your salvation do I long, Hashem,"[36] was a prayer specifically for the mighty Shimshon, who would ultimately be blinded, chained, and tormented by his enemies before taking his final revenge on them.[37] The *Be'er BaSadeh* points out that Yaakov did not daven for Shimshon to be rescued or even to be spared from such an experience. Instead, Yaakov davened for Shimshon to die an honorable death, in which he would take vengeance on his enemies and perform a tremendous *Kiddush HaShem*.

These are just some of the lessons for life, and for death, contained in *Parshas Vayechi*. May we only experience *chaim* and *simchah* among Klal Yisrael, and may we merit speedily in our days the coming of Moshiach who will usher in the time of "בִּלַּע הַמָּוֶת לָנֶצַח, וּמָחָה אֲ-דֹנָי יֱ-ה-וָ-ה דִּמְעָה מֵעַל כָּל פָּנִים – He will swallow up death forever, and Hashem Elokim will wipe the tears away from all faces."[38]

Yaakov Was the First to Ever Become Sick

The Gemara[39] teaches that prior to Yaakov becoming sick,[40] there was no such thing as illness in the world. Yaakov was the first to become sick, and in fact had davened to Hashem specifically requesting that he fall ill before he died so that he would be aware of his impending death and

---

[34] *Rashi, Bereishis* 47:29, from *Kesubos* 111a.
[35] *Rashi, Bereishis* 49:18.
[36] *Bereishis* 49:18.
[37] *Shoftim* 16.
[38] *Yeshayahu* 25:8.
[39] *Bava Metzia* 87a.
[40] *Bereishis* 48:1.

CHAPTER 12: VAYECHI & TEHILLIM 41

thus have the opportunity to bless all of his sons in the precious moments before his passing.

While illness seems like a horrible curse, it can be viewed as a blessing. For prior to Yaakov's request, people would just pass away suddenly. For example, Chazal tell us that a simple sneeze would cause one's soul to suddenly leave the body.[41] Instead, having a warning that death may be approaching enables a person to put his affairs in order, to bless his loved ones, and even to pray to be healed. Illness and suffering also serve as an automatic *kaparah*, atonement for one's sins. And perhaps most importantly, illness enables one to do *teshuvah* – to actively and sincerely repent for one's sins, which in turn may bring healing or at least allow the *baal teshuvah* to return his soul to Hashem in its original pristine condition.

In the *Haftarah* to *Parshas Chayei Sarah*, we are told that Dovid HaMelech became old, could not be warmed, and was in terrible discomfort.[42] Chazal teach that his discomfort was a *kaparah* for his having cut off a portion of Shaul HaMelech's clothing or tzitzis.[43] In addition, the *Haftarah* seems to indicate that while Dovid's vulnerability may have contributed to the premeditated attempt of his son Adoniyahu to usurp his throne, it also provided an opportunity for righteous people such as Dovid's wife Batsheva and Nosson HaNavi to visit Dovid at his bedside and ensure that Dovid would be properly succeeded by Shlomo. Additionally, who can forget the poignant parting blessing of Batsheva to Dovid, blessings from a loving wife to her dying husband and from a faithful queen to her fading king: "יְחִי אֲדֹנִי הַמֶּלֶךְ דָּוִד לְעֹלָם" – May my lord, King Dovid, live forever!"[44]

---

[41] *Pirkei D'Rabi Eliezer, perek* 52.
[42] *I Melachim* 1:1.
[43] *I Shmuel* 24:6; *Brachos* 62b.
[44] *I Melachim* 1:31.

Such vital interactions and lessons were only possible because infirmity served as a signal that time was of the essence to all those involved in the last days of the lives of Yaakov Avinu and Dovid HaMelech.

Delving Into the Description of "*Dal*"

It should be noted that the use of the word "דַּל" here is unusual in this context. Because the context refers to one who is sick or dying, why use the word "needy" or "poor" at all? We can answer that the word דַּל hints specifically to both Yaakov Avinu and Dovid HaMelech, and thus further synthesizes *Tehillim* with the *Parshah*.

Chazal tell us that when Yaakov was forced to flee from his parents and childhood home due to Eisav's bloodlust in *Parshiyos Toldos* and *Vayeitzei*, Yaakov was further pursued by Eisav's son Eliphaz who sought to kill him. However, they reached an agreement in which Eliphaz refrained from murdering Yaakov[45] in exchange for stripping Yaakov of all his worldly possessions.[46] The Gemara states that there are four categories of people who have the halachic status of one who is dead, including a person who is an *ani*, poor.[47] As such, by impoverishing Yaakov and rendering him as if dead, Eliphaz was able to rationalize leaving Yaakov alive by technically accomplishing the mission Eisav had demanded he fulfill.[48] Thus, Yaakov knew full well what it felt like to be "dead" due to being rendered a "דַּל."

Dovid HaMelech had his share of ups and downs as well, and often referred to himself as a "דַּל," such as in the famous *pasuk* of "מְקִימִי מֵעָפָר דָּל, מֵאַשְׁפֹּת יָרִים אֶבְיוֹן – [Hashem] Who raises the poor out of the dust, and lifts the impoverished out of the trash heaps."[49] Famously, the very name

---

[45] In truth, it was Yaakov who was the more powerful of the two and who refrained from killing Eliphaz in self-defense.
[46] *Rashi, Bereishis* 29:11, from *Bereishis Rabbasi*.
[47] *Nedarim* 64b.
[48] *Rashi, Bereishis* 29:11, from *Bereishis Rabbasi*.
[49] *Tehillim* 113:7.

דָוִד itself is symbolic of this, as it contains the letter ד (דָּלֶ״ת) twice, a letter whose spelling and pronunciation literally contains the word דַל within it and which thus epitomizes what it means to be a "דַל."

Furthermore, regarding Dovid himself:
- the first ד of his name represents Dovid's modest and lowly younger years;
- the ו represents his constant connection to Hashem (i.e., the ו is referred to as the וָ״ו הַחִבּוּר that "connects") and the kingship and greatness that he attained (since the letter ו is one of the letters of Hashem's Divine Name י-ה-ו-ה); and
- his name then culminates with the letter ד yet again to show that his original modesty and humility remained unchanged despite his righteousness, fame, and glory; for Dovid knew that all his qualities and blessings were not his own but rather gifts so graciously granted to him by Hashem.[50]

Finally, the Jewish People are called יְהוּדִים because, like יְהוּדָה the son of Yaakov from whom the Davidic Dynasty began, all Jews are gloriously connected to the Name of Hashem "י-ה-ו-ה" together with the letter ד that represents our continued connection to the modesty and humility of a דַל despite our special closeness to Hashem.

Pasuk 3:

ה' יִשְׁמְרֵהוּ וִיחַיֵּהוּ,
וְאֻשַּׁר בָּאָרֶץ;
וְאַל תִּתְּנֵהוּ בְּנֶפֶשׁ אֹיְבָיו

**Hashem will preserve him and restore him to life,
and he will be happy on earth;
and You will not give him over
to the desire of his enemies.**

---

[50] See also *Megillah* 11a.

Appreciate Life

In this context of sickness and death, we must pause to appreciate life. While not identical wording, the phrase "ה' יִשְׁמְרֵהוּ וִיחַיֵּהוּ" contains a very similar message to the blessing of "שֶׁהֶחֱיָנוּ וְקִיְּמָנוּ וְהִגִּיעָנוּ לַזְּמַן הַזֶּה" – [Hashem] Who has kept us alive, sustained us, and brought us to this time."

While שֶׁהֶחֱיָנוּ is a *brachah* reserved for only a handful of special occasions, in truth twice a day in *Shemoneh Esrei*'s *Modim d'Rabbanan*, we praise Hashem with very similar wording: מוֹדִים אֲנַחְנוּ לָךְ... עַל שֶׁהֶחֱיִיתָנוּ וְקִיַּמְתָּנוּ, כֵּן תְּחַיֵּנוּ וּתְקַיְּמֵנוּ – We thank You... for You have given us life and You have sustained us. So may You continue to give us life and sustain us."

Whether in davening and/or simply in our daily personal thought and behavior, we must recognize Hashem's kindness in granting us life itself. As Dovid HaMelech tells us in the very last *pasuk* in all of *Sefer Tehillim*, "כֹּל הַנְּשָׁמָה תְּהַלֵּל יָ-הּ הַלְלוּ-יָהּ – Let all souls praise God, Halleluy-ah,"[51] which Chazal teach also means that for every נְשִׁימָה וּנְשִׁימָה, every single breath we take, we must be thankful and praise Hashem.[52] Let us appreciate everything that we have, and let us not take life and Hashem Who constantly gives us that life, for granted.

Pasuk 4:
ה' יִסְעָדֶנּוּ עַל עֶרֶשׂ דְּוָי;
כָּל מִשְׁכָּבוֹ הָפַכְתָּ בְחָלְיוֹ
**Hashem will support him on the bed of misery;
even when all his restfulness
You have upset by his illness.**

---

[51] *Tehillim* 150:6.
[52] *Devarim Rabbah* 2:37.

Yosef at Yaakov's Deathbed

The phrase "הֹ' יִסְעָדֶנּוּ עַל עֶרֶשׂ דְּוָי" is *Tehillim* 41's most explicit reference to Hashem providing support to one who is on his actual "deathbed." In *Parshas Vayechi* this pasuk was literally fulfilled by Hashem for Yaakov during his final moments, as he merited to be surrounded by his sons and to have the lucidity to properly bless them.

Such support and care were promised to him by Hashem in advance in the immediately prior *Parshas Vayigash*. For when Hashem blessed Yaakov and confirmed that it was proper for him and his family to go down to Egypt to reunite with Yosef, Hashem included an unexpected statement: "וְיוֹסֵף יָשִׁית יָדוֹ עַל עֵינֶיךָ – And Yosef will put his hand on your eyes,"[53] which Chazal say was a guaranty to Yaakov that Yosef will be alive and present at Yaakov's death, and that Yosef will close Yaakov's eyelids when he passes away.[54] This was all fulfilled by Yosef in *Parshas Vayechi* in the presence of all of Yaakov's other sons as well.[55]

The *Zohar Hakadosh*[56] reveals that Yosef was chosen for this task because he was the most beloved of Yaakov's sons. The Zohar then adds another reason: if a father merits to have a son in this world, the son should be the one to close his father's eyes at the time of his passing, which is a great honor for the father. In addition, the closing of the eyelids has deep symbolic meaning. It symbolizes that although the father's "sight" in relation to this world has been taken away, it will be replaced with a new, deeper "sight" in the World to Come. Finally, when performed specifically by the son, the closing of the eyes symbolizes that the son remains alive to continue his father's "sight" – his vision and legacy – among the living, and that the son is willing and able to undertake the responsibility of filling the void left by his father's empty place in this world.

---

[53] *Bereishis* 46:4.
[54] E.g., *Tzror HaMor, Bereishis* 46:4.
[55] E.g., *Bereishis* 49:33–50:1.
[56] *Zohar Hakadosh, Parshas Shelach*.

The above experience was so important that Hashem Himself had reassured Yaakov seventeen years in advance that this would happen; that his precious son Yosef would be there at his side to close his eyes and ensure the transition of Hashem's holy, Torah-true values from father to son precisely in the moment that Yaakov Avinu's *neshamah* left this world.

Pasuk 5:

אֲנִי אָמַרְתִּי: ה' חָנֵּנִי;

רְפָאָה נַפְשִׁי כִּי חָטָאתִי לָךְ

**As for me, I said: Hashem, show me grace;
heal my soul for I have sinned against You.**

A Time to Die

Chazal tell us that at the age of seventy Dovid HaMelech attempted to ward off the Angel of Death by studying Torah without pause, relying on the merit of Torah to protect him.[57] It seems that Dovid always sought life and hoped to merit "רְפָאָה נַפְשִׁי" and healing even to the last second.

Regarding Yaakov Avinu, however, there is no indication that Yaakov resisted death or asked to be healed. Although he was still thirty-three years younger than his father Yitzchak had been at the time of his passing, it appears that Yaakov was ready to move on to the World to Come. He knew it was his time to die, and he accepted it.

In addition, by willingly relinquishing his soul to Hashem when it was so demanded, Yaakov was able to avoid the physical and spiritual difficulties of "dying" and is actually considered in Jewish tradition to be one of the few human beings who never died, a topic that will be discussed

---

[57] *Shabbos* 30a–b.

in more detail below in connection with Chazal's teaching that "יַעֲקֹב אָבִינוּ לֹא מֵת – Yaakov our father did not die."[58]

Healing Through *Chein*

Nonetheless, *pasuk* 5 reveals to us important elements for those wishing to be healed.

In addition to the protective power of Torah study (as noted above) and the mitzvah of giving charity in order to merit the promise of "צְדָקָה תַּצִּיל מִמָּוֶת – charity saves from death,"[59] *pasuk* 5 focuses on a panacea in the form of "חָנֵּנִי ה'," asking Hashem to heal by showing חֵן, Divine grace and favor, and/or through bestowing a מַתְּנַת חִנָּם, a free gift that is completely independent of one's own personal merits.

The concept of God-given חֵן as an enabling element of healing is also emphasized later in *pasuk* 11 of *Tehillim* 41, which states: "וְאַתָּה ה' חָנֵּנִי וַהֲקִימֵנִי; וַאֲשַׁלְּמָה לָהֶם – But as for You, Hashem, show me חֵן – grace – and stand me up; then I shall repay them."

Healing Through *Teshuvah*

Pasuk 5 also describes a second avenue for healing: "רְפָאָה נַפְשִׁי כִּי חָטָאתִי לָךְ – Heal my soul for I have sinned against You," which expresses the recognition that the sickness may very well be a Divine response to the person's own sins. Thus, when the person does *teshuvah*, which in its most complete form consists of performing the four required actions of (1) regretting having done the sin (*charatah*), (2) verbally confessing to having done the sin (*vidui*), (3) desisting from doing the sin (*azivas ha'cheit*), and (4) promising to never repeat the sin in the future (*kabbalah al ha'asid*),[60] then the *teshuvah* process is completed and one is forgiven

---

[58] *Taanis* 5b.
[59] *Mishlei* 10:2 and 11:4.
[60] E.g., *Rambam, Mishneh Torah, Hilchos Teshuvah, perakim* 1 and 2.

for his sins, possibly even transforming the sins into merits![61] As a result, when the sin, which may be the true underlying cause of the sickness, disappears, so may the sickness. The above expression of "רְפָאָה נַפְשִׁי כִּי חָטָאתִי לָךְ," if not a complete microcosm of the *teshuva* process, is certainly indicative of a willingness to begin the *teshuva* process.

While we cannot comprehend Hashem's *cheshbonos* and reasons, and while the above approaches of seeking חֵן and doing *teshuvah* are thus not guaranteed to be effective, they are proven approaches that also bespeak a yearning for continued *deveikus* with and connection to Hashem that is so vital when a Jew is confronted with the challenges of illness or death.

Pasuk 6:
אוֹיְבַי יֹאמְרוּ רַע לִי; מָתַי יָמוּת וְאָבַד שְׁמוֹ
My enemies speak evil of me: "When will he die and his name perish?"

Ha'malach Ha'goel: Protection from All Evil

This *pasuk* is one of three in *Tehillim* 41 in which the word or *shoresh* of "רַע – evil," is used.[62] Here, enemies are spewing words of the utmost evil and wickedness, wishing for the untimely death of the *tzaddik* and for the eradication of his name and memory.

Such derision was unfortunately an experience that Dovid HaMelech had to endure, not just from his enemies, but even from common Jews who were critical of him.[63]

Yaakov Avinu as well was the victim of such horrible hopes. For example, Chazal tell us in *Parshas Toldos* that after Yaakov took the

---
[61] *Yoma* 86b.
[62] See also *Tehillim* 41, *pesukim* 2 and 8.
[63] E.g., see commentaries to *Tehillim* 122:1.

CHAPTER 12: VAYECHI & TEHILLIM 41

blessings from Eisav, Eisav was so committed to the death of Yaakov that Yaakov was already dead in his eyes, and Eisav had even already "drunk a cup of consolation," which was really a cup of celebration over his death.[64] Lavan HaRasha, too, explicitly spoke of the ability to do "רַע" to Yaakov[65] and had the gall to do so even after Hashem had warned him to stop.[66] Although Lavan's evil might have been more of a spiritual attack than a physical one, it would have been no less destructive, and perhaps even more so.

As noted, in *Tehillim* 41 the emphasis on "רַע" is also found in *pasuk* 2: "בְּיוֹם רָעָה, יְמַלְּטֵהוּ ה'" – On a day of evil, Hashem will rescue him," as well as in *pasuk* 8: "עָלַי יַחְשְׁבוּ רָעָה לִי" – Against me they plot my harm."

The unifying point is that no matter what form the רַע takes, whether it be violence, *lashon hara*, illness, or even death, the righteous Jew who trusts in Hashem will be protected. In fact, *Parshas Vayechi* contains Yaakov's famous praise which we, too, echo each evening before going to sleep to protect us against the dangers of the night – a praise of Hashem for protecting Yaakov from all רַע: "הַמַּלְאָךְ הַגֹּאֵל אֹתִי מִכָּל רָע, יְבָרֵךְ אֶת הַנְּעָרִים וְיִקָּרֵא בָהֶם שְׁמִי וְשֵׁם אֲבֹתַי אַבְרָהָם וְיִצְחָק וְיִדְגּוּ לָרֹב בְּקֶרֶב הָאָרֶץ" – May the angel who redeems me from all רַע – evil, bless the young men [Ephraim and Menasheh], and may my [Yaakov's] name be declared upon them, and the names of my forefathers Avraham and Yitzchak, and may they reproduce abundantly like fish within the land."[67] With those words, Yaakov thanked Hashem for repeatedly sending him an angel who protected him in his many times of רַע and *tzarah*, distress and problems, and beseeched Hashem to ensure that Yosef's two sons, and all Jewish People who follow, will be blessed with the same constant protection "מִכָּל רָע – from all evil" that even Yaakov himself received.

---

[64] *Rashi, Bereishis* 27:42, from *Bereishis Rabbah* 67:9.
[65] *Bereishis* 31:29.
[66] *Bereishis* 31:24.
[67] *Bereishis* 48:16.

PARSHAH & TEHILLIM HAND IN HAND

Death Should Not Be Confused with Evil

However, if we remember the context in which Yaakov was speaking, Yaakov's statement of "הַמַּלְאָךְ הַגֹּאֵל אֹתִי מִכָּל רָע" – The angel who redeems me from all evil" raises an important question. For, at that moment when Yaakov was on his deathbed and he declared his confidence in Hashem Who always protected him, he was facing what many would consider to be the ultimate רָע – the ultimate "evil," or at least the ultimate "bad" in the form of death itself. Yet, neither the angel nor Hashem saved Yaakov from death. How can this be reconciled?

The answer is that death is not intrinsically רָע. The Gemara tells us "יַעֲקֹב אָבִינוּ לֹא מֵת" – Yaakov our father did not die."[68] Certainly, Yaakov passed away, as the Torah descriptively tells us that he "expired and was brought in to his people,"[69] was embalmed,[70] and ultimately was buried.[71] Yet the Torah refrains from using the expression of "dying" in connection with Yaakov. Rav Tzaddok HaKohen succinctly explains this Gemara as follows:

> Man, during his life on earth, is formed of two components, body and soul. The more man focuses his life upon the material, the more the soul becomes embedded in his body. Death is the tearing apart of soul from body. In the materially oriented, this is an agonizing process. It is a rupture of their very being. But our forefather Yaakov, even in his earthly life, existed on a completely spiritual plane. His soul was not torn from his body at all, for his body was not a manifestation of his true self. When his soul departed his body,

---

[68] *Taanis* 5b.
[69] *Bereishis* 49:33.
[70] *Bereishis* 50:2.
[71] *Bereishis* 50:13.

CHAPTER 12: VAYECHI & TEHILLIM 41

it was doing no more than taking off a garment. Thus, "יַעֲקֹב אָבִינוּ לֹא מֵת – Our father Yaakov did not die."[72]

With this outlook, it is clear that for Yaakov Avinu at the old age of 147, blessed with twelve righteous sons and many grandchildren who would ultimately form Am Yisrael in his name, the statement of "הַמַּלְאָךְ הַגֹּאֵל אֹתִי מִכָּל רָע" was not intended to include the רָע of death; for Yaakov had lived his life fully through spiritual connection to Hashem at all moments. Therefore, for Yaakov death was not רָע, nor was he going to experience the difficulties of "death" at all.

To summarize, death is not intrinsically evil, nor is it intrinsically bad. Even for those who may be more physically connected and who certainly are not as purely spiritual as Yaakov Avinu was, we know that death is an inevitable part of life. Death serves as a *kaparah*, atonement, for our sins. And Death is a prerequisite path to the afterlife in *Olam Haba*, the real reason why Hashem placed us on this earth in the first place. As taught in *Pirkei Avos*: "הָעוֹלָם הַזֶּה דּוֹמֶה לִפְרוֹזְדוֹר בִּפְנֵי הָעוֹלָם הַבָּא. הַתְקֵן עַצְמְךָ בַּפְּרוֹזְדוֹר כְּדֵי שֶׁתִּכָּנֵס לַטְּרַקְלִין – This world is like a corridor before the World to Come. Prepare yourself in the corridor so that you may enter the banquet hall."[73] Additionally: "יָפָה שָׁעָה אַחַת שֶׁל קוֹרַת רוּחַ בָּעוֹלָם הַבָּא מִכָּל חַיֵּי הָעוֹלָם הַזֶּה – Better one hour of spiritual bliss in the World to Come more than the entire life in this world."[74]

Finally, since *Techiyas Ha'meisim* is a fundamental belief of Judaism, even death itself is only a temporary state, as the dead will, *b'ezras Hashem*, be brought back to life on earth in the Era of Moshiach.[75]

---

[72] *Sefer Resisei Lailah*, perek 56 (English translation taken from the ArtScroll Interlinear Chumash).
[73] *Pirkei Avos* 4:21.
[74] *Pirkei Avos* 4:22.
[75] *Rambam*'s Thirteen Principles of Faith, *Ani Maamin* #13.

Pasuk 7:
וְאִם בָּא לִרְאוֹת, שָׁוְא יְדַבֵּר,
לִבּוֹ יִקְבָּץ אָוֶן לוֹ;
יֵצֵא לַחוּץ יְדַבֵּר

**And if one comes to visit, insincerely does he speak,
his heart gathers evil for himself;
upon going out he speaks it.**

The Brothers Doubt Yosef's Sincerity and Fear Him

Amazingly yet sadly, this *pasuk* which describes apparent kindness disguising hatred and evil can refer to the impression the brothers had of Yosef following the death of Yaakov in *Parshas Vayechi*.

The Torah states: "וַיִּרְאוּ אֲחֵי יוֹסֵף כִּי מֵת אֲבִיהֶם וַיֹּאמְרוּ לוּ יִשְׂטְמֵנוּ יוֹסֵף וְהָשֵׁב יָשִׁיב לָנוּ אֵת כָּל הָרָעָה אֲשֶׁר גָּמַלְנוּ אֹתוֹ — And Yosef's brothers saw that their father was dead, and they said: 'Perhaps Yosef will nurse hatred against us and then he will surely repay us all the evil that we did to him.'"[76] Chazal reveal that prior to Yaakov's death, the brothers were accustomed to dining at Yosef's table where Yosef was generally friendly toward them, but this all ceased once Yaakov died.[77]

The *Maharal* explains Yosef's true motivation. After Yaakov's death, the Egyptians began subjugating the family of Yaakov, and Yosef was concerned that showing any favoritism toward his family would only increase Egyptian hostility toward them and endanger them. This is why Yosef changed his loving practices by keeping his distance from them.[78] However, the brothers were unaware of Yosef's reasoning and feared the worst. The Torah reveals that they were so concerned that they even altered facts for the sake of peace by telling Yosef that one of Yaakov's

---

[76] *Bereishis* 50:15.
[77] Rashi, *Bereishis* 50:15, from *Tanchuma Yashan, Shemos* 2; *Bereishis Rabbah* 100:8.
[78] *Gur Aryeh, Bereishis* 50:15.

CHAPTER 12: VAYECHI & TEHILLIM 41

dying wishes was for Yosef to forgive them for the evil they had done to him, which brought Yosef to tears. The brothers even offered themselves as slaves to Yosef before Yosef reassured them that he meant no harm and would continue to support them and their families, which finally gave them the comfort and reassurance they needed.[79]

While the above was simply a gross misunderstanding, it does reveal that even after seventeen peaceful years of apparent *achdus* and unity among the sons of Yaakov, there was still a serious underlying concern and apprehension on the part of Yosef's brothers that Yosef had not truly forgiven them.

Considering the above, we can explain *pasuk* 7 from the perspective of Yosef's brothers as follows:

- "וְאִם בָּא לִרְאוֹת – And if one comes to visit," i.e., even when the brothers frequently visited Yosef and consistently dined together, and even when all twelve of the sons of Yaakov visited their father and stood by his deathbed together;

- "שָׁוְא יְדַבֵּר, לִבּוֹ יִקְבָּץ אָוֶן לוֹ – insincerely does he speak, his heart gathers evil for himself [toward his brothers]," which describes the suspicion and concern the brothers had about Yosef;

- "יֵצֵא לַחוּץ – upon going out," i.e., following Yaakov's passing from this world and following the brothers' unexplained rejection from dining at Yosef's table;

- "יְדַבֵּר – he speaks it," i.e., the brother's feared that Yosef would then articulate and reveal his hidden hatred of them to mete out upon them his long-awaited revenge.

---

[79] *Bereishis* 50:16–21.

Pasuk 8:
יַחַד עָלַי יִתְלַחֲשׁוּ כָּל שֹׂנְאָי;
עָלַי יַחְשְׁבוּ רָעָה לִי

Together, against me whisper all my enemies;
against me they plot my harm.

The Greatness of Yaakov and Yosef Amidst the Evil

Like Dovid HaMelech who understood that so many overt foes and false friends were determined to undermine him, so too Yaakov Avinu was acutely aware that his life of *tzaros* was filled with enemies and ordeals from within and without in the forms of Eisav, Lavan, Dinah, Yosef, Shimon, and Binyamin.[80]

The expression here of people plotting "רָעָה," harm and evil, parallels Yaakov's statement to Pharaoh in *Parshas Vayigash* in which Yaakov said: "מְעַט וְרָעִים הָיוּ יְמֵי שְׁנֵי חַיַּי – few and רָעִים – evil/bad, have been the days of the years of my life."[81]

In addition, the double use of the word "עָלַי" in *pasuk* 8 and especially in the phrase "עָלַי יַחְשְׁבוּ רָעָה לִי" alludes to another *tzarah* and tragedy with which Yaakov was challenged: the loss of his beloved mother Rivkah Imeinu who died just prior to his return home after twenty-two years apart from her.[82] Earlier in *Parshas Toldos*, when Yaakov questioned Rivkah about the propriety of deceiving Yitzchak to take the *brachos* from Eisav, Rivkah stated: "עָלַי קִלְלָתְךָ בְּנִי – Your curse will be עָלַי, on me, my son."[83] This promise of a concerned mother shielded and protected Yaakov but was also a dramatic declaration that may have put Rivkah in harm's way[84]

---

[80] Rashi, *Bereishis* 43:14, from *Midrash Tanchuma, Mikeitz* 10. See also Chapter 7, *Parshas Vayeitzei* & *Tehillim* 3.
[81] *Bereishis* 47:9.
[82] Rashi, *Bereishis* 35:8, from *Bereishis Rabbah* 81:5.
[83] *Bereishis* 27:13.
[84] E.g., *Brachos* 60a: "אַל יִפְתַּח אָדָם פִּיו לַשָּׂטָן – A person should not open his mouth to the Satan."

and may have even contributed to her premature death by unleashing "עָלַי יַחְשְׁבוּ רָעָה לִי" upon her.

That Chazal tell us that many of Yaakov's challenges were repeated by Hashem in the form of challenges to Yosef,[85] and the fact that Yosef, too, lost his own mother Rochel Imeinu at an even younger age than Yaakov, strikingly demonstrates the greatness of Yaakov and Yosef, despite having been beset by harm and heartbreak.

Pasuk 9:
דְּבַר בְּלִיַּעַל יָצוּק בּוֹ;
וַאֲשֶׁר שָׁכַב, לֹא יוֹסִיף לָקוּם

**"The result of his lawlessness is poured over him,
and now that he lies [ill], no more will he rise!"**

Hints to the Original Dispute Between the Brothers and Yosef

To see the word "יוֹסִיף" used here in *Tehillim* 41 in the context of *Parshas Vayechi* strikes the reader as a clear allusion to יוֹסֵף the son of Yaakov.

The brothers sought to kill and ultimately sell Yosef not out of evil, hatred, or jealousy, but rather from their perspective within the framework of *halachah*, asserting that it was Yosef's own fault and impropriety that had made him deserving of death,[86] or as stated here: "דְּבַר בְּלִיַּעַל יָצוּק בּוֹ" – The result of his lawlessness is poured over him."

In addition, as previously discussed,[87] the brothers also felt that although they would keep Yosef alive, once he "fell" into the pit and then "fell" into the hands of the merchants to whom he was sold, he would

---

[85] *Rashi, Bereishis* 37:2, from *Bereishis Rabbah* 84:6.
[86] E.g., *Rashi, Bereishis* 37:17 and *Rashi, Bereishis* 37:33.
[87] E.g., Chapter 9, *Tehillim* 112:6.

never again be able to ascend, similar to the statement here: "וַאֲשֶׁר שָׁכַב, לֹא יוֹסִיף לָקוּם – and now that he lies, no more will he rise."

However, Yosef was the righteous Yosef HaTzaddik and thus the curse of "לֹא יוֹסִיף לָקוּם" was something he was able to transcend. For, as Yosef "HaTzaddik" he was subject to the famous blessing of the tzaddik: "שֶׁבַע יִפּוֹל צַדִּיק וָקָם – The righteous will fall seven [i.e., innumerable] times and rise up again,"[88] a promise that was truly fulfilled in יוֹסֵף.

The Life and Death of Eisav HaRasha

In addition, this *pasuk* more appropriately describes Yaakov's twin brother and nemesis: the truly wicked Eisav HaRasha, who in *Parshas Vayechi* was killed by a grandson of Yaakov.[89]

With this background, *Tehillim* 12:9 can be explained as follows:

- Eisav's "דְּבַר," his own "דִּבּוּר – words," led him to his death when he publicly challenged Yaakov's claim to Me'aras Hamachpeilah;[90]

- Words of he who was a "בְּלִיַּעַל," a lawless person who lived "בְּלִי עֹל," without the "עֹל מַלְכוּת שָׁמַיִם – yoke of Heaven" upon him, having vehemently cast it off from upon himself;[91]

- Eisav, of whom it can be said "יָצוּק בּוֹ," when he gluttonously had Yaakov "pour into him" the lentil soup straight down his throat;[92]

- Eisav HaRasha, who "וַאֲשֶׁר שָׁכַב," once he was killed and laid down to rest;

---

[88] *Mishlei* 26:14.
[89] See Chapter 8, *Tehillim* 140:10 for a lengthy discussion of the circumstances surrounding Eisav's death.
[90] *Sotah* 13a.
[91] E.g., *Rashi, Devarim* 13:14, from *Sifrei, Devarim* 93.
[92] *Bereishis* 25:30.

- "לֹא יוֹסִיף לָקוּם," no more will he rise, for he will never get up again; not in this world, not in the time of Moshiach, and not even in עוֹלָם הַבָּא.[93]

Pasuk 10:
גַּם אִישׁ שְׁלוֹמִי אֲשֶׁר בָּטַחְתִּי בוֹ, אוֹכֵל לַחְמִי, הִגְדִּיל עָלַי עָקֵב
Even my ally whom I trusted in, who ate my bread, has raised against me his heel.

The Origins of Yaakov and Eisav

The use of the word "עָקֵב" here alludes to Yaakov, whose very name was derived from the word עָקֵב as the famous *pasuk* describing his birth states: "וְיָדוֹ אֹחֶזֶת בַּעֲקֵב עֵשָׂו, וַיִּקְרָא שְׁמוֹ יַעֲקֹב – And his hand was holding on to the heel of Eisav, and he called his name Yaakov."[94]

Furthermore, the negativity contained in this *pasuk* can be understood as a further description of the betrayals that Yaakov suffered due to the wickedness of Eisav:

- "גַּם אִישׁ שְׁלוֹמִי – Even my ally," my brother;

- "אֲשֶׁר בָּטַחְתִּי בוֹ – whom I trusted in," or at least wished I could trust and rely upon, as brothers naturally should;

- "אוֹכֵל לַחְמִי – who ate my bread" when the *bechorah* was rightfully purchased by Yaakov from Eisav only in exchange for lentil soup, yet Yaakov voluntarily added לֶחֶם, bread, to the meal;[95]

- "הִגְדִּיל עָלַי עָקֵב – has raised his heel against me," first even at birth by trying to push Yaakov back into the womb to usurp the

---

[93] *Midrash Tanchuma, Tzav* 2.
[94] *Bereishis* 25:26.
[95] *Bereishis* 25:34.

bechorah and/or to terminate his life, and continuing as they "וַיִּגְדְּלוּ – grew up"[96] (which has the same *shoresh* as הִגְדִּיל) with Eisav consistently trying to tread upon and stomp upon Yaakov.

The Serpent Is the Heel, At the Heel, Who Does Not Heal

The *Baal Haturim*[97] says that the word "עָקֵב" appears three times in *Tanach*, and each time has a snake-related connection. First, in *Parshas Bereishis*: "וְאַתָּה תְּשׁוּפֶנּוּ עָקֵב – And you [the Serpent] will hiss at his heel"[98] in reference to the enmity that will forever exist between snakes and mankind in the aftermath of the *cheit* of the *Eitz HaDaas*. Then in our *Parshas Vayechi*: "וְהוּא יָגֻד עָקֵב – And he will march back on his tracks,"[99] as part of Yaakov's deathbed blessing to his son Gad that his Tribe's warriors would return alive from battle. Finally, we see this word again here in *Tehillim* 41:10's phrase "הִגְדִּיל עָלַי עָקֵב."

The *Baal Haturim* starts his explanation by connecting the phrases in *Parshas Bereishis* and *Tehillim* 41 based on the Gemara[100] that states: "Woe over a great *shamash*, attendant, that has been lost to the world, for if the original Serpent had not sinned, every single Jew would have had two fine snakes at his disposal to bring him precious stones and pearls." Thus, the snakes, who were originally intended to be an "אִישׁ שְׁלוֹמִי – a trusted ally," instead became an enemy and "הִגְדִּיל עָלַי עָקֵב – raised his heel against me" so to speak, to attack mankind and bite him on the heel – all because of the *cheit* of the *Eitz HaDaas* and Hashem's resultant curse of the Serpent.

The *Baal Haturim* then focuses on the use of the word "עָקֵב" in *Parshas Vayechi* and explains that in Yaakov's blessings to his sons, even though

---

[96] *Bereishis* 25:34.
[97] *Baal Haturim, Beresishis* 3:15.
[98] *Bereishis* 3:15.
[99] *Bereishis* 49:19.
[100] *Sanhedrin* 59b.

he explicitly blessed only five of his twelve sons with animal-like qualities and talents (e.g., he compared Yehudah's strength to a lion and Naftali's swiftness to a deer), Yaakov later included all his sons in all the blessings so that each son possessed the strength of a lion, the swiftness of a deer, etc.[101] As a proof of this idea, the *Baal Haturim* says that while Dan was blessed with the powers of a snake, which includes an expression similar to the word עָקֵב in the form of the phrase "הַנֹּשֵׁךְ עִקְּבֵי סוּס" – [a snake that] bites a horse's heel,"[102] just two *pesukim* later the Torah states about Gad: "וְהוּא יָגֻד עָקֵב,"[103] thus associating Gad with Dan in both the proximity of the *pasuk* and the similarity of the *shoresh* of the word עָקֵב. This, says the *Baal Haturim*, clearly shows that Gad, too, was blessed with the powers of the snake.

It is surely no coincidence that *Parshas Vayechi* and *Tehillim* 41, which work in tandem and focus upon sickness and death, contain the common link to snakes and to the Serpent of the *cheit* of the *Eitz HaDaas*, whose wickedness first brought death itself into the world.

Pasuk 11:
וְאַתָּה ה' חָנֵּנִי וַהֲקִימֵנִי;
וַאֲשַׁלְּמָה לָהֶם

But as for You, Hashem, show me favor and stand me up; then I shall repay them.

Metaso Sheleimah: His Bed Was Whole

In the words "וְאַתָּה ה' חָנֵּנִי וַהֲקִימֵנִי" – But as for You, Hashem, show me favor and stand me up," we find a request for health and life to be restored. It is a request for a *refuah sheleimah*.

---

[101] See also *Rashi, Bereishis* 49:28.
[102] *Bereishis* 49:17.
[103] *Bereishis* 49:19.

Surprisingly, the *pasuk* continues by connecting the healing with a strong *justification* of "וַאֲשַׁלְמָה לָהֶם" – so that the requestor can "repay" his enemies with the punishments they so richly deserve. This request is surely not for for vengeance, but rather to be *Mekadesh Shem Shamayim* through the victory of good over evil.

Yet, while Dovid HaMelech and Yaakov Avinu were certainly no strangers to waging war on behalf of Hashem and the Jewish People even at the risk of dying *Al Kiddush HaShem*, another way of sanctifying Hashem's Name is to **live** *Al Kiddush HaShem* in a Torah-true way, including raising a family that values, follows, and exemplifies these same holy characteristics.

The Gemara[104] tells us that when Yaakov wanted to reveal to his sons the *Keitz HaYamim*, the End of Days deadline for the coming of Moshiach, Hashem removed His *Shechinah* from Yaakov so that Yaakov forgot the date because it was not supposed to be revealed. However, Yaakov was worried that Hashem had caused him to forget because one of his sons had a *p'sul*, a flaw, that rendered him unfit. Therefore, to prove their allegiance to Hashem, all twelve of Yaakov's sons proclaimed the most famous of declarations: "שְׁמַע יִשְׂרָאֵל ה' אֱ-לֹהֵינוּ ה' אֶחָד".[105] In this context, *Shema Yisrael* meant "Hear, our father whose name is Yisrael: Hashem is our God, Hashem is one" – we are all pure and God-fearing and there is no defect among us! Upon hearing this, a relieved and proud Yaakov then declared "בָּרוּךְ שֵׁם כְּבוֹד מַלְכוּתוֹ לְעוֹלָם וָעֶד" – Blessed is the Name of His glorious kingdom forever and ever," thereby concluding the formula that would become an indelible part of Jewish prayer, life, and even death, for all time.

This episode proved once and for all that Yaakov's children were *zera kodesh*, holy offspring unblemished by sin, and is referred to by Chazal

---

[104] *Pesachim* 56a.
[105] *Devarim* 6:4.

with the expression: "מִטָּתוֹ שְׁלֵמָה – his bed was *shaleim* – whole and perfect" – as there was no spiritual flaw among Yaakov's progeny.[106]

Thus, the above expression "וַאֲשַׁלְמָה לָהֶם" and its *shoresh* of "שָׁלֵם" are connected to Yaakov on many levels:

- The *tzaddik* discussed in *pasuk* 11 davens for his own רְפוּאָה שְׁלֵמָה – a full recovery.

- On what grounds? To be מְשַׁלֵּם and repay his enemies in the form of vengeance.

- However, while this vengeance may be realized through war at certain times, it is realized at *all* times through the living *Kiddush HaShem* of the *tzaddik's* own personal שְׁלֵמוּת and self-perfection.

- Additionally, this *Kiddush HaShem* is fulfilled by virtue of his מִטָּתוֹ שְׁלֵמָה and the pride of righteous children who follow in the ways of Hashem just like their holy father.

Pasuk 12:
בְּזֹאת יָדַעְתִּי כִּי חָפַצְתָּ בִּי; כִּי לֹא יָרִיעַ אֹיְבִי עָלָי
By this I will know that You desire me; that You would not let my foe shout gleefully over me.

Torah Is the Ultimate Protection

One of the primary attributes of Yaakov Avinu is that he embodied the characteristic of Torah. He was the original "יֹשֵׁב אֹהָלִים" who dwelt in the tents of Torah as a young man and then later immersed himself

---

[106] E.g., *Rashi*, *Bereishis* 47:31, from *Sifrei*, *Devarim* 31. See also *Vayikra Rabbah* 36:5.

in Yeshivas Shem V'Eiver learning Torah day and night.[107] Later, regardless of his location Yaakov maintained this designation and is forever the symbol of the *Amud HaTorah*, Pillar of Torah, supporting the entire world.[108] This is alluded to here in *pasuk* 12 with the use of the word "זֹאת," which correlates to Torah per the famous *pasuk*: "וְזֹאת הַתּוֹרָה אֲשֶׁר שָׂם מֹשֶׁה לִפְנֵי בְּנֵי יִשְׂרָאֵל – זֹאת – And – this is the Torah that Moshe placed before Bnei Yisrael."[109] The lesson here in *Tehillim* 41 is that we, like Yaakov before us, must trust and know with certainty that Hashem desires us and will not let our enemies shout gleefully over us. Why? In what merit do we benefit from the protection of "בְּזֹאת יָדַעְתִּי כִּי חָפַצְתָּ בִּי?" In the merit of "זֹאת!" In the merit of "וְזֹאת הַתּוֹרָה!"

Pasuk 13:
וַאֲנִי בְּתֻמִּי תָּמַכְתָּ בִּי,
וַתַּצִּיבֵנִי לְפָנֶיךָ לְעוֹלָם

**And I, because of my wholeheartedness,
You have supported me,
and You have stood me upright before You forever.**

Yaakov Remained the *Ish Tam* Forever

This *pasuk* as well mentions a characteristic fundamental to Yaakov Avinu's greatness. The word "בְּתֻמִּי" is a reference to Yaakov who is famously praised by the Torah as an "אִישׁ תָּם," a man who was wholehearted and complete in his faith and trust in Hashem.[110] This was true of Yaakov when he had only just turned thirteen years old, and this remained true of Yaakov until his very last breath at the age of 147 in

---

[107] *Bereishis* 25:27 and *Rashi there*, from *Bereishis Rabbah* 63:10; and *Rashi*, *Bereishis* 28:11, from *Bereishis Rabbah* 68:11.
[108] E.g., *Pirkei Avos* 1:2.
[109] *Devarim* 4:44.
[110] *Bereishis* 25:27.

Parshas Vayechi. In that merit, "וַתַּצִּיבֵנִי לְפָנֶיךָ לְעוֹלָם" – Yaakov proudly "stood upright before Hashem forever," with the emphasis on "forever" because (as discussed above) "יַעֲקֹב אָבִינוּ לֹא מֵת" – Our father Yaakov never died but rather continues to live through his righteous and faithful children and descendants, including us, to this very day.[111]

Supporting the Wholehearted

The phrase "וַאֲנִי בְּתֻמִּי תָּמַכְתָּ בִּי" – And I, because of my wholeheartedness, You have supported me," is such a powerful statement that the *Sifrei*[112] even equates it with the Torah's famous instructions: "תָּמִים תִּהְיֶה עִם ה' אֱ-לֹהֶיךָ" – You shall be wholehearted with Hashem Your God."[113]

Just as striking, the words "תָּמַכְתָּ בִּי" – You supported me" possess a parallel in *Parshas Vayechi* where the Torah uses the same *shoresh* in the word "וַיִּתְמֹךְ" when stating "וַיִּתְמֹךְ יַד אָבִיו לְהָסִיר אֹתָהּ מֵעַל רֹאשׁ אֶפְרַיִם עַל רֹאשׁ מְנַשֶּׁה" – [Yosef] supported his father's hand to remove it from upon Ephraim's head to Menasheh's head."[114]

In contemplating the connection, my family and I were blessed with two somewhat opposite explanations. The first is based upon the meaning of the word "וַיִּתְמֹךְ," which means that Yosef "supported" Yaakov's hand in an attempt to take control of it and move it. Similarly, one who is a true "תָּמִים" with Hashem will relinquish control to Hashem and acknowledge Hashem as his "תָּמַכְתָּ," his complete supporter, mover, and director of every aspect of his life.

The second explanation is based upon the *Netziv*, who explains that "וַיִּתְמֹךְ יַד אָבִיו" means that Yosef did not have the heart to overtly move his father's frail hand but rather added just enough extra support to it. By

---

[111] *Taanis* 5b.
[112] *Sifrei, Devarim* 173.
[113] *Devarim* 18:13.
[114] *Bereishis* 48:17.

doing so, Yosef hoped to thereafter gently transfer Yaakov's hand to the proper place slowly and discreetly[115] in an attempt to make it seem as if the switch was Yaakov's idea all along. Similarly, one who is a true "תָּמִים" with Hashem, will receive "תָּמַכְתָּ בִּי" in the form of support from Hashem in a discreet and subtle manner in which the person feels as though he himself is accomplishing something by functioning together with Hashem, even as a partner with Hashem. Interestingly, this approach is alluded to by *Rashi* on the *pasuk* of "תָּמִים תִּהְיֶה עִם ה' אֱ-לֹהֶיךָ," which he so beautifully explains includes the following: "...הִתְהַלֵּךְ עִמּוֹ בִּתְמִימוּת – Walk with Him [Hashem] wholeheartedly…" to rise to the level of being "עִמּוֹ וּלְחֶלְקוֹ – with Him and part of His portion,"[116] in partnership with Hashem.

Pasuk 14:
בָּרוּךְ ה', אֱ-לֹהֵי יִשְׂרָאֵל,
מֵהָעוֹלָם וְעַד הָעוֹלָם, אָמֵן וְאָמֵן

Blessed is Hashem, the God of Yisrael,
from all times past to all times to come, *Amen* and *Amen*!

Concluding Connections to Yaakov and the World to Come

The phrase "בָּרוּךְ ה', אֱ-לֹהֵי יִשְׂרָאֵל," is a declaration that contains a dual meaning: (1) Baruch Hashem, the God of the Nation of Israel; and (2) Baruch Hashem, the God of Yaakov Avinu, who is himself named Yisrael.

Furthermore, the phrase "מֵהָעוֹלָם וְעַד הָעוֹלָם" is itself a double declaration of (1) our recognition that Hashem is blessed in the past and in the future; and (2) our recognition that Hashem is blessed in both this world and in the World to Come. As discussed, this latter understanding centering

---

[115] *Haamek Davar, Bereishis* 48:17.
[116] *Rashi, Devarim* 18:13, from *Sifrei, Devarim* 173.

around *Olam Haba* was a focal point of Yaakov's life and should be a focal point for every Jew.

Finally, there is yet another double expression in the words "אָמֵן וְאָמֵן," which is also very much a phrase consistent with yearning for the World to Come. As the Gemara states: "כָּל הָעוֹנֶה אָמֵן בְּכָל כֹּחוֹ פּוֹתְחִין לוֹ שַׁעֲרֵי גַן עֵדֶן – All who answer *Amen* with all his strength will merit to have the gates of Gan Eden opened up for him,"[117] and as the Midrash states: "כָּל מִי שֶׁעוֹנֶה אָמֵן בָּעוֹלָם הַזֶּה זוֹכֶה לַעֲנוֹת אָמֵן לֶעָתִיד לָבוֹא – All who answer *Amen* in this world, will merit to answer *Amen* in the future time"[118] of Moshiach and *Olam Haba*.

Chazzak Chazzak Ve'nischazeik

In addition, *Tehillim* 41's final words of "אָמֵן וְאָמֵן" are by definition an affirmation of all that was previously proclaimed in this *kapitel*.[119] These words provide finality and serve as a powerful exclamation point for *Tehillim* 41.

These words also mark the completion of the first of the five books of *Sefer Tehillim*, the symmetry of which must be appreciated since *Tehillim* 41 is also the companion psalm to *Parshas Vayechi*, which is the *Parshah* that marks the completion of the first of the five books of the Torah, *Sefer Bereishis*!

As such, the expression "אָמֵן וְאָמֵן" as used specifically here parallels so beautifully the proclamation of "חֲזַק חֲזַק וְנִתְחַזֵּק – Be strong. Be Strong. And may we be strengthened," which we joyously declare in unison in shul upon the completion of each of the *Chamishah Chumshei Torah*, including, of course, *Sefer Bereishis* with the finishing of *Parshas Vayechi*.

---

[117] *Shabbos* 119b.
[118] *Devarim Rabbah* 7:1.
[119] *Radak*, *Tehillim* 41:14.

As we conclude this *sefer* שִׁירֵי יְדִידוֹת: *Parshah & Tehillim Hand In Hand* on *Sefer Bereishis*, may we, too, proudly proclaim חֲזַק חֲזַק וְנִתְחַזֵּק, and may we continue to recite and study each *Parshas HaShavua* and its corresponding *kapitel Tehillim* as we journey through the rest of Hashem's precious Torah, אָמֵן וְאָמֵן!

CONCLUSION TO SEFER BEREISHIS: *V'ZAKEINU L'GADEL*

Baruch Hashem, our study of each *Parshas HaShavua* in *Sefer Bereishis* and its interplay with a specific *kapitel* of *Tehillim* has revealed many intricate connections between the two, and has provided us with a new lens, the lens of Dovid HaMelech in *Tehillim*, through which to learn and view Hashem's infinite Torah as conveyed in the *Parshas HaShavua*.

Along the way, we have learned many important teachings and lessons from Tanach, Chazal, and modern-day Torah commentators, some of which the reader of this *sefer* may have found to be review, while some of which may have been novel.

Among the beauty in what we have learned is the deeper insight and connection we have developed in understanding and emulating the Avos HaKedoshim – Avraham, Yitzchak, and Yaakov; the Imahos – Sarah, Rivkah, Rochel, and Leah; Yosef HaTzaddik, Dovid HaMelech, Shlomo HaMelech, and even Moshe Rabbeinu and Aharon HaKohen, who are not the focus of *Sefer Bereishis*, but to whom the focus of the *Parshiyos HaShavua* dramatically shifts in *Sefer Shemos*.

Thus, as a parting thought on *Sefer Bereishis*, allow me to share with you an original insight on the beautiful *Yehi Ratzon tefillah* that many Jewish women and mothers have a custom to recite each Friday night immediately after kindling the holy Shabbos candles. There, standing in front of the lit candles in the first moments of the holy Shabbos, the Jewish woman davens as follows:

PARSHAH & TEHILLIM HAND IN HAND

"יְהִי רָצוֹן מִלְּפָנֶיךָ ה' אֱ-לֹהַי וֵא-לֹהֵי אֲבוֹתַי שֶׁתְּחוֹנֵן אוֹתִי..." — May it be the will before You Hashem, my God and the God of my forefathers, that you grant favor to me [and, as applicable, to my husband, to my son(s), to my daughter(s), to my father, to my mother] and to all of my relatives..."

The prayer continues as the Jewish woman davens for a life that is good and lengthy for herself, her family, and for all the Jewish People. She asks for all to be remembered by Hashem for goodness and blessing, and to be considered by Hashem with salvation and compassion; to be blessed with blessings that are great; with complete/whole/perfect households; and that the *Shechinah* dwell among us.

The Jewish woman then recites a sentence that is very powerful and has become popularized in recent years by Rabbi Baruch Levine and other song writers and singers. Her prayer will also become the focus of this Conclusion to Sefer Bereishis: the words of "וְזַכֵּנוּ לְגַדֵּל":[1]

"וְזַכֵּנוּ לְגַדֵּל בָּנִים וּבְנֵי בָנִים חֲכָמִים וּנְבוֹנִים, אוֹהֲבֵי ה' יִרְאֵי אֱ-לֹקִים, אַנְשֵׁי אֱמֶת זֶרַע קֹדֶשׁ בַּה' דְּבֵקִים, וּמְאִירִים אֶת הָעוֹלָם בַּתּוֹרָה וּבְמַעֲשִׂים טוֹבִים, וּבְכָל מְלֶאכֶת עֲבוֹדַת הַבּוֹרֵא

Grant us the merit to raise children and grandchildren who are wise and understanding, who love Hashem and fear God, people of truth, offspring that are holy, who are attached to Hashem, who illuminate the world with Torah and with deeds that are good, and with every labor in the service of the Creator."

The prayer then concludes with the following statement:

"אָנָּא שְׁמַע אֶת תְּחִנָּתִי בָּעֵת הַזֹּאת בִּזְכוּת שָׂרָה וְרִבְקָה וְרָחֵל וְלֵאָה אִמּוֹתֵינוּ. וְהָאֵר נֵרֵנוּ שֶׁלֹּא יִכְבֶּה לְעוֹלָם וָעֶד וְהָאֵר פָּנֶיךָ וְנִוָּשֵׁעָה, אָמֵן — Please hear my supplication at this time, in the merit of Sarah, Rivkah, Rochel, and Leah, our Matriarchs, and shine our light that it not be extinguished forever

---

[1] Some texts read "וְזַכֵּנִי – Grant me the merit" in singular, but others are "וְזַכֵּנוּ – Grant us the merit" in plural.

and ever, and shine Your Countenance so that we may be saved, *Amen*."

Amidst the beauty and intensity of this prayer, some have pointed out that the final sentence is very unusual, as it calls upon the *zechus* of the Imahos only, and even mentions them by name: Sarah, Rivkah, Rochel, and Leah but does not mention the Avos at all.

Some have answered that the very beginning of the prayer already alludes to the Avos in the phrase "my God and the God of my forefathers." Others have said that when a Jewish woman lights her Shabbos candles, which has become the woman's special mitzvah that she and not her husband performs, it is more logical for her to call upon the merit of such women as the Imahos at that time rather than call upon the merit of men, even the Avos.

Nonetheless, others have countered that the Jewish woman is still davening on behalf of men such as her husband, sons, father, her male relatives, and all males among the Jewish People, so to limit the merit to just the Imahos is perplexing. Doing so seems not only restrictive but also seemingly disconnected from the broader context.

In any event, it cannot be denied that calling upon the merit of the Imahos and mentioning them by name is beautiful but also extremely uncommon, as it is the Avos HaKedoshim who are always mentioned – such as in the first *brachah* in *Shemoneh Esrei* – and who are certainly never excluded.

However, an astonishing answer lies in the words of the immediately preceeding statement of "וְזַכֵּנוּ" itself, which contains within its requests hidden references that will soon become clear references to the Avos and to all the other male Torah personalities whom we have been studying throughout this *sefer* and throughout *Sefer Bereishis*. The connection is both obvious and incredible:

וְזַכֵּנוּ לְגַדֵּל בָּנִים וּבְנֵי בָנִים – Hashem, please merit us to raise children and grandchildren who are –

חֲכָמִים – **Wise** is a reference to Shlomo HaMelech, who was blessed to be "וַיֶּחְכַּם מִכָּל הָאָדָם – wiser than all men"[2] (see Chapter 10 of this *sefer*);

וּנְבוֹנִים – **Understanding** is a reference to Yosef HaTzaddik, who even Pharaoh could not deny was wise and נָבוֹן when he said: "אֵין נָבוֹן וְחָכָם כָּמוֹךְ – There is no one as wise and understanding as you"[3] (see Chapter 9 of this *sefer*);

אוֹהֲבֵי י-ה-ו-ה – **Those who love Hashem** is first and foremost a reference to Avraham Avinu whom Hashem referred to as "אַבְרָהָם אֹהֲבִי – Avraham, who loved Me,"[4] and for whom love of Hashem, as well as the merciful and kind Divine Name of י-ה-ו-ה, was paramount (see Chapters 3 and 5 of this *sefer*);

יִרְאֵי אֱ-לֹקִים – **Those who fear God** is a famous reference to Yitzchak Avinu, to whom both fear of God and the Divine Name of אֱ-לֹקִים was paramount, as he served Hashem through יִרְאָה as well as דִּין and מִשְׁפָּט, which are expressed by the Name אֱ-לֹקִים (see Chapter 6 of this *sefer*);

אַנְשֵׁי אֱמֶת – **Men of truth** is a reference to Yaakov Avinu, to whom the Divine characteristic of אֱמֶת was paramount and who is called an אִישׁ by virtue of being an "אִישׁ תָּם יֹשֵׁב אֹהָלִים"[5] who dedicated his life to the study and practice of the תּוֹרַת אֱמֶת (see Chapters 6, 7, and 8 of this *sefer*);

זֶרַע קֹדֶשׁ – **Holy offspring** refers to the *Shivtei Kah,* all twelve of the sons of Yaakov whose bed and progeny were perfect in holiness (see Chapter 12 of this *sefer*);

בָּהּ' דְּבֵקִים – *Deveikus ba'Hashem*, attachment, cleaving and connection to Hashem is a goal of all *tzaddikim* and all Jews everywhere for all time,

---

[2] *I Melachim* 5:11.
[3] *Bereishis* 41:39.
[4] *Yeshayahu* 41:8.
[5] *Bereishis* 25:27.

both in this world and the World to Come (see Chapters 4 and 9 of this *sefer*);

וּמְאִירִים אֶת הָעוֹלָם – **Bringing light to the world** is a reference to the Maccabim, who are alluded to throughout the Torah and *Tehillim*, and through whom Hashem brought אוֹר, light, into the world by means of the military victory of Chanukah and the miracle of the Menorah (see Chapters 6, 8, and 9 of this *sefer*);

בַּתּוֹרָה – **Torah** is a reference to Moshe Rabbeinu, through whom Hashem gave the Jewish People the Torah, both Written and Oral, atop Har Sinai;

וּבְמַעֲשִׂים טוֹבִים – **Good deeds** is a reference to Aharon HaKohen, who is renowned as being the quintessential "אוֹהֵב שָׁלוֹם וְרוֹדֵף שָׁלוֹם, אוֹהֵב אֶת הַבְּרִיּוֹת וּמְקָרְבָן לַתּוֹרָה – one who loved peace, pursued peace, who loved mankind, and drew them close to the Torah,"[6] which succinctly describes the ultimate in doing good toward others;

וּבְכָל מְלֶאכֶת עֲבוֹדַת הַבּוֹרֵא – **And all the labor of the service of the Creator** is a reference to Dovid HaMelech, who was involved in the worldly "work" of wars, politics, and leading the Jewish People but whose every action was motivated by a desire to perform עֲבוֹדַת ה', the service of Hashem (see Chapter 11 of this *sefer*).

Thus, while the Friday night *Yehi Ratzon* of the Shabbos candles may only explicitly call upon the merit of the Imahos, the Avos and other Torah greats are not *chas v'shalom* ignored but are very much interwoven into the very fabric of the words of the prayer itself.

In this respect, the Friday night *Yehi Ratzon* is much like the overarching theme of this very *sefer* that begins to reveal the many connections between each *Parshas HaShavua* in *Sefer Bereishis* and its once cryptic corresponding *kapitel* of *Tehillim*. For both the שִׁירָה that is the Torah and the שִׁירָה that is *Tehillim* are very much שִׁירֵי יְדִידוֹת: they are

---

[6] *Pirkei Avos* 1:12; *Sanhedrin* 6b.

songs that intertwine in beautiful harmony יָד בְּיָד – hand in hand with one another. And they are שִׁירֵי יְדִידוֹת – Songs of Belovedness, binding us ever closer to our יְדִיד נֶפֶשׁ – our Beloved of the soul, Hashem.

בָּרוּךְ ה', תַּם וְלֹא נִשְׁלָם.

ABOUT THE AUTHOR

Yerachmiel (Jeremy) Goldman was blessed to be raised in a Torah-true home in Lawrence, New York, where *middos tovos* were paramount amidst an environment of laughter, music, and adventure. Yerachmiel learned at Yeshivat HaKotel in the Old City of Yerushalayim before being drawn to Yeshiva Sh'or Yoshuv, where he became a *talmid* of Rabbi Shmuel Brazil *shlita*. After majoring in English and graduating *summa cum laude* from Queens College, Yerachmiel attended the University of Pennsylvania School of Law, where he earned his Juris Doctor degree. As a practicing attorney, Yerachmiel worked in a large law firm before he and his wife, Naomi, a great-granddaughter of Rav Moshe Feinstein *zt"l*, relocated their growing family to Baltimore, Maryland.

For nearly a decade, Yerachmiel served as in-house counsel for The Johns Hopkins Hospital and Health System, and he continues to practice healthcare law. Simultaneously, Yerachmiel was *zocheh* to give *shiurim* both locally and beyond, and is now in his fifteenth year of giving *shiurim* at the Baltimore Community Kollel and on TorahAnytime. These *shiurim* cover a wide variety of topics, including *tefillah*, *Parshah*, *Tehillim*, and *shalom bayis*, and are inspired by the teachings of Rav Shimshon Pincus *zt"l* and the writings of the *Bilvavi Mishkan Evneh*.

Yerachmiel can be reached at ParshahandTehillim@gmail.com and welcomes your feedback and dialogue.

Proudly dedicated in memory of our dear parents

Yerachmiel and Gittel Goldman ob"m

Their dedication to raising a Jewish family on American shores continues to bear fruit in their many accomplished descendants.

Michael and Ann Renee Friedman

גמלה חסד כל ימי חייה
אהבה וכיבדה את הוריה
לימדה סיפרות לתלמידיה
דאגה לצרכי בעלה וילדיה
אדיבה ונאצלת למכריה

בביתה תורה למדו חבריה
ראתה נחת מיוצאי חלציה
כלילת יופי לכל רואיה
היא דוגמא לכל יודעיה

Dedicated to Dr. Barbara Gail Reich Gluck,

who would have loved Yerachmiel Goldman's
magnificent work and creative ideas.

Simon B. Gluck and Family

לזכות
בריאות והצלחה
בגשמיות וברוחניות
בשביל הנדיבי לב:

אברהם חיים
יוכבד חיה ורדה
בן-ציון מרדכי
ציפורה שירה
אלעזר ישראל
רפאל שמחה

In Loving Memory

of

Sylvia and Sam Reiter

&

Adele and Paul Englander

Talia and Steven Englander
and Family

In Honor

of

Ronald and Janet Goldman

May they only have *simchas*
from their children,
grandchildren,
and great-grandchildren!

Alissa and David Hersh

Mazel Tov

to our Dear Friend

Reb Yerachmiel Yitzchak Goldman

on this beautiful *Sefer*.

May Hashem continue to *bentch* you and Naomi with *nachas*, *bracha*, and *hatzlocha*.

May the sweet songs of Dovid HaMelech bring continued health to our parents:

Jonathan and Nina Herschberg
&
Charles and Esther Spirgel

Daniel and Etty Herschberg

🎼

Mazel Tov

Yerachmiel

on completing your first *Sefer*!

Can't wait to learn from the entire set.

May this *Sefer* be a *zechus* for my Mother,

חיה רחל בת שרגה אריה ז״ל

May this *Sefer* be a continued *zechus*
for my wife and children

שורי פסל בת חיים צבי

חנה רבקה בת צבי יהודה

ברוך אריה בן צבי יהודה

חיה רחל בת צבי יהודה

שינדל פנינה בת צבי יהודה

Last but not least, may this *Sefer* be a continued *zechus*
for the entire Nachamu Crew and their families.

צבי יהודה רינזלר

🎼

"One man's candle is light for many."

— *Masechet Shabbat*

Yasher koach to

Yerachmiel Goldman

on this milestone.

May the light of this *Sefer* serve to illuminate and guide all those fortunate enough to embrace its wisdom.

With appreciation, we dedicate this *Sefer* to the memory of

Chaya Esther bat Sarah

Wife, mother, and friend.

Hillel, Deena, Eliana, Noah, and Ezra Goldman

In Memory of

Tziporah Leah bat Shlomo Zalman

Leah took all of her hardships
and made them her motivation for helping others.
She dedicated her time, resources, and heart to making
sure the people around her were protected and loved.
She opened her heart and home to all in need.
She treated everyone like family
and gave everyone unconditional love.
She led her life with love and care.
She had a kind soul, and it will never be forgotten.
T'hei zichra baruch.

The Zoldan Family

IN LOVING MEMORY OF

Avraham Schwartzbaum

אברהם בן דוד ז"ל

ויאמר ה' אל אברם לך לך מארצך וממולדתך ומבית אביך
אל הארץ אשר אראך

Israel Goldstein

ישראל אלטר בן יעקב ז"ל

קולו נעים ומעורב בדעת עם הבריות

By their loving grandchildren and great-grandchildren

Avi and Shayna Goldstein

Tamar, Eitan, Eliana and Ashira

WISHING

YERACHMIEL GOLDMAN

CONTINUED SUCCESS

SHAUL AND CHANITA KANE

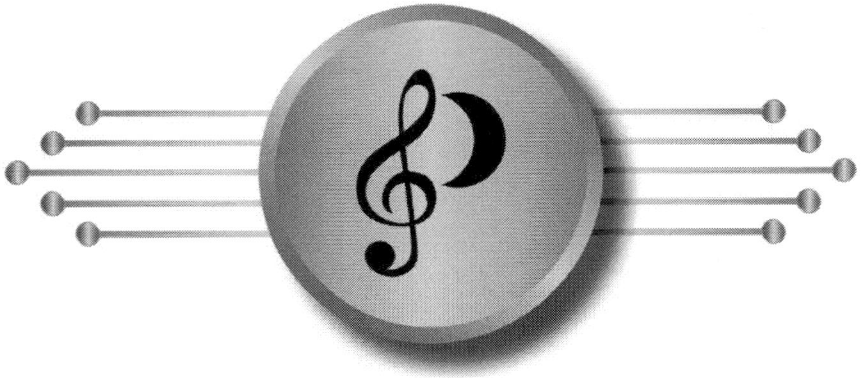

Made in the USA
Las Vegas, NV
30 September 2024

9da35b86-f0e8-41b6-90fc-0ca47a9e0a56R01